FAITH IN THE
BYZANTINE WORLD

Faith in the
Byzantine
World

Mary Cunningham

Downers Grove, Illinois

To Richard, Emily and James

This mosaic panel above the central door of the narthex of Hagia Sophia in Constantinople shows an emperor kneeling before Christ as if in supplication. Art historians have suggested that this figure may be the emperor Leo VI (886–912), kneeling in supplication before Christ, the symbol of Divine Wisdom.

Previous pages:
Wall painting of the *Anastasis* or resurrection scene (1316–21) in the side chapel of the Chora Monastery in Constantinople.

Page one:
The Barberini Ivory (sixth century).

InterVarsity Press
P.O. Box 1400, Downers Grove, IL 60515-1426
World Wide Web: www.ivpress.com
E-mail: mail@ivpress.com

©2002 Mary Cunningham

ISBN 0-8308-2352-2

Printed and bound in China

Library of Congress Cataloging-in-Publication Data has been requested.

P 15 14 13 12 11 10 9 8 7 6 5 4 3 2 1

Y 08 07 06 05 04 03 02

Contents

Introduction

From obscure roots in Palestine, Christianity slowly became the dominant religion in the territories of the later Roman empire and beyond. In this earliest period, the Christian Church was one entity, united by a network of bishops, as well as a shared faith and sacraments. It is out of this unified Church of the early centuries that the two main branches of Christian tradition, the Roman Catholic and the Eastern Orthodox Churches, developed. The former was based primarily in the region of Western Europe, whereas the latter developed in the empire which we now call 'Byzantine'; this had its centre in the capital city of Constantinople (now Istanbul, in modern Turkey). It is important to remember that the two halves of Christendom remained officially joined throughout the whole of the first Christian millennium.

The decisive split occurred in 1054, although a growing separation between Latin-speaking and Greek-speaking Christians had been visible long before this date. Nevertheless, we can speak of unity throughout the Christian world even after this time. Western and Eastern Christians shared essentially the same doctrine, methods of worship and objects of veneration – such as the cross and the Bible. Minor differences did exist, however, in musical traditions, disciplinary matters and the formulation of doctrine. The Orthodox use of holy icons, for example, remained foreign to Western Christians even though they also sponsored religious art in their cathedrals and homes. Perhaps the greatest source of friction lay in the issue of authority: Roman popes increasingly felt that they should represent the highest source of power in the Christian Church. Eastern bishops and patriarchs, on the other hand, believed in a pentarchy, that is, five ancient leading dioceses, or patriarchates, namely Rome, Constantinople, Alexandria, Antioch and Jerusalem. Although Eastern bishops acknowledged the pope as the first in importance among bishops, they were unwilling to grant him complete supremacy in the Church.

This book covers the history of the Byzantine Church between the dates 330 and 1453. To some extent these boundaries, especially that which is usually regarded as the beginning of the Eastern Roman empire, are open to debate. Nevertheless, Constantine's foundation of a new capital city at Constantinople in Asia Minor may legitimately be seen as the start of this new Christian empire. The fall of the city to the Ottoman Turks in 1453 effectively ended the long and varied history of Byzantine dominion. The title of the book, *Faith in the Byzantine World*, is also in some ways inaccurate. People of many different faiths lived in Byzantium at different times, including not only Christians, but also Jews, Samaritans, 'heretics' or those who deviated from the 'right' faith, and even pagans in the earlier period. Nevertheless, Orthodox Christianity had become the dominant faith in this empire by the end of the fourth century. Not only were the daily lives and attitudes of most citizens shaped by this faith, but the government and official Church were imbued with its teachings. Various aspects of this Christian civilization will be explored in the chapters which follow, including the close relationship between Church and State, doctrine and worldview.

The Byzantine empire has traditionally been viewed as a conservative and repressive society. Churchmen, scholars and politicians alike looked to a classical past and attempted to preserve its culture, laws and values – although, of course, within a Christian framework. Historians, beginning with Edward Gibbon in the 18th century, have stressed not only the traditionalism of this society, but also its corruption and lack of creativity. In fact, this view of Byzantium is inaccurate in many respects. If we study the texts and artefacts of the Byzantines carefully, it is clear that creative thought and religious views did flourish and develop in the course of 11 centuries. Most of these productions also reveal a deeply Christian view of the world, a sense of God's immanence and involvement in creation and human history. The expression of Orthodox Christian faith by means of the tools and ideas of classical civilization was consistently both innovative and successful.

Furthermore, the Eastern Roman empire contained in most periods a diverse, multi-ethnic population. The governing elite in Constantinople and a few other cities represented a tiny minority within the population as a whole. Perhaps as many as 90 per cent of the Byzantines were peasants living in rural areas, most of whom were probably illiterate. Not all of these people even spoke Greek; at the outer frontiers of the empire there were Armenian, Slavic and Syriac or Arabic-speaking communities, to name only a few. We are thus attempting to describe in this book a period and culture in Christian history which almost escapes precise definition. At the same time, however, it is clear on the basis of the surviving literary texts and artefacts that Byzantine Orthodoxy provided most of its adherents with a unified and comprehensive worldview. Belief in the triune God, whose definition was established by biblical revelation and in the course of the ecumenical councils, formed the basis of this worldview. Beyond this basic Christian doctrine, the cults of the Virgin Mary, the saints and holy symbols such as icons and relics, as well as religious practices such as attendance at church, keeping the fasts and celebrating the feast days, helped to define Byzantines' sense of cultural identity.

It is with some regret that I have decided not to cover in detail other faiths in the Byzantine world within this book. The reasons for this are primarily those of space. Separate books on Byzantine Judaism, 'heretical' groups such as the Paulicians and Bogomils and, perhaps even more importantly, all the Churches now called the 'Oriental' Orthodox, which survive to this day in Syria, Lebanon, Israel, Egypt, Ethiopia, India and Armenia, are required for each of these topics. This book, like *Faith in the Medieval World*, which also appears in this series, is concerned primarily with the dominant religion in the region that it covers, in this case Orthodox Christianity. The first two chapters provide a broad chronological outline of the history of the Byzantine Church and State; after these, a more thematic approach is adopted. It is inevitable that some repetition will occur in a book of this format; nevertheless, it is hoped that each chapter may be read on its own as well as in conjunction with others. It would be impossible to cover every subject in detail in a book of this size. Suggestions for further reading are therefore provided at the end, including both primary and secondary sources.

Finally, it is necessary to add a word about the technical terms and spellings that are used in this book. It seems impossible to avoid using certain terms which have very precise meanings when writing a book about the Byzantine Church. Many of these, such as 'patriarch', 'ecumenical' council or 'liturgy', in fact represent transliterations of Greek words. Most have been adopted for practical use in English both by scholars and writers of books for the general public. A short explanation of the meaning of each word is provided in this book the first time it occurs in the text. Whenever possible, however, simpler terms are substituted. Spellings follow the conventions of most books published on Byzantine topics. That is, names of people or places which have a well-known English equivalent, such as 'Rome', 'Antony' or 'Michael', appear in that form. Those which have not previously been translated, such as 'Herakleios' or 'Kosmas Indikopleustes', are spelled according to Greek, rather than Latin, conventions.

I would like to acknowledge here the generous help of Augustine Casiday and Zaga Gavrilović, who both read through earlier drafts of the text and suggested a number of changes. Morag Reeve, the commissioning editor at Lion Publishing, has also improved the book in many ways by her judicious comments and criticisms. I would like to express my thanks to both of these kind critics, as well as to the supporting team at Lion, while accepting full responsibility for any mistakes that may remain. I would also like to thank Claire Sauer for her meticulous work in improving the book.

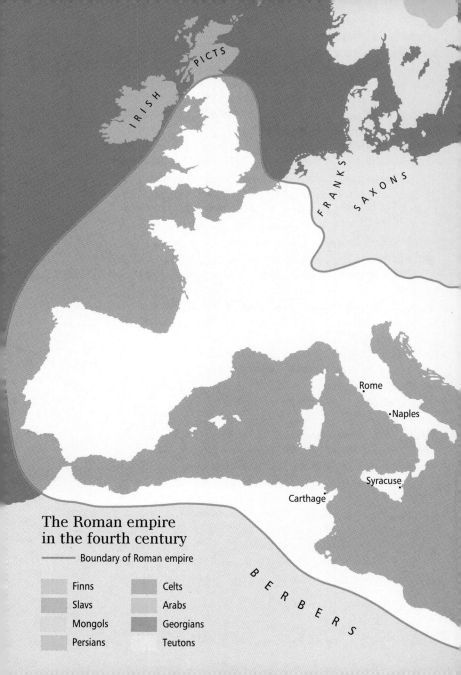

IRISH

PICTS

FRANKS

SAXONS

Rome

Naples

Syracuse

Carthage

The Roman empire
in the fourth century

—— Boundary of Roman empire

Finns
Slavs
Mongols
Persians

Celts
Arabs
Georgians
Teutons

BERBERS

The Byzantine empire
in the eighth century

	Turks		Teutons
	Mongols		Latins
	Magyars		Balts
	Slavs		Georgians (Basques and Abasgians)
	Finns		Arabs
	Celts	——	Boundary of Byzantine empire

IRISH

PICTS

NORTHUMBRIA

WELSH

MERCIA

WESSEX

NORSE

SWEDES

DANES

SAXONS

BRETONS

FRANKISH KINGDOM

GALICIA

BASQUES

UMAYYAD EMIRATE

LOMBARD KINGDOM

PAPAL STATE

BENEVENTO

Rome

Naples

Syracuse

Carthage

A B B A S I D

S L

Europe in the
15th century

Byzantine empire

R K
NOVGOROD
VLADIMIR
TEUTONIC KNIGHTS
SMOLENSK
KHANATE OF THE GOLDEN HORDE
POLAND–LITHUANIA
MOLDAVIA
GARY
mium
WALLACHIA
RBIA
GEORGIA
TREZIBOND
OTTOMAN SULTANATE
Constantinople
Thessaloniki
LATIN STATES
Nicea
Kaisarea
TIMURID EMIRATE
Edessa
Ephesus
Athens
Nisibis
Antioch
RHODES
(Knights of St John)
CRETE
(To Venice)
CYPRUS
Ctesiphon
Damascus
Cyrene
Jerusalem
Alexandria
MAMLUKE SULTANATE

A Christian
Roman Empire
(330–843)

When did the Byzantine Church, or for that matter the Byzantine empire, begin? The time when it ended, at the sack of Constantinople by the Ottoman Turks in 1453, is indisputable, but the point of transition between the later Roman and the Byzantine empires is less obvious. Some historians indeed would argue that there is no beginning: Byzantium represented (and its own citizens in fact adhered to this idea) the continuation of the Roman empire in the East. Many, however, would signal the reign of Constantine the Great, who finally gained sole authority as Roman emperor when he defeated Licinius in 324, and whose dramatic conversion to Christianity ended the period of persecution by pagan emperors, as the starting point for both empire and Church.

Opposite page:
A 12th-century
image of the
ascension of
Christ in a
manuscript
containing
homilies on the
Virgin Mary by the
monk, James of
Kokkinobaphos.

Constantinople, the 'New Rome'

Constantine's decision to found an administrative capital, or 'New Rome', at the site of the ancient city of Byzantion shifted the centre of gravity eastwards in the empire. Several ideas seem to have motivated Constantine in this decision. First, the site was strategically well placed. At a vantage point which divided not only Asia Minor from the rest of Europe, but also the Black Sea from the Mediterranean, Constantinople represented a link between all the territories of the Roman world. Second, it is likely that Constantine saw political advantages in distancing

Constantine's
vision of the
cross as seen in a
15th-century wall
painting in the
Church of the
Holy Cross,
Platanistaza,
Cyprus. The text
reads, 'By this
conquer.'

Constantine's conversion

Although it may be purely legendary, the story of Constantine's
dramatic conversion at the Milvian Bridge outside Rome and
the successful defeat of his first main rival, the usurper
Maxentius, in 312 was regarded even by contemporary
historians as the starting point for a new, Christian Roman
empire. The true sequence of events before this famous battle
remains obscure and was embroidered in subsequent years. An
account written by the Christian historian Lactantius sometime
before 324 relates that Constantine, following instructions he
had received in a dream the night before, instructed his troops
to inscribe the chi-rho sign, ✳, representing the first two letters

in the name of Christ
in Greek, on their shields.
Nearly 30 years later, Eusebius
elaborated this story in his
biography of Constantine,
saying that the emperor had
a vision of a luminous cross in
the sky, accompanied by the
inscription 'Conquer by this'.
After this battle, Constantine
went on to defeat his other
rivals and by 324 had become
sole ruler of the entire Roman
empire. He also decided to
introduce Christianity as the
state religion, providing the
Church for the first time with money and imperial backing.
The extent of Constantine's own conversion remains open to
debate. It is likely that while viewing the Christian God as the
most powerful force in the universe, he continued to express
allegiance to the ancient gods of pagan Rome. Constantine
was finally baptized on his deathbed in 337, and was buried
with much pomp in a mausoleum which he had built in
Constantinople.

himself from the power structures and traditions of the old Rome. In Constantinople, he was able to establish a new order, with a newly appointed senate and administration. Henceforth, Constantinople would represent the centre of the largely Greek-speaking, Eastern Roman empire which slowly and inexorably became separated, both culturally and politically, from the Latin West.

The Christianization of the empire

Perhaps the most important effect of Constantine's conversion was on the Christian Church itself. As a result of Constantine's active patronage and legal reforms from the 320s onwards, the Church began to develop as an institution with wealth and property at its disposal. For the first time, churches on a monumental scale could be endowed and built.

Constantinople

Constantine founded his new capital city on the site of Byzantion, an ancient Greek city-state or *polis*, located on the Bosphorus between Golden Horn, an inlet which leads to the Black Sea, and the Sea of Marmara. Byzantion was insignificant before Constantine chose it for the 'New Rome', but he added

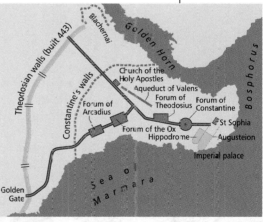

or enlarged all the necessary ingredients of a late-Roman city: wide avenues bordered by colonnades, squares or forums, public baths, a racecourse or hippodrome, a palace and several new Christian churches, including the two central basilicas, Hagia Sophia (Holy Wisdom) and St Irene. Constantine also moved the city walls outwards to allow for expansion; a further set of defensive walls, about 1.5 kilometres beyond Constantine's, was added by the emperor Theodosius II at the beginning of the fifth century. These outer walls proved virtually impregnable on various later occasions, when enemies laid siege to the 'Queen City'.

*'It is our will
that all the
peoples who are
ruled by the
administration
of our clemency
shall practise
that religion
which the
divine Peter
the Apostle
transmitted to
the Romans...
according to
the apostolic
discipline and
the evangelic
doctrine, we
shall believe in
the single Deity
of the Father,
the Son, and the
Holy Spirit,
under the
concept of equal
majesty and
of the Holy
Trinity.'*

AN EDICT ON THE
PROFESSION OF THE
CATHOLIC FAITH, 380

Basilicas intended for large urban congregations, shrines in honour of martyrs or saints, and churches built on holy sites of pilgrimage began to proliferate in Eastern and Western Christendom. The internal organization of the Church also changed in response to imperial patronage and protection. Although bishops had led the Christian community in its decisions since as early as the second century, their organization into various ranks and dioceses seems to date from the period of Constantine. It is interesting to note that Christian dioceses followed closely the secular organization of the state and its division into local provinces by Diocletian and his successors. Each province had its principal bishop, who was responsible for organizing meetings and ordaining all the clerics under his jurisdiction. A hierarchical power structure for the Church came into being at the same time that it began to exert significant influence and authority within the secular state.

The Christianization of the Roman empire continued after the death of Constantine I. Laws which date back to Constantine's successors, such as his son Constantius, reveal increasing restrictions on pagans and more favourable conditions for Christians. The conversion of the masses to Christianity did not happen immediately, however, and the emperor Julian (361–63) initiated a brief return to paganism as the official state religion. By the end of the fourth century, and with the return of Christian rulers, legislation in favour of Christianity became increasingly pronounced. The *Codex Theodosianus*, published between 429 and 438, but incorporating laws promulgated during the reigns of Constantine I and his successors, reveals an ever-increasing intent on the part of emperors to promote Christianity and eradicate paganism. Sundays and important Christian feast days were declared holidays, with the prohibition of secular lawsuits and business transactions. By the end of the fourth century, laws forbidding pagan sacrifices and ordering the closure of temples were being enforced. Pagans were forbidden to hold jobs in the imperial court or in military or civil service. Increasingly, all non-orthodox citizens, including pagans, Jews and heretical Christians, became second-class citizens throughout the empire.

The beginnings of political and religious disunity

After Constantine's brief rule as sole Christian Roman emperor, the empire was divided into Eastern and Western territories under his sons. The shape of late-Roman Christendom began to change irrevocably in the fifth century, owing to military and political upheavals in the West. As Goths, Vandals and Huns invaded the Balkans and Western Europe, Christians in these regions increasingly looked to Rome or Constantinople for protection and spiritual direction. There can be no doubt that the political instability of this period contributed to a need for religious authority,

Jews in the later Roman empire

Jewish communities survived and even flourished in the later Roman empire after the destruction of the Temple (AD 70) and their expulsion from Jerusalem in 135. New communities were established in Palestine and Jews were allowed to govern themselves. Jewish communities in many Eastern cities such as Antioch thus remained strong and vibrant for several centuries, even attracting converts from among the Christian population. After the beginning of the fifth century, however, life in the Roman empire became increasingly difficult for Jews as imperial legislation began to restrict their rights. Privileges such as holding slaves, teaching in public institutions, building new synagogues or serving in the army were henceforth barred. Outside Palestine, a Jewish *diaspora* existed in most of the major cities of the Roman empire. Here the Jews tended to live in small enclaves; in Constantinople they were located in the commercial quarters and worked as dyers, weavers, furriers, glass-makers and even merchants and physicians. Prejudice against the Jews was strong in all periods of Byzantine history, however, and was frequently expressed both in devotional literature and in legislation. Byzantine Christians regarded themselves as the New Israel and believed that the Jews deliberately refused to acknowledge Christ as Messiah. The emperors Herakleios, Leo III and others all ordered the compulsory baptism of Jews at various periods of military stress or economic hardship. There is evidence, however, that some bishops in the Byzantine Church consistently opposed such measures and upheld the right of Jews to practise their ancestral religion.

based now primarily in the main episcopal dioceses of the Roman empire. It is also important to recognize, however, that the barbarian invasions in the West did not topple Roman civilization or the Church. In most cases, the invaders were keen to adopt the culture and institutions of the Roman world; many of them had been converted to Christianity earlier (although, in the case of the Visigoths and Ostrogoths, this was the heretical Arian form of the faith).

Disunity and eventually schism were introduced into the Christian Church as controversy over theological doctrines developed. In the fourth century, the main issue of contention had been the formulation of ideas concerning the Trinity. In the fifth century, discussion moved on to Jesus Christ himself and to the manner in which two natures, the divine and the human, came together in his person. The unfortunate result of the controversy is that after the ecumenical councils of 431 and 451, bishops who felt that their views had not been represented began to split away from the mainstream Church. The Assyrian, or 'Nestorian', Church of the East, which still exists in parts of Iran, Iraq and Northern Syria, remains out of communion to this day with mainstream Orthodox Christianity because of the irregularities which its members perceived in the organization of the third ecumenical council of Ephesus (431). Similarly, the so-called 'Monophysite' churches began to be formed after the Council of Chalcedon (451) as bishops mainly from Egypt, Palestine and Syria found that they could not accept the formulations of that council. The effect of these early schisms on the Christian Church as a whole, but especially on the Chalcedonian Byzantine Church, was significant. Emperors of the fifth, sixth and seventh centuries expended much energy on attempts to heal the schisms, only abandoning the effort after most of the Near East fell to the Arabs in the middle of the seventh century.

Reunification under Justinian

The reign of the emperor Justinian I (527–65) represented the last attempt at political reunification of the Eastern and Western halves of the Roman empire. By his reconquest of

North Africa, Italy, and even a small part of Spain, Justinian aimed to regain the territories which had been under Roman jurisdiction. At the same time, he hoped to rebuild a unified Church in the course of his reign. This would be accomplished by various means, including the building of many more churches and monasteries throughout the empire, attempts to resolve the disputes which still divided bishops within the Church, and finally, by suppressing religious minorities within the empire, especially such 'outsiders' as pagans, Jews and Samaritans.

Justinian's contributions to the development of the Byzantine Church were significant and far-reaching. Due to the increase of commerce and industry during his reign, imperial patronage of art and architecture was carried out on an unprecedented scale. The Great Church of Hagia Sophia, completed in 537, represents a stupendous feat of engineering for the period. Justinian is said to have exclaimed after the completion of the church, 'Solomon, I have surpassed you!' Contemporaries marvelled at the building, with its massive, centralized interior and huge dome, which appears to be balanced on nothing. As Constantinople's main cathedral, Hagia Sophia came to represent for Byzantines of all periods the archetypal church building, a veritable 'heaven on earth'.

Justinian's other achievements include the codification of Roman law, a process which drew on the writings of classical Roman jurists, but which also created an orderly and up-to-date system out of their sometimes contradictory rulings, the further elaboration of the liturgy and the creation of an even closer relationship between Church and State than had existed previously. Building on the ideal image of the Christian emperor established by Eusebius in the fourth century, Justinian was fully conscious of his role as a divinely sanctioned ruler. He summoned Church councils, wrote theological treatises and composed hymns.

The Byzantine 'Dark Age'

Soon after the death of Justinian, the territories which he had worked so hard to reconquer began to crumble. The

empire's resources had been exhausted by the years of military campaigns, making it impossible for Justinian's successors to maintain his achievements. The first area to be lost was Italy, when the Lombards invaded from the north in 568. The Visigoths in Spain began a counter-offensive and by the end of the sixth century had recaptured all of the territories they had lost to the Byzantines. Even greater threats soon appeared in the north and the east, when Turkic peoples such as the Avars, who had originated on the steppes of Asia, began to invade the Crimea and the Balkans, and when Justin II (565–78) broke a peace treaty with Persia. The late sixth and early seventh centuries thus represented a period of great stress for the East Roman, or Byzantine, empire. Increasingly, people looked to God as their only source of protection and consolation.

A catastrophic event for the Byzantines in symbolic terms was the loss of the relic of the true cross when the Persians captured Jerusalem in 614. The newly enthroned Herakleios, one of the few emperors of this period who was able to reverse the tide of military defeats for the Byzantines, did not rest until he had conquered the Persians and restored the relic to Jerusalem. Ironically, however, Herakleios' achievements in the East were swiftly reversed when a new and much more formidable invader overthrew first the Persian empire and then the remaining Byzantine territories in Syria, Palestine, Egypt and even North Africa. The rise of Islam after 632 represents one of the most remarkable and dramatic events in the history of the world. The success and rapid spread of this new and highly unified religious movement completely changed the aspect of the Mediterranean basin and what remained of the later Roman empire.

Iconoclasm

At the beginning of the eighth century, a combination of usurpations, invasions by the Muslims and natural disasters helped to create even more chaos and uncertainty in the Byzantine world. Historians have long debated the possible

Opposite page:
The interior of the sixth-century Great Church of Hagia Sophia, Constantinople, built by the emperor Justinian. 'The church has been made a spectacle of great beauty, stupendous to those who see it and altogether incredible to those who hear of it' (Procopius, *On the Buildings***).**

reasons why Leo III (717–41) decided to introduce Iconoclasm (literally, the breaking of icons or images), the policy of destroying the holy icons within the Church and forbidding their veneration. Whatever the emperor's personal motivations may have been, it is clear that he was backed by a powerful lobby within the Church, which opposed the growing devotion to holy images, seeing this as a return to the idolatrous practices of pre-Christian times. It is also likely that contact in this period with Muslims, Jews and a heretical sect called the Paulicians contributed to the

The rise of Islam

The religion of Islam originated in northern Arabia, a desert region which had been ruled for centuries by competing Arab tribes with pagan beliefs. Owing both to Arabia's importance on the trade routes to the Far East and to the presence of Christian and Jewish communities, its inhabitants had come into contact with monotheistic religions before. In the middle of the seventh century, the prophet Muhammad began to teach the existence of one, transcendent God. Born in the holy city of Mecca and orphaned at the age of six, Muhammad had been trained as a merchant by his grandfather and uncle. At the age of 24 he entered the service of a rich widow named Khadija and eventually married her. Although he continued his job as a merchant, Muhammad became increasingly drawn to religious contemplation and prayer. Some time after 600 (the traditional date is 610), he began to receive revelations from Allah, the supreme God. These teachings, which were collected into the 114 chapters of the Qur'an, commanded the destruction of pagan idols and the worship of one God. In 622, when this new religious group lost support in Mecca, Muhammad was invited to move to the city of Yathrib. This migration, called the Hijra, represents the beginning of the Muslim era. The name of the new city was changed at this time to Medina, 'the city of the prophet'. By 629 Muhammad and his followers took control of Mecca. After his death in 632, the Muslims fought internally for a brief period, but went on to spread into Persian and Roman territories. Partly due to their exhaustion after years of warfare, both powers collapsed in the Middle East in a remarkably short space of time. In 636 the Persian capital Ctesiphon fell to the Muslims; 10 years later the Arabs had conquered most of Syria, Palestine, Mesopotamia and Egypt. The Muslim *caliphate* became Byzantium's most formidable enemy on the Eastern frontier for several centuries after this date.

belief that representational art contravened God's second commandment in Exodus 20:4–5.

Although the extent and severity of Leo III's iconoclastic policy is open to question, his son, Constantine V (741–75), undertook to enforce the edict against images actively and at times aggressively. This emperor considered himself a theologian and wrote several treatises arguing the case against the use of icons in the Church. Constantine V adopted extreme measures in order to eradicate icons and their cult from the empire. According to the chroniclers Theophanes and Nikephoros, both of whom were writing at the beginning of the following century, the emperor persecuted iconophiles in the civil services, the army and the Church. He seems especially to have targeted monks and monasteries, although it is not clear whether this was specifically because of their defensive stance towards the holy icons. For whatever reason he undertook this anti-monastic policy, there is evidence that he systematically razed monasteries or turned them into secular public buildings. Monks and abbots were publicly humiliated and forced to take up professions in secular life. During Constantine V's reign a number of monks and other iconophiles fled to Rome where they received protection from the pope, who publicly supported the cause of the holy images.

The campaign against icons was already losing impetus when Irene, widow of Constantine V's successor, Leo IV, called the seventh ecumenical council at Nicea in 787 to overturn the official iconoclastic policy. At this council the defenders of icons amassed numerous arguments against the charges which had been brought against them, basing these on scripture, tradition and the writings of the Fathers.

Unfortunately, political and military setbacks under Irene's successors in the early ninth century, including the major defeat and death of the emperor Nikephoros I at the hands of the Bulgars, paved the way for a return to iconoclastic policies in 815. Leo V, perhaps associating strong imperial rule and military victory with the iconoclast emperors of the eighth century, summoned a council at

'You shall not make for yourself an idol, whether in the form of anything that is in heaven above, or that is on the earth beneath, or that is in the water under the earth. You shall not bow down to them or worship them.'

EXODUS 20:4–5

'In every village and town one could witness the weeping and lamentation of the pious, whereas, on the part of the impious, one saw sacred things trodden upon, liturgical vessels turned to other use, churches scraped down and smeared with ashes because they contained holy images.'

LIFE OF ST STEPHEN THE YOUNGER, EARLY NINTH CENTURY

The persecution of
iconophile monks
by the emperor
Theophilos
(829–42).
From *The Skylitzes
Chronicle*
(probably second
half of 12th
century).

Hagia Sophia which reversed the decisions of the Council of Nicea. Leo and his successors appear to have acted more moderately than Constantine V in their suppression of religious images, however. Enforcement of the ban on images seems to have been confined to Constantinople and its immediate environs during this period, even during the reign of Theophilos (829–42), who enforced these policies the most rigorously.

The formal restoration of holy images in the Byzantine empire occurred in March 843; this is still remembered and celebrated in the Orthodox Church as the 'Triumph of Orthodoxy' on the first Sunday in Lent. The arguments in

Opposite page:
This icon, recently acquired by the British Museum in London, declares the importance of icons in Orthodox worship and commemorates the men and women who defended them during the iconoclast period between c. 730 and 842.
Icon of the Triumph of Orthodoxy (second half of 14th century).

defence of icons were this time expressed in a document called the *Synodikon*, which proclaimed not only the validity, but even the *necessity* of images in Christian worship. To deny the legitimacy of images of Christ is to undermine the significance of his incarnation, when God willingly put on human flesh and involved himself in the created world. The Orthodox belief in the potential for material creation to be divinely transfigured is also reaffirmed in the *Synodikon*. From this time onwards, the Byzantine Church formally accepted the importance of material symbols such as icons in Christian worship, along with their veneration through physical acts such as kneeling before them or kissing them.

The first five centuries of the Byzantine empire, lasting from approximately 330 to 843, represented a period of enormous transition and change. Beginning as the

continuation of the Roman empire in the East, the state underwent internal changes as it embraced Christianity as its official religion, and began to resolve theological controversies within the Church. Externally, the Eastern empire first extended its dominion under the sixth-century emperor Justinian, and then shrank to only a remnant of its former territories due to invasions by Slavs, Persians, Arabs and other enemies. The seventh and eighth centuries are usually seen as a period of transition from the Roman empire to a vulnerable, medieval state centred on its capital city, Constantinople. The self-questioning that accompanied this change manifested itself in the official policy of banning religious images in the Church, or Iconoclasm. After the restoration of icons to the Byzantine Church, or the Triumph of Orthodoxy, in 843, a new period of confidence and expansion began.

The Parting
of the Ways
(843–1453)

I n the later period of Byzantine history, we see the flowering of this remarkable and unique civilization, as well as its continuing interaction with the other two dominant cultures in the Mediterranean region: Western Christendom and Islam. The Byzantine Church experienced successes and failures in this period: perhaps the most difficult crisis was the period (1204–61) when the Latins occupied Constantinople and surrounding Byzantine territories after the disastrous climax of the Fourth Crusade. The Byzantines survived this setback, however, and their Church, officially in schism with the Roman papacy since 1054, flourished once more after the Latins were finally thrown out of the occupied territories. The period between 1261 and 1453, sometimes described as the 'twilight' years of Byzantium, was one of extraordinary religious and cultural revival, in spite of the inexorable advance of the Ottoman Turks into Asia Minor, the Balkans and eventually Constantinople itself.

The restoration of Orthodoxy

After the official end of Iconoclasm in 843, a number of significant changes took place both in Byzantine society and the Church. First, and perhaps most important for the population as a whole, the empire began to experience a period of prosperity and military success which lasted nearly two centuries. This allowed commerce, culture and

'By the ninth century the process of separation was complete. Out of the ruins of the Roman world had emerged three quite distinct civilizations... Islam, Byzantium and the West.'

MICHAEL ANGOLD,
*BYZANTIUM: THE
BRIDGE FROM
ANTIQUITY TO THE
MIDDLE AGES,* 2001

religious life to flourish, thus initiating a period of revival which has been called after the dynasty which ruled at the time, the 'Macedonian' Renaissance. Second, it is after the period of Iconoclasm and partly due to the role which monks played in that controversy as the defenders of icons, that monasticism flourished as never before. This led to the formation of a powerful monastic lobby which exerted influence in both the Church and the secular government. Finally, it is in this period that the long-standing cultural and political separation between the Byzantine patriarchate and the Roman papacy began to be felt. This process took place slowly and not, as might appear at first glance, in response to a few isolated events.

To begin with the first of these developments, the cultural renaissance of the mid-ninth century manifested itself in a number of areas. After a decline of higher education and learning in the so-called 'Dark Age' of Byzantine history, the seventh and eighth centuries, a revival began to get underway in the early ninth century. It is possible that this was fuelled to some extent by monasteries, which in turn were influenced by monastic emigration from the Holy Land in the face of civil war among the Arabs who now ruled this territory. Theodore, abbot of the monastery of Studios in Constantinople, undertook to reform his monastery, introducing Palestinian liturgical practices and a return to the coenobitic ideals of Basil of Caesarea, with an emphasis on manual labour and productivity. One area of manual labour in which skilled monks could work was the copying of manuscripts in the monastic scriptorium. It can scarcely be accidental that the new cursive script, which rendered the copying of manuscripts so much faster and more economical, was introduced in just this period, sometime between the middle of the eighth and early ninth centuries. Theodore also set his monks to compose hymns and prayers to fill the hours of the entire liturgical year.

After 843 a revival of secular education in the Byzantine empire also took place. A school in a part of the palace called the Magnaura had been established under the emperor

Theophilos (829–42), which taught the secular disciplines of rhetoric and philosophy, as well as mathematics, astronomy and grammar. Patriarchs in ninth-century Constantinople such as Tarasios, Methodios, Ignatios and Photios tended to be well educated in Greek rhetoric, to the extent that their surviving treatises and sermons are difficult for all but the classically educated reader to understand. Religious art experienced a similar revival after its vindication by the Triumph of Orthodoxy. After the middle of the ninth century, a proliferation of church decoration – such as the splendid mosaic of the Virgin and Child in the apse of Hagia Sophia – manuscript illumination and other examples of artistic production took place.

Monasticism also entered a period of growth and prosperity in Byzantine society from the mid-ninth century onward. Several factors probably contributed to this development. As we saw above, monks were believed to have played a major role in resisting the iconoclast emperors and in bringing about the restoration of holy icons in the Church. After the end of Iconoclasm many of these figures were rewarded with high positions in the Church as the incumbent iconoclast bishops were deposed and disciplined. Soon patronage of monasteries also increased and many became extremely wealthy institutions. As more and more houses were founded and endowed with both land and movable property, monasteries and their leaders formed an important and powerful pressure group within society. By the mid-10th century, a series of emperors were so worried by this phenomenon that they enacted laws aimed at limiting the growth of monastic properties. That this legislation ultimately failed reflects the enormous respect and support for monastic life that existed by this time throughout the Byzantine world.

Growing separation between East and West
Tension had been growing between the patriarchate in Constantinople and the Roman papacy for several centuries before flaring up again in the late ninth century. Culturally, the Eastern and Western halves of the former Roman

This mosaic depiction of the Virgin and Child in the apse of Hagia Sophia in Constantinople is dated to 867. A famous sermon by the patriarch Photios describes the image and celebrates the end of the period of Iconoclasm.

empire had been drifting apart from as early as the fifth century. The political and military disintegration of much of Western Europe provided an important backdrop for this increasing sense of isolation. In addition, however, the main languages of communication, Greek and Latin, had become mutually unintelligible for most members of the population.

Doctrinal disagreements, such as the controversy over holy icons in the eighth and ninth centuries, provoked

further misunderstanding and distrust. During the period
of Iconoclasm, a succession of popes refused to accept the
Byzantine Church's rulings and provided a safe haven for
iconophile monks and bishops fleeing persecution. On this
occasion, the papacy was vindicated in its stance when
these policies were eventually declared unorthodox.

The filioque

In the late ninth century, another issue which might at
first glance appear insignificant began to cause controversy
between Roman popes and Byzantine patriarchates. This
was the issue of the *filioque*, a short clause meaning 'and
the Son', which some Western Churches had been adding
since as early as the sixth century to the section of the
Creed which describes the procession of the Holy Spirit.
The addition of this clause probably originated in Spain in
the sixth century; by the eighth and ninth most Frankish
churches were also reciting the Creed in this way. Although
popes had consistently opposed the official addition of the
filioque to the Creed, they did not take active steps to stamp
out its inclusion in Western Churches. Byzantine patriarchs,
beginning with Photios (858–67 and 878–86), attacked
the doctrine of 'the double procession', eventually even
excommunicating the pope at a local Constantinopolitan
synod.

Papal supremacy

The issue of authority also played a major part in the
disagreement between popes and patriarchs in this period.
One of the reasons that Photios entered into a debate with
Rome over the issue of the *filioque* was probably that the
pope had opposed his appointment as uncanonical. Pope
Nicholas I, an able and energetic leader of the Western
Church, felt that he should have the final say over the
choice of patriarchs in Constantinople. Photios, like many
Eastern patriarchs both before and after, upheld the
principle of five leaders of the universal Church, with the
pope as the first *among equals*. In other words, the pope, as

*'I believe in one
God, Father
Almighty,
Maker of
heaven and
earth and of all
things visible
and invisible…
and in the Holy
Spirit, the Lord,
the Giver of life,
who proceeds
from the Father,
who together
with the Father
and the Son is
worshipped and
glorified.'*

THE CREED IN ITS
ORIGINAL FORM AND
AS IT IS STILL
RECITED IN THE
ORTHODOX CHURCH

successor to the apostle Peter, should be recognized as first bishop in the Church, but to the Eastern bishops this did not imply supreme authority.

Mission

Another cause for increasing tension between East and West from the ninth century onwards was Christian mission. Since as early as the fifth century the Roman empire had been threatened by invasion as waves of Gothic, Slavic and Turkic peoples moved westwards and southwards into the civilized world. By the ninth century, both secular and ecclesiastical leaders had begun to explore methods of civilizing these people as an alternative to remaining in a permanent state of war. In the case of the Byzantines, diplomacy had long been used to pacify one enemy so that the army could concentrate its energy on combating another. In the 860s, during the patriarchate of Photios, the most

serious effort yet to convert neighbouring peoples such as the Slavs and the Bulgars to Christianity got underway. Unfortunately, the drive to convert these groups also led to rivalry with Latin missionaries who were working at this time in many of the same areas.

The Christian baptism of the Bulgarian khan, Boris, in 864 or 865.

Missions to the Slavs

In 863 two Greek brothers named Cyril and Methodios set out, at the invitation of Rastislav, its ruler, to the kingdom of Moravia, a Slavic state which was located roughly in the area of modern Czechoslovakia. Rastislav requested that the Christian missionaries from Byzantium bring scriptures and service books translated into Slavonic so that his people could understand what they were being taught. Cyril and Methodios immediately embarked on this task. Having been raised in Thessaloniki, a city which had been surrounded by Slavic immigrants from the sixth century onwards, the brothers were fluent in the language of this neighbouring culture. The dialect that they used for their translations of Christian texts was that of the Macedonian Slavs: this remains the liturgical language of all the Slavic churches to this day and is now called Old Church Slavonic. Unfortunately, the Greek mission to Moravia soon came into conflict with German evangelists

Basil II 'the Bulgar-Slayer' (976–1025)

In spite of their conversion to Christianity, the Bulgars continued to represent a military threat to Byzantium through the beginning of the 11th century. The tsar Samuel, who established a massive Bulgarian and Macedonian empire extending from the Adriatic to the Black Sea, exerted continuous pressure on the frontiers of Byzantium. However, in July 1014, after a carefully planned series of military campaigns against the Bulgars, Basil II succeeded in defeating Samuel's army by subtle tactics of pursuit and ambush. According to legend (historians now believe this story may have been embroidered by later chroniclers), the entire Bulgarian army, allegedly numbering 15,000, was blinded and sent back to their leader in groups of 100 men. Each group was led by a one-eyed man. When Samuel saw this gruesome procession approaching, he fell into a coma and died two days later (6 October 1014).

In this image of Basil II triumphing over his enemies, the emperor stands above the kneeling Bulgarian chiefs, while Christ hands down a crown, indicating his approval and sanction of Basil's conquests.

who were working in the same area. Cyril and Methodios appealed to the pope in Rome for help, which was granted, but the Germans ignored the papal decision and continued to obstruct the brothers' mission. Eventually, after Cyril and Methodios had died in 869 and 885 respectively, the Germans expelled their disciples from Moravia and eradicated all signs of their mission there.

Although the Orthodox mission to Moravia thus failed, the decision to translate Christian texts into Old Church Slavonic was immensely significant. Soon the Byzantines began to send evangelists to other neighbouring peoples, including the Bulgars, the Serbs and eventually the Rus'. The translations begun by Cyril and Methodios continued to be used in these areas and also to be expanded. Thus the Christian message was presented to these peoples in a way which they could understand and assimilate. The Bulgars, after vacillating for some time between the Latins and the Greeks, eventually placed themselves under the protection of the patriarchate in Constantinople. Boris, the khan of Bulgaria, was baptized in 864 or 865.

The Rus'

The earliest Greek reference to a northern people called the Rus' (ancestors of the Russian people) occurs in a sermon preached by the patriarch Photios, describing their attack on Constantinople in 860. The earliest Rus' were Scandinavians who migrated south and settled initially in the region around Novgorod. During the ninth and tenth centuries the Viking Rus' settled along the river routes of modern Russia and gradually merged with the native Slav population, eventually establishing a capital city in Kiev. With their periodic raids into Byzantine territory, the Rus' represented an increasing threat to the empire and it was not long before the tactics of diplomacy and mission were tried. A first attempt at evangelization in 864 failed, but steady Christian infiltration both from Byzantium and from the neighbouring Bulgarian state eventually had an effect. The Kievan princess Olga, who travelled to Constantinople

and witnessed for herself the splendours of the imperial
liturgy in Hagia Sophia, was baptized probably in 954 or 955.
Although her son Svyatoslav refused to follow her example,
her grandson Vladimir embraced Christianity in 988. This is
accepted in the Russian Orthodox Church today as the date
of its foundation: after being baptized himself, Vladimir set
out to Christianize the whole of his realm.

In addition to adopting the Byzantine Orthodox liturgy
and encouraging the growth of monasticism within his realm,
Vladimir and his followers seem to have taken the social
implications of Christ's teachings seriously. Tenth-century Kiev
represented a model of a true Christian state, with organized
social services and distributions of food to the poor. When
Vladimir introduced Byzantine law codes into Rus' society,
he made sure that the most severe punishments and abuses
were eliminated from them. Thus there was no death penalty
in Kievan Rus' and only rarely did rulers resort to corporal
punishment or torture. The story of Vladimir's two sons, Boris
and Gleb, also exemplifies the new Christian ethos of this
period. On Vladimir's death in 1015, the realm was divided
between these two sons and their brother, Svyatopolk. When
Svyatopolk illegally seized their principalities, Boris and Gleb
offered no resistance, choosing instead to die at his hands.

The conversion of the Rus'

The earliest written record of the Russian nation, called the
Primary Chronicle, was probably composed in the 12th century,
but drew on earlier sources. It describes how the ruler Vladimir
sent embassies to observe many different religions before
deciding which one to adopt. When the envoys returned, they
described their experience in Constantinople as follows: 'Then
we went on to Greece, and the Greeks led us to the edifices
where they worship their God, and we knew not whether
we were in heaven or on earth. For on earth there is no such
splendour or such beauty, and we are at a loss how to describe
it. We know only that God dwells there among men, and their
service is fairer than the ceremonies of other nations.'

Tension between the Roman papacy and the Eastern
patriarchates continued to grow in the course of the
10th and 11th centuries. Rival missions to the Slavs did
not help matters, especially as the differences between the
two religious traditions, minor though they were, seemed
significant in the context of the daily life of the Church. For
example, the Greek Church had always allowed priests to
marry, whereas the Latins enforced celibacy. The Orthodox
Churches used leavened bread in the eucharist, as opposed
to the Latins' unleavened wafers, and the rules of fasting
also differed in the two halves of Christendom. An even
more fundamental problem, as we saw above, was the issue
of papal primacy; while the Eastern Orthodox patriarchs
could accept that the pope wielded sole power in the whole
of the Western Church, they could not admit his authority
over their own affairs.

An official schism between East and West eventually
occurred in 1054. The dispute which led up to this rupture
seems trivial, even petty. Nevertheless, these events
should be seen against a background of political insecurity,
especially on the Byzantine side, which helps to explain
the hasty reactions that led to long-term separation. In
the course of the 11th century, the Normans had occupied
much of what had been Byzantine territory in Southern
Italy and proceeded to force the Greeks still living in
these areas to adopt Latin ecclesiastical customs. The
patriarch Kerularios of Constantinople, a strong-willed
and combative individual, refused to let this pass and
retaliated by imposing similar measures against all the
Latin churches in the imperial city and closing them when
they refused to comply. The pope sent three legates to
Constantinople, one of whom was the rigorous Cardinal
Humbert, a reformer within the Western Church in this
period. When communications broke down between
Kerularios and the Latin delegation, Humbert and his
colleagues left a Bull of Excommunication on the altar of
the Great Church of Hagia Sophia, in which they accused

Opposite page
**Icon of the
Russian princes
Boris and Gleb,
who were
declared
'passion-bearers'
by the Church
after their deaths
at the hands of
their brother,
Svyatopolk, in
1015.**

the Greeks of many breaches of discipline, including the
exclusion of the *filioque* from the Creed.

Mutual excommunications by Roman popes and
Constantinopolitan patriarchs had occurred several times
before; it is perhaps a historical accident that the Schism
of 1054 was not healed soon afterwards. As we have seen,
however, this event should be viewed against a background
of a mutual distrust which had been developing for several
centuries and which inhibited each side's desire for
reconciliation. The final seal of separation in any case was
provided by another major event in Christian history, namely
the four crusades which took place between 1095 and 1204.

The Crusades

A Byzantine emperor, Alexios I, was responsible for initiating
the Crusades. After a series of military reverses, beginning
with the disastrous battle of Manzikert in 1071, the Byzantine
empire stood in grave peril from the relentless advance of
the Seljuk Turks. Alexios, in desperation, turned to the West
for help. In March 1095, his envoys met Pope Urban II
at Piacenza and asked for military aid to save Eastern
Christendom from the threat of destruction and to free
the Holy Land, especially Jerusalem, from the infidels.
The First Crusade began with great success: Antioch was
captured from the Turks in 1098 and Jerusalem in 1099. The
Western crusaders immediately carved out principalities for
themselves and installed Latin patriarchs in both of these
cities. Although this did not perhaps constitute part of the
original bargain, the Greek and Latin populations in these
areas appear to have coexisted fairly harmoniously under the
new arrangements. The next three crusades, however, were
by no means so successful. Tension and distrust between
Greek and Latin leaders increased as the crusaders began to
experience military reverses at the hands of the Turks and
Arabs. Finally, the Fourth Crusade resulted in catastrophe for
the Greeks when, on the pretext of reinstating a dispossessed
Byzantine emperor, the Latins sacked Constantinople for
three days in April 1204. The Greeks viewed the destruction

and pillaging of Constantinople on this occasion as an act of treachery on the part of the Latins. It is fair to say that this event represents the real moment when the schism between East and West became final.

The period of Latin domination

After their capture of the capital city, the Latins ruled the various territories of the Byzantine empire, with the exception of a few small principalities that remained under Byzantine rule, for nearly 60 years. In general, this period of Latin occupation (1204–61) was peaceful as far as the two Churches were concerned. Greek Orthodox priests were allowed to continue their ministry in accordance with their Eastern traditions. However, there can be no doubt that the Roman papacy had as its long-term aim the restoration of unity between East and West. To achieve this goal the Latins hoped gradually to replace the Greek ecclesiastical hierarchy by Latin clergy and gradually to enforce the use of Western customs in the Church. None of these measures helped to overcome the Greeks' distrust and resentment towards their Latin overlords; when Michael VIII Palaiologos succeeded in recapturing Constantinople and ousting the Western leaders from most of the Byzantine territories, Orthodox Christians were jubilant.

'The crusaders brought not peace but a sword; and the sword was to sever Christendom.'

SIR STEVEN RUNCIMAN, *THE EASTERN SCHISM*, 1955

The final centuries

The restored Byzantine empire after 1261 covered only a fraction of the territory that it had once controlled. Confined to the Western half of Asia Minor, Constantinople and parts of what is now mainland Greece, the empire faced a hostile Seljuk Sultanate in the East and various European kingdoms in the West. One of the surprising aspects of this period of Byzantine history is that Orthodox faith and culture flourished as never before. This is the period when some of the greatest mosaic and frescoed wall paintings were created, when philosophical and mystical writings proliferated, and monasticism flourished again. It is possible that a sense of isolation and defensiveness promotes a stronger sense of cultural identity. More and more, Constantinople represented for Byzantine Christians the symbolic centre of their civilization. This city alone stood firm once again against the incursions of a hostile and aggressive world outside.

As Byzantine imperial power declined between 1261 and 1453, the Church, rather surprisingly, gained prestige and authority. This may be partly due to the fact that patriarchs played an important political role in this period, promoting culture, negotiating with the West and lending legitimacy to the newly formed state. Although imperial finances were

reduced, owing to the loss of taxable territories, private patrons funded many new monasteries in Constantinople and also in the Balkans and the Peloponnese.

The sense of isolation and frailty in the face of an ever-advancing Turkish enemy in these centuries led the Byzantines once again to seek reconciliation with their fellow Christians in the West. Even though the humiliation of 1204 and the years of Latin domination must have been fresh in his mind, the emperor Michael VIII Palaiologos sent delegates to the Council of Lyons in 1274. Although the official reunion with the West which was achieved at

A traditional iconographic type called the Deesis shows Christ, the Pantokrator ('All-Ruler'), flanked by the Virgin Mary and St John the Baptist in positions of obeisance. From the South Gallery, Hagia Sophia (created after 1261).

Mosaic panel of
Theodore
Metochites
(1316–21), the
founder of the
Chora Monastery
in Constantinople.
Metochites is
shown wearing a
tall headdress,
characteristic of
the costume
worn by wealthy
Byzantine citizens
in this period. He
is kneeling and
offering the
church which he
has dedicated to
Christ.

this council bore with it the promise of greater security,
both against the Turks in the East and aggressive Western
leaders such as Charles of Anjou, the Orthodox people at
home and their bishops vigorously rejected it.

By the early 15th century the situation in Byzantium
was desperate. A new clan of Turks, called the Ottomans, had
succeeded the Seljuks and conquered the whole of Asia Minor
and much of mainland Greece. By attending the Council
of Ferrara/Florence in 1438–39, the emperor John VIII
Palaiologos hoped to gain Western military aid in fighting
the Turks. In addition to the emperor, two important Greek
theologians attended the council: the unionist Bessarion
and the anti-unionist Mark, metropolitans of Nicea and
Ephesus, respectively. A number of issues were discussed at
this council, including the procession of the Holy Spirit, the
use of leavened or unleavened bread in the eucharist, the
existence of purgatory and the primacy of the pope. The
Orthodox delegation ended up capitulating on almost every
one, although Mark of Ephesus refused to add his signature
to the Decree of Union. Once again, the Greek delegation
met with opposition from the majority of Orthodox Christians
when they returned to Constantinople. When the imperial
city finally fell to the Turks in 1453, the quest for unity, along
with the agreements of this council, were abandoned for ever.
As the Byzantine Orthodox Church began to find its feet
under Ottoman domination, the prospect of reunion with
Latin Christendom no longer seemed relevant.

When studying the later history of Eastern Christendom,
it is worth asking who the Byzantines were and how they
viewed themselves. There can be no doubt that, just as in the
West, the Church represented the most important unifying
aspect of this culture. In spite of the catastrophic loss of their
imperial territories to the Turks and other hostile invaders,
Orthodox Christians in the late Byzantine period also could
view themselves as part of a larger commonwealth. The
neighbouring Slavic nations, including the Bulgars,
the Serbs and the Rus', shared with the Byzantines their
Orthodox beliefs and traditions. Thus, even after the fall
of Constantinople to the Ottomans in 1453, the Eastern
Orthodox Church maintained a sense of its own
independence and identity within a wider Christian world.

Portrait medal of
John VIII
Palaiologos.

CHAPTER 3

Church and State

T he conversion of Constantine I in 312 and the gradual Christianization of the empire throughout the fourth century brought about a number of significant changes in political ideology. For the first time the Christian Church found itself in a powerful position. The emperor, whose job was to defend the state and overcome his political rivals by force, must at the same time live a Christian life according to the example set by Jesus Christ. The need to explain and justify Constantine's new role as Christian emperor appears in the writings of Eusebius of Caesarea, bishop and advisor to the emperor. Eusebius wrote not only a lengthy *History of the Christian Church*, one of the earliest examples of this genre, but also a biography and several orations in praise of Constantine. It is in the latter works, in particular the *Oration on the Tricennalia*, or *Thirty Years' Rule*, of Constantine, that we see the full development of a new and creative ideology justifying the whole concept of a Christian empire.

Marble sculpture of Constantine I, from the Palace of the Curators, Rome.

Byzantine political ideology

Eusebius based his ideas on a tradition of divine kingship which originated in the Hellenistic period and became influential in the later Roman empire. He was able successfully to unite the pagan concept of kingship with a new, specifically Christian, philosophy. Monotheism, according to Eusebius, requires an autocracy: just as one all-powerful God in heaven rules over his subjects, so should one supreme emperor administer justice on earth. The earthly emperor is invested with power by his divine prototype. He is the image, or representative, of the divine Ruler in heaven. The Christian emperor thus embodies not only God's power, but also his benevolence and protection towards humankind. His job is to protect the empire from barbarians and unbelievers and to promote peace within both Church and empire.

The importance of Eusebius' political ideology for the future development of the Eastern Roman empire was incalculable. In their role as God's representatives on earth, Byzantine rulers henceforth wielded absolute power over their subjects. It is important to note that usurpers were not ruled out from assuming this privileged position. If a powerful general or other suitably qualified candidate succeeded in overthrowing a weak emperor and assuming power himself, this could be justified on the grounds that he had gained God's favour. All in all, Eusebius' vision of the ideal political system being based on one, autocratic ruler proved both flexible and lasting, even in the highly unstable political and economic circumstances which prevailed in later centuries.

The link between Church and State was thus much stronger in the Byzantine empire than is the case in most modern nations. A distinction between the two entities would have seemed meaningless to most Byzantines: they viewed the polity, which was made up of both secular and religious powers, as one organic whole. The emperor and his government could not operate without the sanction of the Church, nor could the bishops and patriarch serve their flocks without imperial support. As we shall see later in this chapter, however, this ideal picture of the harmonious relationship between the secular and religious spheres of life did not always prevail in later Byzantine history. On a number of occasions, emperors came into conflict with their highest bishops. It is at times such as these that churchmen expressed the view that emperors should not interfere in matters of the Church. In general, however, it remained the duty of the secular government to enforce and implement ecclesiastical policy. Indeed, Byzantines believed that the security of the empire depended on the successful enactment of God's kingdom here on earth.

The idea of the Christian Roman empire envisioned by

'The only begotten Word of God reigns, from ages which had no beginning, to infinite and endless ages, the partner of his Father's kingdom. And our emperor ever beloved by him, who derives the source of imperial authority from above, and is strong in the power of his sacred title, has controlled the empire of the world for a long period of years.'

EUSEBIUS OF CAESAREA, IN AN ORATION CELEBRATING 30 YEARS OF CONSTANTINE'S RULE, PROBABLY WRITTEN IN 336

Opposite page:
Manuscript
illustration of
Christ crowning
Michael VII
Doukas (1071–78)
and Maria of
Alania. This
image reveals the
Byzantine ideal of
divinely
sanctioned
kingship.

Eusebius and adhered to throughout the Byzantine period was thus a strictly hierarchical structure. At the top stood the emperor, God's representative on earth, who was responsible for maintaining harmony in his name both in Church and State. Michael II, writing to the Frankish ruler Louis the Pious in the early ninth century, speaks of having his power from God. Basil I, who like many Byzantine emperors crowned his own son as his successor, wrote, 'The crown which you receive at my hands comes from God.' Although in theory the legitimacy of emperors' reigns was validated by the people's (in other words, the senate's) and the army's acclaim, in accordance with the customs of the later Roman empire, in practice many later Byzantine emperors were crowned dynastically by their fathers. It was only by the mid-fifth century that the full ecclesiastical ceremony surrounding the coronation of an emperor developed; from the seventh century onwards it

Coronation

The formal acceptance of a Byzantine emperor was a complex event, made up of a number of different elements. The ceremonies also appear to have changed somewhat in the course of Byzantine history. The practice of raising the emperor on a shield and acclaiming him was borrowed from Germanic tradition and was first used for the emperor Julian in the fourth century. By the middle of the fifth century, parts of the ceremony were taking place in church, where the patriarch blessed and participated in the investiture of the imperial candidate. At this period, however, the patriarch's role was not yet seen as lending legitimacy to the emperor's rule. The coronation of Constans II in Hagia Sophia (641) represented the beginning of full-scale ceremonies in the Great Church, which became the practice thereafter. The patriarch would crown the emperor on the ambo, a raised platform in the centre of the church, while the congregation acclaimed him. The coronation ceremony would be followed by a *eucharistic liturgy*, thus fully integrating the secular and the religious spheres. A 10th-century text called the *Book of Ceremonies*, attributed to the emperor Constantine VII Porphyrogennetos, provides detailed accounts of the coronation procedures in this period. According to this source, empresses were crowned not in Hagia Sophia, but in a square called the Augusteion, or in a smaller church.

became customary for the ceremony to be performed in the Great Church, Hagia Sophia.

The role of the emperor

When Eusebius writes that the emperor is God's representative on earth, or that he is a living icon of Christ, he of course does not mean that the emperor himself is

divine. Eusebius' picture of the emperor and state is in fact based on a Platonic view of the world. The emperor represents an image or reflection of divine majesty, but he himself remains firmly in the realm of the created world. It is also important to note that Byzantine emperors did not represent priest-kings such as one would find in a true religious state. The emperor was technically a layman in the Church. It is true that he played an important role in looking after the welfare of the Church, calling church councils and implementing their decisions. He also took part on a daily basis in elaborate religious ceremonies which took place both in the palace and in the main churches of the capital city. Byzantine emperors never, however, fulfilled a priestly role in these liturgies. Although they were allowed to enter the inner sanctuary of the Great Church and to receive communion with the clergy, emperors could not themselves administer the sacraments.

Byzantine emperors also played an important role in helping to resolve the doctrinal controversies which broke out in the Church from the fourth century onwards. Thus we see

A mosaic panel depicting the sixth-century emperor Justinian serving in liturgical celebrations. From San Vitale, Ravenna, Italy.

Constantine I summoning the first universal, or 'ecumenical', council in 325. The fact that he presided over the council and regarded himself responsible for enforcing its decisions represents a highly significant precedent for the religious administration of the Byzantine Church in subsequent centuries. Ecumenical councils, of which the Byzantines recognized seven, beginning and ending in the small town of Nicea (325 and 787) near Constantinople, became the accepted method for discussing and defining religious doctrine in response to opposing, or 'heretical', views.

The ecumenical patriarch

After the emperor, the main leader of the Church in the Byzantine empire was the ecumenical patriarch. The term 'ecumenical' comes from the Greek word *oikoumene*, meaning the inhabited world. The title thus conveys the importance of the Patriarch of Constantinople within the empire as a whole. By the end of the sixth century, five major sees within the Roman world had been officially designated 'patriarchates' and given an order of precedence. These were the dioceses of Rome, Constantinople, Alexandria, Antioch and Jerusalem. Constantinople in fact had the least claim to apostolic foundation, but Theodosius I made sure at the Council of Constantinople in 381 that it should nevertheless be placed after Rome in power and dignity.

Soon political and military developments began to influence the shape and organization of Christendom as a whole. After the Near East and North Africa fell to Islam in the mid-seventh century, the patriarchates of Alexandria, Antioch and Jerusalem ceased to wield any significant influence in the affairs of the Byzantine and Western Churches. The ecumenical patriarch in Constantinople increasingly came to represent the leader of the Eastern Christian Church. As the emperor's right-hand man in all matters of ecclesiastical jurisdiction, the Patriarch of Constantinople ideally operated in a close, symbiotic relationship with the secular head of the empire. It certainly made life easier for both men if they could agree

'The constitution consists, like the human person, of parts and members... and of these the greatest and most necessary are the emperor and the patriarch. Thus the peace and felicity of subjects, in body and soul, depends on the agreement and concord of the kingship and the priesthood in all things.'

THE *EPANAGOGE AUCTA*, A LEGAL HANDBOOK PROBABLY COMPILED IN CONSTANTINOPLE SOON AFTER 912 on important issues of doctrine and church practice. Occasionally in the course of Byzantine history, however, we see the relationship between an emperor and his ecumenical patriarch becoming strained or even breaking down. In order to set the theoretical model of the Byzantine Church, which has so far been set out into perspective, it might be useful to look at a few examples of emperors and patriarchs in conflict.

Tension between emperors and ecumenical patriarchs

As the subsequent events of Byzantine history showed, tension between emperors and their ecumenical patriarchs could develop, thus dividing the body politic and causing great strain within both Church and State. The period of Iconoclasm, which lasted from the early eighth to the mid-ninth century, provides the background for one such rift. When the emperor Leo III decided to introduce Iconoclasm as an imperial policy, Patriarch Germanos I was strongly opposed to the idea. Christian imagery, he argued, was strongly established in the Church since apostolic times; the charge of idolatry could only be levelled at ancient Jews, pagans or barbarians who had not accepted the truth of Christian revelation. It is still not known how seriously Leo III imposed Iconoclasm as an imperial policy. It is likely that severe persecution of the defenders of holy icons only began under his son, Constantine V. Nevertheless, Germanos felt morally incapable of remaining in the office of ecumenical patriarch. In 730 he resigned and went to live on his private estate near Constantinople, where he died three years later.

After a brief period between 787 and 815 when icons were formally reinstated in the Church, the first iconoclast emperor's namesake, Leo V, decided to reintroduce the ban against images. On this occasion, the emperor tried to justify his policies by establishing a small committee of clerics to compile arguments against the use of icons in the Church, backed up with passages supporting this position taken from scripture and the writings of the Church Fathers. The incumbent ecumenical patriarch, Nikephoros, however, refused to have anything to do with this commission. Gathering together a group of supporters just before Christmas in 815, he persuaded them formally to reject the emperor's iconoclast compilation. Leo then summoned him to the palace where Nikephoros continued to defend his position, although strong measures of intimidation were employed. Eventually, after several months in which the patriarch remained virtually under house arrest, he resigned from his office and was exiled on the Asian side of the Bosphorus. Although Nikephoros was by this time an old and sick man, he spent his remaining years writing voluminous treatises in which he refuted Iconoclasm and developed further the theological defence of Christian imagery.

It is clear from contemporary writings that some of the defenders of icons were aware of the political dimensions of the controversy. John of Damascus, for example, in one of the three treatises which he wrote in defence of icons, states: 'What right have emperors to style themselves lawgivers in the Church?' Iconoclasm represented one of a few instances in the Byzantine Church when a series of emperors enacted religious policies which, although supported by many bishops at the time, were later declared heretical. Thus while their interference in Church affairs was generally tolerated and even expected by Christians, Orthodox rulers remained laymen and could frequently make catastrophic mistakes. The conceptual difference between Church and State expressed in a few outspoken texts contrasts strikingly with the more usual contemporary depictions of a deeply symbiotic relationship between the two bodies.

Church discipline as a source of tension

Matters of discipline rather than doctrine could also frequently cause tension between emperors and patriarchs. In 795 the emperor Constantine VI divorced his wife and remarried. Byzantine canon law does not completely ban these actions if there are mitigating circumstances, but Tarasios, the current patriarch, was widely condemned by

'Your responsibility, Emperor, is with affairs of the state and military matters. Give your mind to these and leave the Church to its pastors and teachers.'

THEODORE OF STUDIOS, NINTH-CENTURY MONK AND DEFENDER OF ICONS his colleagues for allowing Constantine VI's remarriage. A highly vocal monastic party, led by Abbot Plato of Saccudion and his nephew Theodore of Studios, called for the excommunication of the priest, Joseph, who had presided over it. The resulting controversy, called the 'moechian' (adultery) affair, rumbled on for a decade or so, with subsequent patriarchs being obliged to take one side or the other. Nikephoros followed the example of Tarasios in overlooking the emperor's transgression; furthermore, he reinstated Joseph in 809, thereby infuriating the Studite monks. It is clear that this early-ninth-century patriarch was diplomatic in his response to imperial policy. He was prepared to give way on a matter of discipline, exercising the principle of compromise, while standing firm on the issue of icons which he regarded as fundamental to Orthodox doctrine. Many subsequent examples of tension between Byzantine emperors and their patriarchs also illustrate the fact that this relationship was not uniformly harmonious. It is noticeable that after the period of Iconoclasm, it was not usually doctrinal issues which divided the secular from the ecclesiastical realms.

Church politics after 1204

One of the most important and lasting rifts between Church and State took place after the period of Latin occupation which followed the Fourth Crusade and the sack of Constantinople in 1204. Under the pretext of driving the Latins out of Byzantine territories, Michael VIII usurped the throne which belonged rightfully to Theodore II, a member of the Lascarid dynasty, and was crowned in Hagia Sophia on 15 August 1261. The patriarch Arsenios, who remained loyal to the Lascarids, excommunicated Michael both because of his usurpation and because five months later he blinded the rightful heir and designated his own son Andronikos as his successor. After several years of tension, Arsenios was deposed from his patriarchal seat in 1264 and exiled to the island of Proconnesus. On this occasion the deposition of the patriarch caused a schism

Condemnation of Leo VI for divorce and remarriage

In the early 10th century, the issue of the emperor Leo VI's
fourth marriage caused controversy. Leo, who ruled between
886 and 912, became worried that he had no male heir.
When his first wife, Theophano, died in 897, the emperor took
a second wife, who also died without issue in 899. According
to canon law, two imperial marriages could be tolerated, but
any further unions were strictly prohibited. Leo was undeterred
by this ruling. He married again, and when this wife died in
901, in connection with childbirth, he took a mistress who
finally provided him with a son, the future Constantine VII. The
current patriarch, Nicholas I Mystikos, although accepting the
illegitimate heir of this union, refused to forgive the emperor
for his immoral behaviour. He prohibited Leo VI from entering
the Great Church, actually turning him back from its doors at
Christmas and Epiphany 906–907. The emperor resorted to
deposing the patriarch and seeking pardon from the Roman
pope. He also secretly married his consort, probably around
the time of Easter 906. After his death in 912, however, the
patriarch Nicholas was reinstated and thus vindicated for his
firm stance in opposition to the emperor.

within the Church which lasted for most of the rest of
Michael VIII's reign. The followers of Arsenios refused to
recognize the patriarchs who replaced him; that many of
them were monks, described as 'zealots' and 'extremists' by
those who opposed them, reinforces the impression that it
was frequently the monastic elements in the Church who
took the lead in moral disputes of this kind.

Church and State thus did not represent one entity
in the Eastern Roman empire. They supported each other,
depending on an active, symbiotic relationship, but it
is fair to say that their values and goals were not always
closely matched. Bishops, along with the metropolitans and
patriarchs who led them, usually backed the political aims of
emperors, but when matters of church discipline or doctrine
were breached, they could oppose their secular rulers. The

A gold coin
stamped with an
image of the
emperor John II
Komnenos being
blessed by Mary,
the Mother of
God.

emperor in turn regarded it as his duty to uphold the decisions of ecclesiastical councils and to maintain stability and harmony within society. If he failed to carry out these functions responsibly he risked incurring the disapproval not only of priests and bishops, but also of an increasingly powerful monastic lobby.

In the whole course of Byzantine history, it is possible to find many instances in which the secular and ecclesiastical realms became divided. On the other hand, the checks and balances of this system ensured that in most cases stability could be restored, sometimes at the expense of a patriarch's career. In spite of the questions concerning the right of an emperor to interfere in the affairs of the Church posed by John of Damascus and Theodore of Studios at the beginning of the ninth century, the Eusebian vision of the emperor as 'God's friend, acting as interpreter to the Word of God' prevailed until 1453, when there was no longer an Orthodox emperor to reign over the Eastern Christian empire.

Service to the Community

The medieval Church, in both East and West, was hierarchical in its organization. The clergy was organized into three major orders: bishops, priests or presbyters, and deacons. Beneath this threefold structure were the minor orders, including subdeacons, readers and all the officials who looked after church buildings or ministered to the public. Each office had its own ceremony of ordination, a sacred ritual which conferred both the blessing of the Holy Spirit and the approval of the Church as a whole. Bishops, at the top of the hierarchy, in theory represented the highest source of authority within the Christian Church. They were led in their decisions, however, by five bishops who presided over the most influential sees in the Roman world. In the sixth century, these five bishops came to be called patriarchs or, in the cases of Rome and Alexandria, popes. The five apostolic sees, or patriarchates, were, in order of their importance: Rome, Constantinople, Alexandria, Antioch and Jerusalem.

'For as in one body, we have many members, and not all the members have the same function, so we, who are many, are one body in Christ, and individually we are members one of another'

ROMANS 12:4–5

The threefold structure

Such a strictly hierarchical structure had not, of course, existed in the earliest Christian Church. During the first and second centuries, texts of the New Testament and the Apostolic Fathers testify to the leadership of self-appointed 'prophets', teachers and even distinguished women in the ministry of the early Church. Charismatic leadership had a place in the Church in this period, as Paul testifies in 1 Corinthians 12:28: 'And God has appointed in the church first apostles, second prophets, third teachers; then deeds of power, then gifts of healing, forms of assistance, forms of leadership, various kinds of tongues.' It is clear even in this passage, however, that Paul envisaged an order of precedence with regard to these various offices. The apostles came first; it was their direct successors, or the men whom they approved and blessed, who in the course of the second century became the leaders, or bishops, of the Church.

Problems and challenges of many kinds assailed the Church in the first few centuries: schism within individual communities, issues of authority and differences over doctrine or discipline represent only a few of the internal problems facing early Christian communities. Persecution by various Roman emperors probably strengthened rather than divided the Church, but it also eliminated some of its most talented leaders. In the course of the second century, various groups collectively called the Gnostics emerged and challenged both the teachings and leadership of the mainstream Church. In response to this threat, Irenaeus of Lyons, a bishop who was active in the 170s, wrote treatises in which he addressed the issue of authority. Irenaeus supported the principle of 'apostolic succession', the idea that Christian bishops follow a direct line of succession from the first apostles. Two main principles emerge from this analysis: first, bishops of the orthodox or right-believing Church possess the authority conferred on them by their apostolic succession; and second, they are unified and consistent in their teaching of the Christian faith.

After the adoption of Christianity as the state religion throughout the Roman empire by Constantine and his successors, bishops continued to be ordained and to function in accordance with this tradition. The organization of episcopal sees followed closely the patterns of secular government. Every major city would have its bishop and, following the administrative division of the empire, provincial capitals would be home to a superior bishop, or metropolitan. Most important doctrinal or disciplinary decisions had to be discussed in councils, at which all bishops had an equal vote. When an issue was judged to be of overwhelming importance within the Church, an ecumenical or 'universal' council would be called. In theory, representatives (these could be any bishops) of all five patriarchates were expected to attend the ecumenical councils in order to render their decisions valid. In practice, owing to the increasingly precarious military position of the Byzantine empire in the fifth to the eighth centuries, bishops from Rome and from the three Near-Eastern patriarchates were frequently absent at the later ecumenical councils.

The five patriarchs each held supreme authority within their areas of jurisdiction. The Bishop of Rome, or pope, as he came to be called, increasingly was sole leader of the whole of the Western Church. In the Eastern Roman empire, it was the Patriarch of Constantinople, called the 'ecumenical' patriarch, who came to dominate church politics, especially after the Eastern territories including Palestine, Syria, Egypt and North Africa were conquered by the Muslims in the course of the seventh century. In addition to crowning the emperor and carrying out with him the numerous liturgical ceremonies which formed an important part of the duties of each, the ecumenical patriarch helped to enforce ecclesiastical policies throughout the empire. Patriarchs were elected by all the metropolitans who met for this purpose in a synod at Constantinople. They would present the names of three candidates to the emperor. He could choose one of these, but if none was acceptable, the emperor had the right to appoint a patriarch of his own choice, subject to the metropolitans' approval.

Under the patriarchs came the bishops, led in each province by their metropolitans. Bishops and metropolitans were concerned with all aspects of religious life and worship. They looked after not only churches and monasteries but all other ecclesiastical properties, including charitable foundations and hospitals. In their administrative roles, bishops were responsible for the smooth running of affairs within their dioceses, as well as for preserving harmony within the universal Church. As ordained priests of God, they also administered the sacraments and acted as teachers of

Previous page:
A bishop serving
a liturgy, as
depicted in the
11th-century
Church of
St Sophia, Ohrid,
Macedonia.

the faith. Many sermons delivered by Byzantine bishops of all periods survive. Although some of these are written in a highly rhetorical and poetic style and have obviously been carefully edited after their first delivery, others, mostly dating from the fourth to the sixth centuries, provide instructive explanations of scriptural readings. We know much less about Byzantine bishops' pastoral work among their flocks: sometimes details are recorded in their biographies, letters or in ecclesiastical histories, but it is often difficult to learn much about their relations with parishioners on the basis of their own preaching. A prerequisite for ordination to the episcopate was monastic status: thus, all bishops were unmarried and ideally celibate. This tradition reflects the idea that bishops were chosen originally from the ranks of holy men or ascetics who had renounced the world and chosen a solitary way of life.

The second order of priests or presbyters (the terms eventually became interchangeable) had, in the early Church, served to assist the bishop in his administrative and teaching roles. By the fourth century, resident priests were being put in charge of parishes and were performing the sacramental rites. Priests were also allowed to preach, although their sermons always followed that of the bishop, if he happened to be present. Unlike bishops, priests in the Byzantine Church were allowed to marry. This later became a point of contention with the West, where celibacy had become the rule for priests as well as bishops. The image of the humble village priest, often employed in another profession, such as farming or teaching, and supporting a family, held true in the Byzantine provinces as it does in some outlying districts of Greece and other Orthodox countries today. The advantage of matrimony among the lower clergy was that it kept priests closely involved in their communities and aware of the joys and difficulties of married and family life.

The duties of the deacon and the deaconess were mostly pastoral. As the title suggests in Greek, deacons were expected primarily to assist priests and bishops in their duties. They helped with baptisms, served at the celebration and administration of the eucharist in the Divine Liturgy, performed administrative tasks and sometimes acted as bishops' secretaries. In spite of the fact that they occupied one of the lower ranks of the Church hierarchy, deacons represented an essential order within the clergy, carrying out many important functions. Female deacons, or deaconesses, were ordained in the Church from a very early period. The initial reason for ordaining women to this office seems to have been their assistance at the baptisms of women. Since baptism took place by full immersion in this period and many of the converts to Christianity were adult women, it was deemed improper and distracting for male clergy to preside at their initiation into the Church. The office of deaconess survived until as late as the 11th century in the Byzantine Church, even though the number of adult baptisms soon declined; in the West, the female diaconate seems to have died out much earlier.

Although the Byzantine Orthodox Church was hierarchical, it remained true to its apostolic origins in considering the laity as the foundation of the Church: 'a royal priesthood, a holy nation' (1 Peter 2:9). Unfortunately we hear little from ordinary laypeople of the Byzantine period, since they did not usually write theological discourses, sermons or religious texts. Indeed, it has been estimated that only a tiny

Church rules

A collection of rules for the Church called the *Apostolic Constitutions*, probably dating from the late fourth century and of Syrian provenance, contains valuable information about the three orders of clergy and their functions in the Church in this period. For example, the appropriate qualities of a bishop are listed as follows: 'Let him therefore be sober, prudent, decent, firm, stable, not given to wine; no striker, but gentle; not a brawler, not covetous.' The passage goes on to state that the bishop may be married, but that he should have had no more than one wife. It later became the custom for bishops to be chosen from the monastic profession and thus to be celibate. The *Apostolic Constitutions* also provide rules for the correct conduct of laymen and laywomen, giving advice on clothing, married life, social conduct and many other topics.

'If we take seriously the bond between God and his Church, then we must inevitably think of the Church as one, even as God is one: there is only one Christ, and so there can be only one body of Christ. Nor is this unity merely ideal and invisible; Orthodox theology refuses to separate the "invisible" and the "visible Church", and therefore it refuses to say that the Church is invisibly one but visibly divided.'

TIMOTHY WARE, *THE ORTHODOX CHURCH*, 1993

percentage of the Byzantine population was literate, even to the extent of reading simple Bible passages. On the other hand, the wealth of surviving biographies of saints and collections of miracle stories provide some information about the beliefs and conduct of ordinary Orthodox Christians. Some of these narratives suggest that lay Byzantine Christians attended church especially when they sought divine protection or help. A familiar theme, for example, is that of the barren mother who seeks God's help in conceiving a child. The mother of a ninth-century Palestinian saint called Michael the Synkellos spent much time in church praying for a child before she became pregnant with Michael. Brief references such as these, even though they may represent conventional set pieces in the biographies of saints, provide precious information about the customs and piety of ordinary Byzantine people.

Although the Church hierarchy was loosely ordered in the early Christian period, it had become extremely well defined by the middle and later periods of Byzantine history. A strong sense of order, called *taxis*, prevailed. Lists of precedence, called the *Notitiae Episcopatum*, were drawn up and revised in successive centuries: these set out official lists of bishoprics and determined the order in which signatures would appear in the acts of Church councils. As we have seen, the ecumenical patriarch wielded ultimate authority in the Byzantine Church, especially as the Eastern, or 'Oriental', patriarchates of Alexandria, Antioch and Jerusalem came under Muslim rule. Beneath him, the bishops, led by their metropolitans, reached important decisions concerning church doctrine or discipline in councils. In spite of this hierarchy, however, it is important to realize that Orthodox Byzantines continued to think of their Church as one, unified body. This communion consisted not only of all ordained clergy and the laity here on earth, but also of God and his heavenly kingdom.

Canon law
Besides making decisions about Christian doctrine, ecumenical councils drew up rules, or canons, dealing with

organizational and disciplinary matters. Canons could also be
established in smaller, local synods and added to the growing
list of ecclesiastical laws. The canons of the Church are thus
contained in the Acts or Definitions of the various councils.
In the later period of Byzantine history, they were arranged
into collections and provided with commentaries. The vast
number of canons, established as they were over a number
of centuries and in response to very different circumstances,
inevitably repeat and even at times contradict each other.
These canons do not possess the same authority as the
formal definitions of doctrine which emerged from the
ecumenical councils. They deal with earthly life, whereas
doctrine is concerned with eternal truths. Nevertheless, the
canons did provide guidelines for the daily administration of
the Byzantine Church and for its response to controversy
over issues such as morality, ethics and discipline.

Emperors also frequently enacted laws on ecclesiastical
matters; here again it is clear that no sharp distinction
between Church and State existed for the Byzantines.
Secular rulers were closely involved with the Church in
dealing with matters of heresy and could attend the synod
in Constantinople where trials of this kind took place. Many
emperors also legislated on matters of church discipline: a
good example of this can be found in the 'new decrees', or
Novels, of the sixth-century emperor Justinian. The late-
ninth and tenth-century emperors, Leo VI and Nikephoros
II, issued laws concerning the foundation and maintenance
of monastic properties or regulating Christian marriage.
Sometimes bishops opposed emperors' ecclesiastical
legislation, but more often it was accepted as a legitimate
part of the imperial prerogative.

Bishops were responsible for dealing with breaches of
canon law and church discipline within their own dioceses.
In effect, they acted as judges within their own courts. The
bishop might also receive appeals from the laity in matters
of discipline or morality. In Constantinople, the synod of
bishops, led by the patriarch, would handle serious cases of
heresy or discipline in the ranks of the higher clergy, as we

saw above. Punishment for breaches of ecclesiastical law
usually could consist in temporary exclusion from the
Church or even excommunication. If members of the
clergy were accused of misconduct they might be defrocked,
relegated to a monastery or excommunicated. In the most
serious cases of all, when penalties of exile or death were
recommended, the convicts were handed over to the
secular authority for punishment.

It is thus clear that the laws and courts of the Byzantine
Church played a significant role in the jurisdiction of the
empire. At the same time, however, the application of canon
law in Byzantium possessed in all periods a certain willingness
to take into account individual circumstances. This feature of
Orthodox jurisdiction is technically known as 'economy', or
oikonomia, which may be roughly translated as 'the working
out of God's Law on earth'. Thus, divorce and remarriage,
although officially condemned, were frequently permitted
for ordinary civilians as well as for emperors. This willingness
to consider the special background of each petitioner when
judging his or her case preserved the Byzantine Church from
the more rigid approach to ecclesiastical law which sometimes
prevailed in the West.

Education and higher learning
Education in the Byzantine empire was effectively divided
into two streams from the earliest period onwards. Christian
learning was understood as knowledge of scripture, either
through reading or memorization of the sacred texts of the
Old and New Testaments. On the other hand, from as early
as the second century, Christian writers had employed the
language and conceptual frameworks of the pagan, classical
tradition. This was justified by the idea that Christian
teaching must be expressed eloquently and persuasively for
its mission to become truly universal. In most periods of
Byzantine history, only a small elite, mostly consisting of
professional people, civil servants and churchmen, received
an advanced education in pagan rhetoric and philosophy.
Nevertheless, these individuals wielded power in society;

their ability to understand and express themselves in the
archaic, classicizing language would have represented a
badge of membership to the upper classes.

Illiteracy was less widespread in the Byzantine empire
than in the medieval West, but even so it is likely that a high
proportion of citizens were unable to read or write. Records
suggest that even some monastic superiors were unable to
sign their names to documents; one of Justinian's laws in
the sixth century prohibits an illiterate person being elected
bishop. It is important to realize, however, that the term
'illiteracy' is in some ways inappropriate for a civilization
that used oral communication to a much greater degree than
do most modern societies. Many Christians who could not
read or write could nevertheless understand the scriptural
readings in church, or even absorb the meaning of a highly
rhetorical sermon. Byzantine sources also stress the
importance of images in this largely illiterate culture. During
the period of Iconoclasm, in the eighth and ninth centuries,
pictorial representations of scenes from the life of Christ
were defended on the grounds that they served an
educational purpose in the Church.

Most monasteries would have run a small school, but
unlike those in the West, these taught mostly at a primary
level. It was sufficient for a monk to be able to read the Bible
or to recite the Psalms from memory. Higher education, on
the other hand, underwent many vicissitudes in the course
of Byzantine history. Justinian closed down the Academy
of Athens in 529 on the grounds that it taught only pagan,
classical culture, and the secular university in Constantinople
seems to have closed by about the seventh century. Pagan,
secular education was provided after this by private teachers,
some of whom travelled about from city to city. In the course
of the ninth century, a revival of higher education began
to take place. A school was established in a part of the
palace called the Magnaura, where grammar, philosophy,
mathematics and astronomy were taught. In the early
12th century, a patriarchal school was established, which
concentrated on scriptural studies. Later in the same century

the field of rhetoric was added to this curriculum. Judging by the writings of bishops and patriarchs throughout the Byzantine period, classical and scriptural literary training represented necessary prerequisites for ordination to important sees.

Philanthropy and social activities

The virtue of love for humankind, or philanthropy, is not an invention of the Christian Church. In classical Greece and pagan Rome, philanthropy was regarded as an essential attribute of civilized human beings. On an individual level it implied a willingness to help one's fellow humans in any way possible, whereas collectively it meant the provisions made by society for its weaker members, especially the sick, the aged, widows and orphans. In a book on Byzantine philanthropy, the historian Demetrios J. Constantelos suggests a fundamental distinction between pagan and Christian views of philanthropy. Whereas pagans were motivated to do good because of shared social values, concern for their fellow citizens, or in some cases, in order to gain honour and approbation from the rest of society, Christians, while sharing many of these impulses,

Christian charity

Some Byzantine saints were remembered and praised for their example of active social service. A seventh-century patriarch called John the Almsgiver established a number of charitable institutions in the Egyptian city of Alexandria and its environs. His biographer records his activities in the following passage:

Once when a severe famine was oppressing the city and the holy man's stewards were, as usual, ceaselessly distributing money or some small gift to the needy, some destitute women overcome with hunger and but lately risen from child-bed were obliged to hasten to receive help from the distributors while they were still in the grip of abdominal pains, deadly pale, and suffering grievously; when the wondrous man was told of this, he built seven lying-in hospitals in different parts of the city, ordered 40 beds to be kept ready in each and arranged that every woman should rest quietly in these for seven full days after her confinement and then receive the third of a nomisma and go home.

LEONTIOS OF NEAPOLIS, *LIFE OF ST JOHN THE ALMSGIVER*

possessed a further reason for practising benevolence. This was the idea that the philanthropist is serving God by assisting other human beings. Christians who do good works are also imitating Christ since 'the Son of man came not to be served but to serve, and to give his life a ransom for many'(Matthew 20:28; Mark 10:45).

Ever since the coming of Christ, his followers had attempted to carry out his injunction to serve others, especially the weakest and poorest members of society. Early Christians organized common meals and raised money for the care of the poor, the widows and the orphans. They also extended their mission to prisoners and travellers, providing food, accommodation and other material assistance to anyone in need. When Constantine and his successors adopted Christianity as the official religion of the Roman empire, such philanthropic work could be carried out on a larger and more organized scale. Canon 70 of the Council of Nicea (325) decrees that hospitals should be erected in every city of the empire. The Council of Chalcedon (451) provides evidence of other Christian foundations in its injunction that hostels for travellers, poorhouses and orphanages should be well administered. It is clear from these and other texts that the Church did not forget its traditional commitment to service after gaining imperial backing in the early fourth century.

It is also clear that philanthropy and social service remained important values in Byzantine society throughout its later history. The motivation to imitate Christ and to serve God through service to the community provided the basis not only for individual donations, but also for the work undertaken by both Church and State. It is important to reiterate here, as in other areas covered in this book, that a strong distinction between individual Christians, the Church and the State did not exist in this society. The Byzantine Church was an all-embracing organism; thus all of these categories were involved in funding charitable institutions throughout Byzantine history. The Church probably represented the most important source for endowments;

as a result, many hostels and poorhouses were located next to churches or monasteries and were administered by their officers.

Charitable institutions

A number of different forms of institution were founded throughout the Byzantine period to serve the weak or poorer members of society. Perhaps one of the most loosely organized of these, which must have developed directly out of early Christian fellowships of service, was the confraternity or *diakonia* (not to be confused with the ordained diaconate). The confraternity was a voluntary organization made up of both lay and clerical members of the Church. Many dioceses, local churches and monasteries supported such organizations. The members of the confraternity were in charge of distributing charity to the community in the form of money or food, ministering to the sick and the poor, and helping any travellers who might visit the parish or diocese.

Other charitable institutions founded throughout the major cities of the empire included hospices, hospitals, orphanages, old peoples' homes and hostels for travellers and pilgrims. Occasionally the sources tell us of imperial foundations, which reflect the obligation felt by Byzantine rulers to display the qualities of benevolence and philanthropy. We hear, for example, of the fourth-century empress Flacilla, who was especially compassionate towards lepers. In the sixth century, the historian Procopius writes that the empress Theodora established a monastery and attached hostel intended for the rescue and rehabilitation of prostitutes. Basil I, the founder of the Macedonian dynasty in the late ninth century, erected more than 100 foundations for the poor, including hospitals, hostels and other institutions, both in Constantinople and in the provinces. The individual dioceses of the Church also funded philanthropic institutions throughout the empire. The money to pay for these foundations came from imperial grants, revenues from land and property, and voluntary donations from individuals. A mandatory system of tithes was instituted only fairly late in Byzantine history.

In the later centuries, that is, from the 10th century onwards, monasteries increasingly took on the responsibility of establishing and maintaining hospitals and other philanthropic institutions. Hospitals were usually built next to the church, or *katholikon*, of the monastery, while hospices for the aged and hostels for travellers were usually located outside the monastery walls. Although professional doctors might be appointed to provide specialized care. the monks would care for the sick and the needy as part of their monastic duties. The monastery of the Pantokrator, which was founded in 1136 by the emperor John II Komnenos and his wife Irene and which still stands as a broken shell in the middle of modern Istanbul, housed a large and complex hospital. Fortunately, we know a great deal about the layout and administration of this hospital because the founding charter, or *Typikon*, still survives. According to this document, the Pantokrator hospital possessed five clinics, each of which had about 10 or 12 beds. These wards were assigned to different groups, including patients suffering from illnesses of the eyes and the intestines, women (the *Typikon* does not specify whether these were gynaecological or maternity cases), emergency and general cases. In this hospital of 61 beds there were 35 doctors, some of whom may even have been female.

The Pantokrator monastery and hospital (12th century) which still stands in Istanbul.

Byzantine Christians, from the emperor downwards, thus believed collectively in the importance of philanthropy and social service. The institutional Church and monasteries came increasingly to administer the larger charitable foundations, but it should not be forgotten that the funding for these institutions came ultimately from individual donors, whether imperial or otherwise. The importance of the role played by emperors and empresses in the support of charitable organizations cannot be overemphasized. The image of the Christian Roman emperor, which was expressed so eloquently by Eusebius in the fourth century, included the idea that as the representative of God on earth the Byzantine ruler embodies the virtues of benevolence and mercy. Byzantines thus expected their emperors to practise philanthropy. Individual Christians could also imitate their ruler's example and donate money for the service of the poor. Imitation of Christ and a genuine desire to act ethically probably represented one aspect of their motivation; the hope of divine reward and eternal salvation may have been the other.

The Byzantine system of social welfare inevitably looks haphazard to the modern eye. The extent and availability of social services would have varied according to the district in which one lived, nor did the weaker members of society possess any 'right' to claim help or treatment. Furthermore, it could be argued that by offering charity to the poor, Byzantines did nothing to improve their situation or enable them to help themselves. Nevertheless, it is undeniable that charitable institutions of all kinds provided relief to many underprivileged members of society in the larger cities of Byzantium. The fact that philanthropy remained such a prized ideal among all wealthy citizens, including the emperor, meant that the system continued to work effectively through the final years of Byzantine sovereignty. Even just after the fall of Constantinople to the Turks in 1453, an eye witness lamented that the city would no longer be able to maintain its many philanthropic institutions.

The Solitary Ideal

One of the greatest legacies of the Byzantine Orthodox Church to Christianity is its spiritual tradition. This tradition has at its core the lives and teachings of the 'Desert Fathers and Mothers' – the early Christian men and women who left the temptations and distractions of everyday life for a life of solitude. These individuals literally entered the deserted places surrounding the urban centres of the later Roman empire. Although monasticism was originally thought to have begun in Egypt, we now know that it developed independently in various regions around the Mediterranean basin, attracting both men and women who felt the call to retire from the world. The object of this life was primarily to seek closeness to God without distraction from material or personal attachments. It is clear from the texts written both by and about monks in every period that they were also conscious of imitating Christ, who demonstrated in his own life complete self-sacrifice and devotion to God the Father.

Monasticism in subsequent centuries took many forms, but the solitary and mystical ideal remained at its heart. Thus we find monks in communal, or coenobitic, monasteries all over the Byzantine empire, reading the *Lives* and *Sayings* of the early Desert Fathers for inspiration and spiritual advancement. Although the completely solitary life was later not permitted for most monks and nuns, abbots might allow those few individuals who demonstrated outstanding commitment to retreat to a hermitage nearby or to a cell within the confines of the monastic walls. In the later centuries of the Byzantine period, monasticism had become important not only as a way of life for committed Christians, but also as an institution endowed with much wealth and property. Such economic prosperity naturally implied power, and there can be no doubt that monastic interests played an important part in later Byzantine history. Nevertheless, the power of the monasteries was based on Byzantines' continuing belief in the importance of the spiritual life and Christian ideals that they represented.

The origins of monasticism

How did Christian monasticism come into being and how did it differ from similar movements in other religions? It seems likely that the earliest Christian ascetics emerged in the context of pagan persecution in the third century. In Egypt men such as Chaeremon, bishop of Neapolis, and a certain Paul of Thebes fled into the desert rather than face persecution at the hands of the pagan authorities. Perhaps having tasted the sweetness of solitude and freedom from the burdens of worldly life, such individuals decided to

A late-10th or early-11th-century manuscript depiction of St Symeon on his column.

pursue this solitary way even after the period of oppression had ended.

Asceticism as a way of life did not, of course, originate with third-century Christians. Antecedents exist in the Greek and Roman pagan traditions, with examples such as the philosopher Pythagorus, who flourished in the sixth century BC, and a more recent follower of his named Apollonius of Tyana, who lived a wandering holy life in the first century AD. Judaism was not a stranger to such spiritual endeavours either, with figures such as John the Baptist and the sect of the Essenes representing the best-known examples. Ascetic

Asceticism

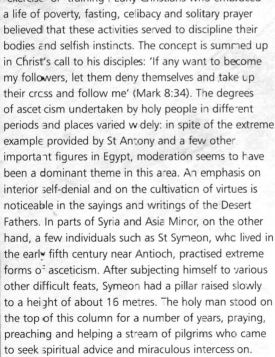

The term 'asceticism' comes from the Greek *askesis*, which means 'exercise' or 'training'. Early Christians who embraced a life of poverty, fasting, celibacy and solitary prayer believed that these activities served to discipline their bodies and selfish instincts. The concept is summed up in Christ's call to his disciples: 'If any want to become my followers, let them deny themselves and take up their cross and follow me' (Mark 8:34). The degrees of asceticism undertaken by holy people in different periods and places varied widely: in spite of the extreme example provided by St Antony and a few other important figures in Egypt, moderation seems to have been a dominant theme in this area. An emphasis on interior self-denial and on the cultivation of virtues is noticeable in the sayings and writings of the Desert Fathers. In parts of Syria and Asia Minor, on the other hand, a few individuals such as St Symeon, who lived in the early fifth century near Antioch, practised extreme forms of asceticism. After subjecting himself to various other difficult feats, Symeon had a pillar raised slowly to a height of about 16 metres. The holy man stood on the top of this column for a number of years, praying, preaching and helping a stream of pilgrims who came to seek spiritual advice and miraculous intercession.

and mystical movements have also featured in other main
world religions, such as Hinduism and Buddhism; these may
well have influenced late-Roman asceticism, including both
its pagan and Judeo-Christian manifestations.

St Antony

The most famous of all the early Egyptian ascetics,
remembered in the Christian Church as the first Christian
monk, is a holy man called Antony. It is worth looking at
his story in detail for two reasons: first, because St Antony's
way of life became the model for all ascetics, both male and
female, who followed in his footsteps; and second, because
his life exemplifies many distinctive aspects of Christian
monasticism. One of the main reasons for Antony's
subsequent fame is that a biography in his honour was
written by the important Alexandrian bishop and theologian,
Athanasius (c. 297–373). The author relates how Antony, a
wealthy young landowner, heard the 19th chapter of the
Gospel of Matthew read out one Sunday in church: 'If you
wish to be perfect, go, sell your possessions, and give the
money to the poor, and you will have treasure in heaven;
then come, follow me.' After reflecting on the meaning of
these words, Antony decided to sell all his property, entrust
his sister to the care of a community of virgins and devote
himself to a life of prayer in the desert.

St Antony trained first with an older ascetic, but then
decided to retreat into greater solitude. First, he shut
himself up in a tomb near his village where, according
to his biographer Athanasius, he spent most of his time
praying and combating the evil beings who inhabited this
place. The late-antique belief in demons, who could take
many forms and devoted themselves to obstructing spiritual
endeavour, remained as strong among Christians as it did
among pagans. The force of their assaults caused physical
harm to the saint but he refused to give up his solitary vigil.
Eventually Antony retreated even further into the desert,
shutting himself up in an abandoned fort on the other side
of the Nile. After 20 years of solitude, during which he

survived on a diet of a tiny amount of bread, the holy man emerged in a purified but apparently completely healthy physical state.

As the biography of St Antony shows, early Christian ascetics drew much of their inspiration from the Bible, and in particular the Gospels. Aspects of their lives, such as temptation by demons and the ability to work miracles, resemble events in the life of Christ. As we see in the *Life of St Antony*, fasting, avoiding sleep and remaining celibate were never viewed as goals in themselves; instead, the early saints regarded these as exercises in physical discipline. Biographers such as Athanasius emphasize that the saints' bodies and souls are involved in the process of transformation from an ordinary existence into holiness. This idea excludes the dualist belief that the material world, which includes the human body, is inherently evil and may never be redeemed.

Pachomios and the rise of communal monasticism

A second, but very different, figure to emerge in the Egyptian desert in the early fourth century was Pachomios, the legendary founder of coenobitic (or communal) monasticism. Pachomios was born into a pagan family and was conscripted into the Roman army during the war of 312/13 between the two emperors Licinius and Maximinus Daia. According to his biographies, which exist in various versions, Pachomios was impressed by the charity of local Christians while billeted in Thebes. The young soldier then prayed to God, promising that he would serve humanity in the same way. After his release from the army he was instructed in the Christian faith and baptized. On the eve of his baptism, Pachomios had a vision 'in which he saw dew falling on him from heaven, spilling into his hand in the form of honey, and flowing from there over the surface of the earth. A voice informed him that this was an augury for his future' (Philip Rousseau, *Pachomios*, 1985).

Pachomios carried out his mission to serve the rest of humanity as well as God by establishing monasteries. In about 320, Pachomios founded a community at Tabennesis in Upper Egypt. This consisted of separate buildings in which 30 to 40

'Antony appeared to [his followers] with an aura of holiness as if he had emerged from some divine sanctuary. They were all stunned at the beauty of his countenance and the dignified bearing of his body which had not grown flabby through lack of exercise; neither had his face grown pale as a result of fasting and fighting with demons.'

ATHANASIUS
(c 297–373) WRITING
OF ST ANTONY'S
EMERGENCE FROM
HIS SOLITARY VIGIL

Opposite page:
A later Greek
fresco of monks
at the Great
Lavra Monastery,
Mount Athos,
dated to 1854.

*'And so there
were on the
mountain
monastic cells
like tents, filled
with divine
choirs of people
singing psalms,
reading and
praying... They
appeared to
inhabit an
infinitely large
area, a town
removed from
worldly matters,
full of piety and
justice.'*

ATHANASIUS, *LIFE
OF SAINT ANTONY,*
FOURTH CENTURY

monks lived together, each subject to a head, or *hegumenos*, who was responsible for the spiritual direction and discipline of the monks. It is possible that Pachomios' military background influenced his vision of monastic life. The emphasis within the monastic houses, which in some ways resembled military barracks, lay on discipline and obedience rather than the pursuit of more individualistic spiritual aims.

In fourth-century Egypt, we thus see the development of two very different strands in Christian monasticism. The first, which was probably the earliest, consisted of individuals living in cells that they had constructed in the desert, sometimes loosely grouped together and sometimes entirely alone, following a life of asceticism, prayer, celibacy and some manual labour. St Antony represents a good example of this style of monasticism and was imitated by many other early hermits. The lives and sayings of many such men and women are witnessed in collections of stories which were first transmitted orally and later written down. Many emerge as distinct individuals who achieved reputations of great holiness and wisdom. The cells and caves of Nitria and Scetis in Lower Egypt must indeed have resembled 'cities' at some points in their history, as when the Western pilgrim Rufinus visited the area in 375, with individual monks continually visiting one another in search of wise 'words' from their elders.

The second tradition, which developed not only in the Pachomian foundations of Upper Egypt, but also independently in various coenobitic monasteries in the Delta region, embraced a much more regulated and disciplined form of religious life. In foundations such as these, the emphasis was on obedience and conformity, rather than on feats of asceticism or solitary prayer. Both of these strands survived in the later Byzantine monastic tradition and continued to be regarded as equally valid forms of Christian life.

St Basil of Caesarea and the development of monasticism in Asia Minor

Another important figure in the history of Christian monasticism is undoubtedly the bishop and theologian Basil

View of
St Catherine's
Monastery, Mount
Sinai, a fortified
foundation
established by the
emperor Justinian
in the sixth
century. The
monastery still
stands in the Sinai
desert, and
contains icons and
manuscripts
dating from all
centuries and in
many languages,
reflecting the
diversity of the
monks who lived
there.

of Caesarea, who, along with his brother, Gregory of Nyssa, and friend, Gregory Nazianzen, became an important contributor to the development of trinitarian doctrine in the Christian Church. Basil was born in about 329 into a large, land-owning Christian family in north-eastern and central Asia Minor (now modern Turkey). He spent most of his life in his native Pontus and Cappadocia, but received an excellent education in classical letters and philosophy at the Academy of Athens.

It is clear from the activities of Basil of Caesarea and others, including his family and friend Gregory, that monasticism was 'in the air' at this stage in Byzantine history. The perfect Christian life, as described and lived out by Jesus Christ himself, represented a way of poverty, charity and, ideally, celibacy. At the same time, Basil recognized that more formal arrangements needed to be made for Christians who wished to live together according to a rule. Sometime between 355 and 358, Basil undertook an extended trip through Egypt, Palestine and Syria. In Egypt, Basil came across the Pachomian monasteries and was deeply impressed by the well-ordered and systematic structure of these houses. It was this form of monasticism,

with its emphasis on discipline and obedience, that Basil
brought back to Asia Minor and which he oversaw in the
numerous monasteries that he founded.

St Basil left a number of writings, which played a
significant role in both Eastern and Western monasticism
in subsequent centuries. These include the 'moral rules', or
Moralia, which were composed early in his career, and the
longer *Asketikon*, a collection of questions and answers
concerning the monastic life, which may have been written
in the 360s. The latter text went through various rewritings
even during Basil's lifetime; later it helped to inspire the
Rule of St Benedict of Nursia in the West and, as we shall
see, the monastic reforms of Theodore of Studios in ninth-
century Constantinople. Basil's vision of organized
monasticism, in which the hours of prayer, manual labour,
eating and sleeping are clearly defined, and obedience to
one's abbot is regarded as the highest virtue, set the tone for
the development of coenobitic monasticism hereafter. This
is not to suggest, however, that the more individualistic and
extreme examples of Christian asceticism did not continue
to flourish throughout the territories of the Eastern empire.

Women and asceticism in the early Byzantine world

Women played an important role in the
development of asceticism in the early
Christian and Byzantine worlds. There can
be no doubt that some women solitaries in
the Egyptian desert, including Syncletica,
Sarah and a few others achieved an equal
status with their male colleagues. The
'desert mothers', as they are called,
attracted disciples of their own and their
teachings survive in the collections of
'Sayings' which developed out of this
milieu.

Somewhat later, however, many
women did struggle with the difficulty of

St Mary of Egypt,
the sixth or
seventh-century
ascetic saint who
was formerly a
prostitute, as
depicted in a
12th-century wall
painting at the
Church of the
Panagia
Phorbiotissa,
Asinou, Cyprus.

breaking into roles that were defined primarily as masculine in this strongly patriarchal society. A group of nuns emerged between the fifth and ninth centuries who achieved sanctity by pretending to be men and entering male monasteries. The biographies written in their honour stress the fact that women such as St Mary/Marinos succeeded in *overcoming* their femininity, becoming like men in their strength of purpose and ascetic prowess. The unspoken assumption behind statements such as these is that women start from a position of greater weakness and vulnerability; both as temptresses and as objects of temptation, they are implicated with Eve more heavily than men in the fall of humankind from grace.

Another feature which is evident in the literary accounts of holy women is the tendency to classify them according to certain stereotypes. Holy virgins such as St Macrina, the redoubtable sister of Basil of Caesarea, and the women who surrounded St Jerome form one class, while another may be identified in the women who renounced prostitution to embrace a life of asceticism, such as Pelagia and Mary of Egypt. From the depths of depravity to the heights of holiness, the latter seem to sum up in their persons the contemporary view of females as 'harlots, witches or saints'. On the other hand, many of the biographies written in honour of these figures are moving accounts of real individuals, struggling to overcome the prejudices of their age and to enter into the spiritual arena on an equal footing with men.

It is interesting that after about the ninth century, asceticism and the undertaking of monastic vows seems to have opened up for women of many different backgrounds, including those who were married or widowed. The pursuit of a solitary, self-directed ascetic life also declined after this time, as women increasingly entered organized, coenobitic monasteries in their pursuit of spiritual aims.

The reforms of Theodore of Studios in the ninth century

After Basil of Caesarea's strong endorsement of coenobitic (communal) monasticism in Asia Minor, houses for both men and women continued to be founded throughout the Byzantine empire and especially in its capital city, Constantinople. The first recorded monastery in Constantinople was established in the late fourth century; by the mid-sixth century about 70 monasteries existed in the capital city alone. Institutional monasticism appears to have gone into something of a decline during the turbulent period of the early iconoclast emperors, Leo III and Constantine V. Accurately or not, later chroniclers and hagiographers linked monks with the defence of the holy icons. For this reason, when icons were reinstated after the Triumph of Orthodoxy in 843, the monastic movement received an enormous boost: in public perception at least, monks belonged to the winning side and deserved extra honour and veneration for their brave opposition to the iconoclast emperors.

Monastic regulation

Institutional monasticism received another important stimulus in the early ninth century from the example and writings of Theodore, abbot of the monastery of Studios in Constantinople. Theodore, who was born in 759, entered with vigour into the task of renovating and reforming the urban monastery of which he became abbot towards the end of the eighth century. Theodore used as his model the surviving rules of his fourth-century predecessor, Basil of Caesarea. Like Basil, Theodore stressed absolute obedience in his monastery, urging moderation in ascetic practice and the importance of manual labour. The monastery became a self-contained economic unit, with workshops in which various necessities such as clothing and shoes were manufactured; it also contained a scriptorium in which manuscripts were copied, and gardens that supplied most of the food for the monastery. Most of Theodore's teachings concerning the coenobitic way of life are contained in a

'Two old men, great anchorites, came to the district of Pelusia to visit [Sarah]... Amma Sarah said to them, "According to nature I am a woman, but not according to my thoughts"... She also said to the brothers, "It is I who am a man, you who are women."'

THE SAYINGS OF THE DESERT FATHERS, TRANSLATED BY BENEDICTA WARD SLG, 1977 series of short sermons which he delivered daily to his monks after the early morning service. These teachings, called the *Great* and *Little Catecheses*, soon came to represent, along with the writings of St Basil, the most influential rules for monasticism throughout the Byzantine empire.

Monasticism after the ninth century

It is impossible to overemphasize the growing importance of monasticism in every aspect of Byzantine social and religious life after the ninth century. In this period, monastic foundations began to proliferate throughout the empire. Everyone from wealthy landowners and emperors to prosperous peasant-farmers wished to bequeath property to existing monasteries, or even to found new ones on their land. In return for the gifts of property and money, monks and nuns could be asked to pray for the souls of the donor and his family, as well as for their descendants. Endowing property to monasteries also represented a way of securing

Monastic Rules

Unlike the monastic houses in Western Europe, Byzantine foundations were not formally grouped into specific orders following standard rules. In Eastern Christendom the monastic world remained much less regulated, with individual monasteries following their own regulations, depending on the directives of their patrons or abbots. The Rule or *Typikon* provided at the time of foundation reflected the unique concerns and needs of each house, but also usually depended on earlier models and especially on the writings of such influential figures as Saints Basil and Theodore. It is also striking that within individual monasteries various styles of spiritual life might be undertaken. Whereas most novices and less spiritually advanced members of the community would follow a communal way of life, the monastery might also contain one or more individuals who were allowed (at the abbot's discretion) to live and pray in solitude. Another striking difference between Eastern and Western monasticism was the lack of stability among monks: in spite of canonical directives which enjoined them to stay in one monastery, many moved frequently from one monastery to another or from monasteries to solitary hermitages.

the survival of an estate or piece of land if a family possessed no obvious heir to manage it. It is clear from the historical sources that people saw monasticism as a calling which could be embraced at any stage in their lives. Deposed emperors, empresses left as widows or divorcées, landowners who had fallen on hard times – all of these groups could, at any age, choose to retreat to the peace and regularity of the monastic way of life.

Monasticism as a landed and wealthy institution finally began to represent a threat to imperial finances by the early 10th century. Monasteries were often exempted from paying the taxes which peasant-farmers had previously supplied. Eventually emperors were forced to introduce legislation aimed at prohibiting the foundation of monastic estates and restricting the growth of new ones. In 964 Nikephoros II Phokas banned all new foundations of monasteries and philanthropic institutions. The reason given to justify this restriction was that existing foundations were being neglected and were consequently falling into disrepair. At the same time, however, the emperor identified and deplored avarice as a motive for the foundation of new monasteries, stressing the importance of poverty in the true Christian life. All such legislation came to nothing in the end, however, which perhaps reflects the irreversible importance of monasticism in both popular and imperial opinion. In 988 Basil II repealed the laws of his predecessor and by the middle of the 11th century, the vested interests of both monastic and lay property owners had prevailed. Many historians view the failure of such legislation against large landowners, including monasteries, as contributing to the long-term financial and military decline of the Byzantine empire.

The close relationship between Byzantine monasteries and the local communities in which they were founded is best described as symbiotic. Far from being completely isolated, both male and female monasteries performed many important services in society which had an impact on most members of the population. Perhaps most importantly, monasteries frequently provided charitable institutions which were served by the monks and nuns themselves. From a spiritual point of view, Byzantine monasteries provided ordinary Christians with guidance, as we know from the records of many laypeople who sought spiritual direction from the abbots of neighbouring monasteries. The importance attached by lay Orthodox to the prayers and commemorations of monastics in return for their patronage has already been mentioned; this represents another example of the close interaction between the secular and religious spheres in the Byzantine world.

Male and female monasteries

Monasteries for both men and women flourished throughout the Byzantine era. It is interesting to note, however, that far fewer convents than male monasteries existed at any given time. It has been estimated, on the basis of a tally of all the known monasteries of Constantinople during all 11 centuries of its history, that there were only 77 nunneries in comparison

A view of
Gregoriou
Monastery,
Mount Athos.

with 270 monasteries. It is also striking that most of the known female monasteries in the Byzantine world were located within cities, rather than in most of the rural areas inhabited by monks. The reasons for this discrepancy are not difficult to find. According to contemporary sources, the founders of convents were worried about the security of nuns in outlying districts; throughout the turbulent Byzantine centuries women in these areas would have been vulnerable to attacks by invaders, pirates and other marauders. In the eyes of pious Byzantines, there could be no worse crime than the dishonouring of a woman who had been dedicated to God. It is also significant that many of the founders of convents, most of whom were imperial or aristocratic laywomen, themselves lived in the capital city. Female monasticism thus remained for the most part an urban phenomenon, closely associated with its benevolent founders and their families.

In the early and later periods of Byzantine history, there are instances of 'double' monasteries, that is, foundations in

'Holy mountains'

One specifically Byzantine phenomenon which seems to have developed at an early date, but also to have flourished with all other forms of monasticism after the ninth century, was the 'holy mountain'. The reason for clusters of monasteries appearing in one area is clear: foundations might break away from their parent houses or a particularly eminent spiritual figure might attract more disciples than could fit into one monastery. In certain areas of Asia Minor and mainland Greece, such clusters were formed on hills or mountains, which henceforth became designated as 'holy mountains'. The choice of mountainous places was certainly symbolic: in both classical and Judeo-Christian traditions these represent both wildernesses and places that are closer to God. Most of the 'holy mountains' which existed in Asia Minor, for example on Mount Olympus in Bithynia, Mount Latros on the south-western coast, Mount St Auxentios, above Chalcedon, and Mount Kyminas, on the border of Paphlagonia and Bithynia, survive only as accounts in literary sources or as ruins. The greatest of all the holy mountains, however, called Mount Athos, was established by a monk called Athanasius in the ninth century on a hilly peninsula in northern Greece. This important monastic centre survives to this day and is still inhabited by Orthodox monks.

which men and women lived in separate communities within one main enclosure. These monasteries tended to be under the supervision of one superior and were supported by the same sources of revenue. On the other hand, every aspect of daily life within these foundations would be carried out separately so as to avoid mutual distraction. The monks and nuns in double monasteries tended to be assigned jobs in accordance with traditional views of gender: whereas the monks might tend the garden and work in the fields, the nuns were responsible for the preparation of food and manufacture of cloth. During the middle period of Byzantine history (approximately from the sixth to the thirteenth centuries), many double houses were closed down in response to imperial legislation against them. There was a resurgence of such houses, however, in the Palaiologan period (13th–15th centuries), sometimes in response to the needs of their founders, who wished to stay together as a family even after entering into the monastic way of life.

It is clear that the position of nuns reflected underlying Byzantine attitudes towards gender. Even in monastic life women could play only a subordinate role, remaining dependent on men for practical needs and for their priestly offices in the running of the convent or double monastery. On the other hand, the responsibility and authority of the female superior and the active participation of ordinary nuns in the life of the convent must have provided these women with some degree of autonomy and self-direction. The important role played by wealthy female patronesses, both in founding monasteries and in overseeing them, reinforces the impression that monasticism provided a significant outlet for female energy in the Byzantine world.

Spirituality in the Byzantine world

At the beginning of this chapter we saw the importance of asceticism and prayer in early Christian spirituality. These ideals remained central to the monastic movement throughout the later centuries in Byzantium, even after the communal, or coenobitic, way of life became the accepted norm. The highest goal for all monks and nuns remained the practice of *hesychia*, which is variously translated as 'solitude', 'stillness' or 'solitary prayer'. Several outstanding figures taught and exemplified this tradition in the course of Byzantine history. These spiritual teachers drew on a large body of writings which began to be collected and disseminated within monasteries as early as the fourth century. The tradition continued to develop, however, as new insights and personal revelations were added over the centuries.

One figure who stands out in the late 10th century is the mystic St Symeon the New Theologian, abbot of the monastery of St Mamas in Constantinople. In his numerous writings, which include short sermons, treatises and hymns, Symeon discusses the steps that lead the mystic to a complete apprehension of God. He describes his own mystical experience, which he attained on more than one occasion, as a vision of divine light. Symeon believed that any human being may, if sufficiently purified and dedicated to prayer, be capable of such a revelation. Symeon, like many monastic teachers before him, believed in the concept of deification (*theôsis*). According to this doctrine human beings, created in God's image and restored after the fall by the incarnation of Christ, are capable of regaining their likeness to God to the extent that they may become by grace what God is by nature. The process is of course a long and slow one: asceticism and prayer form only one part of a journey which is dependent also on the grace of the Holy Spirit.

A community of nuns from the convent dedicated to the Virgin Bebaias Elpidos ('of Good Hope'), Constantinople (between 1327 and 1342).

Another important figure in the history of Byzantine spirituality is the monk Gregory Palamas, who began his career on Mount Athos and then became Archbishop of Thessaloniki in the mid-14th century. Palamas believed that

*'The third
method of
attention and
prayer is the
following: the
mind should be
in the heart...
Keep your
attention within
yourself (not
in your head
but heart).
Wrestling thus
the mind will
find the place
of the heart...
From that
moment,
whenever a
thought appears,
the mind at
once dispels it,
before it has
time to enter
and become a
thought or
image,
destroying it by
repeating Jesus'
name [prayer],
"Lord Jesus
Christ, have
mercy upon
me."'*

GREGORY PALAMAS,
MID-14TH CENTURY

Christians, and especially monks, may achieve complete revelation of God's glory through contemplation. While preserving a completely Orthodox belief in God's complete unknowability and transcendence, Palamas argued that human beings may nevertheless perceive what he called God's 'uncreated energies'. The concept is best exemplified by the vision of uncreated light that shone about Christ at his transfiguration on Mount Tabor (Luke 9:28–36). In most icons of the transfiguration, the three disciples are shown experiencing a divine revelation. They fall down at Christ's feet, covering their faces with their hands. The practical technique for achieving such a mystical experience, which came to be known by the technical term 'Hesychasm', involved deep breathing and quiet repetition of the Jesus Prayer ('Lord Jesus Christ, have mercy on me a sinner'). Like St Symeon the New Theologian, Gregory Palamas based his teachings on the idea that humanity, created in the image of God, is capable and worthy of participation in divine existence.

Controversy over Gregory Palamas' teachings arose when a Calabrian monk named Barlaam entered into an exchange of letters with him. Barlaam objected to the idea that human beings through their own efforts could achieve a revelation of God. Barlaam felt that the Athonite monk's teachings threatened God's transcendence and unknowability, besides stressing too much the role of human endeavour in the process of spiritual enlightenment. A council was called at Constantinople in 1341 to resolve the dispute and decided in Palamas' favour. After his opponents succeeded in the following few years to secure his conviction for heresy and excommunication, however, it took another two councils to reaffirm the orthodoxy of the Palamite teachings. Gregory Palamas was eventually canonized by the Byzantine Church in 1368.

The approval of the teachings of Gregory Palamas in the mid-14th century was a deeply significant event in the history of Byzantine monasticism. Building on centuries of personal endeavour and spiritual knowledge, Palamas summed up in his writings the Orthodox belief in the unknowable transcendence of God, but also the ability of human beings to ascend through prayer to a mystical understanding of his uncreated energies. This positive view of human potential is based on the doctrine that humanity is capable of deification or transfiguration in the presence of God. The mystical writings of Gregory Palamas, Symeon the New Theologian and earlier spiritual teachers continued to provide inspiration for both monastic and lay Orthodox Christians through the difficult centuries which followed the Turks' domination of most Byzantine territories after 1453. These writings, which emerged out of the heart of Orthodox monasticism, represent one of the Byzantium's abiding contributions to the history of Christian spirituality.

C H A P T E R   6

Holy Places,
Holy People

For the Byzantines, the heavenly and earthly worlds
were closely entwined. God's power and mercy could
be experienced at any time by the humblest believer
in various ways, whether through acts of nature or healing
miracles, or in the sacramental rites of the Church. It is
clear that from a very early date some places, objects or
people were seen as channels to divine power. In this
chapter we will explore the various cults which received
special veneration in the Byzantine world. These included
the holy sites in Palestine and Jerusalem, the relics of
martyrs and saints, the Virgin Mary or *Theotokos* ('God-
bearer') as she was more commonly called, and icons.

Holy places
The evidence of Christian visits to the Holy Land begins
very early, with accounts written by important figures such
as Melito of Sardis and Origen in the second and third
centuries respectively. In the fourth century, according
to legend, the mother of Constantine I, the aged Helena,
visited Jerusalem as a pilgrim and funded archaeological
investigations both inside and outside the city. She was
delighted with the discoveries that resulted: the sites of
Christ's crucifixion and tomb represented by far the most
important of these. Constantine immediately set about
building churches to commemorate these sites. A huge
complex incorporating the Anastasis, a circular area
surrounding the tomb itself, Golgotha, a rocky outcrop
believed to be the site of the crucifixion, and a magnificent
basilica was collectively known as the Holy Sepulchre. The

relic of the true cross formed a centrepiece in this holy site. Constantine and Helena also discovered places outside Jerusalem which they believed to be the actual sites of important events in Jesus' life. The cave in which the Christ child was born was honoured by another basilica in the town of Bethlehem. Various places on the Mount of Olives and in Galilee also became centres of pilgrimage and commemoration.

We are fortunate in possessing several early accounts written by pilgrims who visited the Holy Land in the fourth century or later. In 333 an anonymous pilgrim from the west coast of France, probably near Bordeaux, travelled overland to Palestine and, once there, described the sites that he saw. He mentions in his account approximately 21 sites associated with the New Testament and 32 recalling pre-Christian biblical history. Even more fascinating, however, is the account by a Western woman, possibly a nun from Galicia in Spain, called Egeria, who probably travelled eastwards between 381 and 384. She writes in great detail of her leisurely pilgrimage through Palestine, Jerusalem and even the Sinai desert, describing both the sites and the liturgical celebrations that she witnessed in all of these places.

Martyrs and relics

The bodies of martyrs were honoured from a very early period in the Christian Church. People who died in the pagan persecutions represented the ultimate example of Christian sacrifice as they followed the example of the Saviour himself. Inspired by the martyrs' own belief in paradise and the afterlife, Christians believed that these individuals continued to intercede on their behalf in the heavenly kingdom. It is clear from the many texts that were written about martyrs and their cults that their material remains were also imbued with special powers. Shrines were established to honour these holy relics. Many Christians journeyed long distances to venerate the martyrs' graves and to seek healing or other miracles at these sites.

'Here then, impelled by Christ our God and assisted by the prayers of the holy men who accompanied us, we made the great effort of the climb. It was quite impossible to ride up, but though I had to go on foot I was not conscious of the effort – in fact I hardly noticed it because, by God's will, I was seeing my hopes coming true. So at 10 o'clock we arrived on the summit of Sinai, the Mount of God where the Law was given, and the place where God's glory came down on the day when the mountain was smoking.'

J. WILKINSON,
EGERIA'S TRAVELS,
1999

The veneration of relics at the shrines and churches erected in honour of the early martyrs continued throughout the Byzantine period. No city would have been without some share of these precious remains, which were believed to protect the citizens from enemy attack, besides providing miraculous help on an individual basis. Cities which lacked any saintly relics sometimes managed to acquire them as gifts, purchases or even stolen goods. Thus Constantinople, a city that did not feature as the site of any famous martyrdoms at the time of its foundation, nevertheless possessed a huge number of holy relics by the end of the 11th century. A letter which purports to be written by the emperor Alexios Komnenos to a count of Flanders enumerates all of these relics, listing such precious objects as the pillar to which Christ was bound when he was flogged, the lash, the crown of thorns, the head of John the Baptist, and many others.

The veneration of saints

After the end of persecution and the establishment of Christianity as the state religion in the Roman empire, ascetic saints joined martyrs as objects of veneration. The literary accounts of these holy people suggest that most of them achieved special powers even during their lives. Whereas the ascetics in the Egyptian desert practised a more moderate form of asceticism, fasting and praying but also supporting themselves by manual labour, more extreme styles of monastic life emerged in other parts of the empire, especially in Syria. Symeon, the fifth-century Stylite saint has already been introduced in a previous chapter (see illustration on pages 76–77); before erecting the column on which he stood exposed to the elements for a number of years, St Symeon subjected himself to many other physical trials. These included enclosure in a dry cistern and the chaining of his right leg to a stone. Several saints in Asia Minor later imitated Symeon. A slightly younger contemporary, named Daniel the Stylite, had a pillar erected on the outskirts of Constantinople in 460 from which he preached, performed miracles and even advised the emperor.

The historian Peter Brown has studied the phenomenon of holy men and argued that they came to represent the archetypal 'outsiders' in Syrian and, later, Byzantine society. They acquired closeness to God by means of fasting and other ascetic feats, but even more important than this was their self-imposed exile from the rest of society. This enabled these individuals to act as channels between the created and the divine worlds, having direct access to God in a way that even the ordained clergy was denied. Holy men such as Symeon and Daniel were revered after their deaths, since their bodies retained the miraculous powers which they had

Holy fools

One of the most remarkable forms of sanctity to emerge in Eastern Christendom was that exemplified by 'holy fools'. Such figures include the Syrian saint, Symeon of Emesa, and later the Greek saint, Andrew the Fool, as well as many others. This group of ascetics turned all the rules of Christian life, so to speak, upside down. Saint Symeon pretended to be half-witted, acting in outrageous and unpredictable ways. According to his seventh-century biographer, Leontios of Neapolis, Symeon entered a church one Sunday and began throwing nuts at the candles. When the congregation tried to chase him out, he went up into the pulpit and began pelting the women with nuts. As Symeon finally left the church, he overturned the tables of the pastry chefs (presumably selling cakes at the front of the church). Many other incidents in the life of this holy fool seem to mock the customs of the church, but also to recall events in the life of Christ. For example, the saint is said to have first entered the city of Emesa in Syria, where he stayed for the remainder of his life, dragging a dead dog behind him. As he advanced, local children shouted, 'Hey, a crazy abba!' There can be no doubt that Symeon mimics in this scene the entrance of Christ into Jerusalem, reversing the story, however, by making himself an object of ridicule rather than celebration. The holy fool, basing his way of life on the passage 'We are fools for Christ's sake' (1 Corinthians 4:10) experienced humility more completely than even the most impoverished and hungry ascetic could ever do. The tradition of 'holy fools' survived through the later centuries of the Byzantine era and was adopted in Orthodox Russia. St Basil's Cathedral in Red Square, Moscow, is named for a holy fool (Basil of Mangazeia, who died in 1552); in Russian literature the concept is treated most famously in Dostoevsky's *The Idiot*.

An icon of the Mother of God with Christ, flanked by two angels (late 15th century). The Virgin is almost always depicted with Christ in Byzantine art, emphasizing the importance of her role in his incarnation.

acquired through their ascetic labours. Many miracle stories survive, commemorating the cults of both male and female ascetic saints.

Mary the 'God-bearer', or Theotokos

Evidence of Christian veneration of the Virgin Mary before the early fifth century is patchy, but incontrovertible. Although references to the Virgin Mary are infrequent in the New Testament, Christians honoured her from an early date for her role in the incarnation of Christ. By the end of the second century some apocryphal writings, especially a text called the *Protoevangelion* of James, which recounts the story of her conception, birth and childhood, were circulating among the faithful. The bishop Irenaeus of

Lyons stressed Mary's importance in the birth of Christ as the antithesis of Eve: 'for it was necessary... that a virgin, become an advocate for a virgin, might undo and destroy the virginal disobedience by virginal obedience'. The Old Testament books that had prophesied the virgin birth along with every other aspect of the new dispensation provided further backing for the growing cult in honour of Mary.

It is interesting to note that some of the fourth-century texts which honour the Virgin Mary stress her role as a saintly human being. A letter which is preserved only in Coptic, but which was probably written by the patriarch Athanasius, describes Mary as the ideal model for Christian virgins. She was calm and pure, modest, loved good works and prayed constantly to God. She wanted to make progress every day and worked tirelessly to improve her spiritual state. The Virgin is presented in this text as a model of good behaviour, but the author nevertheless stresses her humanity, stating that her good works are not perfect and that 'bad thoughts' occasionally enter her mind. Such a description would be unthinkable several centuries later, when the Virgin Mary had become an object of devotion in the Church second only to Christ himself.

The early fifth century was the period in which the budding cult of the Virgin suddenly acquired official sanction and theological justification in the Byzantine empire. The controversy initiated by Nestorios and Cyril, patriarchs of Constantinople and Alexandria respectively, focused on the title 'God-bearer', or *Theotokos*, for Mary. This was sparked off by their conflicting views concerning the manner in which humanity and divinity were combined in the person of Christ. There can be no doubt that the party led by the Alexandrians, which backed the idea that the Virgin gave birth to God, were motivated in part by their reverence for Mary herself. Nestorios, on the other hand, felt that her exaltation was out of proportion to the role that she actually played in Christ's incarnation. It is likely too that he felt that her true humanity, as well as that of her Son, was compromised by such exalted praise.

After the triumph of the Alexandrians at the Council of Ephesus (431), the cult of the *Theotokos* was allowed to develop unchecked. From this period onward, liturgical praise of the Virgin, which appeared both in poetic sermons and in hymns, proliferated. As feast days in her honour were introduced into the Church calendar in the course of the sixth century, texts extolling her nativity, presentation as a child in the Temple, annunciation and death were composed. More historical sources begin to record the Virgin's miraculous interventions in human history from the late sixth century onwards. It is probably in this period that the city of Constantinople adopted the *Theotokos* as its special patroness.

The most famous story concerning the Virgin's role as defender of the imperial city is that of the siege by the Avars and Persians in 626. With these two enemies mounting a combined and highly organized assault on Constantinople, both from the land and the sea, the situation seemed desperate. The emperor Herakleios was away on campaign in Asia Minor, but Patriarch Sergios, in whose care he had left Constantinople, rallied the citizens by calling on the *Theotokos* for help. The patriarch organized processions around the walls of the city, in which the clergy and people carried icons of Christ and the Virgin and chanted hymns and prayers. This unprecedented involvement of all the citizens in the defence of the city may indeed have played a part in undermining the confidence of the enemies. The Avars and Persians suffered a humiliating defeat and eventually retreated. The Byzantines themselves attributed their salvation to divine protection. According to a contemporary source, the Virgin Mary herself was seen fighting from the walls beside the soldiers. The siege of 626 soon became part of the city's folklore and a popular hymn in her honour, called the Akathistos, acquired a new prologue commemorating these events.

Icons

Scholars are still debating when Byzantine Christians began to use and venerate icons, which mostly took the form of images of holy figures painted on wooden panels. Some argue that this cult developed in the late sixth century, a time when the population as a whole began to sense the breakdown of the civilized, Roman world and to turn to God for reassurance. Others have suggested that the veneration of icons began somewhat later and that holy relics were still viewed in the late sixth and early seventh centuries as the

Windows into the divine realm

The word 'icon' (*eikon* in Greek) simply means 'image'; in other words, a representation in any medium of the artist's vision of reality, whether concrete or imagined. In its more restricted sense, however, an icon has come to mean a religious image which plays a unique and important role in Orthodox Christian worship and doctrine. Anyone who has ever entered an Orthodox church will have noticed the icons, usually paintings of holy people or scenes on wooden panels, which are displayed prominently on stands both in the centre of the nave and on the screen in front of the sanctuary. Regarded in strict theological terms not as objects of devotion in themselves but as windows into the divine realm, icons are kissed and venerated at the beginning and at various points in the course of the service. It is important to recognize, however, that icons occupy a particular place in the hierarchy of holy objects within the church. It is incorrect, for example, to venerate an icon when the elements of the eucharist are being carried in or consecrated; at other times, however, the icon may occupy a central place within a particular sacramental act, such as confession or anointment with holy unction. The earliest icons were believed to have been painted at the time of Christ; the most famous example is the evangelist Luke's painting of Mary, the Mother of God. Later artists regarded the painting of icons as a spiritual act: they would prepare by fasting and prayer, having first completed a long technical training in the art.

Portable icons were usually painted on wooden panels, although they might also be fashioned in ivory, mosaic or enamel. Pigment was applied to a wooden panel, usually cypress, which had been strengthened with cloth and gesso to prevent splits or cracks. In the earliest icons, which survive at St Catherine's Monastery in Sinai, a wax encaustic has been used; this is the same medium that was used in the late-Roman portraits which have been uncovered in the Fayyum district of Egypt. Later pigments mixed with an egg tempera medium were more commonly employed in the manufacture of icons. Gold leaf was applied liberally to the background and the finished painting was protected with varnish.

main channels of divine power. Relics included not only the precious remains of the bodies of martyrs and saints, but also their clothing or possessions, or the substances, such as oil, that flowed from their tombs. No bodily remains, of course, survived from Christ and his mother Mary, since both were believed to have been raised to heaven soon after their deaths. However, from as early as the fifth century, relics such as the Virgin's robe and belt had been discovered and brought with great ceremony to Constantinople.

A group of icons which appeared early, but which may still be classed with relics rather than with man-made images, are those known as icons 'made without hands', or *acheiropoietai*. Perhaps the most famous of these was the icon of Christ found in the city of Edessa, in eastern Syria. According to a legend which is first related in the late sixth century, the king of the city who was contemporary with Christ, named Abgar, fell ill and sent a message to the Saviour, begging him to come and cure him. Instead, Christ gave the king's messenger a towel, or *mandylion*, that he had pressed to his face and which retained the impression of his features. The king was cured by the miraculous image, which was then preserved in the city and used as an object of divine protection, or 'palladium', in times of danger.

Icons 'made without hands' were used to justify the cult of more ordinary icons which was developing in the course of the seventh century. Literary texts of the period suggest that the growing veneration of icons attracted criticism, mainly from members of other religions which were stricter about the use of figural imagery, especially Muslims and Jews. The miraculous icons of Christ, or *acheiropoietai*, were used by defenders of icons to show that God himself approved of representational art. They also employed passages from Exodus and elsewhere in the Old Testament to prove that exceptions to the second commandment were permitted even at the time of Moses. The Jews were commanded to decorate the ark of the covenant with golden images of cherubim, spreading their wings above the mercy seat (Exodus 25:18–22). All of these arguments were later taken

A highly
naturalistic image
of Christ in a
sixth-century icon
from
St Catherine's
Monastery, Sinai.

**Pilgrim flask with
resurrection
scenes from the
period of the
Crusades,
11th–13th
centuries.**

up by defenders of holy images in the iconoclast controversy of the eighth and ninth centuries.

In addition to the literary evidence, material artefacts attest to the diffusion and use of icons in the seventh century. Many early icons were destroyed during the period of Iconoclasm, but some splendid examples survive at the remote St Catherine's Monastery in the Sinai desert. This spiritual centre, which continued to be inhabited by Orthodox Christian monks throughout the period of Arab rule, fell outside the jurisdiction of the iconoclast emperors. A few other early icons survive in Rome and elsewhere in the West: it is likely that these were made by Constantinopolitan artists or by their students.

Stories describing the miraculous intercession of icons in the lives of ordinary Christians began to proliferate from the seventh century onwards. Often these stories are embedded in the biographies of saints, miracle stories or religious chronicles. They suggest that icons were beginning to be regarded as the most accessible channels of divine power that could be tapped at times of need or peril. For example, a collection of stories compiled by a monk called John Moschos tells of a hermit who, before embarking on a journey, would light a lamp and pray to the icon of the Virgin and Child which he kept in his cave. He would ask the Virgin not only to keep him safe on his journey, but also to look after the lamp while he was away. On returning after a journey which may have lasted for as long as six months, the monk would invariably find the lamp well cared for and still burning. Another story in the same collection relates that a woman tried to dig a well on her property and failed to reach water. Eventually she had a vision in which she was told to take the icon of a local saint and lower it into the well. When this was done the water immediately began to flow, filling the well-shaft up to the halfway point. Many other stories of miracles involving icons reveal the increasing popularity of this cult in the centuries preceding the outbreak of Iconoclasm.

After the end of Iconoclasm, the Orthodox Church formally reaffirmed the validity of holy icons and relics. From the late ninth century onward, these objects played a central role in religious worship. Certain standard types of icons began to appear; for example, Mary, the Mother of God, might be depicted in attitudes conveying such qualities as mercy and motherhood. Some churches in Constantinople possessed special icons which became the focus of special liturgical celebrations. At the Hodegon Monastery, for example, an icon known as the Hodegetria ('guide'), in which the Virgin holds the Christ child on her left arm and gestures to him with her right hand, was believed to have been painted by the evangelist Luke himself. This icon was regularly carried in processions around Constantinople. During a siege in 1187, it was taken up onto the walls of the city. According to an account by two Spanish diplomats who visited Constantinople in the early 15th century, a special ceremony took place at the Hodegon Monastery every Tuesday. Special bearers dressed in red, perhaps belonging to a lay brotherhood, carried the icon, which was large, heavy and covered with precious jewels, out into the assembled crowd.

Many icons and other precious artefacts were looted when the Latins stormed Constantinople in 1204, and ended up in the museums and treasuries of Western Europe. Destruction and pillaging took place again when Constantinople finally fell to the Turks in 1453, especially as these invaders did not approve of Orthodox religious art. Nevertheless, enough artefacts and literary records survive to prove the importance of icons and their role in private and public worship throughout most of the centuries of Byzantine rule. Apart from the period of Iconoclasm, which lasted for just over a century, icons featured prominently in this society as channels of communication, or intermediaries, between the divine and the created worlds.

*'The icon is not
just a simple
image, or a
decoration,
or even an
illustration of
holy scripture.
It is something
greater. It is an
object of
worship and an
integral part of
the liturgy.'*

LEONID OUSPENSKY,
*THEOLOGY OF THE
ICON,* 1992

*'Through heaven
and earth and
sea, through
wood and stone,
through relics
and church
buildings and
the cross,
through angels
and men,
through all
creation visible
and invisible, I
offer veneration
and honour to
the Creator and
Master and
Maker of all
things, and to
him alone.'*

LEONTIOS OF
NEAPOLIS, SEVENTH-
CENTURY DEFENDER
OF HOLY ICONS

The world transfigured

One aspect of the formal defence of icons, which became known as the 'theology of images', was its stress on the sanctity of material creation. God created the world, argued the Byzantine theologians; therefore the world is good. God also chose to become incarnate, taking on a human body and thereby re-entering and saving the created world which had fallen away through the deliberate choice of our forebears, Adam and Eve. Iconophile theologians exposed the inherent dualism in the iconoclast position, which argues that man-made, or material, objects are incapable of transfiguration. They argued the opposite point of view, which may be applied not only to icons, but also to holy relics and other material objects. This position is based not only on the biblical idea that creation is inherently good, but also on Neoplatonic philosophy, which teaches that the material world represents a copy of a higher, transcendent reality. Thus, while icons and relics may in themselves be permeated with divine power, they should never be understood as anything more than images or reminders of the figures they represent. Even so, icons, like the saints or martyrs they represent, may be transfigured by the presence of the Holy Spirit and may act as channels of communication between this world and the heavenly kingdom.

The Kingdom of God on Earth

Organized religious worship, which included the daily and weekly services in church, as well as the sacraments of Christian life, affected the lives of ordinary people in the Byzantine world. It is clear that every class of society, including the emperor himself, participated in one way or another in public liturgical life. Weekly church celebrations, festivals commemorating events in the life of Christ and other holy figures, and participation in the holy sacraments all provided structure and meaning to daily life.

The importance of liturgical worship, both public – and this includes not only the services held within churches, but also the numerous processions held outdoors in major cities and towns throughout the empire – and private, throughout the 11 centuries of Byzantine history can scarcely be overemphasized. Religious time, which was organized according to several different cycles, including annual, weekly and daily, gave deeper meaning to the ordinary passage of time. The Christian festivals of Christmas, Theophany (the baptism of Christ), Easter and the Transfiguration, to name only a few of the most important ones, represented liturgically the reliving of major events in the New Testament. By celebrating these feast days, Orthodox Christians felt a continuous sense of renewal and active participation in the life of the Church. In a broader sense, liturgical rites marked the important transitions in the lives of individual Christians, with the sacraments of baptism, confession, marriage, unction and burial. The sense of God's immanence and protection of

Orthodox Christians was reinforced by special services of supplication at times of danger, such as siege, battles or earthquake, and of thanksgiving when these perils had subsided.

Historical development

The origins of the Byzantine liturgy, even after Constantine adopted Christianity as the official state religion, are unfortunately obscure. The reason for this is that no liturgical sources, that is, the texts in which the order and

Interior of a classic Byzantine church of the early 11th century. The monastic church of Hosios Loukas, central Greece, looking towards the apse.

words of religious ceremonies were set out, survive from this early period. The earliest surviving Byzantine liturgical text dates from the middle of the eighth century. Nevertheless, it is possible to draw conclusions about what went on from a number of sources, including sermons, a few surviving liturgical texts from other regions, the accounts of pilgrims and the architecture of churches. We know from these various sources that after the first three centuries of Christianity, during which a variety of liturgical usages developed in different parts of the Roman world, a slow

The symbolism of the church building

In his commentary on the Divine Liturgy, the seventh-century theologian Maximus the Confessor sums up the significance of the church building to Orthodox Christian worshippers both then and now: 'God's holy church in itself is a symbol of the sensible world, since it possesses the divine sanctuary as heaven and the beauty of the nave as earth. Likewise the world is a church since it possesses heaven corresponding to a sanctuary, and for a nave it has the adornment of the earth.' To walk into a church is to enter symbolically the whole cosmos which includes the kingdom of heaven. All of creation worships the trinitarian God unendingly; in church the Byzantine faithful could feel they were participating in the heavenly celebrations, in company with the cherubim, the seraphim and all the other ranks of angels. This cosmos has a hierarchical structure, which is duly represented both in the architecture of the church building and in the ranks of both heavenly and earthly beings engaged in carrying out God's liturgy. In many Byzantine churches, a frescoed or mosaic image of Christ, the Pantokrator ('All-Ruler'), looks down from the central dome, while in the sanctuary, bishops, priests and deacons carry out the most secret and holy elements of the rites. The nave, which according to Maximos represents the created world, is filled with men, women and children, who experience the liturgical celebrations through all their senses: sight, sound, smell, touch and taste.

movement towards the standardization of religious worship began to take place under the emperor Constantine and his successors. The Constantinopolitan liturgical rite was based most closely on the liturgies used in Syria; this is because most of the northern Byzantine territories originally had their closest links with the see of Antioch. The two main texts of the Mass, or Divine Liturgy, that survive in later manuscripts and are still used in Orthodox Church today, are attributed to Basil of Caesarea, who was based in central and north-east Anatolia, and John Chysostom, who came from Antioch.

Between the fourth century, when emperors were engaged in Christianizing the Roman empire, and the reign of Justinian (527–65), the Byzantine liturgy slowly became imperial. Not only were religious ceremonies carried out in the Constantinopolitan churches with increasing splendour and elaboration, but emperors played a central role in these liturgical rites. A tradition of religious processions from one holy site to another, or 'stational liturgies', often with services held along the way, had developed in Jerusalem at an early date. This custom spread to Constantinople and Rome at the same time that these cities were establishing churches and endowing them with relics after the Christianization of the Roman empire. In Constantinople every spectator must have felt involved in these splendid ceremonies, as the patriarch, emperor and clergy processed slowly around the city, probably ending up in the Great Church of Hagia Sophia.

After the splendid and dramatic processional liturgies of the early Byzantine period, however, it appears that religious rites began to move indoors from the eighth century onwards. Historians are not entirely certain of the reasons for this change, but it seems to reflect in some measure the difficult circumstances of the middle centuries of Byzantine history, when the empire was continually beset by both internal and external difficulties. What is noticeable is that after the end of the sixth century, much more attention was focused on the church building as the centre of Christian worship and (as we saw above) as a symbol of the heavenly and earthly cosmos. Liturgical rites which had originally taken place throughout the city now began to be performed within the confines of the church building itself. Thus, in the Divine Liturgy, the processions which introduce the two parts of the service, the Liturgy of the Word and the Liturgy of the Faithful, now moved merely

Manuscript illustration of a procession in Constantinople to pray for relief from a drought. From *The Skylitzes Chronicle* (mid-12th century).

between the sanctuary and the nave, instead of entering through the main doors of the church.

The cathedral and the monastic rites
Another development which seems to have occurred between the sixth and the ninth centuries is the introduction of two separate rites, one of which was intended for cathedral usage and one for the monasteries. The cathedral rite was an

altogether more splendid affair: we may imagine the great spaces of Hagia Sophia echoing to the sound of antiphonal choirs singing highly elaborate musical settings of hymns. The monastic rite, which was developed especially at the important Constantinopolitan monastery of Studios, probably with influence from houses in Palestine, tended to be longer and more repetitive. These services, which took up a major portion of both day and night, especially in the more rigorous monasteries, required ever more hymns and readings to fill the daily hours. In the course of the ninth century, monks at Studios and other Constantinopolitan foundations undertook to compose hymns for every day of the year, commemorating saints and other holy figures.

Both the monastic and the cathedral Byzantine rites continued to be used until 1204, when the Latin crusaders sacked Constantinople in the course of the Fourth Crusade. After this date, the secular clergy appears to have found itself unable to maintain the complex sung office of the Great Church of Hagia Sophia. The rise in monastic power between the ninth and the eleventh centuries also contributed to the gradual supplanting of the cathedral rite by the monastic one. The monastic musical and liturgical tradition had the advantage that it could be performed by a few people as well as by many. During the centuries that followed the restoration of Byzantine rule in Constantinople in 1261, as Turkish domination of Asia Minor and mainland Greece slowly advanced and the empire shrank to a tiny enclave based in the capital, the monastic rite became the only viable method of liturgical celebration. This situation did not change after the fall of Constantinople to the Turks in 1453; while Orthodox Christians continued to carry out their religious rituals under Turkish domination, these offices belonged to the monastic tradition rather than to the elaborate settings of the old cathedral rite.

Liturgical time

The lives of Orthodox Christians were probably dominated most of all by their concept of liturgical time, which operated in various connected cycles, somewhat like the interlocking wheels of a clock. If we start with the smallest of these cycles, the daily one, we already see according to the monastic timetable a series of offices that fill up many of the hours in a 24-hour period. The monastic day began in the evening, according to the ancient Judeo-Christian method of calculating time. Thus Vespers would be the first office in the day, followed by Compline, Orthros (Mattins) and the First, Third, Sixth and Ninth Hours. It is impossible to know how much this monastic schedule would have affected lay Byzantine Christians, but the sources do tell us that many pious laypeople regularly attended morning and evening services, especially during Lent. Some, such as the mother of an eighth-century saint, Stephen the Younger, went to the all-night vigils which were held in some churches on the eves of important feasts or (in her case) in honour of the Virgin every Friday evening. A number of sermons from the eighth century onwards were preached in the course of all-night vigils and their audiences consisted of men and women of all ages and backgrounds.

After the daily cycle, an Orthodox Christian might think of the weekly cycle of services which culminates in the celebration of the Mass, or Divine Liturgy, on Sunday morning. Preparation for this holy rite was intense at all times in Byzantine history; if the faithful planned to receive communion they might fast all week on 'dry foods' – in other words, a vegan diet – attend the vigil that was held on Saturday evening, and perhaps also confession. We do not know how often Byzantine Christians received communion, but it is clear that this represented a most sacred 'mystery' in their lives; theologically, the eucharist represents the unity of all Christians and their participation in the body and blood of Christ. A seventh-century source which records what appear to be genuine questions and answers between laypeople and their spiritual leader reveals some common sources of doubt in relation to the eucharist. Some examples include, 'Should one receive communion if one has inadvertently drunk a cup of water the same morning?'

*'We who
mystically
represent the
Cherubim and
sing the thrice-
holy hymn to
the life-giving
Trinity, let us
now lay aside
all worldly care
to receive the
King of All
escorted unseen
by the angelic
corps! Alleluia!'*

'THE CHERUBIC
HYMN', SUNG IN
THE DIVINE
LITURGY

and 'Should one communicate if one has had conjugal relations the night before?' After the seventh or eighth centuries, both literary and archaeological evidence suggest that the celebration of the Divine Liturgy came to be regarded more and more as a sacred mystery, consecrated behind the templon screen or, later, the iconostasis, and administered only to those who were prepared.

The annual liturgical cycle began on 1 September and finished at the end of August. This 'fixed' progression of feasts follows the solar calendar year and commemorates the major events in the life of Christ and of his mother, the Virgin Mary or *Theotokos* ('God-bearer'). Various feast days, especially those commemorating the Virgin, only gradually came to be added to the calendar, as church officials acknowledged her importance in Christian theology and recognized the need to remember important events in her life. Thus, the Nativity of the Virgin (8 September), introduced into the calendar in the late sixth century, is the first major festival in the calendar; this is followed by the Exaltation of the Cross (14 September), the Presentation of the Virgin into the Temple (21 November), Christmas (25 December) and so on.

Iconography of the major Christian feasts

By about the 10th century, Byzantine religious art had evolved standard ways of depicting the major feasts of Christ and the Virgin Mary. Usually 12 scenes were chosen for the decoration of churches and icons. These were the Annunciation, the Nativity of Christ, the Presentation in the Temple, the Baptism of Christ, the Transfiguration, the Raising of Lazarus, Entry into Jerusalem, the Crucifixion, the *Anastasis* (descent into Hades and resurrection of the dead), Ascension, Pentecost and the death, or *Koimesis*, of the Virgin. However, the choice of scenes could vary, depending largely on those who commissioned these works of art. Each of these subjects represents a major feast in the Church, which would be celebrated by all-night vigils, a Divine Liturgy and feasting.

The major festivals of the Church provided a defining structure in the lives of ordinary Christians. It was a happy coincidence that the Nativity of Christ was celebrated from an early date at about the time of the winter solstice, on 25 December. In 274 the emperor Aurelian also chose this date for the pagan festival of the birth of the Sun god (scholars are still debating whether it was actually Christians or pagans who adopted 25 December for their nativity festivals first). In any case, Christians were able to appropriate much of the symbolism of the pagan festival: Christ was celebrated at this time as the Sun of Righteousness, representing the triumph of light over darkness. Imagery appropriate to the time of year could also be used at Easter, the most important of all Christian festivals. This celebration of Christ's resurrection and Christian rebirth falls at a natural time of renewal, in the early spring.

A second annual cycle, sometimes called the 'movable' liturgical year, centres around Easter, the most important of all the Christian feasts. Beginning with a Saturday in mid-winter, usually sometime in February, called the Sunday of the Publican and the Pharisee, the Easter cycle continues

Mosaic panel showing the Transfiguration of Christ, celebrated as one of the 12 major feast days of the Orthodox Church, from the 12th-century monastery and church of Daphni, near Athens.

after Easter until the feast of Pentecost. This period is termed 'movable', in contrast to the fixed annual cycle, because it is calculated differently every year, in accordance with the lunar calendar. Easter originally followed the Jewish Passover, since according to the Gospels this is when Jesus entered Jerusalem and into the sequence of events that would lead up to his crucifixion. In the early centuries of the Church, however, Eastern and Western Christians disagreed over how closely Easter should follow the Jewish Passover and therefore exactly how the date should be calculated.

The sacraments

Finally, the lifetime cycle of a Byzantine Orthodox Christian, like that of most practising Christians today, was punctuated by a series of sacraments, or 'mysteries', which enabled him or her to participate fully in the life of the Church, as members of the body of Christ (Romans 12:4). It is interesting to note that unlike the Western Catholic Church, the Byzantines never formally committed themselves to a strict number of sacraments, or even to a formal definition of these mysteries. Whereas Theodore the Studite in the ninth century gives a list of six sacraments (baptism, communion, chrismation or confirmation, ordination, monastic tonsure and the service of burial), Nicholas Cabasilas, who wrote a commentary on the sacraments in the 14th century, listed only three: baptism, chrismation and communion. Other later liturgical writers listed as many as 10 sacramental

acts within the Church. This lack of consensus suggests that the sacraments developed more out of the daily needs of the Byzantine Church than as a theoretical construct.

Baptism in the early period represented a truly significant event in the life of an individual who chose to become a Christian. After a three-year period of intensive training, which involved not only catechetical lessons in the mysteries and teachings of the Church, but also rigorous fasting and prayer, the initiate would be baptized on Easter night, thus experiencing in his or her whole being the true meaning of Christ's glorious resurrection. Infant baptism began to supplant the reception of adults into the Church in the sixth or seventh centuries and to some extent the spiritual significance of this most central sacrament in the Church was lost at this time. On the other hand, Orthodox infants and children were considered full, participating members of the Church from the moment of their

The baptism of the son of the Byzantine emperor Leo VI (Constantine VII) by the patriarch, as depicted in a 12th-century Byzantine manuscript.

baptisms, since their confirmation, or chrismation, was performed in the same ceremony. To this day, it is the babies and children in an Orthodox church who wait at the front of the queue to receive communion; if asked whether they fully understand the significance of the eucharist, an Orthodox will answer, 'Would I deny a child its spiritual food any more than its material nourishment?'

After baptism, chrismation and communion, which clearly represented the first three sacraments in the Byzantine Church, the role of confession as one of the 'mysteries' of the Church remained somewhat less clearly defined. The practice of public penance in the early Church slowly gave way to more private confession, followed by a prayer of absolution. The Eastern Orthodox Church differed from the Catholic West in that it never understood sin and salvation in a legalistic way; sin was viewed more as a disease than as a legal crime and absolution represented spiritual healing. A certain informality with regard to confession appears to have existed throughout the Byzantine period: individuals were free to choose their own spiritual guides and confessors. These 'spiritual fathers or mothers' might be lay monastic figures rather than parish priests or bishops.

Marriage

The idea that marriage between two Christians represents a sacred contract appears already in the writings of the apostle Paul: '"For this reason a man will leave his father and mother and be joined to his wife, and the two will become one flesh." This is a great mystery, and I am applying it to Christ and the Church' (Ephesians 5:31–32). This passage expresses two separate ideas concerning marriage. First, Paul reaffirms the Roman understanding of marriage as a legal contract between two consenting individuals. The consequence of this agreement is that they will establish a new home together, sharing everything as if they were one unit. Second, however, Paul suggests for the first time here a Christian view of marriage: the sacred contract between a man and a woman symbolizes the union between Christ and the Church. As a reflection of the eternal kingdom of God, marriage represents an eternal bond which will not be broken even by death.

After the Christianization of the Roman empire, the full involvement of the Church in sanctioning and blessing marriages came about relatively slowly. It was only by the early 10th century that the emperor Leo VI published a law which formally obliged the Church to validate *all* marriages. In spite of the Orthodox Christian belief in the eternal nature of the marriage bond, it was soon recognized that many Christians fell short in upholding this ideal. While not condoning divorce or remarriage after bereavement, the Church frequently allowed that such arrangements might be necessary. The marriage ceremonies of those who were entering into a second or third union were penitential in character and were not combined with the holy eucharist.

The final rites

The office of 'extreme unction', which is administered before every individual Christian's death, evolved out of a more general sacrament known as 'holy unction' delivered at the beds of those who are sick. Both services were composed of scriptural readings and prayers of healing, and would be performed by one or several priests. The ill or dying would also be anointed with holy oil, which symbolized divine mercy and liberation from human suffering of any kind. Along with the funeral service, which was considered a sacrament by many Byzantine liturgical writers, unction expressed also the continuing participation of the individual in the life of the Church. Even in illness and after death, Christians represented members of the living and resurrected body of Christ, into which they had been initiated through baptism and communion.

As we have seen in this chapter, the life of the Byzantine Orthodox Christian was regulated by various liturgical cycles, all of which helped to shape his or her everyday life. The daily practice of liturgical prayer, which lay Christians would carry out before the icons in their own

'The church is heaven on earth, where the God of heaven dwells and moves... It is prefigured in the patriarchs, founded on the apostles, adorned in the hierarchs, perfected in the martyrs.'

ST GERMANOS OF
CONSTANTINOPLE
(c. 634–c. 732), *ON
THE DIVINE LITURGY*

homes, participation in stational liturgies or processions, attendance at church and finally, on a more personal note, participation in the major sacraments throughout their lives – all of these activities would have reinforced the sense of Orthodox Christian life as a structured and symbolic enactment of the kingdom of heaven on earth.

CHAPTER 8

121

DOCTRINE AND
THE SEVEN
ECUMENICAL
COUNCILS

Doctrine and the Seven Ecumenical Councils

C hristianity, like Judaism, is a religion based on scripture. The early Church at first regarded the Old Testament, replete with prophecies foretelling the incarnation of Christ, as their scripture. In the course of the second century, the epistles of Paul, Acts and the four Gospels also gradually acquired the status of divinely inspired writings. Perhaps basing their accounts on oral traditions, the evangelists recorded for posterity what appear to be Jesus' actual words and teachings. But what do the Saviour's indications about himself actually mean? Jesus asks his disciples, 'Who do people say that the Son of man is?' Peter answers, 'You are the Messiah, the Son of the living God' (Matthew 16:13–16). Whatever these words may have meant to Jesus and his disciples, they were understood in many ways by later Christians.

It also may seem that various passages in the New Testament say different things about Christ. 'The Father and I are one' (John 10:30) seems to conflict with the sense of the statement, 'But about that day or hour no one knows, neither the angels in heaven, nor the Son, but only the Father' (Mark 13:32). Scholars today would explain the discrepancies in Jesus' own account of himself as reflecting the different intentions and backgrounds of the individual evangelists who reported his sayings. In the early Church, however, these statements had to be taken at face value and could only be understood as revealing paradoxical aspects of Christian doctrine. The more sophisticated interpreters of biblical texts could also resort to allegory, by arguing that the literal sense of a passage concealed a deeper, symbolic meaning.

The definition of an unknowable God

As we shall see in the course of this chapter, different understandings of the relationship of Christ the Son to God the Father, of the Holy Spirit in relation to both Father and Son, and of the way in which humanity and divinity come together in Christ, led to tragic schisms in the first five centuries of the Church. Nevertheless, it is important to recognize that these controversies did not result solely from intellectual speculations concerning the Trinity and the incarnation of Christ. As many of the early Greek Fathers reveal in their writings on these issues, Christian doctrine has a direct bearing on human salvation. In debating these matters, early Christians thus felt that the correct understanding of trinitarian and christological doctrine could affect their own destiny.

Human beings, since the fall from grace of Adam and Eve, have been separated from God by their participation in this ancestral sin, which also accounts for the difficulties of human existence. But God sent his Son to become one of us and to redeem us by his own death and resurrection. If Christ is successfully to bridge the gap between divinity and humanity, it is essential that he participate completely in both states of being. No one less than God can save humankind; Christ the Saviour therefore must be God. At the same time, however, humanity can only participate in the salvation offered by Christ's death and resurrection if he is fully human. The link between God and humanity can only be secured by a fully human and divine Saviour, the incarnate Christ. The early Greek Fathers took a further step by speaking of the possibility of the 'deification' (*theiôsis*) of humankind as a result of the incarnation of Christ. As Athanasius, bishop of Alexandria, expressed it in the early fourth century, 'God became human that we might become God.'

'If you ask for your change, the shopkeeper philosophizes to you about the Begotten and the Unbegotten. If you ask the price of a loaf, the answer is "the Father is greater and the Son is inferior"; if you say, "is my bath ready?" the attendant declares that the Son is of nothing.'

ST GREGORY OF
NYSSA, FOURTH
CENTURY

Sources of authority

The bishops engaged in resolving controversies concerning
the nature of the Trinity or the humanity and divinity of
Christ relied on various sources of authority to support
their decisions First and foremost, Christian scripture, or
the books of the New Testament which had been accepted
as canonical by the end of the second century, provided the
firmest basis for an understanding of God and of Christ. As
we saw above, however, many biblical passages appear to be
contradictory; both spiritual knowledge and discernment
were needed to make sense of the various evangelists'
accounts of Jesus Christ.

Second, it is clear that from the second century onwards,
bishops and teachers in the Church regarded both written
and unwritten tradition as authoritative within the Church.
The earliest Christian creeds are probably based on local
'rules of faith' which were used in the instruction and
baptismal initiation of new converts. Finally, Orthodox
Christians believed then, and still believe, that God continues
to reveal himself to us through the inspiration of the Holy

Negative theology

A branch of theology which seems to have been in use from the fourth century
onwards, and which draws on Greek philosophical traditions which stress the
unknowable transcendence of God, is known as 'apophatic'. This is sometimes
translated 'negative theology' since it denies that any concept formulated by
human beings can adequately express the mystery of divine being. It is clear that
the apophatic approach remained deeply embedded in the Eastern Orthodox
tradition throughout the Byzantine period. Whereas scholasticism, the idea that
the human intellect may formulate systematic definitions of theology, gained
adherents in the West in the course of the 11th and 12th centuries, Byzantine
Orthodox theologians always regarded the apophatic approach as the best and
deepest expression of our human apprehension of God. On the other hand, it was
necessary to formulate doctrine in order to counter the heresies which continually
challenged the Church. A tension thus existed in Orthodox theology between the
affirmation that God is essentially unknowable and the need to formulate creeds
in which the natures of all three members of the Holy Trinity are precisely defined.

Previous page:
**The descent of
the Holy Spirit at
Pentecost in a
mosaic panel
from the 11th-
century monastic
church of Hosios
Loukas, central
Greece.**

Spirit. The ideas expressed in the seven ecumenical councils
of the Church, which took place between 325 and 787, may
go beyond biblical sources in their formulation of Christian
doctrine; nevertheless, this reflects God's continuing
involvement in human history and the gradual process of
divine revelation. As Gregory Nazianzen argued in the fourth
century, some doctrines, such as the divinity of the Spirit,
were revealed only gradually since Christ's disciples and
their followers were not yet capable of fully understanding
them. 'You perceive', writes Gregory, 'periods of illumination
gradually enlightening us and an order of revelation which
it is better for us to preserve, neither appearing in a single
burst nor maintaining secrecy to the very end'.

The seven ecumenical councils

Controversy over the precise relationship of Christ the
Son to God the Father, which initiated a long period of
dispute concerning the Trinity, developed at the beginning
of the fourth century. The timing of this debate and the
repercussions that it caused throughout the Roman world
(which in this period represented territories all around
the Mediterranean Sea) are in fact no accident. Unity and
shared definitions of doctrine became a high priority
within the Church as soon as Constantine I adopted
Christianity as the state religion of the Roman empire.
Disagreements within the Church had occurred before,
but had tended to be settled by local councils or by the
rulings of individual bishops. Now that the Church
acknowledged one emperor as its temporal head and as
the ecclesiastical hierarchy came to be attached to five
important sees, or patriarchates, the need for universal
councils, whose decisions would be binding on the entire
Church, arose.

Constantine I summoned and presided over the first
ecumenical council, held in Nicea in 325, in response to the
teachings of an Alexandrian priest called Arius. Either due to
a literal understanding of scripture or because he wished to
maintain the complete transcendence of God the Father, Arius

taught that Christ the Son is inferior to God the Father. In one of his few surviving letters, Arius wrote that 'the Son, begotten by the Father, created and founded before the ages, *was not* before he was begotten'. In other words, although created by the Father even before the beginning of time, Christ the Son did not exist co-eternally with God; *there was a time when he was not*. Alexander, bishop of Alexandria, who seems to have been the first churchman to take exception to Arius' teachings, used passages from the Gospel of John to show that the Father and the Son are inseparable and of one being. He argued that by proposing a division between God the Father and Christ, Arius was suggesting that Christ was a mere creature. If this is the case, he no longer represents a link between humanity and divinity: thus, our chance of salvation through Christ does not exist.

At the Council of Nicea, the assembled bishops worked out a formula to express the divinity of Christ and his oneness with God. A new term, *homoousios*, which may be translated 'one in essence', was borrowed from Greek philosophy to express the indissoluble unity of Father and Son. The Nicene Creed stresses the co-eternal and uncreated being of Christ

One way of depicting the Trinity in later Byzantine icons was to portray the three angels who visited Abraham.

the Word: 'God from God, light from light, true God from true God, begotten not made, *homoousios* with the Father'. According to the historical and theological accounts written soon after the Council of Nicea, some bishops, although they may have signed the Acts of the council, remained uncomfortable with the expression *homoousios*. The term could be understood in various ways, but even more worryingly, it represented an innovation which departed from the purely scriptural definitions of Christ. Controversy over this word and the anti-Arian decisions of Nicea themselves rumbled on for nearly a century, especially under the pro-Arian successors of Constantine I. The debate was finally

resolved at the second ecumenical council of Constantinople in 381, when the decisions of Nicea were reaffirmed and the term *homoousios* upheld.

The theologians who contributed most to the development of doctrine in the fourth-century East include Athanasius and the three Cappadocian Fathers, Basil of Caesarea, Gregory of Nyssa and Gregory Nazianzen. Athanasius, who spent much of his career as bishop of Alexandria exiled from his see under a succession of Arian emperors, defended the divinity of Christ in various works, including a treatise, *On the Incarnation*. In addition to their contributions to trinitarian doctrine, which were considerable, the Cappadocian Fathers helped to defend the divinity of the Holy Spirit against a new heresy which questioned his equal status with Father and Son in the Trinity. Basil of Caesarea wrote a treatise, *On the Holy Spirit*, in which he used the authority of both scripture and tradition to argue the equality of the three persons of the Trinity, Father, Son and Holy Spirit. The emended Creed, which was agreed at the second ecumenical council of 381, contained the longer definition of the Holy Spirit: [I believe]… in the Holy Spirit, the Lord and life-giver, who proceeds from the Father, who with the Father and the Son is together worshipped and glorified.'

The Council of Constantinople also built on the work of the first ecumenical council in dealing with the external organization of the Church. It assigned a new order of precedence to the five administrative and spiritual centres of Christendom, or patriarchates. For the first time since Constantine's foundation of the city as 'the Second Rome' in 330, Constantinople was pronounced to be second in importance after Rome, followed by the more ancient sees of Alexandria, Antioch and Jerusalem. The continuing power struggles between the sees of Constantinople, Alexandria and Antioch played a significant part in the events leading up to the next great religious controversy, which dominated the fifth century. This was the debate over the two natures of Christ, contested mainly by proponents of the theological schools based in Antioch and Alexandria.

Opposite page: **Gregory Nazianzen, one of the three Cappadocian Fathers, composing a sermon at his writing desk. From the frontispiece of a manuscript in St Catherine's Monastery, Sinai (dated to between 1136 and 1155), believed to have been produced at the Pantokrator Monastery, Constantinople.**

Trouble began when Nestorius, an Antiochene monk who was appointed bishop of Constantinople in 428, preached against the use of the term *Theotokos* ('God-bearer') for the Virgin Mary, arguing that she gave birth to the incarnate Christ, not to God. Nestorius was probably reacting to an already flourishing cult of the Virgin at this time, but he also based his arguments on christological teaching which he had assimilated in Antioch. The Antiochene school of theology interpreted scripture from a literal point of view, emphasizing the humanity of Jesus Christ and the reality of his historical existence. Cyril, the forceful bishop of Alexandria, on hearing of Nestorius' opinions, began writing letters to important figures in Constantinople, as well as to Nestorius himself. Cyril was informed by the Alexandrian school of theology, which stressed a more allegorical approach to scripture and which also traditionally emphasized the divinity of Christ, as the Word, or *Logos*, of God. Whereas Nestorius wished to uphold the diversity of the two natures in Christ, thereby safeguarding his true humanity, Cyril started from the position of unity, arguing that the divine and human natures are inseparable in the Son of God. Passages such as 'The Word became flesh' (John 1:14) and 'The Father and I are one' (John 10:30) justified the idea that the Virgin Mary, or *Theotokos*, in fact gave birth to God.

The emperor Theodosios II called the third ecumenical council, which was held in Ephesus in 431, in order to resolve this dispute. Cyril and the Alexandrian party dominated this council, which deposed Nestorius and upheld the Virgin Mary's title as *Theotokos*. The Council of Ephesus did not represent the end of the christological debate, however, as the emperor and his bishops struggled to reconcile the Antiochene and Alexandrian parties. Soon after the council, Cyril of Alexandria was forced to sign in 433 a 'Formula of Reunion', which had actually been drafted by the Antiochene theologian, Theodoret of Cyrus. This document, which incorporated the phrase 'a union of two natures' in describing Christ, seemed to Cyril's followers a wholesale sacrifice of Alexandrian theology. In the years that followed, influential clerics in both Alexandria and Constantinople pushed Cyril's Alexandrian theology even further, eventually declaring that there is just one, divine nature in Christ. Another council was held in Ephesus in 449, which was dominated by these hardline 'Monophysites', but which also alienated the eminent Pope Leo I, who had composed a doctrinal statement, or 'Tome', in which he expressed his adherence to a definition of Christ in two natures.

Eventually the need for unity and concord within the Christian empire as a whole decided the issue. After the death of Theodosios II in 450, his successor Marcian called for a new ecumenical council, the fourth, to be held at Chalcedon in 451. The decisions of this council represent a masterpiece of ecumenical compromise in the history of the Church. The Chalcedonian definition of christological doctrine succeeds in accommodating the divergent theologies of Antioch, Alexandria and Rome, as expressed by Pope Leo:

We all with one voice confess our Lord Jesus Christ one and the same Son, the same perfect in Godhead, the same perfect in manhood, truly God and truly man, the same consisting of

This unique image of the Christ child sitting alone may reflect an unwillingness to refer explicitly to his relationship with Mary, since the issue was still being debated when this mosaic panel was executed. Image of Christ sitting as an infant on a throne (432–40), Santa Maria Maggiore, Rome.

*a reasonable soul and a body, of one essence with the Father
as touching the Godhead, the same of one essence with us as
touching the manhood... born from the Virgin Mary, the*
Theotokos... *to be acknowledged in two natures, without
confusion, without change, without division, without
separation; the distinction of natures being in no way
abolished because of the union but rather the characteristic
property of each nature being preserved, and concurring into
one person and one hypostasis.*

THE DEFINITION OF THE COUNCIL OF CHALCEDON, 451

Sadly, however, the first major schisms within the Christian
Church were not averted by the ecumenical councils of the
fifth century. A large group of Christians based in the Near
East (modern Syria, Iran and Iraq) broke away from the
wider Church. They could not accept the decisions of the
Council of Ephesus, with its condemnation of Nestorius and
other Antiochene theologians and its upholding of the title
Theotokos for the Virgin Mary. This Church, which is often
misleadingly called 'Nestorian' (it prefers to call itself 'the
Assyrian Church of the East') survives to this day, remaining
out of communion with the Chalcedonian Orthodox
Churches. A second schism occurred after the Council
of Chalcedon, when adherents of Dioscorus and other
'Monophysite' followers of Cyril of Alexandria, felt betrayed
by the definitions reached at that council. The so-called
'Monophysite' Churches, which still represent the majority
in Egypt, Western Syria, Armenia and Ethiopia, also remain
outside communion with the Western Catholic and Eastern
Orthodox Churches which accepted Chalcedon.

Efforts at reconciliation

The development of doctrine within the Byzantine empire
through the sixth and seventh centuries reflects a continuing
effort on the part of both emperors and bishops to heal the
schisms which had resulted from the councils of Ephesus
(431) and Chalcedon (451). Efforts at compromise included
the re-examination of the teachings of Cyril of Alexandria in

The Virgin and
Child portrayed
in a Coptic wall
painting, dating
probably from
the seventh
century.

the sixth century, the introduction of new ideas such as the 'Theopaschite' formula, which stated that Jesus as God suffered on the cross, and the reappraisal of terms such as *physis* ('nature') and *hypostasis* ('substance'). Eventually, the emperor Justinian called a fifth ecumenical council at Constantinople in 553, which officially registered such compromises in its formal definition of the faith. As so often happened at ecumenical councils, condemnation of one contending group, in this case a group of three Antiochene theologians of the fourth and fifth centuries, was also aimed at reconciling their opponents.

The compromises effected by successive ecumenical councils only had a limited effect in healing schisms within the Church, however. Some historians have argued that theological differences between the various groups were compounded by linguistic, ethnic and political separation. It is certainly true that the non-Chalcedonian Churches were largely based in the Eastern territories of the empire and composed of the non-Greek-speaking peoples of those areas. It is also possible that many of their members felt cut off and alienated from the bishops who represented the Church, who were based in the distant capital city of Constantinople. On the other hand, it is important not to underestimate the importance of 'right belief' or orthodoxy to Christians in this period. As we saw earlier, the doctrines concerning the humanity and divinity of Christ had implications for human salvation, both individual and collective. The fact that the differences between Monophysite, Antiochene and Chalcedonian christology seem in retrospect to reflect subtle variations in emphasis rather than major contradictions should not obscure the fact that their adherents held them to be matters of life and death. The separation of the Churches was further accentuated in the sixth century as rival bishops were ordained and separate ecclesiastical structures began to develop.

The resurrection, or *Anastasis*, of Christ. The iconography of this scene is Byzantine, but there are clearly Oriental elements in the style. Illustration in a Syrian liturgical book from the 13th century.

The doctrine of 'one will', or Monotheletism

Further efforts to reconcile the Monophysite and Chalcedonian Churches took place in the first half of the seventh century, especially during the reign of the emperor Herakleios. Sergios, Patriarch of Constantinople between 610 and 638, devised the 'Monothelite' doctrine, which he hoped would present enough concessions to draw the various Monophysite Churches back into the fold. According to the Monothelite teaching, which was published as an imperial *Ekthesis* (statement) in 638, Christ has two natures but only one, divine will. Although this formula seems to have worked for a time, enabling the agreement of various Eastern bishops to reunion with the imperial Church, two notable Byzantine theologians, a monk named Maximos the Confessor and Sophronios, Patriarch of Jerusalem, denounced it as heretical. Although Maximos did not live to see the success of his efforts against Monotheletism, the doctrine was eventually abandoned at the sixth ecumenical council of Constantinople held in 680–81.

Monotheletism represents the last attempt to heal the major schism within the Eastern Churches that had resulted from the Council of Chalcedon in 451. After the 630s, the imperial need to restore unity to the Church as a whole was rendered irrelevant by the unexpected loss of most of the Near East and North Africa to the Muslims. Christianity survived in these areas, both in Chalcedonian and non-Chalcedonian communities, but Byzantine emperors no longer felt the need to draw them back into the orbit of the Constantinopolitan patriarchate. It is thus correct to say that trinitarian and christological doctrines reached their full elaboration by the end of the seventh century and that no further attempts at compromise were made after that. Nevertheless, one more issue which was soon seen to have a christological dimension remained to be debated: this was the defence of holy images in the eighth century, in response to an iconoclastic imperial policy.

Iconoclasm as a theological issue
In the eighth century, a series of emperors, beginning with Leo III (717–41), introduced a policy of 'Iconoclasm' on the grounds that the Church was lapsing into idolatrous practices. The use of portable icons and the decoration of churches with images of Christ and other holy figures seemed to Leo and his supporters to contravene God's second commandment (Exodus 20:4). Although the arguments for and against religious images focused first on the charge of idolatry, they

later began to move into the field of christological doctrine. The iconoclasts, as we know from the few surviving texts that they produced, charged the defenders of images with the heresies of both Nestorianism and Monophysitism. In creating an icon of Christ, they argued, one is guilty either of separating his human from his divine nature (Nestorianism) or of confusing the two (Monophysitism).

The defenders of holy images, or iconophiles, were fortunate in possessing several distinguished theologians who explored fully in their treatises the implications of the iconoclast charges. John of Damascus, a monk in the monastery of St Sabas near Jerusalem, could write safely from Islamic territories in the early eighth century on the subject of holy images within the Church. John defended icons on a number of grounds, using church tradition, Chalcedonian christology and even Neoplatonic philosophy to justify his arguments. The seventh and final ecumenical council, held at Nicea in 787, compiled a huge scriptural and patristic dossier in defence of holy icons, arguing primarily that their veneration could not be equated with idolatry in the light of Christ's incarnation and the inauguration of the kingdom of God. When Iconoclasm was reintroduced by Leo V (813–20), two more distinguished theologians, the monk Theodore of Studios and Patriarch Nikephoros, developed the christological and philosophical defence of images still further.

The doctrinal importance of the debate which took place in the period of Iconoclasm cannot be overemphasized in the history of Orthodox theology. This is one area in which the Byzantine Orthodox Church diverged significantly from intellectual and spiritual developments in the West. Although the popes who were asked to respond to this crisis supported the use of images, provided refuge for fleeing Byzantine iconophiles and signed the acts of the seventh ecumenical council, it is clear that they viewed icons from a very different spiritual perspective. Religious imagery had been used in the West for centuries, but was seen as fulfilling primarily educational purposes. The degree of cultural separation is indicated especially by the reaction

of Frankish theologians to the Council of Nicea: at the
Synod of Frankfurt (794) they stated that icon veneration
was not an issue of true faith, worthy of discussion in an
ecumenical council.

To the Byzantines, on the other hand, the 'theology
of images' which developed in response to Iconoclasm
represented the final stage in the definition of trinitarian
and christological doctrine, which is summed up in the
proceedings of all seven ecumenical councils. Precise
definitions concerning God were of course inadequate, as
he remains transcendent and uncircumscribed by either
word or image. On the other hand, Byzantine Orthodox
bishops and theologians recognized that the formulations
agreed in ecumenical councils are necessary for two main
reasons: first, one must define the faith in response to the
heresies which threatened the integrity and meaning of the
faith at various times in history; and second, the incarnation
of Christ radically altered humanity's relationship with God.
In taking on our nature, Christ, the Son of God, allowed
himself to be circumscribed, thus forming a link between
the divine and the created worlds.

The development of doctrine after 787
To Byzantine Christians the period of the seven ecumenical
councils (325–787) represented the golden age of Orthodox
theology in which trinitarian and christological doctrine were
fully formulated. This is not to say that further problems did
not arise in subsequent centuries. What is clear, however, is
that later doctrinal developments were concerned largely with
finer points of definition, in response to challenges from both
inside and outside the Eastern Church. After the restoration
of icons in 843, called the Triumph of Orthodoxy in the
Byzantine Church, differences in doctrine and practice arose
between the Constantinopolitan patriarchate and the papacy
in Rome. Ultimately these differences led to complete
schism, formally initiated in 1054. Certain churches in the
West had taken to inserting a short phrase, *filioque* ('and the
Son'), after the statement in the Nicene–Constantinopolitan

Creed concerning the Holy Spirit, 'who proceeds from the Father'. As attitudes concerning the *filioque* clause began to harden in East and West from the mid-ninth century onwards, Byzantine theologians such as the patriarch Photios wrote treatises elaborating the doctrinal significance of this issue. The Byzantines objected to the addition of the *filioque* on two grounds: first, that it represented an innovation that had not been agreed by the Church as a whole; and second, that the statement is false, since the Holy Spirit proceeds from the Father alone.

Other heresies emerged after the ninth century and helped further to define the boundaries of Orthodoxy. In the 10th and 11th centuries, a dualist sect called the Bogomils spread from Bulgaria through the Balkan peninsula and into

The Bogomils

Like the Cathars in Western Europe, the Bogomils were dualists. Dualism is based on the idea that two opposing forces of good and evil are perpetually at war in the universe. Goodness is associated with an unseen, spiritual God who has nothing to do with the created world which we inhabit. A few individuals, called the 'elect', contain a 'spark' of divinity which separates them from the rest of creation. Matter and the physical body, on the other hand, are controlled by the forces of evil. The spiritual and the physical worlds are diametrically opposed and salvation consists in escaping the bondage of human flesh after death. Only initiates with a 'spark' of divine spirit, however, were believed to be destined for salvation. According to Byzantine accounts of the heresy, its adherents led a strict, ascetic life, eschewing meat, wine and sexual intercourse. Anna Komnena, the royal 12th-century historian, described them as follows: 'Your Bogomil wears a sombre look; muffled up to the nose, he walks with a stoop, quietly muttering to himself – but inside he is a ravening wolf'. Reading between the lines of Anna's account, it is possible to detect that, as in the case of most other reforming religious movements, Bogomilism had a strong appeal for those who felt that the established Church had fallen away from the purity of its apostolic origins. The serious difference in doctrine between this sect and Orthodox Christianity, however, lay in their understandings of God and the created world. Whereas the Bogomils like other dualists believed that matter was essentially evil, Orthodox theology declared the whole of the created world to be the handiwork of a good and benevolent God.

Asia Minor, eventually reaching Constantinople itself. This movement may represent a link between earlier dualist heresies such as Manichaeism and the Cathar movements in Italy and Southern France, which appeared in the 12th and 13th centuries.

Palamism and the uncreated essence of God

In the 14th century, a new controversy arose concerning the nature of God and the ability of human beings to apprehend him mystically through prayer, as we saw in chapter 5. The debate between Gregory Palamas and his opponents, most notably a Calabrian monk named Barlaam, also touched on doctrinal issues concerning the nature of God. When Gregory, building on a long tradition of Byzantine mystical writings, asserted that it is possible for human beings to attain divine visions through prayer, Barlaam retorted that this is inconsistent with the doctrine of the transcendence and unknowability of God. Gregory Palamas responded that there is a distinction between God's unknowable essence and his energies. Citing Christ's transfiguration on Mount Tabor as an example, Palamas argued that what the disciples saw was a vision of uncreated light which represents the uncreated energy of God. The Christian mystic who experiences such a vision, both by means of his own efforts and by the grace of God, has directly encountered the living God. Another term for this experience is 'deification' (*theiôsis*); it is only possible because human beings are made in the image and likeness of God. The eventual acceptance of Gregory Palamas' teachings and the condemnation of Barlaam's point of view by the Byzantine Church represents an important stage in the development of Orthodox mystical theology. As in the case of religious images, the debate that accompanied this process helped to develop and clarify the dogmatic issues which were at stake.

Orthodoxy versus heresy

It is clear that the definition of doctrine in the Byzantine Church took place over many centuries and was beset by numerous controversies. The major definitions of doctrine, which took place in the course of the first five centuries of the Church and were ratified by a series of ecumenical councils, provide a dogmatic foundation which is shared by Eastern and Western Christendom alike. Such formal definitions of faith became necessary in response to intellectual challenges which arose within the Church. It is important to stress here that bishops would have preferred to avoid making such formal declarations about the nature of God if that had been possible. As questions arose concerning the nature of the Trinity or the relationship of Christ the Son to God the Father, Orthodox bishops felt that what they viewed as authentic Christian doctrine, based both on scripture and on the living experience of the Church, must be defended.

Faith and Worldview

Whent we say that everyone was religious in the Byzantine empire or, for that matter, in the whole of the medieval world, it is important to understand exactly what we mean by this concept. Belief in one, transcendent God formed the basis of Orthodox Christians' belief, along with a basic understanding of scripture and trinitarian doctrine. However, Byzantine faith also encompassed an entire worldview. The formation of the universe, the playing out of history and humanity's final destiny were all understood from a Christian perspective which may seem alien in many ways to our modern, largely secular culture.

Other aspects of this medieval culture may also strike us as remarkable and deserve closer scrutiny. Byzantines of all periods felt that supernatural forces were present and active in everyday life. These included not only the power which came from God himself, channelled through holy people or objects in the created world, but also malevolent forces which usually took the form of demons. Perhaps because of the fragility of human life in a world which was threatened continually by invasions, epidemics and natural disasters, the Byzantines' belief in the afterlife was also strong. Finally, Orthodox Christianity, the dominant religion in this culture, provided people with a sense of belonging and identity. The perpetual castigation of minorities such as the Jews, heretics or external enemies such as Muslims in Byzantine texts reinforces the feeling of a tight-knit, well-defined group which is pitted against the rest of the world.

Previous page:
Mosaic image of
the creation of
Adam and Eve
executed by
Byzantine-
influenced artists
at St Mark's
Cathedral, Venice,
in the early 13th
century.

The cosmos

Early Christians inherited a number of different intellectual traditions, all of which had to be amalgamated somehow into a sensible explanation of how the world was created, why human beings were put into it and how their history would end. The Greek Fathers of the second through to the fourth centuries built mostly on Judaic tradition, using the biblical account in the first chapters of Genesis. At the same time, however, there were obviously problems with this account from a literal point of view. How, for example, could God separate light from darkness on the first day when he created the sun and the moon only on the fourth? A bishop called Theophilos of Antioch, writing in the second century, provided the first cosmological explanation of these verses. According to him, the universe was fashioned rather like a box: the earth (which is flat) represents its foundation and the sky, or firmament, is stretched out above it. The heaven which God made on the first day was not this visible sky, but an even higher one which lies above it and is invisible from the created world. This has the form of a roof or a vault, as suggested in the passage, 'It is he... who stretches out the heavens like a curtain, and spreads them like a tent to live in' (Isaiah 40:22). The suggestion here is that the visible world represents only a small part of God's creation; sources of light are therefore not confined to the celestial bodies that humans are permitted to see.

Origen, a Christian writer of the late second and early third century, ventured even more deeply into cosmology, constructing in his treatise, *On First Principles*, an elaborate explanation of the universe which was deeply influenced by Middle Platonism. Unlike Theophilos of Antioch and most later Christian theologians, Origen's system does not attempt to explain the physical universe. We find no box-like structures here: instead, the hierarchical structure which is topped by the transcendent God out of whom emanated the Word, or *Logos*, and all the angels and other created beings seems to exist in a purely conceptual framework. Origen's writings, especially *On First Principles*, fell into disrepute about a century after his death, owing to some unorthodox aspects of its teaching. The subordination of the *Logos* to God, even though Origen did affirm the Son's co-eternity with the Father, and the idea of restitution, or *apokatastasis*, at the final Day of Judgment for all, even conceivably the devil, were both ideas that seemed inconsistent with Christian doctrine as it was later formulated.

Perhaps one of the best examples of a biblical view of the cosmos occurs in the *Christian Topography*, a book written by a sixth-century Alexandrian merchant known as Kosmas Indikopleustes. Kosmas had a wealth of experience with which to write about the physical universe. In the course of his career, he had travelled down the Red Sea and visited Ethiopia as well as many other countries. He does not appear to have sailed as far as India, but he had certainly seen more of the known inhabited world than most of his Byzantine contemporaries. Kosmas provides a strictly Christian picture of the universe, in which the created world (described in detail on the basis of his travels) is surmounted by the heavenly kingdom, according to the box-like structure suggested by earlier Christian writers such as Theophilos of Antioch. Like Theophilos, Kosmas creates his picture of the physical structure of the universe in accordance with a literal interpretation of the Bible, especially Genesis.

As we can see from the helpful diagrams which accompany the text of Kosmas' account, he pictures the cosmos as a three-dimensional box surmounted by a vaulted lid. The earth, which is rectangular, forms the base of this receptacle and is surrounded on all four sides by an uncharted ocean. A narrow strip of land encircles the oceans and it is to this that the four walls of the universe are fastened. These walls hold up the sky, which is rather like the ceiling of a house. Above this, the walls curve inwards, forming the vault which contains the heavenly kingdom. The whole structure replicates on a gigantic scale the tabernacle of Moses, with the earth representing the table for the Bread of the Presence (Exodus 25:30), and the firmament taking the place of the veil (Exodus 26:31).

'To the Byzantine man, as indeed to all men of the Middle Ages, the supernatural existed in a very real and familiar sense. Not only did that other world continually impinge on everyday life; it also constituted that higher and timeless reality to which earthly existence was but a brief prelude. Any account of the Byzantine "worldview" must necessarily begin with the supernatural.'

CYRIL MANGO,
*BYZANTIUM: THE
EMPIRE OF NEW
ROME*, 1980

It is of course impossible to know whether Byzantine Christians of all periods believed in such strictly biblical notions of the universe as this. It is clear, however, that Kosmas' *Christian Topography* was recopied and read by many Byzantines in later centuries. Intellectuals such as the ninth-century patriarch Photios were scornful of its content, but we may imagine that many pious Christians found this neat formulation of cosmology satisfying. At the same time, however, more scientific explanations of the structure of the universe were circulating throughout the Byzantine period. These were based on ancient Middle Eastern and Greek astrology and, although condemned by the Church, they must have informed the more educated members of the population. Ancient Greek science pictured the universe as circular, with the earth forming a spinning core at its centre. The distant night sky was seen as the inside of a fixed sphere which revolved around the earth. The stars were attached to this surface and circulated with the sphere, keeping their characteristic groupings in the form of constellations. Meanwhile, within the space between the outer sphere and the earth, the planets, which included the sun, circulated according to their own specific routes. The Greek word *planetes* in fact means 'wandering', thus denoting 'stars' which followed their own paths.

The heavenly court

The heavenly and earthly realms mirrored the imperial Byzantine system in their strictly hierarchical structure. Christ, the incarnate God, is pictured in numerous Byzantine texts and images as an all-powerful ruler. He sits in majesty, surrounded by a court which is made up of such exalted figures as his mother, the Virgin Mary, cherubim and seraphim, archangels and angels, martyrs and saints. This very hierarchical structure replicates the imperial court on earth, except that God rules over the heavenly, as well as the earthly, cosmos. Byzantine texts vary in their depictions of God: he may appear as Ruler, Judge or merciful Father.

The angels who served God were infinite in number, but

were also organized into a strict hierarchy. Some remained in the heavenly kingdom, endlessly praising God, while others were dispatched on missions to the created world, where they helped people in various ways: guarding them from danger, delivering messages or assisting their souls in the dangerous passage to the afterlife. Veneration of specific angels had been discouraged in the early Church, but the cult appears to have survived strongly into later centuries, judging by the numbers of churches dedicated to the archangel Michael throughout the empire. A theoretical and highly mystical treatise covering angelology was compiled by a shadowy fifth-century writer called Pseudo-Dionysios the Areopagite, who was influenced by Neoplatonic philosophy. However, it is unlikely that this difficult text was widely read, in spite of the fact that the Byzantines believed it to have been written by a disciple of the apostle Paul. Most Christians would have assumed the protection of a guardian angel who watched over them at times of danger. The archangel Michael, who was visualized as a military officer, was probably the most popular of all the angels among ordinary people.

Saints were also believed to be present in God's court, although the exact process by which they gained access to the heavenly kingdom after death was never fully explained. Most religious texts, including the *Lives* of saints and visionary accounts, suggest that these holy individuals were spared the long wait for the final Day of Judgment and taken straight to heaven after death. There they were pictured serving in the heavenly court or nestled in Abraham's bosom. From this privileged vantage point, a patron saint might intercede with God on behalf of human beings. Prayers and votive offerings to these holy figures thus played an important role in the everyday lives of Byzantine Christians. It is likely that the faithful felt a special bond with the saints because these were human beings who had crossed the boundary from the created to the divine world.

A large population of demons inhabited the created world, along with humanity and other living creatures.

Opposite page:
Late-12th-century
icon of the
heavenly ladder
visualized by
St John Klimakos,
St Catherine's
Monastery, Sinai.
The monks climb
up the ladder
towards heaven
while small black
demons attempt
to pull them off.

Byzantine texts, especially of the earlier periods, are unequivocal about the presence of these supernatural beings. They are subservient to their master Satan, but many seem to be harboured in pagan tombs and shrines. According to monastic treatises, the demons are usually invisible and work at tempting Christians to sin, gaining access through the five senses or the mind. Some demons are assigned to particular vices; thus there is a demon of pride and vainglory, a demon of fornication and so on. Demons also sometimes take on the form of a human being or an animal, such as a serpent, a dog or a dormouse. In this shape they may confront individuals, reserving their strongest attacks for the ascetic saints, seeking to distract, tempt or frighten them. Demons also

Stories of demons

One of the best sources of information on Byzantine demons is the seventh-century *Life of St Theodore of Sykeon*, an ascetic saint who lived and travelled in Asia Minor. On various occasions, according to this biography, Theodore was summoned by Christians villagers to help them exorcise or banish demons from their communities. As a man of God who had undergone rigorous ascetic training, Theodore was uniquely qualified to help in this endeavour. Once the citizen of a small village, while extending his threshing floor, levelled a small hillock in which a number of demons were lodged. The unclean spirits poured out of the hole and entered the animals and even some of the people in the village. The elders eventually sent for St Theodore, begging him to free their village of this infestation. He arrived and instructed them first to enlarge the hole in which the demons had been housed. On the following day he led a procession around the village and on reaching the site of the hole, prayed and commanded all demons to return to its shelter. He also exorcised them from the individuals who had been possessed. When the demons had re-entered the hole, it was sealed up and a cross was placed on top of the mound. The demons in the *Life of Theodore of Sykeon* represent a nuisance and threat to local populations, but they are easily subjugated by the saint. Interestingly, they appear to have local allegiances themselves – in one passage the demons in the region of Gordiane claim that they are tougher than those of Galatia. They appear in various forms, sometimes taking the shape of flies, sometimes as hares or dormice.

frequently enter into the souls of people and animals, inhabiting them like parasites and driving them mad. Exorcisms similar to those recounted in the Gospels occur frequently in the early *Lives* of saints; by making the sign of the cross or laying his hands on the afflicted individual, the saint expels the demon, who usually emerges with a loud, tearing sound.

Death and the afterlife

The Byzantine view of what occurs after death is not in fact a unified or consistent one. Many accounts emerge from different sources: it is clear that the Church's official line on this matter did not always agree with popular ideas. The prayers, hymns and homilies intended for use at funerals and memorial services generally convey the standard Christian belief that the soul is separated from the body after death. After a period of waiting, the final Day of Judgment will arrive and every individual will be judged by Christ and sent to his or her final destination in heaven or hell. It is the period between death and the Final Day, however, that causes difficulties for most theologians. Does the soul go somewhere else when it is separated from the body and, if so, where? As we saw above, the souls of the saints were believed to go straight to paradise; does this mean that sinners waited in some other, less attractive place? The Byzantines did not at any period formulate an official doctrine concerning purgatory, as occurred in the West in about the 12th century. In fact, this represented one of the issues of contention at the Council of Ferrara/Florence in 1438–39. Nevertheless, some kind of intermediate, third place between heaven and hell is implied in Byzantine texts from a very early period. This represents in effect a place of waiting, where repentance and the reversal of an unfavourable sentence may take place. The prayers of intercession offered by the living were believed to have an impact on an individual's final destiny.

Popular literature, that is, the texts that appear to have been written for and read by ordinary people, convey a somewhat different and occasionally amusing account of life after death. The idea that sinners were immediately punished for their sins was obviously an attractive one. A typical story of such punishment occurs in the seventh-century collection of miraculous tales compiled by John Moschos, a Syrian monk who travelled around Egypt and Palestine. In this account, John tells us that a monk was careless about carrying out the disciplines imposed on him by his superior. Some time later, the monk died and the elder prayed to God to reveal to him what had become of his disciple's soul. He went into a trance and saw a number of people standing in the middle of a river of fire. The monk was there too, submerged up to his neck. When the elder reproved him, saying that he had warned him repeatedly of the likelihood of this retribution, the monk responded, 'I thank God, father, that there is relief for my head. Thanks to your prayers I am standing on the head of a bishop'.

An even more remarkable idea concerning the fate of souls after death is that of the 'toll houses'. This concept was clearly not endorsed officially by the Church, but it appears in a number of sources, and is even hinted at in the highly reputable biography of St Antony, written by the patriarch Athanasius in the fourth century. According to these accounts, the human soul, after being detached from the body at the moment of death, was obliged to travel through the air, stopping at a number of toll houses along the way. The soul would be questioned about its actions during life at each of these staging posts. If the individual had sinned, he or she was obliged to pay an appropriate due, consisting of the good deeds performed during his or her life. According to the 10th-century *Life of St Basil the Younger*, there were 21 toll-houses in all, each of which represented a particular vice. These included pride, anger, avarice, lust and many others. Demons and angels fought at the moment of death for the right to accompany souls along this perilous journey. This is why the prayers of the living could play a pivotal role at this difficult moment.

An image of the
damned being
tormented in
hell, a Last
Judgment scene
executed in
mosaic according
to Byzantine
techniques in the
11th-century
cathedral of
Torcello (an island
near Venice).

Beliefs concerning the final Day of Judgment were based primarily on apocalyptic texts, especially the book of Revelation attributed to the evangelist John. Christ would sit in majesty, flanked by the Virgin Mary and John the Baptist, and surrounded by all of his angels, prophets and apostles. Seven angels (the number seems to vary in pictorial

representations) would blow their trumpets and all of the dead would arise from their graves. This was the moment when the souls of the deceased would be rejoined with their bodies. According to the apostle Paul, this will not be a physical body, but a 'spiritual body' (1 Corinthians 15:44). To some extent the fate of these individuals had been

'Grant her angels who will keep her soul safe from the spirits and beasts of the air, evil and unmerciful beings who endeavour to swallow up everything which comes into their midst.'

PRAYER OF THE
SEVENTH-CENTURY
SAINTLY FOOL,
SYMEON OF EMESA,
AT THE DEATH OF
HIS MOTHER

predetermined since the day of their deaths: in images of the scene they are already lined up on the left or the right side of Christ as they await judgment. Each would then be weighed and dispatched to his or her appropriate destiny, whether this was the heavenly city or eternal damnation. This great event was thought to be imminent by many Orthodox Christians at various points in Byzantine history. Nevertheless, even after the fall of Constantinople to the Turks in 1453 (a catastrophe that some had predicted as heralding the advent of the anti-Christ), human history continued and Christians continued to wait for the Final Day.

Illness and healing

Conventional medicine in the Byzantine empire was remarkably advanced for the period. The Greco-Roman tradition provided the background for Byzantine physicians, who drew on a number of treatises, including those of Hippocrates and Galen. The many copies of these medical texts which survive from the Byzantine period suggest not only that they were widely used, but also that doctors rearranged and added to them on the basis of practical experience. Many hospitals existed not only in Constantinople, but also in the provinces. It is clear that the use of drugs was sophisticated and that remedies could be prescribed for diseases of the chest, heart, digestive system and other organs. Surgery was also remarkably well advanced. Lists of surgical instruments suggest considerable scope in the number and variety of operations performed; we also have accounts of dissections and autopsies performed by Byzantine surgeons in order to advance their understanding of the human body.

At the same time, however, it is clear that many Byzantine citizens sought miraculous healing when conventional medicine had failed. Numerous collections of miracle stories survive, usually in association with the cult of a particular saint. Some saints specialized in healing certain types of illness and would therefore attract many people suffering from similar ailments to their shrines. Cures could

be effected by means of pilgrimage to a holy site, for
example the tomb of a martyr or saint, anointing with the
holy oil that flowed from some tombs or icons, drinking oil
or water associated with a holy site, or incubation. The last
of these methods, which involved sleeping overnight at the
tomb of a saint, may have links with the pagan cult of
Asclepios, who also cured people in this way.

Judging by the accounts of supernatural healings and
other miracles, Byzantine Christians believed strongly in the
presence of both divine and demonic powers in the world.
Faith in God played an important part in the efficacy of
these cures: we hear of the failure of some individuals to
receive divine aid because of their lack of belief. The power

Miracle cures

A good example of a healing cult is that of St Artemios, a Christian official who
had been martyred during the reign of the pagan emperor Julian, probably in
about 362. A collection of miracles stories recounting the miraculous cures which
occurred at the Church of St John the Baptist in Constantinople, where Artemios'
relics had been deposited, was probably compiled in the middle of the seventh
century. St Artemios specialized in diseases of the digestive and reproductive
organs, especially those of the testicles. People suffering from hernias, tumours
and other ailments, would come and sleep in the church. The saint would usually
appear in a vision to these patients as they slept and cure them either by direct
intervention or by offering medical advice. One man, named George, who had
suffered from a testicular disorder for many years, had been advised to have
these organs amputated. Instead he went to sleep in the Church of St John and
dreamed that Artemios, in the guise of a butcher, pierced him with a knife in
his lower abdomen. After removing and cleaning all his intestines, the saint
rearranged them into one coil and put them back into George's body. When the
sick man awoke, he realized that he was completely cured. Another individual was
afflicted with a boil on his testicles which conventional doctors had been unable
to treat. When he went to the Church of St John, the saint appeared to him in
a vision and made an incision on the boil with a scalpel. Immediately the boil
burst and the man was healed. It is interesting to note that in both of these cases
St Artemios used the methods of conventional medicine to heal his patients, while
at the same time drawing on supernatural power.

that came directly from God, even when channelled through saints, relics or icons, was infinitely superior to that of the demons. It was sufficient for a saint to make the sign of a cross, say a prayer or touch those who had been possessed by these evil beings for them to be cured. The healings, exorcisms and other miracles described in Byzantine texts worked to restore the natural order according to God's plan. Disease and death both represented aberrations from this order, which God alone was able to remedy.

Orthodox identity in opposition to 'others'

Another aspect of the Byzantine worldview lies in the concept of collective identity. Orthodox Christians in every period of Byzantine history identified themselves above all by their religion. Obviously they were 'Romans', but that term denoted allegiance to a vast (although rapidly shrinking) political dominion inhabited by a multi-ethnic and multilingual population. In return for being citizens of the Eastern Roman empire and paying their taxes to the centralized, imperial government, Byzantines received military protection but not much else. The Christian religion, on the other hand, provided an entire worldview, encompassing both the earthly and the heavenly kingdoms, as well as life and the afterlife, as we have seen in this chapter. By reading scripture, attending church, praying before icons and visiting the shrines of martyrs and saints, Orthodox Christians participated in a community which shared a sense of collective identity and purpose.

The sense that this Christian identity was threatened both from outside and by forces within also emerges to a greater or lesser degree in every period of Byzantine history. Orthodox Christians felt that their beliefs and way of life were under threat by opposing ideological systems. The first step in combating these forces was to express what they believed in the doctrinal formulations which emerged from ecumenical councils and later in such documents as the *Synodikon* of Orthodoxy. The second was to castigate those who deviated from these doctrines both inside and outside the empire.

It is a striking, although unfortunate, fact that in many periods the group which was singled out for the most criticism was the Jews. There may be various reasons for this long-standing prejudice on the part of Byzantine Christians. Jews had been regarded from as early as the second century as the ideological adversaries of Christianity *par excellence*. Early Christians, many of whom were converted from Judaism, sought to distance themselves from their former brethren, who seemed to them to reject the new message which Christ had come to proclaim. Furthermore, the fact that Jewish communities continued to exist in most of the major cities of the Eastern Roman empire, and that they were allowed for the most part to govern themselves, meant that they appeared as 'outsiders' at the heart of Byzantine society. It was especially during periods of military and economic pressure, such as the seventh and early eighth centuries, that Jews became scapegoats and were subjected to persecution of various kinds. It is clear both in Byzantine texts and images that Jews came to represent symbolically every ideological adversary. Thus, heretics such as Arians or iconoclasts are typically denounced as 'Jews'. Sermons and hymns, especially those associated with the services leading up to Good Friday and Easter, denounce the Jews for their part in the crucifixion of Christ.

Collective identity is constructed in every society not only from people's sense of who they are, but also who they are not. The Byzantines perhaps needed to identify themselves as a group more than do most societies, owing to their frequently precarious political and military situation. As we have seen in this chapter, this identity was based above all on their Orthodox Christian religion, which included not only an agreed set of doctrines and liturgical practices, but also ideas about the formation of the cosmos, the purpose of history and the close proximity of divine power in this world. The sense of belonging to a well-

'Arguing the Christian position through the condemnation of the Jews made perfect sense: over the centuries the process of Christian self-definition had always involved differentiating Christianity from Judaism, and the Christians often condemned their enemies by comparing them to the Jews.'

KATHLEEN
CORRIGAN, *VISUAL
POLEMICS IN THE
NINTH-CENTURY
BYZANTINE
PSALTERS*, 1992

defined group also represented an important part of this worldview. It is unfortunate that this led to the oppression of religious minorities living within the Byzantine empire, but it also probably bolstered the confidence of a society that was frequently under threat of extinction.

Art as an Expression of Faith

An important legacy of the Byzantine Church is the art it produced, much of which still survives in the former territories of the empire, especially Turkey, Greece, the Near East and the former Yugoslavia. Western tourists often visit these sites and are inspired by the wall paintings, mosaics and church buildings that they see. Many of the most precious Byzantine artefacts may be found in the art museums, libraries and treasuries of Western Europe. Some of these were stolen from Constantinople after the crusaders' sack of the city in 1204; others represent the purchases of later Europeans who travelled to the East. This chapter will

The exterior of a typical Middle Byzantine 'cross-in-square' church. The 11th-century monastery church at Hosios Loukas, central Greece.

explore the history of Byzantine art and architecture for two reasons: first, because these traditions represent an important expression of Byzantine spirituality; and second, because they remain probably the most accessible heritage of this extinct civilization for travellers and scholars alike.

Early Christian art

Assigning a beginning to Byzantine art is as difficult as determining a date of origin for the empire. Christian art in the early fourth century, when Constantine was founding Constantinople as his capital city, was still in its infancy. Although scholars still debate whether representational art of all kinds was banned during the first two centuries of the Church on the grounds that it was idolatrous, it is clear that very few images were created in this period. The earliest decorated Christian building, a baptistery at the site of Dura Europas (now in Syria), which is dated to before 256, contains paintings of Adam and Eve, Christ, the Good Shepherd, and the visit of the three women to Christ's tomb just after his resurrection. This monument suggests that a tradition of depicting carefully chosen biblical scenes symbolizing important Christian teachings was already in existence by the mid-third century. It is perhaps even more surprising that a Jewish synagogue contains many wall paintings of Old Testament stories at the same site. It is clear that both Jews and Christians living in this region at this time did not interpret God's commandment against religious imagery (Exodus 20:4) entirely literally.

Another important example of early Christian art may be found in the catacombs, which were used as burial places outside the city walls of Rome by Christians and pagans alike in the early centuries of the Church. The Christian catacombs are believed to date from the third through to the fifth centuries. What is perhaps most striking in the wall paintings that decorate these underground chambers is their ability to convey, in a striking and symbolic manner, a simple but fundamental message of Christian faith: salvation and resurrection in Christ. The choice of scenes, including Abraham's sacrifice of Isaac, Moses crossing the Red Sea, the three men in the fiery furnace and the raising of Lazarus, had all by this time become symbols of Christian resurrection. The catacombs in Rome reveal a fully developed ability to convey Christian truths by means of simple but effective pictorial images, expressing not a narrative, but a theological interpretation of events in the Old and New Testaments.

Another phenomenon which may be related to the rise of Christian art in the third and fourth centuries, but which also reflects a general shift in aesthetic values, is the movement away from classical realism towards abstraction in late-Roman art. Scholars have speculated that an abstract style is frequently used deliberately by artists and that it does not necessarily reflect falling standards in artistic technique. Sculptures such as the porphyry statue of the four emperors (tetrarchs) who ruled at the end of third century, which now stands outside St Mark's Cathedral in Venice, convey a deeper, symbolic message at the expense of a purely realistic image. The abstract, even primitive, style of this sculpture reveals key characteristics associated with these rulers: solidity, unity and military strength.

Late-third or
early-fourth-
century porphyry
statue, probably
of the Tetrarchy,
St Mark's
Cathedral, Venice.

As Constantine promoted Christianity within the Roman empire, it became possible for the Church to build and adorn official places of worship. The decoration of churches soon got under way and various methods of depicting biblical scenes and holy figures developed. Two very different systems of monumental church decoration are evident by as early as the fifth century. The first of these is the method, mentioned above in connection with the Roman catacombs, of portraying theological doctrine symbolically. The image of Christ seated on a globe, surrounded by angels, in the apse of the sixth-century Church of San Vitale in Ravenna, represents a good example of this trend. This mosaic conveys unequivocally the message that Christ, the All-Ruler, has come to save humanity.

The other style of decoration, which also seems to have

developed early, is the more detailed, narrative scene, whose purpose is to tell the biblical story by means of a picture. We find examples of this style of decoration in the fifth-century Church of Santa Maria Maggiore in Rome, which contains detailed scenes from the Old and New Testaments. We know that the Church recognized the educational value of religious imagery and that this may indeed have been seen as the primary purpose of church decoration of this type. Various early Fathers extol the educational value of religious imagery, which they see as useful for the many Christian faithful who were unable to read or who lacked access to books.

Mosaic decoration of church walls and ceilings was widely in use throughout the empire by the fifth and sixth centuries. Ever more fragile and expensive materials were used for the

Christ sitting on a globe surrounded by angels. Apse mosaic in the sixth-century Church of San Vitale, Ravenna.

individual tesserae as this artistic technique was perfected.
A mosaic mural might be made up of pieces of terracotta for
the darker sections, but also translucent glass and even semi-
precious gems. Gold and silver tesserae were created by fitting
thin wafers of these precious materials between layers of
translucent glass. The tesserae would be cut to different sizes,
with the finest and smallest being saved for the depiction of
human faces and other important details. Artists, as they
planned and executed mosaic images high up in churches,
would carefully consider the issues of perspective and light.
A mural was planned so that it would look realistic from the
ground, even if this meant foreshortening individual figures.
The most splendid examples of sixth-century Byzantine
mosaics survive in the areas of the empire that were not
affected by Iconoclasm. The beautiful image of the
transfiguration of Christ in
the apse of the church in
St Catherine's Monastery,
Sinai, or the various churches
established by fifth and sixth-
century rulers of Ravenna,
including Justinian, probably
represent the finest examples
of this 'de luxe' form of
monumental decoration.

Detail of Christ's
head in mosaic at
the sixth-century
Church of San
Vitale in Ravenna.

Portable icons

Between the fifth and eighth
centuries, especially in the
Eastern half of the Roman
empire, still another form of
representational art was becoming increasingly
popular in both public and private worship. These
are the holy icons, images usually painted on wooden
panels, although they could also be fashioned by
means of a number of other media, such as ivory and
enamel. The earliest examples of painted icons are
dated no earlier than the sixth and seventh centuries.

'Represent a
single cross in
the sanctuary…
Fill the Holy
Church on both
sides with
pictures from
the Old and New
Testaments,
executed by an
excellent
painter, so that
the illiterate
who are unable
to read the holy
scriptures may,
by gazing at the
pictures, become
mindful of the
manly deeds of
those who have
genuinely
served the true
God, and may
be roused to
emulate their
feats.'

ST NEILOS OF SINAI
(DIED c. 430)

The largest collection to survive from this period, which consists of about 27 icons, is preserved at St Catherine's Monastery in the Sinai desert, now in Egypt.

A famous icon from the Sinai collection, which is usually dated to the sixth or early seventh century, depicts the Mother of God holding the Christ child on her lap, flanked by two saints, St George and St Theodore. Behind them stand two angels, half turned away and gazing up towards heaven. The different artistic styles evident in this icon have been noted by scholars and are generally thought to be deliberate on the part of the artist. The Virgin, while appearing as a solid, human figure, looks slightly away from the viewer as if to convey her association with divinity. The two angels, who are painted in an impressionistic style, reveal an ethereal quality which is appropriate to their status as 'bodiless' ones. The soldier saints, on the other hand, gaze fixedly at us since they represent the most immediate point of contact between the divine and the human worlds. The severe frontal pose and abstract style revealed here is typical of depictions of saints in this period. It is likely that this was used in order to convey a sense of the spiritual detachment from worldly society of these holy figures.

Art after the end of Iconoclasm: the 'Macedonian Renaissance'
Byzantine art experienced a revival after the end of the period of Iconoclasm, when religious imagery had been suppressed for just over a century. Churches were again decorated with mosaics and wall paintings; icons were produced, and manuscripts illustrated with miniatures and other decoration. This is the period when standard methods of depicting certain biblical themes, called iconography, began to be formulated and employed. At the same time, original and creative artistic approaches are visible in many different media. In this section we will confine our discussion to just two of these categories: the illustration of manuscripts and monumental wall decoration, especially in mosaic.

The production of manuscripts increased markedly after

Sixth-century icon
of Mary, the
Mother of God,
flanked by two
saints,
St Catherine's
Monastery, Sinai.

the early ninth century. This is the period in which a new,
more cursive script, known as the minuscule, was invented.
The defeat of Iconoclasm and increasing importance of
monasteries in the Byzantine world may also have spurred on
this enterprise. Although most surviving Greek manuscripts
are not illustrated with miniatures, those that were
commissioned by rich patrons or emperors often contain
beautifully executed images decorated with gold leaf. Gospel

books and collections of biblical readings called lectionaries are the most numerous among these illustrated manuscripts. Many of these contain full-page illustrations of the evangelists writing their books, as well as images of individual scenes in the life of Christ. Another liturgical book which was frequently illustrated was the Psalter, which contained the 150 psalms attributed to David. Some of the earliest examples of illustrated Psalters are dated to the ninth century. The images which accompany individual Psalms appear in the margins of these manuscripts; interestingly, they refer not only to the content of the verses that they accompany, but also to contemporary events such as Iconoclasm.

David composing the Psalms from the *Paris Psalter* (c. 950).

The illustrations in some ninth and tenth-century manuscripts suggest a return to the classicizing style of Hellenistic and late-Roman art. The modelling of the figures, the depiction of the folds of drapery, attempts at perspective and the use of pagan personifications in these images have led to these works being viewed as products of a cultural renaissance. The use of the term 'renaissance' is perhaps somewhat misleading, however. The pagan, classical past was always present in the Byzantines' memories and was never in need of deliberate revival. It is perhaps more helpful to view classicizing images and literary texts as representing a particular branch of Byzantine culture which never ceased to be important. It was quite acceptable to portray a Christian message by means of pagan rhetorical or artistic techniques. Indeed, these may even have provided a stamp of legitimacy for those readers and viewers who were capable of appreciating their background.

Church decoration in the Middle Byzantine period

The cathedral of Hagia Sophia, designed and constructed early in the reign of the emperor Justinian (527–65), became the ideal model for all subsequent ecclesiastical architecture in the Byzantine empire. Hagia Sophia is a domed basilica which is built on a square foundation. This provides a huge central area in which the eye is drawn upwards by means of a series of arches to the great dome at the top. The eighth-century patriarch Germanos' statement that a church represents 'heaven on earth' was probably written with Hagia Sophia in mind, as he pictured the huge interior of the 'Great Church'. After the period of Iconoclasm, churches constructed in the Byzantine empire tended to be planned according to an architectural type known as the 'cross in square'. These churches, like Hagia Sophia are centralized in structure: the dome on top is supported by a series of pendentives and vaults which lead downwards towards a square foundation. Later Byzantine churches tend to be fairly small in size, however, compared to Hagia Sophia. This gives them a much more enclosed and intimate atmosphere than is found in the great cathedrals of Western Europe.

The decoration of Middle Byzantine churches is uniquely suited to their architectural structure. The wall paintings or mosaics convey by their choice of subject-matter the hierarchical structure of the universe. In the dome at the top appears the bust of Christ, the Pantokrator or All-Ruler, both the Judge and the Saviour of humankind.

The Virgin and Child usually appear in the apse, symbolizing the mystery of the incarnation, which is the central teaching of Orthodox Christianity. On the upper walls and squinches that surround the dome we find scenes from the life of Christ. The choice of scenes usually reflected the important feast days in the Church. Such key feasts as the Annunciation, the Nativity, the Transfiguration, Palm Sunday and Easter were always included, but some flexibility was allowed in their choice and arrangement. On the lower walls of the church appear the portraits of individual saints, martyrs and other important figures. As in the case of the feast day scenes, the choice of saints varies considerably in individual churches. It is clear that the decoration of churches reflects to a large extent the wishes

Image of Christ
the Pantokrator
('All-Ruler') in the
dome of the 12th-
century church of
the monastery of
Daphni, near
Athens.

and specifications of their donors; each church is unique, representing the ideas of its patron, architect and painter or mosaicist, who have together planned its structure and decoration.

Later Byzantine art

Art and architecture continued to flourish in the later period of Byzantine history, in spite of the many vicissitudes experienced by the empire until its final destruction in 1453. A huge variety of artistic media,

including not only wall paintings, mosaics and icons, but also manuscripts, ivories, enamels, silk tapestry and metal work, addressed religious themes. There is unfortunately no space in this chapter to treat each of these topics in detail; instead, it may be useful simply to provide a very general discussion of a few trends and issues in late-Byzantine art.

Returning to the field of wall paintings and icons, it is noticeable in the 11th and 12th centuries that a new, more realistic style was occasionally adopted. This contrasts with the more abstract style of many earlier representations. There is a reason for the choice of different artistic styles. More abstract renderings convey the sense of detachment and tranquillity which is appropriate for devotional art. The more realistic style which appears in some, although not by any means all, later icons seems to express narrative action or emotion on the part of the depicted figures.

This trend is apparent in a fine 12th-century icon of the Annunciation which belongs to St Catherine's Monastery in Sinai, but which may have been created in Constantinople. As the archangel Gabriel approaches the Mother of God, his half-turned body in its swirling draperies convey his anxiety concerning the success of his mission; this idea also appears in a number of homilies commemorating the feast of the Annunciation. The Virgin herself is depicted as a humble young woman spinning her scarlet thread, according to the account in the *Protoevangelion* of James.

Another famous example of realism and emotion in the art in this period may be seen in the wall paintings of the monastery of St Panteleimon at Nerezi, near Skopje, in modern Macedonia. This monastery is dated by an inscription to 1164; its central church contains a number of wall paintings with about 20 scenes, including a detailed Passion cycle. The founder was a Byzantine, Alexios Komnenos, nephew of the emperor John I, who perhaps owned estates in the region. It is clear that he employed Byzantine artists to decorate the main church of the monastery; these highly skilled craftsmen

Late-12th-century icon of the Annunciation, St Catherine's Monastery, Sinai.

provided a sure and delicate touch in their rendering of the story of Christ's passion. In the scene of the lamentation, in which the Mother of God clasps the dead Christ to herself and lays her cheek against his, her grief is strikingly rendered (see illustration on p. 173). Many scholars view 12th-century monuments such as this as the direct precursors of the famous 13th-century Italian wall paintings by Giotto and others.

The period between the recapture of Constantinople from the Latins in 1261 and the final fall of the Byzantine empire in 1453 witnessed a flowering of culture which found expression in both literature and art. Icons

The nativity scene, Hosios Loukas

In order to appreciate the content and meaning of festal scenes in middle Byzantine art, it might be useful to analyse one typical example. The mosaic depiction of the Nativity scene in the late-10th-century monastery church of Hosios Loukas in central Greece serves to illustrate a number of points concerning Byzantine liturgical art. First, it is important to note the economy with which the artist has constructed the scene: the Virgin Mary is shown sitting in a cave next to the Christ child. On her right are the shepherds adoring him and on the left, the three magi. Angels overlook the scene, while Joseph sits rather disconsolately some distance away from the central figures of Mary and Christ. Just to the right of the manger, as if in a separate scene, the child is being washed by two midwives. As we look at this scene it is immediately clear that it does not merely represent the illustration of a biblical story. Every element in the picture has symbolic meaning and may be drawn from a number of textual sources in addition to the Gospels. For example, the ox and the ass, who always appear in Nativity scenes, represent both the animal world and the uneducated classes who first accepted Christ's teachings. The presence of the ox and ass was seen as the fulfilment of Isaiah's prophecy: 'The ox knows its owner, and the donkey its master's crib; but Israel does not know, my people do not understand' (Isaiah 1:3). The story of the washing of the infant by the midwives comes from an apocryphal text known as the *Protoevangelion* of James. The scene is included because it conveys the true humanity of Christ and the reality of his birth as a baby. Many other aspects of the scene are inspired by Old Testament prophecy or by theological considerations such as this. Above all, however, the careful structure of the image and its focus on the symbolic meaning of the events is evident.

proliferated, reflecting the continuing devotion of Orthodox Christians to these portable symbols of divine power. Exquisite mosaic icons, fashioned out of minute tesserae, represent a technical innovation of this period. Illustrated manuscripts, richly decorated with gold leaf and drawing on well-established iconographical traditions, also survive in great numbers. Churches and monasteries adorned with mosaic or frescoed wall paintings were built not only in Constantinople, but also in those outlying provinces which were still under Byzantine rule.

Wealthy private patrons were often responsible either for

Nativity scene at the 11th-century monastery church of Hosios Loukas, central Greece.

restoring or founding religious buildings. In Constantinople
we hear of a number of such figures in the final centuries of
the empire. A senior imperial official named Michael Glabas
refurbished the monastery of Theotokos Pammakaristos,
which still survives as a mosque in Istanbul known as the
Fethiye Camii. Probably in the 1290s Glabas built a small
domed chapel with a mosaic of Christ the Pantokrator at
its summit. Another important example of a late-Byzantine
patron is the scholar and statesman, Theodore Metochites,
who sponsored the restoration of an ancient monastery
called the Chora on the outskirts of Constantinople (see
the illustration on page 46). This refurbishment involved
rebuilding and decorating the vaults of the earlier church with
mosaics, building an inner and outer vestibule, or narthex, as
well as an adjoining chapel called the *parekklesion*. The
mosaics and wall paintings which decorate these various
structures survive to this day and bear witness to the
extraordinary ability of the artists who executed them. The
economy and theological symbolism of earlier Byzantine
iconography has been preserved, but in addition to these we
see a sophisticated depiction of human bodies, emotion and
movement.

The legacy of Byzantine art

Although much Byzantine art has been lost, a great deal
survives throughout the Mediterranean region. Many
modern tourists to these areas find the remains of the
Eastern Roman empire as beautiful and inspiring as the
more renowned monuments of classical civilization. What
many Western travellers may not realize, however, is how
widely the influence of Byzantine art and its craftsmen
spread. The 12th-century churches in Palermo and Cefalù,
Sicily, for example, represent in many ways classic examples
of middle Byzantine decoration. There can be no doubt that
although commissioned by the Norman kings who ruled this
area between the 1140s and 1180s, these churches were
constructed and decorated by Byzantine workmen. The style
and arrangement of the mosaics, from the figure of Christ

the All-Ruler in the dome to the biblical scenes and figures in the nave below, are almost entirely Byzantine in their inspiration. At the same time, however, differences do emerge which probably reflect the wishes and perspectives of the Western patrons. In the Cappella Palatina in Palermo, for example, the placement of a second Pantokrator in the apse, with a seated Virgin below, is unusual in Byzantine iconography. Other variations emerge in the choice of scenes and their arrangement on the walls around the central nave.

In Venice, a city which had maintained close ties with the Byzantine empire even after the fall of northern Italy to the Lombards in the eighth century, the rebuilding of St Mark's Cathedral in the late 11th century was strongly influenced and perhaps executed by Byzantine architects and mosaicists The plan of St Mark's was based on the famous Church of the Holy Apostles in Constantinople, which unfortunately does not survive. The mosaics, like those of the small 11th-century church on the nearby island of Torcello, are entirely Byzantine in style.

The influence of Byzantine art and architecture is thus evident not only in the areas which remained under Byzantine rule, but also in neighbouring states to the north, east and west. Many of the medieval churches of Macedonia, Serbia, Bulgaria, Romania, Russia and the Ukraine may have

Wall painting of the lamentation at the death of Christ on the north wall of the church of the monastery of St Panteleimon, Nerezi, near Skopje, Macedonia.

Previous page:
The monastery
church,
decorated in
Byzantine style in
about 1600, of
Sucevita in
Romania.

benefited by the skills of Byzantine architects and artists; others were built by local builders who had been taught by them. Byzantine influence also continued in Eastern territories, such as Armenia and Georgia, even after these areas were no longer governed by Constantinople. Cultural and religious influence brought with it the time-honoured traditions of church architecture and decoration; these arts were not abandoned, even after political influence had waned.

CHAPTER 11

The Legacy

Constantinople, the capital city of the Byzantine empire, was finally captured by the Ottoman Turks on 29 May 1453. On the night before this attack, the Christian citizens of the city, including both Greeks and Latins, gathered in the Great Church of Hagia Sophia for a final service. The assault on Constantinople began in the early hours of dawn. Eventually the Turkish troops succeeded in scaling the walls and storming the capital city. The Byzantine emperor Constantine XI died in the attack; his body was never recovered. For three days and nights, Sultan Mehmed II allowed his troops to plunder the city. During this period priceless works of Orthodox Christian art, including icons, manuscripts and ecclesiastical treasure, were destroyed. Finally Mehmed II made his triumphal entry into the conquered city and Constantinople became the capital of the Ottoman empire.

Did these tragic events mean the end of the Byzantine empire? Undoubtedly the fall of Constantinople signalled the end of political and military rule in the Eastern Roman empire. The last remaining territories of the Greeks fell shortly after this: the Ottomans soon captured the remaining Aegean islands, and the Despotate of Morea in southern Greece fell in 1460. Finally, Trebizond, on the northern shores of the Black Sea, which had been ruled by a Byzantine dynasty called the Grand Komnenoi, fell to the Turks in 1461. After this date the empire which had defended itself from enemies on all fronts for over 1,000 years finally came to an end.

The Orthodox faithful and their Church did not cease to exist after 1453, however. The Turkish Sultans in Constantinople were in fact tolerant of the Christian beliefs of their Greek subjects during the centuries of Ottoman

rule. In accordance with the earliest traditions of Islam, Christians were viewed as 'people of the book', sharing with Muslims and Jews a common Old Testament heritage. Muslims also venerated Jesus Christ as a prophet, although they could not share Orthodox Christians' belief in his status as Messiah and Son of God. Soon after the fall of Constantinople, Mehmed II appointed the scholarly Greek monk Gennadios patriarch of Constantinople. Gennadios was a determined opponent of the Roman Church and he soon overthrew the agreements which had been reached at the Council of Ferrara/Florence in 1438–39. The Greek-speaking Orthodox Church thereafter maintained an independent existence from the churches of Western Europe, led by the ecumenical patriarch of Constantinople. Christians under Turkish rule were to a great extent allowed to govern themselves in what became known as the *millet* system. Since the Muslims did not make a formal distinction between religion and politics, their Orthodox Christian subjects were allowed to govern themselves independently in almost every sphere except the military. This system continued in Turkey until 1923 and in Cyprus until the death of Archbishop Makarios III in 1977.

Opposite page: A 16th-century view of Constantinople under Ottoman rule.

In addition to Greek-speaking Christians in the former territories of the Byzantine empire, Orthodox Churches survived in the Slavic nations which had been converted from the ninth century onwards. Many of these nations, such as Serbia and Bulgaria, and eventually even Russia, had gained autonomy and self-governance for their Churches during the later centuries of Byzantine history. Whereas formerly the patriarch of Constantinople had appointed bishops and directed their church affairs, now these independent Churches possessed their own patriarchs or 'autocephalous' archbishops. Orthodox Christianity became closely entwined with a sense of national identity in some of these countries, especially as they began to win independence from the Turks in the course of the 19th century. None of these individual Churches ever lost the sense that their roots and traditions were based in the history of the Byzantine empire, however;

as we have seen, their art, religious literature and monastic spirituality all reveal strong links with this medieval heritage.

All of these independent Orthodox Churches survive to the present day, now incorporating over 100 million adherents, not including the 27 million or so non-Chalcedonian Christians who make up the so-called 'Oriental' Orthodox Churches. Eastern Orthodox Christians are based mainly in Constantinople and Greece, as well as in the Slavic-speaking Churches of Eastern Europe including Russia, Bulgaria, Romania, the former Yugoslavia, including especially Serbia, and parts of the Ukraine. One important feature in the survival of the Orthodox Churches is their conservatism, which has led to the preservation of ancient liturgical services, doctrine and monastic spirituality. In contrast to the West's radical revisions of Christian worship, the Orthodox Churches have preserved and continue to use the liturgical texts which were mostly compiled for the universal Church in the fourth and fifth centuries. Many Christians today, including those from Protestant backgrounds, value the contribution which the Orthodox Church has made in preserving this early Christian tradition.

It is impossible in a book of this size to describe fully the development of Byzantine art, or indeed any other aspect of this society's beliefs, liturgical worship and institutional Church in adequate detail. It is hoped nevertheless that readers will have gained a broad understanding of these various legacies of the Byzantine Orthodox Church and that they will wish to continue reading in the field. As in the case of the medieval West, the best sources are those created by the people who actually lived through these centuries. Not only literary texts, but also artistic monuments tell us as much as we will ever know about how Byzantine Christians viewed the world, what they believed and how they expressed these ideas.

Chronology

306–37: Constantine I, 'the Great' (sole ruler from 324).

312: Constantine's vision and subsequent victory at the Milvian Bridge, Italy.

325: Council of Nicea, first ecumenical (universal) Church council. This council formally rejected the teachings of Arius and stated that the Son is *homoousios* (of one essence) with the Father.

330: Inauguration of Constantinople as the 'New Rome'.

337: Baptism and death of Constantine I.

381: Second ecumenical council: the Council of Constantinople. This council again rejected Arianism as a heresy and affirmed the divinity of the Holy Spirit. It also established Constantinople as the second most important episcopal see after Rome.

431: Third ecumenical council: the Council of Ephesus, at which the title *Theotokos* ('God-bearer') for the Virgin Mary was approved.

450–51: Fourth ecumenical council: the Council of Chalcedon. This council affirmed 'two natures' in Christ, a doctrine which some bishops, especially in the Eastern patriarchates, felt that they could not accept. Major schisms eventually developed as a result of the definitions formulated at the Council of Chalcedon.

527–65: Reign of the Byzantine emperor Justinian.

537: Dedication of the new Church of the Holy Wisdom (Hagia Sophia) in Constantinople.

553: Fifth ecumenical council held in Constantinople. Attempts were made to reconcile the Monophysite Churches.

614: The Persians occupied Syria, Palestine and Egypt (formerly Roman territories).

The relic of the true cross was taken to Ctesiphon, the Persian capital.

622: Muhammad left Mecca for Medina. (Muslims call this journey the Hijra.)

622–7: Campaigns of the Byzantine emperor Herakleios against the Persians.

626: Failure of the combined siege of Constantinople by the Persians and the Avars. The Byzantines viewed this victory as divinely ordained, especially due to the help of Mary, the Mother of God.

626–28: Byzantine defeat of the Persians.

630: The relic of the true cross was restored to Jerusalem amid great rejoicing.

634–46: The Muslims conquered Syria, Palestine, Mesopotamia and Egypt.

638: The *Ekthesis*, a statement published by the emperor Herakleios and his ecumenical patriarch, Sergios, which attempted to reconcile Monophysites and Chalcedonians.

655: Pope Martin I and the Byzantine theologian Maximos the Confessor were found guilty of treason for opposing the imperial 'Monothelite' ('one will' in Christ) doctrine. Both were exiled and died shortly afterwards.

680–81: Sixth ecumenical council held at Constantinople. The doctrine of Monothelitism was officially rejected.

717–18: The Muslims besieged Constantinople. Leo III, formerly a general, seized power.

730: The patriarch Germanos resigned. This was due to the introduction of the imperial policy against holy icons, called 'Iconoclasm'.

741–75: Reign of the iconoclast emperor Constantine V. More active persecution of the defenders of icons (called iconophiles) began. Monks and monasteries especially were targeted.

754: The iconoclast Council of Hiereia, at which the policy against images was formally stated.

787: The seventh ecumenical council, held at Nicea, ended the iconoclast policy. The use and veneration of icons in Orthodox Christian worship was affirmed.

800: Papal coronation of the Frankish king Charlemagne, as Roman emperor in the West, took place in St Peter's Basilica, Rome. The Byzantines refused to recognize his claim.

811–13: Bulgarian victories over the Byzantines in the Balkans. The emperor Nikephoros was defeated and killed in battle.

815: Reintroduction of iconoclast policy under the emperor Leo V.

843: The Triumph of Orthodoxy. Iconoclasm was overturned for the second time; holy icons were reintroduced into the Church. The *Synodikon*, a document expressing the doctrines of Orthodox Christianity, was formally published.

860: Rus' (Viking) attack on Constantinople.

863: The Byzantine missionaries Cyril and Methodios set out to convert Moravia to Orthodox Christianity. They took copies of the Gospels and other religious texts which they had translated into the Slavonic language.

864 or 865: Baptism of Boris, khan of Bulgaria.

Early 900s: Expansion of the Bulgars under Tsar Symeon.

922: Peace with the Bulgars.

954 or 955: Baptism of the Kievan (Rus') princess Olga.

963 onwards: Major Byzantine campaigns in the East. Reconquest of territory from the Arabs.

988: Baptism of the Rus' ruler Vladimir into Orthodox Christianity. He brought the new religion to the whole of the Rus' nation.

990–1019: Basil II ('the Bulgar slayer') overcame the Bulgar threat. Bulgaria was reincorporated into the Byzantine empire, with the Danube as the new frontier in the North.

1015: Death of the Rus' princes Boris and Gleb at the hands of their brother, Svyatopolk. They were revered in the Russian Church henceforth as 'passion-bearers' for their nonviolent response to his aggression.

1054: Official schism between the Western Church (led by the Roman papacy) and the Eastern Churches (under the patriarchates of Constantinople, Alexandria, Antioch and Jerusulem).

1071: The beginning of Seljuk Turkish domination of Central Anatolia. The Normans moved into southern Italy.

1081–85: Norman invasion of Western Balkan provinces.

1095: Beginning of the First Crusade.

1098–99: Jerusalem was captured; Latin principalities and a kingdom of Jerusalem were established in Palestine and Syria.

1146–48: Second Crusade.

1186: Rebellion in Bulgaria. After the defeat of Byzantine troops, a second Bulgarian empire was established.

1187: The end of the Third Crusade, as Jerusalem was retaken by the Arab leader Saladin.

1203–1204: Fourth Crusade, ending in the sack of Constantinople.

1204–61: A Latin empire ruled over much of the former Byzantine territories. Independent Greek states survived, however, in Nicea, Epiros and Trebizond.

1261: Constantinople was recaptured from the Latins. The emperor Michael VIII became emperor, but was opposed by supporters of a rival emperor. Schism within the Church resulted from this, only to be healed by the death of the ex-patriarch, Arsenios.

1274: Second Council of Lyons, at which a union of the Eastern and Western

Churches was agreed. However, this union was not accepted by most Byzantine Orthodox Christians.

1280–1337: The Ottoman Turks were taking the remaining Byzantine territories in Asia Minor.

1341: Synod in Constantinople discussed the complaints of the traditionalist monk Barlaam of Calabria against the Hesychast teachings of St Gregory Palamas. Palamas's doctrine was upheld.

1331–55: Height of the Serbian empire under its ruler, Stefan Dušan.

1347: The plague ('Black Death') reached Constantinople. A local council reaffirmed the decisions agreed at the Synod of 1341.

1365: Ottoman Turks took Adrianople, which became their capital city.

1389: Battle of Kosovo. The end of the Serbian empire and advance into the Balkans by the Ottoman Turks.

1393: End of the Bulgarian empire, as the Turks moved further into the northern Balkans.

1397–1402: Bayezit I, the Ottoman sultan, besieged Constantinople. He was forced to withdraw, however when the Turks were defeated by the Turkic leader, Timur (Tamerlane), at the Battle of Ankara (1402).

1430: Thessaloniki was taken by the Ottoman Turks.

1438–39: Council of Ferrara/Florence, attended by the Byzantine emperor John VIII, agreed union between the Eastern and Western Churches once again, in return for military aid against the Turks.

1444: Hungarian and Western crusaders, led by Vladislav of Hungary and Poland, were defeated at the Battle of Varna.

1451: Mehmet II became Sultan of the Ottoman Turks.

1453: Constantinople was conquered by the Ottomans under Mehmet II. The last Byzantine emperor, Constantine XI, died in the battle. The Greek Orthodox Church was allowed to continue under Ottoman rule, with a new patriarch, Gennadios II, appointed.

Suggestions for Further Reading

The best way to learn more about Byzantine faith is to read texts written by people who lived in the period. The series *Classics of Western Spirituality* includes many Eastern authors. *Penguin Classics* and the translations published by St Vladimir's Seminary Press (Crestwood, NY), Cistercian Publications (Kalamazoo, MI) and Holy Cross Orthodox Press (Brookline, MA) also provide access to Orthodox writers. For spiritual treatises intended for both monastic and lay readers, see the ongoing translation of the collection known as the *Philokalia*, which contains extracts of writers dating from the fourth century onwards:

G.E.H. Palmer, Philip Sherrard and Kallistos Ware, *The Philokalia*, vols I–IV, London: Faber and Faber, 1979–95.

For translations of the biographies, or Lives, of saints, see especially:

E. Dawes and N.H. Baynes, *Three Byzantine Saints*, Oxford: Mowbray, 1948, and many subsequent editions.

A.-M. Talbot (ed.), *Byzantine Defenders of Images: Eight Saints' Lives in English Translation*, Washington DC: Dumbarton Oaks, 1998.

A.-M. Talbot (ed.), *Holy Women of Byzantium: Ten Saints' Lives in English Translation*, Washington DC: Dumbarton Oaks, 1996.

A collection of hymns by the great sixth-century hymnographer Romanos the Melodist may be found in:

Archimandrite E. Lash (tr.), *Kontakia on the Life of Christ by St Romanos the Melodist*, San Francisco and London: HarperCollins, 1995.

The best introductory books on the Byzantine Church and Orthodox faith remain the following:

J.M. Hussey, *The Orthodox Church in the Byzantine Empire*, Oxford: Clarendon Press, 1986.

J. Meyendorff, *Byzantine Theology: Historical Trends and Doctrinal Themes*, New York: Fordham University Press, 1974, and subsequent reissues.

T. Ware, *The Orthodox Church: New Edition*, Penguin Books, 1993.

More specialized studies of the topics covered in this book may be found in the following bibliography:

D. Constantelos, *Byzantine Philanthropy and Social Welfare*, New Brunswick, NJ: Rutgers University Press, 1966.

R. Cormack, *Byzantine Art*, Oxford: Oxford University Press, 2000.

R. Cormack, *Writing in Gold: Byzantine Society and its Icons*, London: George Philip, 1985.

K. Corrigan, *Visual Polemics in the Ninth-Century Byzantine Psalters*, Cambridge: Cambridge University Press, 1992.

F. Dvornik, *Early Christian and Byzantine Political Philosophy*, vols I–II, Washington, DC: Dumbarton Oaks, 1966.

J. Herrin, *The Formation of Christendom*, Oxford: Basil Blackwell, 1987.

J.N.D. Kelly, *Early Christian Doctrines*, 1977, fifth revised edition, London: A. and C. Black.

V. Lossky, *The Mystical Theology of the Eastern Church*, Crestwood, NY: St Vladimir's Seminary Press, 1998.

A. Louth, *The Origins of the Christian Mystical Tradition from Plato to Denys*, Oxford: Oxford University Press, 1981.

J. Lowden, *Early Christian and Byzantine Art*, London: Phaidon, 1997.

C. Mango, *Byzantium: The Empire of New Rome*, New York: Charles Scribner's Sons, 1980.

J. Meyendorff, *Christ in Eastern Christian Thought*, Crestwood, NY: St Vladimir's Seminary Press, 1975.

R. Morris, *Church and People in Byzantium*, Birmingham: The Centre for Byzantine, Ottoman and Modern Greek Studies, 1990.

R. Morris, *Monks and Laymen in Byzantium, 843–1118*, Cambridge: Cambridge University Press, 1995.

D.M. Nicol, *Church and Society in the Last Centuries of Byzantium*, Cambridge: Cambridge University Press, 1979.

J. Pelikan, *Imago Dei: The Byzantine Apologia for Icons*, New Haven and London: Yale University Press, 1990.

P. Rousseau, *Pachomios: The Making of a Community in Fourth-Century Egypt*, California: University of California Press, 1985.

S. Runciman, *A History of the Crusades*, vols I–III, Cambridge: Cambridge University Press, 1951–54.

S. Runciman, *The Eastern Schism*, Oxford: Clarendon Press, 1955.

K.M. Setton (ed.), *A History of the Crusades*, vols I–IV, Madison, WI: University of Wisconsin Press, 1969–89.

A.-E. Tachiaos, *Cyril and Methodius of Thessalonica: The Acculturation of the Slavs*, Crestwood, NY: St Vladimir's Seminary Press, 2001.

R.F. Taft, *The Byzantine Rite: A Short History*, Collegeville, MN: The Liturgical Press, 1992.

L. Ouspensky, *Theology of the Icon*, tr. Anthony Gythiel, vol. I, Crestwood, NY: St Vladimir's Seminary Press, 1992.

J. Wilkinson, *Egeria's Travels*, Warminster: Aris and Phillips, Ltd, 1999.

Index

Picture and Text Acknowledgments

Pictures

Picture research by Zooid Pictures Limited.

AKG London: pp. 1 (Erich Lessing), 2–3 (Erich Lessing, from the Kariye Camii Museum, Istanbul), 24 (Erich Lessing), 40, 44–45 (Erich Lessing), 46 (Erich Lessing), 108 (Erich Lessing), 114–15 (Erich Lessing), 142–43, 149 (Erich Lessing), 165 (Erich Lessing), 170–71.

Biblioteca Nacional, Madrid: pp. 36, 110–11 (from *The Skylitzes Chronicle*, vitr. 26–2), 116–17.

Bibliotheca Apostolica Vaticana: pp. 16, 76–77.

Bibliothèque Nationale: pp. 51, 166.

Bodleian Library, University of Oxford: p. 91 (copyright Lincoln College, Oxford, ms. gr. 35, fol. 12 recto).

British Library: p. 134.

British Museum: pp. 29, 47, 104.

Corbis UK Ltd: pp. 28 (Archivo Iconografico, S.A., from *The Skylitzes Chronicle*, vitr. 26–2, fol. 49r., Biblioteca Nacional, Madrid), 34 (Paul H. Kuiper), 48 (Hubert Stadler), 52 (Archivo Iconografico, S.A.), 58 (Gianni Dagli Orti), 73 (Ruggero Vanni), 81 (Chris Hellier), 82–83 (Michael Nicholson), 88–89 (Chris Hellier), 98 (David Lees), 127 (Archivo Iconografico, S.A.), 133 (Andrea Jemolo), 152–53 (Vanni Archive), 159 (Vanni Archive), 161 (Paul Almasy), 163 (Sandro Vannini), 168 (Archivo Iconografico, S.A.), 173 (Archivo Iconografico, S.A.), 174–75 (Janet Wishnetsky).

Dumbarton Oaks, Washington DC: p. 84.

Photostock: pp. 103, 128 (from Mount Sinai codex no. 339 [dated between 1136 and 1155], now belongs to St Catherine's Monastery, Sinai, Egypt), 169.

Scala: pp. 62–63, 131, 162–63.

Sonia Halliday Photographs: pp. 18, 124–25, 178 (Museo Correr, Venice).

Werner Forman Archive: pp. 4, 37 (Venice, Bibl. Marciana ms. gr. 217, fol. 111r.).

Derek West: maps on pp. 10–11, 12–13, 14–15, 19.

Text

Lion Publishing

Commissioning editor: Morag Reeve

Project editor: Jenni Dutton

Insides designer: Nicholas Rous

Jacket designer: Jonathan Roberts

Production controller: Charles Wallis

D0802392

Lady Escándalo

books4pocket

Jo Beverley

Lady Escándalo

Traducción de Pilar Cercadillo Villazán

EDICIONES URANO

Argentina - Chile - Colombia - España
Estados Unidos - México - Uruguay - Venezuela

Título original: *My Lady Notorious*
Copyright © 1993 by Jo Beverley

© de la traducción: Pilar Cercadillo Villazán
© 2003 by Ediciones Urano
        Aribau, 142, pral. – 08036 Barcelona
        www.edicionesurano.com
        www.books4pocket.com

1ª edición en Books4pocket enero 2009

Diseño de la colección: Opalworks
Imagen de portada: Fort Ross
Diseño de portada: Enrique Iborra

Impreso por Novoprint, S.A.
Energía 53
Sant Andreu de la Barca (Barcelona)

Fotocomposición: Books4pocket

ISBN: 978-84-92516-37-7
Depósito legal: B-50.222-2008

Impreso en España – *Printed in Spain*

1

El magnífico carruaje blasonado iba dando tumbos a lo largo
de la carretera de Shaftesbury, sobre unos surcos que se habían vuelto duros como la piedra a causa de aquella rigurosa
helada del mes de noviembre. Repantigado en su interior,
con las lustrosas botas sobre el asiento de enfrente, se hallaba un joven caballero de mirada indolente que vestía un traje azul oscuro con encajes plateados. Sus delicados y bron-
ceados rasgos eran de una belleza algo femenina, pero su
gusto para la decoración era más bien escaso. Los argénteos
calados ribeteaban solamente la parte delantera de su chaquetón y sus únicas joyas eran un zafiro que lucía en la des-
mayada mano derecha, y un alfiler de perlas y diamantes
prendido en el corbatín de nudo flojo. El cabello castaño sin
empolvar, aunque caracterizado por irreprimibles ondulaciones, iba contenido en una pulcra cola de caballo sujeta por
sendos lazos negros en su parte superior e inferior.

Este peinado era obra de su *valet de chambre*, un hombre de mediana edad que iba sentado muy derecho junto a su
amo, estrechando con firmeza un pequeño cofre de joyas en
su regazo.

Al producirse un nuevo y chirriante vaivén, lord Cynric
Mallorer suspiró y decidió alquilar un caballo de montar en la
siguiente parada. Tenía que escapar de aquel maldito encierro.

Estar impedido era un verdadero suplicio.

Finalmente había conseguido persuadir a su solícito hermano, el marqués de Rothgar, de que se hallaba en condiciones de viajar, aunque sólo durante el moderado trayecto de dos días que le llevó hasta Dorset para visitar a su hermana mayor y su nuevo retoño. Y, únicamente, en aquel monstruoso vehículo, provisto de mantas de piel para sus piernas y ladrillos calientes para sus pies. Ahora regresaba a casa, del mismo modo que lo haría una frágil abuela a quien le esperaran el cuidado de la familia y los paños calientes.

La orden proferida a gritos resultó meramente un bienvenido alivio, en contraste con todo aquel tedio. Cyn necesitó un segundo para darse cuenta de que estaba siendo asaltado. Su *valet* palideció, se persignó y empezó a murmurar un torrente de oraciones en francés. Los ojos de Cyn perdieron su perezosa caída.

Se incorporó y lanzó una rápida mirada hacia su florete envainado, situado en el asiento de enfrente, pero rechazó la idea. No le pareció muy verosímil que los asaltantes de caminos fueran a batirse con sus víctimas en un combate de esgrima para disputarse el oro. Lo que sí cogió, en cambio, fue la pistola de dos cañones, sacándola de la funda que había junto a su asiento y comprobando con pericia que estaba limpia y tenía cargados los dos conductos.

Era un arma más atroz que una espada, pero, en semejante situación, bastante más eficaz.

El carruaje se detuvo finalmente, quedándose ladeado. Cyn estudió la escena que se apreciaba en el exterior. El corto día estaba ya bien avanzado y los pinos cercanos arrojaban profundas sombras en el fulgor rojizo de la puesta de sol, pero aún pudo ver a los dos bandoleros con toda claridad.

Uno de ellos se hallaba retirado, entre los árboles, cubriendo la estampa con un mosquetón. El otro estaba mucho más cerca, e iba armado con dos elegantes pistolas de duelo cuya montura era de plata. ¿Robadas? El caballo en el que iba montado, que ahora exhalaba vapor, era de buena raza.

Cyn decidió no disparar a nadie por el momento. Aquella aventura le resultaba demasiado vivificante como para acabar con ella tan pronto. Además, tuvo que admitir que, con la menguante luz del anochecer, incluso alguien como él, podía errar el tiro destinado al bandido más lejano.

Los dos pistoleros iban cubiertos por capas negras y sombreros de tres picos. La parte inferior del rostro la llevaban envuelta en sendas bufandas blancas. Si lograban escapar, no sería fácil describirlos. Pero Cyn tenía alma de jugador, aunque raras veces apostara por dinero. Así que decidió dejar rodar aquellos dados.

—Bajen del pescante —ordenó con aspereza el hombre que estaba más cerca.

El cochero y el mozo de cuadra descendieron obedientemente. A una nueva orden, se tumbaron bocabajo sobre la helada hierba del borde de la calzada. El segundo bandolero se acercó para vigilarlos.

Los caballos, carentes de dirección, se revolvieron, haciendo que el carruaje se bamboleara. Jerome gritó alarmado. Cyn extendió una mano para sujetarse pero sin perder de vista a los dos bandidos. Los corceles estarían a esas alturas demasiado cansados para desbocarse. Su apreciación resultó correcta y el coche se quedó nuevamente en calma.

—Ahora los de dentro —gruñó el bandido más próximo, apuntando con ambos cañones en dirección a la puerta—. Fuera. Y sin trucos.

Cyn consideró la posibilidad de dispararle —a esa distancia estaba seguro de poder meterle una bala en el ojo derecho— pero se contuvo. Podía poner en peligro a los otros, y, ni su orgullo ni sus objetos de valor, merecían el sacrificio de una vida inocente.

Depositó la pistola al lado de su espada, abrió la puerta y se apeó. Tras volverse para ayudar a su *valet*, que tenía una pierna mala, abrió con un chasquido su caja de rapé color gris, se retiró hacia atrás el encaje de Mechlin que remataba el puño de su camisa y aspiró un pellizco. Cerrando la caja de golpe, encaró las pistolas del salteador de caminos:

—¿En qué puedo ayudarle, señor?

El hombre se quedó pasmado al observar esta reacción, pero se sobrepuso:

—Para empezar, puede alcanzarme aquel bonito cofre.

A Cyn le costó trabajo mantener el rostro inmóvil. Tal vez fuera por la conmoción que le había causado su laxa reacción ante el robo, pero el ladrón se había olvidado de controlar la voz. Ahora había sonado como la de alguien joven y de buena familia. Debía ser poco más que un chaval. Cualquier deseo de verlo colgado se esfumó, y su curiosidad iba en aumento.

Abriendo de nuevo la caja, se le aproximó:

—¿Te apetece probar mi mezcla? Es bastante aceptable.

No era su intención arrojar los polvos en la cara del ladrón, pero éste, que no era ningún tonto, retrocedió a lomos del caballo.

—Mantente a distancia. Me quedaré con la caja —incluida su aceptable mezcla— así como con tu dinero, las joyas y otros objetos de valor.

—Desde luego —dijo Cyn, encogiéndose de hombros despreocupadamente. Y tras coger el cofre al que Jerome se aferraba, que contenía sus alfileres, relojes y otras alhajas, colocó en su interior la caja de rapé y después añadió algunas monedas y billetes que se sacó de los bolsillos. Con cierto pesar se quitó el anillo de zafiro y se soltó el alfiler de perlas y diamantes: tenían un valor sentimental.

—Seguro que necesitas todo esto más que yo, buen hombre. ¿Pongo al arca junto a la carretera? Así podréis cogerla cuando nos hayamos ido.

Se produjo otro aplastante silencio. Y después:

—¡Lo que puedes hacer es tumbarte en el lodo con tus criados!

Cyn levantó las cejas y se sacudió una pelusa de la manga del chaquetón.

—Oh, me parece que no. No tengo ningunas ganas de mancharme de polvo —dijo encarando con calma al hombre—. ¿Vas a matarme por eso?

Vio cómo la mano del bandido se tensaba y se preguntó si, por primera vez, no habría jugado mal sus cartas, pero no hubo disparo. Tras un violento silencio, el joven dijo:

—Pon los objetos de valor dentro del coche y súbete al pescante. Voy a llevarme el coche conmigo y tú vas a ser mi cochero, señor Arrogante.

—Muy original —enunció Cyn con lentitud levantando las cejas—. Pero ¿no crees que resulta un poco difícil traficar con carruajes robados?

—¡Cierra la boca o te la cierro yo!

Cyn tuvo la innegable sensación de que el bandolero estaba perdiendo la paciencia —una reacción que él llevaba toda su vida suscitando.

—Haz lo que yo te diga —ladró el bribón—. Y diles a tus hombres que tarden un rato en ir a buscar ayuda. Si alguien nos da alcance, el primer disparo será para ti.

Cyn se dirigió obedientemente a sus lacayos.

—Llegad hasta Shaftesbury y alojaros en el Crown. Si no tenéis noticias mías durante la jornada de mañana, haced llegar un mensaje a la Abadía y mi hermano se ocupará de vosotros. No os preocupéis por esto. Es sólo un viejo amigo que me gasta una broma y a mí me apetece sumarme a la diversión. —Y, dirigiéndose al cochero, añadió—: Hoskins si la pierna de Jerome no aguanta, tendrás que adelantarte y encontrar algún medio de transporte para él.

Después se volvió hacia el cuatrero:

—¿Tengo permiso para ponerme el gabán y los guantes, señor, o va a ser esto una especie de tortura?

El hombre dudó pero dijo:

—Venga, adelante. Pero no voy a dejar de cubrirte ni un solo instante.

Cyn cogió del coche su amplia capa y se introdujo en ella. A continuación se puso sus guantes negros de cabritilla, mientras pensaba con sarcasmo que se echarían a perder con la conducción. Durante un instante, consideró la posibilidad de coger la pistola, pero después rechazó la idea. Quería seguir adelante con aquella inesperada travesura un rato más.

Protegido de esta guisa contra el aire helado, se subió al pescante y asió los cuatro juegos de riendas con sus competentes manos. Enseguida se familiarizo con las marcas de cada uno de ellos, que servían para identificar a los caballos que iban en cabeza y a los de varas.

—¿Y ahora qué, buen hombre?

El bandolero le lanzó una feroz mirada entrecerrando los ojos.

—Tú eres un tipo raro, seguro. —Como Cyn no contestara, el bandido enganchó su caballo a la parte trasera y, subiendo por encima del carruaje, fue a sentarse a su lado—. No sé cuál es tu juego, pero conmigo no te van a valer los trucos. En marcha.

Cyn hizo arrancar a los caballos.

—Sin trucos —prometió—. Pero espero que esa pistola no tenga un gatillo muy sensible. Esta calzada es muy irregular.

Tras unos instantes, la pistola se movió un poco y dejó de apuntarle directamente.

—¿Te sientes más seguro? —se mofó el hombre.

—Infinitamente. ¿A dónde vamos?

—Eso no te importa. Yo te diré cuándo debes girar. De momento, limítate a cerrar el pico.

Cyn obedeció. Percibía la confusa furia que emanaba de su captor y no tenía ningunas ganas de incitarle con sus burlas a que disparara. En realidad, no deseaba provocar a aquel infeliz en absoluto. Más bien le apetecía besarle en ambas mejillas por romper la monotonía de sus días. Estaba harto de que lo mimaran.

Miró a su alrededor y descubrió que el segundo bandido se había adelantado. Supuso que, aunque aquello era una maniobra arriesgada, habían pensado que la amenaza de una pistola bastaría para mantenerle bajo control.

Bien podía ser así. Se sentía amablemente dispuesto a ello.

Tener a sus hermanos revoloteando en torno a él podía haber resultado tolerable si hubiera resultado herido en acto de servicio, pero, la causa de su caída había sido una simple fiebre… Y ahora, ninguno de ellos estaba dispuesto a creer que se había recuperado lo suficiente como para reintegrarse a la vida de su regimiento. Se le pasó por la cabeza saltarse a la torera el plan acordado y ordenar a Hoskins que se dirigiera a Londres, donde podría solicitar un médico del ejército. Sin embargo, aquello no tenía ningún sentido, porque, en cuanto Rothgar abriera la boca, seguro que descubrían que todavía no estaba del todo repuesto.

Del mismo modo que había sido palabra de Rothgar lo que había conseguido que le transportaran de inmediato a la Abadía y le otorgaran los mejores cuidados médicos a lo largo del trayecto, mientras que hombres más valiosos sudaban sus fiebres o morían en los abarrotados hospitales de Plymouth. O lo hacían allá, en las primitivas condiciones existentes en Acadia. Rothgar podía hallarse incluso tras el hecho de que fuera embarcado desde Halifax, para empezar.

Maldito Rothgar con sus mimos.

Nadie en su sano juicio describiría al formidable marqués, el hermano mayor de Cyn, como una gallina clueca, pero, tras la muerte de sus padres, él había acogido a sus hermanos bajo su despótica ala y pobre de aquel que intentara hacerles daño. No se detenía ni ante las fuerzas de la guerra.

Rothgar parecía proteger particularmente a Cyn. En parte, porque era el pequeño de la familia, pero también por aquel aspecto suyo, del que no podía librarse. A pesar de todos los datos que afirmaban lo contrario, la gente seguía viéndole como alguien frágil, incluso su familia, que, desde luego, debería conocerle mejor.

Él era el único de la familia que había heredado de su madre todo el esplendor de su delicada constitución, sus ojos verde miel, su pelo castaño rojizo y sus exuberantes pestañas. Sus hermanas —en especial su hermana gemela— había preguntado con frecuencia a los cielos por qué tenía que haberse producido un hecho tan injusto.

Cyn se hacía con frecuencia la misma pregunta con el mismo grado de desesperación. Cuando era niño, pensaba que con la edad su aspecto se endurecería, pero a los veinticuatro años, y tras haber luchado en Quebec y Louisbourg, seguía siendo asquerosamente guapo. Para afirmar su virilidad, tenía que batirse en duelo con casi todos los nuevos oficiales del regimiento.

—Métete por ese desvío. —La voz del bandolero sacó bruscamente a Cyn de sus meditaciones. Obedeciendo, hizo que los caballos se introdujeran por aquel estrecho camino, en dirección al sol poniente.

El resplandor le hizo entrecerrar los ojos.

—Espero que no quede mucho —comentó—. Pronto oscurecerá y esta noche hay muy poca luna.

—Ya estamos cerca.

Hacía cada vez mas frío y el vapor que exhalaban los caballos parecía el humo de una hoguera. Cyn hizo restallar el látigo para apremiar a los cansados caballos.

El joven cuatrero se repantigó hacia atrás, abriendo las piernas con despreocupada comodidad, como si tratara de transmitir la impresión de tener más edad y ser un endurecido villano. Pero no fue un gesto acertado. La capa le cayó abierta por los lados y la esbeltez de sus piernas, puesta de manifiesto por la posición recostada, reforzó la sospecha de Cyn de que se trataba de un simple mozalbete. Se percató, no obstante, de que la pistola seguía dispuesta y se dijo que eso hablaba a favor del muchacho.

El tipo no era tonto.

Entonces, ¿qué había llevado a aquel joven a emprender una aventura tan temeraria? ¿Un desafío? ¿Deudas de juego que no podía confesar a papá?

Cyn presentía que no corría gran peligro, y su olfato para estas cuestiones estaba muy desarrollado. Desde los dieciocho años, había sido soldado en tiempos de guerra.

Recordó el revuelo que se organizó en su familia cuando se escapó para alistarse. Rothgar no había querido comprarle el grado de oficial, así que se alistó como soldado raso. El marqués lo había traído de vuelta a casa, pero tras numerosas disputas, que hacían estremecerse a cualquier espectador, su hermano se había rendido y le había comprado un alferazgo en un buen regimiento. Cyn nunca se había arrepentido. Necesitaba estímulos excitantes, pero, al contrario de lo que les ocurría a muchos otros vástagos de la aristocracia, el alboroto absurdo no le interesaba lo mas mínimo.

Echó un vistazo a su captor. Tal vez una carrera en el ejército le sentara bien a aquel joven bribón. Un curioso pensamiento le rondó por el fondo de la mente y le hizo recorrer al joven con la mirada. Entonces lo supo con certeza. Contuvo el rictus de sus labios y se concentró en los caballos mientras absorbía la nueva información. A juzgar por la lisura que se apreciaba en la conjunción de sus muslos, el asaltante de Cyn era una mujer.

Empezó a silbar. La situación le parecía prometedora.

—¡Deja de hacer ese maldito ruido!

Cyn obedeció y miró pensativamente a su acompañante. Las mujeres no solían hablar en aquel tono áspero y cortante. Además, la pulcra peluca y el tricornio que llevaba la criatura no dejaban espacio para que pudiera haber mechones de pelo recogidos por debajo. ¿Estaría equivocado?

Como quuien no quiere la cosa, deslizó la vista de nuevo hacia abajo y supo que sus sospechas eran correctas. Ella llevaba uros calzones ajustados que le llegaban hasta la rodilla, y, bajo éstos, no había equipamiento masculino. Además, aunque las piernas de la mujer tenían aspecto esbelto y atlético, los pantalones y las medias con bordados ponían de manifiesto una redondez que era más femenina que otra cosa.

—¿Cuánto queda? —preguntó Cyn, tocando a uno de los guías con el látigo, para salir de aquel tramo particularmente duro—. Este camino es de armas tomar.

—Es aquella cabaña que se ve al fondo. Entra hasta el huerto para esconder el carruaje. Los caballos pueden pastar allí.

Cyn miró hacia la verja, donde había una hondonada tan profunda como una zanja, y se preguntó si aquel carruaje conseguiría pasar. Pero apartó de sí semejantes preocupaciones. Estaba demasiado impaciente por saber cuál sería el siguiente paso de la aventura.

Usando el látigo y la voz, apremió a los cansados corceles para que entraran, manteniéndose con dificultad sobre su asiento mientras el vehículo vibraba al hundirse en el surco y después remontaba el curso del camino. El eje maltratado emitió un chirrido amenazador pero no se partió. Cyn condujo a los caballos al otro lado de los árboles con la sensación de haberlo logrado, preguntándose si la muchacha se daba cuenta de lo hábil que había sido. La pasión que había tenido en sus años escolares por los carruajes estaba dando sus frutos al fin.

—Puede pasar —dijo ella displicentemente.

Empezaba a pensar que su misteriosa dama iba a resultar ser el antídoto para sus males. Todo lo que podía ver de su rostro por encima de la bufanda eran sus duros ojos grises. Supuso que sus labios estarían trazados con la misma dureza.

—¿Qué estás mirando? —le espetó ella.

—Parece razonable que intente quedarme con tus rasgos para poder describirte a las autoridades.

Ella le apuntó con la pistola directamente a la cara.

—Eres un idiota, ¿lo sabes? ¿Qué me iba a impedir dispararte?

Él le sostuvo la mirada sin perder la calma.

—El juego limpio. ¿Eres de la clase de persona que dispara a un hombre sin ningún motivo?

—Salvar el pellejo podría ser una razón suficiente.

Cyn sonrió.

—Te doy mi palabra de que no haré nada para ayudar a las autoridades a prenderte.

La pistola descendió y ella le miró fijamente.

—¿Quién demonios eres?

—Cyn Malloren. ¿Quién demonios eres tú?

Él se dio cuenta de que ella había estado a punto de caer en la trampa y contestar la verdad, pero se contuvo.

—Puedes llamarme Charles. ¿Qué clase de nombre es Sin?

—C-Y-N. Cynric, de hecho. El nombre de un rey anglosajón.

—He oído hablar de los Malloren... —Se irguió—. Rothgar.

—El marqués es mi hermano —reconoció él—. Pero no lo tengas en cuenta en mi contra.— Adivinó que, en aquellos momentos, ella deseaba haberlo dejado al borde del camino. A nadie le convenía contrariar a Rothgar.

Ella se recobró enseguida del golpe:

—Te juzgaré por tus propias obras, milord. Te doy mi palabra. Ahora, desengancha los caballos.

Cyn saludó irónicamente:

—A la orden, señor.

Después se apeó, se quitó el gabán y la entallada levita y, remetiéndose el espumoso encaje de los puños para que no le estorbara, se dispuso a trabajar.

El sol se había puesto y había muy poca luz. Un húmedo frío se le metió hasta los huesos a pesar de la dureza de la tarea. La labor le llevó algún tiempo y ella no le ayudó, se limitó a quedarse allí sentada, apuntándole con la pistola. En cierto momento, la mujer dirigió la vista tras él y dijo:

—Vuelve a la casa Verity. Todo está en orden. Enseguida vamos nosotros.

Cyn volvió la vista y vislumbró un pálido vestido que se daba la vuelta para regresar a la cabaña. Hubiera apostado cualquier cosa a que se trataba del otro bandolero. Todo lo relativo a aquella situación le intrigaba.

¿Qué hacían dos mujeres jóvenes, y al parecer de buena cuna, en aquella cabaña?

¿Por qué se habían metido a bandoleras?

Y, en nombre de Dios, ¿qué era lo que pretendían hacer con el carruaje?

Frotó a los caballos con manojos de hierba seca y los cubrió con las mantas que Hoskins tenía preparadas para los descansos.

—Les iría bien beber agua —dijo.

—Hay un arroyo al final del huerto. Lo encontrarán ellos mismos. Coge el botín y vamos a la casa.

Cyn reunió sus prendas, sin molestarse en volver a ponérselas. Entró en el carruaje y cogió el estuche de las alhajas. Consideró seriamente la posibilidad de coger la pistola. Le resultaría grotescamente fácil coger aquella arma de fuego y disparar contra su captor. Mientras la dejaba allí, se preguntaba si más tarde lamentaría su estupidez.

Al cabo de media hora, la respuesta era afirmativa.

Desde la cama de bronce en la que yacía, con las extremidades extendidas y sólidamente atadas a los postes de sus esquinas, miraba furioso a las tres mujeres que revoloteaban por encima de él.

—Cuando consiga soltarme, voy a estrangularos a todas.

—Por eso estás amarrado —dijo la que todavía simulaba ser un hombre—. Si te dejáramos suelto, no tendríamos ni un solo minuto de paz.

—Os he dado mi palabra de que no tenéis nada que temer de mí.

—A fe mía que no lo has hecho. Lo que has dicho es que no nos entregarías a las autoridades. Pero podrías tramar alguna otra fechoría contra mi hermana o mi nodriza, por ejemplo.

Cyn la miró pensativo. «Charles» estaba resultando ser un enigma fascinante. Al entrar en la cabaña se había desprendido de la capa, el sombrero y la bufanda. Al poco rato, se había quitado distraídamente la peluca. Aquello le agradó. A Cyn tampoco le había gustado nunca llevar peluca: prefería tomarse la molestia de arreglarse su propio cabello.

Incluso desprovista de su disfraz, podía pasar por un joven. El traje de terciopelo marrón trenzado le encajaba perfectamente y, si éste ocultaba la protuberancia de unos pechos, el volante de encaje de la camisa escondía el hecho de maravilla.

No llevaba la cabeza completamente rapada, sino que su cabello formaba un bruñido casco de color castaño claro, salpicado de oro, con tenues ondulaciones. Era un peinado portentoso para una mujer, pero no resultaba tan atroz como podría suponerse, tal vez porque no se trataba de una dama de rasgos suaves. Su aspecto era el de un atractivo joven.

Tenía la piel delicada, desde luego, lo que le hacía aparentar unos dieciséis años, aunque él suponía que debía estar más cerca de los veinte. Su voz era más bien grave. Sus labios no carecerían de encanto si se relajaran formando una sonrisa, pero ella los mantenía apretados e iracundos. No tenía ni idea de por qué demonios estaba tan enfadada con él.

Sus acompañantes le resultaban igualmente desconcertantes.

Verity, presumiblemente la hermana, tenía el pelo largo, brillante y ondulado, de un color entre dorado y miel. Su boca era suave y femenina. En contraste con Charles, tenía una figura exuberante. Charles debía llevar los pechos vendados, pero la generosa silueta de Verity, que quedaba bien a la vista con un escote bajo y un amplio *fichu*, no podría anularse ni con bandas de hierro. Su indumentaria, no obstante, era más propia de una criada que de una dama de alcurnia.

Verity parecía el epítome de la mujer femenina. Prueba de ello era que estaba mucho más nerviosa y era más amable que su hermana.

—No podemos mantenerlo así indefinidamente —señaló.

—Claro que no, pero, de este modo, no nos causará problemas mientras nos vestimos y nos preparamos para marcharnos.

—Pero la… pero Charles —dijo la nodriza con inquietud—, ya sabes que no te está permitido salir.

Esta mujer era mayor, muy mayor. De figura menuda y encorvada. Tenía gafas de media luna y el pelo suave y plateado. Ella había sido la perdición de Cyn. Cuando Charles le ordenó que fuera a la cama para que lo ataran, él se había negado. La anciana, sin embargo, obedeció la orden de llevarlo hasta allí y él había tenido tanto miedo de romper sus huesos de pájaro que terminó por no oponer resistencia.

Cyn se dio cuenta del desliz. La anciana casi había llamado a la joven lady algo. De alta cuna, pues. A pesar de que la una estuviera plausiblemente vestida de hombre y la otra de criada.

—Me importa un rábano si me está permitido salir o no —dijo lady Charles—. Hasta ahora no he tenido motivo para ir a ningún sitio y sí muy buenas razones para esconderme. Ahora todo ha cambiado. Supongo que volveré a su debido tiempo. ¿A qué otro sitio podría ir?

—Te quedarás con Nathaniel y conmigo —dijo Verity.

—Tal vez —dijo Charles, suavizando el gesto—. Pero él ya va a tener bastante trabajo ocupándose de ti y de William, querida. —Desde el piso de arriba llegó un sonido quejumbroso—. Ya está otra vez. Es una pequeña bestia hambrienta, ¿a que sí?

Verity se apresuró a subir por un tramo de estrechas escaleras mientras Cyn encajaba el hecho de que uno de sus asaltantes era madre y, según parecía, desde hacía poco. Así se explicaba la excesiva exuberancia de su figura. La incomodidad y el fastidio dieron paso nuevamente a la fascinación. Ya se veía a sí mismo contando aquella historia a sus compañeros oficiales. Durante los acantonamientos invernales, siempre era de agradecer un buen relato.

La mujer más mayor desapareció en el interior de la cocina, la única otra habitación de la planta baja. Cyn supuso que había otra estancia bajo el alero del tejado, en la que debían dormir las hermanas y el bebé. El dormitorio de la anciana, que era donde se encontraba él, estaba siendo usado como saloncito provisional a la vez que contenía diversos bultos, cajas y baúles.

¿Por qué estaban allí las hermanas, y por qué a Charles no le estaba permitido marcharse?

La chica estaba buscando algo en un arca, ignorándole por completo.

—¿Vais a darme de comer? —preguntó Cyn.

—Más tarde.

—¿Qué es lo que os proponéis hacer conmigo?

Ella se puso en pie y se acercó a la cama. Apoyó el pie sobre el armazón de ésta y dejó descansar el codo sobre la rodilla. Él tuvo la indudable sensación de que estaba disfrutando de su situación de poder.

—A lo mejor simplemente te dejamos aquí así.

Él enfrentó aquellos enfadados ojos grises:

—¿Por qué?

—¿Por qué no?

—No he intentando lastimaros. Hice lo que pude para asegurarme de que mi gente no daba la voz de alarma.

—¿Por qué hiciste eso?

Cyn estaba sorprendido de lo mucho que ella desconfiaba de él Seguramente le tenía miedo. Eso explicaría que lo hubieran atado de aquella guisa. No por crueldad sino por miedo. Con aquella apariencia engañosamente delicada, Cyn no estaba acostumbrado a que las mujeres se comportaran de forma tan cautelosa con él.

Eligió las palabras con cuidado.

—Me pareció que no erais malvados, que no ibais a hacerme daño. No me gustaría veros en la horca. De hecho, quisiera ayudaros.

Ella bajó el pie y dio un significativo paso hacia atrás.

—¿Por qué?

—Sospecho que tenéis una razón muy buena para vuestros actos, y yo hace tiempo que espero una aventura.

Aquello pareció exasperar sobremanera a la chica.

—Hace tiempo que deberías estar en un sanatorio mental.

—No lo creo. Simplemente tengo un bajo nivel de tolerancia al tedio.

—El tedio tiene sus encantos, créeme.

—Aún no he sido capaz de descubrirlos.

—Entonces, considérate afortunado.

Por primera vez, él se preguntó si no se hallaría ella en algún apuro serio. Hasta ahora había pensado que tal vez se tratara de una travesura de niñas, pero no le parecía verosímil que aquella formidable joven fuera a ponerse tan solemne por un asunto trivial.

—Estáis en peligro, ¿no es cierto? —dijo Cyn.

Ella abrió desmedidamente los ojos, pero no dijo nada.

—Razón de más para confiar en mí y dejar que os ayude.

Ella levantó con decisión la barbilla.

—No me fío —y después de contener el aliento añadió—: … de la gente.

Él sabía que había estado a punto de decir, no me fío de los hombres.

—Puedes fiarte de mí.

Ella soltó una amarga y breve carcajada

Antes de responder, él esperó a captar su escondida mirada.

—Hay una pistola cargada en el asiento del carruaje. No la usé al principio porque tu hermana estaba cubriendo a mis hombres. No la usé cuando recogí tu botín porque no quise. Soy un tirador excelente. Podía haberte desarmado, lisiado o matado si se me hubiera antojado.

Ella le miró ceñuda, giró sobre sus talones y se marchó. Cyn oyó el golpe de la puerta de la calle y supo que ella había ido a comprobarlo.

Unos minutos más tarde, la anciana entró de puntillas en la estancia con una taza provista con una cánula.

—Estoy segura de que le apetece beber algo milord —le dijo y empezó a administrarle con cuidado una taza de té dulce y sorprendentemente fuerte. No era como el que él estaba acostumbrado a beber, pero, de todos modos, lo agradeció.

Cuando terminó, la mujer le secó con un paño blanco las gotas que le habían caído.

—No tiene que preocuparse —le dijo, dándole una palmadita en una de sus manos atadas—. Nadie va a hacerle daño. Ch… Charles está un poco inquieto últimamente. —Sacudió la cabeza y la sombra de una genuina ansiedad cubrió sus ojos—. Todo ha sido bastante terrible…

Una vez más, Cyn tuvo la cierta sensación de que lo que se traían entre manos no eran asuntos de poca monta.

—¿Cómo debo llamarla? —preguntó.

—Oh, soy simplemente Nana. Así es como todos me llaman, de modo que usted también puede hacerlo. ¿Le duelen las manos? Espero no haberle atado demasiado prieto.

—No —le aseguró él, aunque sentía punzadas en las manos, como si las tuviera llenas de agujas. No quería que Charles volviera y lo encontrara suelto, no fuera a ser que sospechara que él había querido alejarla de la casa. Trató de conseguir un poco más de información.

—¿Y cómo tengo que llamar a la señorita Verity?

—Oh —dijo la anciana, que evidentemente no era tonta—, Verity puede servir, ¿no? Debe excusarme, milord. Tengo la comida en el fuego.

Chastity Ware atravesó deprisa el huerto en penumbra hasta llegar a la sombría silueta del carruaje. Se había detenido en la cocina para coger las pistolas de duelo y el mosquetón. Ya tendría que haberlas devuelto, junto con los caballos. Pero su principal propósito, así lo reconoció, era comprobar las palabras del prisionero.

En su mente bullían oscuros pensamientos. ¿Qué es lo que le había arrastrado a secuestrar a Cyn Malloren?

Lo de quedarse con el coche había tenido sentido, aunque fue fruto de una inspiración repentina. Verity y el bebé viajarían mucho mejor en un vehículo privado que en la diligencia.

Lo de hacer que él lo condujera también había tenido sentido. No había querido distraer su atención de los hombres durante el tiempo que hubiera necesitado para conducirlo ella misma. No tenía mucha fe en la capacidad de Verity para disparar contra nadie, cualquiera que fuese la circunstancia.

Pero, incluso habiéndole hecho conducir un trecho, podía haberlo abandonado en algún lugar desierto. Ella ya había conducido una calesa. Seguramente, conducir un carruaje de cuatro caballos no era muy diferente.

Lo que menos les hacía falta era un truhán.

De hecho, lo que la había exasperado había sido su insufrible arrogancia masculina.

Se había quedado allí plantado, con su traje azul de ribetes plateados y floridos encajes —demasiado bello para ser decente— y sin asustarse de sus pistolas. Cuando le ofreciera una pizca de su rapé, ella había querido desbaratar su amor propio, viéndolo tumbado en el barro. Sin embargo, como él había adivinado, ella no había sido capaz de dispararle por aquel motivo. Después, él había dado la vuelta a la situación con aquellas amables palabras que había dirigido a sus criados. De funcionar, aquello demoraría la persecución, o puede que incluso la evitara.

Se preguntaba cuál sería su juego, pero al menos ahora resultaría inofensivo durante un tiempo. ¡Cómo detestaba él aquello! Ella sonrió para sus adentros, inflexible, mientras abría la puerta del carruaje.

El interior del vehículo se hallaba a oscuras y Chastity tuvo que buscar el arma a tientas, pero la encontró. Allí estaba, tal y como él había dicho. Sacó la pistola al exterior y, a la incierta luz del cuarto de luna, verificó que estaba cebada y que tenía los dos cañones cargados. Había sido una presunción por su parte decir que podía haberla desarmado, herido o matado —ella también estaba armada—, pero reconoció que había tenido una oportunidad que no había querido aprovechar.

Lo que la hizo estremecerse fue pensar en lo descuidada que había sido al ofrecérsela. La desesperación le hizo cerrar los ojos. Tal vez no estuviera a la altura de la tarea que se había impuesto a sí misma: poner a salvo a su hermana y a su sobrino.

Hacía tan sólo un día que había llegado Verity, aunque sus problemas habían empezado algún tiempo antes. Su esposo, sir William Vernham, un hombre de mediana edad, había muerto hacía casi dos meses, pocos días después del nacimiento de su hijo. Este hecho había desencadenado una batalla por la custodia del niño entre el tío de la criatura, Henry Vernham, y su abuelo —el padre de Verity y Chastity, el conde de Walgrave.

Henry había ganado la primera escaramuza legal y había llegado a Vernham Park para hacerse cargo de todo. Verity enseguida temió por su hijo, puesto que aquella pequeña vida era lo único que se interponía entre Henry y sus aspiraciones: heredar el título y la fortuna. Su temor se había acrecentado cuando Henry trató de mantenerla apartada de su familia y sus amigos. Entonces había resuelto huir con el bebé y llegar hasta allí.

Ahora tenía miedo de Henry, pero no quería buscar la protección de su padre. Lord Walgrave sin duda la mantendría a salvo, pero planificaría de inmediato otro matrimonio pensando en su propia conveniencia. Habiendo tenido que soportar la desdicha de vivir con sir William, Verity había decidido que su próximo marido sería su amor de la infancia, el mayor Nathaniel Frazer. Chastity había decidido ayudar a su hermana a alcanzar este fin.

La dificultad estribaba en que las dos hermanas no tenían apenas dinero y en que Verity era ya objeto de una intensa persecución.

Henry Vernham había visitado la cabaña hacía un par de días para interrogar a Chastity y a Nana; Chastity había tenido el tiempo justo de ataviarse con indumentaria femenina. No les había costado mucho convencerle de que no tenían ni idea del paradero de Verity, porque ésta todavía no había llegado. Su ansiedad y su azoramiento habían sido auténticos.

Chastity apretó los puños al recordar aquella confrontación con Henry Vernham, porque éste no era únicamente el verdugo de su hermana, sino también el hombre que había destrozado su propia vida y había hecho que acabara allí, con la cabeza rapada y vestida de hombre. Se había negado a hablar con él, de lo contrario podía haberse dejado llevar por el impulso de sacarle las tripas, pero el comentario final que aquél le había lanzado casi le hizo olvidar su decisión.

—Estoy seguro de que lamenta haber rechazado mi oferta de matrimonio, lady Chastity, pero ya es tarde para pensar en eso. Ahora se ha convertido usted en una indeseable.

Una ardiente rabia se apoderó de ella en aquellos momentos; de haber tenido una pistola, le habría disparado. Sin embargo, cuando llegó Verity y le contó su historia, la ira de Chastity se enfrió y se canalizó hacia un objetivo. Vernham no iba a arruinar también la vida de Verity.

No había habido tiempo de hacer planes minuciosos ni de pensar las cosas detenidamente, puesto que él podía regresar en cualquier momento. Pero lo que sí habían tenido claro era que necesitaban dinero para sobrevivir y que tendrían que robarlo. Aquella última maniobra de coger el coche había sido una decisión impulsiva. Ahora se daba cuenta de que podían pagarlo con sus vidas.

Maldito Cyn Malloren. ¿Por qué no podía haber sido el mercader gordo y timorato que esperaran ellas?

Ahora, al mirar el florido y reluciente blasón de los Malloren en la puerta del carruaje, murmuró algunos deseos funestos en relación con el destino de su propietario. Después, hizo una mueca y arrancó una piedra del muro del huerto. Se sintió muy satisfecha al utilizarla para raspar la pintura y el oropel de ambas puertas hasta hacerlos desaparecer.

Cuando hubo terminado, sin embargo, la satisfacción la abandonó y arrojó la piedra lejos de sí. Deshacerse del escudo de armas había sido lo correcto —al día siguiente todo el país podía estar buscando el carruaje de los Malloren, —pero sus sentimientos eran confusos e impropios. Apoyó la cabeza contra el vehículo, tratando de contener las lágrimas y maldiciendo en silencio a los hombres que habían sido la causa de su amargura.

Su padre, su hermano y Henry Vernham.

En la callada oscuridad de la noche campestre, dejó escapar una imprecación:

—¡Que los abismos del infierno se lleven a todos los hombres!

Pero enseguida recuperó el control de sí misma. Iba a necesitar tener la cabeza bien fría y estar vigilante para poder abatirlos a todos.

Se aseguró de que la pistola tenía puesto el seguro y la metió en el bolsillo de su abrigo. Pensó en tomar el florete, pero lo dejó allí.

Llevándose con ella los caballos de montar, caminó hacia su verdadero hogar, Walgrave Towers. La gran mansión estaba a oscuras, porque ninguno de sus familiares se hallaba en ella. Su padre y su hermano mayor pasaban la mayor parte del tiempo en Londres y, ahora, seguramente se hallarían persiguiendo a Verity; su hermano pequeño, Victor, estaba en el colegio. Dejó los animales en los establos y se coló en el interior por una puerta lateral.

Dentro reinaba el silencio, exceptuando el tictac de los relojes en las habitaciones desiertas, pero, para Chastity, en aquel lugar se escuchaban las resonancias de recuerdos amargos y dolorosos. Recuerdos recientes. Cuando era niña no había sido desdichada allí. Su padre estaba ausente la mayor parte del tiempo y su tímida madre nunca había ocasionado ningún problema. Pero allí era donde su padre la había llevado hacía pocos meses. Allí era donde había tratado de obligarla a casarse con Henry Vernham.

Chastity se dirigió a oscuras hacia la habitación de las armas y, una vez allí, usó yesca y pedernal para encender una vela. Descargó y limpió las pistolas de duelo y las devolvió a su estuche con forro de terciopelo. Su hermano mayor se saldría de sus casillas si cayera en la cuenta de que la condescendiente educación que le había proporcionado era lo que le había permitido trazarse aquel plan. Las manos de Chastity se quedaron paralizadas al recordar la última vez que había visto a Fort, su rabia, las duras y crueles palabras que le dirigiera…

Tras tensar el gesto, continuó con su trabajo: limpió el mosquetón y lo colocó en su estante. No hacía falta que fuera especialmente sigilosa. Los criados sabían, sin duda, que estaba allí y lo que estaba haciendo, pero preferían hacer la vista gorda. A ella le gustaba pensar que era porque le tenían cierto cariño. Bajo un punto de vista cínico, suponía que no querían verse envueltos en aquella cruel batalla entre sus superiores.

La atmósfera de la casa la oprimía y sintió la necesidad de escapar. Apagó la vela de un soplido y recorrió apresuradamente oscuros y fríos pasillos hasta llegar a la puerta de la torre oeste y salir a respirar el aire fresco y la libertad del exterior. Caminó a grandes zancadas de vuelta a la cabaña, usando deliberadamente aquel andar masculino tan logrado.

Tenía que regresar lo más pronto posible, antes de que su hermana y su nodriza, tan compasivas ellas, hicieran el tonto con aquella hermosa víbora de dulce aspecto que habían atrapado.

2

Chastity encontró a Nana inocentemente atareada en la cocina.

—La comida estará lista en seguida, querida —le comentó su vieja nodriza—. ¿Vas a soltarle o tendré que darle de comer con la cuchara?

Aunque el tono de Nana era suave, Chastity percibió la desaprobación que había en él.

—No podemos fiarnos de él, Nana, y tenemos demasiadas cosas que hacer como para estarle vigilando en todo momento. Podría escaparse y traer hasta aquí a las autoridades.

Nana levantó la mirada de la cacerola.

—Tal vez deberías haber pensado en eso antes de traerlo aquí.

Chastity levantó la barbilla.

—Necesitaba un cochero.

—Ah. —La anciana sacó algunos platos del aparador y empezó a poner la mesa. Chastity se percató de que estaba colocando cuatro cubiertos y de que, con tan sólo dos meses, el bebé de Verity aún no estaba preparado para comer en la mesa—. Creo que puede fiarse de él, lady Chastity —dijo Nana.

Chastity suspiró:

—Recuerda, mi nombre es Charles.

Y se fue a consultarlo con su hermana. Atravesó la habitación de la entrada ignorando por completo al prisionero. Se limitó a depositar la pistola encima de una de las cajas. Después subió con ligereza por las empinadas escaleras. Verity estaba vistiendo a su niño, después de haberlo cambiado, diciéndole tonterías y haciéndole cosquillas.

—No sé cómo puedes comportarte así teniendo en cuenta quién es su padre —le espetó Chastity.

—No pienso para nada en su padre —dijo Verity sencillamente y, después de atar la última cinta del camisón, cogió al chiquillo y lo colocó en los brazos de su hermana—. Míralo. No tiene nada que ver con sir William Vernham.

Chastity afirmó el delicado bulto en sus brazos, cautivada sin querer por la magia del bebé.

—Él es sir William Vernham —señaló mientras hacía muecas para agradar al niño.

Verity dejó de recoger la ropa sucia.

—Ya lo sé. Pero él es diferente —y añadió con fiereza—: Él no será la misma clase de hombre. Yo me encargaré de ello. Y ahora que sir William está muerto va a ser mucho más fácil.

Chastity levantó la vista con viveza.

—Ten cuidado, Verity, no se te ocurra decir eso delante de nadie que no sea yo. De lo contrario, tu cuñado podría acusarte de asesinato.

Verity palideció.

—¿Cómo podría hacer algo así? William murió cuando se le paró el corazón en brazos de su amante.

—Cierto, pero los hombres son capaces de cualquier cosa para conseguir lo que quieren, en especial Vernham. Las autoridades podrían creer fácilmente que tú te valiste de un veneno demasiado sutil como para ser detectado.

—No todos los hombres son crueles —dijo Verity reposadamente—. Nathaniel es un buen hombre.

—Supongo que sí, pero si el mundo fuera un lugar justo, tendrían que haberte permitido que te casaras con él.

—Oh, Chastity…

—Nuestro padre sabía que tú amabas a Nathaniel y, a pesar de ello, te obligó a casarte con sir William, un viejo y gordo hacendado con más dinero que clase. —Irguió al bebé apoyándolo sobre su hombro y le dio unas palmaditas en la espalda.

Verity se mordió el labio.

—El deber de una hija es casarse con quien su padre decida.

—Eso dicen, pero si una pudiera ver el sentido del sacrificio, al menos podría sentir cierta satisfacción. Padre no sólo te casó a ti con sir William sino que también quiso hacer que yo me casara con su hermano. ¿Qué podía sacar él de semejante alianza?

Verity puso la ropa sucia en un cubo.

—No lo sé —admitió.

—Una cosa está clara —dijo Chastity—. Tu ya has cumplido con tu deber. Ni se te pase por la cabeza el hecho de volver a complacer a padre de nuevo. Tú vas a casarte con Nathaniel.

Verity asintió.

—Estoy resuelta a ello, aunque mi conciencia me atormenta. Me gustaría ser tan decidida como tú.

—A decir verdad —dijo Chastity con un escalofrío—, lo que me dio fuerzas para resistirme al matrimonio que me organizó padre fue ver cómo era el tuyo. Sir William era un hombre vil, y su hermano, aunque es de apariencia más amable, está cortado por el mismo patrón. Lo creo capaz de tramar el asesinato de un pequeño.

—Pues yo no sé de dónde sacaste el coraje para hacer frente a padre. Mírame a mí ahora. La única manera que tengo de oponerme a él es huyendo.

Chastity se levantó, colocó al adormilado bebé en su cuna y lo cubrió después con una manta. Luego caminó hacia la diminuta ventana con gablete y se quedó absorta mirando el jardín, iluminado únicamente por el recuadro de luz procedente de la ventana de la cocina.

—Sinceramente, Verity, de haber sabido todo lo que podía ocurrir, no sé si hubiera tenido el valor suficiente. Nunca imaginé que padre llegaría tan lejos. Pero, una vez que empecé a resistirme, había algo que me impulsaba a no detenerme…

Verity rodeó a su hermana con los brazos y las dos mujeres se estrecharon mutuamente.

—Hace tan sólo dos años —dijo Verity—, éramos felices y estábamos llenas de esperanza. ¿Qué es lo que ha ocurrido? —Pero enseguida recobró la compostura—. Hemos de bajar a cenar. — Cogió el barreño y echó una mirada a su hermana—. ¿No crees querida que, habiendo un hombre aquí, deberías ponerte un vestido?

Chastity se secó las lágrimas y enderezó la espalda.

—Desde luego que no. No sería sensato dejarle saber que se las está viendo con tres mujeres.

—Oh, Chastity —protestó Verity—. Es un caballero.

—¿Cómo es posible que eso te parezca algo recomendable? Sir William era un caballero. Se supone que Henry

Vernham y padre también son caballeros. Además de ser un caballero, nuestro prisionero es también un Malloren. Son hombres atractivos y de aire fascinante, pero capaces de cortarte el cuello antes de apartarse si te cruzas con ellos en la carretera. No te dejes engañar por las encantadoras pestañas de Cyn Malloren.

Verity se rió entre dientes:

—¿A que son asombrosas? La verdad es que no puedo sentir miedo de un hombre que tiene ese aspecto.

El tono de Chastity era ahora brusco:

—Estoy segura de que mucha gente ha cometido ese mismo error. Un error fatal.

—En serio, Chastity. A mí me parece inofensivo. Seguramente lo más dañino que ha hecho en su vida es disparar contra los faisanes.

Chastity sacudió la cabeza.

—Es peligroso, Verity. Lo noto. Por favor, intenta llamarme siempre Charles, o por lo menos Chas. Y no reveles nuestro nombre completo. Rothgar y padre llevan años enemistados. Si Cyn Malloren se entera de que somos Wares, se habrá desatado la caja de los truenos.

Al oír este comentario, Verity sacudió la cabeza pero no puso ninguna objeción. Comprobó que William dormía y, tras soplar la vela, encabezó la marcha hacia las escaleras. En lo alto del empinado tramo, se detuvo unos instantes, presa de la duda.

—Chas, ¿qué pasaría si tratara de casarte otra vez?

—¿Padre? —rió Chastity con aspereza—. Eso es lo único bueno de todo esto. Mi desafío le empujó a hundirme en la más absoluta ignominia. Ningún hombre va a querer casarse jamás con la infame Chastity Ware.

Cyn la vio cruzar la habitación a grandes zancadas y subir al piso de arriba. Había encontrado la pistola, por lo que supuso que se habría convencido de que no tenía malas intenciones. Aunque no parecía haberse ablandado mucho.

Quería verla sonreír. Quería que hablara con él, que le contara sus problemas para poder aligerar su carga. Él mismo se sorprendía de haber llegado a sentir, en tan breve espacio de tiempo, una cálida estima por el espíritu de su captora y por su aspecto tan poco convencional.

Aquel peinado bruñido, similar a la piel de una nutria, era extremadamente insólito, pero dejaba al descubierto un cráneo bellamente modelado. ¿Por qué nunca antes se había dado cuenta de la belleza que podía haber en un cráneo? Acariciaba la idea de pasar la mano por aquella lisa cabeza, del mismo modo que anhelaría hacerlo a través de una mata de sedosos rizos.

Aquel cabello ponía así mismo de relieve los diáfanos y fuertes rasgos de su rostro: la alta y lisa frente, la nariz recta, como trazada con cincel, y la rotunda barbilla. Incluso aquellos ojos color azul grisáceo tan normales, cuando adquirían la expresión adecuada, resultaban inolvidables. Desde luego, no se trataba de una mujer corriente, pero a él nunca le habían ido las cosas corrientes.

Ella se conducía con el desenvuelto orgullo de un varón —los hombros rectos, el paso firme y resuelto—. A él le resultaba sorprendentemente erótico y lamentaba el hecho de que aquel atuendo masculino tal vez sólo apareciera en escena con motivo del robo. Se preguntaba qué aspecto tendría ella con un vestido.

Pero no iba a obtener respuesta. Ella seguía llevando pantalones cuando bajó por las escaleras.

Mientras las dos hermanas cruzaban la estancia para ir a la cocina, Cyn dijo:

—¿Te has convencido de que no voy a hacerte daño, Charles?

Ella se volvió y le miró:

—Mientras sigas atado a mi cama, señor mío, desde luego que sí.

—Tienes miedo de vértelas conmigo si estoy libre, ¿no?

Ella puso las manos en jarras.

—En absoluto. Pero ¿por qué habría de tomarme esa molestia?

Estaba gloriosa.

—Juego limpio —dijo él en tono amistoso—. No he hecho nada deshonesto.

Ella sonrió:

—Ayudar a unos salteadores de caminos no es algo precisamente honesto, señor.

Él sonrió con el mismo fingimiento.

—Pido disculpas. No me he dado cuenta de que querías que te estiraran el cuello. Me ocuparé de ello en cuanto pueda.

—Lo sé. Por eso estás atado de pies y manos en esa posición.

Cyn tuvo que reprimir la carcajada. Aquel duelo de evasivas ero lo más divertido que le había ocurrido en muchos meses. Menuda mujer. Aquello le había sugerido una nueva forma de ataque.

—Extraña manera de atar a un hombre —dijo—. Charles, ¿no serás de esos a los que les gusta comerse con la mirada los cuerpos de otros hombres?

Aguijoneada por estas palabras, Chastity le echó un vistazo y se ruborizó: el color le subía a la cara a pesar del disfraz.

En ese momento su aspecto era totalmente femenino: el de una hembra inocente y turbada. La situación le estaba provocando a Cyn una erección.

—Vosotros dos, dejadlo ya —dijo Verity, caminando hacia él con un cuchillo de trinchar. Al percatarse del abultamiento bajo sus pantalones, se limitó a arquear las cejas—. Creo que el hombre tiene mucha razón —le dijo a su hermana—. No ha hecho nada para merecer semejante trato. Puede venir a comer con nosotros.

—¡Verity, estate quieta! —le espetó Charles. Pero Verity ya había cortado las tiras de tela que ataban a Cyn a la cama, y él se había colocado de golpe en posición vertical y trataba de desentumecer las muñecas.

—Querido señor —dijo Cyn, encantado de poder presentar batalla desde una posición de igualdad—. Agradezco la amabilidad de su hermana, pero siendo usted quien está al mando de esta casa, ¿no debería ser capaz de controlar un poco mejor a las mujeres que tiene a su cargo?

Un destello cruzó por los ojos de Chastity.

—¿Con un látigo, acaso?

Cyn guiñó el ojo en dirección a Verity.

—¿Tan díscola es su hermana?

—Oh, basta ya, señor —dijo Verity, aunque haciendo esfuerzos por contener la risa—. Sólo tratáis de provocar su enfado. Si seguís comportándoos así, tendré que ataros de nuevo.

Él levantó las manos dando a entender que se rendía y siguió a las hermanas hasta la aromática cocina. Se preguntaba cuánto tardaría alguien en cometer un inevitable error, revelando que Charles se llamaba en realidad… ¿cómo? ¿Charlotte? Miró a la chica de gélido rostro. «Charles» le pegaba mucho más que «Charlotte».

Nana sonrió al verlo libre e intentó sentarlo en la cabecera de la mesa.

—No, no —dijo Cyn, haciendo gestos en dirección a Charles—. Éste debe ser seguramente su sitio, señor, como el cabeza de familia que es. —Y les dedicó una sonrisa, utilizando con descaro su considerable encanto—. ¿Voy a tener el gusto de conocer el nombre de la familia?

—No —dijo Charles bruscamente, tomando posesión del sitio—. Date por satisfecho con la comida.

Nana colocó sobre la mesa una gran cacerola con estofado de conejo.

—Estupenda comida, además —dijo Cyn con una embelesada sonrisa.

Nana se iluminó.

—Es una gran satisfacción poder alimentar a un hombre.

Cyn lanzó una mirada burlona a Charles.

—Pero si vosotros, los mozalbetes que estáis acabando de crecer soléis ser unos comedores voraces.

Charles se puso rojo.

—Yo no soy ningún mozalbete.

—Mi querido señor, le pido disculpas. Ya sé que a algunos hombres tarda en salirles la barba...

—Permítame que le sirva, milord —dijo Verity apresuradamente y puso una gran ración de estofado en su plato—. ¿Patatas?

Cyn tuvo la delicadeza de abstenerse de tomarles el pelo durante el resto de la comida.

—Y ahora —dijo cuando se hallaban sentados delante de las tazas con el té—, ¿por qué no me contáis qué es lo que os traéis entre manos para que pueda ayudaros?

— Y ¿por qué iba a hacer usted tal cosa? —preguntó Charles inflexible.

—Ya te lo he dicho, tengo afán de aventuras. No puedo existir sin ellas. Siempre he querido ser un caballero andante.

Esta vez fue Verity quien respondió.

—Pero ¿por qué piensa usted que yo soy una damisela en apuros, milord?

Él la miró:

—¿No lo es?

Ella sonrió con tristeza.

—Las damiselas son por lo general doncellas, y yo desde luego ya no lo soy, aunque estoy en un apuro considerable…

—¡No sigas, Verity! —dijo Charles abruptamente—. No te fíes de él. ¿Por qué tienes que ser siempre tan confiada? Si se lo cuentas, él se pondrá de parte de todos los demás.

—¿Qué otra cosa podemos hacer? —preguntó Verity—. Necesitamos a alguien que nos ayude con el coche, y yo me sentiría mejor con…

Cyn sintió que las palabras «con un hombre ayudándonos» flotaban en la estancia y vio cómo la furia acudía a los ojos de Charles. ¿Se trataría sencillamente de una de aquellas rudas y latosas muchachas que querían ser hombres? Esperaba que no.

—Te sentirías mejor con alguien más mayor —dijo él con delicadeza, suministrándole las palabras que faltaban—. Querido Charles, deja ya de fastidiar. Está claro que estás haciendo todo lo que puedes para apoyar a tu hermana a salir del lío en el que debe encontrarse, pero no es nunca sensato rechazar un sincero ofrecimiento de ayuda. Debo tener casi diez años más que tú, y tengo mucha más experiencia. Si me decís dcnde queréis ir, haré lo que pueda por llevaros allí sanos y salvos.

—A Maidenhead —dijo Verity con firmeza—. Mi prometido, el mayor Nathaniel Frazer, está destinado allí.

¿Se trataba del padre del niño? Cyn lo dudaba. Ella llevaba una alianza matrimonial, pero podía ser falsa. .

—Eso no parece muy complicado —se aventuró a decir—. No creo que haya ningún problema.

—Excepto el del dinero —dijo Charles, articulando con lentituc.

—Ah. Eso explica lo del asalto en la carretera.

—Ciertamente.

Nadie parecía dispuesto a ofrecerle más información, así que Cyn siguió tanteando.

—Comprendo que el hecho de viajar en mi comodísimo carruaje resulte atrayente, pero hacerse con él presentaba ciertos riesgos. ¿No habría sido más sensato conformarse con la diligencia, o incluso con esos pura sangre que montabais?

—Los caballos no eran nuestros —explicó Verity—, y si nos los hubiéramos quedado la habríamos liado. Tengo que admitir, sin embargo, que lo de la diligencia hubiera sido una idea más prudente.

—Sí —dijo Charles abruptamente— Tienes razón. Mañana usaremos el coche de su señoría para ir hasta Shaftesbury y compraremos asientos en la diligencia. —Volvió la fría mirada hacia Cyn—. Es decir, si podemos contar con usted hasta ese punto.

—Podéis contar conmigo para ir hasta el fin del mundo —contestó él simplemente—, pero sólo si me dejáis un papel en vuestra aventura. No quiero quedarme fuera.

—¡Esto no es un maldito juego!

—¿Hay peligro de verdad?

—Sí.

—¿Procedente de dónde?

Pero, llegados a este punto, ella cerró con firmeza los labios.

—Creo que deberíamos decírselo, querido —dijo Verity.

—Hablaremos de eso después. —Charles dio por finalizada la discusión poniéndose de pie—. De momento la cuestión es ¿dónde va a dormir?

Cyn no pudo resistirse.

—¿Por qué no duermo con vos, señor?

Charles se quedó helado y a Verity se le atragantó el té.

—¿Hay algún problema? —le preguntó Cyn a Charles—. Le aseguro que no ronco.

—Pero yo sí —se apresuró a decir ella.

—Ah. Dígame señor, ¿dónde duerme?

—En el piso de arriba —dijo ella incautamente. El rubor delataba su agitación, así que añadió—: Hemos dividido el espacio con una cortina.

—Tu hermana y el bebé deben tener un sueño muy profundo, por suerte para ellos. —Como ella parecía no comprender añadió—: Por lo del roncar.

A Cyn le costó mucho esfuerzo reprimir una sonrisa. Santo cielo, si los ojos pudieran escupir fuego, él se vería ahora reducido a cenizas. Aquellos ojos ardientes, aquellos labios puros y firmes y el rubor de la furia en sus mejillas: todo ello contribuía a crear una insólita belleza.

Una oleada de lujuria se apoderó de él por sorpresa. Sintió deseos de desnudarla en aquel mismo instante y de encontrar sus secretos femeninos bajo aquel aspecto varonil. Quería ver aquellos ojos encendidos por la pasión en lugar de por la rabia, que sus mejillas se encendieran por obra del deseo. Menos mal que ya no estaba tumbado con las piernas y los brazos extendidos, porque si no, ella se pondría cardiaca al contemplar su cuerpo. Se apresuró a velar la mirada pestañeando, pero con la firme determinación de llegar hasta el final de aquella aventura.

Se decidió rápidamente que él dormiría en la cocina, aunque sólo había una manta disponible para amortiguar la dureza del suelo de piedra. Puesto que estaba claro que no les quedaba más remedio que confiar en él, le permitieron ir hasta el carruaje a coger su baúl. Con algunas de sus ropas y su enorme gabán, se hizo una cama aceptable, mucho mejor de las que a veces había tenido con su regimiento. La cocina, después de todo, era un lugar caliente y seco.

Nana y Verity estaban retirando los platos de la cena. Charles salió al exterior y trajo agua del pozo. Después se sentó a leer un libro. Cyn trató también de ponerse cómodo.

Se quitó las botas y las limpió con un trapo. ¿Quién sabía cuánto tiempo tendrían que pasarse sin los amorosos cuidados de Jerome? Colgó su chaleco y su chaqueta en el respaldo de una silla. Se desató los lazos del pelo y se lo cepilló. Tras vacilar unos instantes —al reparar en la presencia de las damas— se quitó el corbatín y se soltó los botones de la camisa.

Nana y Verity no le prestaban ninguna atención, pero a quien él observaba era a Charles. Vio cómo, en una ocasión, levantaba fugazmente la vista del libro pero sin mostrar ninguna reacción en particular. Tendría que emplearse más a fondo.

Nana se retiró a su dormitorio. Verity estuvo ofreciendo sus atenciones a Cyn durante un par de minutos y después se fue al piso de arriba. Cyn bostezó y se deslizó dentro de su provisional cama. Esperó a ver qué hacía la muchacha.

Ella cerró el libro y se acercó hasta donde estaba él, quedándose allí de pie. Estando sin atar, a Cyn no le importaba que ella se irguiera por encima de él, si eso le hacía sentirse cómoda. Colocó las manos detrás de la cabeza y le envió una sonrisa a las alturas con toda la capacidad de seducción que poseía.

—¿Quieres compartir el lecho conmigo después de todo?

Ella contuvo el aliento y retrocedió, pero recobró la compostura de inmediato.

—Sólo quiero dejarle claro, milord, que le mataré si intenta engañarnos. Las otras dos son unas blandas, pero yo no.

No era un pendón entonces, ¡qué pena!

—¿Has matado alguna vez a alguien, Charles?

Al responder, sus temblorosos labios delataron su debilidad:

—No.

—Yo sí.

—Me cuesta creerlo.

—¿Sí? Soy capitán del regimiento 48.

Ella se quedó ligeramente boquiabierta.

—Ahora estoy de baja por enfermedad, pero he tenido ocasión de ver lo que es la muerte. Matar no es tan fácil como piensas, a no ser que uno tenga un motivo muy poderoso.

Cualquier rastro de debilidad se esfumó.

—Entonces, yo no debería tener ningún problema —fue la respuesta de Chastity, quien, tras soplar las velas, le dejó solo en la estancia, con el resplandor lateral del fuego por única luz.

Cyr se sosegó. Se quedó mirando las oscuras vigas del techo en penumbra. Se preguntaba quién habría herido tan profundamente a aquella chica para que sintiera ganas de matar. ¿Quién era el responsable de que estuviera allí sin dinero, vestida de hombre y asustada? Sin saber las respuestas, decidió abrazar su causa.

Había encontrado a su damisela en apuros, pero no era la dulce Verity. Era la complicada, airada y bella Charles.

3

Nana le despertó a la mañana siguiente al entrar de puntillas en la cocina para poner el agua a hervir y dejar los huevos que había cogido del gallinero.

—No hace falta que se levante todavía, milord —dijo ella rápidamente, pero él ya había saltado de su cama provisional y la estaba quitando de en medio.

Descubrió que, desde que no estaba en el ejército, se había vuelto un blando. En otros tiempos, no le importaba dormir en el suelo envuelto en su capa, para después levantarse y dirigirse a la batalla. Ahora se encontraba entumecido y con la sensación de no haber descansado lo suficiente. Anhelaba un baño caliente y ropa que no fuera con la que había dormido. Cuanto antes regresara a su oficio, mejor.

—¿Podría darme un poco de agua caliente para afeitarme? —preguntó.

La anciana se la proporcionó encantada.

Cyn se puso manos a la obra delante de un pequeño espejo rajado que había en la pared de la cocina, agradeciendo el hecho de que su barba no fuera particularmente espesa o recia, porque no estaba acostumbrado a realizar esa tarea. Jerome siempre se encargaba de ello, incluso cuando Cyn estaba en el ejército.

Jerome era el único capricho que Cyn había dejado que Rothgar le proporcionase cuando se alistó en su regimiento. En los seis años que llevaba como soldado, Cyn había hecho las cosas a su manera. Había ganado sus promociones, en lugar de comprarlas. Rothgar le había propuesto muy en serio comprarle un regimiento, pero Cyn había rechazado la oferta, demostrándose a sí mismo y a su hermano que podía apañárselas solo.

Hasta ahora.

Hizo una mueca frente al espejo, todavía asqueado de que la fiebre pulmonar hubiera podido con él.

Recordó su lucha por seguir en la brecha, sintiéndose más enfermo cada día que pasaba, pero negándose a admitirlo. Después de aquello, todos los recuerdos se le volvían borrosos: las rudas atenciones de sus hombres; el hospital militar de campaña de Halifax; aquel agujero infernal en el barco, donde deseara estar muerto...

Y, después, de pronto, como si fuera un sueño, se halló en la Abadía de Rothgar, al cuidado de su familia —Rothgar, Brand, Bryght y la mas consternada de todos, su hermana gemela, Elfled. Al sentirse débil y pensar que tal vez fuera a morir, había encontrado solaz en su hogar y sus seres queridos, en los sonidos, los sabores y los rostros de su infancia.

Sin embargo, una vez recuperado, los mimos de sus hermanos le resultaron irritantes. Dios santo, no sabía qué era lo que ellos consideraban buena salud, pero al parecer era un estado demasiado perfecto para que lo alcanzara un simple mortal. Habían llegado incluso a hablar de que dejara el ejército y se dedicara a otra profesión.

Ni soñarlo.

Su mano se tensó y se hizo un corte en la barbilla. Reprimió un juramento y cogió un pañuelo para restañarse la sangre. Terminó la faena sin ningún otro percance y deseó que aquello fuera un buen augurio para la aventura que le aguardaba. Al darse la vuelta, apretando la tela contra la herida, descubrió que Charles había entrado en la cocina. La pilló observándole. Ella se ruborizó, bajó la vista y después volvió a levantarla con descaro.

—¿Te tiembla el pulso esta mañana? —se burló.

—Siempre me afeita mi *valet*. Supongo que todavía no tienes este problema. Dichoso tú. Resulta tremendamente aburrido. A veces añoro los tiempos en los que se llevaban las barbas.

Y, tras arrojar a un lado con saña el paño ensangrentado, se dirigió hacia su baúl para sacar una camisa limpia. De espaldas a la chica, se quitó al desgaire la que llevaba puesta.

Se estiró, volviéndose ligeramente para verla por el rabillo del ojo. El rubor la estaba delatando de nuevo y ella lo sabía. Trataba de concentrarse en cortar rebanadas de una barra de pan casero. Una de dos, o aquella tarea no se le daba muy bien o su mente se hallaba en alguna otra parte, porque las rebanadas le salían en forma de fragmentos y cuñas.

Él descubrió que podía observarla en el espejo mientras simulaba —todavía desnudo de la cintura para arriba— estudiar el pequeño corte de su barbilla. La vio levantar la vista con cautela y después mirarle a través de las pestañas. Él se estiró de nuevo, sabiendo que esto era algo más que una simple broma: se estaba luciendo como un pavo real que despliega su cola.

Ahora ella le miraba abiertamente. Podía sacar sus armas más eficaces. Tenía una cicatriz que le cruzaba el pecho y que, al parecer, ninguna mujer podía ignorar. Procedía de una herida poco importante, un corte superficial producido por un sable, pero tenía un aspecto dramático. Pero, hallándose Nana también en la estancia, no le pareció el momento oportuno para comprobar el efecto que producía sobre su damisela.

Se puso la camisa limpia y se dio la vuelta. Charles se dedicaba a untar de mantequilla las rebanadas que había cortado.

—Haces bien ayudando a las mujeres —dijo Cyn con tono aprobador mientras se ajustaba unos volantes limpios en los puños—. Muchos jóvenes lo encontrarían muy humillante.

Las atareadas manos vacilaron un instante, pero después reanudaron su tarea.

—Muchos jóvenes son unos burros.

Sus manos, observó él, eran lo suficientemente angulosas como para pasar por las de un joven, pero por muy poco. Hacía bien en llevar guantes durante sus correrías.

—Eso es bien cierto. —Esperó que se produjera alguna reacción pero no la hubo. Sacudió la cabeza. Era la muchacha más reservada que jamás había conocido—. Voy a usar el retrete.

Cuando regresó, Verity estaba también en la cocina, con el bebé en brazos. Nana estaba friendo huevos y beicon en el fogón. Se imaginó que Charles, en circunstancias normales, estaría ayudando a la anciana. No se la veía muy feliz en aquel papel pasivo. Ser un macho perezoso requería cierta práctica.

Cyn se acercó a contemplar al bebé. Tras visitar a su hermana mayor, Hilda, y a su nuevo retoño ya tenía alguna experiencia. Se sorprendió al comprobar que este bebé era casi del mismo tiempo.

—Debe de tener tan sólo un par de meses.

—Nueve semanas —dijo Verity, pasando una mano protectora sobre la blanda y rubia pelusa de la criatura.

—Un poco joven para viajar.

La mano titubeó.

—Era necesario.

Cyr descubrió que no era capaz de importunar a la dulce Verity. En lugar de ello, se dedicó a provocar a Charles acudiendo en ayuda de Nana: primero le alcanzaba los platos calientes y después, una vez llenos, los llevaba a la mesa. Tras unos instantes, Charles se dispuso a colaborar. Llenó la tetera con el agua hirviendo y localizó tarros de confitura y mermelada, así como una jarra de leche colocada al fresco, en el alféizar de la ventana. Sus movimientos tenían la desenvoltura que da la familiaridad, pero él no dijo nada.

Nada más hubieron empezado a comer, Cyn habló:

—Bien. ¿Estáis preparados para contarme vuestra historia?

Durante unos segundos, Charles se comunicó en silencio con su hermana. Después dijo:

—Te diremos lo que necesitas saber. —Le clavó una mirada inflexible—. Supongo que piensas que el niño de Verity fue concebido en circunstancias impropias.

Era la explicación obvia.

—¿Y no es así?

—No. Es completamente legítimo, nacido dos años después de la boda en Hannover Square, auténtico hijo de su padre.

—Eso debe ser muy tranquilizador para todo el mundo —dijo Cyn en tono conciliador.

—Su padre ha muerto.

Cyn escrutó a Verity, quién, además de no llevar luto, estaba ansiosa por reunirse con su prometido. Levantó las cejas.

—Diantre —dijo Verity—. No sé cómo a vosotros dos os resulta tan difícil contar una historia en su justo orden. —Encaró a Cyn—. Mi marido murió hace casi dos meses. Mi cuñado tiene la custodia de mi hijo. Cuando llegó a hacerse cargo de nosotros, me di cuenta de que no confiaba en él y, por tanto, ahora estoy buscando al hombre que nos va a proteger a ambos.

Las preguntas se le agolpaban en la cabeza. Cyn planteó la que le resultaba más desconcertante:

—Has dicho que ese protector es tu prometido. ¿Cómo puedes estar prometida en matrimonio si acabas de enviudar?

Verity se puso colorada.

—Nathaniel y yo estábamos comprometidos, aunque mi padre no aprobó nuestra unión. No ha habido ningún hecho indecoroso, pero nuestro compromiso sigue teniendo validez.

Charles irrumpió en la conversación:

—Así que ya ves, se trata simplemente de llevar a Verity y a William sanos y salvos hasta Maidenhead.

Pero Cyn tenía sus dudas.

—¿Y qué pasa con el asunto de la custodia?

—Una vez que Verity y Nathaniel se hayan casado, solicitarán que sea este último quien ejerza de tutor del niño.

Cyn intuía que había mucho más detrás de todo este asunto.

—Y ¿qué pasaría si la justicia decide que esta huida y este matrimonio tan precipitados muestran que tanto Verity como Nathaniel no son dignos de tener un niño a su cargo?

Verity palideció y estrechó contra sí al bebé.

—¡Eso no ocurrirá!

—Entra dentro de lo posible. Lo que quiero decir es que tal vez fuera más sensato regresar a casa y mandar un mensaje a tu Nathaniel para que fuera a ayudarte de un modo más convencional.

Las hermanas se miraron. Cyn percibió la ansiedad que flotaba en la estancia. Fue Charles quien habló:

—A Verity no le permitirían casarse con Nathaniel, y ella cree que Henry V... —se interrumpió; después continuó—: Ella cree que el marido de su hermano quiere matar al niño.

Cyn vio en los ojos de Verity que Charles decía la verdad.

—¿Por qué?

—Porque entonces él lo heredaría todo.

Cyn permaneció en silencio mientras consideraba el asunto. La codicia podía ser una fuerza muy poderosa y, seguramente, a un hombre ambicioso le resultaría exasperante que un recién nacido se interpusiera entre él y todo lo que anhelaba.

Por otra parte, tenía entendido que algunas mujeres se volvían un poco raras después de haber dado a luz.

Se dirigió a Verity.

—¿Cómo murió tu marido?

Ella bajó la vista.

—Su corazón se paró.

—¿Cuál era su nombre?

—¡No respondas a eso! —interrumpió Charles. Después se volvió hacia Cyn—. ¿Qué derecho tienes a interrogarla así? Ya te hemos contado lo principal. Ahora decide si vas a ayudarnos o no.

Cyn tomó su decisión sin ninguna dificultad.

—Por supuesto que os ayudaré. —No pensaba que fuera una empresa muy difícil. Debían ser poco más de cien millas. Un sencillo trayecto de tres días de duración—. Os garantizo que os llevaré sanos y salvos hasta Maidenhead. No obstante, me gustaría saber qué tipo de persecución cabe esperar. ¿Está ya Henry, el tutor legal, efectuando batidas en las carreteras?

—Sí.

—Pero ¿no se le ha ocurrido mirar aquí?

Charles le dirigió una mirada furiosa ante aquella manifestación de su incredulidad.

—Vino hace tres días. Le convencimos de que no sabíamos nada porque era cierto. Verity tuvo que venir andando hasta aquí. Llegó cuando él ya se había ido.

Cyn miró a la joven madre con renovado respeto. Viendo su delicada naturaleza nunca hubiera imaginado que fuera capaz de realizar un viaje tan agotador, con el bebé en brazos y en noviembre. Empezó a pensar que tal vez tuviera un exceso de confianza en la facilidad de aquella empresa. Desde luego, era evidente que Verity creía que el peligro era real. Ahora podía captar el aire de desesperación con el que sostenía al niño junto a ella.

—¿Sabe lo de Maidenhead? —preguntó Cyn.

—Creemos que no —contestó Charles.

Cyn se volvió hacia Verity.

—Entonces, ¿dónde creerá que has ido?

Ella se encogió de hombros.

—Supongo que andará muy despistado. Primero pensó que vendría aquí y, ahora, tal vez que me dirijo a Londres. No creo que sepa nada de mi vida antes de que me casara con su hermano.

—Y, ¿qué pasa con tu familia? —preguntó Cyn—. ¿No pueden ayudarte?

Las hermanas cruzaron una nueva y reveladora mirada. Fue Charles quien contestó:

—¿Qué crees que iba a estar haciendo yo en esta cabaña si tuviera una familia que sirviera para algo?

—¿Has caído en desgracia? ¿Acaso te han echado del colegio?

Había dado en el clavo, aunque ella lo disimuló bien.

—Ya se lo hemos dicho, milord. No queremos pedir ayuda a nuestra familia porque no permitirían que Verity se casara con Nathaniel.

Cyn tenía una norma para la supervivencia que hasta ahora le había sido muy útil: actuar como si fuera a ocurrir lo peor. Se levantó y caminó por la reducida estancia.

—El tutor legal del niño tiene la ley de su lado. Sin duda habrá dado parte, incluso puede que haya colocado carteles en las garitas de peaje y en las principales posadas. Aunque no sepa nada de Maidenhead, las carreteras de pago estarán estrechamente vigiladas. No llegaríais muy lejos en esa diligencia.

—Habíamos planeado usar un disfraz —dijo Charles.

—¿De qué clase?

Nuevamente, las hermanas se miraron con inquietud.

—Verity va a ir vestida de niñera —dijo Charles—. También vamos a oscurecerle el cabello.

—¿Y tú?

—Yo no necesito disfraz.

Cyn se inclinó hacia delante sobre la mesa.

—Henry *el Terrible* registrará de nuevo esta cabaña Cuando averigüe que te has ido, sabrá que tiene que buscarte a ti también.

Ella le miró de frente.

—Para entonces, ya estaremos en Maidenhead.

Ahora que Cyn podía servir de escolta a Verity, la solución obvia era que Charles se quedara al margen, pero, dejando aparte el hecho de que la muchacha no iba a estar de acuerdo, a Cyn no le parecía bien aquella opción. Pretendía seguir explorando a su damisela.

Volvió a pasearse por la habitación mientras sopesaba las alternativas.

—Así que Henry *el Terrible* está buscando a una mujer rubia con un niño. Tan pronto como inspeccione este lugar, sabrá que está buscando a la citada mujer y a su joven escolta. —Hizo una pausa, esperando una corrección que no se produjo.

Contempló a Charles.

—Qué pena que no puedas hacerte pasar por una dama… —E, ignorando la crispación de los labios de Verity y el sonido ahogado que emitió Nana, simuló estudiar a la muchacha—. No, creo que no lo lograrías. No te imagino sonriendo sin ton ni son.

Ella se puso colorada.

—¡Menos mal!

—A ver, entonces, ¿podrías hacer de mozo de establo?

Con un destello de interés, Charles asintió.

—¿Estás seguro?

—Sí. Sé cuidar de los caballos. ¿Harás tú de cochero, en ese caso?

—No. Cabalgaré hasta Shaftesbury y, como supongo que Hoskins estará todavía en el Crown, le pediré que nos lleve.

—Hará un montón de preguntas.

—Por supuesto —dijo Cyn—. Sobre todo cuando le diga que llevaré enaguas. —Lanzó una mirada benevolente a los tres estupefactos rostros—. Burlaremos, sin duda, a cualquier perseguidor, porque yo voy a ser la madre del bebé.

—¿Vas a hacer de mujer? —dijo Charles presa de la incredulidad.

—A menos que seas tú quien quiera tener ese honor. —Cyn hizo aletear sus exuberantes pestañas—. Pero creo que es más sensato así. Yo soy más guapo que tú y sé cómo sonreír sin motivo.

A él le encantó la batalla que se desencadenó en el rostro de Charles: el natural despecho por el menosprecio de su hermosura se veía desplazado por un resplandor de maliciosa diversión, causada sin duda por la perspectiva de verlo vestido con corsé y enaguas.

En eso, él tenía toda la razón. Chastity estaba perpleja y furiosa por la aparición de este maldito hombre que había invadido su vida y parecía que estaba a punto de hacerse con el mando. Deseó que los encajes le irritaran y que tuviera un aspecto ridículo dentro de un vestido.

En cuanto a lo de que no era bella ni capaz de desempeñar el papel de una mujer, no tenía ni idea de lo que hablaba. Las dos hijas del conde de Walgrave habían sido educadas y entrenadas para comportarse como unas auténticas damas, conocedoras de todas las artes femeninas. ¿Cómo, si no, iba a esperar su padre fortalecer su red de influencias políticas a través de sus matrimonios?

Lord Cyn, se dijo a sí misma malhumorada, no era más guapo. Chastity había estado considerada como una belleza durante el tiempo que estuvo en Londres. Había tenido media ciudad a sus pies, incluido —a su tibia manera— el hermano de Cyn, el marqués de Rothgar, el trofeo matrimonial de la década.

De repente, la comicidad de la situación la sobresaltó y tuvo que morderse el labio para reprimir una carcajada. Ella de apuesto galán. Él de hermosa dama. Hubiera querido estar a solas con Verity para poder reírse a gusto. Hacía mucho tiempo que no lo hacía.

Cyn observó el temblor de sus labios y el centelleo de sus ojos. Le hubiera gustado que expresara libremente su regocijo. Sospechaba que debía estar bella cuando reía.

Acto seguido, trató convencer a sus secuestradoras para que le dejaran cabalgar hasta Shaftesbury para tratar con sus criados y comprar ropa de señora. Charles fue a regañadientes a por un caballo —presumiblemente a la gran mansión que había en las inmediaciones, que era el legítimo hogar de aquellas damas.

Cuando regresó, traía dos monturas.

—¿Vas a acompañarme? —preguntó Cyn—. ¿Crees que es prudente?

—Creo que lo prudente es no perderte de vista, milord.

—Seguramente será fácil que alguien te reconozca estando tan cerca de tu casa.

A ella parecía divertirle aquello.

—¿Por qué crees que eso iba a suponer un problema? Verity es la fugitiva, no yo.

—Aún así —dijo Cyn—, puede que fuera mejor que nadie se percatara de que existe una relación entre tú y yo. Vamos a convertirte ya en mozo de establo. ¿Tienes ropa menos elegante?

—No —dijo ella con aire de desamparo.

—Entonces, vamos a ver qué es lo que hay en el carruaje. —Y partió hacia el huerto a paso apresurado. Al ver el espectáculo de las puertas mutiladas, se detuvo.

—¿Era esto realmente necesario?

—Pensé que lo buscarían por todas partes —Chastity se reprochó el estremecimiento nervioso de su voz.

Él la miró con frialdad.

—Eres un demonio, ¿no? ¿Has hecho esto para hacerme daño a mí? Este coche es de mi hermano y no mío. Si Rothgar lo descubre, no vas a poder sentarte en toda una semana. —Contempló el vehículo—. Compraremos pintura para que puedas cubrir la parte dañada. Un coche normal no suscitará comentarios. Uno con signos de ensañamiento, sí.

Sin esperar a que ella respondiera, subió y buscó en el arca que había debajo del asiento. Sacó un fardo de ropa y la dejó caer al suelo.

—Es de Harry —dijo mientras se apeaba—. El verdadero mozo de establo. Es una pizca más alto que tú, pero no mucho. —Deshizo el paquete y mostró una tosca camisa, un par de pantalones remendados y un pañuelo de cuello—. Y todo limpio —comentó mientras le arrojaba las prendas—. Qué suerte. Tendrás que llevar tu abrigo, tu sombrero y tus botas. Si quieres mi consejo, haz que parezcan más viejos.

—Con mucho gusto —Chastity se dio la vuelta—. Volveré donde Nana y me cambiaré.

Cyn se apoyó contra el carruaje con los brazos cruzados.

—¿Eres de naturaleza pudorosa —preguntó— o es que albergas sucias sospechas? Te aseguro, Charles, que mi gusto a la hora de elegir compañía en la cama es… convencional.

Chastity notó que se ruborizaba y sintió rabia por ello.

—Nunca he pensado otra cosa —dijo, batiéndose en retirada—. Como tú dices, sencillamente soy pudoroso.

La voz de Cyn flotó tras ella:

—¿Estás seguro de que has estado en el colegio?

• • •

Chastity caminó hasta la cabaña y cerró la puerta de golpe.

—¡Ojalá hubiera dejado a este hombre al borde de la carretera!

Verity levantó la vista del baúl que estaba empacando. Sus ojos tenían un brillo innegable.

—Creo que nos puede venir muy bien. Nadie va a estar buscando a una mujer más mayor, de pelo oscuro, con un bebé y su ama de cría.

—Yo podía haber hecho de madre.

—Tu no pareces tan mayor como para que no te confundan conmigo, y tu pelo es un problema. Las pelucas resultan arriesgadas. Muchos hombres se afeitan todavía la cabeza y llevan peluca, pero las damas no.

Chastity se paso la manó por la sedosa pelusa, donde hacía tan poco crecieran brillantes rizos.

—Oh, Chastity —dijo Verity, levantándose para ir a su encuentro—. Siento haberlo mencionado. ¡Ya verás cómo crece, querida!

—Ya está creciendo —dijo Chastity—, pero no puedo olvidar cómo me sentí cuando padre me lo afeitó. Y las cosas que decía… —Se estremeció, despés alejó de sí los recuerdos—. Pero, verás, padre me ha hecho un favor. Como mujer, mi aspecto es ridículo, pero como chico estoy impecable y nadie sospecha nada. ¿Quién va a pensar que una mujer se iba a cortar el pelo así?

—Padre entrará en razón…

—No —dijo Chastity con brusquedad—. No pronuncies su nombre. Ha sido capaz de repudiarme y yo he renegado de él.

Verity suspiró.

—Estoy segura de que lo hacía con buena intención.

—Pues yo no. De lo que estoy segura es de que quería salirse con la suya, como siempre.

—Pero es nuestro padre, querida...

—Entonces, ¿por qué no has ido corriendo a sus amantes brazos?

Verity cogió un par de medias y las enrolló.

—Te confieso que no puedo sentir el debido respeto hacia él después de ver cómo te ha tratado a ti.

Chastity la abrazó, comprendiendo lo duro que era para Verity comportarse de este modo tan poco filial. A ella misma le había costado mucho retirarle su confianza al poderoso conde de Walgrave.

—Estás haciendo lo correcto. Créeme, padre no es infalible, y tampoco incorruptible, aunque le den ese nombre.

Verity la sorprendió.

—Me temo que tienes razón. He estado pensando en lo que dijiste ayer. Mi matrimonio con sir William no tiene mucho sentido. Y, si a eso le unimos el intento de padre de casarte con Henry, obtenemos el colmo del absurdo. ¿Crees que, tal vez, las facultades mentales de padre estén menguando con la edad?

Chastity soltó una carcajada.

—¡Desde luego que no! Padre es tan astuto como siempre y, sin duda, tiene, como siempre, sus razones, relacionadas con su ansia de poder. Ya sabes lo obsesionado que ha estado desde que el príncipe Frederick muriera hace diez años.

Hizo una mueca sombría al recordarlo. El conde de Walgrave era de la misma quinta que Frederick, el príncipe de

Gales, y había sido muy amigo suyo. Tenía puestas todas sus ambiciones en él, de modo que sólo tenía que esperar a que el viejo rey muriera y que Frederick ascendiera al trono. Sin embargo, Frederick, con muy poco tacto, había muerto antes que su padre, dejando a su pequeño hijo como heredero. Este joven vástago, el actual rey George III, se hallaba bajo la firme influencia de su madre, la Princesa Augusta y ese apuesto escocés, lord Bute.

El conde de Walgrave quedaba excluido de los círculos del poder.

—Pobre padre —dijo Chastity con falsa compasión—. Tendría que haberle prestado más atención a Augusta, ¿no crees?

—En lugar de convertirla en su enemiga acaparando tanta porción del tiempo de su marido. Pero claro, padre siempre ha tendido a infravalorar a las mujeres.

Chastity frunció el ceño al repasar aquel asunto.

—Con todos sus planes por la borda, supongo que no es de extrañar que padre haya adoptado métodos… extremos. Pero eso no explica lo de la alianza con los Vernham. Supongo que sir William le ofreció a cambio su influencia.

Verity metió las medias en al baúl.

—¿Influencia sobre quién? Sobre Augusta no serviría de nada. Su enemistad con padre es demasiado profunda y, además, está sinceramente ligada a Bute.

Chastity levantó las cejas y sonrió con ironía.

—Algunos dirían inmoralmente ligada.

—¡Chastity!

—¿No lo crees así? Pues serás la única que no piensa eso dentro del mundo elegante. Y Bute es un hombre muy apuesto, aunque tenga el espíritu y el cerebro de un mismísimo conejo.

Verity trató de contener una delatora risita pero no lo consiguió.

—Vale, Chastity. Pero tengo que admitir que es comprensible que padre se escandalice de que un hombre así sea el consejero del rey. Bute podría ser desastroso para la nación y, sin embargo, parece tener bajo su control al joven rey y a su madre.

—Y padre haría cualquier cosa por quebrantar esta situación...

—Pero, Chastity, ¿cómo iban a ayudarle sir William o Henry en este empeño?

—No parece muy posible, ¿verdad? —dijo Chastity—. En una ocasión oí a padre decir que estaba buscando pruebas de que Bute simpatizaba con los jacobitas y que había apoyado al príncipe Charlie *el Bello* en 1745. Se dice que mucha gente coqueteó con los jacobitas cuando parecía que podían tener éxito en su intento de restaurar la monarquía de los Estuardo.

Verity torció el labio.

—Y después, cuando la revuelta fracasó, se convirtieron en leales partidarios de los Hanover. Detesto esa hipocresía interesada.

—¿No era sir William uno de los investigadores especiales que debían poner al descubierto a esos jacobitas ingleses clandestinos?

—Sí —dijo Verity con un escalofrío—. Solía contar historias que llegaban a hacerme tener lástima de esos canallas. Él disfrutaba de veras ejerciendo el poder y aterrorizando a la gente y sospecho que debió reunir bastante dinero haciendo la vista gorda de vez en cuando. Desde luego, en esa época, pasó de ser un modesto hidalgo a convertirse en uno de los leones locales.

—¡Qué hombre tan extremadamente odioso! —dijo Chastity, con la mente en otra parte—. ¡Tal vez sea eso! Tal vez él tuviera pruebas contra Bute, y padre nos utilizó a nosotras como soborno para obtenerlas. Después de todo, Bute es escocés.

Verity interrumpió su trabajo para considerar esta posibilidad, después sacudió la cabeza.

—De verdad, Chastity, lo dudo mucho. Bute es bastante estúpido, pero es leal. Es escocés, pero no todos los escoceses son jacobitas, diga lo que diga la gente.

Chastity suspiró.

—Me temo que tienes razón. —Le pasó a Verity una pila de pañales. Al sentir que algo duro crujía en su interior, metió la mano y sacó un documento lacrado con un pesado sello—. ¿Qué demonios es esto?

Verity parecía la viva imagen de la culpa.

—Oh, eso.

Chastity inspeccionó el documento. Al parecer, constaba tan sólo de un par de hojas de papel, dobladas y selladas por cuatros sitios. Miró a su hermana.

—Yo no sabía qué debía hacer —explicó Verity con evidente nerviosismo—. Hace algún tiempo, sir William me enseñó este escrito, así como el lugar donde lo guardaba, haciéndome jurar solemnemente que, cuando él muriera, yo se lo entregaría inmediatamente al juez Mansfield, el Justicia Mayor. William me hizo jurarlo sobre la Biblia…

—Verity —dijo Chastity con firmeza, sabiendo lo responsable que era su hermana—, tú no vas a ir a Londres hasta que no te hayas casado con Nathaniel y estés completamente a salvo.

—Por supuesto que no —dijo Verity, aunque con cierta inquietud—. Me digo a mí misma que, después de todo, me dirijo hacia a Londres.

—Exacto —Chastity dirigió una mirada al documento—. ¿Qué crees que es?

—No lo sé. Pero como sir William no quería que estuviera en poder de su hermano, me he preguntado si no podría ser una rectificación de su testamento…

—¿Privando a Henry de la custodia? —preguntó Chastity con viveza—. Veamos…

Verity se lo arrebató.

—¡No debemos abrirlo! Oh, Chastity. Estoy segura de que quedará invalidado si se rompen los sellos.

—Pero… —Chastity se interrumpió—. Bueno, supongo que da igual. Lo principal es llevarte hasta Nathaniel. Después ya decidiremos que hacemos con esto.

—Tal vez deberíamos preguntarle a lord Cyn.

—Santo cielo, no —dijo Chastity—. No sabemos de qué trata este documento. No vamos a entregarle munición a un Mallorer. Escóndelo bien. Voy a cambiarme al piso de arriba.

Cuando Chastity se hubo marchado, Verity puso el papel a buen recaudo y suspiró al considerar el apuro en el que se hallaba su hermana. Verity tenía la esperanza de que su propia situación se solucionara de buena manera, pero no había fuerza humana que pudiera arreglar la vida de Chastity.

Que el conde de Walgrave hubiera ordenado a Chastity que se casara con Henry Vernham le resultó chocante; que, para conseguirlo, se hubiera mostrado dispuesto a arruinar la vida de un peón tan valioso —la vida de su hija—, le parecía sencillamente increíble.

Cuando tuvo lugar el escándalo, Verity se hallaba en el campo, pasando allí las últimas semanas de su embarazo. La historia llegó hasta ella, no obstante, de labios de su esposo, salpicada de comentarios rabiosos y humor grosero. Sir William estaba lleno de resentimiento por el hecho de que Chastity hubiera despreciado a su hermano y le había pintado el peor de los cuadros. Ahora Verity había oído el relato en boca de la propia Chastity.

Henry Vernham era diez años más joven que su hermano. Todo lo que William tenía de codicioso y grosero, Henry lo tenía de lisonjero y calculador. No era mal parecido, pero tenía una renta exigua y un cargo insignificante en la corte. Era, de hecho, un don nadie que no se habría ni atrevido a soñar con encontrarse con lady Chastity, a no ser por su vínculo familiar.

Pero, no sólo la había conocido, sino que había tenido el valor de pedir su mano. Y el poderoso conde de Walgrave, en lugar de reírsele a la cara, había ordenado a Chastity que lo aceptara.

Ella se había negado, tomándose el asunto a la ligera en un principio. La rabia del conde había corregido aquella impresión, pero Chastity siguió rechazándolo. Aceptó estoicamente pequeñas restricciones y tuvo que soportar sermones sobre el cumplimiento del deber. No se doblegó siquiera cuando su padre le prohibió asistir a la gran fiesta anual de los Ware si no lo hacía como pareja de Vernham.

Chastity le había comentado que se sintió más aliviada que otra cosa cuando la encerraron en su habitación, puesto que la alternativa era tener a Henry Vernham manoseándola durante toda la velada.

Se había ido a dormir pacíficamente, pero se despertó cerca de la media noche, cuando su padre irrumpió en la alcoba, seguido de media docena de invitados. Ella se sentó en el lecho alarmada y, sólo entonces, se percató de que Henry Vernham yacía a su lado en la cama, completamente desnudo. Se había dado cuenta enseguida de que aquella trampa sólo podía haberse tendido con el pleno consentimiento de su padre. La puerta de su habitación había sido cerrada con llave desde el exterior.

Sin duda, él había esperado que aquello iba a hacer que dejara de resistirse al enlace. ¿Qué otra cosa podía hacer una señorita? Chastity, sin embargo, proclamó en voz alta su inocencia y siguió oponiéndose a la boda. El asunto se había vuelto entonces muy desagradable: todo el mundo creía lo peor, y el conde perdió por completo los nervios. Sin embargo, ni siquiera los azotes o el hambre habían conseguido que Chastity cambiara de opinión.

Al final, el conde se rindió. Se había lavado las manos en lo tocante a su hija y la había desterrado, haciéndola vivir en aquella cabaña. Se había asegurado de que permanecería en su exilio dejándola sin dinero —sólo le proporcionó toscas ropas— y rapando su bella cabellera.

Aquello no había sido necesario, porque, ¿a qué otro lugar podía ir la infame Chastity Ware? Las hijas del conde de Walgrave no habían sido educadas para trabajar por un salario y ningún hombre respetable le ofrecería su nombre. Y aquello era una vergüenza, pensó Verity, porque Chastity había sido siempre una chica muy alegre, hecha para ser esposa y madre.

Cuando Chastity volvió a aparecer en la estancia, había sufrido una transformación. Se había asegurado los flojos pantalones de paño con un cinto, consiguiendo así que sus piernas parecieran más voluminosas. La camisa de piel de topo también encubría su figura, mientras que el pañuelo moteado ocultaba su menudo cuello, su rasgo más delatador. Llevaba la peluca de color marrón oscuro, cubierta por un trasegado sombrero de ala ancha.

—¡Genial! —exclamó Verity—. Mucho mejor disfraz que si llevaras ropa más elegante. Lord Cyn tenía razón.

—Muy propio de ti pensar eso —rezongó Chastity, aunque con una sonrisa.

Un nuevo problema inquietaba a Verity.

—Chas, ¿crees que padre sabe que he desaparecido?

Chastity dirigió a su hermana una mirada penetrante.

—Tarde o temprano se enterará, a no ser que Henry Vernham lleve el asunto en secreto, a causa de sus abominables motivaciones.

—Oh, cielos. ¿Por qué iba a hacer Henry una cosa así? Todo lo que quiere es a William, para poder controlar los bienes. —Verity se estremeció—. ¡Henry *el Terrible*! Esa expresión lo retrata a las mil maravillas. Me gusta lord Cyn.

—A ti te gusta todo el mundo —dijo Chastity con severidad—. Oye, ¿queda sitio para mi traje en ese baúl?

Pero Verity no pasó por alto aquel comentario.

—No me gusta todo el mundo. Siento una profunda aversión por Henry. Pero me gusta lord Cyn, y me siento muy segura sabiendo que es oficial del ejército. Nuestro plan entraña muchos riesgos, querida, pero, estoy segura de que si alguien puede llevarlo a cabo, ése es él.

—¡Él está en esto para divertirse, Verity!

Verity sacudió la cabeza.

—Tienes que aprender a ver lo que hay por debajo de la superficie de las cosas. Recuerda que es un militar, igual que Nathaniel. —Interrumpió por unos instantes la labor de introducir el traje marrón en la bolsa ya casi llena—. El que me preocupa es padre, Chas. Él sabe lo de Nathaniel y no le será demasiado difícil descubrir donde está apostado...

—Y con sus contactos —dijo Chastity tranquilamente—, podría poner a casi toda la nación en pie.

—Chas, tenemos que decirle a lord Cyn quiénes somos y en el lío en el que se ha metido. Padre podría hundirlo con una sola palabra.

Los ojos de Chastity se abrieron alarmados.

—¡Pero eso significaría que se enteraría de quién soy yo! Oh, qué importancia tiene eso al lado de tu seguridad...

—No —dijo Verity rápidamente—. ¿Qué ganaríamos con ello? —Sabía el espanto que le producía a Chastity tener que encarar a alguien como la infame Chastity Ware.

Se miraron la una a la otra.

—No creo que sea para tanto —dijo Chastity—. Estoy segura de que podemos llegar a Maidenhead sin tener que vérnoslas con padre...

—Seguro que sí —dijo Verity con firmeza, después se mordió el labio—. Pero ¿qué pasará con Nathaniel? Si padre es un peligro para lord Cyn Malloren, todavía lo es más para Nathaniel. Podría arruinar su carrera. Han echado a muchos oficiales del ejército por el simple motivo de votar contra el gobierno en unas elecciones... —Las manos de Verity apretaron las de Chastity—. ¿Y qué me dices del bebé? ¿Crees que podrían llevarse a William? ¡Antes preferiría morirme!

—Estoy segura de que no pueden —le tranquilizó Chastity—. Nathaniel nunca lo permitiría. Y, si crees que no sacrificaría toda su carrera por tu felicidad, es que te has olvidado de su verdadera naturaleza. Pero las cosas no llegarán a ese punto —se apresuró a añadir, sabiendo que Verity sería capaz de inmolarse a sí misma antes de hacer daño a su amado—. Nathaniel es un oficial de mucho prestigio, y estamos en tiempos de guerra. Una vez que el vínculo este sellado, nadie podrá pretender llevarse a tu niño.

A decir verdad, no sentía la misma seguridad que manifestaban sus palabras. Notaba cómo le flaqueaban las rodillas ante la perspectiva de desafiar nuevamente la voluntad del conde de Walgrave. Pero ¿qué otra opción tenían?

Necesitaban que las amparara alguien tan poderoso como Walgrave. Era como pedir la luna.

4

Chastity cabalgó hasta Shaftesbury con lord Cyn, atenta a cualquier movimiento furtivo que éste pudiera hacer. A pesar de su manifiesto afán por ayudarlas, ella no se fiaba ni un pelo: su actitud ante la vida era demasiado frívola y hacía que las cosas más indecentes sonaran razonables.

Como por ejemplo, aquella absurda idea de ir de compras a la ciudad.

O lo de devolverle parte del dinero que le habían robado.

Después de todo, había dicho él, su intención era adquirir ropa, y quedaría raro que fuera el mozo de establo quien pagara a los dependientes. La idea era sensata y ella no había podido negarse, pero tenía la irritante sensación de que, con mucha habilidad, él se estaba haciendo con las riendas de la situación.

Dejaron los caballos en la puerta del Crown y encontraron al cochero de Cyn en la taberna. Hoskins era un hombre corpulento, con el rostro rubicundo y curtido de quien ha pasado gran parte de su vida en el pescante.

—Envié a los demás a la Abadía, milord, puesto que había sitio en la diligencia de Exeter. —Apuró la cerveza que Cyn le había pedido y se secó la boca con la manga—. Me pareció que lo mejor que podía hacer era quedarme, por si usted necesitaba ayuda. Además, no puedo irme a casa sin mi carruaje, ¿a que no? —miró a Chastity de un modo muy poco amistoso, pero del que no se desprendía que pensara que era una mujer o un tipo verdaderamente malvado.

Ella tomó un trago lo más grande que pudo de su propia jarra y se esforzó por parecer un joven y petulante rufián.

—Entonces, seguro que te parece bien mi plan, Hoskins —dijo Cyn—. Quiero que nos lleves en él.

—En eso consiste mi trabajo, milord —asintió el hombre, aunque entrecerrando los ojos—. En eso y en evitar que usted se meta en líos.

Cyn sonrió:

—¿Y cómo piensas lograrlo?

—Sólo Dios lo sabe. Es usted carne de horca, de eso doy fe.

Cyn le dio una palmadita en la espalda.

—Anímate. Las cosas no están tan mal como crees, desde luego no hay razón para ahorcar a nadie. Lo primero que tienes que hacer es alquilar un caballo para que puedas volver con nosotros. Después —añadió despreocupadamente—, consigue una pinta de pintura cuyo color se parezca lo más posible al del coche. Tiene un pequeño arañazo. Estate listo para cabalgar con nosotros dentro de una hora o así. Mi amigo y yo tenemos que comprar algunas cosas.

A continuación, Cyn arrastró a Chastity fuera de la pieza, antes de que el hombre, alarmado, pudiera empezar a farfullar preguntas inconvenientes. Chastity trataba de contrarrestar la fuerza que la mano de Cyn ejercía sobre su brazo, pero la presión era demasiado fuerte. No la soltó hasta que no estuvieron bien lejos de la posada.

—Créeme muchacho —le dijo—, no creo que te hubiera gustado tener que describir el daño que ha sufrido el coche. Sobre todo teniendo en cuenta que has sido tú quien lo ha causado.

—Son sólo unos pocos rasguños.

—He visto a Hoskins sulfurarse por una cagada de pájaro que estropeaba el barniz. Cuando vea lo que has hecho reclamará sangre.

—Entonces, ¿por qué quieres que venga con nosotros?

—Necesitamos que alguien conduzca el coche. No te preocupes. Si intenta azotarte, te defenderé hasta la muerte. —Miró el nombre de la calle pintado sobre un edificio y se metió por un callejón.

Chastity había supuesto que se divertiría viendo cómo su señoría intentaba procurarse en poco tiempo ropa de mujer en una población que no conocía. Pero, resultó que la que no tenía ni idea de cómo funcionaban las cosas era ella y no él.

Las señoritas Walgrave habían sido clientes de una sola modista en Shaftesbury, miss Taverstock, a la cual habían encargado únicamente prendas de gran sencillez. Cyn había sondeado al posadero y ahora tenía la dirección del comercio de ropa de segunda mano de la ciudad.

Chastity recorría aquellas zonas de Shaftesbury que le eran desconocidas con aire fascinado. Había callizos con pequeñas tiendas y calles estrechas y tortuosas festoneadas con ropa tendida. Había casas tan oscuras y ominosas como la Armada y otras que parecían sonreír al mundo. Delante de las primeras, merodeaban sucios pillastres. Delante de las últimas había mujeres sentadas que cocinaban o tejían, mientras vigilaban a sus hijos y charlaban con los vecinos.

Algunas calles eran secas y saludables, en otras se oía el ruido de las cloacas desaguando en el conducto principal.

Una tienda de trastos viejos, llena de llamativos cachivaches, captó la atención de Chastity. Después, se fijó en una herboristería que parecía seguir funcionando según las reglas del *Tratado de botánica* de Gerard. Pero Cyn no la dejaba demorarse en estos lugares, la apartó incluso de una encantadora librería.

—No tenemos prisa —protestó ella.

—Le dije a Hoskins que estaríamos de vuelta en una hora. Si no lo hacemos, probablemente pensará que te has deshecho de mí. Mira, ya hemos llegado.

El almacén de la señora Crupley exhibía una fachada estrecha y descolorida en la entrada de un callejón especialmente deprimente. Chastity apreció el asqueroso desorden que había en medio de aquel oscuro pasaje —con un gato muerto incluido— y dio gracias por no tener que atravesarlo. Obviamente, habían llegado al límite de la zona respetable de Shaftesbury. No estaba segura de que pudieran encontrar algo útil en un establecimiento semejante.

Empujaron la puerta y la nariz de Chastity se arrugó al percibir un mohoso olor a podrido y a sudor rancio. El lugar estaba lleno de prendas de vestir, sombreros, calzado y otros accesorios. Había artículos sobre estantes apoyados contra las paredes o en el interior de cajas que descansaban sobre el suelo. La mayor parte de la ropa colgaba de cuerdas que atravesaban la estancia.

La señora Crupley estaba sentada junto a una estufa en una mecedora que había cerca de la puerta. Tenía un gato en su regazo y una taza en la mano. Chastity sospechó que tal vez contuviera ginebra.

No obstante, no le quedó más remedio que sonreír cuando vio el modo en que aquella mujer rolliza de mediana edad disfrutaba con su mercancía. Llevaba un exuberante vestido amarillo de seda y encaje, que se había pasado de moda por lo menos hacía veinte años y estaba lleno de manchas. Sobre sus erizados y grises rizos descansaba un tocado de encaje de elaborado diseño, estilo reina Ana.

—Buenos días tengan ustedes —dijo la mujer—. ¿Puedo ayudarles en algo, encantos?

La señora Crupley conocía bien su género. Cuando Cyn le dijo, sin darle ninguna explicación, que necesitaba ropa de señora de calidad para una mujer más bien y alta y de constitución robusta, ella dejó la taza, se quitó de encima al malhumorado gato y se dirigió a la parte trasera de la tienda. Chastity y Cyn tuvieron que abrirse camino tras ella, esquivando las innumerables cuerdas con ropa colgada.

—Guardo las cosas buenas aquí atrás, claro —dijo la mujer—, fuera del alcance de los manilargos.

Una vez que llegaron a las oscuras y mohosas profundidades del lugar, ella empezó a descolgar muestras y a elogiar sus virtudes.

—Éste es un primor —dijo, haciendo oscilar un vestido azul de hilo de seda mientras les lanzaba rápidas miradas para captar todas sus reacciones.

—Una dama de gran alcurnia podría llevarlo tal y como está, o también hacerle algún arreglo.

Más bien lo último, pensó Chastity, porque el vestido estaba hecho jirones en la parte de debajo de los brazos y tenía cachos descoloridos. No obstante, era bien grande. De hecho, más bien gigantesco. Con algunos recortes, seguramente podría convertirse en un vestido aceptable para una dama esbelta. Ella, que nunca se había planteado estas cosas, comenzó a sentir curiosidad por las posibilidades de la ropa de segunda mano.

Después de todo, parecía bastante probable que a ella misma le aguardara un futuro lleno de privaciones.

Esperaba que le pidieran consejo, pero Cyn la ignoró por completo. Recordó entonces que él la tenía por un joven. De todos modos, no parecía necesitar ayuda. Rechazó varios artículos de etiqueta y algunas prendas vulgares que a la señora Crupley obviamente le parecían el no va más, y eligió dos feos trajes de excelente calidad.

Uno de ellos era un vestido de viaje marrón con cintas color beige, estilo Brunswick; el otro era un abrigo abierto de tela estampada color azul Prusia que iba sobre una enagua gris acolchada y una pechera de trenzado azul y negro. A lo que añadió una capa azul oscuro con caperuza y como complemento un sencillo sombrero campesino de paja.

Era evidente que a la señora Crupley no le parecían muy buenas elecciones y que compadecía a la pobre mujer que se viera obligada a llevar aquellas prendas tan sosas, pero realizó un último intento.

—Éste quedará estupendo poniéndole algunos lazos nuevos —dijo en tono cantarín, mientras acariciaba el liso sombrero—. De color amarillo o verde vivo, diría yo. —Miró a Cyn astutamente—. Se lo dejo todo por guinea y media.

Él regateó implacable hasta conseguir que se lo dejara por dieciocho chelines y seis peniques, y que añadiera al lote una zarrapastrosa peluca negra y un enorme manguito. Chastity se quedó asombrada cuando vio que la mujer sonreía al coger el dinero.

Cuando salieron al callejón, exclamó:

—¡Dieciocho chelines y seis peniques por todo eso! Has timado a la pobre vieja.

Él se echó a reír.

—Le he pagado más de lo que ella esperaba. Si le hubiera pagado demasiado, habría sospechado algo. La gente que es tan pobre como para comprar ropa usada mira cada penique que gasta. —Y, tras dedicarle una rápida e indulgente mirada, colocó en sus brazos uno de los grandes bultos envueltos en papel de periódico—. Me parece que aún no has salido del cascarón, ¿eh, Charles?

Chastity le lanzó un gruñido, pero él ya había emprendido a buen paso el camino de regreso. Chastity le siguió a toda prisa y no tuvo más remedio que admirar su sentido de la orientación. A ella le habría resultado muy difícil encontrar el camino de vuelta al Crown sin ayuda de nadie.

De pronto, él se detuvo delante de una de las tiendas que le habían causado a ella tanta fascinación, una diminuta mercería abarrotada de mercancía: hilos, lazos, tocados y ropa interior de señora ya confeccionada. Ella entró tras él en el establecimiento de ropa íntima.

Mostrando una asombrosa pericia en tales asuntos, y sin el menor asomo de vergüenza, Cyn compró un camisón, una camisola adornada con encaje, dos pares de medias de algodón y unas ligas con lazos rosas.

Parpadeando, alzó las ligas y las sostuvo delante de Chastity.

—¿Qué te parece, Charles? ¿Crees que le gustarán a mi hermana?

Chastity se dio cuenta de que se ruborizaba.

—Mientras le sirvan para sujetar las medias —dijo—, supongo que serán de su agrado. ¿Para qué otra cosa valen si no?

Cyn le hizo un guiño a la chica que se hallaba tras el mostrador.

—Estos jovencitos vergonzosos. —La chica soltó una risita. Chastity hizo rechinar los dientes.

Cyn echó una mirada a su alrededor: por toda la tienda se veían colgadas diversas prendas de muestra. Su sonrisa se ensanchó.

—Veo que tenéis también medias de seda. Déjeme ver uno de esos pares, querida.

La joven subió por una pequeña escalera de mano, bajó una caja y la abrió, dejando al descubierto medias de diversos colores, algunas incluso a rayas.

—Su hechura es de lo mejorcito —dijo la chica, sonrojándose ante sus cortesías—. Mire la calidad del bordado.

Cyn, dando muestras de admiración, sostuvo en alto uno de los pares de medias, unas de seda rosa con rayas rojas de fantasía.

—Oh, en mi opinión, no hay que ser tacaño con estas cosas —dijo afablemente, haciéndole una mueca a Chastity.

Ella le devolvió una mirada furibunda.

—Santo cielo —le dijo Cyn a la dependienta—, he ofendido al muchacho. Me parece que no da su visto bueno a las medias de fantasía. Dígame, querida, ¿qué opina usted de este asunto?

La chica, pensó Chastity con repugnancia, parecía incapaz de tener algún pensamiento que no fuera lujurioso. Además, le parecía increíble que un hombre exhibiera ropa íntima de manera tan desvergonzada delante de extraños…

—Oh, señor —estalló efusivamente la joven mercera—. A mí me parecen maravillosas.

Cyn volvió a contemplar admirativamente las medias.

—Me llevaré este par. Y cinco yardas de lazo amarillo ancho, por favor.

Chastity carraspeó. Cyn la miró y después volvió a mirar a la dependienta.

—Creo que no le gusta el amarillo. Será mejor que me ponga aquel ocre de rayas.

Cuando salieron de la tienda, él se echó a reír.

Chastity le miró con furia.

—¡No tiene usted decencia, señor!

—Cierto. ¿No das tu aprobación a las medias de seda a rayas? Dan un gran realce a un tobillo bien modelado.

—No es un asunto al que yo le dedique ninguno de mis pensamientos —dijo Chastity con frialdad. Y echó a andar arosamente en la dirección que creyó que era la correcta.

Él la alcanzó, con la risa todavía en la voz.

—¿No piensas en los tobillos de las mujeres? Vaya, si que eres un joven extraño.

Chastity decidió que lo más sensato sería no recoger aquel guante. De todas maneras, iba a tener que dejarle que dirigiera la marcha otra vez, porque ella volvía a estar desorientada.

A pesar del brusco paso que llevaba, había muy pocas cosas que escaparan a la atención de lord Cynric Malloren. Camino del Crown, entró en otra tienda, una que anunciaba jabones y productos de belleza. Éste era un establecimiento completamente distinto, con el que Chastity sí estaba familiarizada. Walgrave Towers llevaba años haciendo sus compras de jabón y ungüentos en Travis & Mount. ¿Qué demonios buscaría aquí Cyn Malloren?

Nuevamente, sin asomo de vergüenza, el joven compró un bote de colorete, una caja de polvos blancos y, tras aspirar el aroma de varias muestras, un pequeño frasco de perfume. A juzgar por el extasiado aspecto del rostro del señor Mount, Chastity dedujo que debía ser caro.

Una vez que estuvieron fuera, ella le dijo:

—¿Por qué estas derrochando todo este dinero si, de verdad, quieres ayudarnos?

—No es un derroche. Es importante ser minucioso en las imposturas y te aseguro que nos queda todavía un buen capital. Tienes que aprender a no preocuparte tanto, Charles. —Le dedicó una seductora sonrisa—. A lo mejor tienes hambre. Seguro que hasta un joven tan afectado como tú aprecia los dulces.

A Chastity no le quedó más remedio que decir que sí. En realidad, era bastante golosa. Su corazón se sobresaltó cuando vio hacia dónde se dirigía él. Aún así, protestó.

—No tenemos ni tiempo ni dinero para pasteles.

Pero él ya estaba en el interior de la repostería y pastelería de Dunn & Carr. Chastity decidió que, en resumidas cuentas, el aroma de la panadería superaba incluso al de la tienda de perfumes.

Al poco rato, salieron de allí con una empanada de ciruelas y una bolsa de galletas tostadas. Cyn hizo malabares con los paquetes y sacó dos bizcochos de Shrewsbury. Circulando de espaldas por la calle, puso uno de ellos dentro de la boca de Chastity.

Ella lo cogió. Él le recordó entonces a un escolar que estuviera de excursión, y por un momento se sintió su igual, de su mismo sexo, con su misma insolente seguridad y su mismo despreocupado enfoque de la vida. Ella sonrió al mismo tiempo que recolocaba sus propios paquetes para poder sostener el dulce y saborearlo a gusto. Todavía conservaba el calor del horno: una delicia.

Cyn dio un mordisco del suyo, mientras seguía caminando lentamente de espaldas. Ella dio asimismo un bocado del que tenía entre manos. Él atrapó su mirada y Chastity se descubrió contemplando sus labios mientras él tomaba un nuevo trozo y masticaba. Tenía unos labios hermosos, con un arco perfecto...

Los músculos de la garganta se le movían al tragar. Su lengua se deslizó hacia fuera. Lentamente, lamió los restos de migas doradas hasta hacerlas desaparecer de aquellos labios, dejando tras de sí un húmedo brillo.

Cyn bajo los párpados con aire somnoliento y sensual. Luego sonrió.

Chastity sintió que el corazón le latía con fuerza y se quedó boquiabierta.

Se dio cuenta, entonces, de que ya habían llegado a la posada y que estaban allí de pie como dos estatuas, mirándose el uno al otro. Sabía que tenía que moverse pero se sentía como atrapada dentro de una red, una red pegajosa y caliente. Sólo había dado un mordisco del bizcocho, pero aún tenía en la boca su dulce y hormigueante sabor.

—Sabor, textura, calor —dijo él suavemente, al parecer tratando de incitarla para que diera otro bocado—. La vida pone a nuestra disposición unos placeres tan sencillos y tan espléndidos a la vez. Paladéalos conmigo, Charles... —y se llevó a la boca el último de sus bizcochos.

Chastity se percató de que había dado otro obediente mordisco y de que estaba masticando en sincronía con él... Estuvo a punto de atragantarse. Un calor mareante le recordó vivamente que no eran del mismo sexo. Y que no enfocaban la vida de misma manera.

Él era el enemigo. Era un hombre. ¡Se suponía, maldita sea, que era su prisionero!

Se tragó el bocado de golpe, miró desconsoladamente el resto de la galleta y la tiró al suelo. Después se dirigió al interior de la posada.

Cyn la observó marchar, desanimado pero sin amilanarse. Durante un instante había vislumbrado el fuego que sabía que había dentro de ella. En la cama, tenía que ser una mujer maravillosa, pero, por algún motivo, tenía miedo a los hombres. Tal vez algún amante la había traicionado.

Con habilidad y paciencia conseguiría hacerla entrar en el juego; él tenía ambas cualidades y tres días para utilizarlas.

Mientras la seguía, admitió que el asunto podía resultar más sencillo si ponía fin a aquella mascarada, pero eso levantaría entre ellos nuevas barreras: las del decoro. Con las cosas tal y como estaban, habría más oportunidades y más divertidas.

Antes de marcharse de allí, consideró la posibilidad de hacer preguntas acerca de una hacienda situada a cinco millas de Shaftesbury, en dirección norte. Podía averiguar el nombre de la familia en cuestión de minutos. Pero desistió.

En parte por precaución. Si luego alguien hacía preguntas, no quería que nadie recordara que él se había mostrado interesado en la familia de aquella damisela.

En parte por su espíritu quijotesco, quería que fuera Charles quien algún día le contara toda la verdad.

Cuando Chastity, Cyn y Hoskins regresaron a la cabaña, hallaron a Verity bastante alterada, convencida de que Henry Vernham los había cogido o, cuando menos, que los había visto. Chastity se dedicó a calmar a su hermana y Cyn llevó a Hoskins hasta donde estaban el carruaje y los caballos.

Los cuatro rocines tenían agua y hierba en abundancia, aunque el cochero refunfuñó un poco a este respecto. Cuando vio el daño que había sufrido su coche, se quedó atónito.

—¿Quién demonios ha hecho eso? —preguntó, pasando una afligida mano por encima de las muescas.

—No estoy seguro —mintió Cyn—. Si te explico lo que está ocurriendo, tal vez comprendas algo.

Hoskins escuchó sin dejarse aplacar.

—Si ese joven demonio le ha hecho esto a mi carruaje, le daré a probar mi látigo.

—No, no lo harás. Déjamelo a mí.

El hombre sacudió la cabeza.

—¿Y que le va usted a decir al marqués? No puede largarse ahora, sin más.

—Sí que puedo. No soy un niño, Hoskins. Si se han cumplido mis órdenes, mi hermano pensará que estoy corriendo una aventura. Que, de hecho, es lo que estoy haciendo.

—Una aventura que a mí me huele a problemas. ¿Quién es esta joven que necesita llegar a Maidenhead con tanta urgencia y de manera clandestina?

—No lo sé muy bien —admitió Cyn—, pero es una dama y yo me siento caballeroso. Ahora escucha con atención, Hoskins. No sé si la persecución irá en serio o no, pero yo voy a tomar todas las precauciones posibles. No quiero que se te escape nada cuando hables con la gente por ahí.

—Sé controlarme, amo Cynric, como usted bien sabe.

Cyn se dio cuenta de que si Hoskins le llamaba amo Cynric era que no estaba de buenas con él.

—Ya sé que sabes —dijo en tono apaciguador—. Y, en cuanto al viaje, yo voy a hacerme pasar por una mujer, la madre del niño de Verity. Verity será el ama de cría y Charles el mozo de establo.

Cyn había esperado encontrarse con alguna objeción al hecho de que él fuera a hacerse pasar por una mujer, pero la mente del cochero estaba ocupada en otros asuntos.

—Ese bribón no va a acercarse a mi carruaje —dijo Hoskins con ferocidad.

—¡Al diablo con eso, Hoskins! No va a causar más daños, te lo prometo.

—No quiero que se acerque ni a mi coche ni a mis animales —repitió Hoskins, y volvió a pasar la mano sobre las cicatrices del reluciente vehículo.

Cyn suspiró. Podía imponer su voluntad pero no quería que Hoskins descargara su ira sobre Charles. Después de todo, el hombre no sabía que se trataba de una chica.

—Muy bien —dijo—. Puede viajar como mi hermano. Pero, entonces, tendrás que hacer tú todo el trabajo.

—Me las arreglaré —gruñó Hoskins—. ¿Dónde está la pintura?

Cyn dejó al cochero haciendo lo posible por subsanar los daños. Al entrar en la cabaña y encontrar allí a las tres mujeres, dijo:

—Yo que tú me mantendría apartado de Hoskins, joven Charles. Quiere sacarte las entrañas.

Ella se ruborizó.

—No podíamos andar por todo el país con el escudo de armas de Rothgar adornando uno de los laterales del coche.

—¿Por qué no? Yo estoy en esto voluntariamente y nadie me relaciona con vosotros.

Ella tenía la expresión de alguien que está decidido a no admitir un error.

—¿Cómo voy a mantenerme alejada de él si tengo que ser su mozo de establo?

—Ya no lo eres. Ahora eres mi hermano pequeño. Será mejor que te agencies ropa de más calidad.

Ella se puso de pie al instante.

—¿Tengo que recordarte, milord, que eres nuestro prisionero? ¿Tendrás la amabilidad de dejar de darnos órdenes?

Cyr se sentó.

—Muy bien. Lo dejo en vuestras manos.

Ella le lanzó una mirada furibunda.

—Viajaré como el mozo de cuadra.

—Como quieras. Aunque, entonces, estarás bajo la autoridad del cochero y, Hoskins no es un hombre delicado, ni siquiera en las mejores circunstancias. Siempre ha estado muy orgulloso del perfecto acabado de su carruaje.

Ella tragó saliva pero se mantuvo en sus trece.

—Le ordenarás que no me toque.

—¿Haré yo eso?

—Sí.

Él se encogió de hombros.

—Muy bien, pero es el cochero de mi hermano y no el mío. Él nos ha enseñado a todos a llevar las riendas. Nos ha abofeteado cuando pensaba que lo necesitábamos y contigo hará lo mismo. Supongo que no tiene mayor importancia —añadió despreocupadamente—. Ya te habrán zurrado más de una vez en el colegio. No creo que Hoskins vaya a ser peor.

Verity dijo rápidamente.

—Charles, querido, piénsalo bien. No servirá de nada disgustar aún más al pobre hombre.

Charles se dejó caer en la silla.

—Oh, muy bien. —Le clavó a Cyn una tempestuosa mirada—. Pero soy yo quien da las órdenes en este viaje.

Cyn reprimió una cortante réplica. ¿Dónde estaba aquella mujer encantadora que se había iluminado con motivo de un bizcocho caliente? Después, se recordó a sí mismo que ella estaba herida y, probablemente, asustada. Tenía que ser capaz de controlar aquella lamentable propensión suya a tomarle el pelo.

—Como quieras —dijo él, con tanta moderación como consiguió reunir—. Pero yo conozco el mundo mejor que tú y, además, me temo que Hoskins sólo aceptará órdenes mías. Me parece que también habría que tener en cuenta la opinión de Verity, puesto que todo esto le incumbe directamente a ella. Aparte de que, seguramente, será algo mayor que tú.

—Por supuesto que consultaré a Verity. ¿Cómo has podido dudarlo?

—Los jóvenes a menudo ignoran a sus hermanas —se mofó él, después dio un respingo al darse cuenta de lo poco que le habían durado las buenas intenciones.

—Pues yo no —respondió ella poniéndose en pie—. Voy a hacerme con otras prendas de vestir. —Se detuvo en la puerta y preguntó de mala gana—: ¿Se te ocurre alguna otra cosa que podamos necesitar? ¿Armas o algo por estilo?

Cyn tuvo que conceder que ella había sido capaz de tragarse su orgullo.

—No se me ocurre nada. Tenemos la pistola del coche y mi estoque. Eso debería bastarnos. Después de todo, no vamos a la guerra. —y añadió—: ¡Espera! Una cosa que no tengo para mi disfraz son alhajas femeninas. ¿Puedes conseguirme alguna?

—Veré lo que puedo hacer.

Al cabo de una hora, regresó con camisas de repuesto y un par de botas altas. También trajo un joyero con forro de piel. Era una hermosa pieza con una sólida cerradura, destinada obviamente a contener adornos caros. Al abrirla, resultó que sólo contenía una breve colección de baratijas.

La explicación obvia era que se hallaban en la indigencia y habían tenido que vender todos los objetos de valor. Pero no le satisfacía del todo, porque no aclaraba lo de la ropa de hombre de buena calidad, lo de los caballos de pura casta y lo del par de pistolas con montura de plata. La curiosidad picaba a Cyn cual si se tratara de una cama llena de pulgas.

5

A la mañana siguiente, temprano, se dispusieron a partir. Hoskins fue a preparar a los caballos. Cyn empezó a lidiar con su vestimenta femenina. Charles se vistió con la ropa de calidad y estuvo ayudando a su hermana con su indumentaria hasta que Cyn, taimadamente, puso en tela de juicio el decoro de esa situación. Entonces, ella fue de mala gana a asistirle a él.

Cyn tuvo cuidado de no ofender su pudor y, cuando ella apareció en la cocina, llevaba puestos los calzoncillos. También se había colocado las medias de rayas y las ligas de encaje. Charles le echó un vistazo y estalló en carcajadas. Era una risa muy femenina, pero él no hizo ningún comentario. Se limitó a disfrutar de ella.

La chica estaba estupenda; el humor la hacía sonrojarse. A pesar de la ropa y el cabello, ya sólo podía verla como una prodigiosa hembra. Y esto era peligroso, pensó Cyn, desplazando su atención a su muda.

Cuando levantó la vista, ella había dejado de reírse. Ahora contemplaba horrorizada su cicatriz.

—¿Qué demonios te ha pasado ahí? —preguntó.

—Un sable —dijo él despreocupadamente, interesado en observar su reacción. La lívida cicatriz le atravesaba el pecho como una bandolera. Todas las mujeres que habían tenido ocasión de observarla se habían visto impelidas a tocarla. La mayoría la habían recorrido, algunas con el dedo y otras con sus lenguas.

—Por suerte, me alcanzó de refilón, y el corte fue superficial.

Cyn vio cómo ella estiraba la mano hacia arriba y después reprimía el movimiento.

—Así que eres un soldado de verdad —dijo Chastity.

—¿Dudabas de mi palabra?

—Es que no lo pareces.

Él suspiró jocosamente.

—No puedo disimular mis seductores encantos.

Ella seguía fascinada por la cicatriz. Se adelantó un paso.

—Debiste sangrar mucho.

—Como un odre acuchillado. Puse perdido mi mejor uniforme.

Como ella parecía estar paralizada, él acortó la distancia que había entre ambos dando un paso al desgaire. Al cabo de unos instantes, tuvo que reconocer que, lamentablemente, ella no iba a ceder a la tentación de recorrer la trayectoria de la cicatriz desde el hombro izquierdo hasta la cadera derecha.

Dejó caer la muda de lino por encima de su cabeza y se ató las cintas en la parte inferior del cuello. Después, forcejeó con el vestido estilo Brunswick. Había sido diseñado pensando en la sencillez y la comodidad que requieren los desplazamientos y se componía de una sola pieza. Cuando se lo ajustara, tendría el aspecto de un vestido amplio cayendo sobre un corsé trenzado, pero, en realidad, el peto formaba parte del corpiño y se ceñía alrededor del cuerpo mediante cintas que iban por debajo de la espalda. Era una vestimenta muy adecuada para viajar, pero el principal atractivo que tenía para Cyn era que no llevaba ballenas.

Trató de anudarse él mismo las cintas, pero no pudo encontrarlas bajo la amplia y pesada falda.

—Se me escapan los lazos. Necesito tu ayuda, por favor Charles.

Era obvio que ella se resistía. No obstante, se le acercó por detrás y le levantó la falda.

—No los veo. Deben haber caído hacia la parte de delante.

Ella rebuscó en los costados de su torso. Aquellos fugaces toques la hicieron estremecerse.

—Ya los tengo —dijo ella—, pero creo que están anudados al frente.

Sus manos siguieron las cintas hasta llegar a la parte frontal. De repente, dio un respingo hacia atrás.

—No puedo desatarlas —dijo con voz asfixiada—. Tendrás que quitarte el vestido.

—Oh, seguro que puedes —dijo Cyn en tono despreocupado—. Será mucho más fácil que volver a sacarme todo esto. —Su voz también estaba tensa, pero porque se estaba aguantando la risa. ¿Sabía ella dónde acababa de poner las manos? Sospechaba que sí.

Se produjo un silencio que le hizo pensar que la muchacha se iba a negar, pero, entonces, Chastity volvió a rodearle con sus brazos. Juntándolos en la parte delantera, cogió los lazos anudados y comenzó a soltarlos. No tuvo el menor cuidado de vigilar donde ponía las manos.

Cyn respiró profundamente. ¡Dios santo, le había salido el tiro por la culata! Aquella lagarta sabía exactamente lo que estaba haciendo.

Le había levantado la falda del todo y apretaba el vientre contra sus nalgas. Rodeándole la cintura con los brazos, le frotaba una y otra vez con las manos mientras trataba de soltar los nudos…

Los primeros síntomas de lujuria le incendiaron el cerebro. Se imaginó que se daba lentamente la vuelta entre sus brazos y la besaba; que se hundía hasta el suelo mientras exploraba su boca, sus pechos, la calidez del interior de sus muslos; sintió la oscura intensidad de sus ojos al deslizarse dentro de ella…

Tuvo un escalofrío que le advirtió que estaba yendo demasiado lejos. Su pene erecto forcejeaba contra sus calzoncillos como si buscara el solaz de las manos de ella. Esas manos se quedaron heladas al acariciarle levemente. Cyn sintió cómo se quedaba rígida por el pánico.

A menos que, pensó con desesperado optimismo, se hubiera tratado de una seducción premeditada y su tensión fuera fruto del deseo…

Se soltó de sus brazos y se dio la vuelta. No. Ella estaba colorada. Horrorizada. Asustada.

Cyn se obligó a relajarse y trató de controlar la respiración.

—No me mires con esa cara de espanto, chico. Es una reacción perfectamente natural después de tanto toqueteo. No es nada personal.

Y, apartándose de ella, se levantó la parte delantera de la falda para terminar la tarea.

—Teníamos que habernos dado cuenta de que yo mismo podía hacer esto por delante. —Empujó los lazos hacia atrás—. Ahí los tienes. Si puedes anudarlos, ya hemos terminado.

Ella mostró el mismo entusiasmo que alguien que tuviera que meter la cabeza en la boca de un tigre hambriento, pero volvió a ponerse tras él, le levantó de nuevo las faldas y cogió las cintas. Las ató enseguida y se retiró. Él deseó que los sentimientos que ella le había provocado pudieran retirarse con la misma rapidez.

¿Qué iba a hacer con aquella chica, que, de pronto, se mostraba atrevida y, a continuación, se tornaba mojigata?

—Dime, Charles —preguntó jovialmente—, ¿eres virgen?

—¡Sí! —Se había puesto de nuevo colorada, esta vez con más intensidad—. ¡No creo que sea asunto tuyo!

—Por supuesto que no —dijo él tratando de aplacarla— Sólo estaba pensando en ofrecerte mis servicios para enmendar el asunto.

Ella se quedó boquiabierta. Él sabía que, por unos instantes, ella se había olvidado de que iba disfrazada pero se daba perfecta cuenta del estado del cuerpo de Cyn.

—¿Qué demonios quieres decir?

Él sonrió con amabilidad.

—Simplemente que, a menudo, un hombre más maduro toma a su cargo a otro más joven y le muestra el camino, presentándole al tipo adecuado de mujer. Si vamos a embarcarnos juntos en esta aventura…

Vio cómo ella volvía a la realidad de sopetón. Deseó que lo hiciera también con cierta decepción. Entre ellos se instaló una capa de hielo.

—Lo que nos ocupa es un asunto muy serio, milord. No nos dejará tiempo para visitar burdeles.

—¿Y si no es así?

Antes de que ella pudiera ocultarlo, él percibió un malicioso destello en su mirada.

—Tal vez me interese. Pero, de momento, se supone que le estoy ayudando a vestirse.

A Cyn le encantó aquel toque de picardía. Ella se comportaba con excesiva sobriedad, aunque seguramente aquélla no era su verdadera naturaleza. En el fondo, debía ser una criatura salvaje, muy similar a él, pero, por algún motivo, estaba asustada. Tenía que dejar de atormentarla.

—¿Qué aspecto tengo? —preguntó, volviéndose hasta quedar frente a ella.

Chastity hizo una mueca.

—Lisa por delante y lisa por detrás.

Cyn bajó la vista. La falda le caía flácida y el corpiño le quedaba flojo sobre su pecho plano. Obviamente, había sido diseñado para una dama de formas generosas. Nadie creería jamás que aquel vestido era suyo.

—La enagua gris servirá de relleno para la falda —dijo él—, pero no sé que hacer con el corpiño. ¿Se te ocurre algo?

—Seguro, pero dame tiempo. Espera un poco.

Charles abandonó la estancia y él, mientras tanto, trató de controlar su cuerpo. Hizo algunas inspiraciones con la intención de calmarse y ocupó su mente con pensamientos desprovistos de lujuria.

A medida que su organismo regresaba a un estado más pasivo, iba reflexionando, lleno de satisfacción, sobre el encuentro con su damisela. Habían hecho progresos, desde luego que sí. ¿Era ella realmente virgen? Eso supondría algún que otro problema, aunque, de ningún modo, insuperable. Evidentemente, no era una señorita convencional.

Tal vez no fuera muy deportivo por su parte permitir que Charles pensara que ignoraba cuál era su verdadero sexo, pero la muy tunanta acababa de demostrar que también ella era capaz de explotar aquella situación. Se sonrió admirado, deseando que regresara pronto.

Empezó a forcejear con la acolchada enagua gris, tratando de introducirse en su interior. Para cuando hubo atado los lazos ya se sentía sofocado dentro de todo aquel material. Al intentar caminar, tenía que apartar las faldas de en medio a patadas. Pensó que, después de todo, tal vez fuera preferible usar aros, pues éstos impedirían que la tela se le enredase entre las piernas.

No tenía ninguna intención de llevar calzado de segunda mano, así que se puso un par de zapatos suyos, unos de etiqueta —de cabritilla negra con altos tacones rojos y hebillas de plata. Aunque las mujeres ya no llevaban aquel tipo de calzado, simplemente daría la impresión de estar anticuada.

Caminó un poco más, tratando de acostumbrarse a aquellas prendas, al modo en que se movían mientras andaba y a la manera de caminar dentro de ellas. ¿Había pasado Charles por todo aquello la primera vez que se puso ropa de hombre? Desde luego, había aprendido a moverse con aplomo masculino.

Su damisela regresó con una gran cesta y le tendió un pañuelo de cuello.

—Ponte esto.

Era un triángulo de tela corriente y burda, muy diferente de aquellos finos y ondulados tejidos que llevaban sus hermanas. Se lo colgó obedientemente sobre los hombros, preguntándose qué hacer con sus extremos sueltos.

Ella hizo chasquear la lengua con exasperación.

—Oh, siéntate.

Él obedeció y Charles le remetió la tela con mucha destreza por el cuello del vestido, le cruzó las puntas por la clavícula y se las introdujo por debajo del peto. Él se abstuvo de hacer ningún comentario acerca de su pericia y se limitó a disfrutar con el roce.

Cuando ella dio por terminada la operación, él bajo la vista. El corpiño seguía quedando flojo.

—¿Qué me sugieres? ¿Pañuelos? No estoy seguro de tener los suficientes para llenar esta amplia caverna.

—No. Quedarían muy apelmazados.

—Querido Charles —dijo Cyn con coquetería—, ¿quién crees que se va a dedicar a palparme el pecho?

Ella le lanzó una asqueada mirada.

—Todo el mundo, si te comportas como mujer del mismo modo que lo haces como hombre. Eres un descarado, milord Cyn. Desde luego, haces honor a tu nombre.[1] Mira —ella le señalaba en dirección a la bolsa, que contenía lana sin hilar—. La próxima manta de Nana —le explicó, pasándole un ovillo.— Métetelo por dentro de la pechera.

Él se sentó y se tiró del corpiño.

—Creo que tendrá que ir dentro de la muda para mayor seguridad. —Después de un par de madejas, añadió—: Quedará mejor si eres tú quien lo metes y le das forma, pues podrás ver lo que estás haciendo.

Ella le miró con suspicacia, pero se le acercó obedientemente y empezó a empujar la suave lana gris, apretándola contra la piel de Cyn, puñado tras puñado. De vez en cuando, se detenía para ajustarla a la forma del corpiño.

Cyn sabía que no era prudente hacer que ella le tocara de aquella manera, pero la imprudencia en aquellos asuntos era para él una segunda naturaleza. Se relajó sobre el

---

1. Se refiere a que Cyn fonéticamente es igual a *sin*, que significa pecado.

asiento y se dedicó a estudiar los severos rasgos de su damisela.

Dios, sí que era guapa. Tenía la piel tan delicada como el satén y los trazos de la nariz y su mandíbula eran tan perfectos como los de una estatua de mármol. Sus pestañas no eran tan gruesas ni tan largas como las de Cyn, pero la pureza de su oscuro arco era el único marco posible para aquellos ojos de color gris claro.

Se sintió un poco golfo por tener pensamientos lascivos hacia un ser tan prístino, hacia una madona de aquellas características.

A ella se la veía concentrada. En un momento su boca se abrió. Con la punta de la lengua se humedeció el labio superior. Él contuvo el aliento.

Chastity le miró.

—¿Te he hecho daño?

—No —dijo él, tragando saliva—, cosquillas.

La muchacha le observó con cautela. Él se percató de la reveladora ojeada que había echado a su entrepierna, pero cualquier respuesta física quedaba bien oculta bajo la seda acolchada y la pesada tela. Él sonrió imperturbable y ella reanudó su tarea.

Cyn no sabía por qué estaba decidido a continuar con aquella tortura. Antes de que terminaran, estaría hecho un pingajo.

Chastity vigilaba nerviosamente a Cyn, temiendo que su lujuria regresara, pero entonces se dio cuenta de que no era de él de quien debía desconfiar. Cada vez que rozaba su piel con las manos, eran sus propios nervios los que se incendiaban. En cada inspiración, notaba un olor almizcleño que le dejaba la boca seca y hacía que se le humedecieran los labios.

¡Esto no podía estarle ocurriendo a ella! Los hombres eran criaturas del reino animal cuya lascivia se estimulaba con facilidad. Las mujeres eran más refinadas. No se ponían calientes por el mero hecho de rozar el pecho de un hombre.

Con severidad, llamó al orden a sus insensatos sentidos. Después, utilizando los puños, dio forma al busto de Cyn.

Él trataba de aparentar aburrimiento. No era fácil. Su damisela se apretaba contra él, respirando agitadamente, con los húmedos y carnosos labios anhelando ser besados…

Y él apostaría cualquier cosa a que ella ni siquiera lo sabía.

Chastity, con las manos temblorosas por el contacto con su cuerpo, le miró a los ojos durante un revelador instante…

Después, recobró la compostura y se retiró.

—Ya está. Creo que parece auténtico.

Cyn suspiró pensando en lo que podía haber sido.

—¡Cierto! —exclamó—. ¡Voy a incitar al pecado!

Chastity estaba obnubilada. Su mente se hallaba llena de pensamientos turbulentos, pero este comentario consiguió arrancarle una carcajada.

—No si lo proyectas hacia delante y miras con fiereza —le dijo—. Entonces dirán que eres una arpía. Y es mejor que sea así. Si alguien te toca las tetas, notará que no son de verdad.

Él la miró con un destello perverso.

—Me parece que me has estado haciendo creer lo que no era, joven Charles. ¿Cómo sabes tú cómo son las tetas al tacto?

Chastity no encontró una respuesta inteligente.

—¿Sabes cuál es problema? —se apresuró a decir.

—No.

—Que mañana tendremos que repetir toda la operación.

Ella vio cómo le brillaban los ojos, divertidos ante la perspectiva. Después Cyn se incorporó

—*Il faut sufrir pour être femme* —dijo él, articulando lentamente las palabras. Después, se dio una nueva vuelta—. Bueno. ¿Estoy bien?

Y, ojalá Dios la ayudara, porque ella también iba a disfrutar con aquel juego al día siguiente. Sin duda, debía estar loca.

Volvió a poner en funcionamiento la mente y le echó un vistazo:

—Puede pasar —le dijo, frunciendo el ceño.— Pero me parece que no resultas tan guapa de mujer como te habías imaginado.

—¿Quieres que cambiemos los papeles?

Ella se quedó callada y Cyn sonrió. Después se miró fijamente en el espejo.

—Se me ha olvidado comprar un tocado. Una matrona debería llevar un tocado.

—Te traeré uno —dijo ella y se fue.

¿Que no estaba guapa? Cyn se dio cuenta de que Charles estaba en lo cierto. Su mandíbula era demasiado angulosa y sus mejillas más bien enjutas. Se esmeró en la tarea de aplicar colorete sobre ellas y se consoló pensando que, por una vez, su aspecto era demasiado masculino.

Se espolvoreó el cuello, el pecho y la cara con los polvos blancos, disimulando así su bronceado. Después se puso carmín en los labios y los frunció delante del espejo. Se quitó el lazo del pelo y se peinó las cobrizas ondas, dejándoselas caer alrededor del rostro. Se sacó unos ricitos junto a las sienes, como había visto que hacían sus hermanas.

Después cogió el perfume y se aplicó un poquito al lado de las orejas. Era un aroma almizcleño y tórrido, que haría perder el sentido a cualquier hombre que se acercara. Eso, junto con su enorme busto, iba a hacer que tuviera que defender su honor diez veces al día.

Sin embargo, él había comprado sobre todo aquel perfume con la esperanza de que su damisela lo llevara algún día para él. Por unos instantes, cedió a la tentación de imaginársela desnuda y empapada de un sudor lujurioso, con su fragancia personal mezclada con aquella otra artificial...

Cuando la oyó regresar, se dio la vuelta y, haciendo sobresalir sus encarnados labios, le dijo:

—Bésame, marinero.

Chastity se sobresaltó al constatar el aspecto tan femenino que presentaba. Se había ahuecado el pelo y se había puesto colorete en las mejillas. Pero no eran sólo los cosméticos o la figura. Era algo que tenía que ver con su porte, con la ligera inclinación de su cuello y la seductora manera en que usaba las pestañas. Era un mimo consumado.

Una vez más, sintió que era un tipo peligroso. Al entregarle el sencillo tocado de algodón, se prometió que renunciaría a cualquier futura escaramuza.

Él lo cogió con dos dedos y lo contempló del mismo modo que lo haría una dama desdeñosa.

—¿Sin volantes? ¿Sin encaje? Es espantosamente soso —dijo lentamente con voz bronca pero muy femenina—. Supongo que, no obstante, hace juego con el pañuelo de cuello, que es igual de soso. ¿A quién pertenecen estas prendas tan tediosas?

Chastity no quería responder a aquella pregunta.

—Eso es todo lo que hay —dijo en tono cortante—. Verity no tiene más ropa que la que lleva encima. Si te molesta su simpleza —añadió con dulzura—, puedes hacerle algún bordado en el coche. Ésa será una ocupación muy adecuada para una matrona.

—Menudo desastre —dijo él, imitando su tono—, estoy seguro de que incluso tú manejas la aguja mejor que yo. —Se dio la vuelta para ponerse el tocado delante del espejo. Estaba diseñado para cubrir todo el pelo, pero él se las arregló para asentarlo sobre su cabeza, dejando al descubierto la parte frontal de su cabellera. Cuando se ató las cuerdas bajo la oreja derecha, incluso aquel deprimente sombrero llegó a parecer atractivo.

Chastity descubrió que las resoluciones arrogantes no siempre funcionaban. Ella se había prometido renunciar a todo tipo de escaramuzas, pero todavía se encontraba en medio de la refriega. Ella y Cyn no se estaban tocando, ni siquiera se estaban mirando. De hecho, por el momento, la apariencia de él era la de una mujer. Y ella seguía albergando pensamientos frívolos.

Era imposible que se sintiera así. Nunca antes había reaccionado ante un hombre de aquella manera y, últimamente, los odiaba a todos. Se preguntaba si las mujeres podían estar en celo, como los caballos. Eso era lo que ella parecía. Una yegua atolondrada olfateando a su primer semental.

Pero él no era el primer macho con el que había tratado.

Se había topado con muchas clases de hombres, especialmente en Londres. Estaban aquellos que citaban poesía y los que hacían insinuaciones furtivas e indecentes. Los que le besaban las manos con reverencia y los que le palpaban el cuerpo con el disimulo del baile. Después, apareció

Henry Vernham, quien se creyó con derecho a manosearla por todas partes con sus heladas manos hasta que ella le demostrara que estaba equivocado clavándole un par de afiladísimas tijeras.

Ninguno de aquellos hombres le había hecho sentir nada parecido a lo que Cyn Malloren provocaba en ella. Y, al parecer, sin proponérselo.

Era insensato.

Era imposible.

Era extraordinariamente peligroso y no había que permitirlo.

Por todos los santos, ella había llegado incluso a coquetear con Rothgar sin que de ello se derivara ninguna consecuencia. Y Rothgar era el tipo de hombre contra el que las madres prevenían a sus hijas. Todo lo que Cyn tenía de guapo, él lo tenía de apuesto: poseía un halo de misterioso poder que le confería un gran magnetismo.

Recordaba un encuentro en un oscuro emparrado de un jardín, en el transcurso de un baile. Había sido consciente de que era un atrevimiento irse a un aparte con él y se había preguntado cómo se comportaría.

Sonriendo, él le había puesto un dedo bajo la barbilla y se había limitado a rozarle los labios con su boca. Ella se había sentido inflamada, maliciosa y deliciosamente inflamada, de una manera mucho más potente que con los besos vacilantes que había permitido a otros hombres consumar.

Chastity había disfrutado con la excitación de rozar algo tan peligroso, aunque que no sentía nada especial por Rothgar. Y, como aquello era recíproco, ella se había sentido segura. Pero, aquella aguda y obsesiva conciencia de cada movimiento del hombre, aquella mareante vibración al producirse el más mínimo toque, eran sensaciones completamente diferentes.

En silencio, hizo una plegaria. Pidió que Cyn nunca descubriera que era una mujer, porque, en tal caso, podía desatar contra ella todo el poder de sus tretas. Y, entonces, seguramente estaría perdida.

Cyn hizo una mueca mientras se ponía aquel burdo y simple tocado. Supuso que tanto el sombrero como el pañuelo debían pertenecer a su damisela. ¿Qué es lo que le había hecho elegir aquellas prendas tan horrendas? Parecían más propias de la inquilina de un correccional.

Al pensar que, además de haber elegido aquellas toscas prendas, ella iba vestida con ropa masculina, se preguntó si no odiaría su propia feminidad. Había que verla en aquellos instantes. Su rostro tenía la misma calidez que una mascarilla de mármol.

¿Por qué demonios se sentía atraído por aquella rara avis? ¿Por qué le resultaba tan incitante como la más habilidosa de las prostitutas o como la más encantadora de las damas? Debía de ser la abstinencia. No había estado con una mujer desde antes de ponerse enfermo. Tal vez esta reacción demostrara que estaba completamente recuperado.

En ese caso, todo lo que necesitaba era una ramera lasciva y dispuesta, y su obsesión por su damisela desaparecería.

Pero se dio cuenta de que le resultaba difícil imaginarse que le excitaba cualquier otra mujer que no fuese ésta. Aquello era tremendamente alarmante.

Rebuscó entre la patética colección de alhajas y se pinzó los lóbulos con un par de pendientes de hojalata pintada. Desechó el resto y reclamó sus propias joyas. Tras distribuirlas por encima de las sobrias prendas, dirigió su atención al liso sombrero de paja.

Enrolló unas cuantas yardas del lazo color ocre alrededor de su baja copa y después, usando buena parte del mismo material, formó un nudo de amor en la parte delantera, sujetándolo con el alfiler de perlas y diamantes. Hizo pasar el resto de la cinta por las dos ranuras laterales y, tras colocarse el producto en la cabeza, se ató los extremos formando una amplia lazada.

Chastity se había quedado realmente estupefacta ante aquella presta destreza.

—¿Te vistes así con frecuencia?

Él se dio la vuelta y le sonrió. Tenía un aire desconcertantemente femenino.

—No, pero he tenido ocasión de vestir y desvestir a unas cuantas mujeres. —Hizo aletear sus escandalosas pestañas—. No te preocupes, joven Charles. Ya te llegará el turno.

El cuerpo de Chastity respondió a un mensaje que no podía ser intencionado. Durante unos instantes, la visión de los largos dedos marrones del hombre despojándola de la ropa le nubló el entendimiento.

Él le tocó el brazo y ella se retrajo. Cyn aparentó no darse cuenta y la empujó suavemente hacia delante, haciéndole atravesar la puerta.

—Vamos a ver qué es lo que piensa Verity de esta transformación.

Cuando entraron en el saloncito, Verity levantó la vista y le miró con asombro.

—¡Santo cielo! Si no lo supiera, no lo adivinaría jamás.

—Esperemos que le pase igual a todo el mundo. —Cyn examinó a su vez a Verity.

Tenía el aspecto de una doncella más bien desaliñada. Seguía llevando la sencilla camisola de manga larga, una falda de un barato tejido a rayas y un corpiño de encaje de un práctico color tierra. A lo que había añadido un delantal y un pañuelo de cuello anudado al frente. Casi todo su cabello estaba cubierto por un tocado. El tocado, el pañuelo y el delantal eran sospechosamente parecidos a los que él mismo llevaba. Por la cabeza de Cyn desfilaron conjeturas no muy agradables.

—Me temo —dijo, tanteando con suavidad—, que la gente va a pensar que soy una dama cruel por vestir a mi doncella con la ropa que tiran en el hospicio.

El revelador rostro de Verity le indicó que estaba muy cerca de la verdad. Pero ¿cuál era la verdad?

—No tenemos nada mejor —dijo Charles con viveza—. ¿Crees que su aspecto ha cambiado lo suficiente?

Para oscurecerse el cabello, Verity había utilizado grasa en lugar de tinte. Algunos mechones dispersos le sobresalían por la parte frontal del bonete. El cambio era notable.

—Creo que servirá —dijo él—. Si nos topamos cara a cara con alguien que la conozca bien, no funcionará, pero el principal peligro reside en los carteles que se habrán colocado y en las autoridades, que estarán alertadas. Andarán buscando a una joven mujer rubia con un niño. Yo soy más moreno, y, vestido de mujer, debo aparentar más años de los veinticuatro que tengo. ¿Cuántos? ¿Alrededor de treinta?

Verity asintió y sonrió.

—Lo conseguiremos, ¿verdad?

Él le devolvió la sonrisa del mismo modo que lo haría con un recluta novato que necesita ánimos antes de la primera batalla.

—Sin duda alguna.

De manera espontánea, ella extendió las manos. Cuando él se las cogió, Verity le besó levemente en los labios.

—Gracias. Qué contenta estoy de que te hayamos encontrado.

—De que le hayamos capturado —corrigió Charles con viveza.

Cyn se volvió hacia su ceñuda damisela. La sujetó por los hombros y, antes de que ella pudiera reaccionar, la besó del mismo modo que Verity le había besado a él. Ella dio un respingo hacia atrás y se frotó la boca.

—Querido señor —dijo Cyn con voz trémula, cosa que le resultó fácil pues se estaba aguantando la risa—, le pido mil disculpas. ¡Me he dejado llevar por mi papel!

—Vuelve a dejarte llevar así —le espetó su damisela—, y te sacaré las tripas. —Y, cogiendo uno de los baúles, echó a andar airosamente en dirección al coche.

Hacia el mediodía, Cyn había llegado a la conclusión de que aquella aventura era mortalmente aburrida. ¿Dónde estaba el reto? ¿Dónde estaban los peligros? ¿Dónde estaban los dragones contra los que luchar?

Todo lo que estaba experimentando era el conocido movimiento oscilante del carruaje, el frío helador de un riguroso día de noviembre y la incomodidad de su disfraz. Las faldas le sofocaban las piernas, el relleno de lana le picaba y las bastas cuerdas del tocado le irritaban la piel. Antes pensaba que un alzacuellos rígido era insoportable, pero aquello era indudablemente mucho peor.

Se había quitado el sombrero tan pronto como estuvieron dentro del coche, pero pensó que debía llevar puesto el tocado por si algún viajero con el que se cruzaran miraba al interior del carruaje. Ya habían decidido que correr las cortinas podía despertar sospechas. Se soltó las cuerdas del bonete y las dejó colgando.

—¿Por qué diantre —preguntó— harán una gorra con un percal tan basto? —A pesar de su irritación, hablaba en voz baja porque el bebé estaba durmiendo.

—Para que dure más —dijo Charles secamente—. Después de unas veinte lavadas, se vuelve más suave.

—Sería mejor, seguramente, comprar la tela ya suave.

—Pero sale más caro.

La curiosidad azuzó de nuevo a Cyn.

—¿De dónde han salido estos tocados?

—Los teníamos por ahí —dijo ella, esquivando la pregunta. Después, sonrió con frialdad—. Siento mucho que no hayamos podido ofrecerle algo más apropiado para su delicada piel, milord.

—Ya. Y ¿cómo es que no teníais nada mejor?

Ella le lanzó una cortante mirada.

—¿Por qué habríamos de tener caras bagatelas?

Cyn echó un vistazo a Verity. Parecía considerablemente inquieta.

—Porque tú y tu hermana sois de buena familia. Tus ropas, señor, aunque algo pasadas de moda, han sido confeccionadas por un buen sastre. Así que, si hay ropa de mujer, cabe esperar que sea de la misma calidad.

El rubor de Charles delataba la agitación que sentía, pero respondió con mucha calma.

—Verity tuvo que huir disfrazada y yo, obviamente, no llevo tocados.

Cyn no se daba por vencido.

—Entonces, ¿de dónde ha salido esto?

Ella tensó la mandíbula.

—Nana y yo las estábamos haciendo para la Magdalena de Shaftesbury.

Era una explicación plausible, aunque Cyn no se la tragó. Recostándose hacia atrás, se relajó y se abanicó con su tocado.

—Muy caritativo —murmuró—. Especialmente por su parte, señor.

Ella se mordió el labio.

Fue Verity la que salió al paso.

—Se está atribuyendo más merito del que tiene. Estoy segura de que todo lo que Charles ha hecho ha sido cortar la tela.

El coche entró dando tumbos en el patio de una posada y la conversación llegó a su fin sin que Cyn hubiera averiguado nada nuevo.

El cambio se realizó con lentitud puesto que Hoskins no tenía a nadie que pudiera ir a por un nuevo tiro o ayudar a los mozos de cuadra. Aunque se hallaban todavía en la ruta que Cyn tenía prefijada, éste había decidido no usar los caballos de Rothgar, que le estarían aguardando. También le había indicado a Hoskins que evitara aquellas fondas en las que pudiera ser conocido.

Por lo que Cyn sabía, Rothgar estaba en Londres y no en la Abadía, pero en cuanto se enterara de la desaparición de su hermano, no le cabía la menor duda de que iniciaría su búsqueda. No quería ir dejando un rastro fulgurante. Lo último que le apetecía era «ser rescatado» por el marqués por segunda vez.

Ahora tendrían que alquilar caballos de postas para cada etapa, y postillones para que se ocuparan de ellos. Hoskins murmuraba que aquellos tiros eran meros caballos de carretas.

En resumidas cuentas, nadie estaba contento con el estado de las cosas.

Cyn inspeccionó despreocupadamente el patio de la posada, tratando de detectar algún cartel o algún observador que no les quitara ojo. Nada. Tal vez no les estuvieran persiguiendo. Parecía que tenían bastantes probabilidades de llegar a Maidenhead en un par de días sin el menor incidente.

Qué aburrido.

Entonces, vio el rostro pálido de Verity. En todas las paradas, y cada vez que se cruzaban con algún jinete en la calzada, el miedo la hacía tensarse. Cuanto antes se reuniera con su Nathaniel mucho mejor.

Al arrancar, el bebé se despertó y empezó a llorar. En pocos instantes, el lamento se transformó de un gimoteo en un aullido, un sonido sorprendentemente penetrante para salir de alguien tan pequeño. Verity se sonrojó cuando comenzó a darle el pecho, después de taparse con un chal. Cyn tuvo la cortesía de apartar la vista, aunque no se veía nada. No obstante, la imagen mental de un niño al ser amamantado le resultó fascinante. Los suaves ruidos que el niño hacía al sorber contribuían a realzar este efecto.

Se preguntó qué sentiría uno al observar a la madre de su hijo alimentando a su bebé, qué se sentiría al succionar de unos pezones que producían leche. Miró de refilón a Charles

Parpadeó, asustado de sí mismo. ¿Hijos? ¿Matrimonio? Esas cosas no cabían en su vida. La vida matrimonial y la militar no encajaban. Como decían los veteranos «Cuando un soldado se pone la gorra, debe comprender que su familia está a cubierto».

En todo caso, si se le pasara por la cabeza casarse, no estaba tan loco como para pensar en su damisela en apuros. No parecía tener muchos atributos femeninos. Aunque, Dios Santo, estaría bien tener una esposa con aquel valor…

El ruido del chupeteo cesó y el bebé empezó de nuevo a berrear. Verity trataba de acallarlo parloteando y dándole palmaditas en la espalda. El niño pataleaba y lloraba, con la cara roja y lleno de furia. Verity estaba casi tan roja como él. Cyn se puso a mirar por la ventana, como si no le afectara aquella escandalera, pero deseando poder taparse los oídos con las manos.

El llanto bajó ligeramente de volumen y él volvió a mirar. Charles tenía ahora al bebé. Sostenía a William con más seguridad de la que cabría esperar de un joven. El niño gemía ahora sólo de cuando en cuando, lo que muy bien podía ser un preludio del sueño. Todos suspiraron aliviados.

Pero William debía haberse parado únicamente para recobrar el aliento. De pronto, pateó con fuerza y empezó a chillar todavía más fuerte, como si tuviera un dolor terrible. Cyn no era capaz de imaginarse en qué consistía el problema, pero empezó a temer que la criatura expirara delante de él. Continuamente morían niños a causa de problemas triviales.

Verity, sin embargo, parecía estar más abochornada que aterrorizada.

El ruido siguió y siguió. Charles meneaba al bebé y tenía aspecto de estar tan alarmada como Cyn. Verity volvió a coger al niño y se lo puso otra vez en el pecho, pero el pequeño William lo rechazó con furia. Ella lo sentó erguido, lo volvió a tumbar, se lo arrimó al hombro…

Cyn decidió que estar recluido en un coche con un bebé que llora era una forma de tortura muy eficaz. Para poner fin a aquel alboroto, sería capaz de desvelar secretos de estado.

Verity parecía a punto de ponerse a llorar.

—Oh, lo siento. Debe tener gases, pero no consigo que los saque…

Aunque no entendía de bebés, Cyn sabía mucho de caballos, perros y soldados novatos. Le pareció que, en aquellos momentos, Verity, más que ayudar, estaba entorpeciendo las cosas.

—Oh, déjamelo a mí —dijo, con más viveza de la que hubiera deseado.

Ella dudó, pero él cogió de todos modos a la aullante criatura. Le sorprendió la fuerza con la que el diminuto chiquillo se contorsionaba y, como había cogido más manta que bebé, estuvo a punto de dejarlo caer. Por causas totalmente fortuitas, William terminó de morros contra su rodilla, dándose un porrazo. El niño soltó un eructo, dejó caer una baba sobre la camisa de Cyn y se calló.

Los tres miraban al bebé esperando que comenzara de nuevo aquel ruido ensordecedor. Reinaba la calma y William ni siquiera parecía tener ninguna objeción respecto a su postura. Cyn le dio la vuelta con cautela. El crío era un perfecto querubín que incluso parecía sonreír de gratitud a medida que se adormecía.

Verity se inclinó hacia delante para frotar con un trapo la camisa de Cyn, disculpándose nuevamente.

—Le he debido poner nervioso —dijo—. Estoy segura de que por eso tenía retortijones. Normalmente es un niño muy bueno. —Volvió a sentarse—. Estoy bastante asustada…

Charles le cubrió la mano.

—Tranquila, cielo. Mira, ya estamos cerca de Salisbury y todavía no hemos visto ninguna señal de que nos busquen. Nos hemos agobiado sin motivo.

—Oh, eso espero.

—Pronto pararemos a almorzar. —Charles miró algo desafiante a Cyn, pero, cuando vio que no ponía ningún inconveniente, preguntó en tono más moderado—: ¿Cree que llegaremos a Basingtoke esta noche, milord?

—No, si no nos apuramos mucho —dijo Cyn—. La carretera no es nada buena y no veo razón para que nos apresuremos.

Las hermanas se miraron.

—Entonces, ¿hasta dónde llegaremos?

—La calzada entre Andover y Basingtoke es un lugar desolado, por el que no conviene viajar después de que oscurece. Hay una posada, White Hart, en Worting y otra en Whitchurch. Las dos están bien. Propongo que veamos hasta dónde podemos llegar sin tener que forzar la marcha.

—¿Cómo es que conoces tan bien esta carretera? —preguntó Charles con recelo.

—No hace muchos días que he pasado por aquí. Un viajero solitario no tiene más entretenimiento que el de ir mirando el mapa. —Sacó uno del bolsillo de su asiento y se lo tendió.

Ella lo estudió y encontró Salisbury.

—¿Venías desde Rothgar Abbey?

—Sí.

—¿Dónde está exactamente?

—Cerca de Farnham.

—Entonces, en Basingstoke nos salimos de tu ruta, ¿no?

—Sí.

—¿Llegaremos mañana a Maidenhead? —preguntó Verity.

—Eso depende de las calzadas. Mi propuesta es que vayamos en dirección norte hasta Basingstoke para coger la carretera de Bath en Reading, que es de peaje. Estará en mejor estado que ésta.

Para sorpresa de Cyn, las hermanas no parecían tener ganas de discutir. ¿Estaría Charles por fin ablandándose?

La calma que había seguido a la tempestad ablandaría a cualquiera.

Bajó la vista hacia el bebé, asombrado de lo agradable que era sostener a aquel chiquitín durmiente. Había visto con frecuencia a la hija de Hilda pero nunca, dada su condición de varón, se la habían confiado a su cuidado. Su suave y manejable peso, el ritmo constante de su respiración, los movimientos de succión que realizaba con sus carnosos labios mientras dormía: todo le cautivaba.

Y no se trataba de un niño perfecto. Tenía una roncha en la mejilla, tal vez causada por la manta mojada con sus lágrimas. Verity ya lo había cambiado en una ocasión, pero emanaba de él un olor agrio. Cyn no sabía quién era el padre, pero sospechaba que la criatura nunca haría fortuna valiéndose de su cara.

Detalles sin importancia: el bebé, que dormía dulce y confiadamente, le había llegado al corazón y le hizo pensar de nuevo en tener hijos propios…

—¡Alto!

La orden les cogió a todos desprevenidos. Charles llevó la mano en dirección a la funda de la pistola. Verity hizo ademán de recuperar a su retoño.

Cyn se aferró al bebé.

—Simulad inocencia, maldita sea.

Obviamente, aquello no era un intento de robo. Sólo podía tratarse de una patrulla militar. La puerta se abrió bruscamente. Cyn se volvió hacia ella con expresión atónita.

—¡Por favor! —dijo en un susurro—. El niño está durmiendo.

El joven oficial se quedó desconcertado. Después aguzó la vista. Cyn supo entonces que andaba a la caza de una madre y su hijo.

Una complicación añadida era el hecho de que Cyn conocía muy bien al teniente Toby Berrisford.

6

—Le pido disculpas, señora —dijo Toby sosegadamente, poniéndose colorado. Aquel estado iba muy bien con su piel clara y su cabello rojo, pero Cyn sabía que nunca permitía que interfiriera en el cumplimiento de su deber.

—Tengo órdenes de estar alerta ante el posible paso de una joven madre con un niño de dos meses. Debo preguntaros vuestra identidad.

—Soy Sarah Inchcliff —dijo Cyn en tono apacible—. La señora de Richard Inchcliff de Goole, Yorkshire. Le confieso, señor, que es cierto que mi bebé tiene poco más de dos meses, pero me halaga que me considere usted joven. —Sonrió a Toby provocativamente—. Ya no volveré a cumplir los treinta y éste es mi sexto hijo. ¿Por qué buscan a esos dos?

Toby miró ceñudo a Cyn pero con más desconcierto que recelo.

—La joven dama ha perdido el juicio a causa de la muerte de su esposo y ha huido con su hijo. Nos tememos que intente hacerle daño.

Verity emitió un minúsculo sonido.

—Vaya —dijo Cyn, rápidamente—, es terrible, ¿no? Pero, si ella está tan trastornada, ¿creen que viajará en un coche particular?

—Puede que la esté protegiendo alguna persona desencaminada, señora, y esa persona podría estar en peligro. ¿Quién sabe lo que es capaz de hacer una mujer que ha enloquecido? —Seguía con su ceñuda expresión—. Discúlpeme señora, pero ¿nos conocemos?

Cyn encaró a Toby sin inmutarse.

—Me parece que no, teniente, pero me dicen que me parezco mucho a mis primos. Mi nombre de soltera era Malloren.

El rostro del oficial se iluminó.

—¡Eso es! Tiene usted el mismo aspecto que lord Cyn, de veras.

—Eso es para mí un cumplido —dijo Cyn, y añadió con cierto descoco—: Él es demasiado atractivo.

—¿A que sí? —dijo Toby con una pícara sonrisa—. Y es un demonio con las mujeres. No hay ninguna que se le resista. Bueno, señora Inchcliff, le pido disculpas por interrumpir su viaje. Si se cruzan con esa pobre infeliz, den parte al magistrado local. El tutor del niño y el padre de la mujer se encuentran en la zona y se harán cargo de ellos.

A continuación, el teniente Berrisford cerró la puerta de golpe y William empezó a llorar. Cyn vio cómo su amigo se ruborizaba mientras se dirigía a toda prisa hacia su caballo. Después, le dio el bebé a Verity y, cuando el carruaje echó a rodar, agitó la mano con coquetería, saludando a los soldados.

Verity, con los ojos dilatados por el miedo, le daba el pecho nuevamente al bebé.

—¡Padre y Henry andan los dos por aquí! Santo cielo.

—Esos soldados no han sospechado nada —le tranquilizó Charles.

—Pero ¿y si nos encontramos a padre o a Henry en una posada? ¡No debemos parar en ninguna parte!

—Tenemos que parar —dijo Cyn con una calma deliberada que dejaba patente su autoridad—. Para empezar, Hoskins no puede conducir todo el día sin pausa. Para seguir, todos necesitamos comida y descanso. Además, si te pones nerviosa, William se disgustará de nuevo. —Le sostuvo la mirada hasta que ella se relajó un poco. Entonces, le sonrió. Ella le devolvió el gesto temblorosa y volvió a prestar atención a su niño.

Cyr observó a Charles, quien, indiscutiblemente, tenía una extraña expresión. Debía ser a causa de las palabras de Toby acerca del efecto que Cyn tenía sobre las mujeres. Se preguntó si aquello sería bueno o malo para lo que se proponía con su damisela.

—Me gustaría haberle preguntado a Toby dónde han establecido su cuartel general vuestros perseguidores.

—Entonces, ¿le conoces? —preguntó Charles.

—Y bastante bien, pero no nos hemos visto en los tres últimos años. No te preocupes. No lo descubrirá. Es verdad que tengo una prima que se llama Sarah Inchcliff que vive cerca de Goole.

Ella asintió y volvió a contemplar con adusta expresión el cambiante paisaje.

Por fortuna, el exhausto bebé volvió a conciliar el sueño. Cyr miró en torno a sí, buscando algo que hacer, y vio el ordenado montón de hojas de periódicos. Se trataba de las páginas con las que la señora Crupley había envuelto sus compras. Nana, con su espíritu austero, las había guardado y luego las había incluido en el equipaje por si podían serles de alguna utilidad.

Él las cogió y las alisó.

—Una mezcolanza prodigiosa. Tres hojas de la *Gazzete*, dos del *Morning Post* —cada una de una fecha diferente— y otra del *Grub Street Journal*. No sé si habrá alguna noticia interesante, pero ¿habéis oído hablar del último pasatiempo? Hay que leer las líneas a lo largo de la página y ver qué disparate sale. De vez en cuando, se descubre algún tesoro. Vamos a coger una hoja cada uno.

Al distribuir los periódicos, se dio cuenta de que Charles se había tensado cual si fuera un arco. ¿Qué es lo que podía resultarle alarmante ahora? La muchacha cogió su hoja, una de las del *Morning Post*, y lo primero que hizo fue mirar la fecha. Después, se relajó.

—Virgen santa —dijo—, son muy antiguas. Ésta es de 1759.

Así pues, pensó Cyn, en una más reciente podía haber alguna noticia reveladora. ¿Algo relativo a Verity, o a su propia damisela?

Cyn examinó su pliego.

—Aquí hay una. Va de las esquelas a las noticias de Gloucestershire: «Era una dama virtuosa conocida como… la mayor vaca lechera del condado».

Charles dijo:

—¡No me lo creo!

Cuando Cyn le enseñó la línea, admitió su triunfo y se aplicó al estudio minucioso de su propia hoja.

—Yo tengo una —dijo Verity—. Mirad. Discurre a lo largo de tres columnas: «Wentworth, el salteador de caminos… tras concebir un fuerte afecto… ha acrecentado la población».

—Es muy probable —dijo Cyn con una mueca—. Ese Wentworth arrastró tras de sí una procesión de llorosas mujeres cuando lo llevaron a la horca.

—Aquí tengo una —dijo Charles—. «Un niño de tres años... ha capturado un barco mercante al estilo pirata»... y si hago trampas y me voy dos líneas más abajo puedo añadir: «¡Mediante el juicioso uso de sales olorosas!».

—La Armada debería aprender ese truco —dijo Cyn, disfrutando al ver cómo se relajaba y se divertía su damisela. Podría dedicar toda su vida a la tarea de hacerla sonreír...

Desde luego que sí, aunque, si estuviera en su sano juicio, abandonaría el coche en la siguiente parada y se perdería en el bosque antes de volverse completamente loco.

Pronto se hallaron entrando en Salisbury y divisaron su alta torre.

—Deberíamos parar aquí, si es que es un sitio seguro —dijo Cyn—. Confieso, sin embargo, que si yo tuviera que establecer mi cuartel general en esta zona, elegiría Salisbury. Está en un punto bastante central y cualquiera que viaje desde el área de Shaftesbury hasta Londres o Maidenhead se ve abocado a pasar por aquí. Lo mejor será que hagamos primero algunas pesquisas.

Hoskins había entrado en el Black Horse, una ajetreada casa de postas. Aunque no era allí donde aguardaban los caballos de los Malloren. Cyn le dijo a voces que tal vez pararan allí y después se inclinó hacia fuera y trató de captar la atención de uno de los mozos de cuadra. Un chelín fue lo que atrajo la mirada del nervudo hombre.

—¿Qué desea su señoría?

—Parece que hay mucho jaleo hoy en el Black Horse —dijo Cyn—. ¿Podremos conseguir que nos den un saloncito privado?

—Esto no es nada para el Black Horse, señora —dijo él con presunción—. No tenga cuidado, encontrará habitaciones privadas. —Trató de hacerse con la moneda, pero Cyn la retiró.

—¿Es ésta la clase de posada donde se aloja la gente de alcurnia?

—Tenemos mucha gente importante que viene aquí con regularidad —dijo el hombre con orgullo—. El duque de Queensbury se hospeda aquí, y también el Conde de Portsmouth. Ah, y el gran conde de Walgrave —al que le llaman el Incorruptible— estuvo aquí anoche mismo, y hace sólo tres horas que se ha marchado. —Adoptó una expresión convenientemente sobria—. Está buscando a su pobre hija. La joven dama se ha vuelto loca y recorre el país completamente desnuda con su bebé muerto en brazos.

—Entonces, no será difícil encontrarla —dijo Cyn con sequedad y soltó la moneda. Tan pronto como el hombre se hubo marchado, volvió la vista hacia sus aprensivas acompañantes.

Así que su padre era el conde de Walgrave, uno de los grandes señores de aquella tierra, conocido por todos a causa de su riqueza, su poder y su rectitud casi puritana. No era de extrañar que hubiera dado el nombre de Verity a una hija suya.[2] Tal vez Charles no era Charlotte sino Constance.

Entonces, ¿por qué las hermanas no buscaban la ayuda de aquel dechado de virtudes?

Aquel nuevo elemento, sin embargo, hacía que su empresa le resultara muchísimo más interesante. El conde de Walgrave podría movilizar sin dificultad a las autoridades —ejército incluido— para tratar de encontrar a su hija. Cyn

---

2. Chastity significa castidad. Verity, por otra parte, significa veracidad.

no pudo menos que poner en duda que la boda de Verity con su mayor pudiera poner fin a todo el problema. Se podía destruir a un oficial con mucho menos motivo. La propia carrera de Cyn estaría en peligro si su participación se llegaba a descubrir.

Había algo más, algún otro detalle que tenía que ver con Walgrave. Pero ese algo rondaba en las profundidades de la memoria de Cyn y se negaba a salir a la superficie.

Se encogió de hombros. La suerte estaba echada, y él nunca había abandonado ninguna empresa a causa del posible peligro. Dedicó una sonrisa a sus compinches:

—Por lo menos, hace mucho que el tipo se ha marchado. *En avant, mes enfants.*

El mozo de cuadra estaba en lo cierto. Aunque la posada parecía atetreada, todavía quedaban buenas habitaciones privadas. Cyn cogió una alcoba, además de un saloncito.

Tan pronto como estuvieron a solas, Verity dijo:

—Teníamos que habértelo dicho. Lo siento.

—Me hubiera dado igual. Pero tenéis un adversario colosal, si es que es vuestro adversario.

—Sí que lo es, y ahora irá de camino a la cabaña y pronto averiguará parte de la verdad. Sólo le pido a Dios que Nana sea capaz de no desvelar tu papel en esta trama, señor. No me gustaría que tuvieras a mi padre por enemigo.

Cyn echó una ojeada a Charles. Tenía pinta de estar angustiada y perturbada, pero él ya no tenía necesidad de preguntarse a quién temería. Deseó saber más cosas. Desde luego, el conde no podía estar muy contento con una hija a la que le gustaba hacer de hombre, pero ¿era ése el resumen de todos sus pecados?

Cyn le hizo una pregunta directa a Verity:

—El conde de Walgrave podría protegeros a ti y a William de Henry *el Terrible*. ¿Por qué huís de él?

Verity se mordió el labio.

—Es cierto. Tal vez debiera acudir a él..., no puedo hacer que William corra ningún riesgo..

—Bobadas —dijo Charles en tono tajante—. Padre ha partido en la dirección equivocada y, cuando se dé la vuelta, seguirá sin saber a quién está buscando. Henry V... Henry *el Terrible* sabe todavía menos. Antes de que padre pueda inmiscuirse, te habremos llevado hasta Nathaniel. —Se volvió hacia Cyn—. Padre ya impidió una vez a Verity que se casara con Nathaniel y volvería a hacerlo de nuevo.

—Ah, y en lugar de ello, ¿con quién hizo que te casaras? —Como ellas dudaban, él añadió—: El conocimiento es poder, y creo que nosotros necesitamos todo el poder que podamos conseguir.

—Con William Vernham —dijo Verity—. Su hermano es Henry Vernham.

—Nunca he oído hablar de ellos —contestó Cyn, con la arrogancia propia de la alta nobleza y muy sorprendido—. ¿Cómo es que este caballero resultó ser más idóneo que tu mayor?

Las hermanas se miraron durante un fugaz instante.

—No lo sabemos —dijo Verity.

—¿Era rico?

—Bastante, pero no creo que a padre le importara eso. Él posee una enorme fortuna. Lo que ansía es influencia política. Aspira a controlar las altas esferas de poder. Cree que él es el único que posee las cualidades necesarias para conducir a la nación hacia la gloria.

—¿Y sir William poseía esa influencia política?

—No. —Por primera vez, Verity perdió la paciencia—. No me atosigues más. No es que yo me resista. Mi matrimonio tenía importancia para mi padre, pero yo nunca le encontré ningún sentido. Lo mismo que al de...

Cyn captó el cruce de miradas entre las hermanas y se dio cuenta de que ocultaban algo, algo que tenía que ver con su damisela. Decidió dejar el tema, aunque se hacía muchas preguntas respecto a aquel fascinante enigma.

Dedicó a Verity una reconfortante sonrisa y le dijo:

—No te preocupes por tu padre. Como dice Charles, está corriendo en la dirección equivocada. Eres mayor de edad y tienes derecho a casarte con quien quieras. Parece que ahora mismo estamos a salvo, así que ¿por qué no vas a atender al joven William?

Verity entró en la alcoba, con los ánimos renovados por aquel repentino alarde de confianza. Cyn se quitó el bonete y se sirvió un vaso de vino.

—¿Te pongo a ti, Charles? —preguntó.

Ella estaba de pie junto a la ventana, contemplando la calle. Al oír aquellas palabras se volvió.

—No gracias.

De todos modos, él vertió una pequeña cantidad de vino dentro de su vaso. Cómo ella le dirigió una mirada interrogante, Cyn comentó:

—Pretendo dar al traste, si no con toda, al menos con la mitad de esta botella. Tendrá que parecer que tú te has bebido tu parte.

—¿Piensas en todo, no?

—¿Te parece eso admirable? Mi querido Charles, en condiciones normales, soy un oficial que tiene a su cargo las vidas de numerosos hombres. No puedo permitirme ser descuidado.

Chastity levantó la barbilla ante aquel reproche antes de apartar la vista.

—Crees que soy un chiquillo.

—No —dijo con suavidad—. Creo que eres muy valiente, teniendo en cuenta tus circunstancias. Me gustaría que confiaras en mí y me consideraras tu amigo.

Ella le sostuvo de nuevo la mirada, y él vislumbró en sus ojos una minúscula señal de ablandamiento.

—Tú no sabes nada nada en absoluto de mis circunstancias.

No estaba seguro de cómo debía conducirse, pero, obviamente, se trataba de un momento crucial.

—Deduzco que tu padre y tú no tenéis una relación muy estrecha.

Ella se rió estrepitosamente.

—No, no la tenemos.

Cyn se sentó y trató de sonar relajado.

—Yo tampoco la tenía con el mío, pero le admiraba. ¿Qué es lo que sientes hacia el conde?

Vio cómo la tensión se apoderaba de ella.

—¡Eso no es asunto tuyo!

Aquello era miedo. Podía olerlo. Estaba familiarizado con los diversos regustos del miedo. ¿Qué era lo que Walgrave le había hecho?

Antes de que pudiera continuar con su interrogatorio, los criados trajeron la comida y la dispusieron sobre la mesa. Una vez que se hubieron marchado, Verity volvió a reunirse con ellos. El tiempo para despojar a su damisela de las capas que cubrían su alma había llegado a su fin. Todos se dedicaron a comer, aunque hizo falta animar a Verity para que consumiera suficiente alimento.

—Padre nos reconocería con un simple vistazo —dijo angustiada, mientras esparcía los fragmentos de la empanada de carne por su plato.

Cyn le cubrió las inquietas manos con las suyas

—La gente normalmente ve lo que cree ver. Pon una expresión desgarbada y estúpida y, con la ropa que llevas ahora, puedes cruzarte con tu padre por la calle y no te reconocería.

Verity se sintió sólo un poco reconfortada.

—Tal vez debiéramos escondernos aquí y escribirle una carta a Nathaniel.

—No lo creo conveniente —dijo Cyn—. Comprobarán periódicamente las posadas y, por lo que decía Toby, sospecho que tu padre y Henry *el Terrible* han hecho circular un bonito cuento. Puesto que el conde sabe todo lo relativo al mayor Frazer, sin duda también le habrá contado a él la historia. Y él podría creerle.

—¡Jamás! —exclamó Verity.

—No podemos arriesgarnos. Tan pronto como tu mayor te vea, sabrá la verdad.

—Pero padre tendrá alguien vigilando continuamente Maidenhead y a Nathaniel —dijo Charles.

—Sí pero ya pensaremos algo. En eso —dijo Cyn con una sonrisa—, yo soy vuestra mejor baza. El conde estará esperando que Verity trate de entrar a hurtadillas a los aposentos del mayor, pero el capitán lord Cynric Malloren puede toparse con el mayor Nathaniel Frazer por la calle sin despertar ninguna sospecha. Sólo tendré que volver a adquirir mi verdadera personalidad. Mi uniforme, que está en el equipaje, le dará a todo el asunto un aire más solemne.

Ambas se quedaron pasmadas ante aquella incontestable solución. Cyn miró a Verity.

—¿Por qué no te echas y descansas durante una hora? No sería sensato tratar de llegar hoy hasta Basingstoke, así que tenemos mucho tiempo.

Con una lánguida sonrisa, ella se fue a la otra habitación.

Cyn observó a Charles. Le pareció que era consciente de que él había arreglado deliberadamente las cosas para quedarse a solas con ella. En su interior, había un conflicto entre las intenciones nobles y los deseos carnales. Quería averiguar la verdad para poder ayudarla. También quería explorarla en cuerpo y alma, desmantelar sus reservas y hacerle el amor hasta que no quedara ninguna barrera entre los dos. En ocasiones como aquella, deseaba que ella llevara faldas y que estuviera segura detrás de la barrera de la decencia.

¡Cristo! De repente cayó en la cuenta de que el objeto de sus lujuriosas fantasías era la hija de uno de los hombres más importantes del país. ¿Qué demonios hacía la hija del conde de Walgrave viviendo en una cabaña y llevando pantalones?

Cyn le llenó el vaso de vino, con la esperanza de que le desatara la lengua.

—¿Qué haremos para pasar el rato, Charles? —preguntó—. ¿Jugar a las cartas? ¿Contar aventuras de guerra? ¿O historias de burdel?

Ella encajó bien la pregunta.

—Como ya sabes, no puedo compartir contigo esas materias.

—¿Ni siquiera las cartas?

—Nunca he jugado por más que unos pocos peniques.

—Entonces ya tenemos algo en común. Yo no suelo hacer apuestas altas.

Aquello captó la atención de Chastity.

—¿De verdad? Todo el mundo lo hace.

—A mí no me divierte. No me hace gracia tener que dar a otras personas mi dinero y tampoco quedarme con el suyo, en especial si eso les va a causar problemas.

Ella se relajó y bebió del vaso. Aquel gesto indicaba la existencia de una tregua, pero, antes de que él pudiera sacar partido de su ventaja, la muchacha se le adelantó.

—Entonces, háblame de tus aventuras. Me refiero a las del ejército —puntualizó con sarcasmo—. ¿Dónde has prestado servicios?

—Sobre todo en las Américas y en las guerras de Francia e India.

Los ojos de ella se iluminaron.

—¿Has conocido al general Wolfe?

—Sí. —La miró burlonamente—. ¿Es tu ídolo? Era un hombre con un carácter muy difícil, pero un soldado excepcional.

—Creo que tenía una salud muy precaria —protestó ella en su defensa.

—Cierto.

—¿Estuviste en Quebec?

—Sí y también en Louisbourg, que es, te lo aseguro, uno de los lugares más remotos del planeta. Creo que a los soldados franceses no les importó mucho perderlo.

—¿Qué batalla fue la peor?

—Ninguna —dijo él con una mueca—. Ganamos las dos.

—Pero hubo gran cantidad de muertos y heridos.

—«La sangre es el dios al que sirven las suntuosas galas de la guerra» —dijo él, repitiendo una cita. Y como ella se quedara perpleja, añadió—: Marlowe.

—Te gusta la vida de soldado —dijo ella con sorpresa.

—Si no me gustara me dedicaría a otra cosa.

—Pensé que al ser hombre y de la familia Malloren...
Él hizo girar el vino de su vaso.

—Tú también eres de buena familia, y pronto serás un hombre. Tal vez debieras alistarte también en el ejército.

A Chastity le resultaba muy chocante tener aquella conversación con alguien que tenía la apariencia de una verdadera dama y que estaba dando buena cuenta de una alarmante cantidad de vino. Lord Cynric Malloren tenía la rara habilidad de embrollarle las ideas. Había que admitir, sin embargo, que, en aquella extraña situación, cualquiera se haría un lío.

—Me parece que no me gusta la sangre —dijo ella.

—Te asombrarías de lo que somos capaces cuando nos ponen a prueba.

—Me resulta difícil imaginarte como alguien peligroso.
Él levantó la vista desde debajo de aquellas ridículas pestañas y sonrió.

—Ponme a prueba y verás.

El vino le estaba afectando. Chastity lo vio en sus ojos y aquello la asustó. Todos los temores que le habían asaltado aquella mañana se apoderaron de ella de nuevo. Se puso de pie de un salto.

—Creo que voy a darme una vuelta por el pueblo.

Y antes de que Cyn pudiera detenerla ya se había marchado. Él maldijo aquella lentitud de reflejos que la bebida le había provocado. Ella no debía haber salido. Ni siquiera había cogido la peluca y el sombrero. Ir por ahí con la cabeza rapada ya era bastante llamativo. Él había tenido la culpa. La conversación había sido en principio inocente pero, como le ocurría siempre que estaban juntos, ciertos pensamientos impúdicos se habían adueñado de él. Ella se había dado cuenta y había huido.

Si la perseguía precipitadamente, sólo conseguiría empeorar las cosas. Llamaría la atención sobre ambos. Se puso su infame tocado y su sombrero, y fue a echar un vistazo a Verity. Ella y el bebé estaban dormidos. Entonces, cogió la peluca y el tricornio de Charles, se los metió en el manguito y salió. Se acordó de dar pasos pequeños y de mantener la cabeza recatadamente baja. Al principio, lo de fingir que era una mujer había sido novedoso y divertido. Pero se estaba convirtiendo rápidamente en un aburrimiento supino.

En el recibidor de la posada, un corpulento caballero le saludó quitándose el sombrero y le miró disimuladamente el pecho. A Cyn le dieron ganas de soltarle una bofetada.

La calle principal de Salisbury era amplia y abierta, pero no se veía ni rastro de la chica. Cyn se detuvo a charlar con una mujer que vendía castañas.

—¿Ha visto usted pasar por aquí a un joven con la cabeza descubierta?

La mujer curvó el pulgar con elocuencia.

—Se fue hacía el río, encanto.

Cyn se metió por el callejón señalado. Se encontró dentro de una maraña de caminos tortuosos separados por cabañas, huertos y establos. Por detrás de los muros de tres jardines, que se elevaban hasta la altura de los hombros, vislumbró a Charles. Tras ella se hallaba el río Devon.

Partió en aquella dirección, pero aquella barriada era un auténtico laberinto y las calles pronto le alejaron de su presa. Él siguió sumergiéndose en ellas, decidido a hacer que Charles regresara al saloncito antes de que se encontrara con alguien conocido. De pronto, se percató de la cara de asombro del trabajador de un almacén de cereales y se dio cuenta de que estaba avanzando a grandes zancadas. Murmurando un juramento, empezó nuevamente a conducirse con afectación.

Pocos instantes después, su senda giraba siguiendo el curso de unas parcelas y pudo ver con claridad a Charles, que se hallaba de pie en la orilla del río arrojando hojas muertas al agua. Su aire triste y retraído le cautivó. Su mayor deseo era poder consolarla y protegerla. Ella se alejó caminando hasta que se perdió de vista. Tenía que conseguir que confiara en él y le contara sus problemas.

Unas voces que se acercaban le sacaron precipitadamente de sus pensamientos.

—Te digo que he visto a esa golfa —dijo alguien cuya pronunciación era refinada. Cyn se deslizó inmediatamente a través de la puerta de un jardín, para no ser visto.

—Ésta no es la hermana que buscamos, señor. —El que hablaba era de clase baja y, según supuso Cyn, londinense.

—Pardiez, no tiene sentido que la una esté aquí si no está la otra. Desde que cometió semejante infamia es prácticamente una prisionera. —Cyn pensó que quien así opinaba podía ser Henry Vernham.

¿Qué infamia?

Parecía que los dos hombres se habían detenido por allí cerca.

—Pero ya registramos la cabaña hace dos días, señor, y no encontramos ni rastro de lady Verity.

—Una de dos, o estaban mintiendo o mi cuñada todavía no había llegado. —Definitivamente, se trataba de Henry Vernham—. No se la ve por ningún lado. Pero yo he visto a esa rapaza caminando en dirección al río. Vete por allí que yo iré por aquí. Con un poco de suerte la atraparemos sin armar jaleo. No quiero que se organice ningún alboroto. Una vez que la tengamos a ella, tendremos también a lady Verity.

Cyn repasó sus opciones con toda la claridad mental que le asistía en las batallas: con la rapidez del rayo y la agudeza de un estoque. Al mismo tiempo, registraba la conversación.

—¿Cómo la reconoceré, señor? —gimoteó el criado—. ¿Se parece al retrato de lady Verity?

—En absoluto. Es un osado ejemplar de la especie femenina, una hembra llena de arrogancia. Por lo menos antes. —Henry Vernham soltó una risita—. Pero no tendrás problemas para reconocerla: no tiene pelo.

—¿No tiene pelo, señor?

—Eso he dicho. Su padre se lo rapó cuando la pilló *in flagrante delicto*.

La atención de Cyn se dividió.

¡Rapada!

¿In flagrante delicto?

¿Con quién la habían cogido? Y, ¿por qué, en nombre de Dios, aquel hombre no había permanecido a su lado? Su mano trató de agarrar la espada. Pero no había espada. Aquello le devolvió violentamente la conciencia de su disfraz y de su propósito.

—… sólo la he visto del torso para arriba —decía Vernham—. Lleva indumentaria de hombre, ropa de montar o algo así. Pero su cabello es inconfundible. Parece un auténtico bicho raro. Walgrave pensó que así permanecería recluida donde él quería, lo mismo que si estuviera entre rejas. Además sólo le permitió quedarse con un mísero vestuario.

Ninguna mujer verdadera asomaría su cabeza por la puerta con semejante aspecto.

Cyn se dio cuenta de que había cerrado los puños y que no deseaba otra cosa que saltar la valla y zurrar a Henry *el Terrible* hasta dejarlo sangrando en carne viva, a causa de la presuntuosa satisfacción que captó en su voz.

En cambio, tan pronto como los dos hombres se marcharon, lo que hizo fue sujetarse las malditas faldas y atravesar la removida tierra del jardín hasta llegar al siguiente muro.

No había verja y descubrió que saltar una tapia con aquellas pesadas faldas presentaba algunos problemas. Oyó que algo se rasgaba, pero hizo caso omiso de ello. Tal y como había esperado, el siguiente huerto tenía una cancela que daba a un prado junto al río. Casi la había atravesado cuando oyó que una mujer gritaba:

—¡Eh!

Cyn se dio la vuelta y vio a una fornida ama de casa mirándole con furia, con los brazos en jarras. Él fingió tener miedo.

—¡Oh, por favor señora! Mis hermanos…

La mujer se le quedó mirando boquiabierta. Cyn le puso rápidamente una moneda de seis peniques en la mano.

—Dios la bendiga, señora —murmuró y, después, cruzó corriendo la verja. Un rápido vistazo le indicó que sus perseguidores no estaban por allí. Se recogió las faldas y se lanzó a la carrera hacia donde estaba Charles. Junto a ella, había un rústico banco.

Agarró a la muchacha y le dijo entre jadeos:

—¡Henry *el Terrible*!

La arrastró hasta el banco, se arrojó sobre él y, de un tirón, hizo que ella quedara sentada en su regazo.

Entonces la besó.

Se limitó a apretar los labios contra los de ella, pero la muchacha se puso rígida como una tabla. Por lo menos no se resistió. Cyn tuvo tiempo de embutirle la peluca y el sombrero. Nadie se sorprendería de verlos enroscados en aquella situación. Por encima del hombro de Charles, Cyn estaba al acecho de sus perseguidores.

Un hombre de rostro cetrino y nervudo salió de un callejón al mismo tiempo que otro apuesto y con clase salía por el otro. Ambos miraron hacia los lados y, después, en dirección a ellos.

Cyn concentró su atención en su damisela. Colocó su enorme manguito sobre la espalda de ésta, de modo que le cubriera parte de la cabeza. Después se dedicó a la tarea de besarla. En su conciencia se encendió una señal de alarma, pero él la silenció fácilmente. Después de todo, aquélla podía ser su única oportunidad.

Ella trató de mantener los labios apretados, pero, a medida que él le aplicaba los suyos, se le volvían dulces y tiernos. Cyn trataba de ser delicado, aunque el sabor de ella se le metió dentro y actuó como un afrodisíaco.

Vio cómo la muchacha cerraba los ojos y sintió su respuesta, los sutiles movimientos de su cuerpo contra la largura que surgía de él, aferrada a sus hombros con las manos. Él la estrechó contra sí aún más, hundiéndose en el goce de causarle placer a ella.

Cyn anhelaba explorar su boca, pero sabía que encontraría resistencia, entre otras cosas porque ella pensaba que la tenía por un hombre. Tal vez se acordó de ello entonces. Porque gimoteó y se puso tensa. El deleite de Cyn se esfumó. Se sintió un sinvergüenza por aprovecharse así. Cuando oyó que alguien se aclaraba la garganta, se sintió aliviado al poder interrumpir el beso.

La figura de Henry *el Terrible* se alzaba frente a ellos.

Cyn soltó un alarido y apretó con firmeza el rostro de Charles contra su pecho.

—¡Adrian! ¡Nos han descubierto! No, mi querido chiquillo, quédate tranquilo entre mis brazos. No van a hacerte ningún daño. —Atravesó a Henry Vernham con lo que esperaba que fuera una mirada trágicamente intensa y declaró:

—¡Sólo la muerte podrá separarnos señor!

—¡Pardiez, mujer! No tenemos ningún interés ni en usted ni en su amante. ¿Ha pasado por aquí una joven? ¿Una muchacha con el pelo muy corto?

Cyn calibró a su enemigo. Era alto y moreno. Podía resultar apuesto a primera vista. Tenía los ojos estrechos pero vivos. Cyn estuvo tentado de despistarlo, mandándole en cualquier dirección, pero se limitó a decir con una sonrisa tonta:

—Estoy segura de que, en estos últimos minutos, aunque hubiera pasado el rey, yo no lo habría visto. ¿Decís la verdad? ¿No os han enviado para arrancar a Adrian de mis brazos?

La única respuesta de Henry Vernham fue una mueca que expresaba repugnancia. Se dio la vuelta y echó a andar con brío hacia el centro de la población. El otro hombre miró maliciosamente a los «amantes» y le siguió los pasos. Cyn apretó contra sí a su damisela hasta que los dos desaparecieron.

Dejó que el contacto con ella le envolviera y se le metiera dentro. Sus terminaciones nerviosas y su alma le decían que podría hacerle el amor a aquella mujer de manera sublime. Podía verse en la forma que ella había adoptado al apretarse contra él y acurrucarse bajo sus manos. Y también en el recuerdo que el sabor de ella le había dejado en los labios. Se percibía en el tenue aroma de su cuerpo, un aroma más potente que el mejor perfume francés.

Le pareció que podía sentir el ligero abultamiento de sus pechos vendados contra su torso cuando ella respiraba. El muslo de su damisela había ido a descansar entre los suyos, lo que suponía una fuente de deliciosa tortura. Movido por un irreprimible impulso, le pasó una mano entre la peluca y la cabeza, para sentir la sedosa suavidad de su cabello.

Ella se estremeció de pies a cabeza.

Cyn recordó lo que Henry había dicho. Walgrave la había rapado y la había obligado a llevar aquellos toscos vestidos de penitente porque la había pillado en la cama de un hombre. No le extrañaba que prefiriera llevar ropa de hombre. Pero eso significaba que la chica no era virgen.

Aquello no le gustó. A pesar de los sentimientos voluptuosos que tenía hacia ella, no quería que fuera una fresca.

—¿Se han ido? —preguntó ella en voz baja.

Cyn se dio cuenta de que le estaba acariciando suavemente la nuca, ofreciéndole consuelo en lugar de lujuria. Su instinto le decía que en el fondo era inocente. Debían haberla sorprendido en su primer desliz. Sin duda, debía de haberse dejado llevar por el amor.

Entonces, ¿qué había sido de su amante?

De mala gana, de muy mala gana, la soltó. Ella se puso de pie un tanto aturdida, sin mirarle para nada, y se enderezó la peluca y el sombrero.

—¿A qué ha venido todo esto?

—Les oí decir que te iban a atrapar. Vernham te había visto. Me pareció que tendrías una oportunidad si te convertías en el joven Adrian. Y parece que ha funcionado. —Sobre todo porque lo que andaban buscando era una mujer, pensó él, pero no dijo nada. Tuvo la impresión de que se estaba haciendo necesario poner fin a aquella mascarada si no querían que su empresa peligrara.

—Lo mejor será que recojamos a Verity y nos vayamos —dijo ella.

—Sí, pero con cautela. ¿Hasta que punto te conoce Henry?

El abatimiento se apoderó del rostro de Chastity.

—Me conoce muy bien.

Cyn estuvo a punto de preguntar ¿Ha estado en tu cama?

—Si te ve bien, no se dejará engañar. —Cyn le subió el sencillo cuello todo lo que pudo y le caló un poco más el sombrero. El tricornio, sin embargo, no era lo más indicado para ocultar el rostro.

—Lo mejor será que vayamos del brazo —dijo Cyn—, y hablando. Así tus rasgos quedarán un poco escondidos.

Ella hizo algún remilgo pero accedió. Caminaron tan deprisa como se atrevieron, haciendo el camino de vuelta a la posada con las cabezas agachadas, como si estuvieran compartiendo algún secreto. Cyn vio al criado de Henry merodeando por la calle mayor, pero no había ni rastro del propio Henry. Eso tal vez no fuera un hecho tan halagüeño: podía hallarse registrando la fonda.

El corazón de Cyn latía con fuerza. Pero no a causa del miedo sino de la excitación. Eso era lo que había echado de menos durante aquellos tediosos meses de convalecencia: el límite del peligro, la inminencia de la acción.

Llegaron sanos y salvos a su saloncito, y él se echó a reír alborozado.

—¡Basta! —dijo Charles—. Esto no es un juego, idiota. ¡Se trata de la vida de mi hermana y de mi sobrino!

Él lo intentó, pero sabía que no podría serenarse del todo.

—¿Y no los estoy protegiendo? Además, no nos habríamos metido en este lío —señaló él—, si no hubieras salido en estampida sin motivo alguno.

Ella levantó la barbilla.

—Muy bien, acepto la responsabilidad. Ahora tenemos que irnos.

—Tal vez. —Cyn fue a mirar por la ventana, aunque la vista de la calle mayor no era especialmente iluminadora. Una panorámica del patio de los carruajes sería más útil—. Aunque quizá fuera conveniente esperar hasta que Henry se marchara.

—Puede que establezca su cuartel general en Salisbury —replicó ella—. Y que, cuando no me encuentre, decida peinar la fonda milímetro a milímetro.

Cyn la observó con un renovado respeto.

—Me encanta tener un compañero con las ideas claras. Despierta a Verity. Proseguiremos con la comedia de Adrian y su amante, y simularemos que nos damos a la fuga, sintiéndonos culpables.

Al oír aquello, se puso colorada pero fue hacia la puerta de la alcoba. Se detuvo con la mano sobre el pomo.

—¿Cómo has podido hacerlo…? —preguntó muy rígida, sin volverse para mirarlo—. Un hombre besando a otro hombre…

—Ha sido un simple beso, mi querido muchacho —dijo Cyn con ligereza—. Los hombres continentales se besan con mayor libertad que nosotros los británicos. Además, ¿no has descubierto que siempre hay un cierto grado de experimentación en los colegios de chicos? No te preocupes. Hace mucho que decidí que la sodomía era un vicio que no iba conmigo.

Las sonrosadas mejillas de Chastity se volvieron encarnadas, y ella entró a toda prisa en el dormitorio.

7

Chastity cerró suavemente la puerta y se apoyó contra ella.
Verity y el bebé dormían y no se sentía con ánimo de des-
pertarlos. O tal vez fuera que necesitaba unos instantes para
pensar.

Se dirigió al tocador, se quitó la peluca y el sombrero, y
contempló el espejo móvil de cuerpo entero. Últimamente,
no se miraba mucho, porque hacerlo le recordaba el pasado
y todo lo que su padre le había hecho.

Al principio, cuando su pelo apenas asomaba, había evi-
tado los espejos y se había puesto voluntariamente aquellos
feos tocados. A medida que fue creciendo, aprendió a aceptar su imagen. Todo resultó más sencillo desde que se le ocurrió llevar la ropa vieja de su hermano Victor. Podía pasar
por un apuesto muchacho.

Su padre había hecho sacar de Walgrave Towers toda la
vestimenta de Verity y Chastity, para que esta última no pudiera usarla, pero no había pensado en las prendas de Victor
y de Fort. La ropa de Fort era demasiado grande, porque su
hermano mayor, lord Thornhill, tenía veintiocho años y era
un hombre corpulento. Victor, sin embargo, era un chico esbelto de dieciocho. Su vieja indumentaria había necesitado
únicamente pequeñas alteraciones.

Pero ella aborrecía aquella indumentaria.

Suspiraba por volver a llevar otra vez vestidos de seda, con sus aros, y aquellas bellas y poco prácticas chinelas de satén. Quería tener unos largos y brillantes rizos que le rozaran los hombros, un lunar postizo junto a la boca y un abanico. Cogió el peine de Verity e imaginó que era un abanico. Lo extendió cerrado. ¿Me quieres? Hizo como que lo abría y lo cerraba. Eres cruel. Se lo llevó a los labios. Puedes besarme. Se lo pasó despacio por la mejilla. Te quiero, lord Cyn.

Dejó caer el abanico. ¡No, eso no! ¿Cómo podía haber llegado a sentir eso hacia Cyn Malloren cuando pensaba que nunca más iba a volver a confiar en un hombre? Tal vez había sido la expresión de su rostro al sostener a William. O su amabilidad hacia Verity. O su amabilidad hacia el arisco Charles.

Tal vez fuera su espíritu alegre, el puro deleite con el que encaraba la vida, su gusto por los retos...

Se apartó del espejo, tratando de combatir aquella locura. No había tiempo para la fantasía en aquellos momentos de peligro. Además, en cualquier caso, no quería que le rompieran el corazón. Si le daba a conocer que era una mujer, sería un bicho raro con el pelo rapado. Probablemente tendría que contarle que ella era esa furcia, Chastity Ware. Incluso si llegaba a interesarse por ella, sería sólo para darse un rápido revolcón en la cama más cercana.

Dios, debía tener alma de ramera, porque aquella idea imposible había hecho que la recorriera un hormigueo de deseo.

Todo era culpa de aquel beso fingido.

Nunca le habían interesado demasiado los besos. Cuando Henry Vernham le había dado un beso a la fuerza, había sentido nauseas. Se lo había dicho a su padre, esperando que

Vernham fuera castigado por ello, pero Walgrave le había dicho que no fuera tan remilgada con su futuro esposo. La siguiente vez que Henry Vernham lo había intentado, Chastity le había clavado sus tijeras de bordar.

Aquel recuerdo puso una torva sonrisa de satisfacción en su rostro. Como castigo, ella había tenido que soportar la heladora cólera de su padre, pero Henry Vernham no había vuelto a agredirla de aquella manera.

Chastity tenía que admitir, sin embargo, que, mientras la besaba Cyn Malloren, no había sentido ganas de luchar. Precisamente lo contrario. Su beso le había hecho sentirse cálida y tierna, y había deseado hacerlo más profundo para poder seguir explorando al hombre.

Se apretó las manos contra la cara. Incluso si él, milagrosamente sentía algo por Chastity, y lo seguía sintiendo cuando supiera la verdad, ella no podía dejar que ocurriera nada entre ambos, porque aquello destrozaría a Cyn. Jamás encontrarían la felicidad entre las burlas y el escándalo y, peor aún, él no toleraría que la insultaran. Tarde o temprano la cosa terminaría en un duelo. Ella sería la causa de su muerte.

Chastity había tomado una severa decisión. Tenía que dejar de lado sus sentimientos y concentrarse en su propósito, llevar a Verity y a William sanos y salvos a Maidenhead. Después, dejaría que Cyn Malloren siguiera su camino libre de trabas.

Suavemente, despertó a su hermana y le explicó el problema. Aplacó sus temores y le ayudó a preparar al bebé. Le sonrió para darle ánimos.

—¿Estás lista? No te preocupes. Estaremos fuera de aquí en un abrir y cerrar de ojos, y Henry pensará que se ha confundido cuando ha creído verme.

Verity trató gallardamente de devolver la sonrisa, y ambas salieron a reunirse con lord Cyn.

—¿Preparadas? —preguntó él. Como ellas asintieron él añadió—: El carruaje está esperando y yo le he contado a una criada chismosa la historia de mi fuga romántica con mi joven amante. —Hizo aletear las pestañas—. Creo que le he dado envidia, una gallina vieja con un gallo tan tierno. ¡Así que, agachad las cabezas y en marcha! Vayamos derechos al coche.

Bajaron apresuradamente las escaleras. Cuando cruzaban el recibidor en dirección al patio de los carruajes, Cyn dijo:

—Seguid adelante. Yo voy enseguida.

Chastity se preguntó con desasosiego qué es lo que estaría tramando, pero aquél no era el momento de ponerse a discutir. Condujo a Verity hasta el vehículo que les estaba aguardando. Desde su interior, se dedicó a vigilar ansiosamente la llegada de Cyn.

Escondió la cabeza cuando vio que Henry Vernham se acercaba a la posada. Por la esquina de la ventana vio salir a Cyn y tuvo ganas de gritar para advertirle. Cyn se detuvo. Vernham también.

Cyn hizo una perfecta representación de una mujer que se sentía culpable y estaba aterrorizada. Se echó hacia atrás, se medio tapó la cara con el periódico que tenía en la mano y, después, pasó corriendo junto a Vernham y se metió en el coche. Vernham hizo una mueca burlona a su paso y siguió caminando hacia el interior de la fonda.

Cyn se instaló en su asiento, un mozo de cuadra cerró la puerta de golpe, Hoskins hizo restallar el látigo y el coche salió por la calle mayor.

Verity estaba apretujada en una esquina, agarrando a William con excesiva fuerza.

—¿Me ha visto?

—Por supuesto que no —dijo Cyn, arrojando el periódico arrugado sobre el asiento de Chastity—. Y ya nos hemos largado.

—¡Pero nos perseguirá!

—¿Por qué? Él cree haber visto a Charles, y eso le hace pensar que tú también estás en la zona. Preguntará en todas las posadas de Salisbury pero no encontrará ni rastro de Charles ni de nadie que encaje en tu descripción.

—Pero —dijo Chastity—, ¿qué pasará si se le ocurre preguntar por un bebé?

—Buena pregunta —dijo Cyn con una viva mirada de apreciación—. Si sigue esa pista pronto descubrirá que la licenciosa mujer del prado tiene un bebe de la edad adecuada. Podría sumar dos y dos. —Miró a Verity—. ¿Es muy listo este hombre?

—No es ningún tonto. Es un despilfarrador egocéntrico, pero, cuando le interesa, puede ser muy astuto.

Cyn abrió la trampilla.

—Aprisa, Hoskins.

El vehículo traqueteó y salió disparado cuando los caballos emprendieron el galope.

Verity estaba blanca como la leche.

—¡No podremos escapar! Si nos cogen, lord Cyn, prométeme que harás todo lo que esté en tu mano para que no atrapen a William.

—Claro que nos escaparemos—dijo él con firmeza—, pero te prometo que no le ocurrirá nada a tu niño. —Puso su mano sobre la de Verity y la miró a los ojos—. Confía en mí.

Chastity sintió un dolor en el pecho, un verdadero dolor físico. Deseó que Cyn la mirara de esa manera tan directa y que le prometiera que cuidaría de ella. Oh, se hallaba en un estado lamentable.

Recordó cómo él le había explicado que en su trabajo como oficial era responsable de las vidas de muchos hombres. Se dio cuenta de que debía hacerlo bien. Podía ser frívolo en el momento oportuno y tratar de tomarse las cosas con humor pero, bajo aquella superficie, siempre se escondería el aplomo del coraje y la eficiencia.

Se recordó a sí misma que había tomado una decisión, pero la toma de conciencia de sus sentimientos la había cogido desprevenida y no podía dejar de observarlo y de asimilar cada detalle...

Apartó la vista y la dirigió al periódico que él había arrojado sobre el asiento libre que había junto a ella. Se sobresaltó. Cyn se había demorado para comprar un ejemplar reciente de la *Gazzette*. La página frontal estaba doblada hacía atrás y Chastity pudo leer el titular de uno de los artículos. Desaparecidos la viuda y el heredero de un baronet.

Oh, santo cielo.

Los nombres estarían disimulados de la manera habitual..., viuda de sir W***m V****m, de Gloucestershire..., pero todo el mundo sabría de quien se trataba. ¿Se referiría el periódico a los anteriores escándalos de la familia? Era más que probable, pensó con un estremecimiento. ¿Qué publicación podría resistirse a comentar un chisme tan jugoso?

Según sus razonamientos, Cyn no había relacionado al conde de Walgrave con Chastity Ware. Él debía hallarse enfermo cuando estalló el escándalo. Sin embargo, seguramente debía haberse enterado de algo durante los meses que había pasado en Inglaterra. Si el apellido Ware entraba en juego, no tardaría en establecer la conexión.

Los chismosos inveterados y los caricaturistas habían vinculado rápidamente a Chastity Ware con la mercancía de Haymarket: las prostitutas. ¡Y menudo cachondeo se trajeron con su nombre de pila! Tan pronto como Cyn leyera aquel periódico, lo sabría todo. La despreciaría o, todavía peor, la consideraría una presa fácil.

El periódico adoptó la naturaleza de una pistola cargada que corriera el riesgo de dispararse en el siguiente tropiezo de la carretera. Ella trataba desesperadamente de encontrar una excusa plausible para arrojarlo por la ventana…

—¡Charles!

Dio un salto al oír la aguda voz de Cyn y supuso que llevaba un rato tratando de captar su atención.

—¿Sí?

—Tienes que sobreponerte. Es comprensible que Verity esté un poco trastornada, pero espero que tú estés hecha de una madera más firme. Estamos haciendo planes.

Al menos, eso quería decir que no estaba leyendo el periódico. Chastity utilizó su apariencia viril como armadura.

—Bien —dijo con viveza—. ¿Qué vamos a hacer?

Cyn la observó intensamente durante un instante y luego inclinó la cabeza en señal de aprobación.

—En mi opinión, incluso si Vernham sale en nuestra persecución, no nos dará alcance hasta bien entrada la tarde. Tendrá que pararse y mirar en todas las posadas, por si nos hemos detenido, y eso hará que vaya más despacio. Podemos relajarnos y hacer planes.

—Pero ¿qué pasará si alerta al ejército?

—Es un riesgo que corremos, aunque también ese tipo de persecución se demoraría bastante. Estoy seguro de que tenemos una ventaja considerable, pero, si Vernham llega a sospechar, no conseguiremos llegar a Maidenhead. Si intentamos detenernos a pasar la noche en esta carretera, nos alcanzará. Y estas noches sin luna son demasiado oscuras para viajar.

—Entonces, ¿qué podemos hacer? —pregunto Verity con una calma que decía mucho a favor de la capacidad de Cyn para inspirar confianza.

—Propongo que dejemos la carretera de Londres y nos dirijamos a Winchester.

Las hermanas se miraron perplejas.

—¿Winchester? —repitió Verity—. ¿Por qué?

Él se apoyó contra el respaldo del asiento.

—Porque nadie esperará que vayas en esa dirección y porque tengo allí un amigo que nos dará cobijo. Las fondas son lugares muy arriesgados cuando la búsqueda se halla tan extendida.

—Cierto —dijo Verity—, pero si Henry llega a darse cuenta de que es a nosotros a quien tiene que perseguir, nos seguirá la pista, registrando un coche tras otro.

En los labios de Cyn se dibujó una pequeña sonrisa.

—Sí, pero estará buscando a una dama madura, un joven y una doncella con un niño. Puede que sospeche que Charles es Adrian, pero es menos probable que se dé cuenta de que yo soy un hombre. Por lo tanto, propongo que nos transformemos en otros nuevos personajes.

Aquello cautivó la imaginación de Chastity. Dios Santo, aquel tipo era un astuto bribón.

—¿Qué tipo de personajes?

—Un caballero militar que viaja con su esposa.

—¿Voy a ser tu esposa? —preguntó Chastity, con el corazón tembloroso sólo de pensarlo.

Cyn levantó las cejas.

—¿Tú señor? ¿Por qué complicar las cosas de ese modo?

Chastity recordó de sopetón su impostura.

—Verity puede hacer ese papel —continuó él—. Después de todo, no estamos tratando de ocultarla a los ojos de quienes la conocen, sino simplemente de oscurecer su pista. También nos desharemos del bebé.

—¿Qué? —gritaron Chastity y Verity al unísono.

—Bueno, no de verdad —dijo él con una mueca—. Pero, si sir William coopera, lo colocaremos en mi baúl cuando nos hallemos en público. Si no es así, estoy seguro de que nadie se sorprenderá de que un militar y su mujer tengan un niño.

—¿Y qué pasará conmigo? —preguntó Chastity, ridículamente herida ante la perspectiva de esta familia feliz que la dejaba excluida.

—Supongo que, una vez más, deberías ser el mozo de cuadra. El sombrero de ala ancha oculta muy bien el rostro.

—¿Tendré que ir en el pescante?

Cyn frunció el ceño.

—No. Y no sólo por la hostilidad de Hoskins, sino porque estarías muy visible allá arriba.

Verity arrugó la frente.

—Pues yo no veo cómo esto va a llevarme hasta Nathaniel. Y yo no pienso renunciar a mi propósito, milord.

—Por supuesto que no, pero ahora está claro que las carreteras que van a Londres y Maidenhead están en el centro de la búsqueda. Si la persecución es tan exhaustiva como parece, no me parece probable que podamos llevarte cerca de tu mayor, nos disfracemos de lo que nos disfracemos. Yo visitaré a Frazer y le contaré la historia, entonces, él se reunirá contigo en Winchester.

Verity se echó a reír.

—¡Es genial! ¡Creo que funcionará!

—Desde luego que sí —dijo él con gran aplomo—. Así que yo me pondré mi uniforme, lo que supondrá un alivio, os lo aseguro. Tú llevaras el otro traje de mujer que adquirí y serás mi esposa, y Charles se convertirá en el mozo de establo. Tu presencia dentro del coche quedará sin explicar, Charles.

Chastity había estado repasando aquel ingenioso plan y había detectado un fallo.

—Pero ¿cómo vamos a efectuar el cambio sin que nadie se dé cuenta? Si un grupo de gente entra en una posada y sale otro distinto, es fácil que alguien lo advierta.

Cyn arqueó las cejas.

—Querido Charles, con semejante cabeza para los detalles, deberías considerar la posibilidad de colocarte como oficial de intendencia. Y tampoco podemos parar el coche —dijo en tono meditativo—, y cambiarnos en la orilla del camino, porque los postillones lo verían todo.

—Tendremos que hacerlo dentro del coche —dijo Chastity lentamente, con la mente ya ocupada en la resolución de los detalles—. En la próxima parada, sacaremos del maletero los baúles necesarios. Eso no despertará sospechas. Bajaremos las persianas y todos procuraremos transformarnos como sea durante las siguientes diez millas. Mantendremos las persianas bajadas cuando cambiemos de caballos, y Hoskins hará saber a los nuevos postillones que sus pasajeros son un militar y su familia. Enseguida, descubriremos las ventanas otra vez y lo habremos logrado.

Cyn se rió.

—¡Genial! La licenciosa dama y su Adrian, junto con la doncella sospechosa y el bebé, habrán desaparecido de la faz de la tierra. Con la cantidad de tráfico que hay en esta carretera, dudo mucho que Henry *el Terrible* llegue a descubrirlo, pero con un poco de suerte, pasará varios días intentándolo Te doy la bienvenida, joven Charles, desde luego que sí. Si estás interesado en emprender una carrera militar, encontraré un lugar para ti a mis órdenes en cualquier momento.

Era ridículo, pensó Chastity, sentir un ardor tan cálido ante una oferta tan singularmente absurda. Sólo muy poco a poco fue dándose cuenta de que su plan tenía un fallo: ella tendría que cambiarse de ropa delante de Cyn en la estrecha intimidad del coche.

Se encogió de hombros. Se limitaría a ponerse la ropa de mozo de cuadra encima de la de su hermano. Aquello tendría la venta_a añadida de proporcionarle una mayor corpulencia.

Ahora que ya habían terminado con la planificación, su atención se centró de nuevo en la *Gazette*. El periódico descansaba en el asiento vacío que había junto ella. Estuvo tentada de deslizarse hasta allí y sentarse encima, pero así llamaría la atención de Cyn. Por el momento, él parecía haberse olvidado del diario.

Al Legar a Norton, se detuvieron en la posada y pusieron el plan en marcha. Cyn se lo explicó a Hoskins, pero tuvo que ser Chastity la que ayudara al hombre a sacar los bultos del portaequipajes.

El cochero la miró con furia.

—No se cuál es tu juego, jovencito —murmuró Hoskins—, pero como metas al amo Cyn en líos, pienso retorcer tu maldito cuello.

—¿Qué es lo que te hace pensar que soy yo quien está al mando? —replicó Chastity—. Él es ahora quien manda.

—Pero si no le hubieras enredado con tus trucos, él estaría ahora a salvo en la Abadía.

—No es ningún bebé.

—No, pero este verano casi la palma. Y, si tiene una recaída, todos los Malloren se te echaran encima. Si es que el marqués no ha empezado ya a buscarlo.

Encontraron el baúl de Cyn y la caja que contenía las otras prendas, y las pusieron dentro del carruaje. Hoskins le dirigió una última y malévola mirada de advertencia antes de volverse a subir al pescante.

Chastity se instaló nuevamente en el coche, sin saber por dónde empezar a preocuparse: por la salud de Cyn, por el periódico, o por el hecho de que el formidable marqués de Rothgar probablemente se habría sumado a la persecución. Al empezar a alejarse de la posada fue cuando se dio cuenta de que se había olvidado de deshacerse de la maldita *Gazette*.

—Hoskins dice que Rothgar andará tras tu pista —dijo.

Cyn le dirigió una fugaz e ilegible mirada. Después se quitó el bonete y el sombrero.

—Puede que ni siquiera sepa que me he escapado del nido.

—Tal y como lo dices, suena como si te retuviera con cadenas.

—Los lazos del afecto pueden ser tan fuertes como las rejas.

Chastity percibió que se estaba metiendo en un terreno delicado, pero insistió.

—Yo hubiera dicho que tal vez no fuera tan malo que el marqués nos capturara. Su poder podría sernos de gran provecho.

—Sí, pero para eso habría que saber con certeza de que lado estará.

Aquello hizo que Chastity se tomara una pausa. Tener a Rothgar en su contra sería verdaderamente desastroso.

—Lo mejor será que sigamos adelante —interrumpió Verity con firmeza—. Baja las persianas, Chas, y coge a William.

Chastity obedeció. Después, en la penumbra del coche, su hermana ayudó a Cyn con las infames cintas. Chastity sonrió al evocar el recuerdo de la aventura que habían corrido juntos con el vestido, recuerdo que pensaba atesorar...

Rápidamente, pasó a concentrarse en el bebé, que estaba despierto y tenía ganas de jugar. Le dio el periódico, con la esperanza de que lo mascara hasta deshacerlo o que lo convirtiera en trizas, pero el niño no quiso saber nada de un objeto tan aburrido. Le llamó la atención, sin embargo, la espada envainada de Cyn que descansaba en un rincón. Chastity la cogió y le dejó jugar con los brillantes lazos y la empuñadura dorada.

Cyn les echó un vistazo.

—No le dejes tocar el filo.

El hecho de que William estuviera mordisqueando los cordeles no parecía molestarle lo más mínimo. De hecho, su despreocupación la embelesó. Sería un padre maravilloso...

Basta ya, Chastity.

Cyn enseguida se desprendió del vestido, la muda y las medias —prendas que hicieron que Verity soltara una risita— y se quedó en calzoncillos. Chastity no había considerado este riesgo adicional de aquel improvisado cambiador: que él tendría que desnudarse y vestirse delante de ella.

Chastity se sorprendió a sí misma estudiando las piernas y el torso de Cyn y retiró rápidamente la vista. Él sacó el uniforme y empezó a intentar colocarse los blancos pantalones. Tuvo que introducir primero una pierna desnuda y después la otra, justo al lado de Chastity. No había otra manera. Ella se apresuró a devolver el bebé a Verity, antes de que recibiera una patada.

Después se fue hacia la orilla y terminó, casi por casualidad, encima del periódico. Pero no le fue posible alejarse de las piernas de Cyn. La visión de aquellos duros músculos salpicados de dorado vello hizo que se le secara la boca. Él flexionó un poco la rodilla para poder coger el dobladillo y meter el talón. Verity chilló porque le había clavado el codo.

—Vaya, lo siento. Esto es bastante más complicado de lo que había pensado. Charles, ¿querrás pasármelo por el talón?

Chastity tragó saliva pero obedeció. Primero, tuvo que sujetarle la pantorrilla y después el caliente y desnudo pie, lo que no resultó muy recomendable para su estruendoso corazón. Nunca había prestado la menor atención a los pies, pero ahora tenía en sus manos un bello ejemplar. Le asaltó el extraño deseo de besarle el empeine.

Después, el otro pie reclamó su atención. Volvió a hacer pasar el talón por la pernera del pantalón, suspirando aliviada al finalizar la tarea.

Él se incorporó ligeramente y se subió la prenda hasta la cintura.

—Gracias. Quizá me puedas ayudar también con las medias.

Chastity levantó velozmente la vista y le vio sosteniendo unas medias blancas de seda. Colorada por el bochorno, se las pasó por sus largos y elegantes dedos, por los arqueados empeines y por encima de su dura pantorrilla.

—Estíralas un poco —dijo él con bastante aspereza.

Chastity le lanzó una rápida mirada, pero él parecía estar muy ocupado con su camisa. Decidió mandar a la porra la cautela. ¿Cuántas oportunidades más iba a tener de tocarle el cuerpo a placer? Mantuvo la vista hacia abajo mientras le recorría las piernas con las manos, alisando cada pequeña arruga lenta y meticulosamente. Después, repitió la operación con la otra pierna.

El corazón ya no le latía aprisa. Palpitaba de un modo profundo que le hacía sentir vértigo. Una pesada calidez le oprimió la parte inferior del abdomen…

Después de unos instantes, se dio cuenta de que provenía del pie derecho de Cyn, que descansaba sobre su vientre mientras ella estaba atareada con el izquierdo. El talón se apretaba contra la conjunción de los muslos de Chastity. Una parte de ella muy cercana a aquel talón palpitaba como si fuese una herida, y la muchacha sintió la apremiante necesidad de extender las piernas y apretarse contra él.

Pero se puso rígida y apartó de su lado el pie.

—Ya estás —le dijo.

—Gracias —dijo él, articulando despacio. Luego se aseguró él mismo los jarretes.— Te aseguro, querido Charles, que algún día haré con mucho gusto lo mismo por ti. —Se remetió la camisa—. Ah, esto está mucho mejor. Me siento como si mis piernas volvieran a estar en funcionamiento. —Se metió dentro del largo chaleco blanco, se ajustó los seis botones plateados y se ató la banda escarlata.

A continuación, sacó el chaquetón del regimiento. Era bastante llamativo —color carmesí con bocamangas de ante y relucientes galones dorados en los puños, bolsillos y ojales de ambos lados. Tuvo que realizar un buen número de contorsiones y hubo de rezongar alguna que otra maldición, pero, finalmente, la ajustada prenda quedó en su sitio. Ahora parecía un soldado de verdad.

Se ató un corbatín negro alrededor del cuello y se colgó la gorguera plateada con el distintivo de rango. Sonrió.

—Tengo que decir que hacía una eternidad que no me sentía tan bien en mi propio pellejo. Creo que, no obstante, no me pondré las botas hasta que paremos. Si intento ponérmelas ahora, probablemente os daría a alguna una patada en la cara. —Abrió su neceser y utilizó un pequeño recipiente con agua para frotarse el colorete hasta hacerlo desaparecer. Luego, cogió un peine, un espejo y un lazo.

Le pasó el espejo a Chastity.

—Sosténmelo, querido muchacho, mientras lidio con mi pelo.

Chastity le observó mientras se peinaba los tostados rizos y se los recogía convenientemente en la nuca. Siempre se había burlado de las jóvenes damas que parecían estar en el séptimo cielo cuando veían un chaquetón escarlata, pero ahora era ella quien estaba aquejada de ese mal. El capitán Cyn Malloren tenía un aspecto espléndido con el uniforme de su regimiento. Aunque, para ella, él tendría un aspecto espléndido con cualquier cosa.

Vestido así, sin embargo, había perdido aquel aire de delicadeza que le caracterizaba. Parecía investido de una gran autoridad, capaz de desenvolverse en cualquier emergencia y dispuesto a cualquier peligrosa heroicidad. Chastity tuvo que admitir que era un soldado y que las hazañas arriesgadas eran su cometido. Sí, el peligro y el riesgo eran sus compañeros. ¿Qué había dicho él? «La sangre es el dios al que sirven las fastuosas galas de la guerra...»

En menos de un par de días se separarían. Él se olvidaría pronto de un arisco joven llamado Charles. Ni siquiera llegaría nunca a saber que era una mujer. Una mujer que... que albergaba sentimientos cálidos hacia él.

Ella, por otra parte, no le olvidaría jamás. Durante el resto de su vida, estudiaría las noticias del ejército, esperando encontrar alguna que hiciera referencia a él. Examinaría las listas de fallecidos, temiendo que su nombre apareciera algún día, triste reconocimiento de que aquella risa había sido cruelmente interrumpida...

La voz de Cyn la sacó repentinamente de sus sombríos pensamientos.

—Ahora —dijo él—, transformemos a Verity.

—Tú no vas a participar en eso —dijo Chastity—. Sería indecente.

Él torció los labios.

—Me parece que tu hermana no es tan sensible como tú en estos asuntos, señor.

—Yo...

—¡Paz! —gritó Verity divertida—. Sólo me voy a quitar la ropa hasta la muda y, aunque eso es bastante escabroso, soy perfectamente capaz de hacerlo yo sola. Sin embargo, creo que lord Cyn debería sostener a William. —Le pasó el bebé y éste se quedó inmediatamente embelesado con los galones dorados.

—No me parece probable que vaya a soltar aguas menores sobre su magnífica indumentaria, milord, pero no puedo garantizarlo.

Cyn no pareció desanimarse.

—Siempre he sostenido que un uniforme impecable tiene un aire sospechoso. Rothgar pensaba que mi traje deslucido por la guerra no estaba a la altura de la dignidad de un Malloren, especialmente después de haber sido recortado con vistas a su utilidad práctica en la sierra. Hace unas semanas, insistió en encargar que me hicieran éste. Necesita un poco de ajetreo. Si no me tomarán por un novato.

Sin vergüenza aparente, Verity se despojó de sus burdas prendas de sirvienta y se puso el otro conjunto de Cyn: la enagua gris, el peto azul y negro, y el chaquetón azul Prusia. Se puso de rodillas para que Chastity pudiera atarle las cintas del peto, pero se las apañó ella sola para abrocharse el vestido.

El abundante pecho de Verity llenaba aquel corpiño sin ninguna ayuda. Cyn guardó la lana dentro de su baúl.

No se podía hacer otra cosa con el grasiento pelo de Verity que peinarlo en un apretado moño. Con el sombrero y el tocado estaba elegante aunque severa. Aquella severidad la hacía irreconocible, pero no conseguiría engañar a un familiar cercano.

—No te expongas a la vista —le aconsejó Cyn—, y cuando estés en público, mantén la cabeza gacha. Recuerda, andan buscando a una fugitiva, no a una respetable matrona, y la gente generalmente ve lo que espera ver. —Miró a Chastity—. Ahora tú, joven Charles.

Chastity se despojó del chaquetón de terciopelo y se sacó los pantalones y la camisa que llevaba encima de la ropa de su hermano. Se quitó el corbatín y, en su lugar, se anudó alrededor del cuello el pañuelo de lunares. Sobre la peluca, se encasquetó con firmeza el sombrero de lisa ala.

—Ya estoy —dijo.

Cyn sonrió torciendo el gesto.

—Cualquier día de estos tu recato te va a traer problemas, Charles.

Chastity se dedicó a meter en el baúl todas las prendas desechadas.

Se hizo el silencio, y el sombrío coche se volvió desconcertantemente íntimo. El bebé se quedó adormecido en brazos de Cyn. Ambos parecían muy cómodos con la situación.

Chastity se recostó en su asiento, simulando descansar, aunque en realidad observaba a Cyn Mallcren a través de las pestañas De sus relativamente cortas pestañas. Le ofendía que las de Cyn fueran tan exuberantes, pero las codiciaba para sus propios hijos.

Basta, Chastity.

Pero no servía de nada. Sus ojos seguían absorbiendo la imagen de Cyn y almacenándola con vistas al desolador futuro. Él tenía la cabeza ligeramente vuelta. de modo que ella podía recorrer con la vista el firme trazo de su perfil. Para su sorpresa, detectó un cierto parecido con Rothgar. ¿Dentro de unos diez años, resultaría Cyn igual de intimidante? Lo dudaba. No creía que Rothgar hubiera tenido jamás aquella faceta temeraria y despreocupada que constituía el rasgo más característico de Cyn, y que ella adoraba.

Sus manos eran hermosas. La suavidad con la que mecían al bebé lo ponía de relieve. ¿Cómo es que no se había fijado antes en aquel rasgo? Tenían largos dedos y parecían capaces tanto de usar la fuerza como de obrar con delicadeza. Recordó cómo habían acariciado su cabeza y su cuello durante aquel extraño beso, anheló ser tocada por ellas nuevamente Sólo de pensarlo, la recorrió un estremecimiento de deseo

Cyn sentía la mirada de Chastity como si se tratara de un tórrido roce. Unas cuantas miradas robadas le habían indicado que ella lo estudiaba como lo haría una artista que trabajara en un retrato. Él deseó poder permitirse la misma indulgencia. Ya habría otras ocasiones. Además, se daba por satisfecho al ver que ella no le quitaba ojo.

Había al menos una parte de él que estaba complacida: su parte perversa. Anhelaba jubilosamente la llegada del momento que les diera la oportunidad de explorarse el uno al otro por completo.

Su parte noble le decía a gritos que debía decirle que sabía que era una mujer, para que ella pudiera recobrar el recato propio de una doncella.

Salvo por el hecho de que ella no era una doncella.

Desde el principio había sospechado que ella no era fría ni carente de sensualidad. Ahora lo sabía con certeza. Hacía unos instantes, ella le había tocado las piernas con tacto de amante y a él le había costado mucho mantener el control. De no haber sido por la presencia de Verity, hubiera podido rodear a su damisela con los brazos y arrebatarle un beso. O probablemente algo más.

El coche hizo el siguiente cambio sin ningún problema. Cyn y Verity se apearon unos instantes para que todo el mundo pudiera ver al capitán y a su señora. Nadie les preguntó nada, pero Chastity descubrió a un hombre que merodeaba por allí, cuya mirada le pareció muy inquisitiva. Sin embargo, no tenía aspecto sospechoso.

Nada más arrancar, ella dijo:

—¿Has visto a…?

—Sí —dijo Cyn tranquilamente—. Seguramente no hay de qué preocuparse. Creo que al haber virado hacia el sur, estamos fuera del ámbito de la persecución. Una cosa está clara. No podemos arriesgarnos a detenernos en la carretera. Nunca podríamos ocultar la presencia de un bebé en el interior de una posada.

—Pero si ya está oscureciendo —dijo Verity, pálida a causa del miedo y el cansancio.

—Nos las arreglaremos con las luces del coche —dijo Cyn—. Ya no estamos demasiado lejos. En Winchester, seremos unos pocos más entre muchos miles de personas y tendremos un lugar privado en el que alojarnos. En la carretera llamaremos la atención en cualquier parte que nos paremos

Para provenir de Cyn Malloren, era un discurso muy ponderado. Chastity se percató de que estaba tan preocupado como ella por la impenetrabilidad de la red tendida por todo el sur de Inglaterra. Más que la búsqueda de una persona desaparecida, parecía la caza de un fugitivo. Estaba segura de que aquello era obra de su padre.

El bebé se despertó y hubo que alimentarlo. Verity se distrajo así de sus temores. Chastity deseó poder decirle algo tranquilizador a su hermana, que temía por la vida de su hijo. No se le ocurrió nada excepto que estaban haciendo todo lo que podían y que tenían probabilidades de salir airosas de aquel lance. Fundamentalmente gracias a Cyn. Sin él, haría horas que las habrían cogido.

Cyn reflexionó sobre la intensidad del cerco y dedujo que aquella escapada tenía un trasfondo mayor del aparente. Estudió a las dos hermanas, preguntándose cuál de ellas estaría mintiendo, sobre qué asunto y por qué.

Tras un rugido de caldosos ecos se hizo evidente que había que cambiar a William. Muy evidente. Con anterioridad, se habían detenido en la calzada para permitir a Verity que lo hiciera al aire libre. Sin embargo, en aquellos momentos, el tiempo se les echaba encima y no querían que los postillones supieran que llevaban un bebé, así que ella tuvo que realizar aquella indecorosa tarea dentro del coche, con las ventanas abiertas. El olor era sorprendentemente caseoso, pero muy fuerte. Desgraciadamente, Verity sólo contaba con una pequeña botella de agua para limpiar al niño.

Después de todo, pensó Cyn, tratando de no poner cara de matrona afrentada, los bebés no eran un asunto romántico. Un hombre tendría que estar loco siquiera para plantearse tener una familia mientras está en el ejército.

Cuando terminó, Verity contempló los trapos pringosos.

—El coche va a apestar con esto—dijo en tono de disculpa.

—Tíralos por la ventana —sugirió Cyn—. Los mozos de postas ni se enterarán.

Cuando él vio la vacilación con la que ella se preparaba para hacerlo, suspiró.

—Dámelo a mí.

¿Por qué sería, se preguntaba Cyn, que nada de lo que él se había encontrado en la guerra parecía ni la mitad de nauseabundo que aquel viscoso y agrio paquete? Afinó la puntería y lo lanzó por encima del seto en movimiento hasta el campo que había detrás. Después deseó tener los medios para lavarse las manos.

—Si queremos que después se duerma— dijo Verity—, será mejor que ahora juguemos con él.

La joven madre cantó varias melodías al tiempo que hacía a William batir las palmas al ritmo de la música. Le hizo saltar suavemente sobre su rodilla. Le tumbó de espaldas y le recitó «Este pequeño cerdito» mientras jugaba con los dedos de sus pies. William se reía y gorjeaba agradecido. El entusiasmo de Cyn por la continuidad de la especie revivió. Echó un vistazo a su damisela. Ésta contemplaba el juego con una sonrisa completamente femenina y maternal. Sería una buena madre.

Algo se tensó en el interior de Cyn.

No quería de ninguna manera que ella tuviera hijos con ningún otro hombre que no fuera él. Al diablo con todo. ¿Cómo había podido meterse en semejante lío?

Mentalmente, ensayó unas cuantas frases. Mi querida lady… ¿Lady qué? ¿Charlotte? Si su nombre era Charlotte, le prohibiría que volviera a usarlo. Mi querida lady Charles, me siento profunda y desenfrenadamente atraído por la idea de casarme contigo y llevarte a la guerra. Me temo que buena parte de tu vida la pasarás sin mí en los acantonamientos de una tierra extranjera —espero que se te dé bien aprender las lenguas y las costumbres foráneas—, aunque yo me reuniré contigo con tanta frecuencia como la contienda me lo permita. Desde luego, podrías quedarte con el regimiento, si no te molestan las pulgas, el barro y las interminables obligaciones de atender a los heridos y enfermos…

Suspiró. Seguro que ella se mostraría tremendamente entusiasmada.

También podía retirarse del ejército. Rothgar no hacía más que insistir en ello por culpa de aquellos estúpidos médicos, pero Cyn no tenía ningunas ganas de llevar una vida tranquila. Echaría de menos la camaradería, los proyectos, el reto, la excitación y las tierras extranjeras. La vida ociosa de Londres o el cultivo de los tulipanes en el campo le aburrirían mortalmente y, sin duda, le llevarían a meterse en líos.

Después de todo, había sido el aburrimiento lo que le había enredado en aquella aventura.

Su damisela reía con el bebé: en su rostro se reflejaba el radiante deleite del niño. No tenía nada de fría o de dura.

Al diablo con todo.

Cyn buscó alguna distracción y vio el arrugado periódico.

La luz se estaba extinguiendo, así que prendió una mecha y encendió uno de las velas del candelabro de pared. Después se estiró para coger la *Gazzette*, y buscó las noticias relativas a la guerra.

Los americanos permanecían tranquilos y parecía que el poder francés en aquellas tierras había sido aplastado. Había cierta inquietud en las colonias en relación con los nuevos impuestos fijados para financiar su reciente defensa. Pero aquello volvería pronto a su cauce. La mayoría de las noticias tenían que ver con la escandalosas zarina Catalina de Rusia y el avance prusiano contra Austria. Tal vez él mismo acabara destinado en Hanover o en algún otro sitio por el estilo. Después de la imprevisible y selvática naturaleza del Nuevo Mundo, temía que aquello le resultara insípido.

Al terminar las noticias bélicas, levantó la vista hacia las mujeres.

—¿Queréis que os lea algunas noticias?

—Sí, por favor —dijo Verity.

—¡No! —exclamó Charles.

Interesante, pensó Cyn. Una vez más, vetaba la lectura de un periódico. ¿Qué podía haber hecho ella para atraer el interés de la prensa? Empezó a leer en alto. Leyó un fragmento sobre los disturbios de Rusia y otro sobre los avances en la fundición del hierro, pero examinaba todo el rato las páginas tratando de encontrar algo relacionado con su damisela.

Y lo encontró.

Se saltó el artículo crucial para leer una noticia sobre un incendio en Dover y otra acerca del juicio de un asombroso asesino que, al parecer, había envenenado a la mitad de su familia antes de ser capturado. Pero leyó despacio y se las arregló para ir mirando la otra historia al mismo tiempo.

Tenía que ver con la desaparición de Verity, y no con Charles. Y no se contradecía con lo que ellas le habían contado. ¿Dónde estaba entonces el problema?

Según decía el periódico, se había extendido la preocupación por el paradero de la viuda y el hijo de sir W****m V****m. Se temía que lady V****y V****m hubiera perdido la cabeza a causa de la muerte de su esposo y su reciente parto, el cual, afortunadamente, había producido un heredero para el difunto noble. Tanto el padre de la dama, como la familia de su esposo ofrecían una importante recompensa a cambio de cualquier información que hiciera posible que la desconsolada señora volviera con los suyos para recibir sus amorosos cuidados.

El resto del artículo eran referencias genealógicas.

Lady V****y había sido, antes de su matrimonio, lady V***** W***, hija del conde de W****e, y hermana de lady C*****y W***…

Cyn dejó de leer. Finalmente, su memoria se había activado, y podía rellenar los huecos con las letras que faltaban.

El nombre de su damisela era Chastity Ware.

La infame Chastity Ware.

Cyn se dio prisa en seguir leyendo. Eligió un artículo al azar, que resultó ser un árido ensayo sobre la traducción al alemán que Weiman había hecho de Shakespeare. Le costaba encontrarle sentido, porque la mayor parte de su mente estaba ocupada tratando de asimilar su descubrimiento. Cuando terminó la reseña, ofreció el periódico a las hermanas. Ambas declinaron la oferta, así que él lo dejó a un lado. Notó alivio en el rostro de su damisela.

En el rostro de Chastity Ware.

Le llevaría algún tiempo hacerse a la idea de que se llamaba así, y no Charles; sin embargo, a pesar de su reputación, aquel nombre le pegaba. No obstante, ¿a qué debía atenerse en lo tocante a su reputación?

Recordaba que Henry Vernham había dicho que Walgrave le había rapado la cabeza después de encontrarla en la cama de un hombre. Todo encajaba, pero sólo hasta cierto punto. No cuadraba con lo que él conocía de ella. No podía creer que su damisela fuera una tunanta desvergonzada que fuera de cama en cama.

Y, sin embargo, aquello era lo que el mundo creía.

Cuando Cyn había estado enfermo, su hermano Bryght había venido desde Londres con una selección de entretenimientos, entre los que se incluían las últimas tiras cómicas.

Las había que hacían referencia a los rumores sobre lord Bute y la madre del nuevo rey. Otras retrataban ambiciosos escoceses que dejaban a Inglaterra seca mientras seguían flirteando con los Estuardo. Una muy divertida y obscena sobre el depuesto zar de Rusia, de quien se decía que nunca se había acostado con su mujer, Catalina, aunque todos los demás hombres sí lo habían hecho.

Y le había llevado una sobre el gran escándalo del verano, protagonizado por lady Chastity Ware.

Supuso que el conde de Walgrave, *el Incorruptible*, tenía enemigos que se habían dado el gusto de atacarle a través de su hija. Le habían sacado feo e hinchado, retrocediendo tambaleante desde una cama en la que su rolliza hija yacía alegremente desnuda bajo un amante que babeaba, a la par que decía: «No padre, no voy a casarme con él, solo quiero j***r con él».

Dirigió una fugaz mirada a los prístinos rasgos de la joven mujer que tenía enfrente. No se parecían en nada a los de la ordinaria mujer de la caricatura. Probablemente, el ilustrador no la había visto nunca y no le importaba un pimiento como persona. Sólo se trataba de proporcionar un poco de excitación a las masas y un golpe bajo para el poderoso conde.

Sabía que había habido numerosas caricaturas sobre el tema, pegadas en los escaparates para que todos las vieran —a la venta por el módico precio de un penique las de blanco y negro, y por dos las de color—, que habían pasado de una mugrienta mano a otra como fuente de diversión.

¿Había llegado ella a ver alguna? Por el amor de Dios, esperaba que no.

Cyn había oído la historia de labios de Bryght, salpicada de lascivos detalles. Al parecer, a la chica le habían prohibido asistir a la recepción de los Walgrave a causa de su mal comportamiento; los rumores decían que debido a alguna procacidad anterior. La bondadosa lady Trelyn, la favorita de la buena sociedad, había abogado tanto en su defensa que lord Walgrave, junto con un grupo de invitados, había subido a la habitación de su hija para levantarle el castigo.

Y allí la habían encontrado, como Vernham había dicho, *in flagrante delicto*. Con tantas personas como testigos, no había habido manera de silenciarlo, aunque su padre lo había intentado. El escándalo pudo haberse acallado si ella hubiera accedido a una boda rápida, porque la mayoría de los presentes habrían guardado el secreto y, todo lo más, se habrían producido rumores. Lady Chastity, sin embargo, se había negado terminantemente a casarse con el hombre. De inmediato se la redujo al ostracismo, no tanto por haber pecado como por no seguir las reglas una vez pillada.

Lord y lady Trelyn —conocidos por su irreprochable carácter— fueron los que más tiempo la estuvieron apoyando, negándose a confirmar la historia. Pero al final, ellos también habían claudicado, expresando la gran conmiseración que sentían por el afligido padre.

Se acordaba de algo más. ¡El amante había sido el cuñado de la muchacha, Henry Vernham! ¿Su damisela había descuidado toda precaución por un hombre como aquél? La única explicación sería la lujuria enfebrecida e insensata que se apoderaba de algunas mujeres, pero él no había visto ni rastro de aquel rasgo en Chastity Ware.

Cyn la miró de nuevo. Nunca hubiera dicho que fuera casquivana. Ni tampoco que fuera estúpida. Si había jugado a aquel juego y la habían cogido, la única opción razonable era casarse con aquel hombre. Para una mujer así, el matrimonio no sería una prisión muy rígida.

Y, sin embargo, no podía pensar que ella fuera esa clase de mujer. Las contradicciones y las sospechas se agolpaban en su cerebro.

Recordaba otra cosa. A Rothgar no le había gustado la caricatura y la había hecho desaparecer; probablemente, en el fuego más cercano. Rothgar y Chastity Ware se habían conocido pues antes de la debacle. Tal vez Rothgar se dio cuenta de lo poco que aquellas representaciones tenían que ver con la realidad.

¿También Rothgar se había acostado con ella? Cyn estuvo a punto de emitir un sonoro gemido. Rechazaba aquellos pensamientos, pero éstos le invadían el cerebro con insistencia.

No se podía negar que ella había estado envuelta en el escándalo. Además del testimonio de los Trelyn, Cyn contaba con la evidencia que le habían mostrado sus propios ojos y oídos: el enfurecido conde había rapado el pelo de su descarriada hija y la había confinado a la cabaña de su vieja niñera, permitiéndole quedarse únicamente con las ropas de una prostituta penitente.

¡Y ella había encontrado una audaz manera de burlar aquellas restricciones! Usando las ropas de su hermano y adquiriendo una apariencia masculina. Era una idea muy buena, pero, ¡hacía falta valor para llevarla a la práctica!

Tuvo que admitir que el vapuleado padre de Chastity Ware le inspiraba cierta compasión. Pero sólo si ella era la desvergonzada que se decía.

●　●　●

Chastity vio a Cyn dejar de lado la *Gazette*. El alivio que sintió casi la hizo llorar. Había estado esperando que él leyera aquel artículo como si presintiera la caída de un hacha. Trató de acorazarse contra el escarnio y el asco. Viniendo de aquel oficial le resultarían aún más insufribles que si provinieran de la señora Inchcliff.

Qué extraño era lo de la ropa. Aunque no tuviera mucho sentido, le parecía que la señora Inchcliff se hubiera mostrado más comprensiva y le hubiera otorgado el beneficio de la duda, mientras que estaba segura que el capitán lord Cynric Malloren la condenaría al instante.

Y, sencillamente, su corazón se partiría.

Cyn se inclinó de repente hacia delante y golpeó el techo del carruaje. Hoskins detuvo el vehículo.

—Me voy a sentar un rato en el pescante, ahora que soy otra vez un hombre —les dijo a las hermanas—. Relevaré a Hoskins y le explicaré parte de nuestro plan. Cualquiera que nos vea pasar, distinguirá mi chaquetón escarlata, lo que debería despistar a nuestros perseguidores. —Se puso las botas, saltó al exterior y cerró la puerta de golpe.

—Santo cielo —dijo Verity, mientras el coche arrancaba de nuevo—. ¿No es extraño? Desde que se ha puesto el uniforme se ha convertido en una persona completamente diferente.

Chastity también había advertido cierta brusquedad en sus modales.

—Estoy segura de que es un oficial excelente —dijo en su defensa.

Ya había empezado a sentir su ausencia como si ante ella se abriera un profundo abismo. Lo mejor que podía hacer era acostumbrarse. Pronto él estaría fuera de su vida para siempre. Cogió el periódico.

—Voy a esconderlo antes de que vuelva. Lo he pasado fatal, Verity. ¡Mira!

Verity leyó el artículo y se mordió el labio.

—Oh, cielos. A estas alturas, toda Inglaterra debe estar al acecho, así que es mejor que no me vea nadie que me conozca. Y claro, tenían que sacar tu nombre a colación. —Tocó la mano de Chastity—. Yo pensaba que la tempestad amainaría pronto.

—Nunca llegará ese día. —Chastity suspiró—. Una cosa está clara, después de todo esto jamás aceptaré ciegamente ningún rumor.

Verity se cambió al bebé de brazo.

—Tienes que comprender que no se trata solamente de un simple rumor. Un grupo de personas de intachable reputación te vio en la cama con Henry. Es una desgracia que los Trelyn estuvieran allí. Su palabra está fuera de toda duda.

—Pero yo no invité a Vernham a mi cama. ¡Estaba profundamente dormida!

—Eso no tiene importancia a los ojos del mundo.

Chastity miró fijamente a su hermana.

—¿Estás diciendo que debería haberme casado con Vernham?

Verity suspiró.

—En realidad no lo sé, querida. Supongo que yo sí lo habría hecho, pero yo siempre he sido más débil que tú. Lo que pasa es que empiezo a darme cuenta de lo mala que es la situación en la que te encuentras. —Lanzó una mirada a su hermana—. En parte, a causa de lord Cyn.

Chastity se puso tensa.

—¿Quieres decirme qué tiene él que ver con esto?

—No me negarás que hay algo entre vosotros. Me he dado cuenta. Sin duda, él está confundido por que te tiene por un hombre, pero, tan pronto como descubra que eres una mujer, se mostrará interesado. Es una pena que lo vuestro no pueda llegar a buen puerto.

—No existe nada entre nosotros que tenga que llegar a ningún puerto —dijo Chastity con firmeza. —Y no tengo ninguna intención de que se entere de que soy una mujer. Creo que estás desvariando, Verity.

Eran casi las cinco y había oscurecido cuando atravesaron la puerta norte y entraron en la antigua ciudad de Winchester. La carretera estaba tranquila, puesto que la mayoría de los viajeros ya habían llegado a su destino, pero todavía había mucha gente que andaba por la calle.

Tanto Verity como Chastity se mantuvieron fuera del alcance de las miradas curiosas. Cyn levantó la trampilla y les dijo a voces:

—Vamos a evitar las posadas elegantes y vamos a ir al Three Balls. Hoskins me asegura que, incluso si Vernham o tu padre están aquí, nunca se hospedarían en un sitio tan pequeño, aunque es bastante decente. De todas maneras, no os confiéis. Recordad vuestros papeles y mirad a ver si podéis esconder al bebé en la maleta.

Chastity abrió el baúl. Verity colocó una manta doblada sobre la lana sin hilar y después introdujo al adormecido bebé encima. William suspiró y después recuperó el sosiego.

Le cubrieron con una delgada tela de algodón y cerraron parcialmente el arca.

El coche se balanceó bruscamente. Se escucharon saludos. Las hermanas se asomaron al exterior y descubrieron que se hallaban en el patio de una pequeña fonda, iluminado por antorchas. Era un lugar vetusto, con aleros bajos y escasez de ángulos rectos. Tenía encanto, pero no era el tipo de establecimiento que atraería el patronazgo de la alta aristocracia.

La puerta del carruaje osciló sobre su eje y Cyn les indicó que debían apearse. Chastity comprendió que les convenía dejarse ver, para fijar aquella ilusión en las mentes de los postillones. Dejaron el baúl en el suelo del vehículo y se bajaron. Cyn asistió cortésmente a Verity e ignoró por completo a Chastity. Ésta se preguntaba con sarcasmo si tendría que ir a echar una mano con los caballos, pero temió que, si lo intentaba, se descubriera su impostura.

Mientras los mozos desenganchaban los caballos, el rollizo posadero se apresuró a salir para atender a sus clientes. Cyn se puso a charlar con el hombre y, entre tanto, Verity mantenía la cabeza recatadamente baja y permanecía de pie a su lado. Cyn le dirigía de vez en cuando algún comentario, llamándola «querida» y tocándola con suave familiaridad. Apoyada contra una rueda, con el sombrero calado hasta los ojos, Chastity pensaba con desolación que hacían muy buena pareja.

Vio cómo un joven con expresión aburrida asomaba la cabeza por la puerta de la posada y llegaba a la misma conclusión. ¿Tenía su padre un vigía en cada fonda del sur del país? ¿Por qué? Una cosa era estar preocupado por la desaparición de una hija, pero aquello era algo fuera de lo normal. Rezó para que el bebé no se despertara.

Cyn pagó a los postillones y los hombres se fueron con su bullicio a otra parte. Después, convino que dejaría su carruaje durante unos días en la posada y que alquilaría un caballo de montar para poder explorar la zona. Dejó caer que andaba buscando una casa para arrendar. Cogió habitaciones para él y para su cochero, anunciando que su mujer se iba a alojar en casa de un amigo.

Todo salió a pedir de boca.

En un periquete, todos salían a buen paso del patio de la fonda. Cyn portaba el baúl en el que el bebé seguía profundamente dormido.

—Camino despejado. No creo que tengamos ningún problema con Mary Garnet —dijo Cyn animadamente—. Siempre ha sido una mujer con carácter. No quería irse de Canadá, pero cuando tuvo a su segundo hijo, Roger la persuadió para que regresara a Inglaterra. Ella y los niños están viviendo con su padre, un tipo erudito. Esperemos que él no ponga ninguna objeción.

Todo resultó tal y como Cyn había predicho. Cuando llegaron a la agradable casa de ladrillo, en una tranquila calle, Mary se declaró encantada de tener una huésped femenina. Su padre manifestó exactamente la misma hospitalidad. Enseguida todos se hallaron tomando el té en un cómodo saloncito.

Mary era una mujer robusta de mejillas coloradas y sonrisa pronta. Sus dos niños —una vigorosa niña de cinco años y un chiquillo travieso que todavía llevaba faldones— revolotearon tímidamente durante un rato. Pero, al poco rato, el bebé llamó la atención de la niña y el uniforme de Cyn la del niño.

—Mi papá es soldado —le dijo con gravedad a Cyn.

—Lo sé. Conozco muy bien a tu padre. Nos lo hemos pasado muy bien juntos zurrando a los enemigos del rey.

—¿Con espadas?

—Con espadas y pistolas. Montones de maravillosos y ruidosos objetos.

El chico se apoyó contra la rodilla de Cyn con los ojos maravillados.

—¿Tienes un caballo grande?

—Claro que sí. —Cyn le dedicó una sonrisa—. ¿Quieres jugar a los caballitos?

El chiquillo asintió, así que Cyn lo sentó encima de sus piernas y empezó a declamar:

Las mujeres cabalgan al paso,
al paso, al paso, al paso.
Los caballeros al trote y al galope,
al trote y al galope.
Los granjeros montan así:
Tacatá, tacatá, tacatá.
Y cuando llegan a un seto...
¡Saltan por encima!

Y levantó al niño por los aires, mientras éste no dejaba de proferir alaridos

—Y cuando llega a un lugar resbaladizo.... —El pequeño se quedó tenso, rebosante de expectación—. ¡Van a parar al suelo! —Cyn abrió las piernas y dejó caer al escandaloso crío casi hasta el suelo.

—¡Otra vez! ¡Otra vez!

Cyn empezó amablemente la representación desde el principio.

Chastity le observaba, con el corazón en un puño. Además de los bebés, también le gustaban los niños. Sería verdaderamente un padre maravilloso, firme cuando fuera preciso, pero tremendamente divertido.

Basta, Chastity.

También vio cómo la pequeña Caroline miraba con envidia el juego del caballito, obviamente dividida entre los atractivos del bebé en los brazos de Verity y la pura excitación de aquella farsa. Cuando Cyn reclamó una pausa para recobrar el aliento —aunque el que verdaderamente la necesitaba era el pequeño, para poder calmarse y abandonar el estado de efervescencia en que se encontraba— Caroline solicitó su atención.

—Aquí también vamos a tener un nuevo bebé —le dijo.

Los ojos de Cyn emitieron un destello al mirar a Mary Garnet.

—Espero que eso signifique que Roger ha estado de permiso.

La mujer sacudió la cabeza al contestarle.

—Por supuesto que sí, granuja. Él fue quién te trajo a casa, como bien sabes.

—¿Que me trajo a casa? —preguntó Cyn con la mirada perdida.

—¿No te acuerdas? Él tenía sus dudas, aunque decía que a veces parecía que estabas perfectamente consciente.

Cyn sacudió la cabeza.

—No recuerdo casi nada del viaje. Entonces, tengo que darle las gracias por salvarme la vida.

—Oh, no sé si es para tanto, pero se pondrá contento cuando le diga por carta que estás totalmente recuperado. Quiso visitarte antes de embarcarse, pero le dijeron que no estabas en condiciones.

El buen humor se esfumó del rostro de Cyn.

—¡Qué me estás diciendo! Me pregunto a cuántos amigos más les cerró la puerta mi solícito hermano.

—Vamos, Cyn, no te lo tomes así —dijo Mary—. Estabas muy enfermo. Roger dice que habían perdido las esperanzas hasta que apareció Rothgar y se hizo cargo.

Cyn frunció el ceño.

—Que apareció, ¿dónde? ¡Hacéis que suene como una maldita aparición!

Chastity no podía creer que le hablara de una manera tan brusca a la esposa del hombre que le había salvado la vida, pero Mary no parecía sorprendida.

—¿Tampoco te acuerdas de eso? Eso prueba lo enfermo que debías estar. Se presentó en el muelle nada más que llegaste. Roger decía que su presencia allí le había resultado muy misteriosa, como si alguien le hubiera avisado con antelación.

Los labios de Cyn se torcieron levemente. Si aquello era una sonrisa, desde luego carecía de humor.

—Te aseguro que mi hermano no usa una bola de cristal. Sin duda tenía información rápida y precisa. Así que se presentó y me arrancó de las fauces de la muerte, ¿no? Supongo que debería estarle sumisamente agradecido. Intentaré recordarlo la próxima vez que nos veamos.

Después esbozó una chispeante sonrisa, como si aplicara una chispa a una mecha, y empezó a jugar otra vez con el chiquillo. A los pocos instantes, Caroline se puso a su lado.

—Luego me toca a mí —dijo con firmeza.

Cyn terminó una tanda con el chico y miró a la niña.

—¿Estás segura de que es un juego apropiado para una señorita?

Ella asintió.

—Papá lo hace conmigo.

Cyn puso al niño de pie en el suelo.

—Entonces, tal vez sí. Si nos dejamos la parte de «Van a parar al suelo».

Carolina le miro ceñuda.

—¡Pero si eso es lo mejor de todo, señor! ¿Por qué los chicos son siempre los que se divierten?

Cyn dirigió una rápida e inquisitiva mirada a Mary, pero antes de que ella pudiera hacer ningún comentario, Caroline dijo:

—No será descocado, señor. ¡Mire! —y se levantó las faldas de muselina hasta dejar al descubierto unas calcillas con volantes.

Mary dio un horrorizado gemido, pero Cyn se echó a reír. Cogió a la niña para empezar el juego, y lo llevó a cabo todavía con mayor vigor del que había empleado con su hermano pequeño. Muy pronto su engalanada ropa interior se reveló en todo su esplendor.

Finalmente, depositó a la sonrojada niña de pie en el suelo.

—Ya vale, cielo. Eso es todo por ahora. Tengo que ocuparme de ciertos asuntos. Pero pronto volveremos a pasarnos por aquí y podrás cabalgar de nuevo. Ciertamente, no veo por qué los chicos tienen que ser siempre los que se divierten.

Se iba. Aquello era el fin. De repente, Chastity sintió que no podía soportarlo. Su noble resolución le decía que lo dejara marchar. Su amor hacía que deseara estar junto a él el máximo tiempo posible. Había conservado su disfraz hasta aquel momento. Con su ayuda, ¿no podría estar a salvo unos pocos días más?

Él se dirigió a la puerta. Chastity le siguió hasta el recibidor.

—Creo que debería ir contigo.

Él la miró con extrañeza.

—¿Por qué?

—No puedo quedarme aquí. Esta casa es demasiado pequeña. Podrían reconocerme y acaso necesites ayuda para encontrar a Nathaniel. Después de todo, no le conoces. Además, te conviene tener a alguien a tu lado. Creo que no te das cuenta de lo despiadado que puede ser mi padre.

Para su desesperación, Chastity sabía que aquello era, sobre todo, una sarta de tonterías. Aunque lo último era cierto. No creía que Cyn se tomara al conde de Walgrave lo suficientemente en serio.

—Me admira la meticulosidad de la búsqueda de tu padre —dijo él. Su tono era reflexivo e impenetrable—. Pero ¿estás seguro de que será prudente que vengas conmigo, joven Charles?

Chastity respiró profundamente.

—Sí.

Él asintió.

—Está bien. Díselo a Verity.

Chastity le dio a Verity las mismas razones para irse a solas con Cyn Malloren. La preocupación empañó la cara de Verity, quién también le dijo:

—¿Estás segura de que esto es sensato, querida?

—No —dijo Chastity débilmente—, pero no puedo dejar que se vaya solo. Es un inconsciente. Todavía se lo toma a la ligera.

Verity suspiró, pero le caló aún más el sombrero a Chastity y la besó.

—Buena suerte, querida. Ten cuidado. —Había lágrimas en sus ojos.

Chastity abrazó a su hermana con fiereza.

—Pronto estaremos de vuelta con Nathaniel, te lo prometo.

A los pocos instantes, Chastity caminaba junto a Cyn por la oscura calle, con la sensación de haber roto por fin con su vida anterior y de haberse embarcado hacia un misterioso y aterrorizador futuro. Pero el misterio y el miedo se centraban mucho más en el hombre que llevaba al lado que en el viaje que les esperaba juntos.

Le dirigió una mirada.

—Te gustan los niños, ¿no?

—¿Y a ti?

Había vuelto a olvidar que la tenía por un hombre; no se esperaba que a los muchachos les gustaran los niños. Cualquier día iba a cometer algún error que destruyera aquella ilusión y lo terrible es que tenía ganas de hacerlo. Quería poder encararlo honestamente, como una mujer enfrenta a un hombre, incluso si aquello significaba que él descubría que ella era Chastity Ware.

—No entiendo mucho de niños —dijo ella, y no era del todo falso. No había tratado a muchos y, debido a su desgracia, no había conocido al bebé de Verity hasta su precipitada visita.

—Ni yo tampoco —dijo él—. Soy el más pequeño de mi familia. Tal vez si hubiera crecido con un montón de ellos por medio no me gustarían tanto, pero, como no es el caso, los encuentro refrescantes.

—Sí —dijo Chastity pensativa—. Como la brisa en verano o una fuente en un día caluroso. En las tierras de la guerra, debe de notarse la ausencia de los niños.

—Ojalá fuera así. El lugar con frecuencia parece infestado de bribonzuelos hambrientos. Siento lástima por ellos, pero te confieso que no suelo encontrarlos refrescantes. Y, en lo básico, no son diferentes de los pequeños de Mary o de aquel chico que está barriendo el paso.

Chastity miró al pilluelo. Había puesto un cartel al lado de una antorcha. Cuando alguien se aproximaba, iba corriendo a barrer el polvo y los excrementos antes de que sus clientes cruzaran. Después, recogía diligentemente los peniques que le arrojaban. Ella no solía prestar atención a aquellos chiquillos. Bueno, casi no pensaba en ellos como verdaderos niños. Aquel chico tendría unos ocho años —recio, mugriento y de mirada rápida y sagaz.

—¿Se te parte el corazón? —preguntó Cyn con sequedad.

Ella observó cómo el chico inspeccionaba una moneda lanzada por un próspero clérigo y hacía un gesto grosero a sus espaldas.

—No. Pero esa persona tampoco me inspira en absoluto ningún sentimiento.

—El mundo está lleno de niños —dijo Cyn, y se dirigió a cruzar por el lugar en el que trabajaba el chico.

—¿Va todo bien? —le dijo al muchacho mientras pasaban.

El rapaz se reunió con ellos en el borde de la calzada, a la espera de sus honorarios.

—Vamos tirando, capitán.

Cyn le tiró una moneda.

—Eso por conocer la insignia, o por haber tenido suerte y haber acertado.

El muchacho sonrió al ver los seis peniques.

—¡Dios le bendiga, milord!

Cyn se rió y le lanzó otra.

—Has dado en el clavo las dos veces.

Él y Chastity se alejaron, dejando al chico dándoles las gracias extasiado.

—Hacer algo así resulta muy tentador —dijo Cyn—. Y muy fácil. Pero ¿es generosidad noble o simplemente una forma barata de sentirse Dios?

Chastity se encogió de hombros.

—Supongo que al chico no le importa eso. Cenará bien esta noche.

—No me ha parecido que tuviera aspecto de estar desnutrido. Es probable que se gaste el dinero en ginebra.

Chastity se preguntó si estaría bromeando, aunque parecía que no.

Ella pensaba que iban derechos a la posada, pero Cyn se detuvo y llamó a una puerta. Había un letrero que decía que aquel establecimiento era el banco de Darby.

—¿Qué estás haciendo? —preguntó ella.

—Llamar —dijo él, volviendo a golpear.

—Está cerrado.

—Hay gente dentro. —Llamó por tercera vez.

Cielos, pensó Chastity, debe pensar que la nobleza siempre puede salirse con la suya.

Un airado oficinista abrió la puerta y empezó a decirle que se largara. Cyn se limitó a decir:

—Lord Cynric Malloren. ¿Está Darby?

A los pocos segundos, se hallaban dentro, y todo el personal parecía estar a sus pies. Un caballero eminente, alto y con el pelo plateado, se presentó y, tras hacerles una reverencia, hizo pasar a Cyn una estancia privada en el interior.

Sin duda, se trataba del mismísimo señor Darby. Obviamente, la nobleza se salía siempre con la suya, al menos su representación masculina.

Chastity se apoyó contra la pared y disfrutó de las turbias miradas que los empleados le dedicaron por aquella conducta. Sin embargo, enseguida volvieron a agachar las cabezas sobre columnas de números, ansiosos por terminar la jornada de trabajo y marcharse a casa.

Al poco rato, Cyn era conducido al exterior, tras la correspondiente reverencia. Recogió a Chastity y ambos partieron hacia el Three Balls. Se le veía malhumorado.

—¿Qué ocurre? —preguntó Chastity maliciosamente—. ¿No han querido darte dinero?

—Hubieran estado dispuestos a darme hasta las malditas llaves de la caja fuerte —dijo él en tono cortante—. A veces detesto ser un Malloren.

—Sí, pero te has valido de ello para entrar allí.

Él la miró con frialdad.

—Por tu causa.

Chastity se sintió avergonzada.

—Sí, por supuesto. Lo siento.

Él suspiró.

—No debería pagarla contigo.

—¿Cómo es que conocen tu nombre?

—¡Que conocen mi nombre! Vaya, el viejo Darby me ha mecido en sus rodillas. La Abadía está a menos de veinte millas de aquí y mi dichoso hermano es uno de los consejeros.

Chastity tenía unas cuantas preguntas, pero, por su tono, dedujo que sería mejor guardar silencio. Los interrogantes, sin embargo, no dejaban de asaltarla.

¿Por qué cada vez que se mencionaba el nombre de su hermano, Cyn perdía su desenfadada alegría? Si la Abadía estaba tan cerca, ¿no hubiera sido más sensato refugiarse allí? Ni siquiera el conde de Walgrave intentaría pasar por encima de Rothgar. ¿Pensaba Cyn de verdad que Rothgar era capaz de entregarlos a su padre?

Se hallaron de vuelta en la posada con estas preguntas sin formular y sin responder, aunque Chastity estaba decidida a encontrar algunas respuestas antes de partir. Esta desavenencia con su hermano era la única nube que empañaba la vida de Cyn Malloren y, estando enamorada como estaba, ella haría lo que pudiera por despejarla.

El posadero estaba hablando con el joven que había observado con atención su llegada. El patrón sonreía y hacía reverencias, pero, tan pronto como el hombre se hubo marchado, escupió en la chimenea del recibidor.

—Malditos sabuesos. Siempre traen problemas.

—¿Buscan a alguien? —preguntó Cyn—. ¿Hay algún malhechor suelto?

—Oh, no se trata de ningún malhechor, milord. Sólo una pobre mujer que ha perdido el juicio y anda vagando por ahí. Pero este tipo lleva todo el día merodeando por aquí. ¿Creen que si viniera por aquí no se lo diría? Es lo menos que puedo hacer, al margen de la recompensa, ¿no? Bueno, señor, su habitación está lista y pronto tendrá una suculenta cena sobre su mesa. Le aseguro que mi mujer es una cocinera excelente.

Les condujo hacia las escaleras.

—He decidido que mi mozo de establo se quede conmigo —dijo Cyn—. ¿Tiene una habitación para él?

El posadero asintió.

—Hay sitio encima de los establos, junto a su cochero, milord.

Cyn le lanzó a Chastity una rápida y cautelosa mirada.

—Prefiero que duerma cerca de mí. También me sirve de ayuda de cámara cuando lo necesito.

—Oh, vale, señor. Hay un camastro con ruedas bajo la cama.

De nuevo, una ojeada significativa. El rostro de Chastity estaba tan en blanco como su mente. No había considerado aquella posibilidad.

—Preferiría dormir en habitaciones separadas —dijo Cyn—. Es que ronca.

—Señor —dijo el posadero con cierto malestar—. No tengo más habitaciones. Éste no es un sitio grande y sólo dispongo de tres, que ya están cogidas. Tendrá que elegir entre el catre o el establo.

Cyn miró a Chastity para darle la oportunidad de elegir. Pero ella estaba completamente obnubilada. Sabía que debería hacer cualquier cosa para evitar dormir en la misma habitación con un hombre, especialmente aquel hombre...

Cyn se volvió hacia el posadero y le dijo:

—De los dos males, el menor. Usará el catre. Y póngame un plato más. Charles comerá también conmigo.

En pocos instantes, se hallaron en una pequeña habitación, que todavía resultaba más pequeña por la pendiente del tejado.

—Procura no roncar, joven Charles —le dijo Cyn lentamente—, porque como me despiertes, te aseguro que yo te despertaré a ti.

Chastity echó un vistazo a la angosta habitación y reconoció que lo sensato habría sido tratar de evitar aquella situación, pero no se arrepentía de su imprudencia. A pesar de su reducido espacio, era una habitación acogedora y caldeada por un excelente fuego. La sólida cama contaba con sábanas limpias y frescas. No había ni gota de polvo sobre los delicados muebles, ni tampoco sobre el pulido suelo de madera de roble. Un jarrón de flores secas descansaba sobre una pequeña mesa delante de la ventana, y el aire estaba perfumado. En una esquina, detrás de un biombo, se veía un lavamanos, y había una mesa dispuesta para la comida.

Una vez que sacaran el catre, no quedaría apenas espacio, pero por lo demás, el sitio resultaba muy agradable. A Chastity le dio por imaginarse qué pasaría si fuera su noche de bodas y aquella habitación su cámara nupcial. Sería maravilloso Perfecto.

Pero si lady Chastity Ware acabara de casarse con lord Cyn Malloren, estarían en algún lugar mucho más grandioso. Allí eran únicamente el amo y su mozo, y ella debía ceñirse a su papel.

El posadero y una doncella entraron con la comida. Cyn dijo que se servirían ellos mismos y pronto él y Chastity se hallaron frente a una pitanza principesca. Tenían sopa, lenguado, pastel de cerdo y un pollo. Para completar la colación, había tartaletas de manzana y de queso Chastity empezó a comer por hacer algo, pero descubrió que tenía hambre de verdad.

Al cabo de un rato, Cyn dijo:

—El posadero decía la verdad. Su mujer es una excelente cocinera.

—Sí, desde luego. Y toda la posada parece estar muy bien atendida.

—Una joya, eso es lo que es. Tal vez debiera comentárselo a Rothgar. Él podría poner este sitio de moda.

Chastity masticaba un bocado de tierno pollo.

—¿Por qué adquiere tu voz ese tonillo cada vez que hablas de Rothgar? Dicen que es un hermano muy cumplidor.

Ella temía que le saliera con algún desaire, pero él se limitó a decir de manera rotunda:

—Es un hermano extremadamente cumplidor.

—Entonces, ¿por qué hablas de él como si lo odiaras?

Cyn le dirigió una mirada tan penetrante como el filo de un sable.

—Eres un muchacho descarado. Yo no odio para nada a mi hermano.

Chastity engarzó otro trozo de carne en su tenedor.

—Pero estás enfadado con él.

Él dejó caer sus cubiertos sobre el plato y, por un momento, ella pensó que le iba a poner las manos encima. Pero lo que hizo fue coger el vaso de vino y dar un buen trago de su borgoña.

—Estoy disgustado con él porque no quiere que regrese a mi regimiento. Tiene que meterse en todo, eso es muy típico de él. Pero yo ya no soy un niño. Sólo tengo que convencerle de que estoy completamente sano.

Chastity también abandonó la comida por el vino. Tenía los nervios a flor de piel, pero le parecía importante continuar con aquella conversación porque podía ser de gran ayuda para él.

—Es comprensible que estuviera ansioso si estabas tan enfermo como dice la señora Garnet.

Él se encogió de hombros.

—Supongo que lo estaba. La verdad es que no me acuerdo bien. Pero ahora me encuentro perfectamente. El ejército es mi vida, y él no va a apartarme de ella.

Chastity se sintió muy identificada con el marqués de Rothgar. Ella también, si pudiera, trataría de mantener a Cyn a salvo en casa, aunque sabía que no tenía un espíritu sumiso, capaz de acomodarse a la vida de un hombre de granja, de iglesia o de leyes.

—Seguramente no tendrá poder para separarte del ejército si tú estás decidido a irte.

Él soltó una aguda carcajada.

—No conoces a Rothgar. Con esa combinación que tiene de riqueza, encanto y crueldad, hay poca gente en Inglaterra dispuesta a llevarle la contraria. Tan pronto como diga a la Guardia Montada que estoy incapacitado, todo lo que podré esperar será un cargo decorativo, bien lejos de la acción. No pienso aceptar algo así.

—Si se preocupa tanto como dices, te estará buscando.

Él volvió a llenar los vasos.

—Espero que el hecho de que Hoskins esté conmigo aplaque sus temores, pero, sin duda, tienes razón, maldita sea.

—Henry *el Terrible*, sus secuaces, padre y Rothgar. Me sorprende que aún estemos sueltos.

Él hizo una súbita mueca y levantó su vaso.

—Pero lo estamos y mi intención es que sigamos estándolo. No te preocupes, joven Charles. Lo conseguiremos.

Entrechocaron los vasos y bebieron. Después volvieron a ocuparse de la comida. Chastity, sin embargo, estaba pensativa. Buena parte de los motivos que Cyn tenía para ayudarlas tenía que ver con los confusos sentimientos que albergaba hacia su hermano. ¿Qué ocurriría si Rothgar les daba alcance?

Cyn empezó a hablar de nuevo, esta vez de la vida en el ejército; de su lado más frívolo. Sus historias completaron el retrato que Chastity se había hecho de él, pero sin desmerecerlo. No era fanfarrón, pero estaba lleno de coraje y compasión, y no le faltaban recursos. La hizo reír y, en una ocasión, casi le hace llorar.

Después pasó a contar historias sobre las maravillas del Nuevo Mundo y la llevó hasta bosques profundos y ríos magníficos. Describió extraños indios y abundante vida salvaje.

Aquella intimidad era peligrosa, y Chastity lo sabía, pero no podía resistirse a ella, porque le resultaba sencillamente deliciosa. Era como si estuvieran casados y se sintieran cómodos el uno junto al otro, como si aquella noche fuera de hecho su noche de bodas.

Su mirada se deslizo lasciva hasta la incitante cama...

Basta, Chastity.

Pero no podía poner fin a aquello. Se hallaba embelesada contemplando las manos de Cyn sobre los cubiertos y el cristal. Su bronceada y esbelta fuerza la tenía aturdida. Se fijó por primera vez en un hoyuelo que le salía en la mejilla derecha cuando sonreía, y en cómo los ojos le cambiaban de verdes a dorados, en función del estado de ánimo.

El cuerpo de Chastity se había vuelto hipersensible, incluso al movimiento de sus propias ropas. Todo actuaba sobre sus sentidos: el repiqueteo de la leña de manzano en el fuego; el traqueteo de las ruedas en la calle; el bronco cantar en la taberna; la voz de Cyn agradable y sonora al otro lado de la mesa...

Él interrumpió su cháchara.

—No estás comiendo, Charles. ¿Has terminado?

Ella bajó la vista hasta los cubiertos que descansaban en sus laxas manos y los dejó en el plato.

—Creo que sí.

—¿Cómo? ¿Sin postre? —bromeó él, cogiendo un pastelillo—. Tienes que probarlos. Están deliciosos.

Y lo sostuvo delante de ella.

—Abre la boca.

Chastity contempló el pastelillo de manzana. Estaba cubierto por una capa dorada y reluciente, y bordeado por un volante de suculenta crema amarilla. Chastity se relamió y después separó lentamente los labios. Él le puso el dulce entre los dientes y le dijo.

—Muerde.

Sus miradas se encontraron por encima del pastel. Ella se acordó de aquel bizcocho en Shaftesbury...

Hundió los dientes en la suave y dulce fruta y el crujiente hojaldre se desmoronó y absorbió el estallido de sabor. Mientras masticaba, se pasó la lengua por los labios y los notó cubiertos del brillo de la crema. Masticaba un tanto aturdida pues seguía prendida de su aprobadora mirada. Entre un hombre y una mujer, aquello sería coqueteo...

No, entre un hombre y una mujer, aquello sería pura seducción.

¿Estaba Cyn tratando de seducir a Charles?

—Está muy bueno —dijo ella con nerviosismo.

—¿Sí? —preguntó él con suavidad. Después giró el pastelillo y mordió por la parte en que ella lo había hecho. Saboreó y tragó su parte—. Mmmm —murmuró—. Una obra de arte. —Y lamió lentamente algunas migas doradas que se habían quedado sobre sus labios. Dio un nuevo mordisco y después le tendió a ella el dulce con una inquisitiva mirada.

Chastity pensó en Adán y Eva, en las manzanas y en el Paraíso...

Sacudió apresuradamente la cabeza, se puso de pie, dando la espalda a la tentación, y buscó el frescor de la ventana.

—Ha sido una comida estupenda —dijo con rudeza—. Pero estoy llena.

—Hay ocasiones para el desenfreno, mi querido Charles. Esta podría ser una de ellas. —Aquellas sencillas palabras parecían cargadas de multitud de significados.

—Eso sería perverso.

—¿Y tú nunca eres perverso?

Aunque no lo tuviera a la vista, su poder sobre ella no había disminuido. El corazón le saltaba en el pecho. Sus trémulas terminaciones nerviosas anhelaban que la tocara.

—Intento no serlo —dijo ella secamente.

Cyn la miraba. El deseo casi le estaba causando vértigo. Cuando ella se había empeñado en acompañarlo y se había avenido alegremente a compartir con él la habitación, llegó a la conclusión de que era una libertina. Él estaba más que dispuesto a seguirle el juego, si es que era eso lo que ella quería. Tal vez un breve episodio de lujuria fuera lo que necesitaba para librarse de aquella enajenante aflicción.

Se había entretenido preguntándose cuándo y cómo le confesaría ella su condición de mujer y decidió dejar aquel asunto en sus expertas manos. Sin embargo, él se había relajado mucho a cuenta de la buena comida, el vino y la atenta mirada de la muchacha. Enseguida pasó a desnudarle su alma y, a continuación, se puso a coquetear con ella de forma descarada.

Y la chica le tenía confundido.

Temía que sus primeras impresiones hubieran sido correctas. Se trataba de una inocente que simplemente había cometido un desastroso error. Aunque, en ese caso, ¿qué es lo que la había empujado a ir con él allí esa noche? ¿Tal vez un candor de proporciones catastróficas?

Al pensar en su posible inocencia sentía hacia ella un deseo brutal e imperioso y, al mismo tiempo, algo le decía que no debía tocarla. Cuando trató de alcanzar el vino, la mano le temblaba.

La observó por encima del borde del vaso. Podía ver a través de las voluminosas capas de ropa e imaginársela desnuda. Recorrió con la vista la delicada línea de su recta espalda, la firme redondez de sus nalgas y sus largas y bien torneadas piernas. Se moría de ganas de desvestirla lentamente, de explorar con suavidad cada pulgada de su sedosa piel, de degustar su salado sabor y beberse el perfume almizcleño de sus lugares más íntimos. Deseaba observar cómo aquella azorada ingenuidad se transformaba en éxtasis.

Se levantó bruscamente.

—Lo mejor será que nos vayamos a la cama si queremos partir por la mañana temprano. Hay un retrete en el patio. Voy a salir a usarlo.

Chastity se dio la vuelta y vio cómo la puerta se cerraba tras él. Parpadeó sorprendida, pero dejó escapar un largo suspiro. Sabía que ambos acababan de escapar de aquella situación por los pelos y que debería estar agradecida por ello. Pero no lo estaba. Sentía su ausencia como si estuviera en carne viva.

Suspiró. Tal vez el nombre le predestinara a uno. Verity, después de todo, no podía decir una simple mentira. Tal vez llamarse Chastity implicara que ella nunca podría dar rienda suelta a sus deseos.

Irguió la espalda. Habían salido airosos de aquel momento de peligro y tenía que asegurarse de que no se iba a producir ningún otro. Si no iba a ser capaz de acompañarle sin poner al descubierto su disfraz, debía irse ahora mismo a casa de Mary Garnet.

Se dijo a sí misma que todo iría bien. Aquélla sería la última noche que pasaban en la carretera, puesto que, al día siguiente, llegarían a Maidenhead.

Se metió apresuradamente detrás del biombo y utilizó el orinal. Rápidamente, se despojó de sus ropas exteriores, quedándose con la camisa y los pantalones de buena calidad. Después, sacó el estrecho catre y se acurrucó bajo las mantas, simulando estar profundamente dormida.

Él tardó un buen rato en regresar. Ya empezaba a estar preocupada por su seguridad, pero, cuando finalmente apareció, todo parecía estar en orden. Chastity le vio prepararse para irse a la cama a través de los entrecerrados párpados, sabiendo que aquello era una intrusión en su intimidad, pero sin arrepentirse. Para su decepción, él se cambió y se lavó detrás de la pantalla, de donde salió con una camisola para meterse en la cama. Ella se quedó escuchando su tranquila respiración.

Había dormido a menudo con Verity y sabía lo reconfortante que resultaba tener cerca un cuerpo caliente por la noche. Trató de imaginar qué sentiría al tener a su lado el cuerpo de Cyn frotándose contra el suyo, con su particular aroma alrededor. Intentó detener aquellos pensamientos. No le hacían ningún bien, y, desde luego, no promovían el sueño…

Un sexto sentido le había dicho a Cyn que ella estaba todavía despierta y le hizo ser cauto en sus preparativos para irse a la cama. Ahora, se esforzaba por detectar algún sonido que se lo confirmara. Esperaba y temía a la vez alguna clase de invitación. Todavía excitado, a pesar del largo paseo que se había dado, sabía que el más mínimo estímulo bastaría para hacerle vencer todos sus escrúpulos…

Chastity sentía que la atmósfera de la habitación la oprimía pesadamente. Era consciente de la cercana presencia de él, de su respiración. Tenía que detener aquello antes de hacer ninguna tontería. Se imaginó a sí misma de vuelta en la cabaña de Nana, ayudándola en las tareas domésticas, dando de comer a las gallinas, leyendo uno de los libros con los que solía pasar el tiempo. Había descubierto los relatos de viajes, con los que disfrutaba mucho. Encontraba en ellos una manera de escapar a tierras lejanas…

Cyn asumió que no habría ningún gesto incitante y, después de todo, se alegró de ello. No sabía en qué acabaría aquella situación, pero lo que quería obtener de su damisela era algo más que una explosión de lujuria.

Sin duda ella debía estar ya durmiendo y él debería hacer lo mismo. Se concentró en ello. A lo largo de sus años de campañas militares, que a menudo le deparaban dormitorios que dejaban mucho que desear, había desarrollado la capacidad de conciliar el sueño en cualquier circunstancia.

La habitación se sumió en una somnolienta tranquilidad.

9

Chastity se despertó con la grisácea luz del amanecer y escuchó el distante traqueteo de la posada. Durante unos instantes, se preguntó dónde se hallaba y por qué había dormido con la ropa puesta. Después, lo recordó todo.

Verity, Winchester, Cyn...

Abrió un poquito los ojos y miró hacia la cama, pero, desde el bajo jergón en el que se encontraba, no pudo ver a su ocupante. Se deslizó cautelosamente desde debajo de las mantas, ansiosa por terminar de asearse antes de que él se despertara. Se incorporó sobre el suelo silenciosamente en calcetines y...

Vio a Cyn sentado junto a la ventana, con los pies en el alféizar, mirándola.

—Estaba a punto de despertarte, muchacho —le dijo él plácidamente—. Ya he pedido el desayuno. Tenemos que ponernos en camino.

—Vale —dijo Chastity y se escabulló detrás del biombo. ¿Sería distinto el sonido de una mujer al orinar? Esperaba que no.

Se puso su segunda capa de ropas, la peluca, el sombrero y salió con fuerzas renovadas. Él la examinó y pareció que fuera a hacer algún comentario, pero antes de que pudiera hablar, el posadero y una doncella entraron con un copioso desayuno. Cyn se encogió de hombros y le hizo un gesto a la muchacha, indicándole que se sentara a la mesa.

Las aventuras deben abrir el apetito. Chastity pensó que, a juzgar por el aprecio que hizo al jamón, los huevos, los riñones y el pan frito, bien podía pasar por un jovenzuelo hambriento.

—Hoy deberíamos llegar a Maidenhead, ¿no? —preguntó mientras ambos rebañaban los restos de la comida de sus platos.

—Si todo va bien y el tiempo no empeora. Pongámonos en marcha.

Al cabo de media hora, salían trotando de Winchester. Los caballos que habían alquilado no eran precisamente de raza, pero parecían bastante robustos y resistentes. Tanto mejor, porque aquel día tendrían que transportar a sus jinetes durante más de treinta millas.

Había mucha humedad en el aire y Chastity se felicitó por la doble capa de ropa y el grueso manto de montar. El sol se agazapaba detrás de lóbregas nubes sin intención de iluminar los árboles sin hojas y los pelados arbustos que se erguían muy tiesos sobre la oscura tierra labrada. Deseó que el tenebroso día no encerrara ningún augurio sobre la suerte que les esperaba.

A Cyn, sin embargo, le brillaban los ojos. ¿No había nada que hiciera a aquel hombre sumirse en la melancolía?

—Anímate —dijo él—. El día mejorará. Encontraremos a Frazer y pondremos fin a los problemas de Verity. Después, podremos ocuparnos de los tuyos.

Chastity dio un respingo sobre las riendas, haciendo que el caballo se plantara.

—¿Qué?

—Ten cuidado. Sin duda, su boca es fuerte como el hierro, pero eso no es motivo para andarla rozando. No podría enviarte de vuelta a tu encierro en la cabaña sin intentar echarte una mano. Soy un fervoroso caballero andante, ¿no te acuerdas?

—Me parece que yo no soy una damisela en apuros.

Él la miró bastante serio.

—Aún así, me gustaría ayudarte. ¿Qué crimen has cometido para que te enviaran al exilio?

—La desobediencia —dijo Chastity con desolación.

—Tienes un padre tremendamente estricto.

—Así es.

—Y ¿cuánto tiempo va a durar tu castigo?

Chastity no podía soportar aquello. La tentación de contarle sus penas a Cyn era demasiado grande. Le miró con frialdad

—Mis pequeños problemas no son de tu incumbencia, milord. Cuando arreglemos lo de Verity, yo regresaré con Nana y tú te verás libre de ambas.

Él se mostró conforme, pero a ella no le gustó demasiado la intensa mirada que le dedicó antes de apresurar el paso.

Aquel suave galope le sacó el frío de los huesos pero no alivió el que sentía en su corazón. Su asociación tenía las horas contadas.

Chastity decidió no pensar ni en el pasado ni en el futuro y disfrutar del breve tiempo que le quedaba con Cyn. Al pensar en ello, brotó en su interior una carcajada y ella la dejó escapar. Él le sonrió y ella hizo lo mismo. El día estaba mejorando a marchas forzadas.

Una vez más, él demostró que tenía un excelente sentido de la orientación. Con frecuencia, se salían de la ajetreada carretera y tomaban caminos de caballos que atravesaban la campiña, siempre en dirección noreste, hacia Londres, pero vadeando las rutas principales, ya que Maidenhead quedaba al oeste de la ciudad.

Él no imprimió un ritmo demasiado rápido, pero Chastity dio gracias por las numerosas horas que había cabalgado a horcajadas durante su exilio, porque, de no haber sido por eso, no habría sido capaz de mantener el tipo. Así las cosas, cuando pararon al mediodía para dar de comer a los caballos y alimentarse ellos mismos, entró contoneándose en la posada y manteniendo la adecuada compostura.

Comieron en la sala común, donde compartieron la mesa con un carretero, un médico entrado en años y un oficinista de pálida tez. Chastity se preguntaba porque Cyn se aventuraba a comer en público cuando podían haber alquilado una habitación privada, pero disfrutó de la experiencia. Nunca había comido en semejante compañía. Pronto descubrió por qué Cyn había elegido aquel recinto. Por el cotilleo.

—Hay muchos militares por aquí —dijo el recio carretero, tras echar una ojeada al uniforme de Cyn—. ¿Hay algún problema con los franceses?

—Que yo sepa no —dijo Cyn—. Existe cierta preocupación en torno a la posibilidad de que la guerra en curso anime a los franceses y los jacobitas a intentarlo de nuevo, aunque desde luego no aquí, en la costa sur. De ocurrir algo, sería en Irlanda.

—Siempre andan buscando problemas —dijo el carretero y escupió, aunque sin dejar claro si se refería a los jacobitas o a los irlandeses—. De todos modos, varias patrullas nos han estado controlando a lo largo de la carretera de Londres. Algo pasa.

—Yo sé de que se trata —dijo el doctor con rostro afligido, limpiándose los labios con la servilleta—. Una pobre dama vaga por ahí desquiciada. La viuda de un noble caballero. Y lleva con ella al heredero del aristócrata.

El carretero frunció el ceño mientras masticaba un enorme bocado de carne de buey.

—Un montón de casacas rojas por un difunto. Nunca había visto tantos, ni siquiera en el 45.

—No exagere —dijo el médico—. En aquellos días aciagos, apenas podíamos movernos sin que nos interrogaran. No es que me pareciera mal. Si por mí fuera, todos los simpatizantes de los Estuardo deberían ser ajusticiados. Me ofende profundamente saber que hay por ahí muchos tipos sueltos de los que hubieran corrido a congregarse bajo el estandarte de Charles Edward Stuart. ¡Pero, ahora, incluso tenemos a un escocés como mano derecha del rey!

El oficinista intervino en este punto para declarar que su madre era escocesa, y que no todos los escoceses eran traidores. Muy pronto la comida se caldeó con los asuntos políticos y el doctor continuó con su diatriba contra los jacobitas y lord Bute.

Cuando él médico se marchó, el carretero volvió a escupir.

—Ese hombre sería capaz de entregar a su abuela para que la ahorcaran y seguir considerándose una buena persona. Sobre todo si hay dinero de por medio.

—Pero nuestro deber es oponernos a la traición —comentó Cyn.

El carretero contempló su uniforme con inquietud pero no se calló.

—Sí, pero la lucha contra la traición siempre saca a la palestra a aquellos que tienen algún agravio y a quienes pretenden humillar a otros. Muchas fortunas cambian de manos en los tiempos difíciles.

—Eso es bien cierto —dijo el oficinista con amargura—. Y muchos de los vencedores resultarían tan traidores como los perdedores si se supiera la verdad. Mirad los Campbell, por ejemplo. —Él también se puso de pie y se sacudió la ropa—. Debería estar alerta por si se encuentra con la mujer desaparecida, capitán. Yo así lo haré. Se ofrece una considerable recompensa. Y, puesto que ella estará mejor cuando la encuentren, no será dinero manchado de sangre.

—Sí, decís bien —dijo el carretero—. Pero con el estrecho cerco que hay en las afueras de Londres, esa mujer tendría que ser un hada para llegar a cualquier punto al norte de aquí. Da pena decirlo, pero un día de éstos la sacarán de algún río, con bebé y todo. —Se levantó y fue a enganchar su coche de ocho caballos para continuar su lento y largo viaje hacia Somerset.

Cyn y Chastity salieron también a pedir sus caballos. Mientras esperaban a que se los dieran, Cyn dijo:

—Me ha parecido detectar en ti cierta simpatía hacia los jacobitas, ¿es así? ¿Te ha tocado el corazón el príncipe Charlie *el Bello* y sus gallardos soldados montañeses? Si es así, nos hallamos en bandos opuestos.

—No, no soy jacobita. Pero, por lo que he oído, los montañeses fueron valientes y fieles a sus ideales. Las represalias fueron demasiado severas. Demasiadas familias deshechas. Y cada vez que paso por debajo de Temple Bar y veo las cabezas que siguen descomponiéndose allí… —Se estremeció—. Como ha dicho nuestro amigo el carretero, hay sin duda muchos traidores que no han sido descubiertos, los tramposos que esperaron a ver de que lado soplaba el viento, mientras que los hombres valientes pagaron su precio.

—Eres demasiado ingenuo, muchacho. Muchos jacobitas pensaban que se hallaban en el lado ganador. La triste verdad es que la mayoría de los hombres van a ver qué es lo que pueden sacar con sus acciones.

Mientras comprobaba la cincha y se montaba en su silla, Chastity dijo:

—¿Incluso los caballeros andantes?

Cyn le dirigió una furtiva mirada.

—Incluso ellos.

Cuando cabalgaban por la carretera de Exeter, en dirección norte, el cielo volvió a encapotarse de un modo que amenazaba lluvia. En noviembre, el crepúsculo llegaba pronto, pero, aquel día, parecía que iba a adelantarse aún más.

—No tiene buena pinta —dijo Cyn, echando un vistazo al cielo. Apremió a su caballo y Chastity hizo lo mismo.

Poco después, el caballo de Cyn perdió una herradura.

Él soltó una retahíla de vívidos juramentos en varios idiomas.

—Tendré que llevarlo hasta la próxima aldea —dijo—, y esperemos que haya herrero. A lo lejos veo una alta torre de iglesia. Creo que es una buena señal, vamos.

Empezó a lloviznar y ambos se pusieron las capuchas de sus capas.

—Dudo que lleguemos esta noche a Maidenhead —dijo él irritado—. Si hay amenaza de tormenta, será mejor que no lo intentemos. —Después se encogió de hombros—. De hecho, tal vez sea mejor así. Si paramos a pasar la noche en una aldea apartada, llamaremos menos la atención que si aparecemos tarde y llenos de barro en Maidenhead, donde sin duda el cerco es más estrecho.

Él levantó la vista, como invitándola a romper su silencio.

—Sí, tienes razón —dijo Chastity. Otra noche en la carretera. Oh, Señor.

Para cuando llegaron al pequeño pueblo de East Green, la tensión había hecho que la cabeza de Chastity estuviera a punto de estallar. Se detuvieron en el Angel, un sencillo edificio cuadrado de la calle principal, con un pequeño patio contiguo para los carruajes. Al abrir la puerta, su cálida luz y su agradable charla se difundieron por el patio. El cordial posadero les aseguró que quedaban habitaciones y que había un herrero en esa misma calle. Su mozo de cuadra llevaría el caballo a herrar.

No había ningún vigía evidente por allí, pero lo primero que Chastity vio dentro del Angel fue un cartel clavado en un poste.

Desaparecida. Recompensa. Y, debajo, un dibujo bastante bueno de Verity. Estaba sacado del retrato que le hicieron nada más casarse. Se parecía mucho, pero tenía aires de gran dama, con el pelo recogido en alto, el corpiño escotado y el cuello rodeado de diamantes. Chastity sospechó que Verity, con su actual aspecto, incluso el de matrona respetable, no ya el de desaliñada sirvienta, podría estar de pie junto aquel poste sin que nadie la reconociese.

Cyn captó la mirada de Chastity y le guiñó un ojo. Ella le devolvió el gesto, sintiéndose aliviada al comprobar que la persecución tenía sus fallos.

Y el posadero había dicho habitaciones. Esta vez no la tentaría la insensatez.

Todo iba a salir bien.

Se hallaban hablando de los aposentos y la cena con el mesonero, cuando una voz bramó:

—¡Cyn Malloren! ¡Eres tú! ¡Por todos los santos, qué caro eres de ver! ¡Creía que la habías palmado!

Se dieron la vuelta y vieron a un oficial que salía de la cantina. Su aspecto era jovial, con las mejillas regordetas y grandes ojos azules, pero también medía bastante más de un metro ochenta y tenía la complexión de una estatua de piedra. Cuando agarró a Cyn, Chastity pensó que lo iba a romper.

—¡Gresham! —exclamó Cyn, evidentemente complacido a pesar del abrazo—. ¿Qué estás haciendo en el culo del mundo?

—Ajá —declaró Gresham—. Hoy es tu día de suerte, chico. No necesita habitaciones —le dijo al posadero—. El capitán Malloren se alojara conmigo en Rood House.

—¿Rood House? —preguntó Cyn—. ¿Es tu casa?

—No, la de Heather. —Pasó un brazo alrededor de los hombros de Cyn y le condujo hacia la taberna, volviendo la cabeza para soltar:

—¡Pónganos más ponche de ése, patrón, y rápido!

Chastity entornó los ojos y les siguió. ¿Era Cyn Malloren conocido y querido por toda Inglaterra? Los dos oficiales se sentaron en una mesa junto al fuego y la emprendieron con lo que quedaba de un tazón de ponche caliente. Chastity se sentó en un banco cercano. A excepción de una rápida mirada para comprobar dónde estaba, Cyn la ignoró por completo mientras él y su amigo se ponían al día.

En la cantina, había un puñado de lugareños, ocupados en degustar la cerveza casera del Angel. Observaron a los jóvenes oficiales con un leve y benévolo interés, y después volvieron a sus cotilleos y su dominó. El sonido de las fichas calmó los nervios de Verity.

El posadero entró presuroso con otro humeante cuenco a rebosar. Chastity lo contempló con cierta alarma. ¿Se había bebido ya aquel gigante uno como aquél? Por lo que pudo apreciar, contenía principalmente brandy y ron. En un abrir y cerrar de ojos, los dos estarían borrachos como cubas.

Gresham no daba ninguna muestra de fatiga mientras llenaba dos vasos con aquel líquido. Ni de falta de consideración.

—¿Va contigo? —inquirió haciendo un gesto con la cabeza en dirección a Chastity—. ¿Querrá beber?

—La respuesta a las dos preguntas es sí —dijo Cyn, repantigándose en su silla—. Pero no le pongas demasiado. Es un tierno retoño que lleva poco tiempo lejos de su madre.

Chastity hizo una mueca al oír esta descripción pero se solazó con la exquisita y aromática bebida. Notó cómo el caliente licor se le metía en la sangre y la relajaba. Apoyó la cabeza contra la pared y se negó a preocuparse de nada por el momento.

Dios, cuánto daría por tener paz, y amigos, y días normales...

Escuchaba a medias la conversación de los dos hombres, pero sólo oía noticias de la guerra y anécdotas de gente que no conocía. Ambos se reían estrepitosamente de cosas que para ella no tenían la menor gracia.

Empezó a sentirse desplazada, desconectada del mundo real de Cyn. Incluso contuvo una lágrima con un sollozo. Entonces se incorporó de un respingo y contempló con recelo la bebida que había en su vaso. Cielos, ¿iría a darle una borrachera llorona?

En aquel momento, otros dos hombres irrumpieron en la taberna.

—No temas —declaró uno de ellos dramáticamente—. ¡Hemos venido a sacarte de este aburrido lugar para llevarte al Paraíso!

Aquel galán de pelo oscuro no llevaba uniforme, sino un magnífico y desaliñado traje de satén verde, profusamente adornado. Estaba claro que aquel era Heather —lord Heatherington—, el dueño de Rood House. Su acompañante era el teniente Toby Berrisford.

Fue Toby quien dijo:

—¡Cyn! ¡Me habían dicho que estabas recuperado, pero me alegro de comprobarlo con mis propios ojos!

Lord Heatherington, que estaba visiblemente borracho, tenía dificultad para enfocar la vista:

—¡Voto a Dios que se trata del mismísimo Malloren! ¡Bendito día! ¡Tenemos una cosa más que festejar!

La escena degeneró hasta convertirse en puro griterío. Los lugareños miraban sonrientes a los jóvenes, pero Chastity frunció el ceño. ¿No era Cyn Malloren capaz de tener presente una tarea seria si se le presentaba la ocasión de estar de parranda? Tal vez había hecho bien en acompañarle, después de todo.

La situación se resolvió de la siguiente manera: Cyn pasaría la noche en Rood House, para ayudar a lord Heatherington a celebrar la muerte de su abuelo, acontecimiento largamente esperado que, finalmente, había hecho que el vizconde y ex capitán pasara a poseer una gran fortuna.

Cyn se llevó a Chastity a un aparte.

—Si digo que no, daré más que hablar. Lo mejor será que tú te quedes aquí.

—¡No! —dijo Chastity. Sólo Dios sabía cuándo aparecería él y en qué estado.

—Estarás a salvo. Este lugar queda al margen de las rutas principales.

—Necesitas a alguien junto a ti que mantenga la cabeza fría.

—Conociendo a Heather, aquello será un desmadre total—dijo Cyn con tajante autoridad—. Quédate aquí.

Antes de que Chastity pudiera reaccionar ante aquella orden, su conversación se vio interrumpida.

—¡Vaya! ¿Qué tenemos aquí? —preguntó lord Heatherington con la afabilidad que produce la embriaguez—. ¿Es tu criado? ¿Dónde está Jerome?

—Descansando —dijo Cyn—. Le molesta la pierna. Éste es un muchacho de la zona que me sirve de mozo de establo. Puede quedarse aquí tranquilamente.

—¡Ni hablar! Tengo sitio para todos y mis criados están teniendo también una fiesta de campeonato. Ven con nosotros, muchacho. ¡Te saldrá pelo en el pecho y se te atiesará la parte conveniente!

Chastity se vio arrastrada hacia el carruaje de lord Heatherington. Le lanzó a Cyn una mirada de alarma, pero él se limitó a encogerse de hombros, aunque a ella le dio la impresión de que estaba molesto. Sin embargo, tenía razón, protestar sólo serviría para levantar sospechas. Toby Berrisford, por ejemplo, podía reconocer al joven que había ido con la señora Inchcliff y, de ese modo, empezar a pensar en ella y en su bebé.

Los cinco en el coche iban muy apretados, teniendo en cuenta que Gresham y Heatherington eran corpulentos.

—Debería haber dejado que Charles fuera en el pescante —dijo Cyn, empujando a Chastity hasta el suelo. Ella ocultó la cara entre las rodillas—. Quédate ahí abajo muchacho, déjanos a los demás movernos a nuestras anchas.

Chastity refunfuñó interiormente pero sabía que tenía que tener cuidado. Berrisford no era tonto y no parecía que estuviera bebido. Por lo menos, pensó estoicamente, el suelo del carruaje estaba cubierto por una lujosa alfombra y no por mugrienta paja, como era el caso en los coches de alquiler.

Cuando el vehículo empezó a coger velocidad, Heatherington se puso a cantar y los demás se le sumaron enseguida.

> *Aquí va mi canción para un hermoso pecho*
> *Tan hermoso como su dulce y hermosa dueña*
> *Ven, dame tu pecho, mi dulce pequeña*
> *Y todos mis encantos gozarás en el lecho*
> *Trialará, trialará, !ará*

Chastity levantó la vista por entre la rodilla y el ala del sombrero, queriendo compartir con Cyn la diversión producida por esa tonta cancioncilla. Pero él no la estaba mirando sino que entre verso y verso, había aprovechado para dar un buen trago de una botella. El muy puñetero, parecía hallarse en perfecta sintonía con sus compañeros.

Aquellos hombres parecían conocer una ilimitada reserva de canciones similares. Las melodías eran monótonas, las letras no eran nada poéticas y los temas eran todos lascivos. Para poder comprenderlas, Chastity tendría que haber recibido una excelente educación en asuntos picantes.

Al pensar en ello, fruncía el entrecejo. «Agujero de abajo» le pareció que había entendido, aunque no le encontró sentido a la canción en la que lo decían. Pero ¿qué significaba beber de la taza de abajo? La interpretación obvia era demasiado ridícula.

De todos modos, todo sonaba ridículo.

Los hombres emitían rugidos de aprobación por ser atados de pies y manos y comidos, ¡comidos! y por tener cinco mujeres en fila. Chastity se entretuvo pensando en cuál sería el sentido de aquello. ¿Querría decir que hacían cola, se preguntaba, o que se colocaban una detrás de otra?

También bramaron para expresar su conformidad con los hombros delicados, las redondas nalgas y los enormes pechos. Chastity pensó con tristeza en sus modestos senos. Difícilmente sobresaldrían de las manos de nadie.

Cantaron las glorias de un gran y tupido matojo entre las piernas de una moza. Chastity también carecía de eso. Apenas tenía unos cuantos bucles castaños.

En la buena sociedad, los hombres dedicaban hermosos cumplidos a los suaves labios de cereza y los brillantes ojos azul cielo. Pero ¿sería eso lo que realmente querían? Entonces, ¿qué es lo que ella tenía que ofrecer? Nada de pechos como melones, ni abultadas nalgas ni espesuras entre los muslos.

Ahora seguían hablando de besar un culo colorado. Eso sonaba como si a alguien le hubieran dado algún azote.

Vaya, ahora cantaban cosas más normales, como labios de cereza. ¿Labios de abajo de cereza...?

Tiraron de ella hacia arriba y la empujaron fuera del carruaje. Ya habían llegado a su destino. El que la había agarrado era Cyn, que tenía pinta de estar bastante enfadado. En realidad, parecía estar hecho una furia.

—Lo siento —murmuró ella—. No se me ha ocurrido qué es lo que podía hacer para no venir.

—Tampoco a mí —admitió él. Luego la arrastró hacia sí—. Escucha con atención. Voy a encontrar un lugar seguro para ti y, cuando lo haga, vas a quedarte allí pase lo que pase. Te prometo que si no lo haces te voy a poner el culo bien colorado.

Ella le miró fijamente.

—¿Era eso lo que quería decir la canción?

Él levantó brevemente la vista hacia el cielo.

—Limítate a cerrar los ojos y taparte los oídos. —Cyn la asió fuertemente del brazo, y ambos entraron en la casa.

Rood House era un hermoso edificio jacobeo, con ventanas emplomadas y empinados gabletes. Estaba hecho para la elegancia y los madrigales, pero, tras sus puertas talladas, reinaba el desbarajuste.

El acogedor vestíbulo de madera de roble con su amplia escalera estaba iluminado únicamente por un par de resplandecientes y humeantes faroles, pero lleno de gente. Algunos estaban tirados por el suelo o sobre los escalones a causa de la bebida y la lujuria. Otros pasaban zigzagueantes por delante de Chastity con destino a otras habitaciones. A juzgar por los alaridos, los cánticos estridentes y la música discordante, aquella casa estaba siendo el escenario de una bacanal. El aire estaba saturado de humo, vapores etílicos y perfumes sudorosos.

El ruido le resultaba ensordecedor, pero fue el olor lo que hizo que la cabeza le diera vueltas. Se inclinó contra Cyn, cuyo abrazo pasó de ser represor a brindarle apoyo.

Berrisford y Gresham desaparecieron inmediatamente entre el gentío. Heatherington sonreía benévolamente a sus convidados y compañeros de juerga.

—Menuda fiesta, ¿no? Tu muchacho puede ir al piso de abajo y sumarse allí a la diversión.

—No —dijo Cyn—. Prefiero que se quede conmigo.

Heatherington le miró con extrañeza pero se encogió de hombros.

—Entonces, venid. Os voy a enseñar nuestro teatro.

Cyn no se movió.

—No me habías dicho que esto sería una orgía, Heather.

—¿Y qué fiesta que se precie no lo es? —Su anfitrión frunció el ceño y enfocó la vista hacia ellos con cierta dificultad—. ¿Te están entrando remilgos con la edad, Cyn?

—Es sólo que estoy preocupado por mi uniforme —dijo Cyn—. Es nuevo. ¿Hay alguna habitación en la que pueda cambiarme?

—Debe haber alguna… —dijo Heatherington con vaguedad. Una voluptuosa pelirroja se le había enganchado del brazo y se frotaba contra él. Sus senos estaban prácticamente al descubierto, pero el rostro, por encima de los sensuales labios rojos, estaba oculto tras una máscara plateada. Sus atenciones subyugaron al anfitrión—. Este sitio es grande —murmuró—. Debe haber alguna habitación…

No era de extrañar que el hombre no pudiera articular cuatro palabras seguidas a la vista del modo en que la pelirroja lo estaba distrayendo. Chastity contuvo una risita nerviosa. ¡Si alguien la palpaba de aquella manera, estaría en apuros! Insólitamente, la mujer le resultaba extrañamente familiar. Chastity miró a su alrededor. Aproximadamente, la mitad de las mujeres llevaban máscaras. Esto parecía indicar que se trataba de damas de la alta sociedad que andaban a la búsqueda de aventuras amorosas, como se decía que ocurría en el Club Hell-Fire.

—Para, chica —le dijo el anfitrión a su torturadora, dándole un manotazo en la mano invasora—. Estate quieta un segundo —Se volvió hacia Cyn—. Sube las escaleras y búscala tú mismo. La habitación que más te guste. Búscala tu mismo... Usa lo que te parezca... —Se volvió hacia su desobediente acompañante y se olvidó de ellos.

Chastity se arrimó un poco más, tratando de identificar a la mujer, pero Cyn la apartó de un tirón.

—Te va el *voyeurismo*, ¿no? Entonces, te he traído al lugar adecuado, ¿no es cierto?

Cyn se abrió paso en línea recta hacia las escaleras a través de la multitud borracha, y a pesar de que tres mujeres le abordaron para hacerle proposiciones. Se paró con cada una de ellas para ofrecerles amables excusas por tener que posponer su encuentro.

—¡Vaya! Vas a estar muy ocupado —dijo Chastity entre dientes.

Él le apretó aún más el brazo y estuvo a punto de producirle un moretón.

—Todo por una buena causa. No queremos que nadie nos haga ninguna pregunta inconveniente, ¿verdad?

Pasaron por encima de una pareja que había perdido el sentido y permanecía abrazada. Luego, subieron por las escaleras.

Una mujer joven y sin máscara bajaba hacia ellos. La abundante pintura y los muchos lunares no conseguían ocultar las cacarañas de su rostro, pero su figura era asombrosamente curvilínea. Se estiró el corpiño un poco más hacia abajo, cosa que parecía imposible, y balanceó las caderas.

—Vaya, ¿qué tenemos aquí? Dos apuestos amantes para Sal. Qué suerte la mía... —Se pasó la lengua por los labios y los miró con pericia profesional. Se acercó furtivamente con la intención de apretarse contra Chastity. De su cuerpo emanaba un sudor amargo mezclado con un intenso perfume.

—Me gustan jóvenes —susurró—. Mi especialidad son los jóvenes. Deja que Sally te enseñe, encanto. —La mujer alargó la mano. Chastity la esquivó y se arrimó a Cyn.

Él la rodeó con el brazo.

La furcia sacudió la cabeza.

—¿Eso es lo que os gusta? Maldito desperdicio. Los de vuestra clase están en la biblioteca, encantos. —Y siguió deambulando escaleras abajo a la búsqueda de posibles parejas.

Cyn arrastró a Chastity hacia el piso de arriba.

—¿Te das cuenta de que estás arruinando mi reputación? —refunfuñó él—. Tendré que tirarme a todas las mujeres de la casa sólo para demostrar que no soy un maldito sodomita.

Chastity le miró furiosa.

—Tú tienes la culpa de que nos hayamos metido en este lío. ¡Tú eres el que tiene unos amigos indecentes!

A juzgar por su expresión, parecía como si a él le hubieran entrado ganas de asesinarla.

En la planta de arriba, la cosa estaba más tranquila, pero no más decorosa. El ruido de abajo se desvanecía y se mezclaba con los porrazos, lamentos y chillidos procedentes de las habitaciones cercanas. Tal vez algunas personas no hubieran conseguido llegar hasta los dormitorios, porque se veían esparcidas por allí algunas prendas de vestir. Por el suelo había dos zapatos desparejados; un par de medias de rayas festoneaban el marco de un cuadro; una corbata con adornos de encaje colgaba de un candelabro de pared. Alguien había volcado una copa sobre un arca de madera de roble y el charco de vino se había secado, hasta convertirse en una pegajosa mancha.

—¿Desde cuándo dura esto? —preguntó Chastity.

Cyn se pasó la mano por el pelo y miró a su alrededor con expresión distraída.

—Vete a saber, pero parece que se entregan a ello con energías renovadas… —Un ruido y una corriente de aire les hizo a ambos bajar la vista en dirección al vestíbulo. Una nueva tanda de gente se agolpaba para entrar—. O que siempre tienen sangre fresca —añadió Cyn—. Seguramente la noticia de esta fiesta se ha propagado por los condados que rodean a Londres. Una cosa está clara —dijo mirando aviesamente a Chastity—. Sin duda esto debilita la persecución. Toby, innegablemente, ha perdido la concentración…

Chastity no le estaba haciendo caso. El horror la había dejado helada. Uno de los recién llegados era su hermano, Fortitude Harleigh Ware, lord Thornhill. Estaba segura de que lo reconocería al punto, a pesar de su disfraz. Después de todo, su cara era la misma y él ya la había visto con la cabeza rapada.

—¿Qué ocurre? —preguntó Cyn con viveza.

En ese instante, tuvieron que apretarse el uno contra el otro para evitar ser atropellados por una pareja, una moza desaliñada y con máscara, perseguida por un hombre con la cara roja. La muchacha se reía al mismo tiempo que gritaba, y no corría demasiado rápido. Se metió en una habitación, justo enfrente de Chastity. Su perseguidor se abalanzó tras ella.

—¡Ya te tengo, guasona descarada!

La mujer, que ciertamente tenía los ansiados senos del tamaño de melones, y que mostraba este hecho al mundo entero, agitó las manos e hizo aletear sus pintadas pestañas.

—Oh, señor, me temo que habéis…

El hombre se desabrochó los pantalones y saltó sobre ella.

Cyn cerró bruscamente la puerta, mientras murmuraba entre dientes. La pregunta, evidentemente, se le había ido de la cabeza.

Chastity estaba aturdida a causa de las escenas que se sucedían a su alrededor, pero lo que la había hecho palidecer de miedo había sido la llegada de Fort. En nombre de Dios, ¿qué haría su hermano si la encontraba allí? ¿Pegarla? Era más probable que la asesinara. Él había creído que Chastity había invitado a Vernham a su cama y se encolerizó con ella por no detener el escándalo casándose con aquel hombre. Si llegaba a encontrarla en aquel lugar, y vestida de hombre…

Además, tenía que pensar en Cyn. Acabarían peleándose, y Cyn no tendría nada que hacer contra Fort, que era un hombre fuerte, corpulento, y diestro con la pistola y la espada.

—¡Venga! —dijo Cyn bruscamente—. Tenemos que encontrar una habitación para ti.

Aunque no hubiera hecho falta, arrastró consigo a Chastity. Sin el menor escrúpulo, se dedicó a abrir las puertas que no estaban cerradas con llave. Pero todas estaban ocupadas. En la mayoría de ellas, Chastity sólo pudo ver un edredón que se movía —si bien hubiera jurado que, al final de una de las camas, había más de cuatro pies. No obstante, en una de ellas llegó a divisar unas pálidas nalgas que subían y bajaban.

Soltó una risita. Parecía tan estúpido.

Cyn murmuró de nuevo.

Finalmente, abrió la puerta de una habitación libre. Cyn la empujó a su interior y, tras cerrar la puerta, echó la llave.

—Ojalá la peste se los lleve a todos —farfulló con la espalda apoyada contra la hoja.

Una risa histérica se apoderó de Chastity, que se dejó caer sobre la enorme y arrugada cama. Cuando recuperó el control de sí misma, él estaba recostado contra uno de sus postes esquineros, sonriendo de una extraña manera.

—Lo siento —dijo ella—, pero todo esto resulta tan ridículo.

—¿A que sí? —Él se dio la vuelta para echar un vistazo a la estancia—. Si no me equivoco, ésta es la habitación del propio Heather. Dijo que hiciéramos lo que nos apeteciera y eso hemos hecho. —Arrojó al suelo su baúl y, tras sacar su traje azul, lo cepilló con cierto pesar—. A Jerome le daría un ataque si me viera con semejante harapo, pero a esta gente no le importará.

—No —dijo Chastity, orgullosa de su tono despreocupado—. Sin duda te lo arrancarán en cuestión de minutos.

Él le lanzó una rápida mirada pero se limitó a decir:

—Es muy probable. Esas arpías estarán buscando sangre fresca. Estarían encantadas de dar contigo. ¿Estás seguro de que no quieres aprovechar esta ocasión para ampliar tu educación, muchacho?

Chastity se puso las manos detrás de la cabeza.

—Más bien no. Es terreno abonado para la sífilis.

—Después de todo, no eres tan inocente —comentó él—. Al menos las putas habrán tenido que dar garantías de que están limpias antes de venir aquí, aunque vete a saber si lo seguirán estando cuando se vayan...

Se encogió de hombros y se despojó de su uniforme, quedándose en camisa y calzoncillos.

—¿Y qué me dices de las damas? —preguntó Chastity, decidida a no dejar que su cuerpo la distrajera de su propósito.

—¿Qué pasa con ellas?

—Las mujeres que llevan máscara no son putas, ¿a que no?

—Eso depende de cuál sea tu definición de puta. —Se ajustó los pantalones de terciopelo y se puso el chaleco bordado, estirándoselo hasta los muslos.

Después de todo, Chastity no pudo evitar entretenerse contemplando la flexible largura de su entrepierna. A sus ojos acudieron las lágrimas. No tenía ni idea de porqué se sentía tan desgraciada. Había que pensar en Fort, desde luego, una complicación con la que no había contado. Pero lo que él la inspiraba era miedo. No la hacía emocionarse así.

Era Cyn el causante de aquello. Se había encasquetado el chaquetón y se examinaba en el largo espejo, tratando de comprobar si resultaría del agrado de las putas que aguardaban en la planta baja. Chastity imaginó que podía dar la cara y revelar que ella también era una mujer, aunque no le serviría de nada. En aquella casa había bellezas para todos los gustos, de alta y de baja cuna, todas ellas disponibles y bien dispuestas. Chastity Ware no era más que un bicho raro.

Cyn se anudó una delicada corbata de encaje alrededor del cuello y la sujetó con su alfiler de zafiro. Al contemplarse en el espejo, asintió.

—Creo que así servirá.

Se dirigió al tocador y se atusó el pelo, tomando prestada una ancha cinta azul para hacerse el lazo. Y, tras estirarse el encaje del cuello y las muñecas, se dedicó a inspeccionar los frascos y cajas de Heatherington.

Se aplicó polvos blancos para que su rostro adquiriera una palidez elegante. Abrió una caja de lunares artificiales y arqueó una ceja mirando a Chastity.

—¿Qué te parece?

Cyn se estaba convirtiendo en una nueva criatura, en alguien diferente del alocado aventurero y soldado, en un ser frívolo y perfecto para una fiesta.

—Te falta empolvarte el pelo —le dijo Chastity con frialdad.

Él suspiró.

—Tienes razón, pero los polvos son tan sucios… Y cuesta tanto luego quitarlos. —Se dedicó a olisquear los perfumes de Heatherington y echó uno que fue de su agrado sobre un pañuelo bordado con el borde de encaje. Después, se lo metió en el ojal. Por último, se puso sus zapatos negros con altos tacones rojos y le hizo a ella una ceremoniosa reverencia.

—¿Qué te parezco?

Chastity tragó saliva. Estaba espléndido.

—¿Es que alguien te va a mirar antes de desgarrarte la ropa?

Él sonrió levemente.

—Probablemente no, pero uno tiene que mantener su nivel.

Se llegó hasta la puerta de la habitación contigua y a continuación hizo girar la llave.

—En realidad, no es mi intención quedarme enredado por ahí. Para empezar, porque ambos necesitamos dormir bien antes de nuestra aventura de mañana. Y para seguir, porque no tengo ninguna intención de arriesgarme a pillar la sífilis. Pero tendré que dejarme ver un rato. Trataré de hablar con Toby para averiguar qué tal va la persecución. Regresaré tan pronto como me sea posible. —Se detuvo en el umbral, antes de salir al pasillo—. Cierra la puerta y no abras a nadie que no sea yo. —La miró penetrantemente—. ¿Vale?

Chastity levantó la barbilla.

—Vale. Te aseguro que no tengo ningunas ganas de compartir esta cama con nadie.

—Pues me temo, querido Charles, que tendrás que compartirla con alguien: conmigo.

Aunque aquel punto era obvio, Chastity lo había pasado por alto.

—Entonces dormiré en el suelo.

Él sonrió con cierta pereza.

—Eso me ofendería, muchacho. La cama es grande y yo no tengo piojos.

—Es una manía que tengo, lord Cyn. Siempre duermo solo.

—Ya veremos. —Y, dicho esto, desapareció.

Chastity fue corriendo hasta la puerta y la cerró con llave. Tal vez no le abriera ni siquiera a él.

De pronto, todo se le vino encima y se tapó la cara con las manos. ¿Cómo demonios había llegado a esa situación?

Cyn esperó hasta oír el ruido de la cerradura. De momento, ella le había obedecido, pero no sabía hasta cuándo seguiría haciéndolo. Sonrió y sacudió la cabeza. Dios Santo, qué coraje tenía la chica. Aunque desde luego, las circunstancias la estaban poniendo a prueba. ¿Se derrumbaría antes de que él pudiera poner fin a aquella charada y protegerla convenientemente?

Un rugido proveniente del piso de abajo revelaba la ejecución de alguna proeza. No le interesaba lo más mínimo saber de qué se trataba. Si hubiera sabido la clase de fiesta que les esperaba, hubiera puesto cualquier excusa para quedarse en el Angel.

Aún así, sintió que, tras haber puesto a su damisela a buen recaudo, podía relajarse. También estaba tranquilo porque, hubiera ocurrido lo que hubiera ocurrido la pasada primavera, ella, en el fondo, era un ser inocente. Su manera de reaccionar en aquel lugar hablaba por sí sola.

Hubiera querido no tener que dejarla. Ninguna de las mujeres que había allí, por hermosa que fuese, podía competir con su damisela y con la fascinación que ésta ejercía sobre él. Quería que llegara cuanto antes el final de aquella aventura para sacarle la verdad y poder hacer conjuntamente planes de futuro. Bajaba por aquellas escaleras con la intención de mezclarse entre la multitud pero anhelando poder regresar pronto a Chastity y a la cordura.

Chastity deambulaba por la habitación con gran desasosiego. Se imaginaba a Cyn en brazos de una de aquellas arpías: manoseado, cubierto de babas y desvestido, tratando de satisfacer su lujuria. Las manos se le convirtieron en puños. ¡No era justo! En otro tiempo, ella había sido hermosa y a él no le hubiera resultado tan fácil abandonarla.

Se quitó la peluca de un tirón y se quedó de pie delante del espejo. Un bicho raro. Un bicho raro con pantalones y expresión dura. Llena de furia, se quitó la ropa de hombre y desenrolló la banda que le ceñía los pechos. En un decir amén, se quedó desnuda.

Y emitió un estremecedor suspiro.

Se pasó las manos por el cuerpo. No estaba nada mal. Sabía que no era una belleza despampanante, como Nerissa Trelyn, pero tenía un buen cuerpo. Nerissa Trelyn, sin embargo, tenía unos brillantes y rubísimos rizos. Y unos grandes ojos vacunos con unas pestañas más espesas que las de Cyn. Sus tetas eran como melones, aunque la sociedad elegante describía aquello como un pecho generoso…

Las manos de Chastity se quedaron completamente inmóviles. Nerissa Trelyn: hija del obispo de Peterborough; esposa de lord Trelyn y viva imagen del decoro; ilustre personaje de Londres y árbitro social; una de las personas que habían visto a Chastity en la cama con Henry Vernham y la habían condenado.

¡Nerissa Trelyn era la mujer cuyos encantos habían conquistado la atención de Heatherington!

Chastity miró a su alrededor con indecisión. Cogió una bata de satén marrón y se cubrió con ella. Se sentó en un gran sillón junto al fuego y se sirvió un vaso de vino de un decantador que encontró allí.

Mientras bebía lentamente, se preguntaba si estaría equivocada. Parecía absolutamente increíble y, sin embargo, estaba segura. Sobre todo por aquella voz suya tan dulce y característica. Una peluca roja le cubría el rubio pelo, pero era ella. La gran lady Trelyn estaba allí haciendo de puta.

¿Habría reconocido a Chastity?

No, definitivamente, ella tenía los ojos y la mente pendientes de otros asuntos.

Después de todo, Chastity no tenía que extrañarse de que Nerissa tuviera amantes; todos sabían que se había casado con lord Trelyn por su dinero, y que él parecía un hombre frío y seco.

Pero, quien iba a imaginársela en un sitio así…

¡Y ella había tenido la osadía de condenar a Chastity Ware!

¿Cuántos más había allí? ¿Cuántos hipócritas más?

Chastity apuró su vaso y se levantó. Tenía que averiguarlo. Iba a ponerse otra vez la ropa pero se detuvo. Su hermano Fort la reconocería si se topaba con él.

Tenía que llevar máscara. Pero sólo las mujeres llevaban máscara. Si se vestía de mujer, con peluca y máscara, seguramente nadie la reconocería. Chastity había identificado a Nerissa Trelyn por la voz, así que ella trataría de impostar la suya.

Vaciló indecisa. Quería, con todas sus fuerzas, permanecer a salvo en aquella habitación. Pero también quería, con la misma vehemencia, confirmar lo increíble: que Nerissa Trelyn estaba de parranda en el piso de abajo. Porque, de ser así, tal vez pudiera usar aquella información en provecho propio y salir airosa de la situación en la que se encontraba.

Decidió realizar una breve y cautelosa incursión.

Chastity abrió de par en par las puertas del ropero de lord Heatherington, pero descubrió que sólo contenía ropa de hombre. Juntó las manos a causa de la frustración. Seguramente podría reunir un traje de mujer con las prendas sueltas que había tiradas por toda la casa, pero no se atrevía a salir a buscarlas.

La habitación contigua. Sin duda alguna, debía pertenecer a una mujer.

Al instante siguiente, había hecho girar la cerradura y se hallaba dentro. ¡Sí!

Era obviamente la alcoba de una mujer. ¿Le valdría su ropa? Tras echar una ojeada al armario, comprobó que sí. No era exactamente de su talla pero serviría.

No pudo reprimir una carcajada de placer ante aquel conjunto de bellos vestidos. Hacía mucho tiempo que no veía prendas de confección tan exquisita. Se desprendió de la bata y se puso una fina camisola de seda blanca con mangas hasta los hombros, festoneada con una doble capa de espumeante encaje. Se estremeció de placer al sentir cómo se deslizaba sobre su piel: un simple velo sobre su cuerpo, prácticamente inmaterial.

A continuación, eligió una enagua acolchada de satén blanco con cintas amarillas. Se metió dentro de ella y se ató los lazos en la cintura. Encima, se puso un peto bordado con un escote en forma de uve que le llegaba hasta la cinturilla de la enagua. Tuvo alguna dificultad para atarse los cordones a la espalda pero, como la posibilidad de llamar a alguna sirvienta quedaba descartada, lo hizo lo mejor que pudo, sonriendo al acordarse de cómo había vestido a Cyn, y suspirando al pensar que sentiría ella si fuera él quien le ayudara a ponerse o quitarse la ropa.

Apartó de sí aquellos pensamientos.

Se miró en el espejo. El peto apenas le tapaba los pezones y realzaba la rotundidad de sus pechos. La turgencia de éstos sólo quedaba cubierta por la vaporosa camisola. Nunca había llevado un corpiño tan atrevido, pero le gustaba. Tras aquella larga y árida mascarada, ser de nuevo una mujer le hacía sentirse de maravilla.

Descolgó un vestido abierto de seda, con rayas marrones y amarillas, y se lo puso, enganchándolo al peto a ambos lados de la cintura. Por encima y por debajo, se separaba para dejar al descubierto la enagua y el corpiño. Las mangas hasta los hombros mostraban el volante de encaje de la camisola.

Giró sobre sí misma, riéndose a causa del placer que le proporcionaban las cosas buenas y el tacto suave y susurrante de la seda. Las faldas caían sin demasiada gracia y echó de menos unos aros. Pero si la dueña de todo aquello los tenía, debía llevarlos puestos. El acolchado de la enagua tenía cierto cuerpo y, como Chastity debía ser algo más alta que la verdadera propietaria, por lo menos no la arrastraba.

Se le pasó por la cabeza que tal vez aquella fuera la habitación de Nerissa Trelyn. Buscó alguna pista, pero no encontró nada que confirmara sus sospechas. Acallando la voz de su conciencia, realizó un exhaustivo registro. No halló nada en ninguno de los cajones.

Entonces descubrió una pequeña caja de marfil. Contenía dos cartas, dos ardientes cartas de amor. Suspiró frustrada. Probablemente eran de lord Heatherington pero estaban dirigidas a una tal Desirée. Aquel nombre no significaba nada, porque según la costumbre de moda, un hombre llamaba a su amada con un nombre ficticio. Chastity había sido Bella para uno de sus pretendientes y Corinda para otro.

Pero entonces se preguntó dónde guardaría Heatherington sus cartas de amor.

Se apresuró a inspeccionar su habitación. Después de mirar sin éxito en cajas y cajones —la clase de sitios en los que una mujer guardaría meticulosamente sus *billets doux*— encontró finalmente una misiva dentro del bolsillo de una chaqueta.

El estilo de la dama era más florido, aunque igual de escandaloso. Chastity se ruborizo al leer un mensaje tan lascivo. La nota estaba dirigida a Hércules y firmada por Desi-rée. Aquella caligrafía sería seguramente la de la autora. Una carta como aquella no podía dictarse a ningún secretario. ¿Se trataría de la letra de lady Trelyn?

Chastity se metió con cuidado la nota en el bolsillo del chaleco de su traje. Tenía más ganas que nunca de seguir adelante con su investigación. Quería encontrar pruebas contundentes que le permitieran identificar a Nerissa y descubrir a cualquier otro hipócrita que se hallara reto-zando en la planta baja.

Pero necesitaba una peluca y allí no había ninguna. Por unos instantes pensó que tendría que renunciar a aquella aventura y sintió un culpable alivio. Entonces se acordó de la peluca negra que Cyn le había comprado a la señora Cru-pley. ¿Estaría todavía en su baúl?

Allí estaba. Era un triste ejemplar de vasto pelo negro de caballo, pero le sacaría del apuro. Le pasó un peine para atu-sarla un poco y después esparció por sus rizos unos perfu-mados polvos rosáceos, más bien desagradables, que había encontrado en la alcoba de la dama. La sustancia se quedó flotando en el aire y la hizo toser.

No obstante, consiguió el efecto deseado. Cuando se puso aquel amasijo de rizos sobre la cabeza, los polvos habían sua-vizado aquel inverosímil y denso color negro, haciendo que resultara agradable.

Chastity no se cortó a la hora de usar los objetos del to-cador de la dama. Una pata de conejo untada de colorete le proporcionó un color adicional a sus mejillas. Metiendo un dedo en un bote, consiguió carmín rojo para los labios. Se empolvó la cara y se pegó un corazón de terciopelo negro junto a la boca —una invitación al beso.

Chastity se dio el visto bueno frente al espejo. Allí se veía una dama estupenda, lista para el baile o para el cortejo. Tal vez le sobrara un poco de pintura para esto último. Parecía mayor de lo que era, y más atrevida. Definitivamente, Tony Berrisford no reconocería a cierto joven, y Fort no identificaría a su hermana. Chastity Ware siempre se había vestido con recato, como corresponde a una dama bien educada a la búsqueda de marido.

Tenía muy buen aspecto. Su cintura era esbelta, sus hombros blancos y suaves y, aunque sus pechos no eran grandes como melones, se veían muy favorecidos por el escotado corpiño.

Se recordó a sí misma que no pretendía que la admiraran. De hecho, aquella indumentaria podía granjearle más admiración de la que iba a ser capaz de manejar. Por otro lado, la discreción en el vestir destacaría en aquel lugar como una cereza en un cuenco de guisantes. Se estiró el peto un poco más hacia arriba y se dijo a sí misma que andaría entre los juerguistas sólo durante un rato y que tendría mucho cuidado.

No pudo evitar preguntarse que pasaría si se encontraba a Cyn de aquella guisa. ¿La reconocería? Seguramente no. ¿La admiraría? Apartó aquellas especulaciones de su mente. Lo más probable era que le diera algún azote. Por aquella noche, se mantendría a distancia de Cyn Malloren.

Y, en lo tocante a otros posibles galanes, como todos los hombres parecían estar bebidos, ella debería ser capaz de esquivarlos y ser más lista que ellos. No había precisamente escasez de hembras bien dispuestas.

Por último, la máscara. Se ató una de terciopelo negro que le cubría la mitad superior del rostro, y que, además, tenía la ventaja añadida de que servía para sujetar la peluca. Hizo una leve reverencia frente a su imagen en el espejo. Ni ella misma se reconocía.

Sólo había un par de zapatos y eran demasiado pequeños. Nerissa Trelyn estaba muy orgullosa de sus diminutos pies.

Chastity se encogió de hombros. No creía que nadie se sorprendiera al ver a alguien descalzo por aquella casa. Como toque final, cogió un frasco de perfume, pero, cuando lo olió, su mareante y densa fragancia de rosas le provocó una mueca de desagrado.

Se acordó del que había comprado Cyn. ¿Qué había hecho con él?

Volvió a la habitación de Heatherington y, tras cerrar la puerta que comunicaba ambas estancias, se puso a rebuscar en la maleta de Cyn, hallando por fin el botecito de cristal. Lo destapó y olfateó con deleite la sofisticada mezcla de esencias y flores, sobre una base elemental que incitaba a la lujuria. Dudó unos instantes, preguntándose si no sería peligroso llevar ese aroma en aquel lugar. Después se dijo que una invitación a la intimidad tan discreta pasaría desapercibida entre todos los demás olores. Le apetecía ponérselo para ella misma, porque era maravilloso y le hacía sentirse espléndidamente femenina. Se aplicó una pequeña cantidad sobre los codos y entre los pechos.

Un cálido efluvio ascendió desde su cuerpo y le aturdió la mente. Cyn Malloren tenía un gusto exquisito. Pensó que era una pena que los destinos de ambos fueran por caminos distintos.

Chastity admitió la verdad. Parte de su desesperación por averiguar quién estaba allí aquella noche tenía que ver con la remota esperanza de obtener alguna información que pudiera ayudarla a rehabilitar su reputación. De ese modo, podría relacionarse honestamente con Cyn.

Se tragó las lágrimas al pensar en la imposible tarea que le aguardaba, pero no cedió al llanto. Había aprendido a ser una luchadora y aquella oportunidad que se le presentaba era su única arma.

10

Chastity necesitó todavía un buen vaso de vino del Rin para reunir el coraje necesario y aventurarse a salir. Después, tras lanzar una última y tranquilizadora mirada a la extraña del espejo, abrió la puerta con mucha cautela. El pasillo estaba desierto, aunque también quedaba claro que la mayoría de las habitaciones seguían ocupadas. Cerró la puerta de la habitación con llave y dejó caer esta última en el interior de su corpiño, estremeciéndose ligeramente al sentir el frío del metal.

O tal vez fuera a causa de los nervios.

Tenía que mezclarse con la multitud del piso inferior, pero no le apetecía nada bajar por la amplia escalinata principal y que todo el mundo que levantara la vista pudiera verla. Supuso que debía haber otra escalera menor al fondo del edificio y fue en aquella dirección. Tal y como había imaginado, allí estaba ese acceso secundario. Antes de llegar a la planta baja, sólo se encontró con un par de sombríos criados. Un corto pasillo le llevó hasta el borde del recibidor.

La cosa estaba más tranquila que cuando ella había llegado. Sólo media docena de personas, dormidas o borrachas, yacían por el suelo. Avanzó con cautela. Cinco eran hombres y la sexta era una mujer sin máscara que roncaba en brazos de uno de ellos. No reconoció a nadie.

Chastity supuso que los demás participantes de aquella fiesta se hallaban en las diversas estancias. Las risas, el parloteo y la música parecían retumbar por todas partes, pero, sobre todo, se escuchaba el lejano eco de los cánticos, proveniente de la parte trasera de la casa. Iba acompañado de batir de palmas, pataleos y, de vez en cuando, rugidos de aprobación.

Chastity ya había tenido ocasión de presenciar el florido estilo coral de Heatherington y sus amigos, y había tenido suficiente. Se encaminó en la otra dirección, hacia la parte del vestíbulo que quedaba más cerca del lugar en el que ella se encontraba.

Si aquella casa seguía conservando la estructura con la que había sido construida en tiempos del rey James, las habitaciones se comunicarían unas con otras a lo largo de tres de los lados del vestíbulo. Empezó por la parte frontal.

Entró en un pequeño comedor en el que dos parejas rodaban juntas por el suelo. Chastity no pudo ver quiénes eran, pero le faltó valor para acercarse lo suficiente como para averiguarlo. Se apresuró a llegar hasta la siguiente estancia, que estaba mucho más concurrida.

Se trataba de una sala de juego con toda la afilada intensidad que cabía esperar de la gente que prefería las cartas y los dados a los cuerpos. Hombres y mujeres, con máscaras y sin ellas, hacían que las fortunas se movieran por las mesas, contemplando las cartas y los dados con ojos enfebrecidos y chispeantes. Chastity se estremeció. Siempre le había parecido que el asunto de las apuestas tenía un lado perverso.

A pesar de todo, respiró profundamente y se abrió paso por la habitación, examinando a los jugadores. Santo cielo, allí estaba la anciana lady Fanshaw. Sin embargo, aquello no le serviría de nada. Todo el mundo sabía que las cartas la volvían loca y que sería capaz de ir al mismísimo infierno para jugar una partida. De hecho, pensó Chastity, allí no encontraría nada. Si descubriera que la reina en persona estaba allí jugando, cualquiera que la oyese contarlo bostezaría de aburrimiento.

Cuando se dirigía a la siguiente habitación, una mano la enganchó por la muñeca.

—¿Estás sola, querida? —Un hombre de mediana edad la forzó a sentarse en su regazo—. Venga, dame suerte. —Le pasó sus rollizos dedos por los pechos.

Chastity reprimió el impulso de forcejear. Nada llamaría más la atención. Por el contrario, se dejó caer sobre su pecho y le pasó las manos por el cuello. Él rió entre dientes y volvió a prestar atención al juego. Chastity observaba a través de las rendijas de su máscara y cuando vio, por la expresión del hombre, que su mano se aproximaba a un punto crucial, se escabulló provocativamente y le besó en la mejilla.

Tal y como ella había calculado, él la apartó de un empujón.

—Demonios, mujer. ¡No me dejas ver las cartas!

Ella hizo un puchero y se escapó. Aquello había sido fácil. Tenía que admitir que estaba empezando a pasárselo bien. Detrás del anonimato que le proporcionaba el disfraz, se sentía más segura que nunca. No era lady Chastity Ware. No era una mujer deshonrada. Tampoco era Charles. Había vuelto a nacer.

Alertada por un estallido de carcajadas, se detuvo a mirar el juego de otra de las mesas. En ella, no se apostaba dinero.

Una mujer negra echaba los dados contra todos los que llegaban. Los que tiraban los dados eran hombres, pero había unas cuantas mujeres observando el juego. Si un tipo sacaba ocho o menos, la negra añadía sus guineas al montón que tenía delante. Si sacaba más, conservaba su oro y ella se bajaba el corpiño un poco más y se levantaba las faldas unos centímetros. El jubón de seda rosa le colgaba de los pezones, dejando al descubierto la mayor parte de su pecho color chocolate. La falda estaba a medio camino de sus muslos.

El juego se fue calentando. Chastity se vio también atrapada por la fascinación de esperar la caída de aquel corpiño. Tres hombres probaron suerte y perdieron. La negra reía, exhibiendo su blanca y reluciente dentadura.

—¿Quién va ahora, caballeros? Sólo quedan diez minutos para la hora. Cuando suene el reloj, vuelvo a ponerme la ropa y empezamos otra vez.

Dos hombres más se adelantaron para hacer rodar los dados. Y volvieron a fallar.

Una larga mano blanca adornada con un sello de rubíes recogió los pequeños cubos de marfil.

—Tu destino va a cumplirse, Sable.

Chastity ahogó un jadeo.

Era el marqués de Rothgar.

Seguramente acababa de llegar, porque iba impecablemente vestido con un traje carmesí con bordados en negro. En el cuello y las muñecas, lucía níveos y espumeantes volantes de encaje. Su negro pelo estaba sin empolvar, y sus delicados y atractivos rasgos, iluminados por la parpadeante luz de las velas, parecían tallados en mármol.

Sable, la negra, hizo una mueca.

—Yo gano de todos modos, milord, porque si pierdo, vos me ganáis.

Rothgar agitó el cubilete.

—Qué detalle. Tal vez me venga bien una esclava doméstica...

La sonrisa de la mujer se volvió belicosa.

—No creo que sea una buena idea, si es que apreciáis en algo vuestro cuello, milord.

Rothgar sonrió con frialdad y arrojó los dados. Dos seis le concedieron la victoria definitiva. Un rugido de admiración sacudió la estancia.

Sable metió sus ganancias en un saquito que llevaba en el cinto y, después, se puso de pie. Tiró sinuosamente del jubón y la rosada seda se deslizó hasta la cintura, provocando un gemido colectivo por parte de los hombres. Ciertamente, pensó Chastity, eran unos buenos melones morenos. Rothgar, según pudo apreciar, permanecía cortésmente imperturbable.

Sable se subió poco a poco las faldas hasta quedarse desnuda también de cintura para abajo, con la saya remetida por el talle. Se retorció ante las miradas del personal, dejando ver un oscuro y rizado matojo de pelo entre las piernas. Después, se inclinó hacia Rothgar y le recorrió el pecho con los dedos hasta llegar al mentón.

—Bien, milord, ¿desperdiciarías esto, haciéndome fregar suelos? ¡Te he dicho que el premio es sólo por esta noche?

—¡Qué lástima! —dijo él, abriendo una caja dorada que contenía rapé—, y estos suelos ni siquiera son míos. El pie, esclava.

Sable dio un paso hacia atrás y, con un perfecto equilibrio levantó una pierna completamente estirada delante de él. Rothgar le colocó una pizca de aquellos polvos marrones en el empeine y le sujetó el talón. Inhaló la sustancia, primero por una fosa nasal, luego por la otra.

Después irguió la cabeza pero siguió reteniendo el talón de la mujer. Ésta permanecía con la pierna estirada, sin dar ninguna señal de estar física o mentalmente incómoda. De hecho, tal vez siguiendo una indicación de Rothgar, se balanceó hacia atrás, quedándose unos instantes apoyada sobre las manos y, después, volvió saltar sobre sus pies, encarándole de nuevo a él. Aquella maniobra proporcionó a todos los espectadores una diáfana visión de sus partes íntimas, que, natural o artificialmente, eran de un color rojo escarlata. ¡Labios de abajo de cereza!

Chastity se dio cuenta de que se había quedado embobada y cerró la boca de golpe.

Rothgar aplaudió suavemente y, tendiéndole una mano, como si se tratara de la más distinguida de las damas y estuviera correctamente vestida, la condujo fuera de la estancia.

Chastity contuvo el aliento. Nunca había imaginado que pudiera ocurrir algo así, y este hecho había minado toda su confianza. Le pareció que circular entre aquellas personas era como caminar sobre arenas movedizas. Tuvo ganas de volver corriendo a su habitación y meterse bajo las mantas hasta que llegara el nuevo día.

Pero seguía teniendo una misión que cumplir y una nueva preocupación. No creía que Rothgar fuera capaz de reconocerla, a pesar de su maldita fama de ser omnisciente, pero estaba segura de que Cyn no querría tropezarse allí con su hermano.

El problema era que no podía avisar a Cyn sin quedar ella misma en evidencia y revelar su impostura, mejor dicho, sus imposturas.

Una vez terminado el espectáculo de Sable, los espectadores se dedicaron a deambular por la sala comentándolo. Por el momento, parecían saciados. Chastity sólo tuvo que zafarse de dos invitaciones al coqueteo mientras se dirigía al escritorio que estaba situado en una esquina de la pieza.

No estaba cerrado con llave y había papel, plumas y tinta. La pluma no estaba bien afilada y la tinta tenía grumos, pero se las apañó para garabatear «Rothgar está aquí». Dobló la nota y se la metió debajo del peto. A la menor ocasión se la pasaría a Cyn.

Se apresuró a entrar en la siguiente estancia, que resultó ser una galería que recorría la parte trasera de la casa. La estaban usando como sala de baile, si es que a aquellos brincos y retozos se les podía llamar baile. Había un trío que friccionaba instrumentos musicales, pero la bebida se les apoderaba y llevaban un ritmo alocado. Los bailarines se movían con el mismo frenesí.

Por fin Chastity pudo empezar a recopilar nombres para su lista mental. Lady Jane Trece, santo cielo, la cotilla más malvada de Inglaterra. Meg Cordingly, Susan Fellows y Letty Proud.[3] La rolliza pelirroja no estaría tan orgullosa si se supiera que la habían ido arrojando de mano en mano a lo largo de la estancia, con las faldas al aire.

En Londres, Chastity había oído arteras especulaciones en las que se preguntaban si el pelo de Letty sería del mismo color rojo ardiente por todo el cuerpo. Ahora ya estaba claro. Lejos de sentirse triunfante, Chastity se sentía su-

---

3. Proud significa orgullosa.

mamente triste. Sería imposible utilizar cualquiera de los nombres de las personas allí congregadas sin causar un gran dolor.

Además, sentía envidia de los juerguistas. Su comportamiento podía ser obsceno e incorrecto, pero, al menos durante breves momentos, eran felices. Ella casi no podía acordarse de lo que era la dicha.

Un hombre la agarró y la hizo balancearse al ritmo de un alegre baile. Horrorizada, se dio cuenta de que se trataba de Fort.

—Eh, preciosa, no pongas esa cara de susto. Dime cómo te llamas.

Él era ciertamente muy atractivo, con aquellos ojos azules, su rizado pelo castaño y su perfecta dentadura. Exhibía una seductora sonrisa. ¿Cuánto tiempo hacía desde que no le había dedicado a ella un gesto así? No tanto, aunque a Chastity le parecía una eternidad.

—¿Estás de incógnito? —preguntó él—. Dame un nombre falso, preciosa. Me dará lo mismo.

—Chloe —dijo ella, acordándose de una tía suya muy estirada, la hermana mayor de su padre.

Él se echó a reír.

—No es mi nombre favorito pero da igual. —La atrajo hacia sí y la besó.

Chastity se quedó helada. Aquello era un pecado terrible, ¿no?

Él la apartó de su lado bruscamente.

—¿Qué pasa, encanto? ¿No soy tu tipo?

—Lo siento, señor —dijo ella balbuciente y con voz temblorosa—. Es que… no me encuentro bien. ¡Necesito un sitio para vomitar!

—¡Vaya por Dios! —dijo él, soltando una carcajada y conduciéndola hasta la puerta—. Sigue por este pasillo y llegarás al exterior de la casa. Buena suerte.

Y dicho esto, regresó con los danzantes. Chastity sonrió con tristeza. Aquélla era la alegre amabilidad que ella recordaba. Fort era un hombre duro que se irritaba enseguida, pero también era gentil. Consideró las cosas desde su punto de vista. Él había sido uno de los que habían pillado a Vernham en su cama, aunque no se había enfadado de veras hasta que ella se negó a casarse con él. Sólo entonces Fort asumió la misma actitud crítica de su padre.

Chastity se detuvo pensativa unos instantes, mientras observaba a su hermano. ¿Estaba allí únicamente por la fiesta o estaría participando en la batida? Debía estar preocupado por Verity, pero era muy propio de él divertirse cuando se le presentaba la ocasión. Fort encontró otra pareja y, al cabo de un rato, salió de la estancia con ella. Chastity se armó de valor y regresó al baile, con la intención de encontrar alguna prueba más.

Heatherington atravesó la estancia con su querida del brazo, aplaudiendo a sus invitados. Chastity se aproximó a ellos. Era, sin duda, Nerissa. Aquella manera de bambolearse y esa costumbre que tenía de acariciarse el cuello como si tratara de detectar alguna arruga…

Un hombre se plantó delante de Chastity, impidiéndole el paso.

—¿Sola? Seguramente no. Por lo menos, ya no lo estás. —Le tendió la mano invitándola a bailar. Era el enorme capitán Gresham. No se había cambiado de ropa y llevaba el uniforme hecho una pena: el chaleco blanco le colgaba abierto, la corbata había desaparecido y se había desabrochado los botones del cuello de la camisa. También había perdido la peluca, lo que dejaba al descubierto su oscuro pelo rapado.

Chastity fue hacia él. Si permanecía sola, la acosarían constantemente y, ¿por qué no iba a poder ella disfrutar también un poco?

Durante un rato, bailaron moderadamente, pero, después, él la cogió y la hizo girar por el aire. Chastity chilló. Temía que se le estuviera viendo todo y que se le volara la peluca. Estaba también aterrorizada por el tamaño y la fuerza de aquel hombre, que la hacían sentirse como una niña en sus brazos. Se dio cuenta de que nunca antes había salido al mundo sin la protección de su padre, de su hermano o de Cyn. Pero, en aquellos momentos, no había nadie que pudiera salvarla de aquel gigante.

Gresham la fue bajando despacio contra su cuerpo. Ella suspiró aliviada al poder poner otra vez los pies en el suelo, hasta que se dio cuenta de que la maniobra le había dejado levantada la parte delantera de la enagua, de modo que una buena porción de sus piernas estaba a la vista.

Él soltó un gruñido guasón y la besó.

Chastity se hallaba completamente indefensa. Un potente brazo la sujetaba. Con el otro, el hombre le sostenía la cabeza. Su cráneo encajaba dentro de aquella mano del mismo modo que una naranja lo haría en la de Chastity. La ardiente boca de Gresham la asaltó y cuando ella quiso resistirse, él deslizó el pulgar hacia delante para obligarla a abrir la boca, y la invadió con su espesa lengua. Nunca antes le había ocurrido nada así.

Se sintió abrumada, avasallada y vencida, pero sus sentidos estaban anegados y se dio cuenta de que su boca se había ablandado bajo aquella diestra presión. Esto fue lo que más la asustó.

Él se retiró lentamente.

—Eso está mejor, preciosa. ¿Qué ocurre? ¿Hay alguien contigo aquí?

Aprovechando la oportunidad de escapar, Chastity dijo.

—Sí.

—Es una pena. —La mano del hombre ascendió y, con un apretón, le rodeó el pecho.

Demasiado fuerte. Le había hecho daño. Cualquier vestigio de placer había desparecido, dando paso al terror. Iba a ser violada en aquella misma habitación. Nunca la habían manoseado de aquella manera, ni siquiera Henry Vernham.

Ella forcejeó contra el férreo brazo de Gresham, buscando desesperadamente una salida, pero él aprovechó la oportunidad para darle un mordisco en el cuello.

—Sí, es una pena, desde luego —dijo ella jadeante—. Pero me he escabullido de él porque no quería darme de comer. De verdad, señor, me muero de hambre. Yo…no… no puedo pensar en otra cosa hasta que no deje de dolerme el estómago.

Él se echó a reír y le mordisqueó la curva superior de su pecho.

—Ahora que lo dices, yo también tengo un hambre canina, y, aunque tienes una pinta deliciosa, supongo que no debo comerte. —Comer, pensó Chastity un tanto histérica. ¡Eso es lo que querían decir!—. Heather debe tener comida por alguna parte —dijo él—, y los dos necesitamos tener fuerzas ¿a qué sí?

Aturdida y aliviada, Chastity le sonrió.

—Sobre todo yo, señor —le dijo con timidez—. Con lo grande que es usted.

—Nunca podrías adivinar cuánto, preciosa, te lo prometo. —Gresham le agarró la mano y se la colocó sobre su abultado pene.

La incredulidad hizo que Chastity se quedara de piedra. ¡Aquello despedazaría a una mujer!

Él rió entre dientes.

—¿Estás segura de que quieres comida para el estómago? Puedes comerme a mí todo lo que quieras. Te aseguró que te llenaré.

Al oír aquellas palabras, a Chastity se le revolvieron las tripas.

—Oh, sí —dijo rápidamente—. ¡Más segura que nunca! —Todo lo que quería era librarse de él, para poder volver a su habitación y hallarse de nuevo a salvo. Tenía unos cuantos nombres y ya no le quedaban agallas.

Él la condujo a otra estancia, protegiéndola de la gente y aprisionándola al mismo tiempo con el brazo. Era prácticamente imposible soltarse y, de conseguirlo, él volvería a atraparla en un santiamén. ¿Conseguiría algo pidiendo auxilio? Si obraba así, su identidad quedaría al descubierto.

Ese pensamiento le produjo tal horror que estuvo a punto de desmayarse.

Antes prefería ser víctima de una violación.

Tendría que convencer a aquel hombre de que tenía tantas ganas como él y esperar que se apartara de su lado en algún momento, tal vez para traerle a ella comida.

Aunque la habitación estaba abarrotada de gente, ella no había prestado mucha atención a los que la rodeaban, hasta que oyó que emitían un rugido. La muchacha dio un salto.

—¿Qué es eso? —dijo jadeante.

—¿Todavía no has visto el teatro, corazón? —preguntó Gresham. Y, como si fuera una niña, se la subió encima del hombro.

Chastity se dio cuenta de que estaban en el «teatro» de Heatherington. Alguien había construido una peana en un extremo de la sala y dispuesto sillas para el público. La diversión tenía tantísimo éxito que las sillas estaban todas ocupadas y la gente se hallaba de pie por toda la estancia. Supuso que era allí donde antes se habían producido los cánticos, pero ahora la actuación no era musical sino que se trataba de una cópula.

La pareja estaba completamente desnuda salvo por las máscaras que les cubrían todo el rostro. Gruñían y se contorsionaban en una posición tan extraordinaria que a Chastity le costaba creer que fuera físicamente posible.

Forcejeó para bajar al suelo.

—¿No es de tu gusto? —le preguntó Gresham sorprendido.

—Eh… demasiado estimulante —dijo Chastity agitada—. Tengo que mantener el control hasta que coma.

Él soltó una risita ahogada y apoyó la espalda contra la pared. Después, apretó a la chica contra sí.

—¿Estás caliente, eh? —le preguntó—. Es una pena desperdiciarlo… —Le levantó las faldas por detrás y le acarició los muslos.

Chastity se retorció desesperadamente, pero aquello sólo parecía alentar aún más al hombre. Alguien se chocó con ella por detrás, dejándola sin aliento, pero, al mismo tiempo, desplazando la mano de Gresham a causa del impacto.

—Le pido disculpas —murmuró ese alguien. Chastity se tensó al reconocer la voz de Cyn. Una parte de ella quería esconderse y otra parte deseaba gritar pidiendo auxilio.

—Gresham —dijo él distraídamente—, veo que has encontrado una agradable chica a la que abrazar.

—Desde luego que sí —dijo Gresham, haciendo que Chastity se diera la vuelta entre sus manos—. Te presento a lord Cyn, preciosa. —Y le colocó las manos posesivamente encima de sus senos.

Chastity rezó para que se la tragara la tierra. Cyn tenía un aspecto llamativamente incólume para llevar en aquel barullo más de una hora. Era obvio que no sospechaba la verdadera identidad de la mujer que tenía ante él. Dedicó una sonrisa a la dama, haciendo gala de un excelente y despreocupado buen humor, y le hizo una ligera reverencia.

—Encantado, querida.

Chastity no quería que la reconociera, pero tampoco quería que la abandonara en las garras de aquel gigante. Si era preciso, se delataría.

—Lo mismo digo —dijo ella con su falsa voz—. No tengo nada en contra de agasajar a dos, guapo.

Las manos de Gresham se tensaron.

—Eh, de eso nada.

Cyn sonrió.

—Me temo que tampoco es lo mío, preciosa. Si quieres verme en privado más tarde…

«¿Cuántas citas como ésta has acordado? —pensó Chastity—. ¿Y con cuántas has cumplido?»

Gresham se regodeaba:

—Más tarde estará hecha un guiñapo, amigo mío. Yo que tú me buscaría otra pareja.

Chastity sonrió forzadamente.

—Oh, muy bien, pero por lo menos podíamos buscar la comida ¿no?

—Vale, vale —dijo Gresham—, la encontraremos. —Y
en un aparte le dijo a Cyn: —Es una moza con un apetito
realmente feroz.

—Más le vale —dijo Cyn—. A propósito, yo sé donde
está la comida. Vamos, os llevaré.

La habitación que seguía a la del teatro estaba casi vacía y la gente que allí había parecía estar simplemente hablando. Desgraciadamente, uno de los presentes era Rothgar, que ofrecía rapé a nada más y nada menos que el conde
de Bute, el mentor y confidente del joven rey, y supuesto
amante de su madre. ¿Era aquel lugar, entonces, el verdadero rostro de la sociedad? ¿Estaría entre aquellas personas el mismísimo rey?

Chastity echó un vistazo a Cyn, pero éste no parecía haber visto a su hermano, y Rothgar estaba de espaldas a ellos.
Chastity se preguntaba dónde habría dejado a la voluptuosa Sable.

A continuación entraron en la siguiente habitación, en
la que había dos mesas dispuestas con comida y bebida. Sorprendentemente, no había ninguna accesoria, por lo que la
gente tenía que comer de pie. Había alrededor de una docena de invitados dedicados a aquella actividad y, al parecer, se
divertían horrores con ella.

Cuando Chastity, escoltada por sus dos acompañantes,
llegó a las mesas comprendió por qué. Ni siquiera la comida
estaba al margen de la ingenua obscenidad de lord Heatherington. En el centro de cada una de las mesas, la comida estaba dispuesta formando la silueta de un cuerpo —de mujer
en una de ellas y de hombre en la otra—. La mayor parte del
interés se concentraba en la figura femenina. En la intersección de la blanca crema de sus muslos, había un puñado de

perejil y unas guindas servían de pezones a los medios melones que hacían las veces de pechos. Los hombres se inclinaban a mordisquear las cerezas confitadas, que luego eran reemplazadas por otras procedentes de un cuenco próximo.

Chastity miró hacia la otra mesa, donde la cereza, previsiblemente, se hallaba en el extremo de un pepino. Cogió un inofensivo trozo de pan con queso, pensando que nunca más sería capaz de volver a comer pepino. Gresham se acercó a realizar el ritual de las cerezas. Aquélla era su oportunidad de escapar, pero Cyn seguía todavía con ella.

Se preguntó que haría él si ella se escabullía, después de todo no era asunto suyo. Por otro lado, aquél podía ser el único momento propicio para advertirle de la presencia de su hermano.

No sabía que hacer. Tenía que huir pero podía avisarle antes de hacerlo. Él se volvió hacia la mesa para coger un muslo de pollo y ella se sacó la nota del pecho. Se inclinó por encima de él, apretándose contra su espalda mientras se estiraba tratando de alcanzar unas uvas, y le metió el papelito en el bolsillo.

Él se dio rápidamente la vuelta y la observó ceñudo.

—Vaya, ¿qué ocurre, milord? —preguntó ella con nerviosismo.

—Nada —dijo él, al tiempo que trataba de atravesarla con la mirada, como si la viera por primera vez.

Chastity miró a Gresham, quien, tras dedicarle una sonrisa, se inclinó para coger una guinda con los dientes. Estaría de vuelta enseguida.

—Tengo que irme —dijo ella—. ¡Necesito ir al retrete!

Él también miró a Gresham. Después, la agarró por la muñeca.

—Vamos, te enseñaré por dónde se va.

Él la arrastró fuera de la habitación. Gresham dejó escapar un iracundo bramido. Cyn la llevó a través de un corto pasillo hasta la helada noche del exterior.

—¿Qué estás haciendo? —gritó Chastity, jadeando a causa del frío viento.

—Buscarte un sitio para que hagas pis, encanto. Eso es lo que quieres, ¿no? O, ¿es que Gresham era más de lo que podías tragar? —No se parecía en nada a Cyn. Las palabras de aquel tipo sonaban duras e irritadas.

—Pero, ¡aquí hace mucho frío!

Él se quitó bruscamente el abrigo y se lo puso a ella por los hombros, haciendo que quedara aprisionada por la prenda. A continuación, se valió de ella para llevarla aún más cerca de él.

—¡Milord…!

Sus labios la hicieron callar. Eran firmes y no admitían una negativa, pero Chastity se fundió enseguida en ellos. Llevaba tanto tiempo anhelando aquello. ¡Qué importaba que él no supiera quién era ella! Aprovecharía aquel instante y lo atesoraría entre sus recuerdos.

Una vez que se rindiera, estaría perdida. Rodeó con sus brazos el cuerpo de Cyn. Se acopló a cada pulgada de su cuerpo. Acogió su dulce y picante lengua dentro de ella…

De repente, él se soltó y la arrastró un poco más lejos a lo largo del edificio, hasta que quedaron ocultos tras unos arbustos. Conteniendo el aliento, la mandó callar. Chastity estaba aturdida.

Entonces escuchó a Gresham:

—¿Dónde demonios te has metido? ¡Malloren, sinvergüenza, sal de ahí y devuélveme a mi moza!

Tras unas cuantas imprecaciones más, volvió al interior de la casa y dio un portazo.

Cyn se levantó, tirando también de ella.

—¿Quieres reunirte con él?

Chastity sacudió la cabeza. Quería quedarse allí para siempre con Cyn, caliente y a salvo dentro de su abrigo, y dejar que el mundo se hundiera.

Él le levantó la barbilla con los nudillos.

—Entonces, ¿qué es lo que quieres?

Ella seguía percibiendo aquella dureza, pero una cosa estaba clara: aquel momento era un regalo del cielo. Era la oportunidad de amar a Cyn sin ponerle en peligro.

—Te quiero a ti —susurró la muchacha.

Él contuvo el aliento.

—Me pregunto por qué…

No había respuesta para aquella pregunta, así que Chastity se limitó a esperar. Él dejó bajar la mano por el cuello y el hombro de ella y deslizó los dedos por dentro del rígido corpiño hasta tocarle el pezón. Aquella velada había sido demasiado para ella. Sus sentidos estaban trastornados. Se desplomó hacia atrás, apoyándose en la tosca pared de ladrillo y le dejó hacer a voluntad.

Cyn trazó con suavidad un círculo alrededor de la cresta de su aréola y ella se estremeció. Él apretó la cadera contra ella y ella respondió con el mismo gesto.

—Me quieres a mí, ¿no es así? —le dijo él quedamente—. Bien, mi dulce y pequeña libertina, pues yo también te quiero a ti. —Liberó los dedos y la condujo más allá, siguiendo la pared de la casa.

—¿Dónde vamos? —dijo Chastity, que se sentía destemplada en medio de la fría noche.

—A cruzar las cocinas. No quiero batirme en duelo con mi amigo por ti. No vales tanto, ¿no te parece?

Nuevamente, aquella dureza provocó en Chastity un espasmo de intranquilidad.

Se recordó a sí misma que él no sabía quién era ella; la tomaba por una puta, o por una dama de moral relajada. ¿De verdad quería que la tratara así?

Por imperfecta que fuera, aquélla era la única oportunidad que se les ofrecía. Y ella decidió aprovecharla yéndose con él.

11

Cuando entraron en la cocina, el ruido y el calor reinantes impactaron a Chastity de tal modo que pensó que la casa estaba ardiendo. Los sirvientes estaban escandalosamente borrachos, aunque trataban de ocuparse de los asadores y hacer que circulara la comida y la bebida en el piso de arriba. Algunos se habían rendido. Una pierna de cordero se chamuscaba, y una mujer borracha roncaba en un rincón, con los labios entreabiertos.

Nadie se dio cuenta de que Cyn se apropiaba de una cesta y metía en ella algunas rodajas de carne, pasteles de fruta y un tarro de nata montada, antes de llevarse a Chastity de allí. Ella miró hacia atrás y vio cómo un cocinero se giraba y buscaba aturdido la crema.

Pasaron por el cuarto donde se almacenaban las viandas antes de ser servidas, donde, muy oportunamente, había media docena de botellas de vino abiertas. Una de ellas y un par de vasos fueron a parar a la canasta. Esta vez, Chastity protestó.

Cyn la miró.

—Has dicho que tenías hambre, encanto. Me propongo satisfacerte en todos los terrenos.

Lo decía sonriendo, pero ella seguía percibiendo una heladora frialdad tras sus palabras. En cierto modo, se alegraba de aquella displicencia. No quería que él sintiera ternura por aquella mujerzuela de una noche.

Y, una vez más, tuvo que reconocer que estaban viviendo una mentira.

Él la condujo hasta una estrecha escalera de servicio. En su arranque, había una hilera de velas y una lámpara para encenderlas. Cyn prendió una y se la dio a Chastity para que la llevara mientras subían por aquellos escalones.

A Cyn le hubiera costado mucho expresar lo que sentía tras aquel nuevo rumbo de los acontecimientos. Después de todo, ella era una fresca. Él la había dejado a salvo en la habitación y después se la había encontrado, en su verdadera salsa, haciendo de furcia. El único motivo por el que podía haberse sumado a la fiesta era la búsqueda de un hombre.

Le daban ganas de llorar.

Por otro lado, iba a poseerla. Si pensaba burlarse de él del mismo modo que había hecho con Gresham, iba apañada. Se había mostrado dispuesta y le había seguido sin protestar. Pronto aplacaría la lujuria que llevaba días atormentándole. Aquel beso había bastado para dejarle el cuerpo temblando.

Y bien sabía Dios que se encargaría de que ella le recordara. Tal vez hubiera retozado en la cama con la mitad de los hombres de Inglaterra, pero no podría olvidar a Cyn Malloren.

Subieron dos tramos de escaleras y Cyn, que iba en cabeza, abrió una puerta forrada de tela que daba a un pasillo silencioso y polvoriento.

—Tal y como yo pensaba. El ala de los cuartos de los niños. Y lleva mucho tiempo sin usarse.

En aquel tranquilo rincón, la orgía que se desarrollaba más abajo parecía algo irreal. Con todo, hacía frío y, a pesar de llevar puesto el abrigo de Cyn, Chastity tiritaba.

Él exploró las cuatro habitaciones y después se decantó por una de ellas. Probablemente habría sido el dormitorio de la niñera, porque contaba con una estrecha cama que aún estaba cubierta por una manta y un edredón.

Cyn colocó la cesta en el suelo e inspeccionó la chimenea.

—Todavía queda leña aquí, y hay algunos trozos de carbón en el balde. Tal vez podamos hacer fuego.

Chastity dejó la vela en el suelo. Su luz era tenue, incluso en aquella pequeña estancia. Se acurrucó dentro del abrigo de Cyn, ahogándose en su aroma, pero empezando a tener dudas. ¿Qué estaba haciendo lady Chastity Ware en esa habitación polvorienta con aquel hombre? ¿Cómo era que su vida la había llevado a ese punto?

En un estante, había unos cuantos libros mordisqueados por los ratones. Él los hizo pedazos y, aplicándoles la vela, prendió la lumbre. Las llamas arreciaron y después se oyó el chisporroteo de las ramitas. Chastity se acercó instintivamente al fuego.

Él levantó la vista.

—Creo que arderá y el tiro parece despejado. No obstante, tardará un rato en notarse el calor.

—Por lo menos hay luz.

La habitación resultaba más acogedora por el simple hecho de tener la chimenea encendida.

Cyn quitó el colchón, la manta y el edredón de encima de la cama, colocando el primero en el suelo. Extendió la manta sobre él e hizo una elegante reverencia.

—Su sofá, milady.

Chastity se daba cuenta de que una vez se sentara en aquel jergón su destino estaría sellado. Se hundió en él a través del torbellino de sus perfumadas faldas de seda. Y de una buena cantidad de polvo.

Él trajo la cesta y la puso en el suelo antes de sentarse a su lado y echar el edredón por encima de las piernas de ambos.

Ella se apretó aún más el abrigo sobre los hombros.

—¿No tienes frío en mangas de camisa?

Él la miró de soslayo.

—En absoluto.

Chastity apartó la mirada. La expresión de Cyn había hecho que su temperatura aumentara unos cuantos grados.

Él sirvió el vino y le tendió a ella un vaso. Ella dio un sorbo y sintió cómo su calidez se extendía por su cuerpo y le afectaba inmediatamente al cerebro. Esperaba que él saltase sobre ella en cualquier instante y deseaba que lo hiciera antes de que perdiera el aplomo.

—Necesito de veras comer —dijo ella rápidamente.

—¿O te emborracharás? —murmuró él—. Tal vez yo te quiera borracha, encanto.

Ella le miró a través de las ranuras de la máscara y dejó el vaso.

—¿Creéis que es preciso que yo esté como una cuba para que vos hagáis lo que os plazca, milord?

Cyn torció la boca.

—No. Eso sería ridículo, ¿no? —Alargó la mano y le recorrió los labios con un dedo. Un contacto enardecedor. Luego, añadió en tono seductor—: ¿Alguna vez te dijo tu niñera que no jugaras con las cosas de comer? —Cogió una rodaja de carne de ternera y la enrolló lentamente—. A ver, ¿a qué te recuerda esto?

Aquella pregunta hizo que Chastity frunciera el ceño.

—¿Un rollo de carne?

Él se quedó pensativo.

—¿Demasiado pequeño? Tienes razón, sin duda. —Enrolló alrededor dos rodajas más y se lo volvió a enseñar—. ¿Así te gusta más?

Y, tras colocar la carne en la mano izquierda de Chastity, le cogió la derecha y la llevó hasta su entrepierna.

—¿Qué te parece?

Chastity se quedó helada. Nuevamente, comer. Pero, se suponía que ella era una libertina y tenía que comportarse como tal. Sonrió de la mejor manera que pudo.

—Parece normal —dijo con la voz entrecortada. De hecho, todavía parecía más bien pequeña. ¿Todos los hombres la tenían enorme?

—Entonces, come —le dijo él con suavidad.

Tenía las mismas ganas de comerse aquello que de comerse una serpiente, pero no tenía elección. Se pasó la lengua por los labios, se llevó la carne a la boca y mordió. El bulto que tenía bajo la mano brincó como si ella hubiera dado allí el mordisco. Ella se concentró con fiereza en masticar la tierna carne. ¿Qué haría una furcia en aquellas circunstancias?

Ella trató de retirar la mano derecha, pero él se la retuvo allí.

—Quiero un poco de vino —dijo entonces la muchacha.

Él usó la mano libre para coger el vaso de Chastity y levantarlo hasta la altura de sus labios, mientras el bulto se movía como si estuviera vivo debajo de su mano cautiva. A continuación, él bebió también de aquel vaso.

—Come —le dijo él con delicadeza—. Vas a necesitar tener fuerzas.

Chastity estaba aturdida. Había esperado que la agarrara, la besara, la acariciara y la penetrara. No había estado muy segura de que le fuera a gustar, pero se trataba de algo por lo que tenía que pasar. Desde luego, lo que no había esperado era que ella misma tuviera que hacer algo que no fuera rendirse.

Él parecía listo para tomarla, entonces ¿a qué se debía aquella demora? Dejó caer la carne a medio comer.

—Creo que ya he comido bastante.

—Pero, tú eres una dama de feroces apetitos. A lo mejor eres golosa. —Cyn se movió para coger los pasteles y la nata, soltándole la mano para poder hacerlo. Chastity se apartó ligeramente con disimulo y notó en las costillas la llave que llevaba dentro del corpiño. Sospechó que muy pronto resultaría un incordio, así que se la sacó rápidamente y la metió debajo del colchón.

Cyn contemplaba pensativo uno de los pasteles y Chastity adivinó lo que vendría a continuación. La seducción mediante la comida parecía ser su técnica preferida. Y resultaba efectiva. Gracias a sus encuentros previos, ella se hallaba sensibilizada de antemano. Todo el confuso anhelo creado por una galleta de Shrewsbury y un pastellillo de manzana regresaron para inflamar las ambiguas ansias que sentía ahora.

Él mordió el bollo, y un jugo carmesí le chorreó por la mano.

—Cereza —dijo haciendo una mueca—. Perfectamente apropiado.

Se llevó el pastel a la otra mano y le tendió a ella la que estaba manchada de aquel néctar. Obedeciendo la silenciosa orden, Chastity lamió el espeso líquido. Tenía un sabor agridulce, al que había que añadir el gusto salado de la piel de Cyn. Él le pasó la suave carne de su mano por la lengua. Ella aplicó allí la boca y chupó.

Él soltó la mano con suavidad y le tendió el bollo.

—Come.

Ella dio un mordisco. El jugo se escurrió de nuevo. Él inclinó el pastel, haciendo que se derramara sobre los pechos de Chastity. Ella chilló y levantó las manos para proteger el vestido, pero él se las cogió e hizo que se tumbara de espaldas.

Cyn usó la lengua para lamer hasta la última gota, mientras ella yacía sobre el colchón presa de extraños deseos.

Unos dedos hábiles le desabrocharon el traje, le soltaron los lazos del corpiño y se lo quitaron. Una vez abierto el vestido, Chastity quedó tendida debajo de Cyn, cubierta solamente por la fina camisola de seda y la enagua. Ella se preguntó si él la encontraría escasamente dotada.

Le miró a la cara y supo que no era así Inflamado, extasiado, y con una oscura intensidad en la mirada, le recorría con los dedos la curva de sus pechos. Ella se sintió henchida de un arrebatado poder.

—¿Le parezco de su gusto, milord? —murmuró ella.

—Eres bella, como bien sabes —le dijo en un tono de voz que era poco más que un susurro.

A continuación, llevó la mano a los cordeles de la máscara, pero ella se la cogió.

—¡No! La máscara se queda puesta.

—Entonces, ¿tanto valor tiene tu reputación?

—Para mí sí.

Él le recorrió la mejilla con el pulgar siguiendo el borde del negro terciopelo.

—¿Me confiaras al menos tu nombre?

—No —musitó ella—, pero puedes llamarme Chloe.

—¿Chloe? ¿De verdad? ¿Te reirás de mi dolor? —Y citó en voz queda—: «Bésame, querida, antes de que muera. Bésame una vez y alivia mi dolor».

Los tórridos labios de Cyn cayeron sobre los de ella. Santo cielo, ella daría lo que fuera por aliviar su dolor. A sus ojos acudieron las lágrimas. Afortunadamente, la máscara las ocultaba.

Súbitamente, él la dejó. Ella se incorporó, temiendo que algo en ella le hubiera disgustado. Pero él había cogido el tarro de crema chantilly. Sonrió, levantó las cejas y, tras coger una pequeña cantidad, la dejó caer sobre su clavícula.

Chastity se miró y se quedó boquiabierta. Él la hizo tumbarse otra vez y le extendió la nata sobre la curva superior de sus senos. Después, ella sintió cómo él le retiraba la camisola y se supo desnuda. Notó que le ponía y le extendía más crema.

Sin aliento, ella esperaba anhelante su boca. Pero, en cambio, un dedo le recorrió los pechos y se presentó delante de sus ojos.

—Come. Tienes hambre.

Chastity no tuvo que separar los labios porque tenía todavía la boca abierta de la conmoción. Sacó la lengua y tomó un poco de nata. Estaba sazonada con licor de naranja.

—Está muy buena —susurró—. No deberíamos desperdiciarla.

Él sonrió.

—No vamos a desperdiciarla. —Se lamió lentamente el resto de la nata del dedo, después untó más y se la ofreció a ella nuevamente—. Esta vez cómetela toda, dulce Chloe. Toda.

Atrapada totalmente por su mirada, Chastity tomó el dedo de Cyn en su boca, saboreó la deliciosa, escurridiza y refrescante crema y se la tragó. Cuando iba a soltar el dedo, él le dijo:

—No. Quédatelo. Chúpalo. Despacito...

Acto seguido, bajó la cabeza y le lamió parte de la crema de los pechos de una larga pasada. Como si estuviera viviendo un sueño, Chastity siguió sorbiéndole el dedo.

Sintió cómo su lengua le rodeaba primero un pezón y luego el otro. La dulzura de aquella sensación le hizo contener el aliento. Su boca jugueteó con la punta de ambas aréolas.

—Ah, preciosidades —murmuró—. Tenéis envidia de mi dedo, ¿a que sí?

La boca de Chastity se quedó súbitamente inmóvil. Él se agachó y, tras meterse uno de los pezones en la boca, lo friccionó con la lengua. Un estremecimiento sacudió a Chastity y ella hizo lo mismo con el dedo.

—Muy bien, encanto —le dijo él con suavidad—. Enséñame lo que quieres.

Chastity se quedó a la espera de lo que vendría a continuación. Pero él no hizo nada. Entonces comprendió el juego. A modo de prueba, le chupó el dedo. Y él le chupó el pezón. Ella chupó más fuerte. Y él también. Parecía como si ella, de un insólito modo, se diera placer a sí misma. Ella sorbía lenta y profundamente, al tiempo que sentía como una creciente fiebre la abrasaba por dentro.

La entrepierna empezó a palpitarle y ella se agitaba con desazón. Escuchó unos gimoteos y se dio cuenta de que era ella misma la que emitía aquellos sonidos. Y, en realidad, ninguno de los dos se había quitado todavía la ropa.

Él se le colocó encima y se frotó contra ella. Aquello ayudó un poco pero no mucho. Desesperada, Chastity sorbió el dedo de Cyn hasta el fondo de su boca, pero él se rió y lo liberó.

—¡Santo cielo, Chloe! A este paso, uno de los dos acabará sangrando. Ven, desvísteme.

Para sorpresa de Chastity, él se puso de pie y parecía esperar que ella hiciera lo mismo. Ella se quedó tumbada unos instantes, enfebrecida por la lujuria, pensando que él cambiaría de opinión. ¿No sentía la misma apremiante urgencia que ella? Al parecer, no. Mareada y palpitante, se incorporó con dificultad. Bajó la vista y se observó. El abierto vestido le colgaba de los hombros y, de cintura para arriba, era toda jugo lechoso, nata y piel desnuda. Dando un tirón, volvió a cubrirse los pechos con la camisola.

Luego, con dedos torpes y temblorosos, trató de desabrochar los botones del largo chaleco de Cyn, con los nervios a flor de piel al sentir el contacto de su cuerpo. Se rindió a la mitad, poniéndole las manos sobre el pecho y buscando ayuda en su sombrío y penetrante rostro.

Con la intención de apremiarlo, se irguió para darle un beso.

Los labios de Cyn juguetearon con los suyos pero luego él se retiró.

—Cuanto antes acabes, encanto, antes podremos continuar.

La fiebre amainó un poco, aunque Chastity hubiera llorado para hacerla desaparecer. ¿Qué loco juego era aquél? Empezaba a creer que él se proponía mortificarla y que no iban a hacer nunca el amor.

Acabó con los botones rápidamente. Al soltar el último, notó la rígida dureza del hombre. Aquello la tranquilizó un poco. Él necesitaba una mujer, la necesitaba a ella. Se acordó de lo que había pasado cuando tuvo que desatarle los lazos. Vacilante, presionó y frotó con suavidad.

Cyn contuvo el aliento.

—Todo depende de la velocidad a la que quieras que vayan las cosas, Chloe.

Chastity no tenía manera de saberlo. Retiró la mano.

—Ah —dijo él, con una larga exhalación—. Eres una experta. No esperaba menos.

Sonaba algo molesto, pero como todo estaba resultando diferente de lo que Chastity había esperado, ¿por qué habría de sorprenderla aquello? Le sacó la camisa del talle y se la subió por encima del pecho. Descubrió que le encantaba pasarle las manos por los tersos músculos. Se detuvo para recorrer con los dedos el perfil de éstos, extasiada.

Se quitó él mismo las mangas de la camisa y, después, se la sacó por la cabeza.

Chastity recorrió con un dedo la lívida cicatriz que le atravesaba el torso.

—¿Cómo te has hecho esto?

Cualquier mujer haría aquella pregunta.

—Un sable. En Quebec.

—Debiste sangrar un montón.

—Como un odre rajado. Puse perdido mi mejor uniforme.

A Chastity le asaltaron recuerdos agridulces. Sabía que las cosas entre ambos tendrían que ser de otra manera, pero aquello era lo mejor a lo que podían aspirar.

Bajó la vista y observó sus propios pechos, sus pechos desnudos, todavía veteados de nata. Cogió la poca nata que quedaba y la extendió suavemente a lo largo de la cicatriz. Después la retiró con la lengua. Aunque él permanecía inmóvil, ella era consciente de que su respiración se había hecho más profunda.

El bulto que escondía su pantalón se apretó contra el vientre de la muchacha.

—Vamos Chloe —dijo él con viveza—. Una cosa es ir despacio, pero si sigues demorando esto, vas a desaprovechar mis atributos.

Chastity dio un respingo al oír aquello y desabrochó rápidamente los botones del pantalón y de los calzoncillos. Armándose de valor, le bajó ambas prendas. El pene de Cyn emergió libre hacia ella.

Chastity lo agarró con las dos manos.

Al instante siguiente, no sabía por qué lo había hecho. Tal vez fuera un intento por controlar aquella cosa, pero ahora la notaba palpitar entre sus manos y no tenía ni idea de lo que iba a hacer con ella.

Con nerviosa frivolidad, él le dijo:

—Bésala y se portará muy bien contigo.

Ella contempló su húmeda punta y después le miró a él con los ojos muy abiertos. Él sacudió la cabeza y deslizó los dedos de ella, haciéndole soltar su presa. Ella se alegró de dejarla marchar. Cyn se despojó rápidamente de las prendas inferiores y las medias, hasta quedar espléndidamente desnudo allí de pie.

Chastity contempló a su hombre. Cyn Malloren había perdido casi toda su apariencia de delicadeza. Era todo músculos. Hermosos y tensos músculos. La realidad se desvanecía. El disfraz, aquella mascarada en la que se hacía pasar por puta, su pasado, su futuro, todo se convirtió en sombras. En aquel momento, sólo estaban ella y Cyn.

La muchacha jadeó cuando él le cogió la barbilla y la obligó a mirarle a los ojos.

—Necesito hechos, dulce Chloe. Me parece que no tienes tanta experiencia en esto como pretendes hacerme creer, ¿no es cierto?

Chastity quería mentir. Tenía miedo que la echara de su lado y se fuera a buscar a una mujer del estilo de Sable. Pero él exigía la verdad.

—Cierto.

Él asintió y respiró para calmarse.

—Bien, lo que te voy a preguntar es importante y, si me mientes, te juro que te zurraré. ¿Eres virgen?

Chastity vaciló. Supuso que si decía que sí, todo habría terminado y no podría aplacar su feroz apetito. Por otro lado, ella no era fisiológicamente virgen, así que él no se daría cuenta.

Después del fiasco con Vernham, Chastity había llamado a su médico para que la reconociera y certificara su pureza. Cuando su padre se enteró, se apresuró a hacer que la visitara una mujer; ésta decía ser comadrona, pero Chastity sospechaba que regentaba algún burdel. El odioso lacayo de su padre, Lindle, la había sujetado mientras aquella mujer le desgarraba el himen, llevándose la endeble prueba de su virtud.

Cuando el doctor Marsden llegó por fin, ella no quiso recibirlo, pero su padre la obligó a aceptar que la examinara el afligido médico. La advirtieron de que si algún día trataba de contar su versión, el doctor Marsden certificaría su perversidad.

—¿Y bien? —preguntó Cyn con viveza—. No es una pregunta tan difícil.

—No —dijo Chastity—. Por supuesto que no soy virgen.

Él le sondeó la mirada.

—¿Es eso cierto? Hablaba en serio. Te zurraré si me mientes en esto, y sabré si me has dicho la verdad o no.

Chastity tragó saliva pero le miró a los ojos.

—No me harás sangrar, te lo aseguro milord. Antes de hoy, ya ha habido un hombre en mi cama. —Ambas afirmaciones eran completamente ciertas.

Él le soltó la barbilla.

—Sea pues.

Le retiró el abierto vestido de los hombros y lo dejó caer al suelo. Después, hizo que se diera la vuelta para desatarle los lazos de la enagua.

El contacto de los dedos de Cyn en su columna le produjo pequeños estremecimientos. Cuando la enagua cayó, él le pasó los nudillos por las vértebras. Hueso, seda y carne. Ella se bamboleó hacia atrás y él le mordisqueó suavemente la nuca.

Entonces estornudó.

—Maldita sea. ¿Por qué demonios te has tenido que poner polvos? —Pero lo decía en tono jocoso mientras le daba la vuelta.

—Lo siento. Como has adivinado, no tengo mucha experiencia en estos asuntos.

Cyn le cubrió los pechos con las manos.

—No creo que la experiencia tenga nada que ver en eso. He conocido mujeres sabiamente perversas que no parecen darse cuenta de lo mucho que las cremas y los productos para el pelo pueden entorpecer el placer.

Le frotó levemente los pezones a través de la seda. Aquel febril anhelo creció de nuevo en el interior de Chastity, esta vez con más fuerza por haberse visto frustrado antes. Ella hizo ademán de quitarse la camisa pero Cyn la detuvo.

—No, encanto, déjatela puesta. No estoy seguro de estar preparado para verte en todo tu esplendor.

La cogió y la tumbó de nuevo en el colchón.

—Yo sí estoy lista para recibirte.

—¿Ah, sí? Vamos a ver.

Se arrodilló entre las piernas de ella. Le puso las manos en los tobillos y las fue deslizando poco a poco hacia la parte superior de los muslos. Sus endurecidos dedos producían una deliciosa fricción al rozar la suave piel de la muchacha, que se retorcía con desasosiego, abriendo voluntariamente las piernas ante aquella deliciosa invasión. Pero las manos de Cyn se detuvieron a la altura de los muslos. Sus dedos se flexionaron allí, contra la satinada epidermis de su cara interna.

Chastity apretaba la cabeza hacia atrás.

—Santo cielo, ¿qué me estás haciendo?

Notó que él tenía allí la cabeza, entre sus piernas, con los labios en el lugar en el que habían estado los pulgares. Ella se incorporó, apoyándose sobre los codos.

—¿Qué…?

Él la cortó.

—No hagas tantas preguntas. ¿Te gusta?

Ella sintió sus dedos en el vello del pubis, resbalando por el fluido que se había producido allí.

—Claro que te gusta. Parece como si te hubiera puesto crema también ahí.

Sus dedos se deslizaron dentro de ella. Chastity se desplomó hacia atrás con un gemido gutural que la sorprendió a ella misma por su sonido primitivo. Ella empujó contra su mano y él siguió el ritmo de la fricción que ella parecía estar demandando. Cyn se desplazó un poco hacia arriba para atrapar un pezón con la boca y chupar al compás del movimiento de la mano.

Aquello fue la perdición de Chastity. Una parte de su cerebro conservaba la cordura y gracias a ella supo que seguramente estaba expresando a gritos la desesperada necesidad que tenía de dejarse ir. Hubiera preferido estar callada y comportarse como una dama pero le resultaba imposible. Trató de disculparse pero lo que en realidad hizo fue ponerse ancha y apretar su cuerpo contra él.

Entonces, Cyn se movió. Su boca y su mano la abandonaron y ella sintió cómo la rigidez del hombre se apretaba sobre ella.

—Sí —dijo ella jadeante.

Él se deslizó dentro de ella lentamente, casi como de prueba. Chastity gimoteó y se propulsó hacia arriba para absorberlo. Parecía que no iba a poder entrar, porque su gran tamaño contrastaba con lo prieta que estaba ella, pero la plenitud que producía aquel ensanchamiento era deliciosa.

A Chastity le pareció oír un extraño suspiró cuando él se instaló finalmente en su interior. Después, volvió a salir con delicadeza.

Ella serpenteó tras él, temiendo que fuera a dejarla. Él volvió a entrar y ella se estremeció aliviada.

—No tengas miedo, Chloe —dijo él suavemente, pasándole la mano tiernamente por la mejilla—. No voy a dejarte con las ganas. Vamos, vayamos hasta el final.

Cada acometida encontraba su respuesta simétrica. Al principio iban despacio, mientras se estudiaban mutuamente con suavidad y ternura. Pero, luego, la inminencia de la descarga se apoderó de ellos y corrieron hasta alcanzar una explosión que hizo trizas la mente de Chastity.

La muchacha emergió flotando de aquella oscuridad y llenó de aire sus pulmones vacíos con la certeza de que nunca volvería a ser la misma. Se había quedado completamente limpia, llena y vacía a la vez, aturdida, pero más viva que nunca.

Él se quedó tendido sobre ella, respirando profundamente, caliente y sudoroso. Cuando se meneó, se habían adherido el uno al otro a causa de la transpiración, el jugo y la crema, y tuvieron que despegarse para poder separarse. El aire fresco acarició la húmeda piel de Chastity y ella se echó a reír con fruición.

Él se inclinó sobre ella, con los ojos oscuros y misteriosos, pero sonriendo al verla complacida.

—Una cosa está clara, Chloe de mis amores, lo que ha pasado hasta ahora por tu cama no han sido más que patanes. ¿Por qué malgastar todo este esplendor con ellos?

Ella quería contarle la verdad, pero estropearía aquel glorioso momento. Y no estaba segura de que él no fuera a zurrarla por la mentira que le había contado, aunque todo lo que le había dicho fuera cierto.

—No sabía lo que me perdía.

Él apartó la vista y le pasó una mano por el brazo.

—¿Y ahora?

—Ahora ya lo sé.

—¿Y qué vas a hacer con esa información?

Ella supo entonces qué era lo que tenía que hacer. Él no creía haber sido el primero, pero estaba seguro —segurísimo— de haber sido el primero en mostrarle aquel éxtasis. Y ahora se sentía responsable, igual que si le hubiera arrebatado su virginidad. Volvía a surgir el caballero andante. ¿Acaso tenía que intentar ayudar a todas las criaturas extraviadas que se encontrara en su camino? Ya tenía bastante con tener en sus manos a Verity, William y Charles. Sólo le faltaba tener que preocuparse de la lasciva Chloe.

Chastity tenía que liberarlo. Con este pensamiento, se incorporó hasta quedar sentada.

—A partir de ahora, sabré lo que valgo —dijo ella con franqueza—. En el futuro, no otorgaré mis favores con ligereza.

Él apoyó la mano sobre el muslo de ella.

—¿Es eso una promesa?

Ella asintió. Ansiaba desesperadamente poder abrirle su corazón, decirle que le amaba y que no podía imaginarse aquellas intimidades con ningún otro hombre, por habilidoso que fuera. Anhelaba poder sincerarse con él, aunque sólo fuera durante un instante.

Pero aquella noche era todo lo que les estaba permitido tener, y si intentaba ser honesta, la echaría a perder.

Y la noche aún no había terminado.

Ella contempló pensativa su pene, que le caía flácido sobre el muslo. Él se rió entre dientes y dijo:

—No tardará mucho, ya lo verás.

Se sentó y le quitó a ella la manchada y arrugada camisola. Después, echó el edredón por encima de ambos. Estar acurrucada junto a él, era para ella una inesperada dicha. Tal vez la cosa se le estuviera yendo de las manos, porque aquello no iba a poder olvidarlo tan fácil…

Él sirvió dos nuevos vasos de vino.

—Háblame de ti.

El trato de Chastity no incluía la conversación.

—¿Serías capaz de arrancarme la flor de mi misterio?

—Desde luego que sí. Te desnudaría hasta llegar al fondo de tu alma.

Ella se estremeció.

—¿Por qué no me cuentas primero tus secretos, milord?

—Mis secretos... —Él se quedó contemplando el resplandeciente fuego—. ¿Es un secreto que suelo tener miedo antes de la batalla? No lo es entre mis compañeros de armas, porque todos compartimos la misma debilidad. Sólo un tonto no siente miedo. No temo a la muerte, sino a la mutilación.

Chastity apretó con fuerza el vaso que tenía entre las manos. La muerte era la última cosa sobre la que quería hablar.

—¿No tienes secretos menos militares?

Él le lanzó una mirada.

—¿Quieres una lista de mis amantes?

Por supuesto que no.

—¿Así se resumen tus intereses? ¿El amor y la guerra?

—Tal vez. Me pregunto cuánto tiempo hace falta para conocer a alguien. Para enamorarse.

Chastity se quedó mirando fijamente el misterioso mundo del fuego.

—Un instante o toda la vida.

—Muy cierto. Me debes un secreto.

Ella sacudió la cabeza.

—Estoy hecha de secretos y misterios y, si revelo tan sólo uno de ellos, me desmoronaré.

Súbitamente, la hizo ponerse de pie y la arrastró hasta el pequeño espejo moteado que había en la pared y la sostuvo allí. Ella observó la imagen desnuda de ambos, un poco distorsionada por la ondulación del cristal y la luz parpadeante. Él era Cyn, con el pelo cayéndole en ondas hasta los hombros. Ella era un misterio, incluso para ella misma. Desconocía a aquella mujer enmascarada, de pelo oscuro y empolvado, y labios abultados.

—Mira —le dijo él—, y yo te enseñaré tus secretos.

Empezó a tocarla con minuciosa destreza, observando cómo ella contemplaba a aquella extraña libertina derretirse de deseo. Dejó caer la cabeza hacia atrás, sobre el hombro de Cyn. Sus labios se abrieron. Su pecho subía y bajaba al compás de las profundas y anhelantes respiraciones. Chastity miró la imagen de Cyn en el espejo. No estaba poseído por el deseo sino atento a las reacciones de ella.

—No me gusta esto —dijo ella.

—Mentirosa.

—No quiero que te quedes atrás. Acompáñame.

Él le mordisqueó el hombro.

—Puedo descubrir todos los secretos de tu cuerpo y usarlos para hacerte estallar en pedazos, pero no te desmoronarás. Te harás más fuerte.

Ella trataba de resistirse a su hábil roce.

—Eso es otra cosa.

Él incrementó la presión de su mano entre sus muslos y un estremecimiento hizo flaquear la voluntad de Chastity.

—Es la misma cosa —dijo él—. Cuéntame tus secretos.

Una nueva oleada de tormentoso deseo la recorrió. Ella cerró los ojos.

—¿Qué es lo que quieres?

—Lo quiero todo de ti. Confía en mí.

Ella abrió las piernas.

—Confío en ti.

La mano de él se detuvo.

—No me refiero a eso. Confía en mí con todo tu ser.

Ella sacudió la cabeza.

—No tengo nada para ti, Cyn Malloren. —La muchacha se soltó y echó a correr, agachándose para recoger su ropa. Él la derribó sobre el colchón, usando el peso de su cuerpo para doblegar el de Chastity y la sujetó por las muñecas.

—Esto aún no ha llegado a su fin —le dijo con sombría mirada.

—Ya te he dicho que no tengo nada más.

—Sí que lo tienes. Lo quiero todo de ti. Quiero tus secretos.

Chastity forcejeó.

—¡Estás loco!

—Claro que lo estoy. ¿No lo notas tú también? ¿Qué hay en esta habitación, maldita sea? Después de esto, ¿podrás estar con otro hombre?

—¡No pienso estar con ningún otro hombre!

—¡Confía en mí! —Él la besó con pasión. Chastity le devolvió el beso entre sollozos. Esta vez, las lagrimas se escurrieron por debajo de la máscara y él las bebió de sus mejillas.

—Llora, llora por nosotros, Chloe. Pase lo que pase, nunca olvidarás esto.

Él volvió a hacerle el amor, con la boca, las manos y todos los nervios de su cuerpo. Al principio, ella luchó contra aquella pasión, porque tenía miedo de su ferocidad, de la violencia con la que él se entregaba, pero después se rindió.

Él no se lo puso fácil. Por dos veces la llevó hasta las puertas del clímax y, a continuación, se detuvo a pesar de sus súplicas, refrescándola con vino y nata, hasta que volvía a la realidad, una realidad llena de deseo.

Ella le llenó de improperios, incluso trató de pegarle.

Él le dio la vuelta con suavidad y le masajeó la espalda, usando la nata como lubricante, hasta que se quedó flotando, como si estuviera inerte, y encontró cierta paz. Después, la hizo ponerse de rodillas y la acarició desde detrás hasta que volvió a jadear de excitación.

—Que el demonio te lleve, Cyn Malloren —susurró ella—, si vuelves a dejarme colgada otra vez.

Él se echó a reír y se escurrió hasta quedar tumbado debajo de ella, mirándola.

—Entonces, vuela tú misma, Chloe. Cabálgame.

Se sentó a horcajadas sobre él y lo engulló con codicioso apremio, deslizándose arriba y abajo con la fricción más dulce del mundo. Observó cómo él se desmadejaba, pero la muchacha había aprendido bien la lección. Con un supremo esfuerzo de voluntad, se detuvo, quedándose en suspenso encima de él.

Cyn abrió los ojos de golpe y apretó los puños.

—Oh, dulce arpía libertina de los infiernos... ¿Tengo que suplicarte?

—Sí —dijo ella.

—Por favor —susurró él, con lóbrega mirada.

Chastity volvió a acoplarse y ambos se elevaron a las alturas.

Durmieron. Chastity se despertó atravesada encima de Cyn con el edredón más o menos sobre ellos. El fuego se había extinguido, y la luz que entraba por la polvorienta ventana sugería el despunte del alba. Se levantó con mucha cautela, estremeciéndose a causa del aire helado, pero él no se movió.

Apenas podía verlo con aquella luz grisácea aunque se moría de las ganas. Se acercó con la intención de tocarlo pero apartó la mano. Las lágrimas le ahogaron al comprender que aquello era el final. Después de aquella noche, ella tendría que huir.

Sin apenas respirar, se puso la camisola, la enagua y el vestido. Cogió el corpiño, calculando que le resultaría demasiado difícil intentar colocárselo allí. Pensó que no se encontraría con nadie a aquella inerte hora de la noche. Pero, si así era, la ropa que llevaba puesta sería suficiente para atravesar la penumbra.

Rescató la llave de debajo del colchón y abrió con cuidado la puerta, parpadeando al oírla rechinar. Pero él no se despertó. Ella salió con sigilo al exterior, bajó por las estrechas escaleras y emprendió el camino de regreso a la habitación de lord Heatherington.

Cyn abrió los ojos tan pronto como ella se hubo marchado. La noche más tórrida de su vida estaba teniendo un desenlace verdaderamente frío y desolador. Cerró los ojos y la revivió. No se sentía orgulloso de todo lo que había ocurrido pero era consciente de que, al final, había salido bien.

Una cosa estaba clara: ya no podría vivir sin ella. Y no podría dejar que ella viviera sin él.

Había sentido dolor físico al reconocer el perfume que llevaba la furcia de Gresham. Le pareció que todos los placeres de la tierra se habían vuelto escoria al darse cuenta de que su damisela era una libertina y no un ángel injustamente juzgado. Se la había robado a su amigo con más ánimo de venganza que de placer.

Se había mostrado dispuesto a que una ramera le asqueara con sus trucos, pero, en cambio, había sido seducido por una gallarda ignorancia. Entonces, había esperado de verdad que ella le confesara que era virgen y se preparó, con gran perjuicio para su salud mental, para dejarla intacta. Incluso cuando la penetraba, estaba convencido de que descubriría que ella le había mentido.

Y le decepcionó comprobar que ella decía la verdad.

Pero, después de todo, para arrebatarle a alguien la virginidad no hacía falta gran cosa. Y estaba claro que no era una experta mujerzuela. Tal vez Vernham hubiera sido el único…

Sacudió la cabeza y sonrió. Sin duda, ella estaría en aquellos momentos volviendo a adquirir la subrepticia identidad de Charles. Iba a ser duro, pero pensaba abandonarla hasta que hubiera encontrado una solución. El futuro no se presentaba fácil. El mundo no iba a perdonar que un Malloren se casara con una mujer deshonrada, y Rothgar haría lo imposible para impedirlo.

Pero a pesar del mundo, de Rothgar y de todo, él la haría suya, la cuidaría y la haría cantar de júbilo día y noche. Se les presentarían algunas dificultades, pero las dificultades eran el antídoto del aburrimiento.

Se puso de pie y se estiró, sintiéndose el rey del universo. Se vistió y trató de poner en orden su insólito nido de amor. Lo hizo silbando.

12

Chastity conocía sólo dos rutas para regresar a la habitación de Heatherington. Una de ellas la llevaría por fuera de la casa y la otra le haría cruzar el vestíbulo frontal. Cuando abrió la puerta que daba al exterior, una neblina tan espesa que parecía llovizna la dejó helada. Se echó a temblar, cerró la puerta y se encaminó hacia el recibidor. Se miró el pecho casi desnudo y se preguntó si no debía ponerse el corpiño, pero la casa estaba en silencio. Se limitó a tirar de los bordes delanteros del vestido, reduciendo el espacio que había entre ellos, y apresuró el paso.

Se quedó de piedra al oír unas voces lejanas —le pareció que provenían de la sala de juego—, pero decidió que aquellos adictos no representaban ningún peligro y se aventuró a cruzar el vestíbulo.

Todavía ardía una única lámpara humeante y el aire estaba cargado con los espesos olores del sudor y del alcohol. Pero el lugar estaba desierto. Había unas cuantas prendas de vestir esparcidas por el suelo, y, sobre la brillante madera de roble, una gran mancha oscura denunciaba que allí se había derramado algo. Supuso que no sería sangre. Si alguien hubiera perdido tanta sangre, se habría producido una gran conmoción.

Aunque, de haberse producido aquella noche una masacre colectiva, ¿se habrían percatado Cyn y ella?

A pesar de hallarse en una situación desoladora, los recuerdos la hacían sonreír. Nunca había imaginado que hacer el amor fuera así. Habían quedado fundidos por la pasión, igual que el hierro en la fragua. No tenían futuro, pero aquella única noche bien había valido todo el dolor que les acarrearía.

Pero sólo si Cyn nunca llegaba a averiguar la identidad de Chloe. Tenía que desaparecer antes de que él se despertara. Se cogió las faldas y echó a correr hacia las escaleras. Su pie tropezó con un jarro vacío, que rodó hasta chocar con estrépito contra el poste de la escalera.

—¿Qué tenemos aquí?

Chastity se volvió de golpe y vio al marqués de Rothgar plantado en el vano de una puerta e iluminado por el halo de luz de las velas de un candelabro. Tras dejarlo sobre una mesa, se acercó a ella.

Chastity se giró para subir las escaleras al galope, pero él se movió con una velocidad sorprendente y la cogió por el brazo, sin violencia, pero con la suficiente fuerza como para evitar que escapara.

—Por favor, señor —dijo ella, con un impostado acento rústico y apartando el rostro—, deje que me vaya.

Él le hizo volver la cara.

—No ha sido una buena idea tratar de hacerte pasar por una campesina, querida. Sólo las damas de alcurnia llevan máscara aquí.

Chastity se tiró de los extremos del vestido, tratando de juntarlos. Se sentía medio desnuda en más de un sentido.

—Tal vez quiera que me tomen por una dama de alcurnia, señor.

—Me pregunto por qué. A ellas no se les paga.

Él se las había apañado para que ambos se dieran la vuelta, de modo que él se interponía ahora entre ella y las escaleras. Una colosal barrera. El corazón de Chastity empezó a bombear con fuerza dentro de su pecho, a causa del miedo.

Él la contempló, con el esbozo de una leve sonrisa en sus delicados labios. Sus ojos estaban en la penumbra y ella no podía tener la certeza de que el humor hubiera llegado hasta ellos. A la muchacha le temblaron las piernas. Por el amor de Dios, ¿qué era lo que quería?

Rothgar tenía el mismo aspecto opulento e inmaculado que presentara unas horas antes, y no parecía falto de sueño. ¿Era humano aquel hombre? ¿Había venido a Rood House por casualidad o había seguido el rastro de Cyn hasta allí? Era imposible que la relacionara a ella con su hermano, incluso si sabía que éste había llegado hasta allí acompañado de un joven lacayo...

Se sacó un taleguito del bolsillo, lo abrió y arrojó una cascada de guineas sobre la mano.

—He estado pasando el tiempo en las mesas —dijo—. Esta bolsa por el resto de tu noche.

Chastity se apretó aún más el vestido.

—Ya... ya casi ha amanecido.

—Cierto.

Chastity tragó saliva y sacudió la cabeza.

—Estoy demasiado cansada, señor.

Él arqueó una ceja.

—Has vuelto a meter la pata. Una puta no está nunca demasiado cansada. ¿Qué eres tú entonces, una dama o una prostituta?

Presa de la desesperación, Chastity trató de pasar dándole un empujón, pero él se limitó a desplazarse, volviéndole a bloquear el paso y quedándose allí de pie como un muro en su camino.

—Voy a gritar.

—¿Crees que eso te servirá de algo?

Él se había subido al primer escalón, lo que hacía que su impresionante altura resultara aún más abrumadora. Chastity se hizo daño el cuello al tener que levantar la vista para mirarlo.

—¿Qué es lo que quiere, señor?

—Milord —le corrigió él suavemente—. Me preguntaba dónde has pasado la noche.

Chastity le miró a los ojos.

—Con un amante.

—Eso suponía, y te ha debido dejar muy cansada. ¿Es eso una proeza?

Chastity volvió a intentar pasar dando un rodeo, pero él volvió a bloquearle el paso. No podía más. Estaba a punto de echarse a llorar.

Él desenganchó un alfiler de su corbata de encaje —una irregular perla negra incrustada en oro— y lo hizo girar ante ella.

—Este broche a cambio de un beso.

Chastity contempló la rotación de la gema y sintió que se mareaba.

—¿Y después me dejarás irme?

—No pareces muy zalamera, muchacha. Pero, sí, después te dejaré marchar. Si es que todavía lo deseas.

Chastity sabía bastante más de besos que la última vez que Rothgar la besara, y aquella perspectiva la asustaba. Pero, después de todo, se trataba sólo de un beso. Además, Cyn podía despertarse en cualquier momento y salir tras ella.

—Muy bien, milord.

Él le puso las manos en la cintura y la elevó sin esfuerzo a un escalón superior al suyo, de modo que ella estaba ahora sólo media cabeza por debajo de él. Aquella acción hizo que las manos de Chastity se soltaran y que el vestido se le abriera. Ella trató de agarrarlo, pero él llegó primero: junto las dos mitades y las sujetó con el alfiler. Después la miró.

Chastity permanecía en calma, decidida a pagar su deuda con dignidad.

—Deberías haber definido lo que es un beso antes de aceptar el trato— le dijo él con delicadeza.

A la muchacha se le abrieron los ojos.

—Un beso es un beso.

—¿Qué es, según tú, un beso? —Le puso las manos sobre los hombros y le frotó la clavícula con los pulgares. No era una sensación desagradable, pero ella tenía presente en todo momento que Cyn podía aparecer en cualquier instante. De ser así, quedaría al descubierto frente a su hermano, se pelearía con Rothgar a causa de ella y Chastity perdería la oportunidad de escapar.

—Simplemente juntar nuestras bocas —dijo ella con brusquedad.

Él se echó a reír.

—No eres muy generosa, querida. Muy bien, juntemos simplemente nuestras bocas.

Él retiró las manos y se inclinó para aplicar sus labios sobre los de ella. Exploró y tironeó hasta que la boca de Chastity se ablandó. La muchacha sintió la extraña necesidad de aferrarse a él para no caerse pero lo que hizo fue apretar el corpiño contra su pecho. Tenía que haber puesto un límite de tiempo al beso.

La lengua de Rothgar le recorrió la parte interna de los labios y ella sintió que se ablandaba aún más. Cerró los ojos y reconoció la habilidad del hombre, pese a desear que acabara de una vez. Los oídos de la muchacha se agudizaron ante la posible aparición en escena de Cyn, presagiando sus pisadas. Aunque éste bien podía tomar también la ruta exterior.

¡Puede que estuviera ya en la habitación de Heatherington!

La lengua del hombre se introdujo en su relajada boca. Instintivamente, Chastity la escupió y abrió los ojos de golpe, temiendo la represalia.

Él sonreía, aunque con cierto pesar.

—No eres muy generosa, desde luego. —Y retrocedió unos pasos—. Sigue tu camino, pajarillo.

Chastity hizo ademán de devolver el imperdible, pero él le detuvo la mano.

—Quédatelo. Nuestro encuentro me ha resultado de lo más instructivo. Sin embargo, si crees que no te has ganado esta fruslería, puedes contestarme a una pregunta.

Cautelosa, Chastity subió unos cuantos escalones.

—¿Cuál?

—Los besos que te han dado esta noche, ¿te han complacido más que el mío?

—Oh, sí —dijo Chastity, y sólo entonces se dio cuenta de que estaba sonriendo y de que probablemente se había sonrojado.

Él le hizo una elegante y florida reverencia.

—Entonces, te deseo que recibas muchos más de la misma fuente.

Estupefacta, Chastity se dio la vuelta y huyó.

Al llegar a la puerta de la habitación de Heatherington se detuvo vacilante. Tal vez Cyn estuviera ya allí. Y aunque no fuera así, no sería de extrañar que su anfitrión hubiera decidido usar su cama, valiéndose de otra copia de la llave. Hizo girar la cerradura y abrió la puerta lentamente. La alcoba parecía vacía.

Fue a gatas hasta la cama. Definitivamente, no había nadie. Buscó a tientas la caja del pedernal junto a la cama y prendió una llama para encender la vela. No había ninguna señal de que nadie hubiera estado allí desde que ella se había marchado.

Se dejó caer sobre la cama, temblando y a punto de ser desbordada por los acontecimientos. Quería esconderse en un agujero y disponer de mucho tiempo para juntar los pedazos astillados de su persona y reunir el coraje para seguir adelante. Pero no tenía tiempo. Debía volver a transformarse en Charles y marcharse de allí.

Trató de soltarse el alfiler del vestido. No era fácil. Rothgar lo había prendido en la parte más gruesa de la seda. Levantó la vista y se vio en el espejo. ¡Cielo santo, tenía una pinta desastrosa!

Llevaba la peluca ladeada y se notaba que le habían besado exhaustivamente los labios. Los polvos rosados se habían esparcido por la negra máscara de terciopelo y por los hombros del vestido, cuyo aspecto no era muy decente. Sus pechos, sin el corpiño, ofrecían un aspecto más voluptuoso de la cuenta.

¿El exigente de Rothgar se habría sentido atraído por aquella mujer?

Jamás.

Entonces, ¿qué es lo que había pretendido? Mientras se despojaba de la indumentaria de mujer, Chastity le daba vueltas a aquello. Si ella hubiera accedido a venderse por unas pocas horas, sin duda, él hubiera seguido adelante con el trato, pero no había sido un ofrecimiento serio. Aún así, él se había resistido a dejarla marchar y el beso le había salido caro.

No comprendía cuál había sido su propósito y eso le asustaba. Cuando ella había sido lady Chastity Ware en Londres, Rothgar no la había intimidado. Simplemente, le había producido cierta turbación. Pero ahora, al ser una fugitiva liada con su hermano —cosa que él jamás aprobaría— temblaba de miedo. La conducta de Rothgar hacia que la huida le resultara aún más urgente.

Vertió el agua fría de la jarra en la palangana y se enjuagó el sudor, la nata y los cosméticos. Sonrojándose, se limpió las huellas de la cópula de entre las piernas. Sus manos se quedaron inmóviles. ¿Qué ocurriría si estaba embarazada?

Virgen santa, ¿qué haría en ese caso? ¡Debía haberse vuelto loca! Su padre seguramente la mataría. Se colocó las manos sobre el abdomen, como si fuera a notar ya algún cambio. Después, las retiró. Ya se enfrentaría a ese desastre a su debido tiempo. Sin embargo, al pensar que podía traer al mundo un hijo de Cyn, un secreto anhelo se instaló en su interior. Otra razón más para escapar.

Él, sin saberlo, había hecho el amor con una joven dama soltera, y aunque pensara que no era virgen, ella sabía que Cyn Malloren sentiría que tenía que casarse con ella. Un hijo sellaría definitivamente su destino. No podía atraparlo con aquel truco barato. No podía forzarlo a contraer un matrimonio que arruinaría su carrera y lo apartaría para siempre de su familia.

Se apresuró a hacer desaparecer las pruebas de su mascarada. Volvió a meter la peluca en el baúl, pero luego se dio cuenta de que aquello revelaría inmediatamente a Cyn quién había sido la misteriosa dama. La sacó y la arrojó al fondo del armario de Heatherington con la esperanza de que Cyn se olvidara de su existencia. Hizo lo mismo con las ropas y la máscara.

Cogió el alfiler con la perla y se preguntó qué hacer con él. Estuvo tentada de dejarlo allí, aunque sentía que era un regalo que le habían ofrecido honestamente. ¿Qué había querido decir Rothgar con su última pregunta acerca de los besos que había recibido aquella noche? Viniendo de otro hombre, hubiera pensado que se trataba de resentimiento por no haberla complacido. Pero aquél no era el estilo de Rothgar.

Nuevamente, la perplejidad ante aquella conducta le produjo miedo. Se prendió el alfiler en la bocamanga de la chaqueta. Si las cosas se ponían muy mal. tal vez algún día pudiera costearse con él unas cuantas comidas.

Se puso su propia peluca en la cabeza y la cubrió con el sombrero gacho de ala flexible. Otra vez Charles le miraba desde el espejo. Su rostro de la pasada noche, encendido por la pasión, se superponía sobre la imagen real. Casi podía imaginar a Cyn detrás de ella, acariciándola…

Abandonó con esfuerzo aquellas divagaciones y se dijo que debía apresurarse. Rebuscó en el uniforme de Cyn y encontró su dinero. Cogió la mitad.

Durante un instante de debilidad, se aferró a su chaquetón rojo y absorbió su aroma. Santo cielo, ¿cómo iba a dejarlo?

Santo cielo, ¿cómo iba a quedarse?

Después de la última noche, sería imposible mantener la mascarada. Y, ahora más que nunca, no podía decirle la verdad. Sería cómo atraparlo con un engaño.

O tal vez aún peor. Tal vez la misteriosa dama con la que había hecho el amor había llegado a importarle. Recordó la vehemencia con la que él le había exigido que le revelara sus secretos.

Tal vez le diera por buscar a Chloe.

Bien, pues tanto Chloe como Charles iban a desaparecer.

Chastity se quedó helada.

Si ambos desaparecían, ¿se le ocurriría a él relacionarlos? Seguramente, su mente no tardaría mucho en iluminarse. Se cubrió la cara con las temblorosas manos.

¿Correría él más riesgos si ella se quedaba, o si se iba?

Empezó a pasearse por la habitación. Súbitamente, supo lo que tenía que hacer. Debía quedarse. Por el bien de Cyn, tenía que continuar con aquella charada.

Volvió a poner el dinero en su sitio. Se estudió de nuevo en el espejo de cuerpo entero para asegurarse de que no quedaba ni rastro de Chloe. Tenía los labios más rojos y carnosos que de costumbre, pero eso era todo.

Se llevó la mano a la entrepierna. La pasada noche le había enseñado que la virilidad era algo más bien visible. Tenía suerte de que no la hubieran descubierto todavía. Afortunadamente nadie había sospechado nada y la doble capa de pantalones ayudaba mucho. Si Cyn albergaba algún recelo, había que hacer algo para contrarrestarlo.

Volvió al baúl y sacó la lana que había dado forma al pecho de Cyn. Hizo un rollo cilíndrico con ella, pensando en Cyn, duro y flácido, y tratando de calcular el tamaño adecuado. El tamaño flácido valdría. No tenía ninguna intención de que nadie pensara que se hallaba en estado de excitación.

Se dio cuenta de que se había quedado plantada allí de pie, con las manos inmóviles, recordando… No era justo.

¿Por qué no podían tener una oportunidad? Se acordó de los nombres que había recopilado y de la carta. Quizás encontrara la manera de usarlos. Quizá diera con la mujer que le había roto el himen. Quizás Henry Vernham confesara.

Quizá, quizá, quizá.

Eran posibilidades remotas. Una buena parte del mundo no creería jamás en su honestidad, pero ella intentaría que así fuera. Lucharía.

Miró el rollo de lana gris y se lo metió por dentro de los pantalones, añadiendo otra pelota más en la intersección de sus muslos. Volvió a examinarse en el espejo y asintió. La ilusión era sutil, pero si alguien tenía dudas acerca de su género y miraba, o incluso tocaba, cualquier incertidumbre desaparecería. Esperaba que aquello le sirviera también con Cyn.

Comprobó minuciosamente que no quedaba ni rastro de Chloe. Después, desordenó la cama, para que pareciera que había dormido allí, y se sentó a esperar.

Poco después, llamaron a la puerta. Chastity la abrió y dejó pasar a Cyn. ¿La miraba intensamente, o era cosa de sus nervios y de las ganas que tenía de echarse en sus brazos?

—Espero que hayas tenido una noche tranquila, joven Charles.

—Pasable —dijo Chastity con reserva—. Supongo que tú no.

Él la miró desde debajo de unos párpados que le pesaban, a causa de la noche de amor y la falta de sueño.

—¿Por qué supones eso?

—Porque no has regresado aquí. Sólo puedo pensar que encontraste otra cama, pero no para dormir.

Él empezó a quitarse el traje y a ponerse el uniforme.

—Oh, algo he dormido, pero si me adormilo en la carretera, confío en que la mitad virtuosa de nuestra expedición me conduzca hasta Maidenhead.

La palabra Maidenhead[4] hizo que Chastity se ruborizara, lo que fue una solemne estupidez. Para ocultarlo, se puso a meter el traje de Cyn en el baúl y, al hacerlo, notó un crujido en el bolsillo. ¿No había encontrado aquel hombre todavía la nota? ¿Qué podía hacer ella entonces? Rothgar la preocupaba. Difícilmente podía hacerlos prisioneros, pero, si se topaban con él, seguramente les entretendría.

—¿Quieres conservar este papel? —preguntó ella, tendiéndoselo.

Él lo cogió sorprendido y lo leyó.

—¡Cielos!

—¿Qué pasa?

Cyn le lanzó una mirada.

Rotghar está aquí.

—¿Esa nota es suya?

—¡Qué va! Alguien ha querido avisarme. Me pregunto quién habrá sido.

—¿Querrá detenernos?

—No —dijo Cyn tajantemente—. Pero el único motivo por el que puede hallarse en un lugar como éste soy yo. Me temo que nos sigue los pasos muy de cerca.

—¿Por qué te iba a perseguir de ese modo?

—Siempre tiene que meter las narices en todo. —Se estiró el uniforme, inspeccionó la habitación y cerró la hebilla del arcón. Una vez más, la más mínima mención de su hermano le hacía perder los nervios.

---

4. Maidenhead significa virginidad.

—¿Listo?

Chastity se quedó sorprendida de la facilidad con la que habían vuelto a los papeles de Charles y Cyn. Incluso llegó a sentirse un poco celosa de la licenciosa Chloe con la que había pasado la noche. Sacudió la cabeza para espantar aquella idea disparatada y salió de la estancia tras él.

Él se encaminó a las escaleras principales, pero ella, acordándose de Rothgar, le tiró de la manga.

—Hay… Tiene que haber una escalera secundaria al fondo del edificio.

Él arqueó una ceja.

—No somos unos fugitivos. Estamos aquí porque nos han invitado.

—¿Y qué me dices de tu hermano?

La barbilla de Cyn se tensó.

—No voy a salir a hurtadillas por la escalera de servicio para evitar a Rothgar.

—Muy bien —replicó ella—. Vete al infierno por el camino que más te plazca.

Él dudó unos instantes, después, partió en dirección opuesta al vestíbulo principal. Tras bajar todos los peldaños de la otra escalinata, Cyn se metió por un pasillo que les llevó a las dependencias de los criados.

La casa parecía inerte con aquella grisácea luz matutina. La cocina estaba fría y desierta. O casi desierta: descubrieron a tres sirvientes acurrucados en unas mantas junto al fuego.

Cyn sacudió la cabeza, aunque con una leve sonrisa.

—Cuando Heather da una fiesta, al mundo le duele la cabeza. Este acontecimiento pasará a los anales de la historia.

Encontró la despensa y se agenció medio pastel de carne frío, una barra de pan casero, un buen pedazo de queso y al-

gunas manzanas. Sirvió dos jarras de cerveza de un pequeño barril y le pasó una a Chastity.

Ella se la bebió.

—¿No vamos a desayunar en la posada?

—No vamos a ir a la posada. Si Rothgar está aquí, seguramente sabrá que hemos dejado los caballos en el Angel. Y
habrá puesto vigilancia. Intentaremos tomar prestados un
par de caballos de Heather, sin armar mucho jaleo.

Chastity no pudo resistirse.

—Creía que no ibas a andar escondiéndote por temor a
Rothgar.

Él le lanzó una brevísima y desagradable mirada.

—Lo único que hago es tratar de evitar una confrontación directa. Vamos.

En el exterior, la densa llovizna se les metió dentro, con
su gélida humedad. Chastity se estremeció y se apretó la
capa al cuerpo.

Les costó un tiempo encontrar los establos en aquel
mundo gris, pero finalmente, se hallaron en el interior de éstos examinando las hileras de caballos. Aquel lugar, sin embargo, no estaba del todo abandonado. Un anciano se les
acercó renqueante.

—¿Necesitan sus caballos, señores? —Les observó con
el normal recelo—. No contaba con que nadie se levantara
tan pronto esta mañana.

—No creo que lo hagan muchos más —dijo Cyn con desenvoltura—. Soy lord Cyn Malloren y me halló en misión
del gobierno. Lord Heatherington me prometió dejarme
usar dos de sus caballos.

Él hombre se quedó indeciso, pero no tenía ninguna intención de oponerse a una autoridad tan firme. Fue a ensi-

llar dos pura sangre. Cyn le dio a Chastity el baúl y ayudó al hombre.

Cuando hubieron montado, Cyn preguntó, como que no quiere la cosa:

—Creo que está aquí mi hermano, el marqués de Rothgar. Imagino que no se habrá levantado todavía.

—Nadie lo ha hecho, excepto usted, milord.

—Ah, vale. Si acaso lo viera, dígale que lamento no haberle visto.

Tras estas palabras, los jinetes apremiaron a los caballos para que salieran del patio y se dirigieran por la senda que llevaba a la carretera.

Chastity no le iba à la zaga.

—¿No habría sido más sensato sobornar a ese hombre para que guardara silencio?

—Rothgar le pagaría más para que hablara.

—Entonces, lo que has hecho es plantearle un desafío.

Cyn sonrió, dejando ver por un instante el destello de su dentadura.

—Para cuando se levante y desayune, estaremos ya en Maidenhead. Que nos coja entonces, si quiere.

Él apretó el paso y se adelantó, mientras Chastity murmuraba unos cuantos calificativos escogidos a sus espaldas. La inquina que le tenía a su hermano podía resultar catastrófica, pero ella no podía advertirle de que Rothgar estaba ya levantado y al acecho, sin, al mismo tiempo, revelar su propio secreto.

Siguieron cabalgando hasta que encontraron un mojón que arrojaba alguna luz sobre dónde se encontraban.

—Lo peor de todo esto —dijo Cyn—, es que durante ese último trayecto en el carruaje, me despisté y no sé bien dónde nos hallamos.

—Sin duda, te distrajiste a causa de las hermosas canciones.

—Sabes qué te digo, joven Charles, que te vas a convertir en un tipo de lo más aburrido como no aprendas a divertirte un poco.

—Te aseguro que, cuando las circunstancias son propicias, sé disfrutar de lo lindo.

—¿Ah, sí? Me gustaría verlo.

Chastity ocultó una secreta sonrisa.

Cyn ocultó asimismo una secreta sonrisa: el espíritu de la chica parecía tan fuerte como de costumbre. Después, escudriñó el encapotado cielo, que se mostraba más brillante allí donde el sol pugnaba por salir.

—Una cosa está clara, tenemos que ir hacia el norte. En algún punto nos cruzaremos con una carretera que vaya a Londres.

Al cabo de una hora, había dejado de lloviznar y la neblina se había esfumado. Se detuvieron y compartieron la empanada. Cyn bostezó. Chastity tuvo que luchar para no hacer lo mismo. ¿Cuánto habían dormido aquella pasada noche? No más de tres o cuatro horas.

—¿Cansado, milord? — le preguntó ella con dulzura.

—Un poco. ¿Y tú? Te veo un poco rígido. Tal vez no estés acostumbrado a… cabalgar tanto.

Chastity no levantó la sonrosada cara. Él no sabía ni la mitad. Tenía los músculos tensos a causa del viaje a caballo del día anterior, pero, si tenía la entrepierna tan sensible, era de hacer el amor.

—No importa —dijo él, dándole una palmadita de aliento en la espalda—. Ya no nos deben de quedar más de seis millas.

Pronto llegaron a la carretera de Oxford y, en una casa de postas llamada Five Rings, descubrieron que Maidenhead quedaba a tan sólo dos millas al este. Siguieron a medio galope por la concurrida calzada, dejando atrás a carreteros, conductores de ganado y gente a pie, y eran adelantados por diligencias y carruajes privados.

Chastity se quedó súbitamente sin aliento y tiró de las riendas.

—¿Qué pasa? —preguntó Cyn.

—Acaba de pasar el coche de mi padre.

—¿En qué dirección?

—Hacia el este, hacia Maidenhead. Detengámonos pues. Vamos a darle una buena ventaja. —Cyn puso fugazmente su mano sobre la de Chastity—. No te preocupes. Ya sabíamos que andaba por aquí. Y Henry Vernham también, seguro, a no ser que todavía esté peinando la zona más al sur, en busca de la señora Inchcliff. No nos buscan a nosotros —por lo menos a mí.

La visión del carruaje de su padre había hecho que todo el terror que el conde le inspiraba a Chastity volviera a apoderarse de ella. Pero la muchacha sabía lo que tenía que hacer.

—Cyn —dijo ella.

—¿Sí?

—Lo importante es llevarle el mensaje al mayor Frazer. Si, por algún motivo, mi padre me encuentra, tienes que escaparte y continuar con nuestra misión.

Él frunció ligeramente el ceño.

—¿Y dejar que tú sufras las consecuencias de su ira por haber abandonado tu reclusión?

A Chastity se le hizo un nudo en el estómago al pensar en la cólera que dominaría a su padre si la encontraba vagando por el país vestida de chico. Pero consiguió hablar con tono arrogante.

—Me llevaré una regañina por irme de la cabaña de Nana, pero eso no es tan grave.

—Pues Verity parece temer de veras a tu padre. ¿Por qué no quiere recurrir a la ayuda del conde?

—Por que le impediría casarse con Nathaniel.

—Si no fuera por eso, ¿se sentiría segura con él?

Chastity sabía que tenía que tranquilizarlo.

—Sí. ¿Por qué no?

—Simplemente, me lo preguntaba.

—Es un hombre muy estricto, que cree tener derecho a dirigir las vidas de sus hijas. Eso es todo.

—Y de sus hijos —añadió él, puntualizando.

Cyn *el Protector*. Chastity necesitaba que se concentrara únicamente en los problemas de Verity.

—Yo todavía soy un escolar —señaló ella—, y debería estar haciendo lo que me mandan.

—Creo que te pegará.

Ella se encogió de hombros.

—Es muy probable. Pero no me voy morir por eso.

Cyn asintió y ambos siguieron avanzando.

Chastity no sabía lo que el conde podía hacer con ella si llegaba a cogerla. Nunca antes se había visto envuelta en nada tan escandaloso. Después de todo, su padre sabía que ella no había invitado realmente a Vernham a su cama. Los azotes de entonces habían pretendido forzarla a aceptar aquel matrimonio. El conde, obviamente, había esperado que ella se derrumbara al causarle un poquito de dolor.

Chastity había descubierto que él tenía una gran habilidad para causar «un poquito de dolor».

Su padre no había tratado de causarle ningún daño permanente ni de dejarle ninguna cicatriz, aunque en una ocasión, la actitud desafiante de su hija le había producido una ira casi asesina. Eso había sido cuando ella empezó a poner en duda la cordura del hombre y a temer verdaderamente por su vida. Él, no obstante, se había controlado, sin llegar a perder los estribos.

El que había estado más cerca de romperle el cuello había sido su hermano Fort. Tenía un carácter bastante impetuoso y estaba convencido de que ella había mancillado el honor de la familia. Ahora, sin embargo, Chastity se sentía con fuerzas para hacer frente a Fort, incluso si él le echaba las manos al cuello. Pero, la idea de encarar a su padre hacía que le temblaran las rodillas.

—Ya casi hemos llegado —dijo Cyn—. Mantén los ojos bien abiertos y la cabeza gacha.

—Eso parece un poco difícil.

Él esbozó una sonrisa.

—Nunca he dicho que esto fuera a ser fácil.

—Sí, sí que lo has dicho.

Él se echó a reír.

Llegaron a las primeras casitas de Maidenhead cuando el reloj de la iglesia daba las once. Ya no se veía al conde, pero era lógico pensar que se hallaría hospedado en una de las muchas posadas. Maidenhead estaba en la concurrida carretera de Bath y contaba con un buen número de casas de postas. Por su bulliciosa calle principal, se apiñaban diligencias y carruajes. La gente salía y entraba apresuradamente de las tiendas.

Cyn desmontó de su caballo y le indicó a Chastity que hiciera lo mismo.

—Así llamarás menos la atención. Hay que encontrar un lugar seguro para ti. Después podré ir a buscar a Frazer. No hay cuartel aquí, pero, aunque él debe estar alojado en casa de alguien, tiene que haber un puesto de mando.

Chastity quería permanecer a su lado, pero sabía que no era sensato. Ella supondría un gran riesgo para la operación.

—Si pudiéramos saber en que posada está mi padre…

Cyn se detuvo ante el Fleece Inn, en cuya entrada revoloteaba un mozo de establo, atento a los posibles clientes.

—Buenos días —dijo Cyn—. ¿Sabrías decirme si el conde de Walgrave se hospeda aquí?

—No, capitán —dijo el hombre—. Está en el Bear.

Cyn le lanzó un penique y siguió su camino.

—Entonces, evitaremos el Bear. Seguramente, tendrá vigiladas todas las posadas, pero no nos busca ni a ti ni a mí.

Se pararon en el Saracen's Head. Chastity se bajó el ala del sombrero antes de hacer que su caballo entrara en el patio. Los mozos les salieron al paso para hacerse cargo de los caballos y, ellos dos se encontraron pronto en el interior del hostal. Cyn reservó una alcoba privada y un salón y entabló conversación con el posadero. Hablaron de las personas insignes que se hallaban presentes en aquellos momentos en Maidenhead, de la presencia del ejército y del extraño caso de la extraviada lady Vernham, cuyo cartel parecía estar por todas partes.

Para cuando llegaron a sus habitaciones, sabían que el conde de Walgrave había ido de un lado para otro por la carretera de Bath, tratando de encontrar a su hija; que una compañía de infantería que se preparaba para partir a tierras continentales estaba acantonada en la ciudad bajo el mando del mayor Nathaniel Frazer; que el mayor tenía su cuartel general en Cross House, junto al río; y que todo el mundo se temía que la pobre dama estuviera muerta. Se estaba rastreando el curso del río en busca de su cuerpo y el de su bebé.

Cyn instaló a Chastity en los aposentos con todo aquello que necesitaba.

—Tú te quedarás aquí.

—Muy bien. —Ella no pudo evitar la súplica—: No tardes mucho.

—No creo que me lleve mucho tiempo. Podrías ir pensando qué hacer en caso de que Frazer no quiera saber nada de nuestro plan. Podría poner su carrera en peligro.

Chastity levantó la barbilla.

—No le fallará a Verity. ¿Me estás diciendo que pondrías tu carrera por delante de tu amor verdadero?

—¿Quién dice que yo lo tenga? Pero no —admitió el suavemente—, no lo haría. Sin embargo, yo tengo algunas rentas, además de mi paga, y una familia poderosa que me respalda. ¿Qué me dices de Frazer?

—Tiene una pequeña hacienda, pero su familia no se puede comparar a la tuya.

—Bueno, veremos lo que dice. —Parecía que le costaba irse—. Quédate aquí —repitió—. No vayas a inquietarte y salir por ahí. Y cierra la puerta. No hay razón para que nadie te importune.

—Vale —dijo ella con impaciencia—. No soy tonto. Cuanto antes te vayas, antes acabaremos con todo esto.

Cuando él se hubo marchado, ella hizo girar la llave en la cerradura. Aquella acción resultaba extrañamente similar a la de la noche anterior, sólo que esta vez Chastity no tenían ninguna intención de escabullirse de la habitación bajo ninguna apariencia. Se sentó junto a la ventana que daba a la bulliciosa calle. Mientras contemplaba la animada escena, trataba de encontrar alguna salida para su propio futuro.

Si encontraba a la mujer que le había robado su virginidad, tal vez lograra obligarla a confesar. Podía amenazar con poner al descubierto a Nerissa Trelyn si ésta no modificaba su relato de los hechos, y emplazar a otras mujeres presentes en la orgía para que la apoyaran. Todo aquello parecía bastante quimérico. Si las mujeres decían que estaba mintiendo, ¿quién iba a creerla? Y para poder contar su historia tendría que admitir que ella misma había estado en aquella orgía.

Su única prueba sustancial era la carta. La sacó y se puso a estudiarla. Era verdaderamente bastante escandalosa y, tras una noche de amor, Chastity la comprendía mucho mejor.

... *sueño contigo, Hércules mío, Atlas mío, cuando yazgo en la fría cama del deber conyugal. Pienso en tu poderosa vara dentro de mi bolsillo de seda y T. Flojo cree que es él quien me hace gemir. Cuando nos vimos la semana pasada en el teatro, llevaba tu pañuelo entre las piernas. ¿Se te abulta al pensar en ello? Te aseguro que la seda con tus iniciales enseguida se empapó con mi deseo. Volveré a hacer lo mismo, así que piensa en ello la próxima vez que nos encontremos.*

¿Querrás hacer otro tanto por mí? Te adjunto el lazo de mi camisola rosa —esa que no habrás olvidado—. Llévalo atado sobre tu cuerpo cuando vayamos a coincidir, pero no demasiado fuerte, mi noble semental, no vayas a morir por ello.

Oh, suspiro por ti incluso cuando escribo estas líneas. No puedo soportarlo. Iré. Te lo prometo. Me arriesgaré a todo por ti...

Cuando Chastity leyó la nota por primera vez, se sintió asqueada por su tono libidinoso. El hecho de que una matrona de la buena sociedad hubiera perdido de ese modo la discreción la había escandalizado. Pero, ahora, sobre todo sentía envidia. Estaba sin duda escrita por la propia lady Trelyn y podía arruinar su reputación, pero Chastity no estaba segura de ser capaz de causar a otra los sufrimientos que ella misma había tenido que soportar.

Después de todo, ¿qué había hecho Nerissa Trelyn, sino decirle a todo el mundo la verdad: que había descubierto a Chastity Ware en la cama con un hombre? No podía pedirle que mintiera.

Apoyó la cabeza sobre la mano. Lo mejor sería pensar en un lugar en el que estuviera a salvo de su padre. Su institutriz favorita se había casado con un vicario de Westmorland. Un lugar que parecía lo suficientemente apartado.

Se echó hacia atrás de un respingo. Al otro lado de la calle, había visto a un hombre que, tras quedársela mirando, se largaba de allí. No creía que la hubiera reconocido, sin embargo, había percibido algo ruin en los movimientos de aquel individuo...

¡Qué idea tan estúpida la de sentarse al lado de la ventana!

Se puso de pie de un salto. ¿Qué podía hacer ahora?

Le había prometido a Cyn que no se iría, pero no podía quedarse en aquella habitación como un conejo en su madriguera, esperando al terrier. Cogió algún dinero del equipaje y salió corriendo, escaleras abajo.

No había nadie sospechoso en el vestíbulo de entrada. Tal vez alguien estuviera vigilando el lugar, pero nadie mostró ningún interés por su persona. Se metió por un pasillo que llevaba a la cocina y, al abrir la puerta de ésta, sorprendió al posadero sentado a la mesa y cenando. Éste, al verla, se levantó, no muy complacido.

—¿Quería algo, joven? Debería usted haber hecho sonar su timbre.

Chastity sabía que tenía que evitar caer en manos de su padre, pero también debía evitar que la relacionaran con Cyn. Se había inventado una historia. No es que fuera muy creíble: todo dependía de que el hospedero se dejara comprar.

Le dedicó una cándida sonrisa.

—Me temo que debo confesarle algo, señor. Verá, me he escapado de casa. Estoy pensando en alistarme en el ejército pero mi padre no me deja. Dice que soy demasiado joven. El capitán Malloren me ayudó cuando estaba en apuros y ahora va a arreglar las cosas para que pueda unirme a su regimiento. Pero acabo de ver a mi padre en la calle y me da miedo que no entienda la participación del capitán en este asunto. Es un hombre importante y podría ocasionarle problemas. Así que me voy a esconder hasta que el capitán regrese. Por favor, no le diga a mi padre que he estado aquí.

—Y depositó tres guineas sobre la mesa.

El posadero se quedó mirando las monedas durante un instante. Acto seguido, éstas desaparecieron en el interior de su bolsillo.

—Vaya, que me zurzan muchacho. ¡Estar en contra de que su hijo se una al ejército de Su Majestad! ¿A dónde va a ir a parar el mundo? ¿Por qué no sales por ahí y te quedas por la zona de los caballos? Allí estarás a salvo, y yo se lo diré al capitán cuando regrese.

Chastity le dedicó una amplia sonrisa y salió corriendo por la puerta. En el patio había un coche a punto de partir, pero no parecía presentar ningún peligro para ella, así que caminó despacio hasta los establos.

Tan pronto como entró allí, alguien la agarró por detrás. Una mano le cubrió la boca y la otra le enganchó la entrepierna. Esta última retrocedió como si la hubieran mordido y Chastity quedó libre. Hubiera querido echar a correr, pero sabía que, si quería salir airosa de aquel trance, tenía que encararlos.

—¿Qué demonios…? —gritó la muchacha, dándose la vuelta.

Los dos hombres menudos se miraron el uno al otro nerviosos. Gracias a Dios, se trataba de dos completos extraños.

—Lo sentimos, chaval. Andamos buscando a una joven dama que se ha escapado de su casa. Pensábamos que tú eras ella.

Chastity separó bien las piernas y colocó las manos sobre las caderas, tratando de parecer un petulante mozo de establo.

—¿Una joven dama? Iros a la mierda, ¿tengo pinta de ser una joven dama?

—No, muchacho. Y baja la voz. Vas a espantar a esa señorita.

Chastity les examinó.

—No sé que es lo que os traéis entre manos. —Eligió un caballo al azar y simuló estar ocupado reponiendo el heno y llenando el cubo de agua. El corazón le iba al galope de puro miedo. Gracias a Dios, había puesto relleno en los pantalones. Ayer mismo, la hubieran cogido. Le resultaba difícil mantener la calma. Finalmente, retrocedió sobre sus pasos, pasó por delante de los dos individuos, lanzándoles una mirada llena de suspicacia, y continuó andando hasta llegar al ajetreado patio de la posada. No tenía ni idea de lo que debía hacer ahora, pero sabía que tenía que mantenerse apartada de Cyn. Se encaminó a la calle.

La encontró más tranquila que antes, ya que mucha gente debía estar comiendo. Se sintió a merced de las miradas ajenas. ¿Dónde podía ir? A la iglesia. Dirigió sus pasos hacia la torre, tratando de llevar el mismo paso que el resto de la gente que caminaba por la cera, parándose de vez en cuando para mirar un escaparate y comprobar que no la perseguían. Estaba absorta mirando una colección de piezas de porcelana cuando una mano le enganchó por el cuello de la chaqueta.

—¡Maldita sea tu estampa! ¡Cuando padre me lo dijo no me lo podía creer!

Reflejada en el escaparate, Chastity vio la imagen de su hermano Fort.

13

El corbatín le apretaba tanto que Chastity apenas podía respirar, pero Fort debió decidir que no quería montar una escena y la soltó. La muchacha no tuvo ocasión de escapar porque él la sujetó violentamente por el brazo.

A Chastity se le pasó por la cabeza la idea de resistirse, de pedir ayuda a los espectadores curiosos, pero supo que no serviría de nada. Fort le diría a cualquier mediador que se trataba de un criado o un escolar que se había fugado, y todos le creerían.

Miró a su alrededor en busca de Cyn, pero después se esforzó por sacarse aquella idea de la cabeza. Por el bien de Verity, no debía permitir que su familia se enterara de su plan y de la implicación de Cyn. Aunque se puso mala al pensar que tendría que encarar a su padre, dejó que su hermano la remolcara a lo largo de toda la calle principal de Maidenhead.

Echó un vistazo a Fort, preguntándose si sería posible hacer que se pusiera de su lado. En esos momentos, estaba furioso, pero Chastity tenía que admitir que cualquier hermano honesto se pondría así al descubrir a su hermana vagabundeando por Inglaterra vestida de mozo de establo. ¿Lograría convencerlo de que los planes que su padre tenía para Verity no eran buenos?

Recordó al Fort de la noche anterior, amable, a su manera; y al hermano mayor que había sido por lo general indulgente. Dejó de oponer resistencia y él se relajó un poco.

Cuando se metieron por una bocacalle, ella preguntó:

—¿Dónde me llevas?

—Padre ha alquilado aquí una casa.

Eso la hizo dar un tirón, y estuvo a punto de soltarse. Él soltó una maldición y la sujetó.

—¡Fort, por favor, déjame ir!

—¿Por qué demonios iba a hacer eso? ¿Para dejar que seas la fulana de algún otro hombre? No puedo imaginar que tengas otra razón para ir de un lado a otro del país con esa pinta.

Chastity estuvo a punto de protestar y decir que aquello era mentira. Estaba acostumbrada a que las acusaciones que se formulaban contra ella fueran falsas. Pero, la noche anterior, sí que había sido la fulana de un hombre.

—Volveré derecha a la cabaña de Nana —prometió ella, en medio de su desesperación.

—Desde luego que lo harás. Padre se encargará de eso, a menos que haya planeado un confinamiento más duro. —Fort la arrastró hacia delante y ella no tuvo más remedio que ir.

—¡Fort, mi reputación está arruinada! ¿Qué sentido tiene mantenerme encerrada? ¡Deja que me pierda como mejor me parezca!

Él la cogió por los hombros y la sacudió.

—¡Ya has hecho que nuestro nombre sea objeto de escarnio! ¿Voy a dejarte suelta para ver todo lo bajo que puedes caer? ¡Antes prefiero verte muerta!

Siguió tirando de ella por otra calle y a través de un arco, hasta llegar a un pequeño recinto. Cuatro silenciosas casas daban a una diminuta calle. Todas tenían un cierto aire de desolación. De hecho, aquel lugar parecía estar al margen del mundo. Allí podía suceder cualquier cosa sin que nadie lo advirtiera.

Chastity se estremeció y tiró hacia atrás.

—¡Fort, no! ¡Tú no sabes lo que padre puede llegar a hacer!

—¿Ah, no? Espero que te azote y además a conciencia.

La llevó a la fuerza hasta una puerta barnizada de negro y dio unos golpes secos. Chastity abandonó toda esperanza cuando vio que era George Lindle quien la abría.

Aquel hombre era oficialmente el secretario de su padre, pero, en realidad, era un tranquilo empleado el que se encargaba de los papeles. Lindle era más bien su secuaz, su esbirro, aunque con un estilo elegante y refinado. En su redonda y reluciente cara, se dibujó una amplia sonrisa.

—Alabado sea el Señor —declaró el hombre—. Uno de los corderos está a salvo.

Chastity se percató de que, como de costumbre, sus ojos permanecían apagados y fríos. Al verlo, las piernas de la muchacha empezaron a flaquear.

Lindle la había sostenido o atado durante las palizas y durante la desfloración, sin dejar jamás de sonreír. Ella había empezado a pensar que tenía algún problema en la boca y no podía dejar de hacerlo.

O tal vez fuera que simplemente disfrutaba viendo sufrir a la gente.

—Sí, Lindle —dijo Fort—. Hemos rescatado a uno de los corderos, lo que me hace pensar que enseguida encontraremos al otro. Voy a llevarla al piso de arriba. Mándale aviso a mi padre.

—El conde ha ido a planificar la búsqueda con el coronel de la milicia en Slough, milord. Le enviaré un mensaje inmediatamente, pero él tardará unas horas en regresar.

Chastity ofreció una fervorosa plegaria dando las gracias.

Lindle hizo ademán de marcharse pero se dio la vuelta, el vivo retrato del criado discreto y bien dispuesto.

—¿No deberíamos hacer algo mientras tanto para poner a salvo a Verity y a su niño, milord? No estaría bien que les pasara nada malo...

—Cierto —dijo Fort—. Bien —le preguntó a Chastity—, ¿dónde están?

—¿Por qué me lo preguntas a mí? —Tuvo un destello de inspiración—. ¿Por qué crees que estoy aquí? Los estoy buscando.

—¿Por qué aquí?

—Por la misma razón que vosotros: Nathaniel. —Fingió estar alarmada—. ¿Queréis decir que nadie ha encontrado todavía el menor rastro de ella? ¡Oh, cielos! Tal vez se haya arrojado al río. Pero ¿por qué? ¿Por qué? ¡Nadie logrará convencerme de que es a causa de la desesperación por la muerte de sir William!

Había conseguido engañarlos —o al menos desconcertarlos—. Ocultó su satisfacción mientras los dos hombres intercambiaban ceñudas miradas.

—La llevaré arriba —dijo Fort finalmente—. Envía ese mensaje.

Llevó a Chastity a una habitación vacía. Tan pronto como ella la vio sus expectativas de fuga se esfumaron definitivamente. La habitación había sido acondicionada para albergar a un prisionero. Su padre y Lindle no cometían errores en aquellos asuntos.

Sin duda, había sido una alcoba, pero ahora era un caparazón, desprovisto de cualquier cosa que un espíritu ingenioso pudiera utilizar para escaparse. No había nada en las paredes, excepto las marcas que habían dejado los cuadros que antes habían colgado de allí. Y nada en el suelo, salvo una pizca de polvo. La única ventana, de un tamaño mediano, no tenía cortinas y Chastity supo, sin necesidad de comprobarlo, que tendría el marco asegurado con clavos.

Sin embargo, el cristal podía romperse.

Había un hogar, pero no había fuego. Una pena, porque ella no lo habría dudado y habría prendido fuego a la casa. Habían limpiado hasta las más minúsculas cenizas. ¿Se podría subir por la chimenea? Lo dudaba, pero estudiaría el tema. Haría cualquier cosa con tal de salir de aquella casa antes de que regresara su padre.

Su única esperanza consistía en conseguir el apoyo de Fort o, al menos, mantenerlo junto a ella. Su padre no desplegaría toda su crueldad delante de su hijo y, desde luego, se guardaría mucho de dejarse llevar por uno de sus accesos de cólera. Después de todo, el conde de Walgrave era un dechado de dignidad, nobleza y ecuanimidad. El Incorruptible.

Chastity nunca le había tenido cariño, pero había dado crédito a su imagen pública hasta que tuvo que enfrentarse a él.

Fort miró a Chastity y suspiró.

—No sé cómo has llegado a esta situación, Chastity. ¿Es cierto que no conoces el paradero de Verity?

A la vista de su genuina preocupación, a Chastity le resultó difícil mentirle, pero lo consiguió.

—Sí. Esperaba que estuviera en Maidenhead, a salvo con Nathaniel.

—Estaba a salvo en su casa —dijo Fort sucintamente—. No puedo comprender que es lo que la llevó a huir así. Y todo para echarse en brazos de un hombre. ¿Sabes lo que dirá la gente?

Chastity sabía de sobra lo que la gente hacía con la reputación de una persona.

—Debe haberse hallado desesperada, Fort. Debió sentir que estaba en peligro.

—En ese caso habría recurrido a su familia. Padre la habría protegido. A ella y a su hijo.

Estaban entrando en un terreno delicado.

—Parece lógico. Aunque, desde luego, ella siempre ha amado a Nathaniel, así que tal vez él fue el primero que acudió a su mente...

Ford se le quedó mirando.

—¿Fugarse prácticamente en combinación, en noviembre, con un bebé, y para irse con un hombre con el que coqueteó hace unos años? Ni hablar, me temo que además ha tenido que volverse loca. No sé dónde vamos a ir a parar.

—¿Es que no te das cuenta, Fort —le dijo Chastity muy seria—, de que debe haber tenido algún motivo? ¿Qué me dices de Henry Vernham? Él obtuvo la custodia del niño, ¿no? Quizás él la empujó a ello.

Los labios de Fort se curvaron al escuchar aquel nombre.

—Me creería casi cualquier cosa de ese canalla, pero no creo que llegue a hacerle daño a una Ware. Los Vernham son una estirpe nauseabunda, pero no son tan estúpidos.

—¡Nauseabunda! —repitió Chastity—. Entonces, ¿por qué no te opusiste a que Verity se casara con William?

—¿Por qué demonios iba a hacerlo? Él era el hombre que Verity había elegido.

—¿Verity? Tonterías. Era padre quien le había elegido.

—¿Padre? —se mofó Fort—. Dios sabe lo difícil que me está resultando encontrar una mujer con la clase suficiente como para complacerle. ¿Por qué iba a promover él una alianza con sir William y los suyos?

—¿Por qué iba Verity a querer casarse con un hombre como ése? Fort, sabes bien que siempre ha querido casarse con Nathaniel.

Él se encogió de hombros cínicamente.

—No sería la primera mujer que pensara que un título, incluso uno indigno, y una fortuna, obtenida como fuere, valen más que un rostro hermoso. Nathaniel Frazer no tiene prácticamente nada.

A Chastity le dieron ganas de pegarle. ¿No se daba cuenta de las tonterías que decía?

—Te estoy diciendo, Fort, que Verity no quería casarse con sir William y que se hubiera ido de buen grado con Nathaniel con lo puesto. Tú la conoces bien. ¿Alguna vez ha estado interesada en los títulos y en las riquezas?

Fort parecía algo aturdido, pero replicó:

—Todavía tiene menos sentido que fuera padre quien alentara semejante enlace.

—Él promovió el mío con Henry Vernham.

Fort rió amargamente.

—¡Sólo después de que ese reptil fuera descubierto desnudo en tu cama!

Chastity se quedó boquiabierta. ¿De verdad creía aquello? Era obvio que sí. La inutilidad de tratar de sacarlo de su error la abrumó. Era como intentar mover una montaña con una cucharilla, sobre todo porque primero tendría que convencerle de que su augusto padre no tenía nada de noble.

Abandonó aquella discusión y se interesó por algo que Fort acababa de decir. Durante un tiempo había creído que lo que le había sucedido a ella era un simple giro del destino, pero últimamente veía cada vez más claro que todo debía formar parte de un plan. Seguramente era demasiado tarde para defender su propia reputación, pero si lograba entender lo acontecido, tal vez pudiera salvar a Verity.

—¿Qué has querido decir con eso de la fortuna de sir William? —preguntó ella—. Has dicho «obtenida como fuere». ¿Qué quieres decir?

Pero Fort le estaba mirando la ropa con expresión apenada.

—Si no queremos que padre te despelleje, será mejor que te busquemos ropa decente. —Se dirigió a la puerta y llamó a voces a Lindle, pero alguien le respondió que el hombre había salido.

—No importa, Fort —dijo Chastity—. Eso no va a cambiar mucho las cosas. ¿Qué me dices de la fortuna de Vernham?

Él sacudió la cabeza.

—Todo el mundo sabe que se hizo con un montón de dinero después del año 45. Él era uno de los investigadores especiales enviados para examinar a los acusados de simpatizar con los jacobitas. También es del dominio público que muchos partidarios de los Estuardo estaban dispuestos a pagar para que se hiciera la vista gorda.

Chastity recordó que Verity había comentado algo parecido, pero aquello no parecía explicar nada. Se dirigió a la ventana. Daba a un pequeño jardín cuyos altos árboles lo protegían de las miradas de las otras casas. El lugar, desde luego, era de una gran privacidad. Allí de pie, un guardia la vigilaba. Aquella ruta de escape quedaba descartada.

—¿Cómo es que estás aquí? —le preguntó a su hermano.

—¿Dónde querías que estuviese? ¿Haraganeando en un café? Estoy aquí buscando a Verity. Cuando descubrimos que habías desaparecido, pensé que ella estaría contigo y más o menos a salvo. Pero ahora sí que estoy preocupado. ¿Me juras que no conoces su paradero, Chastity?

Chastity se recordó a sí misma que no conocía el lugar exacto en el que paraba Verity. Podía estar en cualquier habitación de la casa de la señora Garnet, o en el jardín, o incluso en la calle, si iba convenientemente disfrazada.

—Lo juro —dijo con firmeza.

Fort aceptó la respuesta y comenzó a andar de un lado para otro.

—Y apostaría cualquier cosa a que Frazer nos dijo la verdad cuando le preguntamos.

—¿Cuál fue su reacción?

—Se quedó muy preocupado. Se quería poner a buscarla él mismo, pero le convencimos para que se quedara aquí por si Verity intentaba pedirle ayuda. Aunque no me explico por qué demonios tendría que recurrir a él y no a nosotros. —Se dio la vuelta y miró a Chastity con furia—. Tampoco entiendo por qué no has podido quedarte donde te dijeron o por qué te metiste en la cama con un gusano como Henry Vernham…

—¡Yo no hice tal cosa!

—Entonces, ¿qué diantre hacía él allí? —bramó Fort.

—¿Cómo demonios quieres que lo sepa? —le gritó ella en respuesta.

Él la abofeteó.

—Cuidado con esa lengua. Pareces una fulana.

Chastity se cubrió la dolorida mejilla, con lágrimas en los ojos. Durante su mascarada se había acostumbrado a expresarse de un modo impropio para una señorita.

—Lo siento —dijo—. La preocupación también me tiene a mí medio desquiciada, Fort. —Después, con toda la intensidad que le fue posible, añadió—: Yo no invité a Henry Vernham a mi cama. Lo juro. Detesto a ese hombre. ¡Él intentó violarme!

Él permaneció imperturbable.

—Eso fue lo que dijiste entonces, pero no cuela, querida hermana. Nadie te oyó gritar hasta que no te pillaron.

—¡Estaba dormida hasta que todos vosotros irrumpisteis en la estancia!

—¿Esperas que me crea que un hombre desnudo se metió en tu cama y empezó a desvestirte sin que tú te despertaras?

—Sí. Puede que los demás no me crean, pero tú deberías hacerlo. Siempre he tenido un sueño muy profundo. ¿No te acuerdas de aquella vez que me llevaste dormida al pasillo y me pusiste debajo de la peana del dragón y yo me puse a gritar como una loca cuando me desperté y vi que sus mandíbulas me querían engullir?

Los labios de Fort se curvaron al sonreír.

—Sí, pero entonces tenías sólo diez años.

—Sigo siendo igual.

Él frunció el ceño pensativo.

—Pero Henry Vernham no podía saberlo. Si tú no le invitaste, lo lógico era que pensara que empezarías a chillar y él sería hombre muerto. Mira, Chastity —le dijo su hermano en tono amable—, sin duda, has cometido un error de juicio. Nadie te va a condenar eternamente por eso. Y él es un hombre atractivo a su manera. Pero deberías haberte casado con él. No tenías elección.

—¿Incluso si él se hubiera metido a hurtadillas en mi cama con ese plan *in mente*?

—¿Cómo podía saber que le iban a interrumpir o que padre no se lo tomaría a la tremenda y pensaría en el matrimonio?

Porque fue padre quien lo planificó así, hubiera querido gritar Chastity. Pero Fort jamás la creería.

—Él había pedido mi mano y padre le había dado su consentimiento.

—Porque tú le querías. No se puede jugar con la gente.

—¿Quién ha dicho que yo le quería?

—Padre.

—Padre estaba… —reprimió la palabra que tenía en la punta de la lengua—. Estaba equivocado. Oh, Fort, créeme. ¿Por qué iba a querer yo casarme con Vernham? No lo encuentro atractivo. Y ni siquiera tiene riquezas o un título para endulzar el trago.

Él frunció el ceño, y Chastity pensó que finalmente había logrado impresionarle.

—¿Me estás diciendo que todavía estás intacta?

Ella abrió la boca para decir sí, pero luego la cerró y tragó saliva. Renunciaría a la pasada noche para poder responder afirmativamente, pero lo cierto era que su inocencia había desaparecido.

—No —susurró la muchacha.

Y vio cómo se instalaba en el rostro de su hermano una afligida desilusión.

—Pero no ha sido Vernham, ¿no? —comentó él con amargura—. ¡Qué ocupada has estado! ¿Quién ha tenido entonces el honor de desflorar a mi hermana? Dame un nombre y le daré muerte.

—No puedo.

Él la agarró.

—¡Un nombre!

Ella no abrió la boca. Fort la sacudió y la arrojó al suelo.

—¿Acaso has rodado por los arbustos con un desconocido? ¿Cuántos ha habido desde entonces? ¡Dios, me pones enfermo! ¿De dónde habrás salido para ser así?

La figura de su hermano se erguía sobre ella, con el rostro oscurecido por la rabia y las manos formando unos enormes puños, capaces de aplastarle los huesos. Ella pensó que la iba a golpear. Entonces, él se dio la vuelta y, dando un portazo, abandonó la habitación. Chastity oyó cómo echaba la llave y hundió la cabeza entre las manos.

A menos que su padre se condenara con sus propias palabras, ni Fort ni ninguna otra persona creería su historia. Sencillamente resultaba inverosímil. A ella misma le costaba darle crédito.

Y ahora tenía que pensar también en Cyn. Si su participación en todo aquel lío llegaba a descubrirse, Fort era capaz de descuartizarlo.

Tenía que salir de allí. No se sentía con ánimos de plantarle nuevamente cara a su padre. Además, no se le podía escapar el nombre de Cyn. Echó un vistazo a la chimenea, pero, tal y como había pensado, era demasiado estrecha. Sólo un deshollinador diminuto podría subir por allí.

Sin demasiadas esperanzas, consideró la opción de la puerta. Miró por la cerradura y vio que la llave estaba aún allí, aunque dudaba que eso pudiera servirle de algo. Para comprobar su hipótesis, dio unos golpes en la puerta.

—Sí milady —le dijo un hombre en tono respetuoso. Como había supuesto, había un vigía en la ventana y otro en la puerta.

—Quisiera beber algo —dijo ella para justificar su acción.

—De acuerdo —dijo el hombre, pero no se marchó. Chastity oyó cómo decía a voces—: Eh, Jackie, lady Chastity quiere algo de beber.

A los pocos minutos, le llevaron una jarra de madera con agua y unas galletas. Sin plato. Tenían mucho cuidado de no darle nada que pudiera resultarle útil.

Sola de nuevo, Chastity contempló con tristeza un bizcocho de Shrewsbury y lo comió lentamente, en honor a Cyn Malloren. No estaba tan bueno como aquellos recién hechos que habían comprado en Shaftesbury, pero le trajo dulces recuerdos.

Pensar en Cyn era un acicate para su ánimo. Ya no era la azorada chica que había sido meses atrás, la última vez que fuera prisionera de su padre. Sus experiencias la habían endurecido, pero había sido Cyn Malloren el que había encendido su espíritu. Ahora sabía que tenía derecho a ser fuerte y a estar enfadada.

Desgraciadamente, aquello no la libraba del miedo. Sabía que su padre era un hombre temible. Cuando se enfrentó a él por el asunto del matrimonio, no sabía hasta dónde podía llegar ni cuál era la profundidad de su crueldad. Había sobrevivido gracias a una especie de aturdido fatalismo. Pero ahora, se echaba a temblar cada vez que pensaba que iba a estar nuevamente en su poder.

Aquella espera la ponía mala, así que se puso a inspeccionar otra vez la habitación, pero no se le ocurrió ningún plan de fuga. Recordó el comentario de Fort sobre su ropa y comprendió que sin duda la obligarían a ponerse algún horrible vestido de penitente. Eso la hizo pensar en la carta de lady Trelyn. No quería que se la encontraran encima. El corazón estuvo a punto de parársele al pensar en las explicaciones que tendría que dar.

Atenta al posible sonido de pasos aproximándose, buscó un escondite en la desolada estancia. No había ningún tablón suelto en el suelo. Tampoco grietas ni rincones ocultos. Empezaba a pensar que tendría que comérsela cuando descubrió que la repisa de madera de la chimenea se había despegado un poco de la pared, dejando un pequeño hueco. Con un escalofrío de alivio, metió allí la carta.

Ya la recogería, si es que podía hacerlo sin correr ningún riesgo. De lo contrario, se quedaría allí, para regocijo de algún propietario de aquella vivienda en años venideros.

Se preguntó desazonada si existía alguna posibilidad de que Fort la reconociera como su pareja de baile de la noche anterior. Aquello sería decididamente su fin. ¿Cómo iba a explicar su presencia en lo que sin duda había sido la orgía más destacada de la década?

Rebuscó de nuevo en todos sus bolsillos, asegurándose de que no tenían nada que pudiera empeorar las cosas. Cuando finalmente se tranquilizó, se sentó y apoyó la cabeza contra una de las paredes. Hacía frío en aquella habitación y se alegró de llevar la ropa de mozo de establo encima de la de Victor. Lamentó no llevar también la capa de montar. Todo estaba en silencio. Se preguntó qué hora sería y, al cabo de un rato, oyó que un reloj distante daba las dos.

Con suerte, Cyn y Nathaniel se habrían puesto ya en camino, pero ella tenía que resistir el máximo tiempo posible, por si se habían retrasado. El día anterior había cabalgado mucho y la pasada noche apenas había dormido. A pesar del miedo, se adormiló. Soñó que naufragaba, que las aguas le lanzaban de acá para allá..

—¡Que te lleve la peste, Chastity! ¡Despierta!

Abrió los ojos tras un parpadeo y vio que Fort la estaba sacudiendo, más preocupado que enfadado. Cuando vio que estaba despierta, la soltó.

—Sí que duermes profundamente, ¿no? —Parecía pensativo. Tal vez estuviera empezando a creer parte de su historia. Pero eso le importaba muy poco ahora a Chastity. Su padre estaba allí, y Lindle asomaba tras su hombro. Ella se incorporó con dificultad.

El conde de Walgrave se había casado ya mayor y tenía ahora más de sesenta años. Pero era un hombre robusto e imponente de astutos ojos azules, nariz noble y carrillos carnosos. La indumentaria que llevaba era sencilla y propia para viajar: de terciopelo marrón con leves encajes dorados y una peluca gris. Pero la simplicidad no empequeñecía su presencia. Aquel hombre llenaba la estancia. Acarreaba un sofisticado aunque ligero bastón de bambú de dorada cabeza. Chastity se acordaba bien de aquel objeto.

—Gracias, Thornhill —dijo el conde con frialdad—. Ya puedes marcharte.

Chastity le envió una súplica a su hermano con la mirada.

Tal vez él lo notara, porque se había quedado pensativo.

—Me gustaría quedarme, señor. Si, como crees, ella sabe dónde está Verity, me gustaría ser el primero en saberlo. Dios sabe los peligros que mi pobre hermana estará corriendo.

—Dios y cualquier hombre con experiencia —comentó el conde con su melosa voz. Sonaba calmado, pero Chastity se dio cuenta de que aquella intervención no le había hecho gracia. Entonces supo que su instinto le había aconsejado bien. A pesar de su violencia, a pesar de que ahora la tenía por una libertina, Fort era su única protección en aquella situación.

El conde dio dos majestuosos pasos al frente hasta quedar delante de ella. Después, apoyó las manos en la empuñadura de su báculo.

—Me entristeces, hija. Confieso que me tienes desconcertado. Verte así, con esas impúdicas prendas, huyendo de la protección de tu hogar… Además, me temo que has contagiado tu perversidad a Verity. No has venido aquí a buscar a tu hermana. La has traído hasta aquí con el mezquino afán de fastidiarme.

Chastity estaba tan aterrorizada como había anticipado, pero descubrió que su padre ya no la paralizaba. Su ingenio seguía funcionando. Esperaba poder conseguir que revelará algo significativo delante de Fort.

—¿Por qué iba a fastidiarte a ti, padre, que yo trajera a Verity aquí?

Con un leve estrechamiento de los ojos y la boca se dio por enterado del cambio que se había operado en su hija, pero no perdió ni un ápice de su dignidad.

—Porque el hecho de que mi querida hija acuda en busca de ayuda a cualquier otra persona que no sea yo es para mí un golpe. Puedo creer que Vernham haya hecho algo que empujara a Verity a abandonar su hogar, pero, sin duda, ella huyó a Walgrave Towers a buscar mi ayuda. Fuiste tú, desdichada criatura, la que la persuadiste para que emprendiera esta loca aventura. ¿Qué esperas sacar con ello?

Chastity estuvo a punto de caer en la astuta trampa y reconocer el plan.

—Vine a Maidenhead —replicó evasivamente—, porque sabía que si Verity iba a algún sitio distinto de Walgrave Towers sería aquí, donde está el hombre al que siempre ha amado. Tal vez pensó que intentarías impedir otra vez que se casara con él.

—¿Impedir? —inquirió el conde atónito—. Ella eligió libremente casarse con sir William.

—¿Libremente? —se mofó Chastity—. ¡Tú la intimidaste para que lo aceptara, hipócrita, del mismo modo que lo intentaste conmigo para que me casara con su hermano!

El conde sacudió la cabeza con expresión triste.

—Ven aquí y extiende la mano derecha con la palma hacia arriba.

Chastity sintió que la recorría un frío helador. Era un juguete en manos de su padre. Antes de vestirse de muchacho, antes de sus andanzas junto a Cyn, nunca le habría hablado así a su padre, bajo ninguna circunstancia. Pero también sabía, que antes o después la esperaba el bastón.

—Padre —dijo Fort por toda protesta, aunque Chastity vio que sus palabras le habían afectado.

—Querido chico —dijo el conde con gesto triste—. Esta muchacha es indómita y cada día lo es más. No puedo permitirlo. Me duele pegarla, pero puedes ver por ti mismo que los métodos más suaves son inútiles. —Volvió a mirar a Chastity—. Obedece o habrá que hacerlo por la fuerza.

Ella obedeció, pero, aunque le costara caro, no estaba dispuesta a que pareciera que era la primera vez que sucedía algo así, como pretendía el conde.

—Está bien, padre —dijo ella vivamente—. Me enseñaste las reglas cuando me golpeaste para que me casara con tu amigo Henry Vernham. No las he olvidado.

Dio unos pasos al frente y extendió la mano. Al darse cuenta de que le temblaba, sintió rabia. No había sido así la primera vez. Claro que entonces no sabía lo mucho que dolía.

El bastón se abatió sobre ella y Chastity sintió que la palma de la mano le ardía. Se la aprisionó contra el pecho, mientras trataba de combatir las lágrimas.

—Esperemos que no vuelvas a ser tan descarada —dijo el conde—. Nunca más vuelvas a poner en duda mi rectitud como padre. Nunca. Y ahora dime dónde está Verity.

—No lo sé.

La muchacha vio que el conde se daba cuenta de que su respuesta era honesta, pero Walgrave era un hombre muy astuto y colocó la empuñadura de su bastón bajo la barbilla de Chastity para obligarla a mirarle a los ojos.

—Entonces, dime dónde la has visto por última vez.

Ella dudó y luego recordó:

—En Semana Santa, en Walgrave Towers.

El conde se volvió hacia su hijo:

—Está mintiendo.

—Sí —dijo Fort—. En nombre de Dios, Chastity, ¿por qué estás haciendo esto? Verity puede estar en peligro y su hijo todavía más. Dínoslo, para que podamos protegerla.

Chastity se dejó de fingimientos:

—Sólo si padre promete que la dejará casarse con Nathaniel.

—Eso es absurdo —dijo el conde—. Hasta que no se pase el año de luto, el matrimonio con cualquier hombre es impensable.

Ella se obligó a mirarle a los ojos, inflexible.

—Promete que se lo permitirás entonces.

Las mejillas del hombre se tiñeron de rojo; una señal de advertencia.

—No voy a prometer nada. ¿Pretendes hacer tratos conmigo, impúdica desvergonzada? Vas a decirme el paradero de tu hermana simplemente porque me debes obediencia filial y vas a confiar en que yo me ocupe de su bienestar.

—¿Cómo cuando la casaste con Vernham? —se mofó ella.

—Extiende la mano derecha.

Al obedecer, a Chastity le temblaban los labios. El bastón se abatió sobre el verdugazo anterior y a ella se le escapó un grito.

El conde se quedó en silencio. Chastity permanecía a la espera. Mientras apretaba contra sí la ardiente mano, las lágrimas le corrían por las mejillas. Sabía que las cosas sólo podían ir a peor. Aquello no era nada y sin embargo ya le parecía mucho. ¿Cuánto tiempo podría resistir antes de contarlo todo? ¿Cuánta ventaja necesitaban Cyn y Nathaniel? Miró a Fort, preguntándose si él la ayudaría, pero sabía que lo había vuelto a perder cuando se dio cuenta de que ella conocía el paradero de Verity.

La muchacha se preguntaba por qué su padre trataba de encontrar a Verity con tanta desesperación. ¿Por la simple necesidad de controlar? Era posible, aunque su instinto le decía que no. Aquella porfiada búsqueda tenía el mismo extraño empeño que el matrimonio de Verity con sir William, y que el que le fuera propuesto a ella con Henry Vernham. Había algo más detrás de todo aquello.

Por improbable que pareciera, Vernham debía tener algún poder sobre el conde de Walgrave.

¿Cuál? ¿Cuál?

Fort se acercó a ella y le cogió con suavidad la mano dolorida. Desplazó a Chastity a cierta distancia de su padre, lo que podía considerarse como una buena señal.

—Duele como un demonio, ¿no? ¿Quieres decir que te hizo esto para forzarte a casarte con Vernham?

—Y otras cosas… —Chastity miró hacia el lugar en el que el conde hablaba tranquilamente con Lindle. Aquello no presagiaba nada bueno—. Fort —dijo ella en voz baja—, hay algo que no está bien en todo esto, algo que no tiene sentido.

—Tal vez —admitió él—. Pero eso no cambia el hecho de que tenemos que encontrar a Verity.

—Ella está a salvo —le aseguró Chastity—. De verdad. Está en casa de una familia muy agradable y digna.

Lindle abandonó la estancia, y Walgrave se acercó a Chastity y Fort.

—¿Te lo ha dicho? —le preguntó a Fort—. A menudo, un poco de amabilidad después de la severidad hace maravillas.

—Dice que Verity está a salvo con una familia respetable.

Chastity lanzó una fugaz mirada a Fort, aunque sabía que aquella maniobra no había sido premeditada, al menos por su parte.

—¡Vaya! —dijo el conde—. Eso hace que mi ansiedad paterna disminuya considerablemente. Sin embargo, sólo se aplacará del todo cuando pueda estrechar a mi hija mayor y a mi único nieto contra mi pecho. La dirección, por favor.

Chastity sacudió la cabeza.

—¿Por qué tienes ese empeño en mantener a Verity apartada de mí?

Chastity sabía que era imposible responder a aquella pregunta sin cuestionar su rectitud como padre. Aunque le iba a hacer falta más valor del que tenía, la muchacha extendió su pobre mano maltratada.

El conde levantó el bastón, pero luego se limitó a colocarlo bajo la temblorosa mano de su hija, rozándolo suavemente contra sus nudillos.

—Me parece que estás poseída por algún demonio, y ahora no tenemos tiempo suficiente para sacarlo de tu cuerpo. Pero no temas, que a su debido tiempo me ocuparé de ello. —Dejó que aquella promesa surtiera efecto—. Pero ¿mi dulce Verity? ¿Qué es lo que la ha hecho desconfiar de su padre? ¿Eh?

Chastity estaba lista para los golpes. Casi deseaba que llegaran ya para acabar cuanto antes.

—Bien —dijo el conde—. Dime cómo has hecho que Verity se vuelva contra mí.

—No ha hecho falta que yo hiciera nada —dijo Chastity—. Ella no huyó a Walgrave Towers sino a la cabaña. Ella no deseaba buscar tu ayuda.

El golpe seguía sin producirse. Ella conocía también aquel truco. Aquella espera, que era casi peor que el dolor.

El conde se lo había explicado en una ocasión durante aquellos terribles días. Cuando había sucumbido a la ira y la había azotado inflexiblemente, el efecto causado había sido extraño. Había alimentado la fuerza de la aterida muchacha y él lo sabía.

—La brutalidad lleva a muchas personas fuera de sí —había dicho entonces—. Además deja señales que pueden resultar inoportunas. Por otra parte, pequeñas cantidades de dolor, aplicadas convenientemente, pueden quebrar a un hombre fuerte.

Ahora el conde pasaba el bastón suavemente por la palma de la mano de Chastity y le frotaba con él. Ella apretó los dientes para aguantar el escozor.

—¿Y por qué Verity no quería buscar mi ayuda?

Verity había roto los lazos con su padre por el modo en que éste había tratado a Chastity. Su previsible oposición al matrimonio con Nathaniel había sido un motivo secundario. Chastity podía decirle eso, pero le llamó la atención la intensidad con la que el conde le hacía aquella pregunta. ¿Por qué era tan importante? ¿Estaría él a punto de decir algo revelador?

Walgrave le dio un par de golpecitos en la mano con el bastón, reclamando la respuesta.

Al tercer toque, Chastity no pudo más:

—Por el modo en que me trataste a mí.

Él la escrutó detenidamente, después usó el báculo para empujar la mano de la muchacha hacia abajo y se alejó unos pasos. Las rodillas de Chastity ya casi no podían sujetarla, pero ella permaneció de pie. Sabía que aquello no había terminado.

En el exterior de aquella aislada casa no se producía ningún sonido y parecía que en el interior de la estancia todo el mundo estuviera conteniendo el aliento. Chastity empezó a contar. Había descubierto que ésa era la única manera de evitar que la desesperación la arrastrara cuando su padre ponía en juego aquel calculado uso del silencio.

Ya había llegado hasta sesenta y cinco cuando el conde se dio la vuelta.

—Una nimia razón para poner en peligro su vida y la de su hijo. No es propio de Verity. Me temo que has debido de largarle una sarta de mentiras. Bueno, todo se aclarará cuando la encontremos. —La puerta se abrió—. Aquí está Lindle con ropa más apropiada para ti. Vamos a dejar que te cambies, hija. Reanudaremos nuestra conversación cuando tengas un aspecto más adecuado.

Chastity no acertaba a colegir que pensaba Fort de todo aquello, pero se dio cuenta de que se resistía a marcharse, dejándola allí. Tuvieron que conducirle hasta la puerta. Luego, la llave giró en la cerradura y Chastity se quedó a solas. Se dejó caer sobre el suelo y se sopló la dolorida mano.

El castigo apenas si había empezado. Su padre ni siquiera había intentado sacarle la verdad sino que, tal y como él había dicho, se había limitado a reaccionar ante su falta de respeto filial. Pero también había sido una manera de aleccionarla para lo que la esperaba, de recordarla cómo había sido la última vez, cuando las palmas de las manos se le llenaron de ampollas y Lindle tuvo que sostenérselas en alto porque ella ya no tenía fuerzas para hacerlo. Cuando su espalda, sus nalgas y sus piernas habían sido un amasijo de cardenales.

Y esta vez iba a ser peor. Porque él era más despiadado y estaba más desesperado. Esta vez no le iba a importar si le dejaba alguna cicatriz o le causaba algún daño irreparable. Ella no sabía por qué estaba tan desesperado pero percibía su enorme cólera. Y pronto estaría de vuelta.

14

Chastity se incorporó. Aquello era lo que su padre quería. Quería que estuviera sola mientras oscurecía, cada vez más llena de miedo. Tenía que hacer algo. Por ejemplo cambiarse de ropa. No tenía inconveniente en volver a ser una mujer.

Al empezar a desvestirse, se preguntó dónde estaría entonces Cyn. Durante un traicionero instante rogó que estuviera cerca, planificando su rescate. Después apartó de sí aquel pensamiento. Tenía que desear que estuviera camino de Winchester y de Verity. Ella le había dicho que, si la atrapaban, él debía escapar y llevar a Verity a un nuevo lugar.

Se desnudó y se apresuró a ponerse aquella indumentaria de mujer —la camisola de seda, la enagua de tafetán y un corpiño con manga. Le sorprendió que las prendas fueran de tan buena calidad, pero supuso que ni siquiera Lindle había sido capaz de encontrar ropa de indigente en tan poco tiempo. Sólo Dios sabía dónde habría encontrado aquellas prendas, porque los colores no estaban buscados para que combinaran. La camisola era rosa, la enagua rojo amapola, y el corpiño a rayas verdes y amarillas.

Tuvo que luchar con los ganchos de la parte delantera del jubón. Éste no sólo era pequeño sino que además tenía un escote indecente. Por mucho que se lo ajustara, apenas le cubría los pezones y, al menor movimiento, se le salían de nuevo, quedando cubiertos únicamente por la camisola rosa, que de puro fina era prácticamente transparente.

Se los metió bien por dentro y, al bajar la vista para contemplarse, se quedó horrorizada. Los colores eran vulgares, el corpiño indecente y la enagua le quedaba varias pulgadas por encima de los tobillos. Aquello no era casual. Su padre la estaba vistiendo como una puta.

Quería volver a ponerse su atuendo de hombre, pero eso sólo serviría para que el odioso Lindle la desnudara. Estaba segura de que su padre y su servil lacayo no regresarían hasta que hubieran encontrado la manera de librarse de Fort.

Le resultaba extraño que su hermano, a quien ella había tenido por su enemigo, resultara ser ahora su único refugio.

Como no le habían dejado ningún calzado, se puso las medias y las botas de chico. Le quedaban ridículas, pero calentaban y eran más decentes que el resto. Además, para estar más abrigada y decente, se echó el chaquetón por los hombros. Y al hacerlo, se pinchó el dedo con algo.

¡El alfiler de Rothgar! Cielos, otra prueba contra ella, y ésta no entraría en la rendija de detrás de la repisa. Tras unos instantes, se lo prendió en el interior de la enagua. Allí sería difícil que nadie lo encontrase, incluso si la desnudaban. Si lo hallaban, siempre podía decir que había venido con la ropa, que, hacía no mucho, debía haberse hallado sobre otro cuerpo. Podía olerlo.

Seguía sin oírse ningún indicio de que alguien se aproximara.

No te quedes ahí, esperando y agobiándote, se decía a sí misma. Haz algo. Se puso a andar por la habitación, pensando en todo lo que había pasado.

Meses atrás, cuando Fort la reprendiera por su conducta, ella le había visto como uno más de los que conspiraron para causar su ruina, pero ahora veía que, aunque no lo supiera, él también era una víctima de su padre. ¿Podría ella abrirle los ojos?

Él había tenido motivos para dudar de su castidad y ahora ella se lo había confirmado. Hecho que no la favorecía nada. Seguramente, Fort no protestaría si la azotaban. Pero no creía que pudiera contemplar impasible la calculada crueldad de Walgrave. El problema era que el conde encontraría la manera de librarse de él antes de empezar a usar esa táctica.

Chastity mantenía la noción del tiempo únicamente gracias a las campanadas de un reloj distante y la paulatina desaparición de la luz. En cuatro ocasiones se tensó al oír pasos que se aproximaban a la puerta, pero no entró nadie. Aquello era simplemente parte del tormento. Intentó sobreponerse.

Entonces, la llave giró. Ella encaró la puerta e hizo acopio de todas sus fuerzas. Alguien volvió a echar la llave. Había sido otro truco. Chastity se echó a llorar, pero se forzó a detener el llanto antes de que nadie pudiera oírla. Decidió aplicar su mente a la búsqueda de soluciones en lugar de aguzar el oído para tratar de detectar pisadas.

Podía provocar a su padre para que perdiera el control. Quizás en ese estado revelara algo significativo, pero, al mismo tiempo, Chastity temblaba al pensar en lo que podría hacerle a ella. Rezó para que Fort se negara a marcharse, pero sabía que era inútil: Fort no se daba todavía cuenta de que el conde era el enemigo.

Había oscurecido por completo, y el reloj acababa de dar las ocho, cuando la llave volvió a girar. Esta vez la puerta se abrió y entró su padre, seguido de Lindle, quien llevaba una palmatoria que enseguida depositó en un rincón. Fort no estaba con ellos. Chastity se temió lo peor.

—Tu hermano ha ido a ver al mayor Frazer —dijo el conde mansamente—. Volverá dentro de un rato. —La examinó—. Esa chaqueta no pega mucho con el conjunto. Quítatela.

No tenía sentido presentar batalla por aquellos pequeños detalles, así que Chastity obedeció.

El conde asintió.

—Puedes quedarte con las botas. No me gustaría que cogieras frío. —La recorrió con la mirada, haciéndola sentirse sucia—. Una indumentaria muy apropiada para ti, querida. Lindle, tengo que felicitarte.

—Gracias, milord.

—Ahora ya puedes llevarte esas prendas inadecuadas, Lindle. Deshazte de ellas.

Chastity observó con desesperación cómo se llevaba la ropa de hombre de la estancia. Intentó ajustarse una vez más el corpiño de rayas; después pensó que era mejor dejarlo. No quería darle a su padre esa satisfacción.

El conde la miró con frialdad.

—Ya debes conocerme a estas alturas, hija. A mí nadie me lleva la contraria.

—Y, sin embargo, yo lo he hecho.

Él estrechó los ojos, dejando ver que las palabras de la muchacha habían surtido efecto.

—Así que crees que has ganado la partida.

—No. Pero tú tampoco.

Él levantó el bastón y ella retrocedió, pero solo llegó a tocarle la cabeza con él.

—Tu pelo empieza ya a tener una pinta aceptable, ¿no? Me temo que habrá que eliminarlo antes de que nos separemos.

Chastity cerró los ojos y tuvo que contenerse para no suplicar. No pudo evitar acordarse de lo mal que lo había pasado cuando se lo raparon, de lo fea que resultaba aquella pelusa oscura.

—Pero no quiero que pienses que soy tan malo, querida —ronroneó el conde, haciendo que Chastity se echara a temblar—. ¿Ves?

Ella abrió los ojos. Lindle había regresado con una peluca, una bonita peluca color miel. Se parecía mucho al tono natural de su pelo. La muchacha miró a su padre vivazmente.

—Claro que sí. Está hecha con tu propio pelo. —El conde la enganchó en la empuñadura dorada de su bastón y se la mostró a su hija—. Dime dónde está Verity y podrás quedarte con ella. Vamos, pruébatela. Lindle, un espejo.

El conde se la colocó delicadamente sobre la cabeza. Chastity se estremeció al entrar en contacto con su padre. Lindle apareció con un largo espejo que dejó apoyado contra la pared. El conde llevó a Chastity frente a éste y ella, por primera vez en muchos meses, se vio a sí misma con el aspecto que debería tener. Tupidas y sedosas ondas le enmarcaban el rostro reproduciendo exactamente lo que había sido su peinado habitual, como si el horror nunca se hubiera producido…

La peluca le fue arrebatada y ella gritó. Volvía a ser un bicho raro. Observó el efecto general de su indumentaria. ¡Un bicho raro y además indecente! Se cubrió el pecho con las manos y se dio la vuelta.

Su padre le sujetó las manos y se las apretó con fuerza por detrás de ella, obligándola a mirar al espejo. Ella cerró los ojos. Él la hizo arquear la espalda, de modo que los pezones se le salieron del corpiño.

—El colorete, Lindle.

Chastity se retorció, pero no pudo evitar que le bajaran la camisola y le frotaran con algo ambas aréolas.

—Mira —le dijo su padre.

Como ella se negara, él le retorció los brazos hasta que obedeció. Las crestas de sus senos estaban teñidas de un violento color rojo. A pesar de la camisola, era como si estuviese desnuda.

—¿Cómo puedes hacer esto? —le gritó a su padre—. ¿Cómo puedes permitir que ese... ese ser me toque?

Él no parecía arrepentirse, pero le soltó los doloridos brazos.

—Tú te lo has buscado —le dijo él alejándose—. Te he dado todo lo que una hija puede desear. Estaba dispuesto a asegurar tu porvenir y tu bienestar, pero tú no tienes ninguna confianza, ni sentido del deber para con tu familia, ni para conmigo, que soy tu padre. Y ahora estás pagando por ello. Ese colorete, por cierto, deja una mancha imborrable. No te lo podrás quitar. Pero puede que acabes encontrándolo apropiado.

Chastity se dio la vuelta lentamente para encararle, presintiendo una nueva estratagema.

Él sacó el reloj de bolsillo de oro y lo abrió con un chasquido.

—Ahora son las ocho y cuarto. Si me dices dónde se encuentra Verity antes de las nueve, te dejaré marchar. Si sigues en tus trece, te entregaré a un burdel que hay junto al río. La abadesa espera ansiosa un bocado tan sabroso y me asegura que elegirá para ti únicamente a los clientes más interesantes. ¿Sabes lo que eso significa? Unos meses atrás hubiera pensado que no, pero ahora ya no sé qué pensar. ¿Qué aventuras has corrido, hija, desde que, insensatamente, te dejé en libertad…?

—¡No puedes hacer eso! —dijo ella jadeante.

—Claro que puedo. Ya no me sirves para nada.

La rastrera frialdad de aquellas palabras dejó a Chastity aturdida pero en el fondo se sentía aliviada. Su padre cumpliría su palabra —siempre lo hacía— y la dejaría irse si le decía dónde paraba Verity. Ella hablaría justo antes de las nueve, Walgrave la soltaría, y para cuando él y sus esbirros llegaran a Winchester, Verity ya se habría marchado. Gracias a Dios, el conde no sabía que había una tercera persona en aquel asunto.

Walgrave señaló la peluca tirada en el suelo.

—Y para darte un aliciente más, si te portas bien, puedes quedarte con ella como premio. —Se volvió hacia la puerta.

Chastity luchó para no manifestar su alivio.

Él hizo girar el pomo.

Ella realizó una larga espiración.

Él se detuvo.

—¿Se me olvida algo, Lindle?

El criado no respondió a aquella pregunta retórica.

El conde se dio la vuelta.

—Ah, sí. Está pendiente el asunto del castigo de mi hija, ¿no?

El miedo atravesó a Chastity como si fuera un verdadero dolor físico. Se había vuelto a burlar de ella.

El conde se dio cuenta y sonrió.

—Vamos a ver. —Y comenzó a contar con sus largos y anchos dedos—. Punto uno, te vas de tu casa sin permiso. Dos, te vistes con ropa indecente. Tres, te dedicas a vagar por Inglaterra e incluso consigues algún dinero. —La miró levantando las cejas—. ¿Vas a decirme de qué manera? ¿No? No importa. Cuatro, has hecho que tu hermana se descarriara y has puesto a ella y a su hijo en peligro. Cinco, te has mostrado desvergonzada y díscola conmigo. Sexto, no te arrepientes. Ponte de rodillas en el suelo.

—¡No, maldito seas! —Chastity miró en torno a sí, tratando de encontrar algo que le sirviera de arma, pero no había nada. Nada.

—Siete, eres una malhablada. Lindle.

El secretario se adelantó, con implacable afabilidad. Esta vez, costara lo que costara, Chastity no se sometería. Ya no quedaba nada de paternal en aquella conducta. Estaba animada únicamente por la rabia y el espíritu de venganza.

Ella se resistió, llegando incluso a morder a Lindle, pero él la redujo, retorciéndole las manos brutalmente detrás de la espalda y doblándole la cabeza hacia atrás debajo de su brazo. A punto estuvo de estrangularla, pero ella no dejó de dar patadas. Aunque no había nada al alcance de sus botas.

El esbirro le levantó las faldas y ella sintió el aire helado en las piernas y en las nalgas, dejando escapar un penetrante alarido de rabia. No podían volver a hacerle aquello. ¡No podían!

Lindle aumentó la presión de su brazo, de manera que ella no pudo emitir ya ningún sonido. El bastón silbó y los muslos le ardieron de pronto.

—¡A ver si aprendes, demonio de mujer! —gruñó su padre y la azotó de nuevo—. ¡A mi no me desafía nadie! ¡Nadie!

Un tercer golpe le mordió las piernas y ella dejó escapar un grito ahogado.

—Santo cielo, padre. ¿Qué estás haciendo? —exclamó Fort, irrumpiendo en la estancia.

Chastity quedó libre y se desplomó sobre el suelo, jadeando por la falta de aire.

—Disciplina —contestó bruscamente el conde—. ¿También tú vas a negarme mis derechos?

Fort estaba blanco a causa de la conmoción.

—No, desde luego que no. Pero esto no es muy decoroso, ni apropiado.

Al conde se le subió el color y estuvo a punto de perder el control. Chastity rezaba para que Fort lo viera al fin cómo realmente era. Pero Walgrave logró sobreponerse.

—Puede que tengas razón, muchacho —dijo con desconsuelo—. Pero el egoísmo y la actitud desafiante de esta chica acaban con mi paciencia. Sigue sin querer ayudarnos a encontrar a su hermana.

Fort se acercó a Chastity y la levantó con delicadeza.

—Tienes que hacerlo —le dijo—. Frazer ha dejado el puesto de mando. Ha dicho que le reclamaba un asunto familiar urgente, pero no creo que sea cierto.

—Lo sabía —rugió el conde— ¡Maldita seas…!

Chastity vio cómo los ojos de Fort se agrandaban al fijarse en la ropa que llevaba puesta, cuya indecencia ella no trató de ocultar.

—Si ha ido a reunirse con Verity, Fort —dijo la muchacha—, ella estará a salvo.

Fort se volvió hacia el furioso conde.

—Supongo que eso es cierto, padre. Frazer se ocupará de su bienestar.

El rostro del conde adquirió un tono aún más purpúreo.

—¿Es que toda mi familia se ha vuelto loca? ¿Tengo que quedarme quieto mientras mi hija mayor se fuga con un oficial a las pocas semanas de enviudar? Después de que esta ramera... —le atizó un agudo golpe en el pecho a Chastity con la punta del bastón, haciéndola gritar—. ha arrastrado nuestro nombre por el lodo, ¿alguien sabe lo que dirá la gente? Sin duda, que Verity asesinó a su primer marido para quedar libre y poder casarse con su amante. Incluso pondrán en duda la paternidad del niño. —Y al acabar de decirlo, la saliva le salía a borbotones.

Fort, horrorizado, en su afán de proteger a Chastity la había rodeado con el brazo, pero ahora la muchacha se había soltado. Su padre estaba a punto de revelar su verdadera naturaleza y ella pretendía provocarlo.

—No —le gritó—. ¡Puede que hayas arruinado mi vida, asqueroso hipócrita, pero no dejaré que destroces la de Verity!

El conde intentó flagelarle la cara con el báculo, pero ella lo interceptó con el brazo. Un verdugón escarlata le brotó al punto.

—¡Basta! —gritó Fort y agarró el bastón. Lo partió en dos y arrojó las mitades a los lados.

—Lindle —aulló el conde—.¡Deja fuera de combate a este traidor!

Todavía sonriendo, el fornido secretario agarró a Fort. El conde, que babeaba de rabia, continuó apremiándole. Por el momento, ambos ignoraban a Chastity. Ella no podía hacer nada por Fort. Además, no creía que su hermano corriera tanto peligro como ella. La muchacha aprovechó su oportunidad y escapó, echando mano de la peluca en su huida.

—¡Detenedla! —bramó el conde. Pero Chastity, que más que correr volaba, ya había bajado las escaleras y había salido al porche. Uno de los hombres del conde estaba allí apostado pero no era muy corpulento. Ella lo cogió por sorpresa y lo derribó.

Corrió velozmente por la estrecha y desierta calle. La escasa longitud de sus faldas era ahora una ventaja. Sin embargo, estaba oscuro y la muchacha se precipitó por encima de un barril que alguien había dejado junto a la entrada de su vivienda.

Se levantó, temblorosa y jadeante, y se obligó a ir un poco más despacio. Detrás de ella, se escuchaban voces, pero la persecución todavía no estaba bien organizada. Pensó en pedir ayuda en alguna casa, pero desechó la idea. Con la indumentaria que llevaba, ninguna persona respetable le dejaría atravesar el umbral de su puerta y, además, casi todo el mundo en Inglaterra entregaría al conde de Walgrave a su descarriada hija.

Se volvió a embutir los rojos pezones bajo el corpiño y se sumergió en un oscuro callejón, después se metió bruscamente en otro y luego en otro, con la única intención de despistar a cualquier perseguidor. No tenía ni idea de adónde ir ni adónde pedir ayuda.

¿Estaría Fort en condiciones de ayudarla?

Se acordó de Cyn y reprimió un sollozo. Le pareció que los dulces días que había pasado en su compañía pertenecían a otra vida. Ojalá él estuviera allí.

Se precipitó por una estrecha calle, raspándose el codo al rozar una pared. Pasó junto a un asombrado basurero nocturno. Se introdujo por otro callizo, jadeante y sin aliento. ¿Estaba dando vueltas en círculos?

De pronto, el callejón la escupió al lado del Támesis, en los muelles. Pequeñas embarcaciones flotaban ancladas y, por allí cerca, el sonido de una canción emergía de una taberna. Durante un instante su animado sonido la reconfortó, pero luego se acordó de lo del burdel junto al río. Se estremeció y se hundió en la sombra de un recodo de la pared, consciente de que aquél no era un buen lugar para ella.

Se tomó unos instantes para recobrar el aliento e intentar deshacerse del pánico que le enmarañaba la mente. Pero no lo consiguió; aquello había sido muy fuerte. Le dolía todo. Le daba pavor pensar que las cosas podían ponerse aún peor. Se sentía como un animal acosado. Sólo buscaba un agujero en el que poder esconderse. Aguzó los sentidos tratando de detectar algún sonido que evidenciara la persecución.

¿Qué debía hacer? Había huido de su padre desesperada, pero ahora estaba sola en medio de la noche, sin un penique y casi desnuda en una ciudad extraña. En el barrio más rudo de una ciudad extraña y, con aquel aspecto, no cabía esperar que la ayudaran.

Se dio cuenta de que tenía la peluca fuertemente agarrada y se la puso en la cabeza. Estaría más segura en otra parte mejor de la villa. Tal vez pudiera esconderse en un jardín o en un cobertizo hasta que se hiciera de día. Y después ya vería.

Oyó voces que se acercaban y se quedó helada, apretando la espalda contra la pared de madera que había tras ella. Pasaron cuatro hombres, quejándose del precio del tabaco con un acento bastante cerrado. Cuando entraron en la tasca, el volumen del canto subió abruptamente, después volvió a bajar. Cuando hubieron desaparecido, la muchacha se combó aliviada y salió vacilante de entre las sombras.

Un farol parpadeante en el exterior de la taberna arrojaba un poco de luz y Chastity pudo ver que en la zona no había un alma, al menos humana. Dos gruesas ratas corretearon en medio de la tenue luz.

Chastity reprimió un gimoteo y avanzó a hurtadillas bordeando el edificio hasta que llegó a otro callejón, un simple hueco oscuro que conducía a las tinieblas. Se metió en sus fauces. Sus botas resbalaban en el viscoso suelo y poco le faltó para vomitar a causa del hedor. Sin duda, los otros callejones habrían sido parecidos, pero ella había estado demasiado aterrorizada para darse cuenta.

Dio gracias al cielo de no poder ver como era aquel pasadizo, temerosa de lo que vendría a continuación. Se acordó del callejón de Shaftesbury y del gato muerto. El que recorría ahora olía como si contuviera unos cuantos.

Contenía uno vivo. Chastity lo pisó y él le arañó la rodilla y huyó dando aullidos.

Santo cielo, pensó a la par que soltaba un gimoteo, ¿quedaba alguna pulgada de su cuerpo que no estuviera herida o amoratada?

Extendió una mano para tocar la fría piedra de la pared que había a su derecha, sin duda el muro del algún patio trasero. Fue recorriéndola con la mano mientras avanzaba tambaleante, porque, en medio de la oscuridad, le devolvía la certidumbre de la realidad. Delante de ella todo era negrura. Sólo por encima, si levantaba la vista, se extendía una estrecha franja grisácea: el cielo nublado.

Empezaba a pensar que nunca más volvería a ver la luz. Oyó un ruido extraño y se dio cuenta que eran sus propios gimoteos jadeantes. Se los tragó.

Entonces vislumbró luz en la distancia. Era tan sólo un tenue y vacilante halo dorado, pero ella avanzó hacia él a trompicones como si fuera la puerta del cielo. El callejón se convirtió en un camino ligeramente más ancho, flanqueado por viejas y estrechas casas inclinadas, básicamente oscuras. Una de ellas tenía una mortecina antorcha en la puerta, y eso era lo que ella había visto.

Era como si la cordura regresara a un mundo desquiciado. Sin embargo, allí no había dónde esconderse. No había huecos entre las casas, ni tampoco escalones. Echó a correr buscando una calle más ancha, tratando desesperadamente de alejarse del río y encontrar un escondite.

¡Voces al frente!

Se quedó helada. Miró a derecha e izquierda, pero todo era en vano. Se hundió contra una pared, rezando para que no fueran sus perseguidores, para que aquellos hombres no le salieran al paso…

Pero ahí estaban. Un paje iluminaba el camino de dos oficiales de chaquetones rojos, el uno menudo y el otro regordete. Los dos iban alegremente borrachos, pero se mantenían firmes sobre sus pies.

Chastity se arrimó hasta una puerta, con la esperanza de que pareciera que se trataba de su casa y los hombres pasaran de largo. Vana esperanza. Los soldados se detuvieron.

El delgado levantó un anteojo y sonrió. Ambos caminaron hacia ella, mirándola socarronamente.

—Vaya, buenas noches, preciosa —dijo el hombre rollizo en tono animado.

Chastity sólo podía hacer lo que haría una dama en caso de ser abordada groseramente. Miró al frente sin hacerle caso. Pero el hombre le agarró con sus toscos dedos la barbilla y la obligó a mirarle. No era feo, pero tenía una expresión abominable.

—¿Dónde están tus modales, tunanta? —le dijo burlonamente.

A Chastity le habían abandonado las fuerzas. Le dolía todo. El cansancio le hacía tambalearse. Se le saltaron las lágrimas

—¡Por favor, caballeros, no soy lo que ustedes piensan! —Vio que su aristocrático acento tenía cierto efecto y se devanó los sesos tratando de encontrar una historia. ¿Y por qué no algo parecido a la verdad?—. ¡Soy una dama noble, a la que han raptado de su casa y vendido en un burdel! Ayúdenme, por favor.

Los hombres se miraron, luego volvieron a observarla. La escuchaban, pero a Chastity le parecía que sus palabras no estaban sirviendo de mucho. La expresión del delgaducho se había vuelto aún más aborrecible. Ella se cubrió los pechos con la mano.

El gordo se volvió hacia el paje.

—¿A ti qué te parece? ¿Es una dama o una puta?

El muchacho contemplaba la escena como si fuera una diversión pensada para su regocijo.

—Yo diría que es una puta en toda regla, capitán.

—Lo mismo pienso yo. —El hombre se volvió hacia Chastity—. Puede que tu historia sea cierta, preciosa, pero está claro que llevas ya algún tiempo en este oficio. ¿Por qué habrías de poner peros a unas cuantas guineas más? Vamos a probar tus mercancías y después te mandaremos a casa con mamá. —Estalló en carcajadas y el flaco celebró la broma con una risita.

—¡Estoy intacta! —imploró ella—. ¡Oh, créanme señores! Acaban de llevarme a ese lugar y me he escapado.

—Vale pues —dijo el flaco arrastrando las palabras con los ojos brillantes—, entonces nosotros somos los afortunados, ¿no? La señora Kelly cobra diez guineas por una virgen. Sujétala, Pog, que voy a lanzar una moneda a ver quien va primero.

—De acuerdo, Stu. —El hombre corpulento rodeó a Chastity con sus rollizos brazos. Chastity gritó, pero sólo consiguió emitir un breve chillido antes de que su gruesa mano, que apestaba a rapé y a cebolla, le tapara la boca. Ella pataleó, pero él se limitó a reírse.

El delgado capitán sacó una corona y la hizo girar por el aire, lanzando destellos en aquella luz mortecina. La tapó sobre el dorso de la mano y miró a su amigo arqueando una ceja.

—Cara —dijo el que la tenía sujeta.

El tipo flaco miró la moneda.

—Mierda, tú ganas. No importa, así me la dejarás bien engrasada.

Su captor le hizo darse la vuelta.

—¡Ven aquí, querida! —Y plantó su cálida y viscosa boca sobre la de Chastity—. Aquello era el fin. Chastity le mordió la lengua y empezó otra vez a dar patadas. Él dejó escapar un juramento y la soltó. Ella se le lanzó a los ojos.

Él la tumbó, dándole un brutal golpe en la cabeza. Chastity se quedó aturdida unos instantes cuan larga era, después gateó y se puso de pie. El hombre intentó agarrarla, pero su amigo había tenido la misma idea. Los dos hombres se enredaron y cayeron al suelo. Al paje le dio la risa.

Chastity le escupió y echó a correr, pero una mano que se agitaba la enganchó la falda y la hizo precipitarse sobre los adoquines. La mano la arrastró de nuevo hacia los hombres. Ella daba patadas y puñetazos furiosos a su alrededor. Casi había conseguido liberarse, cuando un nuevo atacante la agarró por detrás. Ella lanzó el codo hacia atrás y escuchó un jadeo.

—Tranquila —dijo una voz que, a la vez que sonaba divertida, dejaba traslucir el dolor—. No voy a hacerte daño.

Chastity se quedó helada, después se giró.

—Cyn… —susurró la muchacha.

Él abrió los ojos, incrédulo.

Ella se arrojó en sus brazos.

Cyn se había quedado de piedra de la impresión. ¿Aquella sucia, bella y magullada mujerzuela era su damisela? ¿Qué demonios había estado ocurriendo? Llevaba horas buscándola por la villa.

—Oye, ponte a la cola. Es nuestra. —Los dos oficiales se habían puesto de pie y tenían una actitud beligerante.

—Es una picarona, ¿verdad? —dijo el tipo delgado—. Hay de sobra para los tres, pero hemos lanzado una moneda y ha ganado Pog.

Ella se tensó y gimoteó. A Cyn le dieron ganas de matarlo, pero no podía verse envuelto en un drama de esas características. Tenía que evitar que el nombre de Chastity saliera a la palestra.

—¡Qué pena! —dijo Cyn, sonriendo sin ganas—. Pog ha perdido ahora.

—¡Maldita sea, no puedes hacer eso!

—Claro que puedo. Vamos querida.

Casi se había dado la vuelta cuando le alertó el gemido de una espada al ser desenvainada. Volvió a girarse, lanzó a

Chastity detrás de él y sacó su propio florete. No era momento de andarse con delicadezas. Apenas tuvo tiempo de desviar la punta del arma del tipo delgado de su corazón.

Cyn recuperó el equilibrio y se midió con él. Pero no halló adversario. La destreza de aquel hombre era más bien escasa. Además estaba borracho. Podía atravesarle con su espada en cualquier momento, pero no se atrevió. Ya se oía el tintineo de algunas puertas y ventanas al abrirse. La gente quería ver lo que pasaba. Pronto llegaría la Guardia. Se propuso convencer a su adversario para que se retirara sin que mediara derramamiento de sangre.

Al principio, Chastity permaneció aturdida, observando cómo la espada de Cyn parpadeaba en la mortecina luz, cómo las delgadas armas silbaban y se entrechocaban, anunciando la muerte. Entonces, vio un movimiento y miró hacia allí. El otro hombre, Pog, se movía furtivamente hacia ella. Su expresión burlona, de húmedos labios, revelaba sus intenciones.

Chastity agarró la antorcha del paje y se la arrojó al hombre.

—¡Apártate de mí! —él retrocedió tambaleante y soltó una maldición.

—No le prendas fuego —le dijo Cyn, que se movió unos cuantos pasos hasta quedar cerca de ella para lanzarle una mirada de apoyo, con cierto aire divertido. ¡Maldición, aquel hombre era capaz de disfrutar incluso con aquella situación!

—Mira —le dijo a su contrincante, sin que le faltara aún el resuello—. Soy mejor y más rápido que tú, y además estoy sobrio. No tengo ganas de derramar sangre, pero la verdad es que tengo algo de prisa. ¿Cómo lo ves? —Y como si quisiera demostrar su razonamiento, seccionó un botón plateado del uniforme del tipo delgado y lo envió, emitiendo destellos hasta el canalillo de desagüe.

—¡Mierda! —farfulló el hombre, rechazando la espada.

Al instante siguiente, Cyn había vuelto a cercenarle otro botón.

—Oh, déjalo ya, Stu —gruñó Pog—. No te tomes tantas molestias por esa furcia flaca.

Stu rezongó, pero bajó su espadín y dijo, con fingido desprecio.

—Maldita sea, tienes razón, Pog. Sin duda está mas gastada que un trapo viejo. —Envainó la espada y se contoneó con chulería—. Vamos a buscar una mejor. Pero no vuelva a cruzarse en mi camino, señor —le dijo a Cyn—. Porque no voy olvidar esta noche.

Los dos tipos y el paje se marcharon. A los pocos instantes, Chastity estaba a solas con Cyn. Entonces cayó en la cuenta de que él no se había mostrado sorprendido al descubrir que era una mujer. El golpe fue tremendo.

—¡Lo sabías!

Él metió la espada en la vaina y le dedicó una apesadumbrada sonrisa.

—Sí, pero éstos no son ni el momento ni el lugar para hablar de eso. Salgamos de aquí. —La rodeó con el brazo y la apremió a avanzar por el camino en dirección a la calle principal.

Chastity hubiera querido decir cientos de cosas, pero comprendía que tal vez fuera necesario apresurarse.

¿Desde cuándo lo había sabido?

Ya no estaba sola.

Él debía saber que ella era Chastity Ware.

Tal vez lo peor hubiera pasado ya.

¿Lo había sabido él la noche anterior? ¿Lo había atrapado, después de todo?

Aquello acabó con las pocas fuerzas que le quedaban. Las piernas le temblaban y la cabeza le daba vueltas. Si continuó andando fue gracias al fuerte brazo de Cyn.

15

Cyn la llevaba casi en volandas cuando llegaron a un tosco establo que no era el del Saracen's Head. La transportó hasta su interior y la colocó sobre un montón de paja. Había media docena de caballos, todos ellos bestias de carga, excepto los suyos. La única luz era un farol mortecino suspendido en el exterior. Cyn lo metió dentro y lo colgó de un gancho.

—He traído los caballos aquí por si acaso la posada estaba vigilada. —Se volvió hacia ella y la vio por primera vez. Se quedó repentinamente serio y se arrodilló ante ella—. Santo cielo, ¿qué te ha ocurrido?

Chastity trató de meterse los rojos pezones dentro del corpiño. Le temblaban las manos y, de todos modos, era una tarea imposible. Empezó a llorar. La envolvía el abrigo de Cyn —que conservaba el calor de su cuerpo— y luego sus brazos.

—Calla, amor mío, calla. Ya ha pasado todo. No dejaré que nadie te haga daño.

Ella, al oírle, se echó a reír, un tanto frenética. Él murmuró una maldición, después le acercó un frasco a los labios y lo inclinó. El brandy puro abrasó la garganta de la muchacha, que recobró la lucidez pero sin poder dejar de llorar. Él continuó sosteniéndola y calmándola hasta que las lágrimas cesaron.

Al cabo de un rato, la movió para poder verle la cara y le secó las lágrimas con ternura. Chastity esperaba que la interrogara. Ella misma tenía una buena lista de preguntas. Pero él dijo simplemente:

—Tenemos que irnos de aquí. ¿Puedes cabalgar?

Chastity quería descansar, acaso morirse, pero hizo acopio de fuerzas. No quería que su padre y su hermano atraparan a Cyn.

—Supongo que sí… —respondió mirándose la ropa con expresión impotente.

Él siguió la dirección de su mirada.

—¿Qué…? No te preocupes. —Cogió el baúl—. Ponte mi ropa de repuesto. Te quedará grande, pero cualquier cosa es mejor que lo que llevas puesto ahora.

Ella se fue detrás de un tabique y se despojó de aquellas odiosas prendas. Le hubiera gustado quemarlas, pero las metió en la bolsa para no dejar pruebas de su paso por aquel lugar.

Se puso un par de calzoncillos de Cyn, una camisa, sus calzones azules, un chaleco y un chaquetón. La camisa estaba usada y conservaba todavía su olor, que a ella le resultó extrañamente dulce. Los pantalones le quedaban anchos de cintura, pero se los sujetó con un cinturón. Las perneras le llegaban hasta las pantorrillas, pero con las botas no se notaría. Y el abrigo le iba demasiado grande de hombros.

Se hizo un nudo flojo con un pañuelo alrededor del cuello y se dio cuenta de que todavía tenía puesta la peluca. Se la quitó con pesar y la metió en el baúl. Pensaba que ya se había acostumbrado a su casco de pelo, pero después de haber sido ella misma durante un rato, le volvía a parecer chocantemente corto. Enderezó los hombros y salió.

Él sonrió.

—Bienvenido de vuelta, Charles.

Ella cerró los ojos y se rindió ante su ternura, dándose cuenta claramente por primera vez de que todas sus buenas intenciones se quedaban en nada.

Cyn había ensillado los caballos mientras ella se cambiaba y ahora le acercaba a Chastity el suyo. Levantó una mano y se la pasó por el cabello. Ella reculó pero él no la dejó retirarse y le acarició la parte trasera de la cabeza.

—Llevo tanto tiempo queriendo hacer esto… —Dejó caer las riendas del caballo—. La peluca es bonita, pero tu pelo corto también es hermoso.

—No hablas en serio.

La tocaba con cariño y dulzura, y ella sentía que la calidez de aquel roce le recorría la espina dorsal.

—Claro que sí. Tienes un rostro que no necesita adornos ni distracciones. También llevo mucho tiempo queriendo hacer esto…

Y le aplicó los labios, suaves y tiernos al principio, aunque de ningún modo vacilantes. Chastity sabía que debía resistirse, pero aquel era su primer beso sincero y no podía rechazarlo, así que le devolvió el gesto. Él lo hizo cada vez más profundo, abriéndole la boca con calidez, usando las manos y todo su cuerpo para llevarla más allá de la razón, a un mundo gobernado únicamente por los sentidos.

Ella saboreó a su hombre, dulce como la miel y con regusto a brandy. La boca se le volvió puro anhelo y sus manos palpaban con ansia.

Él se echó hacia atrás riéndose.

—Santo cielo, amor, ojalá éstos fueran el momento y el lugar.. —Le acarició la mejilla—. No pongas esa cara de susto. Todo va a salir bien. Confía en mí.

—Soy Chastity Ware. Las cosas no podrán salir nunca bien.

—Soy Cyn Malloren. Confía en mí.

La sensación de exasperación que se apoderó de ella le resultó familiar:

—Ni siquiera un Malloren puede hacer que cambie el mundo.

Él le dedicó aquella indolente sonrisa que tanto la regocijaba.

—Ponme a prueba y verás. Vamos. —Y juntó las manos entrelazando los dedos para ayudarla a montar.

Chastity decidió dejar aquella infructuosa conversación por el momento. Él ya se había enterado de que había ciertas cosas que no tenían remedio y pensó que si ella no le dejaba adquirir ningún compromiso, ni le descubría quién era Chloe, él se cansaría pronto de aquel juego.

Al levantar el pie para apoyarlo en las manos de Cyn, fue cuando se dio cuenta de que cabalgar le iba a causar dolor. Apretó los dientes y no abrió la boca al caer sobre la silla, pero se le saltaron las lágrimas. Gracias a Dios, su padre no había llegado a azotarle en las nalgas. Con las molestias de sus muslos escocidos ya tenía de sobra.

Cyn estaba subiendo a su propio caballo, así que dispuso de unos instantes para sobreponerse. Sin embargo, ¿hasta dónde podría llegar?

No tenía elección. Si le hablaba a Cyn de sus heridas, ambos se quedarían allí y su padre los atraparía. Walgrave era un enemigo terrible en circunstancias normales, conque mucho más ahora que su cordura empezaba a sér dudosa. Si era capaz de volverse contra su primogénito y heredero, ¿qué haría con un extraño?

Chastity cogió las riendas con la mano izquierda, esperando que Cyn no lo notara. Cabalgaron el uno junto al otro por el oscuro camino, siguiendo el rumbo que él marcaba y alejándose del pueblo.

—Antes he explorado esta ruta —le dijo a la muchacha—. Esta calzada parte de Maidenhead hacia la aldea de Woodlands Green. No creo que esté vigilada. Es fácil y llana. Además está delimitada por setos. No debe ser difícil seguirla incluso en la oscuridad, si nos lo tomamos con calma.

Chastity hizo una plegaria dando las gracias por la marcha lenta. Cada movimiento de vaivén del caballo le causaba una punzada de dolor, pero, yendo al paso, podía soportarlo.

—Cuéntame qué ha pasado —le dijo a Cyn.

—Podría decirte yo exactamente lo mismo —dijo él, pero obedeció—. Encontré a Frazer sin problemas. Está totalmente de nuestro lado. Parece tener una opinión bastante pobre de vuestro padre, lo que parece lógico, después de que el conde lo rechazara como pretendiente de Verity. La cosa es que, pretextando que se iba a su casa, está ya camino de Winchester. Si viaja de noche, puede llegar allí al mediodía. Ojalá hubiera más de un cuarto de luna.

—¿Y qué hará entonces?

—Va a llevar a Verity a un lugar llamado Long Knotwell, donde su hermano, Tom, es el párroco. Por suerte, Frazer acaba de pasar allí un par de meses de permiso, recuperándose de una pequeña herida. Como ha establecido en ese pueblo su residencia, no hay ningún inconveniente para que se casen allí.

—¿Dónde está Long Knotwell?

—Cerca de Fleet. Frazer hizo un chiste fácil sobre las bodas rápidas, aunque, desde luego, esas ceremonias apresuradas, hoy en día, son ilegales. Como no hay tiempo para las amonestaciones, necesitarán una licencia pública.

—Dios santo. ¿Cómo se consigue eso?

—La otorga un obispo. En este caso, el obispo de Londres, ya que Long Knotwell se encuentra dentro de su diócesis. Normalmente, hace falta que una de las partes se persone y haga un juramento sobre la legalidad de la unión, pero he decidido tratar de obtener la licencia con la declaración jurada de Frazer en mano, mientras él se ocupa de llevar a Verity hasta Long Knotwell. En caso de apuro, el reverendo Frazer los casará de todos modos. Esos matrimonios suelen tener validez si no existe ningún impedimento legal. En todo caso —añadió con sequedad—, espero que el hecho de que el obispo sea tío de mi madre ayude un poco.

—Otra vez el poder de los Malloren. Pero entonces, ¿no tendrías que estar en Londres?

Él se volvió hacia ella.

—Primero tengo que ponerte a salvo.

—¿Por qué? —preguntó ella exasperada—. El tiempo es vital. Mi padre no ve el momento de ponerle las manos encima a Verity. ¡Te dije que te olvidaras de mí si me cogían!

—Nunca haces lo que te dicen —le dijo él en tono frívolo—. ¿Por qué iba a hacerlo yo?

Ella protestó:

—¡No se te ocurra tomarte esto a broma!

Vio cómo Cyn sonreía —sus dientes relucían en la oscuridad.

—«Aquel que es de corazón alegre vivirá en una continua fiesta» —citó él—. Es mi forma de ser, encanto… Sin embargo, trataré de ponerme serio si eso es, de verdad, lo que quieres. —Su voz adquirió una fría autoridad al añadir—: ¿Por qué no empiezas por contarme tu historia? Comenzando por explicarme por qué abandonaste la seguridad de la posada.

Se oyó un zumbido y el ulular de una lechuza que pasó volando por encima de sus cabezas. Se produjo un nervioso susurro en un arbusto cercano, pero, por lo demás, el campo estaba en silencio. Cyn también guardaba silencio. Un silencio que exigía explicaciones.

—Alguien me vio en la ventana —dijo Chastity de mala gana—. No quería que me cogieran en aquella habitación, porque me relacionarían contigo. Así que me fui. Soborné al posadero para que no dijera a nadie que yo había estado contigo. Le dije que huía para alistarme en el ejército y él se llenó de fervor patriótico, por un valor de tres guineas, para ser precisa.

—Eso supuse. Por lo que te puedo decir, guardó un silencio de por lo menos tres guineas. ¿Qué más pasó?

—Intenté esperarte en los establos, pero algunos de los hombres de mi padre se encontraban ya allí. Me escapé de ellos por los pelos, pero tuve que salir a la calle. Y Fort me echó el guante.

—¿Tu hermano? Está de parte de tu padre, ¿no?

—Ya no lo está. Me he escapado gracias a él.

Era un tanto incómodo mantener una conversación así en la oscuridad. Ella no podía ver su expresión y su voz no dejaba traslucir nada, pero Chastity sentía que, a su derecha, emanaba el poder: el oficial la estaba interrogando.

—¿Escapado de dónde? —preguntó él.

Chastity repasó apresuradamente su historia.

—Mi padre había alquilado una casa y Fort me llevó hasta allí. Me encerraron en una habitación. Convencí a Fort de que no sabía dónde estaba Verity y de que había ido a Maidenhead a buscarla. Sin embargo, cuando mi padre llegó, no se tragó el cuento y me obligó a quitarme la ropa de hombre. —Chastity buscó una manera de eludir aquello, pero no la encontró—. Me amenazó con venderme a un burdel si no se lo contaba todo.

Cyn se giró bruscamente.

—¿Que hizo qué?

—Pero no lo hizo —añadió ella rápidamente—. Lo de venderme, quiero decir. Sin duda sabía que yo cedería antes de llegar a ese punto. —Chastity no trataba tanto de defender a su padre como de proteger a Cyn. Si le decía toda la verdad, él podía empeñarse en regresar para ajustar cuentas con el conde.

Y moriría.

Bajo las palabras de Cyn podía apreciarse la furia reprimida:

—¿Cómo escapaste?

—Fort se interpuso.

—Bien hecho —dijo Cyn con cortante impaciencia.

Chastity sentía verdaderas ganas de defender a su hermano:

—Le costaba creer que padre pudiera ser tan perverso. La cosa es que se pelearon y eso me dio la oportunidad de escapar, pero no tenía dónde ir.

—Y con el aspecto de una furcia de los muelles. Santo cielo. Gracias a Dios que te encontré entonces.

—Amén —dijo Chastity con suavidad—. Pero sigo creyendo que tendrías que haber huido por la mañana, y haber ido a Londres a por la licencia. ¿Es allí dónde nos dirigimos ahora?

—No estoy muy seguro de te encuentres en condiciones.

Tampoco ella, pero sabía que él no la iba a dejar y no quería que por su culpa se produjera ninguna demora.

—Yo estoy bien —dijo la muchacha en tono animado—. Esta tarde incluso me he echado una siesta.

Siguieron cabalgando sin interrupción. Chastity sacó fuerzas de flaqueza. Pensó en los mártires, en Horacio en el puente, en Feidípides en Maratón. En comparación, su tarea era minúscula y sus heridas menores.

Aún así, debían quedar unas veinte millas para llegar a Londres y, después, casi otro tanto hasta Long Knotwell. No sabía si conseguiría llegar. Había aprendido que los humanos tenían una resistencia inagotable cuando se les ponía a prueba, pero la suya parecía estar llegando a su fin. Podía aguantar a aquel ritmo de paseo, pero cuando se hiciera de día y empezaran a trotar, desfallecería.

Incluso aquel paso de tortuga hacía que la tela de los calzoncillos le rozara los verdugones de las piernas. A pesar de sus firmes resoluciones, se movía de un lado a otro buscando una postura más cómoda. Tenía que estarse quieta. La más pequeña señal de malestar alertaría a Cyn, y eso sería el final.

Llegaron a Woodlands Green cuando el reloj daba las nueve, y atravesaron calladamente la aldea dormida.

—¿Adónde vamos ahora?

—Al sur. Al menos eso creo. —La despreocupada hilaridad que lo caracterizaba había vuelto a su voz. Este rasgo exasperaba a la vez que atraía a Chastity. Parecía imposible que le pasara nada malo con Cyn Malloren a su lado.

—¿Por qué hacia el sur? Creía que íbamos hacia Londres.

—Porque si hay vigilancia, estará en la carretera de Bath que pasa por Maidenhead. Si vamos hacia el sur, llegaremos a la carretera de Southampton y desde allí podremos darnos prisa. ¿Cansada?

—Un poco —confesó, sabiendo que una negativa rotunda no colaría. Se preguntaba cuántas millas más añadiría este rodeo a su viaje.

—Me pregunto si no debería dejarte en alguna parte… pero, cada vez que lo hago, acabas metida en algún lío.

Chastity contemplo su sombría silueta. ¿Estaba admitiendo que la había reconocido como Chloe? Seguramente, él tendría algo que añadir…

—¿Qué es lo quieres decir exactamente? —preguntó ella con cautela.

—Hoy te he dejado en el Saracen y te encuentro medio desnuda en brazos de un hombre.

Ella se combó aliviada.

—Lo dices como si yo lo hubiera planeado así. Además, creo que estás exagerando. No siempre me ocurre eso.

—Pero tal vez sea cosa del destino —dijo él jovialmente—. Si has de acabar en brazos de un hombre, prefiero que sean los míos.

Chastity no tuvo valor para insistir en el tema. ¿Qué iba a hacer si descubría que él había reconocido a Chloe? Se derretía al imaginarse otra vez en sus brazos, pero trataba de reprimir aquel deseo egoísta.

Cyn observó la sombría silueta de la muchacha en la oscuridad. Había muchas cosas que estaban mal y él no las sabía todas. Ella parecía tan frágil como el cristal rajado, propenso a romperse al más mínimo impacto. ¿Qué le habían hecho a su damisela? Ella no había contado toda la verdad.

¿Había conseguido de verdad librarse del burdel?

¿La habían violado?

Anhelaba dolorosamente poder verse libre de Verity y su mayor para llevarse a Chastity a algún lugar en el que poder reparar todas sus heridas. No estaba seguro de poder quedarse tranquilo dejándola en alguna parte, ni siquiera en una fortaleza armada que estuviera de su parte. Sentía el loco deseo de arrastrarla delante de él y cabalgar rodeándola con sus brazos. Pero era un desvarío. Ella pensaría que estaba trastornado. ¿Por qué tenía la sensación de que la muchacha estaba llorando? Maldijo aquella oscuridad.

—¿Estás bien? —volvió a preguntarle.

—Por supuesto que sí —replicó ella.

Cyn trató de apartar de su mente estas preocupaciones. No se podía hacer nada.

—Este camino es muy accidentado. Me parece como si en cualquier momento fuera a caer en la ciénaga del desánimo. Voy a ir delante del caballo. —Se apeó.

Apretando los dientes, Chastity hizo lo mismo.

—No hace falta que tú te bajes.

—Lo prefiero —dijo ella muy sinceramente. Caminar no le resultaba del todo indoloro, especialmente ahora que la ropa le había rozado los verdugones, pero era mucho mejor que cabalgar.

Tenían que tener mucho cuidado con cada paso que daban, porque el firme del camino era muy malo y, en algunos sitios, había charcos muy profundos. No podían esquivarlos todos. Chastity se congratuló de que los dos llevaran botas.

Atravesaron dos silenciosas aldeas. En cada una de ellas, la muchacha estuvo a punto de suplicar que se detuvieran y buscaran refugio. Pero venció su debilidad y prosiguió la caminata. Resistiría una milla más, sólo una milla…

Se había propuesto —hacía mucho tiempo, según le parecía, y en otro mundo— garantizar la seguridad de Verity y William. Aquélla era la última fase y no podía fallarles.

Se tropezó y Cyn le cogió la mano. Ella jadeó.

—¿Qué tienes? —Le rozó suavemente con el dedo y descubrió una magulladura—. ¿Estás herida?

—No es nada.

—¿Qué ha ocurrido?

Ella retiró la mano.

—Me he lastimado. Me he raspado con algo.

Ella continuó avanzando y él la siguió. Chastity tenía lágrimas en los ojos, a causa de la fatiga y el dolor. Bendijo la oscuridad que las ocultaba y rezó para que él no la hiciera hablar.

Él se detuvo.

—Me parece, aunque no lo podría jurar, que a nuestra derecha hay un cobertizo. Está a mucha distancia de cualquier granja, así que no creo que tenga ganado. Necesitamos descansar.

Era demasiado tentador. ¿Podría ella volver a moverse si se paraban?

—Yo estoy bien. Tenemos que darnos prisa.

—¿A esta marcha? Mi intención era poner distancia entre nosotros y Maidenhead. Y eso ya lo hemos conseguido. Tanto da que descansemos nosotros y dejemos reposar a los caballos, para coger buena velocidad después, como que sigamos avanzando hasta quedar exhaustos. Además, nos arriesgamos a causarnos heridas. Vamos. Aquí hay un hueco en el seto.

Chastity no tuvo más remedio que seguirle. Ciertamente, una buena parte de ella estaba ya sucumbiendo a la seducción del descanso.

La oscura silueta resultó ser un cobertizo, aunque bastante desvencijado. Había en él algo de heno, sin embargo, y Cyn les puso una buena porción a los caballos. El resto lo apiló y lo cubrió con su capa.

—Vamos soldado. Es hora de acampar.

Chastity se dejó caer, sintiendo que le dolía todo el cuerpo, pero al mismo tiempo, saboreando el sublime alivio del descanso. Él se sentó junto a ella, produciendo un súbito crujido. Ella apenas podía verle, pero notaba su cálida y amada presencia. Cyn echó el manto de la muchacha por encima de ambos, se recostó hacia atrás y le tocó suavemente el hombro.

—Apóyate sobre mí. Estarás más cómoda.

—¿Y tú?

—No puedo imaginarme nada más delicioso.

A Chastity le apetecía, pero tenía miedo de que él quisiera hacer el amor. Estaba demasiado cansada. Y él probablemente descubriría sus heridas. Ella había decidido que no iba a permitir que él se implicara hasta ese punto.

—No estoy intentando seducirte —le dijo él con calma—. Te doy mi palabra. Los dos necesitamos descansar.

La muchacha no podía desconfiar de nada de lo que le dijera con aquella voz tan firme. Chastity se reclinó hacia atrás con cuidado y halló el hueco de su hombro. Parecía estar diseñado para albergar su cabeza. Él la rodeó con el brazo, como si éste fuera un escudo y con el calor de su cuerpo aplacó su frío. La extenuación se apoderó de ella, haciéndola cerrar los párpados y nublándole el cerebro.

—¿No será peligroso que nos durmamos los dos?

—¿Por qué? Para que tu padre nos encontrara aquí, haría falta que fuera brujo. Duérmete, lady Chastity.

—¿No te importa? —masculló ella.

—¿A qué te refieres?

—Que yo sea Chastity Ware.

—Me importa mucho tu bienestar, amor.

Ella intentó hacer un movimiento de protesta, pero estaba demasiado exhausta.

—No puedes amarme.

—No seas tan mandona. Yo puedo hacer lo que me dé la gana. Duérmete.

Lo siguiente que Chastity sintió fue su mano acariciándole la cara.

Se despertó y vio la pálida luz de la mañana colándose dentro del cobertizo a través de los huecos de los tablones. Tenía los ojos picajosos y le dolía la cabeza. O, mejor dicho, le dolía todo. Las escasas horas de descanso no habían servido de mucho.

—Ese hijo de puta te ha llenado de cardenales —dijo él con serenidad—. Debería haberlo matado.

—No fue el tipo con el que te peleaste.

—Debería haberlos matado a los dos.

Ella sonrió lánguidamente.

—Empieza a defenderme, Cyn Malloren, y tendrás que desafiar al mundo.

—¿Y cuál es el problema? —preguntó él con ligereza—. Todo lo que le pido a la vida es que me rete.

Ella cerró los ojos desesperada, pero se forzó a abrirlos. De lo contrario, se habría dormido de nuevo.

Él la besó tiernamente en los labios.

—Es la primera vez que te beso por la mañana. Espero que sea la primera de muchas.

El corazón de la muchacha se estremeció pero ella dijo:

—Difícil lo veo.

Él le acarició con suavidad la barbilla.

—¿Por qué dices eso?

—Una vez que tengamos la licencia y Verity se haya casado, podrás seguir con tu vida.

—Mmm —dijo él, mirándola con ojos indolentes. Ella creyó reconocer esa expresión e intentó apartarse, pero él alargó una mano y la detuvo.

—Prometí que no iba a seducirte, Chastity.

—Sí.

—Yo siempre cumplo mi palabra. ¿Me crees?

No podía negarlo.

—Sí.

—Entonces créeme si te digo que este beso es sólo un beso y no un preludio de otra cosa. —Le rozó sutilmente la mejilla con la mano—. Olvida el pasado. Olvídate de todo. Eres una joven dama de alcurnia que se halla cobijada con un truhán, un truhán que se ve impulsado por tus encantos a robarte un beso, pero que no intentará robar nada más. Puedes relajarte y disfrutar. Incluso si después te sientes obligada a abofetearle por ello.

Él se inclinó sobre ella y la besó con delicadeza. Al principio, los labios de Cyn eran tan suaves como el aliento de la muchacha, pero, después, tomaron posesión de ella con una lenta e hipnótica destreza que hizo que fluyera en su interior un cálido deleite. Su mente se disparó vertiginosa, abandonando la gélida realidad.

Cuando él se retiró, ella no pudo menos que sonreírle.

—Besa así a muchas señoritas, milord, y verás qué pronto acabas en el altar.

—A lo mejor es eso lo que quiero. —Le levantó la mano para besarle la palma. Y se quedó helado.

—¿Qué demonios…? —La miró intensamente—. Esto no son raspaduras.

Ella trató de retirar la mano, pero él no le dejó.

—¿Quién te ha apaleado? ¿Tu padre? —Antes de que ella pudiera responder, él le cogió la otra mano para examinarla y luego la soltó.

—¿Por qué? —preguntó él.

Ella nunca hubiera imaginado que él pudiera tener una mirada tan peligrosa. Se apresuró a aplacar su enfado.

—Fui una insolente. Sin duda, tenía derecho a hacer lo que hizo. —La muchacha sonrió irónicamente al acordarse—. Entre otras cosas, le dije que era un asqueroso hipócrita.

Él se relajó un poco, sacudió la cabeza y le alivió las heridas con un liviano beso.

—Un patriarca muy estricto, de eso no hay duda. ¿Cuántos años tienes?

Le parecía raro que no lo supiera.

—Diecinueve.

—Eres demasiado intrépida y audaz para tus diecinueve años, pero yo no te pegaría por eso. ¿No sabe que tiene un tesoro?

Ella se dio cuenta de que Cyn no entendía lo de su padre. Ni siquiera la propia Chastity comprendía cómo su padre había llegado a ser como era, pero sentía que podía llegar a hacerlo si tenía la ocasión de considerar todas las piezas del rompecabezas. Le contestó así:

—Él no cree que una mujer valerosa sea un tesoro. Él quiere que yo sea dulce y mansa como Verity. Deberíamos ponernos en marcha.

Dijo esto último de mala gana y él le respondió de la misma manera. Ninguno de los dos quería abandonar aquel pequeño paraíso que habían encontrado, pero el deber les reclamaba. Cyn la levantó cogiéndola de la mano izquierda. Haciendo un esfuerzo sobrehumano, Chastity no gritó cuando sus entumecidas piernas flaquearon de dolor. Pero él lo notó.

—¿Qué pasa? —le preguntó.

—Sólo que estoy agarrotada —dijo rápidamente—. Estoy toda magullada, desde que me caí sobre aquellos adoquines. No obstante, me muero de hambre. Creo que no he comido nada desde el desayuno de ayer.

—Dios santo, ¿desde entonces? Yo compartí una estupenda cena con Frazer. Entonces, pongámonos en marcha, y lo primero de lo que nos vamos a ocupar será de que comas.

16

Chastity pensaba que no sería capaz de montarse en el caballo, pero él aceptó la historia de las magulladuras y el agarrotamiento y la ayudó a subir. Al notar las punzadas de las contusiones, la piel raspada y las postillas tiernas, se dijo a sí misma que, al distenderse, la cosa mejoraría. Pero no tenía mucha fe en ello.

Cabalgaron lentamente hasta llegar a una aldea llamada Wickford y se detuvieron en el Brown Cow. Era una posada bastante sencilla, con techo de paja bajo, y no una casa de postas, pero el hospedero les aseguró que podía servirles el desayuno en la taberna. Ésta resultó hallarse vacía a aquella temprana hora del día, pero estaba ya caldeada por un llameante fuego. Chastity se acercó reconfortada, se acomodó en un banco y extendió las manos buscando el calor.

Cyn se quedó de pie al otro lado de la chimenea y estudió a la muchacha pensativo.

—Estás al límite de tus fuerzas, ¿no es así?

—Estaré bien cuando haya comido —mintió ella. ¿Qué otra cosa podía decir? Cyn no iba a estar dispuesto a abandonarla. Él no dijo nada, pero Chastity sabía que no la había creído. Y con razón. Se obligó a sentarse derecha—. No podemos rendirnos ahora.

—No, supongo que no. —Cyn Malloren estaba inusitadamente serio, con el ceño fruncido como si contemplara una perspectiva desagradable.

Entró una doncella y puso la mesa para ambos. Al poco, regresó con una barra de pan caliente, mantequilla y un puchero de café. A Chastity le rugieron las tripas.

Cyn se echó a reír.

—Vamos, empieza con esto mientras esperamos que nos traigan el resto.

La hizo sentarse y le cortó una gruesa rebanada de pan, cubriéndola bien con mantequilla. Mientras ella le hincaba el diente, él le sirvió el café.

—¿Nata? ¿Azúcar?

Ella asintió, con la boca llena. Tan pronto como hubo tragado, bebió un poco de café. Éste se deslizó por su interior como si fuera un reconstituyente líquido, mucho más de su gusto que el brandy. Sintió que volvía de nuevo a la vida. Sonrió a Cyn.

Él le devolvió la sonrisa.

Cuán primitiva podía volverse una. En aquellos momentos, el hecho de obsequiarla con comida le hablaba de amor con mayor elocuencia que las joyas o las flores.

Al pensar en el amor, Chastity se puso seria. Dio otro pensativo mordisco al trozo de pan que tenía en la mano. Temía saber cuál era el ingrato deber que Cyn estaba considerando: el de casarse con aquella joven dama con la que se había comprometido inconscientemente al pasar noche en su compañía. Y eso sin saber que ella también era Chloe. La conmovía pensar que su sentido del honor le llevaría a pedirle matrimonio incluso a la infame Chastity Ware, pero no iba a permitir aquel sacrificio.

—Ésta es mi chica.

Ella le lanzó una rápida ojeada. Estaba sentado, estudiándola con la barbilla entre las manos. Tenía los párpados entornados, pero ella presentía la profundidad de la mirada que ocultaban sus pestañas.

Chastity volvió a bajar la vista, más confundida que nunca. Ansió desesperadamente volver a sentirse segura, como en los días que habían sido Cyn y Charles.

Una vez más, pareció que él le leía los pensamientos:

—Me gusta el hecho de que por fin podamos reconocer la verdad —dijo él con suavidad.

Ella mantuvo la vista fija en el pan.

—¿Desde cuándo lo has sabido?

Se produjo una pausa. Luego, él respondió:

—Desde el principio.

Ella le miró sobresaltada:

—¿Qué?

Se dio cuenta de que Cyn le hablaba con pesar y cautela.

—Lo hacías muy bien, pero yo me percaté de... de... la falta de atributos.

Chastity sintió que las mejillas le ardían, pero en esos momentos, la doncella y el posadero entraron apresuradamente con fuentes llenas de huevos, salchichas, jamón y ternera. Les ofrecieron cerveza y sidra, pero ellos rechazaron ambas bebidas. Cuando se marcharon, Chastity seguía sin saber qué decir.

Se sirvió comida y, a pesar del hambre que tenía, se limitó a mirarla.

—¿Por qué no dijiste nada? —inquirió. Quería preguntarle, ¿sabes lo de Chloe?, pero de ese modo, tal vez se delatara.

Él cortó una rodaja de jamón y después dejó el cuchillo y el tenedor en la mesa. Tampoco tenía ganas de comer nada.

—Sentía que necesitabas aquel disfraz, cielo, mucho antes de que conociera tus problemas. No sabía lo que podía ocurrir si te forzaba a reconocer la verdad, pero sospechaba que no sería nada bueno. Al menos, desde mi punto de vista.

Ella levantó bruscamente la vista.

—¿Qué quieres decir con eso?

Los labios de Cyn esbozaron un amago de sonrisa, pero sus ojos seguían vigilantes.

—Quería —necesitaba— conocerte mejor. ¿Qué hubieras hecho si yo te hubiera desafiado el primer día?

Chastity hizo memoria.

—No lo sé. Probablemente te hubiera dejado atado en la cama.

Él sonreía ahora abiertamente.

—Sabía que mi instinto de conservación era sólido. Y a ti te hubieran cogido antes de que acabara ese día.

—Sí.

El hambre le apremió y Chastity empezó a comer, pero su mente se dedicó a repasar el tiempo que habían pasado juntos. Santo cielo, ¿habían sido sólo cinco días? Admitió que Cyn no lo había tenido fácil. Pero luego se acordó de sus bromas, de las ligas, de la galleta de Shrewsbury, de cómo se había burlado del pobre e inocente Charles. De los malditos lazos. Le miró.

Él dio un respingo, pero sus labios dibujaron un mohín.

—Eres un demonio de hombre —le dijo ella con afable intensidad—. Eres… eres.. —El mohín se convirtió en una abierta hueca. ¡Se estaba burlando descaradamente de ella, maldita sea!

Chastity cogió el plato con la tierna mantequilla y se lo arrojó. Aterrizó pringoso sobre su uniforme de ribetes dorados y luego se escurrió. Mientras él permanecía en su asiento, atónito, ella repitió la operación con la barra de pan y el contenido de la jarra de leche.

Él se puso de pie de un salto, chorreando.

—¡Que la peste te lleve, mujer! —Como ella buscará nueva munición, él la apartó de la mesa de un empujón.

—¡Eres un cerdo viperino!

—Serpiente.

Chastity se quedó boquiabierta.

—¿Qué?

—Los cerdos no son viperinos. Las serpientes sí. —Volvía a reírse de ella.

—¡No me lo puedo creer! Me has mentido, me has atormentado, me has hecho pasar por situaciones terribles. —Ella enfatizaba cada punto dándole un golpe en el pegajoso chaleco—. ¡Y ahora pretendes enseñarme a hablar!

Él dejó que le llevara a empellones hasta la mesa, pero no estaba en absoluto arrepentido:

—Tú me secuestraste, me robaste mis pertenencias, me ataste y me amenazaste. Y, en cuanto a lo de atormentar, mi dulce y libertina arpía del infierno, tu podrías dar lecciones.

Chastity sintió que el riego sanguíneo no le llegaba a la cabeza, pero lo único que consiguió decir fue:

—Oh, cielos.

Él avanzó. Ahora le tocaba a ella retroceder.

—Prefiero tomarme esto como un arrebato cariñoso. —La cogió por los hombros—. Los dos somos parecidos,

Chastity Ware. De no haber conocido a Chloe con mi cerebro, la habría conocido con mi cuerpo.

Ella trató de escabullirse, pero él la envolvió con sus brazos.

—Siento haberte hecho daño. —Le levantó la barbilla con delicadeza—. Pero, qué demonios —dijo Cyn, volviendo a sonreír—, todos y cada uno de esos embrollados momentos han merecido la pena.

Ella quiso mirarle con furia, pero el júbilo que vio en los ojos de Cyn le arrancó una gorjeante risa.

—¿Es que nunca te pones serio?

—Si puedo evitarlo, no. —Le depositó un beso en la punta de la nariz. Después, para sorpresa de Chastity, adquirió una expresión grave y añadió—: Pero no soy ningún idiota, ni un cantamañanas. Soy un hombre. Un soldado. Y he visto cosas que espero que tú no tengas que ver nunca.

Frunció el ceño y se quedó dubitativo. Chastity no sabía que ocurría, pero quiso tranquilizarle. Le estrechó un poco más contra sí, esperando que él interpretara correctamente aquel gesto. Debió de hacerlo así, porque él la abrazó a su vez.

—Recuerdo una batalla —dijo solemnemente—. Hacía un tiempo asqueroso. Caían chuzos de punta. Mientras estábamos en acción, se podía soportar, pero cuando caía la noche, estábamos allí al raso, sin tener donde guarecernos. —Bajó la vista para mirarla—. Construimos un refugio a base de cadáveres, nuestros y suyos, y dormimos bien abrigados…

Chastity tragó saliva y trató de no mostrar el horror que sentía.

Él le buscó la mirada.

—Ésa es mi vida. ¿Podrías compartirla?

—¿Dormir rodeada de cadáveres? —preguntó ella, con una voz más bien chillona.

Él soltó una breve carcajada.

—En realidad son más pacíficos que las ratas o las pulgas... Pero no, supongo que no habrá que llegar hasta ese punto. Pero no quiero prometer nada. —Le puso los nudillos bajo la barbilla, para evitar que bajara la vista—. Te estoy pidiendo que te cases conmigo.

—No puedes casarte con Chastity Ware.

—Ya hemos hablado antes de esto. Nadie va a impedirme que haga lo que me parezca.

—¿Qué me dices de Rothgar?

—Ni siquiera él. Soy mayor de edad y mi renta, aunque no es muy grande, está fuera de su control.

—¿Me estás advirtiendo que eres pobre?

Cyn, divertido, tenía los ojos chispeantes.

—Un Malloren arruinado. ¡Que el cielo nos ampare! Tendremos lo suficiente para vivir con comodidad y elegancia, cuando la guerra nos lo permita. Cásate conmigo, amor mío.

—No tienes por qué hacer esto —protestó ella—. Mi reputación ya estaba arruinada antes de conocerte. Mi aspecto es el de un bicho raro...

Los labios de Cyn la hicieron callar, suavemente al principio, ávidos y ardientes después. Ella respondió con tal fuerza que ella misma se sorprendió.

Cuando por fin la dejó libre, su respiración estaba tan agitada como la de ella.

—No eres un bicho raro, Chastity Ware, a menos que eso quiera decir que eres única. Tu pelo, si es que es eso lo que te fastidia, crecerá. A mí me gusta así, pero si lo prefieres, usa la peluca. —Recorrió el perfil de su rostro con la mano—. No es el deber lo que me lleva a pedirte matrimonio. Para mí eres más bella que ninguna otra mujer, incluso sin acicalar. Eres valiente. Eres de ingenio rápido y lengua vivaz. Eres la única mujer que he conocido cuyo espíritu puede igualárseme. —Le cogió la mano y la apretó contra él—. Provocas mi deseo de un modo que me maravilla y me asusta mucho a la vez. ¿Recuerdas aquel primer día?

Al rememorar la sensación que le produjo notar el sexo de Cyn duro bajo sus dedos, Chastity se sintió invadida por multitud de recuerdos que provocaron sus ansias y la enardecieron, pero se acordó de él, atado de pies y manos sobre la cama. Asintió.

—Incluso entonces —dijo él—, mi cuerpo lo sabía. —Distraídamente, ella lo acarició. Él se estremeció. Ella retiró bruscamente la mano y deshizo el abrazo.

—Es simplemente lujuria —dijo ella—. Se pasará.

—No existe tal cosa. Lujuria es una palabra sucia para designar el deseo. Supongo que el tiempo hace desaparecer todas las cosas, pero el deseo que me inspiras tardará mucho en desvanecerse.

—¿Sabes que nos conocemos desde hace muy poco tiempo? —inquirió ella, que luchaba contra sí misma además de contra él.

—A mí me parece que te he conocido toda mi vida —declaró él.

—Hace sólo cinco días —señaló Chastity inflexible.

Él arqueó las cejas.

—Volví a nacer el día que te conocí.

—¿No puedes hablar en serio?

—No —dijo él con un petulante gesto de las manos—. Ya lo he intentado en serio. Está claro que tendré que hablarte en broma para que te cases conmigo.

Ella hizo acopio de fuerzas:

—No voy a casarme contigo.

Él se limitó a encogerse de hombros.

—Ya lo veremos.

Ella sintió ganas de empezar a arrojar cosas otra vez.

Él la vio mirar el bote de la mermelada y se movió para bloquearle el paso.

—¿Vamos a pelearnos del mismo modo en que hacemos el amor, es decir con comida? Se me ocurren unas cuantas variaciones para el tema. La miel, por ejemplo, resultaría mejor que la mantequilla. Bien pegajosa. Para retirarla a lametones haría falta un buen rato…

Una parte de Chastity hubiera querido golpearle en la cabeza con el atizador. Pero otra parte, mucho más poderosa, quería rendirse a aquella dichosa locura para el resto de sus días

—Tú también te has puesto perdida —le indicó él.

Chastity bajó la vista y vio que tenía la ropa embadurnada de mantequilla.

—Pero no estoy mojada —le contestó.

Él se palpó el empapado chaquetón.

—Cierto. Será mejor que me ponga la ropa que llevas puesta. Es hora de que vuelvas a convertirte en mujer.

—No pienso ponerme esas prendas indecentes.

—Por supuesto que no, aunque tal vez te sirvan como ropa interior. Estoy seguro de que podemos comprarte un vestido.

Él acababa de hacer que se moviera el terreno sobre el que pisaban los inseguros pies de la muchacha.

—Pero, se supone que soy un hombre.

—Ya no hay razón para ello. —Sonrió con pasmosa dulzura—. Quiero que viajes conmigo como mujer, cielo. Si de verdad me vas a dar puerta, es lo menos que puedes hacer, darme unas breves horas de verdad antes de que nos separemos.

Unas breves horas de verdad antes de que nos separemos. Era una noción tan dulce que Chastity se rindió.

—¿Cómo cabalgaré?

—A horcajadas, si así lo quieres. Como una mujer de campo. También podemos intentar hacernos con una silla lateral.

Chastity se preguntaba si las faldas le resultarían más cómodas. Después, miró a Cyn a la cara y supo que éste le había vuelto a leer el pensamiento.

Él le cogió la mano derecha con cariño y la estudió. La marca se había atenuado un poco pero seguía estando roja y tierna.

—Es hora de que me cuentes todo lo que te ha pasado, Chastity.

Ella quiso marcharse, pero él no se lo permitió.

—No tiene importancia —dijo la muchacha—. Deberíamos ponernos en camino. Verity y Nathaniel pueden estar esperándonos.

—Sí que tiene importancia. Te hace daño al cabalgar, ¿no?

—Es que no estoy acostumbrada a montar durante tanto tiempo.

—Ni… a hacer el amor. ¿Es eso?

Ella se puso nuevamente colorada y volvió a intentar soltarse.

—¿Por qué me atormentas así? —protestó—. Puedo cabalgar. —Consiguió liberarse y se encaminó hacia la puerta.

Él le bloqueó el paso.

—Me estás mintiendo.

Chastity se exasperó al ver que nunca conseguía engañarle.

—Si quiero mentirte, Cyn Malloren, lo haré.

—Pero no sobre esto.

Estaba tan serio que su expresión resultaba realmente imponente. Chastity se dio la vuelta. No quería hablar. Odiaba el recuerdo de las manos de Lindle sobre ella, de ser azotada como un chiquillo. No pensaba hablar de ello.

Cyn apoyó las manos sobre los hombros de la muchacha, con suavidad, cariñosamente. ¿Cómo era posible que las manos pudieran seguir expresando tantas cosas maravillosas?

—Debes decírmelo —le dijo con ternura—. Todo irá bien, Chastity. Te lo prometo. Confía en mí.

Ella no pudo resistirse a aquella súplica.

—Él me apaleó… en los muslos. No fue mucho, pero duele… Ya debería estar mejor…

Las manos de Cyn se tensaron y luego se distendieron. La hizo darse la vuelta y le escrutó el rostro.

—¿Es ésa la verdad?

—No parece que se me dé muy bien contarte mentiras. —Él se echó a reír y ella se dio cuenta de que lo hacía con alivio—. ¿Qué era lo que habías pensado?

Él sacudió la cabeza.

—No importa.

Cyn se alejaba y ahora le tocó a ella cerrarle el paso.

—Oh, no, tú no vas a ningún sitio. Me has sacado la verdad con presiones, Cyn Malloren y ahora vas a pagar por ello. ¿Qué era lo que creías?

Él la miró a los ojos.

—Creía que tal vez no habías conseguido librarte del burdel.

Ella le observó con asombro.

—Pero…

—Pero ¿qué?

Chastity no quería acabar la frase, mas sabía que él volvería a insistir al punto.

—Pero ayer no me dolía tanto. Así que, ¿por qué habrías de pensar…?

Él sacudió la cabeza, aunque con ternura.

—Eres una inocente, querida. Me alegro. Dejémoslo así.

Él se disponía a regresar a la mesa, pero ella se aferró a su chaquetón.

—Oh, no, de eso nada. Edúcame.

Un luminoso destello recorrió los ojos verde miel de Cyn.

—Ah, ésa es mi intención. Todo llegará, no te preocupes.

Pero Chastity no abandonaba su hueso.

—Dímelo.

Él se rindió.

—Si te hubieran usado en el burdel o te hubieran violado en cualquier otro sitio, estarías dolorida, tal vez incluso desgarrada.

—Desgarrada —dijo ella, con los ojos en blanco.

—Ahora ya ves porque no puedo dejarte a tu suerte en este mundo cruel, amor mío. Eres demasiado inocente. —El beso que le dio hablaba de miedo y de la necesidad de protegerla. Los botones del chaleco de la muchacha cedieron ante los hábiles dedos de Cyn. Sus pechos sintieron la tierna devoción del hombre...

El sonido de un carraspeo hizo que Chastity se apartara de un respingo.

Al darse la vuelta, vieron al posadero en la puerta.

Chastity miró a Cyn horrorizada, pero él sonreía, sin el menor asomo de vergüenza.

—Ah, nos ha descubierto. Es precisamente lo que usted sospecha, buen hombre, somos amantes a la fuga. ¿Será usted comprensivo con las víctimas de Cupido? —Esta pregunta fue gentilmente acompañada de una guinea.

La guinea desapareció y el hospedero asintió, todavía con los ojos fuera de sus órbitas.

Cyn sonrió a Chastity.

—Mi dueña y señora tuvo que ponerse esta estrafalaria vestimenta para escapar de su tiránico padre, pero estaría más cómoda con un vestido. ¿Tiene usted alguno que nos pueda vender? —Le ofreció otra guinea.

El mesonero asintió.

—Sí, milord. Me ocuparé de ello, milord.

—Y una habitación en la que podamos cambiarnos. Como puede ver, he tenido un pequeño percance.

El hombre se fijó en la mantequilla y la leche, y los ojos se le abrieron aún más.

—Desde luego, milord.

—Y en el improbable caso de que alguien haga preguntas sobre nosotros, ahora o más adelante, usted y su gente no nos habrán visto. —Esta última frase no fue acompañada de dinero. El tono bastaba. Muy propio de un Malloren. Decía claramente que volvería cual ángel justiciero si les causaba problemas.

Pronto se hallaron en una alcoba, con agua caliente para lavarse y un cerrado vestido azul para Chastity. Se trataba probablemente del mejor atavío de alguna de las sirvientas, porque tenía algunos volantes y algún tosco bordado, pero estaba bastante gastado.

Cyn lo sostuvo en el aire a la altura de la muchacha.

—Es más o menos tu talla. Pero algún día no muy lejano, amor mío, me gustaría verte lucir tus propias galas. —Sonrió lentamente—. Entonces, querré despojarte de sus sedosas capas, una por una.

Chastity se sonrojó y no pudo evitar echar una traicionera ojeada a la cama.

—Sí —dijo él con suavidad, y empezó a quitarse la ropa.

Durante unos instantes Chastity se preguntó si le habría entendido mal, pero cuando él se desprendió de los calzoncillos, supo que no.

Él se quedó plantado frente a ella, con las manos en las caderas.

—¿Y bien?

—Bien, ¿qué? —preguntó ella, aferrándose al vestido que tenía delante como si fuera un escudo.

—Quiero hacer el amor contigo, abierta y honestamente, a la luz del día. Sin máscaras ni disfraces.

La erección de Cyn daba fe de su deseo, pero él no avanzó en dirección a la muchacha. Ella sabía que si se oponía, la dejaría tranquila.

Pero también sabía que aquélla podía ser su única oportunidad de aparearse sinceramente, y puesto que él ya sabía lo de Chloe...

Era una muestra de debilidad, pero la muchacha no tenía fuerzas para resistirse. Los planes de matrimonio de

Cyn eran imposibles y ella no creía ser capaz de poder vivir en pecado con ningún hombre. Al día siguiente, tendrían que separarse para siempre, pero, en aquellos momentos, ella le deseaba con toda su alma además de con su cuerpo..

Con las manos temblorosas, ella se despojó de la ropa, quedándose con una única prenda, los calzoncillos de Cyn. Un exiguo escudo. Le costaba levantar la vista para mirarle.

Oyó como él exhalaba aire con suavidad.

—¿Sabes? —le dijo Cyn reverentemente—, no hay nada masculino en ti.

Chastity sintió una oleada de ruboroso ardor recorriéndole el cuerpo. No sabía qué hacer.

—Ven a mí, querida, por tu propia voluntad.

Ella le miró entonces y el tierno amor que vio en sus ojos le hizo olvidar sus miedos. Sofocada por la vergüenza, se arrojó en sus brazos. Él la apretó contra sí y Chastity sintió cómo él también se estremecía de la emoción.

—Querida mía —murmuró él—. Cariño mío. Corazón mío. No llores…

Chastity alzó la vista para mirarle.

—¡Duele mucho!

Él, aunque tembloroso, se echó reír.

—Creo que podremos aliviar parte del dolor.

—¡Cyn! —protestó ella.

Él la calló con un beso y la llevó hasta la cama. La depositó allí boca abajo y, cuando ella quiso girarse, la sujetó para que no lo hiciera.

En el silencio que se produjo, ella se mordió el labio. Entonces, las manos y la boca de Cyn le rozaron levemente los cardenales.

—¿Qué clase de hombre es tu padre? —le preguntó él en voz baja.

—Es peligroso. No te enfrentes a él, Cyn.

—Le mataré, si se me presenta la ocasión.

Esta vez, dejó que ella se diera la vuelta. Chastity le miró fijamente.

—No tendrás ocasión. —Pero no estaba segura. Nunca antes había visto a Cyn así. No se había puesto así ni siquiera con aquellos patanes que se habían peleado por ella.

—Yo buscaré la ocasión.

Ella le agarró el rígido brazo.

—No. Déjalo. Él tiene derecho a castigarme.

—No tiene ningún derecho a aterrorizarte.

Chastity respiró profundamente.

—Cyn quiero que me des tu palabra de honor de que no vas a ir a por mi padre de ninguna de las maneras. —Como no vio ninguna señal de debilidad en su rostro, siguió presionándole—. O dejo ahora esta cama y me visto inmediatamente.

Él se apartó ligeramente.

—Venga.

Chastity sintió el frío del abandono.

Él se puso de pie. La dejó.

—Puedo controlar el deseo que siento por ti. Tu padre merece morir, y no sólo por haberte apaleado y haberte dado esas ropas, amenazándote con llevarte a un burdel. Hay algo más detrás de todo esto, ¿no es cierto?

Aquella punzante pregunta la cogió desprevenida y se dio cuenta de que había respondido sin palabras. La determinación de Cyn la asustaba. Tenía miedo de lo que podía ocurrir si se enzarzaba con su padre, pero lo que más le dolía era que se alejara de ella. Parecía que, después de todo, él no la necesitaba tanto como ella a él.

Cyn había cogido los calzoncillos, pero debió volver a leerle el pensamiento, porque los dejó caer, regresó a la cama, se inclinó y la besó.

—Me muero por tus huesos.

Y la dejó.

Ella se incorporó de un salto y le agarró por la cintura.

—Entonces, ámame. Por favor.

Él se dio la vuelta lentamente y la miró. Chastity se estremeció al ver cómo Cyn cedía a la pasión. La besó de una manera tan profundamente envolvente que acabó otra vez sobre la cama sin saber muy bien cómo.

Esta vez, su ardor era tumultuoso, a la vez que delicado. Le mimó con esmero las heridas y realizó todos los movimientos con un cuidado exquisito.

—Todo va bien —le susurró ella—. Todo va bien. No me vas a hacer daño. Ven a mí. Entra.

Chastity veneró el cuerpo de Cyn con el suyo, enroscándose a su alrededor con la ductilidad de una viña, hasta que los cuerpos de ambos parecieron haberse fundido. Las manos y la boca del hombre estaban por todas partes, lo mismo que las de ella. Su unión tenía la dulzura de la llave que entra en la cerradura adecuada: abrió las puertas de un cielo que estaba por encima de los escándalos, del deber, del dolor…

Pero después, inevitablemente, Chastity fue arrojada de nuevo a la sombría realidad. Supo que aquél había sido un momento que formaba parte de una vida que tendría que vivir sin él. Se cubrió los ojos con un brazo y libró una silenciosa batalla contra las lágrimas.

Él seguía acariciándola con la mano derecha.

—Chastity.

La muchacha tuvo que apartar el brazo y mirarle a los ojos, a sus oscuros y serios ojos.

—Tengo que saberlo —dijo él—. La otra noche, tú no eras virgen. ¿Quién ha sido él? ¿Dónde? ¿Cómo?

—¿Cuántos? —añadió ella con amargura.

La mano de Cyn la tranquilizó.

—No, Chastity. Esto no es una acusación. Simplemente, necesito saberlo. Necesito saberlo todo sobre ti.

—¿No me está permitido tener ningún secreto?

Él suavizó la expresión.

—Ya hemos hablado de esto antes, ¿no es cierto? No quiero que haya secretos entre nosotros. Te hablaré de todas mis amantes, si tú me hablas de los tuyos.

Chastity contraatacó su insistencia desde la retaguardia.

—Me sorprende que puedas recordar todas las tuyas.

Él la besó.

—No saques conclusiones tan rápidamente. Nunca he hecho el amor a una mujer frívolamente y no uso los prostíbulos para soldados. En cualquier caso, sospecho que tu historia es importante para desentrañar el misterio que nos ocupa. Cuéntame lo que te ha ocurrido.

Chastity no quería hacerlo por nada del mundo. Sólo serviría para que él se enojara aún más con su padre. Además, se preguntaba cuál sería su reacción al descubrir que Chloe había sido virgen. Más serio que nunca, había prometido pegarla si le engañaba.

Él frunció el ceño ante el silencio de la muchacha.

—¿No confías en mí? Te doy mi palabra de que nada de lo que me digas podrá hacer que mi amor por ti disminuya. Si te hubiera poseído un regimiento entero, seguirías siendo para mí igual de honorable. Confía en mí, Chastity. Por favor.

—Eso es un golpe bajo —murmuró ella, pero empezó a contárselo todo: lo de la proposición de matrimonio de Henry Vernham, la presión constante para que se casara con él, el incidente de la cama, los golpes y también la ruptura forzada de su himen.

La voz se le quebró al ver cómo él se ponía cada vez más furioso.

—Morirá —dijo Cyn—. Y Vernham también.

—¡No! —Chastity se aferró a él—. Déjalo, Cyn. Ya no tiene remedio.

—Encontraré la manera de arreglarlo y vengarlo. —A continuación, controló su ira y le desordenó tiernamente el húmedo pelo—. Pero por ti, Chastity, no por mí. Te amo y mi amor es más grande al saber lo que has tenido que soportar.

Tras estas afectuosas palabras, a Chastity se le escaparon finalmente las lágrimas.

Él la estrechó contra sí.

—No llores, amor, por favor. Ya pasó. Nunca más tendrás miedo ni estarás sola. Te lo prometo, y yo siempre cumplo mi palabra.

A ella le hubiera gustado poder creerle, pero había aprendido a conciencia la dura lección que le había dado la vida. Se apartó bruscamente de él.

—¿Cómo? —quiso saber ella—. Eres un hombre maravilloso, pero eres eso, sólo un hombre. No puedes cambiar el mundo, y mi padre te aplastará.

Los ojos de Cyn centellearon divertidos, como preludio de una amplia sonrisa.

—Querida, ¿has olvidado que soy un Malloren?

Ella se le quedó mirando atónita hasta que él saltó de la cama y la hizo ponerse en pie.

—Vístete, moza —le dijo, y le dio un manotazo en el trasero. Cuando ella se volvió con la mirada llena de furia, declaró—: Eso es por mentirme sobre lo de tu virginidad. Y —añadió con ternura—, para demostrarte que siempre cumplo mi palabra.

Después empezó a vestirse y ella, todavía aturdida, siguió su ejemplo. Se puso la mugrienta camisola rosa, la llamativa enagua y, encima de ambas prendas, el vestido azul. Sin que ella se lo pidiera, él fue a ayudarla con los corchetes de la espalda. Un dulce y espontáneo gesto de intimidad.

Chastity se acercó al pequeño espejo y se puso la peluca. El vestido era más humilde que cualquiera de los que había llevado como lady Chastity Ware, pero era decente, y a su sencilla manera, favorecedor. La peluca hecha con su propio pelo, sus propios rizos ondulados color miel, parecía borrar todo lo ocurrido en los últimos meses. Sonrió con sarcasmo. Como si eso fuera posible.

Cyn se puso tras ella y le colocó las manos en la cintura, acariciándole los costados.

—Sin ballenas —dijo en tono de aprobación.

—No tengo corsé. Si lo tuviera me lo pondría.

—¿Quieres que te prometa que, si alguna vez te veo llevarlo, te lo quitaré?

Ella se dio la vuelta. El bromista incorregible había regresado.

—Idiota. ¿Cómo quieres que lleve un vestido elegante sin corsé o sin peto?

—Ah —dijo él triunfalmente—. Así que empiezas a pensar en hacer vida de sociedad nuevamente, ¿no?

—¡No! ¡Eso es imposible!

—No hay nada imposible.

Chastity no quiso seguir discutiendo. Ya se daría él cuenta muy pronto. En cuanto se encontraran con alguien del mundo distinguido o en cuanto Rothgar se enterara de su relación. Entonces quedaría claro que la alta sociedad nunca volvería a admitir a Chastity Ware en su seno.

—Debemos irnos —dijo ella—. Ya hemos perdido demasiado tiempo.

Él sacó su reloj.

—Según mis cálculos, veinte minutos.

Chastity se le quedó mirando.

—¿Sólo?

—¿Cuánto tiempo crees que lleva esto? —le preguntó él en tono burlón—. Claro que tendremos muchas largas y lánguidas noches de amor, pero piensa en todos los alegres veinte minutos que nos esperan. O acaso periodos más breves.

—Ella vio cómo su expresión cambiaba y se le encendió una alarma interior.

Cyn volvió a abrir el reloj. Luego llevó a Chastity a la cama y la hizo tumbarse. Antes de que ella pudiera reaccionar, él se soltó los pantalones, le levantó a ella las faldas y la penetró.

El cuerpo de la muchacha brincó a causa de la conmoción y el intenso placer.

—¡Cyn!

—¡Delicioso pecado! —dijo él, con los ojos maliciosamente iluminados. La sedujo lentamente, frotándole los pezones con los pulgares. Después, llevó una de las manos más abajo, entre los cuerpos de ambos y la hizo girar. Chastity jadeó y cerró los ojos enfebrecida. Nebulosamente, oyó sus propios gritos y el resuello de Cyn.

Después, él la volvió a poner sobre sus vacilantes pies y abrió el reloj con un golpecito.

—Cuatro minutos. ¿Lo ves?, las oportunidades son infinitas.

Chastity le puso la mano en el hombro para afianzarse en la vertical.

—Estás loco.

—Loco por ti, oh, bomboncito mío. —Le echó la capa de montar por encima de los hombros—. *En avant.*

Chastity bajaba por las escaleras antes de haber tenido tiempo de recomponerse.

Cyn pidió los caballos y pagó la cuenta. Chastity trató de ignorar las miradas curiosas de los sirvientes de la posada, muchos de los cuales parecían tener una excusa para cruzar el recibidor.

La muchacha vio cómo desaparecían unas cuantas guineas más en el bolsillo del mesonero.

—Por vuestra cooperación —dijo Cyn, y añadió afablemente—. Recordad que no me hace gracia que se contraríen mis deseos. —Se dio la vuelta para ofrecerle la mano a Chastity y, después, se volvió hacia atrás—. Por cierto, mi apellido es Malloren. —Lo dijo con un aire que hubiera sido propio del mismo Rothgar. Chastity vio cómo se le abrían los ojos al hospedero.

Mientras salían a la calle, le preguntó a Cyn:

—¿El apellido Malloren provoca miedo por todo el país?

—Lo dudo mucho. Pero aquí sí.

—¿Por qué?

—Estamos a unas diez millas de Rothgar Abbey. —Observó el caballo, que llevaba una silla normal y corriente—. ¿Estás segura de que podrás apañártelas?

Había llegado el momento de la honestidad y ella no tenía ya nada que ocultar.

—Puedo cabalgar, pero no sé hasta dónde. —Utilizó la plataforma para montar y se colocó bien las faldas.

—No tendrás que ir muy lejos. Te voy a llevar con Rothgar.

—¿Qué? No tenemos tiempo para andar dando rodeos, Cyn, y ¿por qué quieres ver a Rothgar? Llevas unos cuantos días evitándole.

—Debo confesarte —dijo él mientras subía a su montura—, que espero que no esté allí, quiero decir en Rothgar Abbey. Allí estarás a salvo. No te necesito para obtener esa licencia. Y me haces ir más despacio.

Dicho así, ¿cómo podía ella contradecirle? Aún y todo, se estremeció al pensar que la iba a presentar a su familia no ya como la infame Chastity Ware, sino como su actual querida. Si llevara una marca hecha con hierro candente, no resultaría más obvio.

Se puso aún más nerviosa cuando se dio cuenta de que aquel plan tampoco hacía feliz a Cyn. Mientras caminaban sobre los caballos por la calle de la aldea, era obvio que él transmitía cierta tensión.

—No tienes que llevarme a tu casa. Puedes dejarme aquí.

—No. En Rothgar Abbey estarás segura. —Tenía el aire de quien ha tomado una resolución. Chastity suspiró y se concentró en guiar al caballo por entre una manada de gansos.

Cuando la calzada se despejó, ella comentó:

—Si estás dispuesto a llevarme donde Rothgar, también podías haber llevado a Verity allí.

—Probablemente debería haberlo hecho.

—¿Por qué no lo hiciste?

Él la miró de soslayo. Ella vio cómo se crispaba un músculo en la mandíbula de Cyn.

—Porque se me habría terminado la diversión, maldita sea.

Chastity se mordió el labio para reprimir una sonrisa. Se daba cuenta de lo mucho que le había costado admitirlo.

—¿Por qué terminar ahora con la diversión? —le dijo en tono ligero—. Déjame aquí.

Él detuvo el caballo y le cogió la mano.

—No, Chastity. Ya se ha acabado el tiempo de las tonterías.

—Habían empezado a gustarme. —Aquel tono de broma no alteró el aire severo de su caballero andante—. Por favor, Cyn —le dijo ella muy seria—. Creo que no puedo soportar ninguna dosis más de realidad en estos momentos.

—¿Qué quieres decir?

¿Acaso era tonto?

—Soy Chastity Ware, y además tu fulana. No puedo presentarme así ante tu familia.

Cogiéndola de la barbilla le hizo volver el rostro hacia él.

—Eres Chastity Ware, mi futura esposa. Si mi familia no te recibe con los brazos abiertos, romperé con ellos para siempre.

—¡Cyn, no!

—Cabalga —replicó él bruscamente y, dando un palmetazo a la grupa de su caballo, reanudó la marcha. Chastity farfulló unas cuantas opiniones escogidas sobre los hombres, pero él la ignoró.

La muchacha no tuvo problemas para seguir aquella marcha constante. El volumen de sus faldas y el tiempo de recuperación habían eliminado la mayor parte del dolor. Sin embargo, nada podía borrar el miedo que sentía ante lo que la esperaba. Se esforzaba en buscar la manera de prevenir aquel nuevo desastre: que Cyn rompiera con su familia por su culpa.

Antes de que ella pudiera salir de su ensimismamiento, Cyn se desvió hacia la verja de un cercado y la abrió. Chastity le siguió con aprensión, pero sólo fueron a parar a un prado.

—Estamos en las tierras de mi familia —dijo él confirmando sus temores—. Pero aún nos quedan unas cuantas millas. ¿Cómo te encuentras?

—Estoy bien. Pero Cyn —dijo ella antes de que él pudiera acelerar de nuevo la marcha—, ¿no podrías dejarme en alguna cabaña o un sitio por el estilo?

—No —dijo él abruptamente y emprendió un trote ligero.

Chastity detuvo su caballo y esperó. Él tiró de las riendas y retrocedió, con la boca rígida y tenso como un arco.

—Si es necesario, te ataré y te acarrearé, Chastity. Verás que estampa tan bonita.

Y parecía dispuesto a hacerlo.

—Está bien, Cyn, iré, pero sólo con una condición.

—¿Cuál?

—Que me prometas no culpar a tu familia por lo que ocurra.

—¿Por qué estás tan segura de que te van a rechazar? Por todos los santos, ninguno de nosotros somos de una pureza sin mácula —exceptuando quizás a mi hermana.

—Estoy segura de que tu hermana es virtuosa. Si está en casa, tendrá que darme la espalda. Hacer otra cosa, sería caer tan bajo como yo.

—¡Diantre! ¡Deja ya de hablar así!

—¡Es la verdad y tú no puedes cambiarla!

—¡Yo puedo hacer lo que me parezca! Si te presento a mi familia como una dama virtuosa, deberían tratarte como tal.

—¡Virtuosa! ¡Soy tu querida!

Él cerro brevemente los ojos.

—No debería haberte tocado, ¿no es cierto? No debería haberte usado como he hecho esta mañana, ni siquiera de broma. He hecho que pierdas el respeto por ti misma.

—¡Cyn, no!

Él, con un gesto de amargura en la boca, dirigió la vista hacia abajo, donde se encontraban sus manos asiendo las riendas.

—Antes de esa noche en Rood House, dijera el mundo lo que dijera, tu sabías que eras pura. Eso te daba la fuerza que he admirado en ti desde el principio. Y yo te la he quitado.

—¿Estás diciendo que ahora soy débil? —Ella había formulado aquella pregunta a modo de desafío, con la esperanza de sacarlo de su zozobra, pero sabía que, en cierto modo, sus palabras eran ciertas.

Él la miró a los ojos.

—Más débil.

—Gracias —dijo ella tajantemente.

—Es la verdad. Me he llevado tu honor.

—Tú no te has llevado nada. He sido yo la que te lo he dado, libre y gozosamente.

—Pero yo tendría que haber esperado hasta que estuviéramos casados.

—Eso supondría esperar eternamente.

—En absoluto —dijo él con calma—. Me propongo volver con una licencia de matrimonio para nosotros, además de la de Verity.

—Eso es imposible —señaló Chastity, no sin cierta fruición—. Soy menor de edad y padre jamás dará su consentimiento.

Cyn hizo un movimiento brusco y su caballo dio un bandazo.

—Al infierno con todo, me había olvidado de eso. Ya encontraremos la manera. —Se encogió de hombros—. Si no, también podemos esperar hasta que seas mayor de edad. ¿Cuándo es eso?

—El próximo abril; falta un año.

—Ya es esperar —comentó él—, pero no para siempre. Pasarás ese tiempo con mi familia.

—¡Oh, Cyn! —protestó ella—. ¡Ahora resulta que no sólo vas a presentarme, sino que quieres que viva con ellos!

—Sí. —Le acarició la mano—. Chastity, ya sé que tus experiencias hacen que te resulte difícil, pero me gustaría que confiaras en mí, sólo por esta vez.

—Confío en ti, pero…

—Mi familia no te va a rechazar. Estoy seguro.

—Ni siquiera tu hermana.

—Ni siquiera Elf. Se inquietará y sospechará que tal vez no estés a mi altura. Pero sospecharía lo mismo de cualquier mujer sobre la faz de la tierra.

—¿Y Rothgar?

—Lo mismo.

Chastity no creía ni media palabra.

—Entonces, ¿por qué te preparas para la batalla?

Él abrió los ojos sorprendido, pero después se echó a reír.

—Una vez te conté un secreto: que todos los soldados tienen miedo antes de la contienda. No me amedrenta la lucha, sólo tengo cierto temor.

—¿De qué?

Él se encogió de hombros incómodo.

—Tal vez temor no sea la palabra adecuada… Es una renuencia natural a echarme atrás. Una vez le dije a Rotghar a la cara que nunca aceptaría nada de él, que construiría mi vida en función de mis propios méritos. Y ahora voy a tener que rectificar.

Lo había explicado con sencillez, pero ella sabía, por la manera en que la mención de su hermano siempre le ponía los nervios a flor de piel, que aquello no era era nada fácil para él. Aquélla era una gran prueba de amor.

—¿Al pedirle que me acoja? —le preguntó ella con delicadeza.

—No —dijo él sorprendido—. Eso lo doy por descontado. Pero yo no me desenvuelvo bien en el mundo de la alta sociedad. Si queremos desenredar tu situación, vamos a necesitar su ayuda.

—¿Qué? Cyn, ni siquiera Rothgar puede blanquear mi sepulcro.

Una mueca característica le iluminó el rostro.

—Olvidas que él es un Malloren. Igual que a mí, no hay nada que le apasione tanto como un reto. Vamos.

Ella se resistía a moverse.

—Aún no me lo has prometido. Si tu familia no me acepta, no debes echarles la culpa.

Él sacudió la cabeza.

—Muy bien, te lo prometo, pero no será necesario. Confía en mí.

17

Aparecieron en uno de los costados de la casa y cabalgaron directamente hacia los establos. Desde aquel ángulo, Rothgar Abbey tenía el aspecto de una sólida construcción isabelina, pero Chastity pudo apreciar que tenía una fachada más palaciega. El terreno era también una mezcla de jardines formales y ornamentales en los alrededores de la mansión y ondulantes campos más allá. Por entre los primeros, andaban majestuosos los pavos reales, mientras que, en las praderas, discretamente separadas por un foso, se veía pastar a los ciervos.

La Abadía irradiaba un aire de orden y prosperidad que hizo que Chastity se sintiera como en su propia casa. No había esperado que el hogar del hombre a quien denominaban el «oscuro marqués» fuera así.

Dejaron los caballos a cargo de un sobresaltado mozo de establo y entraron por una puerta lateral. Cyn estaba visiblemente tenso y Chastity era un manojo de nervios. La muchacha no quería tener que pasar por aquello, pero, ya que parecía inevitable, por lo menos le hubiera gustado tener algo mejor que ponerse que aquella mezcla de prendas de prostituta y criada.

Él pareció notar su desdicha y se detuvo para besarla.

—Confía en mí, Chastity.

¿Qué podía contestar a eso? Reforzó la frágil confianza que tenía en sí misma recordando que, por lo menos, tenía pelo.

Aquella entrada les condujo a un desnudo pasillo entre habitaciones que servían de almacén y tuvieron que recorrer un buen trecho antes de encontrarse con nadie. Una doncella se detuvo sobresaltada al doblar una esquina e hizo una reverencia.

—Bienvenido a casa, milord —dijo, y se apartó de en medio. Incluso en aquella inesperada situación, puso de manifiesto lo bien enseñada que estaba y sólo se permitió desviar la vista levísimamente durante un instante en dirección a Chastity.

—Gracias —dijo Cyn—. ¿Quién está aquí?

—Toda la familia, milord.

Él asintió y ella se retiró apresuradamente.

Eso, pensó la muchacha, quería decir que también estaría su hermana, a la que horrorizaría la idea de hallarse en presencia de Chastity Ware. Y significaba que también estaría Rothgar, quien —ojalá el cielo la asistiera— podía reconocer a la puta de Rood House. Chastity perdió por completo el aplomo.

—Oh, Cyn —susurró ella—. No tienes que hacer esto. Les pondrás en una situación imposible. —Hizo acopio de valor—. No necesitas la ayuda de Rothgar. Seré tu querida. ¡A quién le importa mi reputación!

—Tú reputación te importa a ti, y no vas a ser mi concubina. —La miró fijamente a los ojos—. De hecho, te doy mi palabra, Chastity. No volveré a acostarme contigo hasta que no seas mi esposa. —Antes de que ella pudiera responder, la cogió por la muñeca—. Vamos.

Si no caminaba, la llevaría a rastras.

Fueron a dar súbitamente a un fastuoso recibidor de mármol, con adornos dorados, en el que montaban guardia dos lacayos con librea, quienes, a pesar de su buen oficio, se quedaron pasmados ante su inesperada aparición.

—¿El marqués? —preguntó Cyn.

—En la Sala de los Tapices.

En la pequeña habitación rodeada de tapices, una mujer pelirroja envuelta en delicada seda blanca ocupaba un asiento y el marqués de Rothgar se hallaba de pie junto al fuego. Al abrirse la puerta, ambos se dieron la vuelta.

—¡Cyn! —gritó la mujer y se levantó para echar a correr hacia él—. ¡Qué poca vergüenza tienes, menudo susto que nos has dado!

Cyn dejó libre a Chastity para abrazar y aupar a su hermana. Cualquiera hubiera podido apreciar que eran de la misma sangre. Chastity recordó entonces que eran gemelos. Sin embargo, no se parecían demasiado, porque lady Elf —con quien ella había coincidido una vez en Londres— era pelirroja y tenía los ojos azules.

Cyn soltó a su hermana y cogió la mano de Chastity.

—Elf, ésta es lady Chastity Ware. La he traído para que se quede durante un tiempo. Chastity, ésta es mi hermana, lady Elfled. La familia le llamamos Elf. Creo que no te he explicado de dónde provienen nuestros extraños nombres, ¿no es cierto? A nuestro padre le apasionaba profundamente todo lo anglosajón. Se las arregló para demostrar que nuestro linaje tiene escasa contaminación normanda, al menos él quedó convencido. Y nos puso a todos nosotros nombres de héroes y heroínas anglosajones.

Un crítico poco amable habría dicho que Cyn parloteaba para posponer el momento de la verdad.

Chastity había visto cómo a su hermana se le habían agrandado los ojos al escuchar su nombre y cómo había lanzado una rápida mirada a Rothgar, pero lady Elf recobró rápidamente la compostura:

—Elfled era la Señora de los mercios —dijo—. Una mujer con carácter que, a efectos prácticos, gobernó Inglaterra durante muchos años. Cynric fue tan sólo un rey menor, aceptable. Rothgar lleva sobre sí la carga de llamarse Beowulf. Él fue, desde luego, otro héroe mítico.

Con esta parrafada, evitó tener que dar la bienvenida a Chastity y dirigió toda su atención a Rothgar, quien todavía no se había acercado, sino que continuaba de pie junto al fuego, esperando. Chastity tragó saliva. ¿Era aquello el preludio del rechazo? ¿Qué haría entonces Cyn?

Los ojos de Chastity cruzaron la estancia y se encontraron con los de Rotghar. Él la escrutaba con una expresión completamente ilegible.

Los tres se movieron entonces hacia Rothgar. Beowulf. Ella nunca se había preguntado cuál sería el nombre de pila de aquel hombre. Wolf,[5] desde luego, le pegaba. Se dio cuenta de que, mentalmente al menos, ella también estaba parloteando.

El hermano mayor de Cyn llevaba un rústico chaquetón marrón y unos pantalones de ante, aunque estaba igual de imponente que con los bordados y encajes.

—Rothgar —dijo Cyn en tono reposado—. Creo que ya conoces a lady Chastity. La he traído aquí para que se quede, puesto que va a ser mi esposa.

---

5. *Wolf*, o *wulf*, significa lobo.

Lady Elfled jadeó. Chastity se obligó a mantener la cabeza alta y a mirar a Rothgar a los ojos, fríos y grises, mientras esperaba la explosión. Pero ésta no se produjo. Él se inclinó cortésmente.

—Entonces, será un honor para nosotros tenerla aquí, lady Chastity. ¿Por qué no sienta? A no ser que prefiera que Elf la acompañe directamente a su habitación.

¿Era aquello una indirecta para que le dejara a solas con Cyn y ambos pudieran discutir? Chastity se sentó con firmeza sobre una silla.

—Tal vez le apetezca té, lady Chastity —dijo Elfled nerviosa—. O algún otro refresco.

—No, gracias. —Chastity sabía que debía prestar más atención a la hermana de Cyn, pero estaba totalmente pendiente de lo que ocurría entre él y Rothgar.

—Estamos muy contentos de tenerte en casa —le dijo el marqués a su hermano—. Espero que estés bien.

—Estoy perfectamente, gracias.

—¿Y mi coche? Perdona que te lo mencione, pero he oído algo de unos bandoleros…

—Una simple broma. El coche y Hoskins se encuentran en buen estado, en Winchester.

—Ah, me quitas un peso de encima. Winchester —dijo Rothgar en tono meditativo—. ¿Un repentino interés por las antigüedades?

—Una repentina huida de los malvados —dijo Cyn bruscamente—. Me he visto envuelto en alguna que otra peripecia. De hecho, la aventura no ha terminado y debo ponerme en camino. Sólo quiero que me des tu palabra de que tratarás a Chastity con el respeto que merece mi futura esposa y de que, bajo ninguna circunstancia, la entregarás a su padre.

Rothgar lanzó una críptica mirada a Chastity.

—¿Walgrave? Eso esta hecho. No nos tenemos mucho aprecio.

—¿Y qué me dices de la primera parte? —insistió Cyn.

—Mi querido muchacho —dijo Rothgar cortésmente—, como huésped en mi casa merece todos los respetos, independientemente de cuál sea su futuro.

Una elegante evasiva. Chastity observó cómo la boca de Cyn se contraía al encajar esta respuesta. Sin embargo, contenía la promesa requerida. Cyn se volvió hacia Chastity.

—Aquí estarás a salvo. Volveré tan pronto como pueda, tal vez incluso hoy. —La miró fijamente—. Prométeme que no te irás, pase lo que pase.

Ella no quería que la abandonara allí. Deseaba poder pedirle una vez más que la llevara con él.

—¿Cómo quieres que te prometa que no me marcharé? ¿Y si hay un incendio en la casa?

—Déjate de chistes.

—¿Y eres tú el que me dices eso? —exclamó ella—. ¿Podré por lo menos pasear por los jardines?

—Sólo si vas acompañada.

—Cyn, realmente…

Él se inclinó hacia delante, arrinconándola en su silla.

—Prométemelo —dijo.

Ella se dio cuenta de que se había puesto terriblemente serio.

—Vale. Está bien. Y ahora, ¿querrás ir a por la licencia de Verity?

Cyn, con el rostro trémulo, se mordió el labio. Estaba claro que no había querido mencionar a Verity.

—Ah —dijo Rothgar—. Así que estás metido en ese asunto. Me complace saber que lady Verity y su niño están bien. ¿Están en Winchester, acaso?

—No —dijo Cyn con frialdad—. Espero que a estas alturas se encuentren en Long Knotwell esperando una licencia de matrimonio.

Rothgar aceptó aquello sin pestañear.

—¿Necesitas ayuda para conseguirla?

—No, gracias. —Pero Cyn dudó, mientras se armaba de valor.

Chastity pensó que el ambiente estaba tan cargado que podía cortarse con un cuchillo. Aquél no era el mejor momento para pedirle a Rothgar que los ayudara en su causa perdida. La muchacha se puso de pie.

—Cyn, márchate ya, por favor. Una vez que Verity esté a salvo ya habrá tiempo para otras cosas.

Él la cogió por los hombros, la llevó hacia sí y le dio un rápido y tórrido beso, de lo más indecoroso. Chastity se quedó turbada y sin aplomo para mirar a su anfitrión a la cara.

Cyn se dirigió a la puerta. Ésta se abrió para dar paso a otro hombre, tan alto como Rothgar, tan vivaz como lady Elfled. Otro Malloren. Lord Brand, pensó Chastity.

—¡Saludos, hermanito! Por fin a salvo en el nido.

—No por mucho tiempo —dijo Cyn con brusquedad pero sin aspereza.

El recién llegado parecía intrigado. Rothgar dijo:

—Creo que lo más prudente será que Brand te acompañe, Cyn —para tratarse de Rothgar, el tono era de lo más comedido.

Cyn se giró.

—¡Maldita sea, sé ir hasta Londres sin necesidad de que venga conmigo una niñera!

—Eso creo yo también. Pero los viajes son siempre azarosos, las carreteras están plagadas de indeseables y tu misión parece importante. Un compañero podría resultarte útil y no va a hacer que vayas más lento.

Se produjo un largo y pesado silencio. Después, Cyn indicó:

—De acuerdo. Si a Brand no le importa. —Por el modo en que lo dijo, parecía que estuviera dando su consentimiento para una amputación.

—Nada podría complacerme más —dijo Brand secamente—. Y aquí me tienes, vestido para montar. Voy a buscar la capa y nos vamos.

Dicho esto, salió de la estancia. Cyn tomó aire de manera ostensible y volvió a acercarse a su hermano.

—Voy a ver al obispo de Londres, con la declaración jurada del novio. Si me escribes una nota, el tío Cuthbert se quedará mas conforme.

Era una sencilla petición, pero Cyn le había dicho que había jurado no aceptar ayuda de Rothgar, lo que, a todas luces, era cierto. La cara de lady Elfled, e incluso la de Rothgar, le decían a Chastity que aquél era un momento muy importante.

—¿No hay ningún impedimento para que se celebre ese matrimonio? —preguntó Rothgar con calma.

Cyn miró a Chastity.

—Que yo sepa no.

Chastity dijo:

—Absolutamente ninguno, excepto la oposición de mi padre. Como Verity es mayor de edad, legalmente eso no constituye ningún obstáculo.

Rothgar se llegó hasta un escritorio, garabateó algunas palabras en una hoja de papel, espolvoreó arenilla y, tras sellarla, se la entregó a Cyn.

—¿Vas a llevar la licencia directamente a Long Knotwell?

—Ésa es mi intención.

—Entonces, tal vez convenga que nos reunamos allí contigo. Lady Chastity querrá asistir a la boda de su hermana y, además, no estará de más contar con testigos influyentes.

Cyn miró ceñudo a Chastity.

—Ella está cansada…

—Estoy perfectamente —dijo Chastity rápidamente—. Quiero estar allí y asegurarme de que todo sale bien.

—En un carruaje —le dijo Cyn con firmeza a su hermano.

—Por supuestísimo. Desgraciadamente, tendrá que ser en mi segundo mejor coche.

Cyn dejó escapar una breve carcajada.

—Será suficiente. Y, como pretendo casarme con Chastity tan pronto como sea posible, te estaría muy agradecido si pensaras en cómo podemos restaurar su reputación y obtener la aprobación de su padre para el enlace.

Brand, que regresaba en esos momentos, alcanzó a escuchar la petición y murmuró:

—¡Cielos!

Incluso a Rothgar parecían faltarle las palabras. Pero finalmente dijo:

—Será un placer para mí. —Detrás de las palabras, parecía haber muchos mensajes implícitos.

Cyn se limitó a inclinar la cabeza, y él y Brand se marcharon.

Chastity se quedó con el marqués y lady Elfled.

Rothgar volvió a observar a Chastity. No era una mirada particularmente desagradable, sin embargo, a la muchacha le dieron ganas de escabullirse. Cyn tenía razón. Aquel momento resultaría mucho más fácil si ella supiera, en el fondo de su corazón, que era pura.

—Tenemos mucho que hacer —dijo él al fin—. Pero sospecho que las ha pasado usted canutas, lady Chastity. ¿Por qué no deja que Elf la mime un poco, mientras yo empiezo a mover algunos hilos?

—No es necesario todo esto, milord —dijo Chastity serenamente—. Sé que este matrimonio es imposible y Cyn acabará también por comprenderlo.

Las cejas de Rotghar se alzaron de súbito.

—¡Querida mía! Tratándose de un Malloren, todo es posible. —Con esa muestra de arrogante sacrilegio, salió de la estancia.

—Oh, querida —dijo lady Elfled.

Chastity tragó saliva.

—Lo siento. No era mi intención provocar esto.

Al punto, lady Elfled se sentó junto a ella en el asiento.

—Por favor, no se disguste, lady Chastity. No es usted la causante de mi inquietud. Somos nosotros, los Malloren. Parece que no podemos hacer nada sin complicarnos… Pero usted ha roto el hielo entre Cyn y Rotghar. Es usted una bendición y no una desdicha.

Chastity pensó que aquel halago era un tanto exagerado.

—Estoy segura de que ambos pueden solucionar sus malentendidos sin mi ayuda.

—Eso parece lo lógico, pero lo cierto es que, en los últimos seis años no lo han conseguido.

Chastity la miró con asombro.

—¿Llevan seis años sin hablarse?

Lady Elfled suspiró.

—No exactamente sin hablarse. Cyn ha venido a casa de permiso porque no sería capaz de dejar de verme a mí, y apenas han discutido. Pero ha habido barreras. Cyn no ha querido nunca aceptar ayuda. Yo no estuve presente, pero tengo entendido que cuando Rotghar impidió a Cyn que se alistara en el ejército, le dio a entender que dudaba de su capacidad para subsistir por sí mismo.

—Vaya tontería —declaró Chastity—. Por parte del marqués, quiero decir. Cyn sabe apañárselas de sobra.

—¿A que sí? —dijo lady Elfled llena de radiante orgullo—. Pero, de verdad, nadie lo hubiera dicho cuando era más joven. Los dos andábamos siempre en algún que otro apuro. Hace años que Rotghar ha aceptado la verdad y está muy orgulloso de él. Pero, ya sabe cómo son la mayoría de los hombres. Una vez que toman estas posiciones, parece que estuvieran a ambos lados de un golfo y no pudieran cruzarlo. Usted, querida, es ese puente que tanto estaban necesitando.

Lady Elfled Malloren era absolutamente encantadora, y el recibimiento que brindaba a Chastity parecía auténtico. Chastity se preguntó cómo era que una mujer tan bella y amable no se había casado a sus veinticuatro años. Era cierto que Cyn era más guapo —sus rasgos estaban más acabados—, pero con aquel pelo entre rojo y dorado y aquella tez clara, lady Elfled no estaba nada mal, y su porte era delicado y resuelto.

Chastity decidió infundir sosiego en la mente de la muchacha.

—Estoy encantada de ser un puente, milady, y no pienso crear un nuevo abismo. Antes hablaba en serio. No me voy a casar con Cyn.

—¿Le ha dicho usted eso a él?

—Sí.

—¿Y qué respondió?

—No quiso aceptarlo, pero lo hará, cuando se dé cuenta de lo imposible que es.

Lady Elfled se echó a reír.

—Querida mía, tiene usted que aprender muchas cosas de los Malloren. Rotghar no conoce el significado de la palabra imposible, y Cyn nunca desiste de sus propósitos. Por eso mismo, llegaron a ese punto crítico. Y ahora, puesto que vamos a ser hermanas, debes llamarme Elf, si no lo encuentras demasiado ridículo, y tratarme de tú. Y yo te llamaré Chastity.

No tenía sentido discutir sobre aquello, así que Chastity se mostró de acuerdo.

—Bien. Me alegro mucho de que estés aquí. No tienes idea de lo aburrido que puede ser estar rodeada de hermanos varones. Los hombres no tienen verdadera sensibilidad.

La expresión de Chastity debió exhibir alguna señal de protesta, porque Elf añadió con una sonrisa.

—¿Vas a decirme que Cyn es todo sensibilidad? Debe ser el poder del amor, porque yo no me había dado cuenta antes. Bien —dijo bruscamente—. Voy a comportarme como una hermana y decirte que me parece que seguro que lo que más te apetece es darte un baño y ponerte ropa más adecuada.

Chastity se sonrojó al pensar en cómo debía oler y el aspecto que debía tener, pero no podía ofenderse por una oferta tan deliciosa.

—Sí, me encantaría.

—Entonces, vamos.

Lady Elfled dio algunas órdenes y condujo a Chastity a su propia habitación, que contaba con un acogedor fuego.

—Creo que somos de la misma talla —le dijo su anfitriona, y con la mano señaló una serie de armarios—. Escoge lo que más te guste. —Entró una doncella y Elf se dirigió a ella—: Ah, Chantal, ayuda a lady Chastity. ¿Te importa si me quedo? —le preguntó a continuación a Chastity.

Chastity recordó los verdugones, los cardenales y los rojos pezones.

—Preferiría bañarme en privado.

Era una petición extraña, tratándose de una mujer que se crió con sirvientes. Chastity vio cómo los ojos de Elf daban muestra de haberse percatado de ello, pero nadie dijo nada.

Aparecieron dos criadas más, portando la bandeja del té y fuentes con carne fría, queso, panecillos y pasteles. Las dos damas se dedicaron a picotear mientras Chantal les mostraba ropa, buscando su aprobación.

—Si vas a viajar para asistir a la boda —dijo Elf—, necesitarás algo elegante pero no demasiado frágil. ¿Qué colores te gustan más?

A pesar de haber decidido no retener a Cyn, al ver tal cantidad de prendas hermosas, Chastity sintió deseos de aparecer ante él siendo ella misma: la bella Chastity Ware.

—Mi color favorito ha sido siempre el rosa fuerte —dijo la muchacha—, pero no creo …

Elf batió las palmas.

—¡Chantal! *¡La langue de la reine!* —La doncella se dirigió a otro armario y Elf le dijo a Chastity—. Hace un año, ese color hacía furor, pero a mi pelo le va fatal.

Chantal extendió un precioso vestido sobre la cama. Era de seda color frambuesa, con bordados en un tono más pálido, y llevaba ribetes con volantes alrededor de la abierta falda. De un cajón, salió una enagua color hueso con bordados rosáceos y un peto con un brocado a un juego y perlitas.

—Cielos —suspiró Elf— cada vez que lo veo me enamoro de él... Pero cógelo—añadió rápidamente—. Me estarás haciendo un favor. ¡Chantal te besará los pies!

—Desde luego, milady —dijo la doncella con una risita—. Una o dos veces al mes, lady Elfled pide que le saquen este vestido y yo sufro lo indecible hasta que decide no ponérselo.

Era obvio que aquel color no le sentaría nada bien a Elf, pelirroja y de piel clara, así que Chastity estuvo felizmente de acuerdo.

La doncella sacó también ropa interior de seda y enseguida les anunciaron que el baño estaba listo en el cuarto de vestir.

Chastity cogió las medias y la camisola y se fue a asearse ella sola, consciente de estar haciendo algo chocante.

Una vez que estuvo desnuda se contempló el cuerpo con claridad. No era de extrañar que Cyn se hubiera enfadado. Tenía más rasguños y moretones de los que creía. Los verdugones de los muslos estaban colorados; en los brazos tenía marcas oscuras de dedos; y tenía un feo chichón en la sien, allí donde Pog la había golpeado cuando la tiró al suelo.

Y además los pezones. ¿Le habría supuesto mucho esfuerzo a Cyn no referirse a ellos al hacer el amor en la posada?

Durante unos instantes, sintió ganas de esconderse en algún agujero, pero luego se acordó de que Cyn nunca la había visto hermosa. Se encargaría de que así fuera. Sólo por esta vez.

Se hundió en la bañera de hojalata pintada con un suspiro de satisfacción. El agua, a la que se había añadido un delicado aceite perfumado, tenía la temperatura perfecta. En un aparador contiguo, había paños y fino jabón. Aquélla era la vida para la que había sido educada.

Se lavó cada pulgada de su cuerpo, después se quitó la peluca y se enjabonó el cabello. Su horripilante poda resultaba práctica en aquellos momentos. Se lo secó con una toalla y se relajó un rato en la bañera.

Trató de encarar el triste futuro que le esperaba. Ahora, ni siquiera tendría acceso a Nana. Su padre la desterraría por completo y ella no podría recurrir a Cyn. Tendría que cuidar de sí misma.

Aquella idea le causaba pavor.

Tal vez pudiera convertirse en actriz… Aunque no poseía ningún talento especial en aquel sentido. Además, de la mayoría de ellas, se decía que eran rameras. Si ella no tenía cuajo para ser la fulana de Cyn, difícilmente podría ser la fulana de ningún otro hombre.

Recordó lo que Cyn le acababa de pedir a Rotghar, que reparara su reputación y obtuviera el consentimiento de su padre. Ojalá… Pero la reacción de todos los presentes había dejado bien claro que aquello era un sueño imposible.

Salió de la bañera por no empezar a llorar. Se secó, cepilló la peluca y se la puso. Dejó caer la camisola de seda por encima de sus hombros, y ésta se deslizó hasta sus pantorrillas. Aquélla era una prenda más apropiada que la que su padre le había proporcionado o la que encontrara en Rood House. Era delicada pero opaca. Ocultaba la mayor parte de sus heridas. Tenía un bello ribete, bordado también en blanco, en los bajos y en el cuello, y en los codos llevaba un primoroso encaje de seda.

Chastity se sentía hermosa por el simple hecho de llevarla puesta.

Se puso con delicadeza las blancas medias de seda, adornadas con capullos de rosa, y se ajustó las ligas rosadas, sonriendo con tristeza al acordarse de las que Cyn había comprado en Shaftesbury. Tal vez pudiera rescatarlas, si es que Verity aún las conservaba, y atesorarlas hasta su solitaria vejez.

Volvió a ella aquel cosquilleante temor. ¿Y si estaba embarazada? No permitiría que esto la hiciera dudar. Tenía que encontrar la manera de devolverle a Cyn la libertad. Ya se ocuparía de los demás problemas a su debido momento.

Cuando regresó al dormitorio, lady Elfled le dedicó una sonrisa:

—Vístete. Tengo muchas ganas de ver cómo te queda el vestido. Seguramente a la perfección.

Chantal ayudó a Chastity a colocarse el armazón de los aros, que sostendría las livianas faldas sin necesidad de voluminosas enaguas. La combinación de seda blanca que se puso encima era ligerísima. Y el peto bordado le rodeaba reconfortantemente el torso y los pechos.

Chastity observaba en el espejo cómo las diferentes capas iban realizando una mágica alquimia sobre su aspecto. Su ánimo se elevó. Era como una armadura, una frágil armadura de gasa, pero armadura al fin y al cabo. Dentro de ella, se sentía muy mujer y con poderío.

—Tienes una figura estupenda —le dijo Elf con sincera franqueza—. Tu cintura es más esbelta que la mía. Para conseguir ese mismo efecto, yo tendría que estar sin resuello.

Cuando Chantal acabó de atarle los lazos del corpiño, sostuvo el vestido en alto y Chastity metió los brazos en las mangas. La doncella abrochó la parte frontal y, con aquel roce de seda sobre seda, el atuendo estuvo completo.

—*Parfait* —opinó Chantal.

—Desde luego —dijo Elf—. Ese color te favorece muchísimo.

Chastity sonrió a la imagen del espejo. El rosa oscuro hacía aflorar el color de sus mejillas y labios; el bello corte del jubón realzaba la curvatura de sus senos sin el menor asomo de indecencia; la opaca seda de la camisola cubría esa curvatura con un suave y tentador velo.

Se movió, sintiendo cómo se balanceaban las livianas faldas de seda, que sostenidas por los aros alcanzaban una envergadura de casi dos metros. Se dio una vuelta y se agachó haciendo una gentil reverencia, riéndose, encantada de ser mujer.

Elf le cogió las manos para levantarla.

—Ch —le dijo—. ¡Cómo me gustaría tener lo que tú tienes!

—¿Qué es lo que tengo?

—Poder sobre los hombres.

Chastity sintió que le ardía el rostro.

—Yo no… Y si lo tengo, no me ha servido de mucho.

—¿No? —preguntó Elf con cierta tristeza—. Pero tienes a Cyn, que está dispuesto a luchar contra los dragones por ti.

Chastity no comprendía el anhelo que veía en los ojos de la otra mujer. Lady Elfled Malloren, con su clase, su dote, su aspecto y su carácter dulce, tenía que haber atraído la atención de muchos hombres.

—Estoy segura de que cualquier hombre estaría dispuesto a pelearse con dragones también por ti, Elf.

—Tal vez —dijo Elf, aunque con un suspiro—. Vamos —dijo bruscamente, antes de que Chastity pudiera añadir nada más—, quiero que Chantal te aplique un poco de maquillaje para ocultar ese hematoma, y después iremos a ver qué es lo que ha planeado mi augusto hermano.

Chastity se sentó obediente, para que la doncella pudiera trabajar.

—No me gusta llevar demasiada pintura —le dijo a la chica.

—*Bien sûr que non* —le respondió ella—. Después de todo, esto es para llevar en el campo: un poco de crema para cubrir el *meurtrissure*, y un poco de colorete para las mejillas y los labios…

Cuando la habilidosa doncella terminó, el cardenal apenas se notaba, y el aspecto de Chastity se vio sutilmente realzado. Chastity sonrió.

—Eres un genio, Chantal.

—*Bien entendu* —dijo la doncella en tono complaciente—. Voy a elegir otras prendas para usted, milady. —Y con una maliciosa sonrisa añadió—: Puede estar segura de que se trata de cosas que lady Elf jamás se pondría.

—Monstruo repugnante —dijo Elf, sin rencor—. Aunque hay que reconocer que tiene razón. Eliminando la tentación me estarás haciendo un favor. Chantal, deshazte de esta ropa vieja.

La doncella recogió las vestiduras que Chastity se había quitado. Acto seguido, dio un pequeño grito.

—¡Me he pinchado!

Antes de que Chastity pudiera decir nada, ya había sacado el alfiler con la perla.

—¿Es esto suyo, milady?

A Chastity se le pasó por la cabeza negarlo, pero se dio cuenta que Elf, que tenía los ojos muy abiertos, lo había reconocido.

—Sí —dijo la muchacha y lo cogió, harta ya de engaños y mentiras. Se lo prendió en la parte delantera del peto y después miró a Elf, que se había puesto muy pálida.

—Rothgar no es mi amante —le dijo.

—Oh —murmuró Elf—. Mejor. Realmente, no sé que pasaría si dos de mis hermanos se pelearan por la misma mujer… ¿Estás lista para bajar?

Chastity volvió a mirarse en el espejo y, a pesar de su aspecto, tembló ante la perspectiva de encarar a Rotghar. Necesitaba un arma.

—Creo que…, de veras creo que me hace falta un abanico.

Al instante, tuvo uno en sus manos, hecho en pergamino pintado de color crema.

Encontraron a Rotghar en la Sala de los Tapices. Estaba mirando el fuego pensativo, pero al oírlas llegar se dio la vuelta. La admiración que Chastity percibió en su rostro era genuina: el hombre le hizo una profunda reverencia.

—Lady Chastity, ya me explico que mi hermano esté *ensorcelé*.

Chastity hizo una genuflexión aún más pronunciada. Abrió el abanico con un chasquido y le miró desde detrás de su protección.

—Tu hermano, Rotghar, nunca me ha visto así.

Él la levantó.

—Entonces, me alegro por él todavía más. —Rothgar vio el alfiler pero no dio ninguna muestra de sorpresa. Ella dedujo que él ya había caído en la cuenta de que Chastity era la mujer a medio vestir que se había encontrado en las escaleras de Rood House. Pero ¿desde cuándo lo sabía?

Elf miraba con ansiedad lo que ocurría entre los dos, hasta que Rotghar le dedicó una cálida y sincera sonrisa, que decía mucho acerca de lo que sentía hacia su familia.

—Si ese vestido estaba en tu armario, querida, es de mucho agradecer que haya venido lady Chastity para librarte de él.

—Eres un hombre horrible. A algunas pelirrojas no les sienta mal el rosa.

—Sí, a algunas, pero no es tu caso. Y menos ese tono, diría yo. —Hizo que las dos mujeres se sentaran—. Me parece que podemos suponer que Cyn entregará hoy la licencia en Long Knotwell. Creo que el carruaje nos puede llevar hasta allí en hora y media. Tal vez debiéramos partir dentro de una hora. Si es preciso quedarse a pasar la noche, habrá sin duda algún lugar en el que podamos alojarnos.

—¿Yo también tengo que ir?

—Desde luego. Yo debo ir a escoltar a Chastity, y tú tendrás que venir de carabina.

La mirada de Elf voló hacia el alfiler. Rotghar suspiró.

—No pienses semejante bajeza, querida. Lady Chastity no hizo nada impropio para conseguir esa fruslería. —Sus ojos estaban llenos de ironía cuando le dijo a Chastity—: Sin embargo, puede que quieras considerar si quieres explicárselo a Cyn o no.

—Para mí se han terminado los subterfugios —dijo ella con evidente frialdad.

—Excelente. —A Chastity le pareció que aquella palabra estaba cargada de significado—. Elf, querida, tal vez puedas preparar algunas cosas más para nuestra invitada, por si tenemos que pasar allí la noche. Si su hermana tampoco dispone de ropa buena, seguramente apreciará que sacrifiques alguna otra prenda de tu guardarropa, en especial algo adecuado para su boda.

La generosa Elf se levantó inmediatamente.

—Desde luego. —En la puerta, dudó unos instantes y añadió arqueando las cejas—: Creía que iba a hacer de carabina, hermano querido.

Rotghar le brindó una sonrisa.

—Te aseguro que no acostumbro a forzar a las prometidas de mis hermanos.

—Ninguno de tus hermanos ha estado prometido hasta ahora —señaló ella.

—Incluso en ese caso.

Tras sacudir la cabeza, Elf se marchó.

Chastity se quitó el alfiler y se lo ofreció a Rotghar.

—Aquí tiene, milord. Será mejor que se lo devuelva. Y no es por Cyn, sino porque yo no lo quiero

Él no hizo ademán de cogerlo.

—Pero ahí queda muy bien. Además, tú te lo ganaste.

Como él no lo quiso tomar, ella lo dejó caer sobre la alfombra.

Él ignoró el valioso objeto y observó detenidamente a Chastity.

—Cuando nos besamos en Londres, me pareciste intrigante —dijo él, haciéndola desplegar nuevamente el abanico a causa del sobresalto—. Veo que mi instinto, una vez más, no me ha fallado.

El corazón de Chastity empezó a palpitar con agitación. Santo Dios, no más complicaciones. Se dio aire de la apresurada manera que advertía a un hombre que el tema de conversación no le gustaba.

—¿Estás queriendo decirme que me amas?

—Oh, no —dijo él con calma, observándola con aquellos fríos ojos grises—. Si te amara, nada de esto habría ocurrido, ¿no crees? Pero me interesaste...

A Chastity le pareció que aquello era un duelo dialéctico y tuvo la sospecha de que su rival era sensiblemente superior. Cerró el abanico de golpe, y ensayó una briosa y despiadada maniobra.

—Yo estaba con Cyn en Rood House.

—Por supuesto —replicó él con indolencia.

Ella intentó una nueva y atrevida estocada:

—Pienso casarme con él.

—Por supuesto —volvió a decir él, cual diestro espadachín que jugara con una novata.

—¿Por qué dices «por supuesto»? —inquirió ella.

—Porque si no lo hicieras —señaló él—, tendrían razón los que te tachan de furcia.

Aquel golpe había ido directamente al corazón.

—Tal vez lo sea —susurró ella.

—Yo no podría dejar que mi hermano se casara con una mujer así.

Chastity sintió que la abandonaba la esperanza, la esperanza de que ocurriera algo que ella había decidido negarse a sí misma, pero a lo que, de todos modos, se había aferrado. Levantó la barbilla para encarar a Rotghar.

—Puede que no seas capaz de detenerlo.

Ella supuso que él se mofaría de semejante desafío, pero, en cambio, lo que hizo fue abandonar la contienda y quedarse mirando el fuego pensativo.

—Tienes mucha razón. Además, yo no me atrevería a oponerme a sus planes otra vez.

Aquello tenía pinta, por increíble que pareciera, de ser la admisión de su derrota. Chastity se dio cuenta de que, de modo completamente inconsciente, se había llevado el abanico abierto frente a los ojos, en señal de simpatía.

—¿Por qué no? —preguntó la muchacha.

—Tengo cierta tendencia al despotismo —dijo él sencillamente. Es lo mismo que decir que un lobo tiene los dientes afilados, pensó Chastity—. Cuando Cyn quiso alistarse como soldado, no me pareció conveniente. No había cumplido aún los dieciocho años y parecía todavía más joven. Yo no creía que por su cabeza hubiera cruzado jamás ningún pensamiento serio. Por otra parte, yo le había sacado de un montón de apuros que podían haber tenido consecuencias graves. El ejército castiga duramente la indisciplina, incluso si ésta proviene de sus oficiales…

Él la miró directamente y el abanico no le sirvió de protección.

—Por supuesto, no habrás visto nunca ningún azotamiento.

Chastity sacudió la cabeza.

—Los hombres reciben azotes incluso por extraviar partes del equipo. Cincuenta latigazos, tal vez. Los oficiales están por lo general libres de ese castigo. Aunque, desde luego, se les puede pegar un tiro. Seguramente recordarás la ejecución del almirante Byng, cuyo crimen fue no aplicar-se lo suficiente en la liberación de Menorca. Como Monsieur Voltaire dijo muy sucintamente, le dispararon «*pour encourager les autres*».

Chastity cerró el abanico y lo dejó caer.

—Me equivoqué al juzgar a Cyn, desde luego —dijo Rotghar contemplativamente—. Era el aburrimiento lo que le hacía meterse en líos. Él ha ordenado y supervisado un buen número de azotamientos y, al menos, dos ahorcamientos. —La miró—. No estoy diciendo que sea tan duro como sufrir el castigo, pero, como magistrado que soy, sé que no es fácil.

Chastity trató de imaginarse a Cyn en una situación así, pero no pudo. ¿Su simpático y despreocupado amante era capaz de semejante crueldad? Entonces recordó la improvisada historia del refugio hecho de cadáveres. Había sido una advertencia deliberada. ¿Acaso le conocía? ¿Cómo podía pretender eso en menos de una semana llena de embrollos?

—¿Por qué me estás contando esto? —preguntó ella. Y era una súplica para que no continuara.

—Para contestar a tu pregunta. Querías saber por qué yo no volvería a oponerme a Cyn. Cuando me negué a concertar su entrada en toda regla en el ejército, él se escapó y se alistó como soldado raso. Le rescaté de allí, por supuesto, y le traje a casa. Pero estaba claro que sólo podría retenerle usando cadenas. Tuve que ceder, pero las prolongadas consecuencias de mis desencaminadas objeciones han sido graves.

—¿Qué quieres decir? Él parece feliz con la vida que lleva.

—En cierto modo. Pero yo erigí ciertas barreras entre él y su familia y, por el mero hecho de interferir, he impedido que se tome las cosas con naturalidad. De hecho, casi le mato.

—No. Tú no has tenido la culpa de su enfermedad.

—No lo tengo muy claro. Él no quería admitir su estado. —Los labios de Rotghar se crisparon formando una mueca irónica—. Yo no he dejado de entrometerme y estoy al corriente de lo que hace. Otro hombre hubiera reconocido que estaba enfermo y hubiera buscado ayuda. Cyn, sin embargo, siente que debe demostrar constantemente su autosuficiencia.

Chastity no sabía que decir. Intuía que Rothgar estaba en lo cierto. Además sabía que al poderoso marqués le había costado mucho ser tan honesto con ella; Chastity no podía ser menos.

—No pienso casarme con él —le dijo.

—¿No? Permíteme que insista.

Chastity le miró con asombro.

—¿Cómo dices?

—Al margen de sus deseos, que son importantes para mí, recuerdo Rood House. Si no te casas con él, es que eres como te han pintado. Me niego a creer que me he equivocado tanto al juzgarte.

Chastity se puso de pie de un salto.

—¡A la porra con tus juicios! ¿Es que mis deseos no cuentan para nada?

Ella casi había esperado recibir un bofetón —como ocurriera con Fort—, pero Rotghar se limitó a levantar una ceja.

—¿Estás diciendo que no quieres casarte con él?

—Sí.

—Que la pasión que habéis compartido era simplemente vulgar lujuria.

Chastity sintió que le ardía el rostro. Quería decir sí y privarle de su victoria, pero no le salían las palabras. Aquello equivalía a una respuesta negativa.

Él la cogió por los hombros. Chastity retrocedió, pero él le dijo:

—Tranquila, querida. Mis intenciones por una vez son honorables y benignas. No puedes negar a Cyn el derecho a casarse contigo lo mismo que yo no debí oponerme a que eligiera su camino en la vida. Si lo intentas, te arriesgas a empujarle hacia el desastre, igual que yo estuve a punto de hacer.

—No puede existir mayor desastre para él que el matrimonio conmigo.

Los labios de Rotghar dibujaron una sonrisa.

—Tiene que haber una manera de solucionar las cosas. Y estoy seguro de que él la encontrará.

Derrotada, Chastity se inclinó hacia delante, apoyándose sobre su hombro. Para su consternación, empezó a llorar. Ya no podía más con toda aquella desesperación. Aparte de Cyn, quien además de un apoyo era parte del problema, aquél era el primer hombre fuerte que se le ofrecía desde que Henry Vernham se metiera a hurtadillas en su cama. Rotghar no dijo nada, pero la rodeaba con brazos firmes. Su misma lejanía era parte de su poder tranquilizador.

Cuando ella pudo controlar las lágrimas, él la hizo sentarse en una butaca y le ofreció un pañuelo.

—Lord Rotghar —dijo Chastity sonándose la nariz—, no puede ser. Incluso si él es capaz de soportar el hecho de estar casado conmigo, ¿crees que a mí me apetece verme obligada a moverme en círculos en los que todo el mundo me dará la espalda?

—Claro que no —dijo él, como si estuvieran hablando del tiempo—. Simplemente, tendremos que enmendar esos desafortunados rumores.

—¡Desafortunados rumores! —Ella se preguntó si se habría vuelto loca—. Mi reputación está completamente arruinada, milord. Ninguna dama de buena cuna en todo Inglaterra querría permanecer en la misma estancia que yo.

—Elf no ha huido. ¿Estás poniendo en duda su alcurnia?

—Desde luego que no. Ella me ha aceptado por el amor que le tiene a su hermano.

—Entonces, esperemos que Cyn sea amado por muchos.

—No seas ridículo. —Ella se asombró de su propia temeridad, pero encaró a Rotghar de todos modos—. No tengo ninguna duda de que Cyn será expulsado de su regimiento si se casa conmigo.

Él levantó sus negras y elegantes cejas.

—Entonces, le compraré otro. A estas alturas, ya debería ser coronel.

Chastity se había quedado sin palabras.

Él se sentó enfrente de ella y estiró sus largas piernas.

—Y ahora, cuéntame qué hacías en la cama con Henry Vernham.

18

Chastity sacudió la cabeza. No quería pasar otra vez por todo aquello. Él no la creería, y, aunque así fuera, no podría hacer nada al respecto.

—¿Quieres resolver este lío? —preguntó él.

—Es imposible.

—Al menos, vamos a intentarlo.

La fuerza de la voluntad de Rotghar acabó quebrando la de la muchacha. Indecisa, ella contó la historia, incluyendo la participación de su padre.

—¿Walgrave hizo eso para obligarte a casarte con un Vernham? —preguntó él.

—Sí.

—¿Por qué?

—No lo sé. —Habían vuelto a establecer un duelo dialéctico. Pero el hecho de que él la desafiara significaba que se tomaba el asunto en serio. Resultaba más tranquilizador que intimidante.

—¿Te parece razonable? —le preguntó—. ¿Esperabas eso de tu padre?

Ella apartó la vista de aquellos indómitos ojos grises.

—Entonces no. Ahora, no lo sé. Creo que está loco.

—¿Por qué dices eso? ¿Qué ha hecho desde entonces?

Chastity no quería hablar de eso.

—Lord Rotghar, esto no tiene sentido. No se puede hacer nada.

—Siempre se puede hacer algo, pero necesito conocer todos los hechos. —Como ella se quedó dudando, él añadió—: ¿No te gustaría volver a ocupar tu legítimo lugar en la sociedad, casarte con Cyn sin que nada empañara tu buen nombre y ser feliz?

Los ojos de la muchacha se llenaron de lágrimas.

—Eso es imposible…

—Para un Malloren —repitió él—, no hay nada imposible. ¿Entonces?

Chastity suspiró.

—Como bien has dicho, el hecho de que padre intentara obligarme a que me casara con Vernham no tiene sentido alguno. Al igual que la desesperación con la que ha estado persiguiendo a Verity. Él decía que es fruto de la preocupación paternal, pero hay algo más. Aunque no sé de qué se trata.

—¿Decía? ¿Cuándo ha sido esto?

Chastity manoseó el abanico.

—Él me atrapó en Maidenhead. Supuse que se enfurecería al encontrarme vestida de hombre… —Se dio cuenta de que Rotghar no debía saber nada de su disfraz, y le encaró con actitud desafiante—. He llevado ropa de hombre durante varios meses.

—Eso sin duda explica la refrescante brusquedad de tus modales. ¿Había una razón para ello?

Chastity tampoco quería hablar de eso, pero, tras unos instantes, se quitó la peluca.

—Ah —dijo él con suavidad—. ¿Tu padre?

Ella asintió y recompuso su aspecto.

—Supongo que no es un castigo desproporcionado para una hija descarriada. ¿Eso fue todo lo que hizo?

Chastity se dijo a sí misma que los azotes, más que un castigo, habían sido un medio para forzarla a ir al altar.

—Y lo de las ropas. —Como él la mirara sorprendido ella dijo—: Procedían de la prisión local.

—Y tú preferiste ponerte algo más adecuado. Te felicito, querida. Así que tu padre no se enfureció por tu indecorosa indumentaria, sino que… ¿qué?

—Él creía que yo conocía el paradero de Verity y él quería dar con ella. Estaba encolerizado conmigo principalmente porque creía que yo la había animado a huir de él. Sé que sus hijas somos para él meros peones de su juego, pero sus comportamiento me pareció desmedido.

Rotghar echó la cabeza hacia atrás y contempló el techo pintado.

—Y lady Verity, ¿por qué se escapó?

—No se fiaba de Henry Vernham. Tan pronto como apareció para ejercer como tutor del niño, ella tuvo miedo de que quisiera causarle algún daño al pequeño William.

Rotghar estudiaba el techo con absorta atención. El tenue eco de un reloj que había dado el cuarto resonó por toda la casa. En la chimenea, rodó un trozo de carbón chispeante. Finalmente, él habló.

—¿Por qué casó tu padre a Verity con sir William? Él también era un don nadie.

Chastity no aguantaba ya más.

—No lo sé. Y no creas que no hemos tratado de entenderlo. Nada tiene sentido, pero lo hecho, hecho está. Si Verity termina a salvo y feliz, yo me daré por satisfecha.

Él bajó la vista.

—Pero eso no resolverá el problema de Cyn, y me temo que incluso la felicidad de tu hermana puede estar en peligro. Si nadie se lo impide, tu padre puede hacer la vida imposible a la nueva pareja.

Aquello era bien cierto.

—Pero ¿qué puedo hacer yo?

—Ayudarme a descubrir qué es lo que hay detrás de todo esto. Tiene que haber algo, algo que podamos usar. Puedo olerlo. Cuéntamelo todo. Necesito todos los detalles.

A favor de su propia causa, Chastity no lo habría hecho, pero por Verity era capaz de cualquier cosa. Repasó cada confrontación con su padre, recordando sus palabras lo mejor que pudo, detallando —con los ojos puestos en el abanico— sus pequeñas y sus grandes crueldades. Explicó con especial claridad lo ocurrido en Maidenhead, puesto que lo tenía muy reciente.

Si su relato había causado impresión al marqués, éste no lo manifestó. Su rostro y su voz seguían imperturbables.

—Así que tu padre insistía en saber por qué Verity no había acudido a él en su huida.

—Sí, parecía sorprendido. Creo que, después de todo, se considera un buen padre.

—¿Qué motivación podría tener Verity que a él le asustase?

—¿Asustarle? —repitió Chastity extrañada.

—Oh, sí, Chastity. Me has estado hablando de un hombre muy asustado. Él debe haber pensado que Verity le evitaba porque sabía algo que podía perjudicarle.

—Ella sabía que me había tratado mal.

—¿Crees que eso le importa mucho a él?

Chastity tuvo que sacudir la cabeza.

—Me parece —dijo Rotghar —que este asunto gira en torno a la muerte de sir William Vernham.

Chastity frunció el ceño.

—No puede ser. Él murió de un ataque al corazón y, además, eso ocurrió después de mis problemas.

—Detrás de ambas cosas, podrían esconderse los mismos factores. ¿Qué relación existía entre sir William y tu padre, antes del matrimonio de Verity?

—Ninguna.

—Piensa un poco —le dijo él vivamente.

Chastity repuso:

—Ninguna, te lo digo yo. Sir William era un don nadie, un hidalgo de medio pelo, con más dinero que clase.

—¿Era rico?

—No si lo comparamos contigo o con mi padre, pero sí más rico que la mayoría de los de su posición. Fort dice que amasó su fortuna como investigador especial después del 45, robando posesiones o aceptando sobornos a condición de que hiciera la vista gorda con algunas pruebas que acusaban a ciertos traidores. Es un hombre tremendamente odioso.

—Pero cuando este odioso hombre pidió la mano de Verity, se la concedieron —reflexionó Rotghar—. Debe haber tenido algún poder sobre tu padre. ¿No imaginas de qué puede tratarse?

—No. Padre es *el Incorruptible,* recuérdalo. No juega, bebe con moderación, nunca he oído ningún rumor que lo relacionara con ninguna mujer...

—¿Podría ser un caso de traición? —Las palabras cayeron como un jarro de agua fría.

—¿Qué?

—¿Sacrificaría tu padre a su hija, mejor dicho, a sus dos hijas, para salvar su cabeza?

—¡Traición! ¡Padre!

Él se puso en pie de un salto y empezó a deambular por la estancia. Chastity pensó que se parecía a una bestia al acecho de su presa.

—Traición —repitió él—. Tiene toda la pinta. La única cosa cierta en relación al conde de Walgrave es su ambición. ¿Y si se hubiera amilanado en el 45, pensando que el príncipe Charlie *el Bello* podía salir victorioso?

—¡Pero él siempre se ha mostrado totalmente en contra de los jacobitas!

—Las palabras cuestan poco. Su amistad con el príncipe Frederick le ligaba a la dinastía de los Hanover, pero cuando los jacobitas se aproximaban a Londres y la familia real hacía las maletas, pudo parecerle que todo se le escapaba de las manos. Aún se recuerda por todo el país lo que ocurrió cuando los Stuart regresaron, en el año 1660, y Carlos II recompensó a aquellos que le habían sido fieles. Pocas oportunidades se le ofrecían en aquellos momentos a un partidario de la república, por ilustre que fuese. No sería de extrañar que tu padre hubiera establecido entonces algún discreto contacto con los jacobitas.

Chastity estaba aturdida por la conmoción.

El marqués continuó, casi cariñosamente.

—¿Y si el investigador especial sir William Vernham se hubiera hecho con pruebas de este hecho y hubiera tenido la astucia de ocultarlas de tal modo que en caso de que le asesinaran, el conde no saliera bien parado? Ya sabes que esos inspectores no solían recibir mucho dinero por su desagradable trabajo. Pocos de los culpables tenían mucho que ofrecer y aquí, en el sur de Inglaterra, había pocas haciendas que pudieran resistir un saqueo de ese tipo. Pero el conde de Walgrave... —Sonrió—. Vernham debe haber estado cobrando su renta del conde durante más de quince años.

—¿Y Verity? —preguntó Chastity.

—Tal vez sir William quiso tener al conde todavía más agarrado. Posiblemente deseaba de verdad a tu hermana. La cuestión de la dote habría que tenerla en cuenta también. Tal vez se tratara de un simple abuso de poder, una nueva ocasión de burlarse del león encadenado. Y algo muy peligroso. Me pregunto si no fue eso lo que desquició por completo a tu padre. El dinero para hombres como nosotros no tiene demasiada trascendencia, pero verse obligado a unir su sangre con la de semejante canalla... —Al pensar en ello, la voz de Rotghar se transformó casi en un gruñido.

—Y le exigieron lo mismo conmigo... Pero entonces, ¿por qué intentó forzarme a aceptarlo de manera tan cruel?

—Porque sir William seguía teniendo la sartén por el mango. —Rothgar tenía la mirada perdida—. Tal vez todavía la tenga, incluso después de muerto.

—¿Qué quieres decir?

—Si existen esas pruebas, ¿dónde están? Tu padre debe de estar desesperado, sin saber por dónde le puede venir ahora el ataque.

—¿Qué me dices de Henry Vernham?

—No creo que se hubiera dedicado a perseguir al niño de haber tenido en sus manos una fuente mayor de riquezas.

Chastity contuvo el aliento.

—A menos que esté buscando esa fuente...

Rotghar se volvió rápidamente hacia ella.

—Tal vez no ha estado buscando al chiquillo para asesinarlo, sino buscando lo que tenía su hermano. Él debe pensar que Verity tiene la clave... ¡Lord Rotghar! —exclamó Chastity—. Verity lleva consigo este documento. Sir William le hizo prometerle que, si él moría, debía llevarlo al Justicia Mayor en Londres. Ella supuso que afectaba al asunto de la herencia, así que, antes de huir, lo cogió...

A Rotghar le brillaban los ojos.

—¿Dónde está ese documento ahora?

—Lo tiene ella. Pero, lord Rotghar —dijo Chastity apurada—, incluso si tus especulaciones son ciertas, no podemos usarlo. No sólo destruirá a padre, sino también a todos nosotros. La Corona confiscará los bienes... Fort...

—Las cosas no llegarán a ese punto —le aseguró él—. Pero si se trata de un documento incriminatorio, será un arma poderosa. Con ella conseguiremos sin duda que el conde acepte tu matrimonio y el de Verity.

—Y evitaremos que trate de destruir a Nathaniel. Pero, entonces, alguien se convertirá en el nuevo enemigo de mi padre. Me temo que serás tú.

—Soy tan capaz de cuidar de mí mismo como sir William. Te lo aseguro. —Sonrió—. El destino es una astuta arpía, ¿no crees? Sir William arregla las cosas para dejar al descubierto a tu padre en caso de que éste le mate, pero no piensa que puede morir repentinamente antes de tiempo. Le da un ataque en brazos de su amante, y toda la situación explota. Tu padre, al sospechar que Verity es la pieza clave, ha revuelto Roma con Santiago para encontrarla. Entonces, te encuentra a ti por medio. No es de extrañar que montara en cólera.

Tal y como decía él, todo encajaba.

—Lord Rotghar, tengo que indicarte que esto no va a hacer que mi matrimonio con Cyn sea más fácil. La oposición de mi padre ha sido siempre la parte menos importante. Lo que he dicho antes es cierto. No quiero arruinar su vida. Antes me mataría.

—No te pongas melodramática. ¿No crees que le destruiría el hecho de ser la causa de tu muerte?

Chastity jadeó ante aquel ataque.

—¡Mire a donde mire no hay esperanza!

—Sin embargo, yo empiezo a ver la luz. —Tocó una campana y entró un lacayo. Rotghar garabateó una nota, la selló y se la entregó al hombre.

—Quiero que un jinete lleve esto a Henry Vernham. Las últimas noticias que tengo de él lo daban en Salisbury, pero también se le ha visto rastreando la carretera de Southampton en busca de su cuñada y el bebé.

El sirviente salió con la nota.

Chastity volvió a fijar la vista en Rotghar. ¿Acaso pensaba que era Dios?

—Vete a saber dónde está ahora. ¿Qué dice la nota?

—Mis hombres están bien entrenados y son perseverantes. Le encontrarán tarde o temprano. La nota le informa de la boda de su cuñada y le invita a esta casa para la celebración. Ya he invitado también a tu hermano…

—¿Aquí?

—Desde luego. Estamos preparando una discreta fiesta, discreta únicamente por el hecho de que tu hermana ha enviudado hace muy poco.

Chastity estaba en medio de un torbellino.

—Pero no podemos estar seguros de Fort —protestó la muchacha—. Por lo que sabemos, podría decírselo a padre.

—Eso espero. Pero ya he enviado una invitación similar a tu padre.

—¿Qué? —Ella se puso de pie de un salto. Su instinto le decía que saliera por piernas.

Él le cogió la mano para calmarla. Le dio la vuelta y estudió las apagadas marcas.

—No volverá a hacerte daño, querida.

Ella retiró la mano.

—Impedirá la boda de Verity —replicó ella—. Sin duda llegará con Henry Vernham detrás, dispuesto a arrancarle el bebé de los brazos. ¡Vas a echarlo todo a perder con esa maldita arrogancia de los Malloren!

—Oh, lo dudo mucho —dijo él y sonrió con un destello de excitación que a Chastity le resultó familiar.

—Oh, Dios —gimió ella—. Cyn tenía razón. Te encantan los retos. No te importa la gente que esté implicada. ¡No sé cuál de los dos es peor!

—Oh, está clarísimo que yo —dijo él marqués y recogió el alfiler de la alfombra. Lo volvió a prender en el peto de Chastity—. El pobre chico es simplemente un mero aficionado.

Chastity se miró el broche.

—Algo terrible va a ocurrir —dijo con un estremecimiento—. Lo sé.

—Han estado ocurriendo cosas terribles; tú lo has sufrido en carne propia. Vamos a poner fin a esto. —Le levantó la barbilla—. Eres una luchadora, Chastity Ware. No te eches para atrás ahora.

Ella tragó saliva.

—Estoy asustada.

—La mayoría de la gente lo está antes de una batalla.

—Eso es lo que dice Cyn.

—Él debe saberlo bien.

Partieron hacia Long Knotwell formando una cabalgata. Chastity, Elf y Chantal viajaban en un carruaje. Obviamente era el segundo mejor coche del marqués, pero era bastante bueno. En éste, los escudos de armas resplandecían con impoluta arrogancia.

Rotgar iba a caballo junto con su otro hermano, Bryght.

—Arcenbryght —susurró Elf cuando se lo presentó a Chastity—. Con un nombre así, es una pena que se haya convertido en una criatura tan melancólica.

Bryght Malloren era tan alto y delgado como su hermano mayor, pero como llevaba una peluca castaña, Chastity no pudo apreciar el color natural de su pelo. Sus ojos tenían un tono verde dorado parecido al de Cyn, pero no tenían la misma calidez. Transmitía la innegable impresión de tener mejores cosas que hacer.

—No le hagas mucho caso a Bryght —le dijo Elf tan pronto como se hubieron instalado—. Últimamente es así con todo el mundo. Tiene el corazón herido. Ya te lo explicaré en otro momento.

Incluyendo a los dos hermanos, iban escoltadas por doce jinetes, todos ellos armados. Aquello le pareció a Chastity un tanto excesivo y así lo manifestó.

—Rothgar está preparado para afrontar cualquier contratiempo —comentó Elf sin darle mayor importancia.

Chastity se estremeció.

—Esto podría terminar en una guerra.

—Oh, no lo creo. Los tiempos de los barones feudales hace mucho que terminaron. Sin duda sólo quiere asegurarse de que tu familia no cause ningún problema.

Pasaron el rato entretenidas hablando de livianos temas de sociedad. Chastity estaba encantada. Habían creado una isla de normalidad en medio de un mar tormentoso. En el mejor de los casos, se trataba de un refugio temporal, pero ella lo agradeció.

Pero entonces Elf dijo:

—Aquí estoy yo, hablando de excitación teatral, con las aventuras que tú has debido correr en la vida real. ¡Cómo te envidio!

—Mis aventuras no han sido particularmente gozosas.

—Sé que ha debido ser horrible… —Elf suspiró—. Pero aún así te envidio. ¿Cómo voy a encontrar jamás un matador de dragones, si jamás me acerco lo suficiente a un dragón?

Chastity no sabía que decir e intercambió una elocuente mirada con la doncella. A pesar de que Elf era algo mayor que ella, en algunos aspectos parecía una inocente chiquilla.

—Tienes una hermana mayor —le dijo Chastity—. Ella debe haber encontrado un hombre que sea de su agrado.

—Oh, sí, pero Hilda ha sido siempre muy apacible. Se enamoró tranquilamente de lord Steen, y tranquilamente se casó con él. Ahora viven tranquilamente en Dorset, produciendo tranquilos bebés. Me temo que a mí me gustan los hombres con más carácter, pero mis hermanos los ahuyentan sistemáticamente. Quieren que me case con otro lord Steen.

Chastity frunció los labios.

—Y tú quieres casarte con un Rotghar…

Elf se echó a reír:

—O un Brand, o un Bryght o un Cyn. Un hombre que sea capaz de hacerle frente al diablo. ¡Ay de mí, me temo que me voy a convertir en una vieja solterona!

Entraron en Long Knotwell a media tarde, causando bastante excitación. La gente salía de sus casas para contemplar boquiabierta el desfile. Los niños corrían parejos a él, tratando de mirar dentro del conche. Chastity oyó a una niña que decía:

—¿Es el rey, Jimmy?

Se detuvieron delante de la vicaría y Rotghar se acercó a abrir la puerta del carruaje y conducirlas al interior de la casa. Era un lugar modesto, que muy pronto estuvo lleno de Mallorens. El vicario, el reverendo Thomas Frazer, se adelantó.

—Ah, lady Chastity, me alegro de que esté usted aquí. —Echó una nerviosa ojeada a los dos altos Malloren que había en su salón—. Su hermana y mi hermano están en el piso de arriba. Ya sólo falta la licencia.

A los pocos minutos, Verity se reunió con ellos y abrazó a Chastity.

—¡Qué buen aspecto tienes! Tenía tanto miedo de que te ocurriera algo terrible mientras yo vivía tan cómodamente. Mary Garnet ha sido toda atenciones. Después vino Nathaniel y me trajo hasta aquí. ¡Ni la más mínima aventura!

Verity parecía un poquito desilusionada. Chastity decidió mantener a su hermana en la ignorancia.

—Yo tampoco he vivido ninguna aventura —dijo—. Cyn tiene que llegar dentro de poco con tu licencia. Ven, que te voy a presentar a lady Elfled Malloren, la gemela de Cyn. Te va a prestar alguna ropa. Puedes elegir la que más te guste para tu boda.

Verity sonrió, con los ojos llenos de lágrimas, y le dio las gracias a Elf.

—De verdad, es un poco tonto pensar en algo así, cuando lo importante es casarme con Nathaniel, pero quería llevar algo especial para la ceremonia.

Chastity se volvió para saludar a Nathaniel, su viejo amigo y vecino. En aquella habitación llena de Mallorens, tenía un aspecto bastante corriente, pero era un hombre apuesto, de rasgos regulares y mirada penetrante. Obviamente, a los ojos de Verity, eclipsaba incluso al marqués.

—Tengo que darte las gracias por cuidar de Verity, Chastity —dijo el mayor—, sé que has debido ser el alma de la operación.

—En serio, Nathaniel, ¿crees que ésta es forma de hablar de tu futura esposa?

Él se puso colorado.

—Sabes que la adoro, pero no creo que nadie pueda pensar que tiene el valor necesario para asaltar un carruaje.

Chastity sonrió.

—Tal vez eso fuera una gran insensatez, más que el producto de un temple de acero. Aunque, después de todo, parece que ha funcionado. —Se lo llevó a un aparte—. Nathaniel, tengo que advertírtelo: Rotghar pretende que tú y Verity vayáis a la Abadía después de la ceremonia, pero ha invitado también a mi padre y a mi hermano. ¡Incluso les ha dicho que la boda va a celebrarse aquí! Con un poco de suerte, no llegarán a tiempo de causar ningún desaguisado, pero...

Nathaniel, irritado, miró de refilón al marqués, formidablemente arrogante con aquel traje de terciopelo gris.

—¡Qué me dices! Pero ¿qué es lo que se trae entre manos?

—Vete a saber. Aunque sus intenciones parecen buenas. Sólo quería ponerte sobre aviso. Pero creo que será mejor no decirle nada a Verity. Le dará un soponcio.

Él levantó una ceja:

—¿Es esa manera de hablar de tu hermana?

Chastity tuvo que concederle aquel tanto.

Elf y Chastity subieron después al piso de arriba con Verity para examinar las cajas que Chantal iba desempaquetando. La doncella miró a Verity y después asintió:

—El azul —dijo—. También le queda bien a lady Elf, pero tratándose de una boda…

Elf silenció las objeciones de Verity con un negligente gesto de la mano.

—Debes ponerte el azul. Tengo muchos más, te lo aseguro.

El traje de novia de Verity, por tanto, era de gorgorán azul cielo, con la falda cerrada, pero abierto en la parte del corpiño, dejando al descubierto un peto ajustado con lazos blancos, estrecho en la cintura, pero que se iba ensanchando hasta llegar a la altura de la clavícula. El amplio escote sacaba buen partido de su bello tórax y sus abundantes senos. Había también una cinta para el cuello a juego, en seda azul con perlas bordadas, que se ataba por delante con un lazo.

Con el pelo recogido en alto, parecía totalmente una gran dama. En la vicaría no disponían de un espejo de cuerpo entero, así que tuvo que aceptar la palabra de las otras mujeres, que le aseguraron que a Nathaniel le encantaría su aspecto.

Llamaron a la puerta y entró la doncella de mediana de edad del reverendo Frazer.

—Me mandan a deciros que abajo esta todo listo, señoras.

Chastity fue presa de la agitación. Eso quería decir que Cyn estaba allí. Se retorció nerviosamente la rosada falda.

Verity le cogió la mano y se la apretó.

—Tú también estás muy bella, querida. Mucho más que antes. En primavera eras una chica guapa. Ahora eres una mujer arrebatadora.

Chastity se sobresaltó, preguntándose si sería tan obvio que ella y Cyn eran amantes.

El salón de la vicaría estaba abarrotado tras la llegada de dos nuevos Malloren. Al abrirse la puerta, Cyn levantó la vista rápidamente y miró a Chastity casi como si fuera una desconocida. Instintivamente, ella abrió el abanico de golpe para proteger su rostro de aquella tórrida mirada.

Oyó cómo Nathaniel dedicaba unas tiernas y admirativas frases a Verity.

Escuchó a Rotghar ultimar los detalles con el vicario.

La vista se le quedó prendida en Cyn.

Él se le acercó.

—De haberte visto así —le dijo suavemente—, no creo que me hubiera atrevido a aspirar tan alto.

Chastity descubrió que la voz la había abandonado y utilizó el abanico, meneándolo de un modo que expresaba agitación e interés.

—Cuando Rotghar solucione todo esto —le dijo muy serio—, no pienso pedirte nada. Puedes conseguir algo mejor que yo. —De repente, Cyn vio el alfiler de Rothgar prendido en el peto de la muchacha y los ojos se le abrieron como platos—. O quizá ya lo hayas hecho.

Chastity dejó de mover el abanico.

—¡Cyn, de veras…!

Pero el reverendo les estaba empujando ya hacia la iglesia. Cyn fue al lado de Chastity, pero era como si estuvieran separados por un muro. Debería haber estado contenta, pero se sentía muy molesta. Necesitaba decir algo para romper aquella barrera, pero aquél no era momento para tratar temas personales. Se acordó de las extrañas invitaciones que Rotghar había mandado a su padre, a su hermano y a Henry Vernham, y se lo contó a Cyn.

—Interesante —dijo él, todavía muy distante—. Tendrá sus motivos y después de haberle pedido ayuda, no debemos tramar ningún subterfugio.

La ceremonia discurrió sin la menor perturbación. Chastity se acordó de la primera boda de Verity, en la que ella pronunciara sus votos muy rígida, mirando al frente. Esta vez los dijo con amor, mirando a los atentos ojos de Nathaniel.

Chastity se tragó las lágrimas y, a base de mucha fuerza de voluntad, consiguió no mirar ni una sola vez a Cyn en toda la ceremonia.

Elf y Rotghar actuaron de testigos, colocando, por lo tanto, todo el peso del apellido Malloren detrás de aquel enlace.

Cuando el rito llegó a su fin, Rotghar dijo:

—Ahora debemos llevaros a todos de vuelta a la Abadía. Hemos planeado una celebración y, si partimos ahora, todavía tendremos luz suficiente.

Teniendo presente que Walgrave podía aparecer en cualquier momento, nadie necesitó que le animaran a marcharse de allí. Incluso convencieron al reverendo Frazer para que les acompañara, con la excusa de que él también tenía que celebrar la boda de su hermano. Pero todo el mundo sabía que no era cosa de dejarlo allí para que lo encontrara Walgrave y descargara sobre él su rabia.

Verity y el bebé se unieron al resto de las damas en el coche. Todos los hombres hicieron el camino cabalgando. Nathaniel iba muy cerca del carruaje, como si no pudiera soportar una distancia mayor.

Elf suspiró:

—Otro matador de dragones.

Verity miró perpleja a Chastity.

Cyn no iba al lado del carruaje, sino que parecía ir conferenciando con Rotghar, quien probablemente le iba informando de sus planes. Chastity se preguntó si debería hablarle a Verity de eso, pero decidió posponer el momento. La idea de que su padre estaba salpicado en un asunto de traición empañaría aquellos instantes de felicidad. Cuando llegaran a la Abadía y el equipaje de Verity estuviera a mano, Chastity le pediría el documento. ¿Resultaría ser tan importante como ellos pensaban o se llevarían una decepción? ¿Cambiaría en algo el futuro de Chastity? ¿Había alguna posibilidad, por remota que fuera, de que su reputación fuera restituida, de que ella tuviera también un día como aquél: el día de su boda?

No se permitiría a sí misma esperar algo tan improbable. Sería como esperar ser virgen de nuevo.

Llegaron a Rothgar Abbey justo cuando se ponía el sol. Pronto estuvieron en su opulento y elegante interior. Enseguida se prepararon habitaciones para Chastity, y para Verity y Nathaniel. Había también una niñera dispuesta a ayudar con el bebé. Y estaba a punto de servirse una cena de celebración.

Cuando Chastity iba a preguntarle a su hermana por el documento, descubrió que los recién casados ya habían desaparecido en la privacidad de su dormitorio. Echó un vistazo en dirección al marqués, pero éste no daba señales de impaciencia.

Pilló a Cyn mirándola, pero él no hizo ningún ademán de querer hablar con ella.

Debería sentirse contenta.

Pero le dolía el corazón.

Buscó refugio en el santuario de su propia habitación, decidida a no llorar. Después de todo, si él creía que ella estaba bajo la protección de Rotghar la dejaría en paz. Se hallaba paseando por la estancia, afianzándose en su resolución de dejar a Cyn en libertad, cuando Verity llamó a la puerta y entró. Una Verity con los ojos brillantes, que irradiaba felicidad.

—¡Casi no me lo puedo creer, Chastity! —exclamó Verity mientras se abrazaban—. ¡Lo hemos conseguido! Y el marqués dice que puede garantizar que Nathaniel no pagará por esto. —Se sonrojó con el arrebol del amor—. Nathaniel no ha querido escuchar mis preocupaciones. Dijo que si había algún problema con el matrimonio, me llevaría al extranjero para que pudiéramos casarnos.

Chastity la besó.

—Me alegro tanto por ti, Verity. ¿Te ha dicho el marqués como piensa manteneros a salvo?

—No —dijo Verity con una pizca de ansiedad—. ¿Dudas de él?

—Oh, no, pero… —Chastity se dispuso a explicar lo increíble—. Esto va a sonarte raro, Verity, pero creo que todo lo que ha ocurrido podría explicarse si sir William hubiera tenido algún poder sobre padre, un poder que se deriva de la traición que cometió padre allá en 1945. Pensamos que sir William debe haber tenido posesión de un documento que relaciona a padre con los Stuart.

—¿Traición? ¿Padre? —dijo Verity, exactamente del mismo modo que Chastity en su momento. Pero luego asintió lentamente—. Lo admito, tenía que ser algo de gran envergadura lo que lo explicara.

—Y creemos —dijo Chastity con cuidado—, que el documento que llevas contigo no era de tipo legal, sino una prueba incriminatoria.

—¡Santo cielo! —jadeó Verity.

—¿Querrás dárselo a Rotghar para ver de qué se trata?

—Desde luego —dijo Verity, pero, a continuación, abrió enormemente los ojos y se puso pálida.

—¡Oh, vaya!

—¿Qué?

—Estaba en el bolsillo de mi vestido de criada.

Chastity recordaba haber hecho un fardo con él cuando se cambiaron dentro del coche.

—¿Qué ha sido de él? ¿No lo habrás tirado?

—No, lo dejé en casa de Mary Garnet. Con la emoción de ver a Nathaniel, me olvidé por completo del documento. —Verity se llevó una mano a la boca—. ¡Le dije que podía dar aquella ropa a los pobres!

Chastity se recogió las faldas y bajó volando las escaleras en busca de Rotghar. Un lacayo le dijo que estaba en su estudio y ella acudió precipitadamente allí.

Rotghar levantó la vista.

—Chastity. ¿Qué ocurre?

Ella le explicó lo de la prueba.

—Ah —dijo él con cierta alarma—. Has hecho bien en preguntarle. No hay tiempo que perder.

—¿Qué vas a hacer?

—Enviar inmediatamente a alguien a buscarlo. Lo mejor será que vaya Cyn, puesto que conoce a esa gente.

—Lleva dos días a lomos de un caballo —protestó ella.

—Es un soldado y él me asegura que se encuentra perfectamente.

Aquello era irse al otro extremo de una actitud sobreprotectora, pero Chastity se distrajo con otro pensamiento:

—Me he acordado de otra cosa.

—¿Sí?

Le habló de la mujer de Rood House, dándose cuenta entonces de que él también había estado allí y sin duda sabía que el lugar había estado lleno de mujeres supuestamente respetables. Continuó, decidida a no dar demasiados detalles, y explicó lo de la nota de Nerissa Trelyn. Aquello no tenía nada que ver con la traición, pero ella había prometido contárselo todo.

Los ojos de Rotghar centelleaban interesados.

—Ah. Dices que la nota era explícita. ¿Recuerdas algo de lo que decía?

Chastity se sonrojó al pensar en ella, pero buceó en su memoria.

—Ella le llamaba a él Hércules... Había algo de un pañuelo entre las piernas de ella en el teatro y un lazo alrededor de su... —Ella le miró y sacudió la cabeza, con las mejillas ardiendo—. No puedo repetir semejantes cosas...

—Es suficiente —le dijo él con gentileza—. Ya veo el tono. Sólo quería estar seguro de que era más explícita que la típica carta de amor.

—Oh, desde luego era algo más que eso.

—¿Y dejaste esa misiva detrás de la chimenea? Dime otra vez cómo encontrar esa casa.

Ella le dio las indicaciones lo mejor que supo y él las anotó. Acto seguido, hizo llamar a Bryght Malloren para enviarle a rescatar aquella prueba. Él pareció alegrarse de poder eludir la celebración.

—¿Crees que servirá de algo? —preguntó Chastity—. No tengo ningún deseo de hacer daño a lady Trelyn. Ella sólo estaba diciendo la verdad cuando confirmó mi deshonra.

—Eres demasiado bondadosa. Nerissa Trelyn sería capaz de hundir a cualquiera en un instante con tal de obtener su propósito. Pero no creo que tengamos que mancillar su intachable reputación. Medio mundo sabe que es una furcia, aunque les divierte simular lo contrario. La mayoría de la gente sabía que tú eras una víctima inocente —esas cosas se sienten—, pero se lo pasaban bien difamándote. De vez en cuando, necesitamos sacrificar una víctima en el altar del decoro. Nos da la tranquilidad de comprobar que todavía existen normas. No es una estampa muy bonita.

—Tú formas parte de ella.

—Y una parte muy importante —reconoció él afablemente—. Pero yo nunca hago daño a quienes son inocentes.

Él se adelantó y le levantó la barbilla para besarla en los labios.

—Casi envidio a mi hermano…

Un sexto sentido le dijo a Chastity que Cyn había entrado en la estancia. Se desprendió de los lánguidos dedos de Rotghar y le encaró.

—¿Es así cómo tu nombre va a ser rehabilitado? —preguntó Cyn con un tono helador, propio del mismo Rotghar—. Muy acertado. Nadie se atreverá a cuestionar el honor de la prometida de Rotghar.

—Por lo menos, delante de mí —dijo Rotghar con calma—. Pero lo que nos preocupa, según creo, es lo que se dice a nuestras espaldas.

Chastity se sintió como un cordero entre dos lobos.

Rotghar miró a su hermano de una manera que hizo a Chastity estremecerse.

—Si dudas, aunque sea durante un segundo, del honor de lady Chastity a causa de ese beso, Cyn, es que no la mereces. Tengo una misión para ti, pero puede esperar unos minutos.

La puerta hizo clic al cerrarse tras él. Cyn y Chastity se quedaron a solas.

—¿Qué demonios hay entre vosotros? —inquirió Cyn.

Chastity sabía que podía utilizar aquel momento para dejar libre a Cyn, pero sería a costa de destruir la relación de éste con su hermano.

—No hay nada entre nosotros —le dijo.

—Entonces, ¿por qué llevas ese alfiler?

Ella lo había olvidado. Temblorosa, se llevó la mano hacia el pecho, como si quisiera ocultarlo.

—Él me lo dio en Rood House.

—¿Por qué?

Chastity no podía soportar aquel helado tono. Aunque hubiera obrado mal, necesitaba su cariño.

—No puedes creer de verdad lo que estás insinuando —protestó ella y se echó en sus brazos.

Él la rechazó.

—¿Por qué? —quiso saber él.

Azorada, ella le acarició la mejilla.

Él apartó de sí la mano de la muchacha.

—Chastity, ¿por qué te dio Rotghar ese alfiler?

—¡Por los servicios prestados! —replicó ella bruscamente, apartándose de él—. ¡Eres el más estúpido de los hombres!

—Seguro que sí, pero me asombra que lograras encontrar tiempo para él.

—¡Cyn Malloren, te has vuelto loco! Sólo me robó un beso.

Él la cogió por el brazo y la arrastró hacia sí.

—Y te pagó con esa perla —se mofó él—. ¿Me tomas por tonto?

Ella le golpeó en los nudillos con el abanico.

—¡Suéltame, señor! No tengo nada más que decirte hasta que no recobres la cordura.

Él la dejó libre, pero volvió a rodearla con sus brazos.

—Nunca volveré a estar cuerdo. Oh, Chastity, no sé que hacer contigo ahora que te veo como una dama elegante. Me das miedo. Serías una marquesa tan estupenda. —Le deslizó suavemente la mano por la mejilla—. Por favor, no vuelvas a dejar que Rotghar te bese.

Estar entre sus brazos le proporcionaba una dulce sensación. O, mejor dicho, agridulce:

—¿De verdad crees que me interesa?

—¡Cómo no iba a interesarte! Ya te lo he dicho antes. Una vez que tu reputación se haya restablecido, no me necesitas para nada. Tendrás muchos pretendientes, entre ellos, sin duda, Rotghar. Él nunca besa a una mujer sin un motivo.

Aquello le resultó muy duro, pero Chastity se deshizo del abrazo y se forzó a decir estas frías palabras.

—Muy bien. Tal vez me case con Rotghar, después de todo.

Él la miró con desamparo, pero asintió.

—Bien. Sin embargo, si tu reputación no es restituida debemos casarnos.

Ella le encaró vivamente:

—¡No permitiré semejante sacrificio!

—Me he aprovechado de ti...

—Yo consentí de buena gana...

Él emitió un gruñido y volvió a llevarla junto él para darle un beso.

Después, sus labios exploraron primero la curva de uno de sus pechos y después la del otro, minando la determinación de la muchacha—. Tienes un sabor delicioso, a frambuesas con nata...

—Cyn, ¿otra vez comida...?

—Mmm.

Chastity trató de permanecer fría, pero el deseo la invadió, acrecentado por sus diestras caricias. Se rindió con un desesperado gemido...

Llamaron a la puerta y ambos tuvieron el tiempo justo de separarse antes de que entrara Rotghar. Él los examinó impasiblemente y dijo:

—Excelente. Cyn, hay algo urgente que hacer en Winchester. ¿Crees que estás en condiciones?

Una rápida mirada le dijo a Chastity que Cyn no tenía ganas de abandonarla pero aceptaba cumplir con su deber.

—Me las arreglaré con un caballo de refresco.

—Bien. —Rothgar le explicó la situación con claridad—. Mandaré dos caballerizos contigo, pero todo será más sencillo si eres tú quien le hace la petición a la esposa de tu amigo. Y si se ha deshecho ya de la prenda, tendrás que encontrarla y recuperar el documento.

—Caramba. ¿Voy a tener que rondar a los respetables pobres, y meterles las manos en los bolsillos?

Los labios de Rotghar se torcieron en una mueca.

—Haz lo que sea necesario. Una vez que lo tengas a salvo contigo, puedes descansar todo lo largo que eres en un lugar seguro, mientras los mozos montan guardia.

Chastity se estremeció al sentir la inminencia del peligro. Si alguien descubría que Cyn tenía ese documento, iría tras él. Henry Vernham sería capaz de matar por hacerse con aquella prueba; el conde de Walgrave destruiría medio mundo con tal de hacerla desaparecer. Aquél no era el momento de retenerlo.

Tomó las manos de Cyn y le besó.

—Ten cuidado. Por favor.

19

El banquete de la boda fue un evento un tanto extraño. Verity y Nathaniel sólo tenían ojos el uno para el otro. Elf tenía aspecto melancólico. Brand y Rotghar charlaron inconexamente sobre asuntos políticos. Chastity estaba preocupada por Cyn.

Aunque se conocían hacía muy poco tiempo, apenas habían estado separados. No estaba acostumbrada a inquietarse por él *in absentia*. Se percató de que Rotghar y Brand estaban hablando de la guerra. Aquello le interesaba, puesto que la seguridad de Cyn dependía de ella.

—¿De verdad creéis que terminará pronto la contienda? —preguntó.

—Casi con toda seguridad —dijo Rotghar—. A raíz de la batalla de Wandewash en la India y de la rendición en Canadá, la expansión francesa se ha detenido. Ahora que el rey George ha retirado su apoyo al rey Frederick, Prusia tendrá que avenirse al dialogo. —Sonrió, al tener en cuenta los sentimientos de la muchacha, y añadió—: Puede que en un futuro cercano no tengas que afrontar la idea de que Cyn está combatiendo.

—Tal vez lo manden a casa durante un tiempo —dijo Elf esperanzada—. Le he visto tan poco en los últimos años, y a ti, mi nueva hermana, acabo de conocerte.

Chastity sabía que debería haber protestado, pero la idea de ser en el futuro la esposa de Cyn era una fantasía demasiado deliciosa como para abandonarla por completo. Permaneció sentada, en una silenciosa ensoñación, mientras Elf se preguntaba dónde se alojaría Cyn, llegando incluso a especular con la posibilidad de futuros sobrinos.

La cena terminó con un brindis por los recién casados. Elf se levantó para conducir a las damas a sus aposentos, pero Nathaniel también se levantó. Tan sonrosado como una novia, indicó que ya estaban listos para irse a la cama. Con una cara admirablemente inexpresiva, Rotghar les deseó que pasaran una buena noche.

Elf llevó a Chastity hasta su saloncito para tomar el té.

—Pronto te tocará también a ti.

—A veces me permito soñar —dijo Chastity—. Pero, sinceramente, no veo que sea posible.

—Rothgar pensará algo —dijo Elf con confianza—, y Cyn no se detendrá por una mera cuestión de reputación. Sin embargo, espero que eso pueda enmendarse, porque todos nos sentiremos mucho más cómodos. Hablando de comodidad, quiero librarme de este corpiño inmediatamente. Estoy segura de que Chantal me lo ha apretado especialmente para poder competir con tu talle. Me siento como si fuera a reventar.

La doncella les llevó enseguida unas encantadoras *negligés*, amplias batas con adornos de encaje y lazos, y las dos muchachas se instalaron tranquilamente para charlar tomando el té.

—¿Por qué no me cuentas más cosas de tu familia, Elf? — inquirió Chastity.

Elf vertió el agua hirviendo sobre las hojas de la tetera.

—Claro que sí, puesto que vas a unirte a ella. Como sabes, somos seis, todos con extraños nombres. La madre de Rotghar no puso ninguna objeción y, desde entonces, la pauta quedó establecida.

—¿Tenéis diferentes madres?

—¿No lo sabías? Ella murió cuando Rotghar tenía cinco años. Nuestro padre se casó poco después. Apenas recuerdo a mi propia madre, porque los dos, ella y mi padre, murieron cuando yo tenía sólo siete años. Dicen que Cyn, el muy tunante, es el que más se parece a ella.

—Lord Rotghar debía ser muy joven cuando heredó el título.

Elf le pasó el té a Chastity en un plato de porcelana china.

—Acababa de cumplir los diecinueve. Además tuvo que asumir la responsabilidad de sus cinco hermanos, dos de los cuales eran unos endiablados gemelos. Se lo tomó muy en serio. Ha sido muy bueno con nosotros.

—Está claro que los sentimientos que le unen a su familia son muy fuertes.

—Sí. Realmente, debería casarse, y creo que está empezando a planteárselo. Aunque ahora las cosas podrían cambiar.

Chastity tomó un sorbo de su taza.

—¿Por qué ahora?

—Ha estado esperando que se casara algún hermano para mantener la dinastía, pero los planes de matrimonio de Bryght fracasaron. Ahora que Cyn va a casarse, temo que Rotghar abandoné su propósito de encontrar esposa.

—No entiendo por qué el marqués espera que sean sus hermanos los que cumplan con su deber por él.

—Ah —dijo Elf, y por primera vez pareció dubitativa—. Bueno, es un escándalo de la familia y tú vas a formar parte de ella. De todos modos, no es algo por lo que te tengas que preocupar. Verás, se trata de su madre.

—¿La madre de Rotghar?

—Parece ser que no era una persona muy agradable.

—Pero ¿se acuerda él de muchas cosas relativas a ella?

—De algunas. Los acontecimientos violentos disparan los recuerdos. Ella tuvo un segundo bebé, una niña. Y la mató.

Chastity derramó sin querer un poco de té.

—¿Qué?

—Es cierto. La criatura tenía apenas unos días, y ella la estranguló. Rotghar estaba presente cuando lo hizo, pero era demasiado pequeño y no pudo impedírselo. Tenía sólo cuatro años, pero se acuerda. Creo que por eso nos protege tanto a nosotros. Está tratando de salvar a su hermana recién nacida.

Chastity depositó en la mesa su platillo con el té antes de que su temblorosa mano lo volviera a tirar.

—Pero ¿por qué hizo una cosa así?

—Nadie lo sabe, pero he oído que se dice que algunas mujeres se vuelven locas después de dar a luz. Tras el trágico suceso, la encerraron, por supuesto, sin permitirle que se acercara a su hijo. Contrajo una enfermedad que la fue consumiendo y, finalmente, murió.

—Es una historia terrible, pero ¿por qué no iba a querer casarse el marqués?

Elf se entristeció.

—Le preocupa que pueda ser algo hereditario. Siempre ha tenido mucho cuidado de no perder el control.

—Creo que no debería darle importancia a eso. ¿Quién sabe como pueden salir los niños?

—Algunas cualidades se transmiten de padres a hijos. Como el color del pelo o de los ojos. O el talento para el arte o la música. —Elf sonrió de forma tranquilizadora—. No debes dejar que esto afecte tus planes, Chastity. Y, ahora, ¿por qué no me hablas de tu familia? ¿Tienes más hermanas aparte de Verity?

—No, sólo dos hermanos. Fort —es decir, Fortitude— y Victor. Como ves, vosotros no tenéis el monopolio de los nombres raros. Fort es el mayor y tiene el título de lord Thornhill. Victor tiene sólo dieciocho años.

—¿Cómo son?

—Oh, Fort es un hombre muy típico. Le gusta montar a caballo y la caza, y un nuevo deporte llamado boxeo. Se ponen unos guantes acolchados y se golpean el uno al otro hasta que uno de los dos cae al suelo. ¿Te imaginas? A pesar de esos gustos tan espantosos es bastante bondadoso, pero poco sensible.

Elf se echó a reír.

—Como dices, un hombre muy típico.

—En cuanto a Victor, llevamos peleándonos desde que nació, así que no puedo juzgarlo. Sin duda, mejorará con la edad. —Ahogó un bostezo y después se ruborizó por ser tan grosera.

Elf dejó inmediatamente su té.

—Qué desconsiderada he sido. Debes estar exhausta.

—Confieso que sí —dijo Chastity—. He dormido muy poco las dos últimas noches.

Elf se puso colorada. Chastity estuvo a punto de apresurarse a corregir la impresión que obviamente había sacado

Elf: que habían sido dos las noches de amor, pero entonces se dio cuenta de que más o menos había sido así. Con una tensa sonrisa, le dio las buenas noches y se fue a su propia habitación. Una vez allí, suspiró.

No estaba hecha para el escándalo. Odiaba la sensación de no sentirse del todo virtuosa. Cyn había tenido mucha razón al decir que su encuentro amoroso la había debilitado. Si no podían casarse, debían separarse, porque, por mucho que su cuerpo suspirara por él, ella se moriría si tuviera que vivir en la deshonra.

A la mañana siguiente, despertaron a Chastity con un delicioso chocolate y la noticia de que había llegado su hermano y estaba ansioso por hablar con ella.

Saltó de la cama, hecha un manojo de nervios. Tuvo la cobarde tentación de llamar a Elf para que la acompañara, pero supo resistirse a ella. A pesar de la amabilidad de los Malloren, ella estaba sola en el mundo y debía obrar en consecuencia.

Descubrió que tenía una amplia selección de ropa, la mayor parte de la cual, como Chantal había dicho, no le quedaría bien a lady Elf. Con la ayuda de la doncella, se puso un recatado vestido de algodón de la India color naranja con estampado marrón. En este caso, el naranja era casi exactamente del mismo tono que el cabello de Elf, y el efecto hubiera sido chocante.

Aquella dama tenía obviamente la costumbre de comprar ropa sin pararse a considerar aquel aspecto. Sin embargo, el vestido le quedaba bien a Chastity y los comedidos volantes del borde del corpiño, aunque adornados con caros bordados, creaban la decorosa estampa que ella deseaba.

¿Estaría Fort todavía de su parte?

Encontró a su hermano en la Sala de los Tapices, paseando de un lado a otro.

—Buenos días, Fort —dijo ella, tratando de mantener la dignidad y la compostura.

Él se dio la vuelta súbitamente y Chastity vio que tenía un ojo morado y una contusión en el labio.

—¡Oh, Fort! ¿Padre te ha hecho eso?

—Ha sido Lindle, para ser exactos. —Hizo una mueca de dolor—. Estoy encantado de comunicarte que él está mucho peor. Le rompí la nariz.

Chastity se echó a reír.

—¡Gracias, gracias, gracias!

Su hermano la miraba cálidamente.

—Tienes mucho mejor aspecto, Chastity.

—Gracias a ti. Siento haberte abandonado...

—No importa. Me alegro de que tuvieras la sensatez necesaria. Pero, después de dejar por los suelos a Lindle y escapar de las garras de padre, recorrí todo el pueblo buscándote. Me imaginé cosas espeluznantes. Estuve a punto de destrozar un par de burdeles.

Chastity fue hasta él y le besó tiernamente.

—Gracias. Pero Cyn estaba haciendo lo mismo.

—¿Cyn? —dijo él frunciendo el ceño con tal desconcierto que ella supo que había entendido «pecado».[6]

Con cierta sensación de ahogo, Chastity se dio cuenta de que Fort no sabía nada de Cyn Malloren. Pero ¿de qué otro modo podía ella justificar su presencia allí? De haberlo pen-

---

6. Nueva alusión a la fonética de Cyn = sin, es decir, pecado.

sado antes, tal vez hubiera podido inventarse alguna historia…

—¿Sin? —preguntó él, algo más calmado.

—Lord Cynric Malloren —dijo Chastity, pasándose la lengua por los labios mientras se preguntaba si no debería requerir protección, después de todo—. Él … él… él fue el que nos escoltó a Verity y a mí hasta Winchester.

—Un Malloren —soltó Fort—. Me preguntaba cómo habrías terminado aquí. ¿Y cómo es que él estaba en Maidenhead?

—Él fue quien me ayudó a encontrar a Nathaniel, por supuesto —dijo Chastity con brillantez—. Creo que se puede entender.

—¿Solos? —En los ojos de Fort brilló la furia—. ¿Vosotros dos haciendo noche en la carretera, solos? —Se llevó la mano a la empuñadura de la espada—. ¿Dónde está él?

—No está aquí —dijo ella rápidamente—. Y, Fort, tú no vas a hacerle ningún daño.

—¿Que no? Acabáramos.

—¡Quiere casarse conmigo!

—¡Ja! ¿Quiere casarse con Chastity Ware? ¡Eres más tonta de lo que pensaba!

Ella golpeó a su hermano en el pecho.

—¡Pensaba que creías en mí!

Él hizo ademán de darle con el puño, pero se controló conteniendo el aliento.

—Tú me has dicho que no eres virgen.

—Sí —dijo ella, mirándole a los ojos—, pero lo era.

—Entonces, él es un canalla.

—No.

Él inspiró profundamente.

—Hermana, está claro que no entiendes de qué van estas cosas.

—Lo entiendo perfectamente. No fui seducida, Fort. Fui a él voluntariamente, porque le amo.

—Es un canalla por haberse aprovechado de ti.

—Él no creía que yo fuera virgen entonces, Fort. Prométeme que no te pelearás con él.

—No te prometo nada. —Se dio la vuelta y se paso las manos por el desordenado pelo—. Voy a sacaros a ti y a Verity de este lugar inmundo. Nadie se fía de los Malloren, sobre todo si hay una mujer por medio. Sin duda, te irán pasando de uno a otro. —Se giró para mirarla burlonamente—. Si no lo han hecho ya.

—¡Fort, basta ya!

Él se detuvo unos instantes y la miró fijamente.

—¡Cyn Malloren! Sabía que me sonaba ese nombre. Él estaba en... —Se interrumpió y después dijo—: En cierto lugar.

Se estaba refiriendo a Rood House.

—¿Has desayunado, Fort? —le preguntó Chastity rápidamente.

—He oído que Cyn Malloren estuvo peleándose por una fulana —se mofó él—. ¿Qué te parece eso querida hermana? Hace apenas tres noches, tu honorable seductor se estuvo disputando una ramera.

Entonces, Fort empezó a contar las noches. Ella lo leyó en sus ojos.

—Ésa era la noche que tú estabas en la carretera con él, camino de Maidenhead... —Su ceño fruncido se transformó en una horrorizada expresión—. Santo Dios bendito...

—Chastity se retiró estratégicamente detrás de un sofá,

preguntándose si le resultaría posible llegar hasta la puerta de la estancia.

—¡Ya me parecía a mí que aquella fastidiosa Chloe me resultaba familiar! —Su voz se inflamó hasta convertirse en un rugido—. ¡Pequeña furcia asquerosa!

—¡Tú también estabas en Rood House! —chilló ella.

Él se abalanzó sobre ella. El sofá, repentinamente, dejó de servir como parapeto. Chastity buscó un arma y agarró un gran jarrón chino, la mejor defensa que encontró a mano.

Fort se detuvo.

Se detuvo porque tenía un reluciente estoque en el cuello. Lo empuñaba Rotghar, que había aparecido como por arte de magia.

—Ah —dijo Fort—. Otro Malloren. ¿Es entonces ella la puta de toda la familia?

—Mi querido Thornhill —dijo Rotghar con suavidad—, ella es, a todos los efectos, una más de la familia. Si la ofendes, me veré obligado a tomármelo personalmente…

Incluso Fort pareció aplacarse al percibir la concentrada animosidad de la voz del marqués.

—Ella no niega que tu hermano la desgraciara —dijo Fort—. Él tendrá que darme una satisfacción.

—Eso es algo entre tú y él. Pero es tu padre el que la ha desgraciado. ¿De qué lado estás tú? —La espada, que permanecía inmóvil en su cuello, enunciaba una promesa letal.

Fort la ignoró y miró fijamente a Chastity. Ella le envió una silenciosa súplica. Él suspiró.

—Del de ella.

Rotghar bajó la espada. Sólo entonces se dio cuenta Chastity de que Brand y Elf estaban también en la habitación.

—Entonces, todos estamos en el mismo bando —dijo Rotghar en tono apaciguador, como si aquella escena violenta nunca hubiera tenido lugar—. Déjame que te cuente algunas cosas sobre tu padre…

El tiempo se arrastraba pesadamente en la Abadía mientras todos esperaban que los planes de Rothgar produjeran algún resultado. Nadie sabía con certeza cuáles eran los hilos que Rothgar había movido, excepto él mismo, y la única señal clara que había dado era ordenar los preparativos de un gran baile de máscaras, que tendría lugar al cabo de cinco días.

—Cinco días —dijo Elf con calma—. ¿Y quién va a asistir?

—Asistirán todos aquellos a quienes he invitado —dijo él enigmáticamente.

Quedó claro que Rothgar había convidado a toda la pequeña nobleza local y a buena parte de la aristocracia.

—¿No les parecerá raro que les inviten a un gran baile con tan poca antelación? —preguntó Chastity.

—Oh, no —dijo Elf—. Siempre hace las cosas así. Se le antoja algo y organiza un evento social. Ya están acostumbrados.

—Supongo que entonces estarán acostumbrados a los actos un tanto desorganizados. A mi padre le llevó semanas preparar el baile de la pasada primavera.

—¿Desorganizado? —dijo Elf con la altanería de los Malloren—. Desde luego que no.

Chastity se vio inmersa en un remolino de eficiente actividad. Se trajeron de Londres numerosos criados suplementarios para la ocasión. Se enviaron mensajes a las demás haciendas de Rothgar, demandando provisiones. Tanto los criados como las provisiones llegaron a través de los medios más rápidos, sin que importara para nada el coste de éstos. Una docena de canastas de gansos llegaron por correo en un calesín.

Fort se quedó en la Abadía. Parecía aceptar la posible culpabilidad de su padre, pero no se mostraba muy cordial hacia los Malloren. Estuvo taciturno mientras aguardaba la llegada de Cyn. Cyn, que traería el documento que podía causar la ruina de la familia Ware al completo. Cyn, que había seducido a su hermana.

Fort tenía toda la pinta de querer matar a alguien.

—¡Qué hermano más odioso! —dijo Elf, mientras dirigía la nueva disposición de los muebles—. No parece que se preocupe por ti lo más mínimo.

—A lo mejor es que se preocupa demasiado —dijo Chastity—. ¿Qué haría Rothgar si te encontrara en la cama con un hombre?

Sólo de pensarlo a Elf se le abrieron enormemente los ojos, pero dijo:

—No se volvería contra mí.

Chastity no quiso discutir, pero le pareció que Elf era demasiado optimista. Esperaba que nadie hiciera nunca pedazos las ilusiones de su nueva amiga.

Al atardecer del día siguiente, Bryght regresó de Maidenhead con la carta. Chastity y Elf estaban con Rothgar en la Sala de los Tapices, cuando Bryght llegó y le entregó la misiva a su hermano.

—La casa estaba completamente vacía, y Walgrave ya no está en Maidenhead. —Con tono sombrío, añadió—: No me dijiste de quién era la carta.

—Tampoco te dije que la leyeras —comentó Rothgar con una inconfundible nota de humor. La ironía de Rothgar solía ser motivo de preocupación.

Chastity vio cómo se tensaba un irritado músculo de la mandíbula de Bryght. No se había afeitado y todavía parecía más enfadado y hosco de lo habitual.

—¿Iba a pelarme el trasero cabalgando para conseguir esa maldita nota sin pararme a comprobar que no se trataba de una lista de la lavandería?

Rothgar escudriñó el perfumado papel y levantó las cejas.

—Con una simple ojeada hubieras visto que no era precisamente eso.

—Una simple ojeada me dijo quién la había escrito. Reconocí la letra y el perfume.

—Ah —dijo Rothgar con una sonrisa definitivamente benigna, y al mismo tiempo heladora.

Bryght apretaba la mandíbula y los puños de un modo alarmante.

—Me enviaste deliberadamente.

Rothgar no lo negó.

—Nunca has querido creer que esa mujer tuviera el más mínimo defecto.

—No sé que creer ahora. ¿Habría ella llegado a esto si se hubiera casado conmigo?

Chastity se dio cuenta con horror de que el amor perdido de Bryght era Nerissa Trelyn.

—Ella eligió a Trelyn por voluntad propia —señaló Rothgar

Bryght giró sobre sus talones y salió de la estancia dando un portazo.

—Como ves —le dijo Rothgar a Chastity—. Tengo una cuenta pendiente con Nerissa Trelyn. Pero aún así, no tengo intención de destruirla a menos de que ella me obligue.

Chastity miró horrorizada a Elf, pero la dama se limitó a encoger los hombros como si aquellos dramáticos hechos fueran una parte habitual de la vida. Cielos, vivir con los Malloren era como vivir en la guarida del dragón, con Fort como águila invasora.

Paso un segundo día y, como Cyn seguía sin aparecer, Chastity empezó a preocuparse por su seguridad. En tres ocasiones estuvo a punto de suplicarle a Rothgar que enviara una partida de hombres a buscarle, pero, si Cyn estaba a salvo, aquello le molestaría. Además, la seguridad de Rothgar era tan abrumadora que temió ofenderle mortalmente si insinuaba que sus planes podían tener algún fallo.

La muchacha enterró sus preocupaciones ayudando a Elf a organizar el baile. Ésta parecía tenerlo todo controlado, excepto un pequeño detalle.

—Necesitamos un tema —le dijo a Chastity—. Un baile debe tener un tema.

—¿Las flores? —sugirió Chastity.

—No pega en noviembre —dijo Elf con una mueca—. Ni siquiera para un Malloren. ¿Medieval? —reflexionó a continuación—. No, porque la gente querría venir disfrazada y no hay tiempo para eso. ¿Veneciano? Eso sería excesivo... Ah —dijo de repente—. ¡Ambiente chino!

—¿Chino? —inquirió Chastity mientras seguía a su anfitriona en dirección a las profundidades subterráneas de la casa.

—¿Cómo no se me ha ocurrido antes? —farfulló Elf alegremente—. Ven conmigo y verás.

Lo que Chastity vio fue un montón de fardos envueltos en arpillera. Cuando un criado los desembaló resultaron ser retales de valiosísima seda roja china pintada a mano.

Tocó uno de ellos con reverencia, después se volvió a Elf horrorizada.

—¡Ni se te ocurra!

—Voy a colgarla alrededor de las paredes del salón de baile.

—No, Elf, no puedes hacer eso —gimió Chastity— ¡Es demasiado cara!

—Oh —dijo Elf—, no para un Malloren.

Entonces Chastity vio la manera en que Elf curvaba los labios. Volvió a mirar la seda. Sin duda era un tejido muy valioso. Desplegó un poco con delicadeza. Era un rollo de imitación muy bien conseguido. En su interior sólo halló un vasto y brillante algodón estampado con el mismo diseño dorado.

—¡Tunanta! —dijo al fin—. ¿De dónde ha salido esto?

—Fue Rothgar quien lo adquirió, en una de sus empresas más misteriosas. Todavía me pregunto qué puedo hacer con la seda buena, pero es demasiado exótica para un vestido… —Miró a Chastity—. Al menos para mí.

—No voy a ir al baile con un vestido que parece que está hecho con las cortinas —dijo Chastity con firmeza.

Elf se rió.

—Desde luego que no. Para más adelante, tal vez. Mientras tanto, vamos a desenrollar y a colgar esto. —Dio unas cuantas instrucciones y se marchó de allí—. Sería de gran efecto pintar el enmaderado del salón con laca negra —reflexionó.

—Pero ¿que sea algo permanente? —señaló Chastity, preguntándose si aquello supondría algún problema para un

Malloren—. Siempre se pueden construir paneles falsos y colocarlos alrededor de toda la estancia. —Tan pronto como terminó de decirlo, Chastity supo que se había contagiado de la perspectiva que los Malloren tenían ante la vida.

—Por supuesto —dijo Elf encantada y dio nuevas órdenes. Lo más asombroso de todo era que la ingente platilla de sirvientes nunca pestañeaba ante ninguna orden, por extravagante que fuera.

Con un Malloren, todo era posible.

Ella había empezado a considerar a Rothgar Abbey como un Versalles en miniatura.

Se hallaba dirigiendo la colgadura de la «seda» cuando regresó Cyn. Éste entró en el salón y se detuvo en seco.

—¡Cielos! ¿Es esto realmente…?

Chastity se giró.

—¡Cyn! —Sin pensarlo se arrojó entre sus brazos bajo la discreta pero fascinada mirada de veinte criados.

Ella recobró la compostura inmediatamente y se separó de él. Él estuvo a punto de soltarla, pero, de repente, casi con desesperación, salió con ella de la estancia hasta el pasillo. Permanecieron allí de pie durante un instante, embebidos en la mutua contemplación. Después, sus bocas se unieron en una apremiante comunión.

Chastity supo entonces que le resultaría casi imposible vivir sin la presencia de Cyn, su tacto, su voz, su amor…

El beso llegó a su fin pero ellos aún siguieron aferrados el uno al otro.

—Dios, cuánto te he echado de menos —gimió él contra su mejilla.

—Yo también te he echado de menos. Estaba muy preocupada…

Él se apartó ligeramente.

—No debemos hacer esto. Tu reputación…

—No me importa…

—A mí sí. —Inspiró profundamente y se separó de ella del todo—. Deja ya de tentarme, mozuela.

—¡Ja! —protestó ella—. Así que me toca hacer de Eva, ¿no? —Pero sonrió con júbilo por su llegada—. Ven a ver el salón de baile.

Él dejó que ella le llevara otra vez hasta la estancia y contempló las paredes.

—Ya veo. Ni siquiera Rothgar haría…

—Es asombrosamente convincente, ¿a qué sí?

Él se acercó y examinó uno de los paneles y exhaló el aliento aliviado.

—Desde lejos es asombroso. Y más a la luz de las velas… La reputación que tenemos los Malloren de hacer cosas increíbles se va a ver reforzada.

—Al margen de lo que ocurra en el baile —en aquellos momentos, el propósito de la celebración se le hizo evidente a la muchacha, como si fuera un jarro de agua fría—, ¿conseguiste el documento?

—Sí —dijo él, y cerró los ojos—. Pero por los pelos. Mary le había dado la ropa a su doncella, que a su vez se la había pasado a su madre. Cuando llegué a casa de la buena mujer acababa de meterla a remojo en una tina de agua caliente con jabón.

Como si no pudiera resistirlo más, él le cogió la mano.

—Oh, Dios. ¿Sobrevivió la tinta? —el tenue contacto de la mano de Cyn estaba destrozando la mente de Chastity.

Él hizo una mueca.

—La mujer había sacado el documento del bolsillo, pensando en devolvérselo a Mary, pero lo dejó sobre una mesa, cerca de un pedazo de carne para asar. Se manchó un poco de sangre.

—En cierto sentido, resulta apropiado —comentó Chastity, entrelazando sus dedos con los de él.

—Muy cierto. Lamentablemente, luego le debió parecer un bocado muy apetitoso al muy canalla del perro de la dama.

Chastity cerró los ojos.

—No quiero saberlo.

—Está sólo un poco mordisqueado.

Ella abrió los ojos y le sonrió, tan complacida por su presencia como por sus noticias.

—¿Le has dado la carta a Rothgar?

—Se la he dado a Verity, puesto que es suya. Creo que ahora se la debe estar entregando a Rothgar. —Levantó la mano de la muchacha y se la besó.

Ella le miró anhelante, pero dijo:

—Entonces, vamos. Estoy en ascuas por saber lo que dice. Y como resulte que se trata de unas meditadas últimas palabras a modo de consejo, me dará un síncope.

Cyn se dejó arrastrar por ella.

—¡Eso me gustaría verlo!

Ella le lanzó una ceñuda mirada que se transformó en una carcajada y lo remolcó tras ella.

Al llegar al estudio de Rothgar, sin embargo, él ofreció verdadera resistencia y la atrapó contra la pared.

—Pareces feliz —le dijo casi con nostalgia.

Chastity se sorprendió al caer en la cuenta de que lo era. Que llevaba días siéndolo. Feliz de ser de nuevo una mujer, en una casa normal, con algo parecido a una familia. Había borrado de su pensamiento los terribles últimos meses y se negaba contemplar su triste futuro.

—¿Te importa?

Él sacudió la cabeza.

—¿Por qué habría de importarme, amor? Esto es lo que yo quiero para ti. Lo que insisto en darte. Si el documento resulta no sernos de utilidad, encontraremos alguna otra solución.

—Oh, Cyn —dijo Chastity—. Rezo para que tengas razón.

—Claro que tengo razón. Tienes a los Malloren de tu parte.

Chastity sacudió la cabeza pero dijo:

—Quiero darte las gracias por traerme aquí, Cyn. Y también por reclutar a Rothgar. Sé que no ha sido nada fácil para ti.

Él estalló en una clamorosa carcajada.

—¡Reclutarlo! ¿Eso ha sido lo que he hecho? ¡Es genial!

Y fue Cyn el que arrastró a una pensativa Chastity al interior del estudio.

Allí encontraron a Rothgar, Verity y Nathaniel —estos dos últimos muy serios. Rothgar pasó el manchado y ligeramente mordisqueado documento a Cyn y Chastity.

—Cielos —dijo Chastity al irlo leyendo.

Era un documento tremendamente incriminatorio, aunque como firmante figurara únicamente un tal «señor Ware.» El destinatario, quienquiera que fuese, claramente había pedido pruebas de con quién estaba tratando. En respuesta, se daban numerosos detalles que apuntaban, sin dejar lugar a dudas para aquellos que lo conocieran, a lord

Walgrave. En una misma frase, se combinaban las palabras vástago, fortitude, chastity, victor y verity.[7]

El señor Ware prometía usar su influencia sobre cierta gente de alcurnia —léase el príncipe y la princesa de Gales— para inducir a la familia real a que huyera, una vez que el ejército jacobita estuviera a treinta millas de Londres.

Declaraba su inmutable lealtad a James III, mencionando un encuentro con el «rey» durante su Gran Gira de 1717.

—¿Pudo tener lugar realmente ese encuentro? —preguntó Chastity—. Puedo imaginarme que padre permitiera que su ambición lo controlara y que diera ese paso, pensando que los Stuart estaban a punto de triunfar. Pero ¿en su juventud, y poco después de la rebelión de 1715?

Rothgar contestó:

—De hecho, ése es el dato menos incriminatorio. Un joven puede andar desencaminado, o estar mal aconsejado. En aquellos días, según tengo entendido, estaba de moda hacerse el bravucón entrando en contacto con los Stuart durante una Gran Gira. El resto, sin embargo, es suficiente para colocar a vuestro padre en una situación muy peligrosa, desde luego. Destruirá para siempre su imagen de incorruptible.

Verity miró a Rothgar.

—Hay que decírselo a Fort. Debe dar su punto de vista.

—Por supuesto. —Rothgar mandó llamar a lord Thornilll.

Fort entró en la habitación con bastante recelo, distanciándose física y mentalmente de aquellos inoportunos alia-

---

7. Aparecen los nombres de los hijos del conde Walgrave aunque no como tales, sino con minúsculas, haciendo alusión a las virtudes que representan: *fortitude*, la fortaleza; *chastity*, la castidad; *verity*, la veracidad y *victor*, la victoria.

dos. Lanzó a Cyn una mirada de encendida furia. Rothgar le tendió la carta.

Fort la leyó y se derrumbó sobre una silla.

—Jamás lo hubiera creído… ¡Debió volverse loco!

—Eran tiempos extraños —dijo Rothgar—. Tú andabas aún con la niñera y no te acordarás de gran cosa. Yo era muy joven, demasiado joven para que los acontecimientos me afectaran demasiado, pero recuerdo que hubo unos pocos días en los que parecía que lo imposible fuera a hacerse realidad. Todo eran rumores y desorden. La realeza de los Hanover había hecho el equipaje y estaba lista para huir a su pequeño distrito en Alemania. Muchos creían que los simpatizantes jacobitas iban a salir a montones desde todos los rincones … Tú padre se acobardó.

—¡Pero jacobita! Yo hubiera jurado que nunca simpatizó con ellos. ¡No puede ser! En asuntos espirituales, él es más puritano que papista. Por eso nosotros llevamos estos nombres.

—Pero más ambicioso que ninguna otra cosa. En 1745, se hallaba en la flor de la vida. Era de la misma edad, según creo, que su amigo Frederick, el príncipe de Gales, es decir, tenía unos treinta y ocho años. Dos hombres ambiciosos, aguardando su momento, impacientes por alcanzar el poder. El gran Walpole había caído unos años antes, sin una mano firme que le sucediera para conducir los destinos de Inglaterra. Todo estaba a punto. Sólo hacía falta que muriera el rey.

—Rothgar sonrió sarcásticamente—. Ninguno de los dos imaginó que el viejo rey George II viviría hasta 1760, sobreviviendo a su codicioso hijo… Ironías del destino.

Pero antes de que la rueda de la fortuna diera ese giro, se produjo otro sucio golpe del hado. Walgrave, que se hallaba al acecho para hacerse con el control de Inglaterra tan pronto como Frederick fuera proclamado rey, ¿iba a permitir que los jacobitas se lo arrebataran? Luchó contra ellos, pero cuando vio que podían salir victoriosos, vaciló, incapaz de contemplar cómo su sueño se iba a la porra. Tal vez ellos se aproximaron a él, le tentaron. Frederick, como sabéis, no era un personaje modélico, sobre el que poder construir un nuevo orden. Era un borracho y un libertino...

Rothgar se encogió repentinamente de hombros.

—Disculpad mis especulaciones. Tal vez el noble conde nos saque de dudas cuando llegue.

—¿Cuando llegue? —preguntó Fort aturdido.

—¿No te lo ha dicho Chastity? Le he invitado al baile. Fort seguía de pie, con la carta todavía en sus manos.

—Podría arrojar esto al fuego.

—Tal vez —dijo Rothgar.

—Tienes la sartén por el mango finalmente, ¿no Rothgar? —dijo Fort con sorna—. Debes estar disfrutando con todo esto. ¿Qué piensas hacer?

—¿Yo? —dijo Rothgar dócilmente—. Voy a asegurarme de que mi hermano pueda casarse convenientemente con tu hermana. Es el único interés que tengo en este asunto. Esta carta desempeña sólo una pequeña función; con ella se podría doblegar la voluntad de tu padre. En cuanto al resto, lo dejo en tus manos, pero yo que tú no le dejaría saber que la tienes en tu poder sin tomar antes alguna precaución.

La habitación se quedó en absoluto silencio mientras Fort consideraba la posibilidad de que su padre le matara para recuperar el documento. Él entregó la carta de nuevo a Rothgar.

—Guárdala. Cuando haya decidido un curso de acción, te lo haré saber. —Fort salió de la estancia con paso majestuoso.

Verity le dijo algo en voz baja a Nathaniel y se levantó. Miró a Chastity y ambas salieron en pos de su hermano.

Le encontraron en su habitación, donde la había emprendido con una botella de brandy. Moviéndose las dos al unísono, se la quitaron.

—Ahora no, Fort —le dijo Verity.

—¡Todo esto es culpa vuestra! —gruñó él.

—¡Vaya! ¿De veras? —declaró Chastity—. En mi vida había oído nada tan injusto. Verity y yo hemos sufrido terriblemente y no porque nos lo hayamos buscado nosotras.

Fort se volvió hacía ella:

—¡Si tú no hubieras caído en la depravación con un maldito Malloren, Rothgar no tendría ahora a nuestra familia con el agua al cuello!

Chastity se colocó los puños sobre las caderas y se inclinó hacia delante:

—¡Si padre no hubiera cometido traición, nada de esto habría sucedido! ¿O te has olvidado de eso?

Él gimió y hundió la cabeza entre las manos.

—Si esto sale a luz, todos estamos perdidos.

Chastity y Verity se sentaron, cada una a un lado de su hermano.

—Fort, ya has oído a Rothgar. No piensa hacerlo público.

Él levantó la vista.

—¿Os fiáis de Rothgar?

—Sí —dijo Chastity—. ¿Tú no?

—Él odia a los Ware.

—¿Cómo es eso, Fort?

—La cosa viene, sobre todo, a causa de un hombre, un tal Russell, que era partidario de los Pitts, a quienes padre detestaba. Ahora me doy cuenta de que padre en realidad detesta a cualquiera que se interponga entre él y el poder. Russell era Comisario General del Ejército. Le acusaron de corrupción y fue juzgado y declarado culpable. Rothgar permaneció todo el tiempo al lado de su amigo. Se decía que había compartido con él los botines, claro. Padre siempre ha presumido de colaborar para que Russell fuera llevado ante la justicia y poner fin a los escándalos que afectaban a nuestros valientes soldados que luchaban con uniformes estropeados y usaban armas en mal estado... —Volvió a hundir la cabeza entre las manos—. Ahora ya no sé qué pensar.

Verity dijo:

—¿Supones que Rothgar tal vez desee vengarse?

—No creo que sea la clase de hombre que olvide las ofensas.

Chastity dijo tranquilamente pero con firmeza:

—Me parece que te equivocas. —Fort levantó la cabeza para mirarla y ella añadió—: Ya sé que piensas que estoy atontada por el amor, o por la lujuria, pero la devoción que Rothgar siente por su familia sobrepasa a cualquier otro impulso que pueda tener. Descubriendo a padre sólo empeoraría mi situación, y él no le haría eso a Cyn.

El ceño de Fort se destensó un poco.

—Espero que tengas razón. Pero, cuando todo esto termine, él seguirá teniendo el documento, o al menos la información... No me fío de él.

Chastity puso una mano sobre la de su hermano.

—Haré que Rotghar prometa devolver el documento y guardar silencio. Él cumplirá su palabra.

Fort se sacudió de encima la mano de su hermana.

—No quiero que te arrastres ante ningún Malloren para pedir favores. Me pregunto —dijo con sorna—, qué pedirá a cambio.

Las hermanas estallaron al unísono:

—¡Fort! —dijo Verity asombrada.

—¡Idiota! —exclamó Chastity.

Esta última se levantó y le miró de frente.

—¡Para tu información, el marqués es como un hermano para mí, y en los últimos días se ha comportado conmigo mejor que mi verdadero hermano en toda su vida! —Chastity giró sobre sus talones y salió de la estancia dando un portazo.

Fort se puso a soltar improperios.

—No hay quien pueda con esta chica. Me dan ganas de pegarla.

—Ni se te ocurra —dijo Verity con firmeza.

Él suspiró.

—Me siento como si estuviera en un torbellino. Chastity deja que estos Malloren hagan con ella lo que les dé la gana. Ella se cree todo lo que le dicen. —Miró a Verity—. Me alegro de que estés casada con Frazer, aunque por ahí también se avecina el escándalo, sobre todo cuando Vernham os lleve a los dos a juicio. Y ahora padre. Lo que faltaba.

—Supongo que tú eres puro como la nieve.

—No —admitió él con pesar—, pero empiezo a parecerlo con estas compañías

Verity le sonrió.

—Yo también confío en Rothgar. Al igual que Nathaniel.

—Estáis todos locos —dijo Fort.

20

—Estáis todos locos —dijo Fort mirando en torno a sí en la Sala de los Tapices aquella misma tarde. Sólo los que no pertenecían a la familia Malloren parecían estar de acuerdo con él.

—Yo no lo creo —dijo Rothgar—. Hay que dar salida al rencor acumulado. Cyn quiere matarte por haber abandonado a tu hermana. Tú quieres matarlo a él por protegerla. Lo que procede es un duelo.

—¡Pero yo no quiero que ninguno de los dos muera! —protestó Chastity.

—Tú eres una mujer —le dijo Rothgar despectivamente—, y no entiendes de estos asuntos. —Pero ella vio el divertido regocijo que se escondía tras aquellas palabras, y eso la tranquilizó. Aunque el regocijo de Rotghar raras veces resultaba inofensivo.

—Entonces, no deberías sacar estos temas delante de una mujer tan ignorante, ¿no crees? —preguntó ella vivazmente.

—¡Ay de mí! —dijo él con una leve reverencia—. Qué torpe he sido, pero ¿no te resulta excitante, monada, saber que se van a pelear por ti?

—No —dijo Chastity, pero algo en su interior le dijo que estaba mintiendo.

—Dime, lord Thornhill —inquirió Rothgar—. ¿Eres bueno con la espada?

—Muy bueno —replicó Fort—. Pero no tengo intención de matar a lord Cynric. No creo que eso me honrara a los ojos de mi familia.

—Pero sí a los ojos de tu padre —señaló Rothgar afablemente—. Pero si eres bueno, creo que tú y Cyn podéis batiros *au naturel*, sin que haya mucho riesgo de que os hagáis un daño irreparable.

—¡Con las espadas sin protección! —exclamó Nathaniel conmocionado—. Yo no quiero participar en esto.

Pero Cyn ya se había puesto de pie, con un destello en la mirada.

—Creo que es una idea estupenda. Ya es hora de que lord Thornhill tenga algunas heridas en su propia carne.

Chastity se puso también de pie:

—Todavía está magullado por defenderme a mí, Cyn. No estás siendo justo.

—Fue lento en el cumplimiento de su deber. —Miró a Fort desafiante—. ¿No es cierto?

—Y tú demasiado rápido —dijo Fort con sorna—. ¿No es así?

Ya habían salido por la puerta.

Chastity se volvió hacia Rothgar.

—Si alguno de los dos resulta herido, tú serás el culpable.

—Tiemblo de miedo —contestó él, dándole un golpecito bajo la barbilla—. Primero pensé en que se batieran a puñetazos, pero de ese modo acabarían llenos de sangre y contusiones. Los dos albergan resentimientos, querida, y quiero que mañana tengan la cabeza despejada cuando empiece la diversión.

—¿Qué diversión? —quiso saber Chastity, pero él ya había salido tras su hermano fuera de la habitación.

Chastity siseó entre dientes mientras le seguía.

Descubrió que el duelo iba a tener lugar en el recibidor. Cyn y Fort se habían descalzado y estaban en mangas de camisa, probando unos ligeros espadines de duelo. Éstos parecían tener cierta fragilidad y una misteriosa belleza, pero, sin nada que embotara las puntas, eran instrumentos mortales.

Se estaban colocando sillas para los espectadores, pero Chastity se acercó a Rothgar.

—¡Por favor, no hagas esto! Puede ocurrir un accidente...

Él bajó la vista hacia ella:

—¿Fanfarroneaba tu hermano cuando ha dicho que era muy bueno?

—No lo creo.

—Cyn también es muy bueno, o tal vez algo mejor que eso. Sería raro que la punta de un estoque llegara sin querer a alguna parte. Los accidentes pueden ocurrir en cualquier momento y en cualquier lugar. Sólo los zoquetes evitan la aventura por temor a ellos.

Chastity farfulló algunas apreciaciones sobre los hombres en general y, en particular, sobre los Malloren, y, contoneándose, fue a sentarse junto a Elf.

—En tu familia están todos locos —le dijo a la muchacha.

—Y también en la tuya —le respondió Elf, con los ojos brillantes de excitación.

—¿No estás ni siquiera un poco nerviosa? —le preguntó Chastity.

Elf la miró sorprendida.

—Desde luego que no. Cyn es verdaderamente muy bueno. Creo que nunca ha sido derrotado, ni siquiera por Rothgar. Rothgar dice que se ha vuelto torpe con la edad y que en su juventud le hubiera superado, pero creo que no lo dice en serio.

Chastity volvió a mirar a Cyn, sorprendida. ¿Por qué él la sorprendía constantemente?

Ya le había visto manejar la espada cuando la rescató en Maidenhead. De hecho, él había jugado con su adversario. Ella se dio cuenta entonces de que era bueno. Pero ¿muy bueno?

Tan pronto como empezó el asalto, supo que sí. Ya había presenciado combates de esgrima con anterioridad y entendía un poco de la ciencia y el arte que requerían. Apreció el ligero juego de piernas de los dos hombres, la elasticidad de sus cuerpos y la fuerza de sus ágiles muñecas.

Pero vio todavía más. Fort lo hacía bien, sin perder el equilibrio y con mucha fuerza. Al ser algunas pulgadas más alto que Cyn, tenía la ventaja de tener mayor alcance. Pero no parecía servirle de mucho.

El filo de azogue de Cyn chocaba y se deslizaba contra el de Fort, con una facilidad que parecía carente de esfuerzo. Daba igual la estocada que Fort intentara, porque el florete de Cyn la paraba con suavidad, haciendo que el combate pareciera una danza —cuya dulce coreografía buscara la armonía— en lugar de una peligrosa contienda.

Chastity notó en el progresivo gesto de concentración de Fort que no era el quién dirigía el baile. Entonces él quebró el ritmo y se movió con menos donaire pero de un modo más brusco y amenazador —fue directo al corazón de Cyn. Chastity jadeó, pero Cyn le atajó y controló igual que había hecho hasta entonces.

Fort hizo una mueca y retrocedió, bajando la espada.

—Vaya, sí que eres bueno.

Cyn bajó también su espada.

—Tú también eres diestro.

Fort se rió con sarcasmo, pero no parecía querer rendirse.

—Podrías desarmarme, ¿no es así?

—Tal vez —dijo Cyn, con la mirada velada tras las pestañas.

—Quiero verlo. —Fort se colocó en posición.

Cyn vaciló.

—Quiero verlo —dijo Fort—, y apoyaré tu boda con mi hermana.

Cyn sonrió y levantó el arma a modo de saludo.

Volvieron a encontrarse, haciendo entrechocar sus aceros.

—Mereces que te hiera —dijo Cyn, y rozó a Fort súbitamente en la barbilla con la punta de su estoque, haciendo brotar una hilera de gotas carmesí.

Fort blasfemó y dio un traspié.

Pero Cyn no lo desarmó inmediatamente, sino que esperó a que Fort se recuperara y, entonces, casi con desgana, en tres movimientos que Chastity vio cómo Fort reconocía y trataba de esquivar, envió la espada de su adversario girando limpiamente por el aire hasta que quedó fuera de su alcance.

—Santo Cielo —dijo Fort —. ¿Dónde has aprendido?

—Aquí y allá —dijo Cyn—, pero sobre todo de Rothgar. Es un maestro más severo que la mayoría de los que se pueden contratar. Me pinchó más de una vez para enseñarme a no bajar la guardia, cuando era todavía un muchacho.

—Nunca he tenido la más mínima intención —dijo Rothgar con helada precisión— de perder un hermano a lo tonto, por culpa de una espada bravucona. —Se quitó el chaquetón—. Hermanito, quiero poner a prueba mi temple. Tal vez hoy pueda hacerte una nueva marca.

Recogió ágilmente la espada caída y encaró a Cyn.

—O tal vez sea yo el que te marque a ti —dijo Cyn, con un destello en la mirada

Rothgar se rió con ganas.

—Inténtalo.

Las espadas volvieron a entrechocarse, pero esta vez podía apreciarse la similitud de estilos. También era obvio que Cyn estaba teniendo que estirarse por completo, pero lo mismo podía decirse de Rothgar. En más de una ocasión, no se hirieron por los pelos. La espada de Rothgar se deslizó una vez hacia el rostro de Cyn, desviándose en el último instante. Chastity se tapó la boca con las manos.

Un instante después la punta del estoque de Rothgar volvió a dirigirse hacia la cara de Cyn, como si pretendiera sacarle un ojo. Esta vez, Cyn controló fácilmente la acometida.

—Me alegro de que por fin te hayas aprendido ésa, Cyn. —Entonces el marqués resopló al tiempo que el florete de Cyn le cortaba la camisa a la altura del corazón y se retiraba. Rothgar retrocedió, sonrió, y saludo con la espada—. He olvidado mis propias lecciones. No hay que perder tiempo regocijándose.

Los dos hermanos se abrazaron. Brand y Bryght se acercaron a ellos para compartir sus comentarios. Pronto, también Fort y Nathaniel formaron parte de una alegre camarilla de varones dedicada a repetir los movimientos y aprender nuevos pasos.

Elf, Chastity y Verity se miraron y se marcharon a comentar extensamente la insensatez de los machos de la especie.

No obstante, el plan del marqués parecía haber funcionado. Fort seguía teniendo sus recelos, pero estaba dispuesto a trabajar con los Malloren. También había garantizado su apoyo al matrimonio de Chastity y Cyn.

Fue sólo más tarde cuando Fort anunció a Chastity:

—No me voy a oponer a tu boda, pero sigo sin fiarme de Rothgar. No es que ponga en duda su honor, sino sus motivos. Puede que su plan no sea del todo bueno para nosotros. Estate alerta, querida. Cuando se trace la línea, espero que estés del lado de los Ware.

El día del baile amaneció despejado y con sol, a pesar del frío. Buen tiempo para viajar y, con la luna casi llena, la gente podría regresar a casa confiadamente.

Chastity sabía que Rothgar esperaba que su padre acudiera al evento, pero no sabía cómo podía estar tan seguro. El conde debía sospechar ya algo. Por su parte, esperaba que su padre no apareciese. No quería tener que volver a encararlo. Seguramente bastaría con decirle que tenían la prueba que podía destruirle.

Ya estaba lo bastante nerviosa con este su primer acto social después del desastre, sin necesidad de añadir ningún otro motivo de terror. Desde luego, le daba cierta tranquilidad el hecho de que se tratase de un baile de máscaras, pero Chastity se estremecía al pensar que iba a moverse entre gente que, de reconocerla, le haría el vacío.

También sabía que iba a ser un momento crucial. No sabía exactamente qué era lo que Rothgar había planeado, pero aquel tranquilo interludio había llegado a su fin. Después de aquella noche, o bien era restaurada a un estado de gracia —lo que parecía bastante improbable— o se vería obligada a decidir qué hacer el resto de su desdichada vida.

Había estado evitando a Cyn. Él parecía haberse tomado en serio su promesa de no acostarse con ella, pero eso sólo hacía que su proximidad fuera aún un suplicio mayor. El mero hecho de verlo, el más leve roce de su ropa contra el cuerpo de la muchacha, era suficiente para dejarla transida de pasión. Pero la razón le decía que pronto tendrían que separarse. Debía prepararse para ello.

No sabía cómo iba a soportarlo.

Había sumergido su deseo en los preparativos del baile y ahora todo estaba ya dispuesto. De Londres, habían llegado brillantes faroles de papel para iluminar el salón manteniendo al mismo tiempo el ambiente exótico. Se había erigido en él una pagoda ingeniosamente iluminada, alrededor de la cual caminaban unos mandarines mecánicos.

Un equipo de muchachos se encargaba de dar vueltas a los autómatas, pero a Chastity casi le parecía que era cosa de magia. El ambiente en la mansión aquella noche estaba cargado de presagios. O tal vez fuera que el acto que iba a tener lugar fuera simplemente un juguete mecánico, cuyo artífice y diseñador era Rothgar.

Mortificada por sus miedos y sus esperanzas, Chastity se echó una capa de piel por encima y rehuyó los preparativos del último momento para pasear por la glorieta oeste y observar cómo el sol poniente doraba la Abadía. Entonces apareció Cyn y se unió a ella. La muchacha pensó marcharse, buscando la seguridad de la compañía de otras personas, pero no tuvo fuerzas para huir de él en aquellos momentos, cuando el final estaba tan cerca. Se estremeció. Y no a causa del frío.

—Noto una sensación extraña.

—Estás nerviosa por el baile —. Simplemente su voz era suficiente para desarmarla.

—No —dijo ella—. Todo el mundo parece tenso, como si alguien les hubiera dado cuerda.—Después pensó en el destino como en un relojero y sintió unas ganas tremendas de hallarse a salvo en los brazos de su amado. Se volvió hacia él.

—¿Crees que mi padre vendrá, Cyn?

—Si Rothgar le ha enviado el mensaje adecuado, lo hará. —Los ojos de Cyn le decían que él deseaba lo mismo que ella. Mucho más que ella.

—¿Y qué mensaje puede ser ése?

—No lo sé, pero Rothgar lo habrá encontrado. —Él la sonrió de pronto—. ¿Qué vas a llevar puesto esta noche?

—Un dominó y una máscara.

—Como todo el mundo. Dame alguna otra pista.

Ella se obligó a guardar silencio.

—No importa —le dijo él con suavidad—, si no soy capaz de encontrarte, Chloe, es que no te merezco. —Él le cogió la mano y, ella, tras oírle pronunciar aquel nombre privado, ya no fue capaz de resistirse más.

Mientras paseaban por la solana, el corazón y el alma de Chastity tenían su atención puesta en el contacto con su elegante mano de espadachín. Ella entrelazó sus dedos con los de Cyn.

—¿Por qué no me habías dicho que eras tan bueno con el florete?

Él la miró de soslayo, jugando a su vez con los dedos de la muchacha.

—No es fácil dejar caer algo así en una conversación: «A propósito, resulta que se me dan muy bien los duelos».

—¿Dársete bien? —repitió ella—. Detrás de una habilidad así hay mucho trabajo.

Él le acarició la mano con el pulgar.

—Disfruto con ello. A menudo tengo problemas para encontrar un adversario a mi altura, pero en Canadá, capturé un prisionero francés que era un digno contrincante. Con él pulí mi destreza.

Ella se detuvo y le miró.

—¿Te batías en duelo con un prisionero?

Él levantó la mano de la muchacha, todavía entrelazada con la suya y la besó prolongadamente.

—Sólo como ejercicio, corazón.

Chastity se estremeció a causa del poder sensual que aquel hombre tenía sobre ella. ¿Cómo iba a sobrevivir sin él?

—Los duelos se están convirtiendo rápidamente en un arte decorativo —dijo él muy calmado, aunque sus ojos estaban encendidos—. Es cierto, como dice Rothgar, que conviene tener destreza, para evitar que algún tipo pendenciero te quite la vida por nada, pero, si lo que se requiere es la muerte, la pistola es más certera.

Muerte. No, no hables de muerte por favor.

Él le rozó los nudillos con los labios.

Chastity se debatía entre la necesidad de ser protegida y la de protegerlo a él de cualquier daño.

—¿Por qué todos los hombres acabáis siempre luchando? —protestó ella débilmente.

Ahora Cyn le raspó ligeramente la piel con los dientes y ella sintió cómo el abismo del peligro le producía un tórrido estremecimiento de deseo.

—A veces los hombres también hacemos otras cosas —le recordó él con suavidad.

—Cyn, no —susurró ella, aunque sin mucha fuerza. Si él la quería en aquel lugar y en aquel momento, sobre las frías piedras, sería suya.

Él contuvo el aliento y se recompuso.

—Tal vez debiera enseñarte a manejar la espada —le dijo con ligereza—. Por si vuelves a querer ir disfrazada por ahí.

—Espero no tener que volver a hacerlo jamás.

—¿No te proporcionó ningún goce? —Aquella pregunta parecía tener un doble sentido.

—Un poco —confesó ella—. Disfruté de la excitación, pero no de los engaños. Y, desde luego, tampoco de la vergüenza. —Ella volteó las manos, para coger las de Cyn—. Lo que sí me gustó fue tener un amigo, un amigo llamado Cyn.

Al igual que las nubes cambiantes, su rostro pasó de la oscuridad del deseo contenido a una oscuridad aún mayor, fruto del remordimiento.

—Hasta que yo lo estropeé seduciéndote.

—Yo no diría que lo estropeaste.

—¿No?

Ella cerró los ojos. ¿Por qué insistía él siempre en saber la verdad?

—Las cosas cambian, Cyn. Sería perfecto si pudiéramos casarnos…

—Nos casaremos —dijo él ásperamente—. Me retracto de lo que dije. Nunca permitiré que seas de ningún otro hombre. —Deslizó las manos por debajo de la capa de Chastity y la apretó fuerte contra él—. No puedo vivir sin ti, Chastity. Me he dado cuenta en estos últimos días. Pero no es tu cuerpo lo que más necesito. Si lo deseas, podemos vivir el resto de nuestros días como hermanos.

—¿Por qué demonios iba yo a querer eso...? —preguntó la muchacha, mientras sus caderas se apretaban contra él como si tuvieran voluntad propia. Pero, entonces, un sonido la sobresaltó, volviendo a traer a escena la realidad y todos sus miedos.

—¡Oigo un coche!

Ella se apartó, pero él no aflojó el abrazo.

—Tranquila. Puede ser cualquiera.

Ella sacudió la cabeza.

—No creo que sea ningún invitado, Cyn. Es demasiado pronto. Tal vez sea padre. —El miedo le puso los nervios a flor de piel.

Él le cogió las manos con un firme apretón.

—Ya te has librado de él. No volverá a hacerte daño nunca más. —Mientras se calmaba, la cogió de la mano y la condujo hacia la casa—. Vamos, amor. Aunque sea el mismo demonio, plantémosle cara con valentía.

Entraron en el recibidor de mármol y escucharon la despaciosa voz de Vernham reclamando a su pupilo.

Cyn siseó entre dientes y le salió a su encuentro. Chastity corrió tras él para impedir que matara al hombre que la había desgraciado, pero Rothgar había llegado antes.

—Ah, Vernham. ¿Tu pupilo? —dijo, colocándose sin esfuerzo en medio de Cyn y su blanco—. Te refieres al joven sir William. Sin duda querrás asegurarte de que está a salvo, pero no creo que desees privarlo de los cuidados de su madre cuando todavía toma el pecho.

Vernham miró en torno a sí, furioso e inquieto, y constató cómo se iban congregando los Malloren. Brand y Elf habían ido al vestíbulo siguiendo a Rothgar, y ahora Bryght salía de la biblioteca. Vernham obviamente percibió la animosidad, pero no podía imaginar que ellos supieran nada de él, al margen de que era el tutor legal del niño.

Él cogió una pizca de rapé.

—Lady Vernham será bienvenida junto con el niño.

—Pero Verity es ahora lady Verity Frazer y hay que tener en cuenta los deseos de su esposo. Y ahora, señor —dijo Rothgar con una bucólica afabilidad que aterrorizaría a cualquiera que lo conociese—. Tómese algún refresco. Si ha venido como respuesta a mi nota, ya sabrá que hemos planeado una fiesta para esta noche. Tiene que quedarse.

A pesar de sus protestas, Vernham se dejó llevar hasta la Sala de los Tapices y se sentó con una taza de té en las manos.

—¡Exijo ver a mi pupilo! —estalló. Después vio a Chastity y palideció.

Ella le sonrió.

La muchacha no había visto hasta entonces unos ojos que se salieran de sus órbitas. Hasta entonces.

—Desde luego que sí. Debes ver a tu pupilo —dijo Rothgar, e hizo que fueran a buscar a Verity y a su niño.

Cuando ambos llegaron, acompañados por un mayor Frazer de mirada dura, Vernham estaba de pie, observando intranquilo a sus acompañantes. Apenas miró al bebé.

—Bien. Entonces, tú te vienes conmigo ahora.

—Por supuesto que no —dijo Verity con firmeza—. Y no te vas a llevar a William, Henry. Tendrás que presentar un recurso en el juzgado, y eso, según creo, puede llevar mucho tiempo.

Los estrechos ojos de Vernham revolotearon por la estancia. Todos los Malloren sonreían, Cyr incluido, pero a

Henry no debió resultarle reconfortante, lo que demostraba que Verity tenía razón cuando lo describía como un hombre astuto.

—Supongo que tienes razón —dijo él intentando parecer calmado—. A estas alturas, no hay nada que yo pueda hacer si el chiquillo se encuentra bien. No quiero entreteneros más. Te pido disculpas si te he atosigado, Verity, pero estaba tremendamente preocupado por ti. No ha sido muy considerado de tu parte marcharte sin dejar ningún mensaje o indicación de a dónde te dirigías.

—Pero si yo huía de usted, señor —dijo Verity sencillamente.

Él se quedó descolocado.

—¿Por qué, por el amor de Dios?

Nathaniel intervino en ese punto, para evitar que Verity, disgustada como estaba, hablara más de la cuenta.

—Puede que fuera una decisión equivocada, Vernham, pero todos debemos alegrarnos de que todo haya salido tan bien. Mi intención es solicitar la custodia del niño, lo que seguramente le parecerá apropiado, y pasar a administrar su propiedad.

Vernham le lanzó una mirada llena de odio pero sonrió.

—Apelaré, como usted comprenderá. Estoy seguro de que la justicia defenderá la voluntad de mi hermano. —Se puso los guantes, mirando todavía inquieto a su alrededor, como si esperara que le impidieran irse—. A propósito, eso me recuerda que ha desaparecido un documento, lady Verity, un documento que mi hermano guardaba en su caja fuerte. ¿No te lo habrás llevado contigo, por casualidad? Creo que es un codicilo del testamento y habría que entregárselo a los abogados.

Chastity contuvo el aliento y se controló para no dejar escapar ninguna información.

—Oh, eso —dijo Verity vagamente—. Sí, lo cogí para ponerlo bajo custodia. Me pregunto dónde lo he puesto. Creo que debo tenerlo por algún bolsillo

Chastity casi pudo sentir cómo a Vernham le crujían los dientes detrás de su sonrisa. El problema era que también se percató de la diversión que había en la mirada de Verity. En cualquier momento podía echarse a reír y poner todo el juego al descubierto. Su hermana nunca había sido capaz de sacar adelante una mentira.

—¿No podrías buscarlo? —preguntó Vernham un tanto tenso.

Fort irrumpió entonces en la estancia, distrayendo la atención de todos.

—Me habían dicho… que eras tú. ¡Tengo una cuenta pendiente contigo, maldito canalla!

Había cogido a Vernham por el cuello y fueron necesarios tres Malloren para soltarlo. Al menos uno de los tres no se sentía filantrópico:

—Tendrás que ponerte a la cola, Thornhill —dijo Cyn—. Yo estoy primero.

—Tendrás que luchar conmigo para merecerlo —gruñó Fort.

Cyn se limitó a levantar una ceja y Fort soltó alguna que otra blasfemia.

Vernham se llevó las manos al magullado cuello.

—¡Me ofrecí a casarme con esa perra!

Fort le dejó dio tal golpe que lo dejó fuera de combate.

—Que barbaridad —murmuró Rothgar, e hizo sonar una campana. El lacayo que acudió a la llamada recibió instrucciones de llevarse al inconsciente caballero y cuidar de él.

Cuando se llevaron a Vernham, Rothgar dijo:

—Tengo que confesar que no sabía muy bien cómo iba a convencerle para que se quedara en la guarida del león. Todos parecíais decididos a ensañaros con él. Te felicito Thornhill.

—A la mierda las felicitaciones —dijo Fort—. Quiero sacarle las tripas.

—Más adelante —dijo Rothgar—. Primero quiero que se produzca una confrontación entre él y Walgrave, a ser posible delante de testigos.

Los primeros invitados comenzaron a llegar al caer la tarde, residentes locales poco sofisticados, emocionados por la invitación a la Abadía. Algunos llegaban ya con la máscara, sobre todo los más jóvenes; otros se ponían los disfraces una vez que se habían desprendido de sus abrigos y capas. Para algunos, el disfraz consistía únicamente en el antifaz que les cubría el rostro, pero la mayoría llevaban también los envolventes mantos de seda con caperuza llamados dominós. En general, no tenían una genuina intención de ocultar su identidad y se saludaban unos a otros constantemente.

Chastity, por otra parte, había hecho grandes esfuerzos para asegurarse de que no la reconocían. Un dominó de seda rosada y una máscara color perla que le cubría la mitad del rostro la encubrían parcialmente, pero, además, se había empolvado profusamente la peluca, que ahora tenía un color gris plateado.

Cuando se contempló en el espejo de su habitación, estuvo segura de que ni siquiera Cyn sería capaz de reconocerla. Se acordó de lo que él le había dicho. ¿Penetrarían los ojos del amor incluso a través de aquel disfraz?

Mientras observaba la escena, vigilante por si aparecía su padre, Chastity escuchó el parloteo de la gente del lugar. Hablaban de niños y de cosechas y —con más regocijo que pasión— de la última moda. Los labios empezaron a temblarle y se dio cuenta de lo mucho que deseaba aquello para sí misma. Una vida normal y corriente, envuelta en asuntos de extraordinaria importancia.

Aquella gente se interesaba por la política, pero no mataría por alcanzar el poder; se interesaba por la moda, pero no se arruinaría por ella.

Escuchó a dos corpulentos caballeros refunfuñar acerca de lord Bute y el influjo de los ambiciosos escoceses sobre Inglaterra, pero ni siquiera aquel tema parecía exaltarles.

A aquellos hacendados les importaba poco que Whitehall se fuera a la porra, si les dejaban seguir ocupándose de su tierra.

Entonces se dio cuenta que había sido la propia presencia de aquel hombre la que había suscitado el tema. La escueta máscara de lord Bute no ocultaba —no era esas su intención— a uno de los hombres más apuestos de Inglaterra. Su acompañante era una mujer que llevaba un dominó rojo y un antifaz que le cubría todo el rostro. ¿Otra dama de la alta sociedad en busca de aventuras?

Él aceptaba sonriente las atenciones de la pequeña camarilla que se había formado a su alrededor y de los lugareños predispuestos a codearse con los grandes. Chastity sacudió la cabeza. Era bien parecido, amable y tenía buenas intenciones. Pero carecía de la talla necesaria para llevar a Inglaterra a su máximo esplendor. Veía con claridad que su manera de ejercer el poder había llevado a su padre a su posición extremista.

Empezó a escrutar a los invitados que llegaban para ver si descubría a su progenitor. Seguramente sería capaz de reconocerlo. ¿Se habría tomado la molestia de ponerse una máscara? No era su estilo.

Le distrajo un caballero que hizo una reverencia ante ella.

—Dulce rosa, ¿querrá pasear conmigo?

Su voz y el terciopelo azul le sonaban de algo.

—Tal vez esté esperando a alguien, señor —dijo ella.

—Entonces, no espere más, mi encantadora flor. Él está aquí.

Ya había caído. ¡Era lord Heatherington! ¿Qué estaba haciendo allí? Ella le golpeó suavemente en la muñeca con el abanico.

—Canalla embustero. Él no tiene vuestra estatura.

—Entonces no os interesa. ¿No me daréis una oportunidad para que os convenza de mis encantos?

Aquel hombre no carecía de atractivo, pero sabiendo lo que sabía, Chastity no estaba dispuesta a irse a un aparte con él ni por toda la corona de Inglaterra.

—Me temo que no, señor —le dijo—. Tendréis que encontrar otro pimpollo.

Él encajó la negativa con donaire, hizo una reverencia y se alejó.

Mientras tanto, habían llegado numerosas personas que ella no había podido observar. Un caballero enmascarado con una túnica de seda dorada pasó a su lado, se detuvo y se dio la vuelta para mirarla. Acto seguido, se le acercó.

—Mi bello camaleón —murmuró Cyn—. Veo que la preocupación ha hecho que te salgan canas.

—¿Cómo me has conocido?

—¿Y cómo no iba a hacerlo? Vamos —dijo él, tendiéndole una mano—, tengo que encontrar a Rothgar.

—¿Por qué? —preguntó Chastity, repentinamente nerviosa.

—Únicamente para decirle que Brand lo ha convencido de que se una a la fiesta.

Chastity no pudo negarse. Le dio la mano y ambos zigzaguearon entre la multitud en busca del marqués.

—¿Cómo demonios lo ha logrado Brand?

—Le dijo que era la única manera de conseguir algo de comer y beber. Vernham es muy aficionado a la bebida. Desde que ha recobrado la conciencia no ha parado de pedir brandy.

—¿Te ha contado Rothgar sus planes?

—No. No te preocupes. No dejaré que nada ni nadie te haga daño. —Parecía darse cuenta de que ella estaba muerta de miedo.

Rothgar no estaba en el vestíbulo, así que se dirigieron a la primera sala de la recepción. Un repentino crujido a la altura de la puerta hizo que Chastity se percatara de que Cyn llevaba una espada.

—Entonces, ¿acabará la cosa de manera violenta? —susurró ella llena de ansiedad.

Él sonrió, un Malloren de los pies a la cabeza.

—Eso espero.

El animado alboroto de la gente feliz, sin más preocupación que la de los hijos o las cosechas, le pareció a Chastity casi macabro al vislumbrar los horrores que se avecinaban.

Encontraron a Rothgar en la habitación acondicionada para el juego, acomodando a Bute en la mesa. Se mostraba particularmente obsequioso con la enmascarada acompañante de Bute. Chastity comprendió que debía tratarse con toda seguridad de Augusta, la princesa de Gales y madre del rey George.

Se quedó muda de asombro. ¿Era aquello casualidad o es que Rothgar estaba apostando muy alto? El hecho de que la princesa Augusta y el conde de Walgrave fueran enemigos encarnizados, ¿formaba parte de la red que Rothgar estaba tejiendo?

Augusta había tenido celos de la proximidad entre Walgrave y su marido, el príncipe de Gales. A la muerte del príncipe Frederick, había puesto a su hijo —el actual rey— en contra del conde.

Cyn le comunicó a Rothgar que Vernham se había sumado al jolgorio y Rothgar asintió. Tenía el pelo empolvado de blanco y llevaba un maquillaje ligero que subrayaba su lado más perverso, pero, exceptuando una pequeña máscara negra, no llevaba ningún disfraz. Todo el mundo podía reconocerle y darse cuenta de que era peligroso. Chastity se había acostumbrado a él, tal y como era con su familia, relajado y con atavío rústico. Pero así, con las fastuosas galas propias de la corte —satén azul oscuro y plateado—, volvía a tenerle miedo.

¿Tendría razón Fort? ¿Aprovecharía Rothgar aquella oportunidad para destruir a un enemigo a cualquier precio?

Tal vez él le adivinó el pensamiento, porque sonrió y le tomó una mano para besársela.

—Empieza a planear tu boda, monada..

—¿Cómo puedes estar seguro...?

Él levantó las cejas.

—Todo está empezando a encajar en su sitio de manera admirable.

Chastity supo entonces que tenía razón. Todos se movían siguiendo sus instrucciones. La muchacha echó una alarmada ojeada en dirección a la princesa.

—No pienso quitarme la máscara —dijo con firmeza.

—Tú harás lo que se te diga. Cyn, quédate con ella y contrólala como haría un buen marido.

—Todavía no estamos casados —dijo Cyn lisa y llanamente—. y, aunque lo estuviéramos, no la obligaría a quitarse el antifaz aquí.

Rothgar no parecía especialmente contrariado.

—Entonces, por lo menos permanece junto a ella.

—Eso concuerda perfectamente con mis deseos. —Cyn se llevó a Chastity de allí.

—Estoy muerta de miedo —susurró ella—. He sido tan feliz y ahora todo va a desmoronarse.

—Pero sólo para abrir la cancela de una felicidad aún mayor. Cuando Rotghar está seguro de algo nunca falla. —Él la llevó hasta una habitación silenciosa y la miró de frente—. Ha dado su visto bueno para que vuelva al servicio activo. Dice que ya estoy recuperado y que no se interpondrá en mi camino.

A Chastity le pareció que el mundo se convertía en un lugar desangelado.

—¿Cuándo te irás? —le preguntó, tratando de ser valiente.

—Después de que nos hayamos casados. O tal vez no lo haga. —Él la atrapó con delicadeza contra la pared—. No estoy seguro de que te vaya a gustar la vida militar.

Chastity, cuyos sentimientos estaban en conflicto, protestó.

—¡Cyn, no puedes renunciar a tu carrera por mí!

—¡Pero tampoco puedo renunciar a ti por mi carrera! —Sus dedos recorrieron los bordes de la máscara de la muchacha—. Hay otras cosas —le recordó él, y el cuerpo de Chastity respondió instantáneamente.

—Pero a ti te encanta ser un soldado. —Chastity estaba orgullosa de su tono firme, especialmente porque la presión que el cuerpo de Cyn ejercía sobre el suyo estaba disparando todas sus ansias.

—He estado pensando en ello, Chastity —le dijo suavemente, mientras su mano deambulaba, al parecer de manera incontrolada, y bajaba por el cuello de la muchacha hasta desatarle el lazo de la capa y dejársela abierta—. No estoy seguro de que sea así. Lo que me gustan son los viajes y la aventura. —Los dedos de Cyn se desplazaron hasta la curva de sus senos, por debajo de la camisola de seda—. Quisiera hacer algo relevante —añadió, al tiempo que el talón de su mano encontraba bajo el corpiño el punto relevante en el que sus pezones se erizaban sensitivos. Ejerció la presión suficiente para dejarla sin aliento. La sombra de las pestañas de Cyn se proyectaba sobre sus mejillas mientras estudiaba pensativo las reacciones de la muchacha—. Pero hay otras cosas —siguió murmurando él—. Si la guerra termina, la vida en el ejército será muy aburrida, pero habrá trabajo interesante que hacer en Canadá: establecer gobierno, hacer los mapas, explorar. ¿Qué más podría desear un hombre, aparte de explorar un lugar tan bello y misterioso? —Su mano se dedicó a explorar la hondonada que había entre sus pechos.

Chastity, rindiéndose, apoyó la cabeza en el hombro de Cyn.

—Me confundes. No creo que quieras eso de verdad.

Los dedos de Cyn se deslizaron por debajo del corsé.

—Me encanta confundirte, y no hay palabras para describir la profundidad de mi sed de ti. —Él encontró entonces la carne sensible de la muchacha y la atrapó.

—¡Ah! —A Chastity se le escapó un grito de deseo y Cyn lo capturó en su boca. Siguió usando la lengua ferozmente para prometer otros deleites, llevándola hacia dentro y hacia fuera al tiempo que ella se estremecía y se derretía. Los endebles aros de la falda estaban aplastados y Cyn metió su muslo entre los de la muchacha para confortarla y atormentarla a un tiempo.

Colgada del cuello de Cyn, sintió que las piernas le punzaban hasta volverse inservibles. Los latidos de su corazón no le dejaban oír nada más. Un feroz calor la envolvió, transportándola más allá del mundo de la razón.

La boca de él la soltó y ella le miró doliente, presa de unas ansias que él seguramente no iba a aplacar.

Entonces, su mano izquierda dejó el corpiño y conquistó sus faldas. Encontró la ardiente comezón y la acarició allí, catapultando su tumultuoso cuerpo hacia alturas imposibles.

—¡Cyn! —jadeó ella, aferrándose a él—. ¡Dios mío! ¡Dios mío!

—Derrítete por mí, Chastity —susurró él—. Aquí y ahora.

Ella no tenía elección. Se agarró a él al tiempo que los estremecimientos la sacudían y ahogó los gritos de su desahogo contra el terciopelo de su hombro. Después, se hizo la calma.

Chastity estaba mareada y pegajosa, y sus piernas todavía parecían las de una muñeca de trapo. Mientras su corazón iba aminorando la marcha, los labios de Cyn seguían susurrándole su tranquilizador mensaje sobre el cuello.

Ella tomó aliento.

—¿Por qué?

Él se retiró un poco hacia atrás para sonreírle y la muchacha pudo ver la pasión que lo marcaba.

—Porque te deseo más allá de los límites de la cordura.

—Pero…

—Pero he hecho una promesa y voy a cumplirla. Espero —dijo él, apoyando su cabeza contra la de ella—, que esta situación no dure mucho.

—Oh, Cyn… —Ella le acarició el pelo con delicadeza—. Yo no necesitaba eso. De verdad.

—Pero yo sí. —Se apartó un poco e hizo una mueca—. ¿Crees que soy un noble mártir? Dulce Chastity, en este mundo sólo hay un placer mayor que hacer que te disuelvas en el éxtasis.

No le quedó más remedio que creerle.

—No tenía ni idea… —Aquella vacilante frase expresaba un mundo de ignorancia.

—Lo exploraremos juntos, al igual que la nueva tierra. ¿Querrás, amor mío?

Ella trató de encontrar sus rasgos bajo la máscara.

—¿De verdad quieres dejar el ejército?

—Sí.

Ella se rindió ante aquel sueño.

—¿Y qué voy a hacer yo?

—Explorar conmigo… dentro y fuera de la cama. —Él empezó a ponerle bien la ropa con mucha pericia—. Podríamos fijar nuestra residencia en Montreal. O también en una prometedora ciudad que se está construyendo, llamada Halifax. Está en Acadia, en la costa este. Tu podrías quedarte allí cuando fuera necesario y viajar conmigo cuando pudieras.

Ella le sostuvo la cabeza y le besó.

—Suena maravilloso. ¿Sabes?, nunca me ha gustado mucho la vida dentro de un salón. —Chastity se estaba preguntando qué ocurriría si ponía a prueba su promesa.

—Claro que lo sé. La primera vez que nos vimos, reconocí en ti un espíritu afín. —Se soltó de los brazos de la muchacha—. Alguien de veras valiente.

—Probablemente fueron las pistolas lo que te dio la pista —murmuró ella, moviéndose otra vez hacia él.

Él sacudió la cabeza.

—Sin duda. Dame tu mano izquierda, ladrona de corazones.

Chastity se detuvo y le tendió la mano. Él le deslizó un anillo en el dedo, un anillo de compromiso de oro compuesto por dos manos enlazadas. Ella lo contempló.

—Oh, Cyn…

Él le colocó otro anillo encima, un arco de diamantes.

—Se llama anillo custodio —le dijo—. El rey George acaba de instaurar la moda regalándole uno a su nueva esposa. Se coloca sobre el otro, para proteger al anillo y a la relación de todo mal. ¿Sabes que el diamante es la piedra más dura?

Chastity palpó las bellas joyas y las lágrimas se le escaparon por debajo de la máscara hasta rodar por sus mejillas.

—Oh, Cyn, tengo tanto miedo. Me da miedo hacerme ilusiones. Sigo siendo la infame Chastity Ware.

Él la besó para ahuyentar las lágrimas.

—Ven, vamos a bailar, mi querida lady Escándalo. Así espantaremos las preocupaciones.

Chastity se dejó ir a través de la danza —la primera vez que bailaba con Cyn— hasta que vio a Nerissa Trelyn en su grupo.

Aquella era Nerissa Trelyn, la líder de la buena sociedad. No se había esforzado mucho con el disfraz. Llevaba la hermosa cabellera rubia sin empolvar y su pequeña máscara de plumas no disimulaba sus facciones. En lugar de un dominó, llevaba un vaporoso vestido amplio de prístina seda blanca Chastity pensó con amargura que tendría un aspecto ciertamente virginal de no ser por el amplio y bajo escote, que sacaba el máximo partido de su espléndida figura. Por si alguien tenía la menor duda acerca de su identidad, llevaba los magníficos diamantes Trelyn, regalo de su afectuoso marido. Ella solía acompañar a su marido con una dignidad casi regia, propia de la Reina de la Buena Sociedad. Lord Trelyn no era un hombre muy mayor —debía tener la edad de Rothgar— pero actuaba como si tuviera sesenta años, y al mismo tiempo se mostraba muy satisfecho de la posesión de aquella gloriosa criatura.

Chastity sintió cierta compasión por Nerissa, hasta que recordó que la propia dama había sido quien había decidido su matrimonio, rechazando, al parecer, a Bryght Malloren mientras tanto, y que ahora era la amante de lord Heatherington.

Chastity volvió a escudriñar a los invitados tratando de reconocer a su padre, pero en la penumbra del salón de baile chino, la vista no alcanzaba muy lejos. Incluso se estaba quemando incienso —o algo por el estilo— y su humo plateado, sumado al de las velas, empañaba el aire.

Cuando el baile terminó, fue con Cyn a la habitación de los refrescos y bebió un poco de vino.

—Es un evento espléndido, especialmente si tenemos en cuenta la premura con la que se ha preparado.

—El personal de la casa está acostumbrado, y pueden hacer algo así en menos que canta un gallo.

—Con mucho trabajo adicional —señaló Chastity.

—Desde luego. Rothgar es inmensamente rico. Considera que es su deber dar trabajo a la gente.

—Mi padre es más rico todavía, según creo. Pero cuenta cada vela y supervisa las comidas que se sirven en la sala de los criados.

—Bueno, compréndelo —dijo Cyn con un pícaro guiño—. Ha tenido que soportar todos estos años a los codiciosos Verrham.

Aquello era traer a colación las cosas a traición.

Chastity se estremeció.

—¿Cuándo va a suceder todo?

—A su debido tiempo. ¿Por qué no vamos a ver el juego?

—Creía que no te gustaba apostar.

Él la condujo fuera de la estancia.

—Dije que no me gustaba jugar por dinero. Resulta muy relajante ver cómo tiran su fortuna los tontos que pueden permitírselo.

Observaron cómo Bute perdía miles de guineas con mucha calma y después recuperaba una pequeña parte; cómo la princesa Augusta casi pierde un brazalete que valía aún mucho más. Chastity no se sorprendió al ver a lady Fanshaw encorvada sobre sus cartas como un buitre. Sin duda, había sido invitada, pero habría aparecido de todos modos, atraída por el rumor del juego, como un ave carroñera seducida por el olor de un cadáver en descomposición.

Un lacayo le llevó una nota a Cyn. Él la leyó y después se la metió en el bolsillo.

—La habitación del jardín —dijo.

El corazón de Chastity empezó a latir con fuerza mientras él la conducía fuera de la estancia.

—¿Padre? —susurró la muchacha.

—No lo dice. —Cyn se detuvo en un silencioso rincón para besarla—. Sé valiente, Charles. Esta vez no estás sola.

21

La habitación del jardín era simplemente un pequeño salón decorado con un papel pintado en el que se veían enrejados cubiertos de viñas en flor. A través de unas amplias puertas de cristal, se podía acceder al invernadero, que daba a una glorieta exterior y al jardín ornamental. En aquella gélida época del año, las puertas de cristal estaban tapadas por una cortina, y un fuego caldeaba la habitación.

Cyn y Chastity entraron en la pequeña estancia y hallaron a Henry Vernham sentado en una silla, bajo la custodia de Brand Malloren. Vernham se sobresaltó.

Cyn lo ignoró mientras acomodaba a Chastity en el sofá y se instalaba después a su lado.

—Señor Vernham —dijo afablemente—, espero que le estén atendiendo bien. ¿Le han dado todo lo que usted necesita?

—Supongo que sí. —A pesar del delator brillo de sus ojos, el hombre era capaz de articular bien las palabras. Rothgar, como siempre, había acertado y Vernham era un bebedor empedernido—. Aunque me sorprende que te importe —dijo Vernham con sorna—. Tu hermano mayor ha debido meterte en cintura, ¿no?

Cyn sonrió.

—Siempre hay que servir una comida abundante al prisionero condenado.

Vernham palideció y trató de ponerse en pie, pero Brand le empujó para impedírselo. Antes de que la cosa pudiera pasar a mayores, la puerta se abrió y el conde de Walgrave entró muy airoso seguido de Lindle y dos fornidos asistentes. Rothgar y Fort entraron tras ellos.

A pesar de la tranquilizadora presencia de Cyn, el corazón de Chastity empezó a latir violentamente.

La pequeña estancia estaba abarrotada, pero su padre creaba un espacio en torno a él como por derecho natural. Chastity se percató de que tenía un nuevo bastón, de ébano con adornos dorados y bastante más sólido que los que usaba generalmente. No exhibía el menor nerviosismo. Pasó la vista sobre ella como si fuera una extraña. Con actitud desafiante, ella se quitó la máscara y se echó hacia atrás la capucha del dominó.

—Bien, Rothgar —exigió Walgrave—. ¿Puedo saber la razón de todo esto? Estoy disgustado, muy disgustado. No tienes derecho a entrometerte en los asuntos de mi familia.

Rothgar se colocó de pie junto al refulgente fuego.

—Pero nuestras familias van a unirse felizmente.

Los ojos del conde atravesaron a Chastity.

—¿Esa furcia desvergonzada? Adelante, pero ella no es hija mía.

La mano de Cyn reconfortó a Chastity y ella sostuvo la mirada sarcástica de su padre. Él apartó la vista, dirigiéndola a Henry Vernham.

El rostro de Vernham evidenciaba un profundo terror. Chastity se dio cuenta de que sin la prueba crucial, Vernham se hallaba desnudo ante la inquina de Walgrave. Sin embargo, la muchacha notó cierto recelo en la manera en que el conde miraba a Vernham. Tal vez no estuviera completamente seguro de que Henry Vernham estaba indefenso.

—Como queráis —dijo Rothgar tranquilamente—. Sólo pretendía ser amable en honor a la familia. —Tomó contemplativamente una pizca de rapé—. De hecho, insisto. A veces me sorprende mi propia generosidad. Creo que el señor Vernham tiene algo que usted quiere.

—Eso pienso yo también —dijo Walgrave con una maliciosa sonrisa—. ¿Debo entender que me permitís recuperarlo?

Rothgar hizo un gesto:

—Por favor.

—Maldita sea —gritó Vernham, tratando nuevamente de ponerse en pie—. No tengo nada. ¡Nada!

El conde, sin embargo, había vuelto a centrar toda su atención en Rothgar.

—Tal vez deba desconfiar de los regalos de los Malloren.

Chastity se dio cuenta de pronto de que los números favorecían a su padre. Allí había tres Malloren y, en el banco de su padre, se contaban cuatro individuos, incluyendo a los dos asistentes. También estaba Fort, pero no podía estar segura de cuál sería su posición cuando lo que estaba en juego era el futuro del título nobiliario. Vernham lucharía por su cuenta.

Llegado el momento, ella también echaría una mano, pero, entre aquellos hombres, Chastity era un peso ligero.

Rothgar cogió otra pizca de rapé y se sacudió algunas motitas.

—Siempre conviene ser precavido, Walgrave. Sin embargo, en este caso, tengo motivos para ser generoso. No puedo permitir que entre una mancha en mi familia con tu hija.

El conde estalló en una sonora carcajada.

—¡Cielos, creo que os vais a llevar toda una cloaca!

—¡Padre! —exclamó Fort. Cyn se puso en pie.

Walgrave se volvió hacia su hijo:

—¿Estás de su lado, chico? Entonces eres idiota. Si no la ha pervertido Vernham, entonces la ha pervertido un Malloren.

La espada de Cyn siseó al salir de su vaina, pero Rothgar levantó la mano. Cyn se detuvo en seco, con la fría mirada puesta en el conde.

Rothgar se volvió hacia Vernham.

—Mi querido señor, ¿sois inocente después de todo? ¿No os aprovechasteis de lady Chastity?

Vernham estaba absolutamente aterrorizado. Miraba fijamente la espada desenvainada de Cyn, a pesar de que no era a él a quien estaba apuntando.

—¡No, por supuesto que no! Apenas la toqué.

—Entonces debió de tratarse de una broma que se os fue de las manos. Y vos os ofreciste noblemente a casaros con ella para reparar el daño que, sin querer, habíais causado.

—Sí, sí. Si la muchacha era virgen cuando yo me metí en su cama, también lo era cuando me bajé de ella.

—¿Sí lo era? —inquirió Cyn, y ahora el estoque apuntaba a Vernham, a pocas pulgadas de sus despavoridos ojos.

—¡Lo era! ¡Lo era! —balbució él—. Le rompieron el himen para que no pudiera demostrar su inocencia. ¡Pero eso fue después!

Todas las miradas se volvieron hacia Walgrave.

Pero él permanecía impasible.

—Monsergas. Si pretendes absolver a la chica de este modo, Rothgar, no vas a conseguir nada. —Bajó la vista hacia Vernham—. Dame ese papel, desgraciado, y te dejaré vivir.

Vernham se hundió en su asiento.

—¡Ya te he dicho que no lo tengo!

—Entonces te voy a hacer pedacitos para asegurarme...

La puerta se abrió.

Todos los presentes se volvieron a mirar a la mujer que entraba. Cyn bajó incluso la espada del rostro de Vernham. Era una extraña. No, de ningún modo, pensó Chastity. La muchacha jadeó horrorizada al reconocer a la matrona que le había robado la prueba de su virtud.

Era alta y bien parecida, si uno no reparaba en la dureza de sus ojos y su boca. Iba tan lujosamente vestida como cualquier otra mujer de la casa.

—Ah, Mirabelle —dijo Rothgar—, bienvenida.

Mirabelle miró en torno a sí con infinito cinismo.

—El conde de Walgrave me pagó —dijo ella con claridad—, para que rompiera la virginidad de lady Chastity, su hija. Todas las pruebas indicaban que ningún hombre la había tocado. —Una ligera sonrisa curvó sus finos labios—. Aunque yo me dedico más bien a reparar lo que ha sido roto de manera poco conveniente...

—¿Se supone que esto tiene alguna validez? —preguntó el conde—. A una mujer así se la puede comprar por unas pocas guineas.

—Al contrario, milord —dijo Mirabelle—. No me molesto ni en ofrecer un pañuelo a un caballero por menos de veinte. —Dicho aquello, inclinó la cabeza frente a Rotghar y salió de la estancia.

Rothgar se volvió hacia Vernham.

—Puesto que sois inocente, ¿por qué no le dais al conde su documento? Así podréis marcharos.

—¡Ya os he dicho que no lo tengo! —exclamó Vernham—. Lo tiene Verity en alguno de sus malditos bolsillos.

—Entonces, tal vez deberíamos ir a buscar a Verity y la carta. Lord Thornhill, ¿le importaría hacernos ese favor?

Chastity vio cómo su padre reaccionaba al oír la palabra «carta», pues significaba que Rothgar sabía de qué documento se trataba. Se volvió y miró a su hijo con sorna:

—Anda chico, ve. Haz de lacayo de Rothgar, ya que no vales para otra cosa.

Los labios de Fort se tensaron, pero él salió de la habitación.

—Mientras esperamos —dijo Rothgar—. ¿Por qué no nos cuenta, señor Vernham, cómo apareció usted en la cama de lady Chastity sin su consentimiento y sin que ella diera la voz de alarma? Es un truco que me gustaría aprender.

El entendimiento de Vernham estaba claramente nublado por la bebida y el miedo, y el giro que daba la conversación no le resultó extraño. Se echó a reír:

—Duerme como un tronco. Un ejercito entero podría meterse con ella en la cama sin que se diera cuenta. Tuve que pellizcarla para que se despertara cuando llegaron los testigos.

—Pero seguramente, ¿vos no podíais contar con que tuviera un sueño tan profundo? —pregunto Rothgar con mansedumbre.

—Walgrave me lo dijo —dijo Vernham y después miró al conde muy nervioso.

El conde le devolvió una mirada llena de rabia pero no dijo nada. Si Rothgar esperaba obligarle a realizar una admisión que lo incriminara, no lo iba a conseguir.

Chastity se preguntó si podría volver a conseguir que su padre perdiera el control.

La muchacha se levantó, sorteando la mano de Cyn que quiso impedírselo.

—Y a mi padre le importaba un pimiento yo, ¿no es verdad, monstruo? —Se colocó con actitud insolente delante de Walgrave y se rió de él—. Debiste pensar que todo te resultaría muy fácil, pero yo he desbaratado todos tus planes.

Ella vio cómo los labios del conde formaban una irritada mueca.

—Si me hubiera casado con Henry Vernham, nada de esto hubiera ocurrido, ¿a que no? ¡Pero yo me reí en tu cara! Así que decidiste forzarme a hacerlo. Le diste a ese hombre la llave de mi habitación y después llevaste allí a la crema y nata de la sociedad para que hicieran de testigos. ¿Cómo has podido caer tan bajo y deshonrar así a tu propia hija?¡Asqueroso hipócrita!

Chastity temió que él usara su bastón para fustigarla y se quitó de en medio. Cyn dio un paso al frente, con la espada preparada.

El conde cogió su báculo y lo retorció, dejando al descubierto un cortante filo. Se lo arrojó a su fiel secuaz:

—¡Lindle!

Cyn sonrió tiernamente:

—Así que tú eres Lindle. No creo que quieras hacerlo, ¿verdad?

Lindle se le acercó. Cyn retrocedió un tanto.

—Somos más —le dijo Cyn—, no creo que podáis salir victoriosos. ¿Merece la pena morir por cumplir las órdenes de este hombre?

La expresión de Lindle no cambió. Seguía exhibiendo aquella extraña sonrisa.

—Deja de cacarear, gallito, y pelea.

Las espadas entrechocaron brevemente y entonces —casi como quien no quiere la cosa—, Cyn hizo un buen corte en la mejilla de Lindle. El hombre gritó y se apretó la mano contra la herida. La sangre le manó por entre los dedos.

La punta del estoque de Cyn descansaba ahora sobre su cuello:

—No creo que tu sonrisa puede volver a ser exactamente la misma de antes. —Cyn empujó el florete y el hombre se tambaleó hacia atrás, hasta que quedó contra la pared y no tuvo dónde ir.

—Y ahora —dijo Cyn—, ¿rompió la señora Mirabelle el himen de Chastity siguiendo las órdenes del conde?

Ciertamente, Lindle debía tener alguna deformidad en la boca, porque seguía exhibiendo una pavorosa sonrisa mientras lanzaba una rápida y desesperada mirada a su amo.

El conde le ignoró, como si nada de aquello tuviera que ver con él.

—Sí —dijo Lindle sofocado.

—¿Estabas tú allí? —preguntó Cyn.

—Sí. —La sangre aún le salía por entre los dedos. Aquel corte fortuito había sido hondo y el hombre parecía estar a punto de derrumbarse.

—Y ¿apañó el conde las cosas para que pillaran al señor Vernham en la cama de su hija?

—¡Sí! —bufó Lindle—. Siguiendo las órdenes del conde, yo le dejé entrar, yo le animé. El miserable gusano no creía que el plan podía funcionar. Pero, una vez que se dio cuenta del sueño tan profundo que tenía la muchacha, pasó un rato muy bueno manoseándola.

Chastity sintió nauseas. Cyn emitió un gruñido y durante un instante pareció que fuera a atravesar a aquel hombre de parte a parte, pero retrocedió y bajo la espada. Le hizo una pequeña reverencia a su hermano.

—Discúlpame por interrumpir vuestra discusión.

—No importa —dijo Rothgar—. ¿Walgrave? ¿Por qué no lo admites? Sin duda tenías tus razones.

Pero Walgrave se mantenía firme.

—Lo niego todo. No creía que Lindle fuera tan cobarde como para vomitar mentiras al dictado, pero veo que estaba equivocado.

Acompañada de Nathaniel y Fort, Verity entró en la estancia. Palideció al ver a su padre y no pudo reprimir un jadeo al ver a Lindle cubierto de sangre.

—Lady Verity —dijo Rothgar—. ¿Has recuperado el papel del que hemos estado hablando?

—Sí —dijo Verity, y sacó la hoja doblada y sellada, al tiempo que se adelantaba para dársela a Rothgar.

Walgrave se lo arrebató y, con un solo movimiento, lo arrojó al fuego y sacó una pistola.

—¡No os acerquéis! —gritó—. ¡Que nadie trate de sacarlo!

Todos contemplaron cómo el papel ennegrecía y, después de arder, se transformaba en cenizas.

Walgrave se echó a reír.

—¡Por fin!¡Libre! Ja, Rothgar, a pesar de todos tus ingeniosos trucos, me has despejado el camino. Puedes quedarte con mi maldita familia, con todos y cada uno de sus apestosos miembros. ¡Que hagan de tu vida un infierno, al igual que lo han hecho de la mía!

—El infierno seguramente sean todas las malas compañías —dijo Rothgar, mientras miraba pensativo las cenizas de la prueba—. No obstante, parece que has ganado. Tal vez quieras ser magnánimo en tu victoria y admitir que tu hija no perdió su virginidad con un hombre.

El conde estaba aturdido por la sensación de liberación.

—Desde luego —declaró—. Aunque no me puedo imaginar para qué diantre os puede servir.

—Tal vez puedas ponerlo por escrito —dijo Rothgar, señalando un escritorio donde había papel y tinta preparados.

El conde vaciló, pero seguía sonriendo como un poseso. Parecía que lo que no habían conseguido las amenazas lo iba a lograr la euforia de su éxito, conduciéndolo a la locura.

—¿Por qué no? Pero pondré que lo hice para forzarla a un matrimonio necesario. Eso no cambia el hecho de que Vernham estuviera en su cama. Y yo niego haber tenido nada que ver en eso.

Chastity tenía la opresiva sensación de haber fracasado. Rothgar lo estaba haciendo lo mejor que podía, pero sin la prueba de la traición, no se podía hacer nada. Nathaniel pronto podría encontrarse amenazado, y nada de lo que allí había ocurrido la beneficiaba a ella lo más mínimo.

—¿Qué? —gritó Vernham, poniéndose en pie—. ¡No me eches a mí la culpa, canalla! Tú lo planeaste todo para evitar que mi hermano usara esa carta. Habrá desaparecido, pero recuerdo lo que decía palabra por palabra. Todavía puedo contarle al mundo…

Walgrave se dio la vuelta y le disparó.

El estallido de la pistola reverberó en la pequeña habitación, y Chastity se cubrió los vibrantes oídos con las manos. Vernham se precipitó hacia atrás sobre su asiento, con expresión de asombro, al tiempo que la sangre se extendía por su pecho. Trató de hablar, después, su rostro se contorsionó súbitamente por la agonía y murió.

Cyn dejó caer la espada para estrechar a Chastity entre sus brazos como Nathaniel hacía con Verity. Chastity se aferró a él, pero después se apartó para mirar a su padre.

—Eso ha sido un asesinato a sangre fría. —Miró a los hombres que la rodeaban—. No podéis dejar que este crimen quede impune.

Su padre empolvó la hoja de papel con arena fina y la limpió delicadamente. Después, se la tendió:

—Ven aquí, chica. Coge esto y cierra el pico. Aprende a mantenerte al margen de los asuntos de los hombres.

Chastity agarró el papel, pero lo arrojó al instante.

—¿Los asuntos de los hombres? ¡Los asuntos de los hombres me han desgraciado!

—Me alegro de que por fin te enteres de la finalidad de todo.

—Y a ti no te importa. A ti, mi padre, no te importa que yo sea injustamente calumniada. ¿Cómo puedes pensar que vas a servir a Inglaterra, cuando no puedes servir a tu propia familia?

—Mi familia existe para servirme a mí —dijo él, levantándose. Con un descuidado empujón, quitó a Chastity de en medio.

Ella cogió la espada de Lindle del suelo y, a pesar del clamor, arremetió contra su padre. Él desvió la hoja con la pistola, pero la punta le hizo un tajo en la manga, hiriéndole en el brazo. El conde gruñó y, lleno de rencor, giró la pistola en dirección a la cabeza de la muchacha. Chastity sintió cómo le rozaba la sien, al mismo tiempo que Cyn se lanzaba sobre ella, haciéndola caer sobre el suelo, a salvo.

—... en la noble casa de los Stuart, vemos la fortaleza (*fortitude*) y la veracidad (*verity*), acompañadas de la victoriosa (*victor*) castidad (*chastity*), todas ellas virtudes dedicadas a la mayor gloria de Inglaterra.

Todos se quedaron de piedra. El silencio se apoderó de la estancia al tiempo que todos se volvían hacia Rothgar, quien, en pie, leía un documento en voz alta. Un documento manchado de sangre y ligeramente mordisqueado.

—No —bufó Walgrave.

Lindle soltó una risita nerviosa.

—Deberías haberla leído antes de quemarla, ¿no crees? —preguntó Rothgar mansamente.

—¡No! —aulló el conde. Levantó la pistola y disparó, pero estaba descargada y se limitó a hacer clic. Entonces, se la tiró a Rothgar. Pero no le dio.

—¡Matadlo! —les dijo hecho una furia a sus dos secuaces. Todavía en el suelo, medio cubierta por Cyn, Chastity vio que su padre había perdido por fin los estribos, pero ¿ocasionaría Walgrave la muerte de todos ellos?

Los dos hombres habían sido unos meros espectadores atónitos de todo aquel jaleo. Ahora se miraban el uno al otro sin hacer nada.

—¡Matadlo o haré que os cuelguen! Os hundiré. Hundiré a vuestras familias…

Los hombres miraron a Rothgar buscando ayuda.

Rothgar sonrió:

—Ahora, milord —le dijo al conde, cuyo rostro estaba amoratado por la congestión—, bailarás a mi son, en lugar de hacerlo al de los Vernham. ¿Crees que te gustará más?

—Eso jamás —gruño Walgrave. Metió una mano en el bolsillo del hombre que tenía más próximo y sacó una pistola. El hombre, obviamente aterrorizado por todos aquellos sucesos, se quedó quieto como un maniquí y no hizo nada.

Sin embargo, para cuando Walgrave levantó el arma con la intención de disparar, tanto Brand como Rothgar le estaban apuntando con sendas armas de fuego.

—Una situación interesante, ¿no es así? —preguntó Rothgar—. Podrías matarme, pero tú, a ciencia cierta, también morirías. ¿Estás listo para encontrarte con tu creador?

La boca de Walgrave se torció en un rictus de odio.

—Prefiero morir antes que concederte la victoria, Rothgar. Llevas demasiado tiempo siendo una espina para mí.

—Estoy encantado de que me aprecies.

—Dame ese documento y nadie tendrá que morir.

—No —dijo Rothgar—. Pero te doy mi palabra de que no lo usaré mientras vivas tranquilo en Walgrave Towers, sin volver a participar en los asuntos del gobierno y sin interferir en las vidas de tus hijos.

—¿Qué? —gritó Walgrave—. ¿Bailar al son que tú toques el resto de mi vida? ¡Jamás, debes estar loco! —Blandió la pistola salvajemente por toda la habitación

¿Dispararía a Rothgar?

¿A Brand?

¿A Fort?

¿A ella misma?

Con un desquiciado cacareo de regocijo, Walgrave retrocedió hacia la puerta.

—¡No intentéis detenerme!

—Puedes irte —dijo Rothgar con calma—. Pero recuerda mis condiciones. Al contrario que Vernham, yo no tengo nada que perder haciendo público este papel.

—Público —gritó Walgrave—. Sí, público… —Abrió la puerta y corrió pesadamente hacia el recibidor.

Cyn se puso en pie de un salto.

—Está loco. Va a herir a alguien. —Y salió corriendo tras él.

Chastity se incorporó con esfuerzo, obstaculizada por las faldas y el dominó, y le siguió junto con todos los demás.

Oyó cómo Walgrave aullaba algo sobre la traición y Rothgar. Estaba tratando de incriminar a Rothgar...

La muchacha corrió al recibidor de mármol y vio a su padre blandir la pistola y despotricar contra traidores y fornicarios como si fuera un predicador loco. Los invitados se agazapaban detrás de las sillas y los pedestales. Chastity vio a Fort entrar por el otro extremo del recibidor y moverse rápidamente para controlar al conde.

Todo ocurrió muy deprisa.

Los ojos desorbitados del conde se fijaron en alguien que se hallaba en la sala de juego:

—¡Tú...! —gruñó él—. ¡Tú! ¡Causante de todas mis calamidades...!

Fort sacó de pronto una pistola.

—¡Padre, no!

El conde apuntó.

Fort le disparó.

El brazo del conde dio un respingo, y su propia bala rebotó inofensiva sobre un pilar de mármol. Se desmoronó torpemente. A Chastity le dio por pensar que a ella no le gustaría nada que la vieran en aquella posición tan poco digna.

Se adelantó corriendo, pero su padre estaba completamente muerto. El disparo le había atravesado el corazón. Levantó la vista y vio a la princesa Augusta, inconsciente y desparramada de forma poco elegante sobre su silla. Las cartas se le habían caído de las manos. Ella había sido el blanco y se había desmayado de miedo.

Chastity miró a Fort, que estaba de pie, blanco y helado, contemplando lo que había hecho. Pronto, Nathaniel y Verity estuvieron a su lado.

En torno a ellos se formo una excitada cháchara, salpicada de llanto. Cyn tomó a Chastity entre sus brazos y la apartó del cuerpo.

Las pistolas de Rothgar y Brand habían desaparecido de la vista. Rothgar se movía con delicadeza, tratando de calmar a los alarmados invitados, pero Chastity se percató de que no hacía nada por evitar que la gente se congregara en el vestíbulo. Elf apareció en escena y corrió a atender la princesa Augusta, desatándole la máscara y aplicándole sales olorosas.

Inmediatamente se corrió la voz acerca de la identidad de la misteriosa dama, causando más agitación entre los presentes que el hecho de que hubiera un cadáver.

Rothgar se acercó y le dio tranquilamente a Cyn instrucciones para que se llevara a Chastity del centro de la acción. Entonces, ambos se retiraron hacia atrás por entre la gente. ¿Y ahora qué? ¿Cuántos de aquellos sucesos habían sido programados por el artífice de la obra? Seguramente, ni siquiera Rothgar era capaz de planear que un hijo matara a su padre.

¿O sí?

La muchacha echó un vistazo, pero Fort había desaparecido de la vista.

—Cyn —dijo ella—. Tengo que buscar a Fort. Debe sentirse fatal.

Pero Cyn la agarró por el brazo.

—Todavía no. Verity está con él. —Cyn la llevó por detrás de la gente hasta un lugar en el que se podía ver y oír lo que ocurría en la sala de juego.

Augusta había recobrado el sentido y estaba siendo instalada con delicadeza en un diván. Rothgar hizo sobre ella una solícita reverencia a la par que se aseguraba de que estaba bien.

La princesa se apretó un paño húmedo sobre la cabeza.

—Ese hombre, Walgrave —dijo en su inglés con acento alemán—, nunca me ha gustado. Era una mala influencia para mi querido Frederick.

—Me temo que se volvió loco, alteza —dijo Rothgar.

Augusta movió ligeramente el trapo, mientras trataba de asimilar lo ocurrido.

—Gritaba algo de una traición. Creo que os acusaba a vos de traición, milord marqués.

—Decía que habías sido jacobita en el 45 —dijo lady Fanshaw—. Ese hombre estaba chiflado. En aquel año tú debías estar aún en el colegio.

—Cierto —dijo la princesa—. Y vosotros, los Malloren, sois tan leales. —Chastity percibió el revoloteo de la mirada de Augusta en dirección a Bute, quien con mucho tacto se había apartado de ella. No era conveniente que los hacendados locales, gente más bien convencional, se diera cuenta que la madre del rey había acudido a aquel evento sin más acompañantes que el hombre de quien se decía que era su amante.

—Completamente leales —dijo Rothgar, sirviéndole un poco de vino—. No sabe cuánto lamento que haya tenido que ocurrir esto mientras usted estaba invitada en mi casa, alteza. Tenemos que encontrar a su doncella. —Él miró a su alrededor—. ¿Dónde está lady Trelyn?

Nerissa era dama de compañía, pero Chastity sabía que aquella noche no había venido con la princesa Augusta. La sugerencia, sin embargo, trasmitía la impresión de un absoluto decoro. Pero ¿cómo pensaba Rothgar hacer que los Trelyn bailaran al son que él tocaba?

La princesa se relajó y tomó un sorbo de su vino.

—Estoy segura de que vos, milord, no habéis tenido la culpa de este descalabro. Me pregunto qué sería lo que le hizo perder el juicio al pobre hombre.

—Mucho me temo que lo consumían los remordimientos, alteza.

—¿Los remordimientos?

—Sí, alteza. Verá, en esta fiesta, se encontró con el canalla que causó la deshonra de su hija, al comienzo de este mismo año. Como el hombre estaba bebido, Walgrave descubrió que su pobre hija era inocente de todo mal.

—¿Habláis de Chastity Ware? —preguntó Augusta con asombrada incredulidad.

—Desde luego. Parece que Henry Vernham obtuvo la llave de la habitación de la dama y se deslizó entre sus sábanas. Sabía, por los comentarios de la familia, que ella tenía un sueño extraordinariamente profundo. Él avergonzó deliberadamente a lady Chastity para conseguir su mano, y su enorme dote.

—Menudo sinvergüenza —dijo alguien entre el gentío—. Habría que azotar a ese desgraciado.

—Me temo —dijo Rothgar— que eso es imposible. La angustia del conde era tan enorme que disparó contra él.

Se oyó un claro murmullo de aprobación.

La princesa se mostró un poco escéptica.

—Es una historia extraña, milord.

—Tremendamente extraña —consintió Rothgar—, pero el conde insistió en dejar constancia de uno de los puntos cruciales de la verdad.

La princesa cogió el papel que Rothgar le tendió y lo leyó.

—Asombroso —comentó—. Esto deja claro que la pobre lady Chastity era más virtuosa de lo que parecía. Tal vez su nombre le vaya mejor de lo que habíamos supuesto.

—Y a mí me gustaría añadir mi palabra —dijo una voz. Nerissa Trelyn se abrió paso hasta allí. Chastity se dio cuenta de que, aunque ahora se esfumaba, Bryght parecía haber estado con ella y, por una vez, tenía aspecto de estar divirtiéndose.

Nerissa aparentaba serenidad, aunque estaba tan pálida como su prístino vestido. Le hizo una profunda reverencia a la princesa:

—Le pido disculpas por no haber estado a su lado cuando tuvo lugar el terrible suceso, alteza.

También Augusta podía ser una buena actriz. Hizo un gesto con la mano:

—Yo te di permiso para que te ausentaras. Pero ¿qué es lo que tenéis que añadir lady Trelyn? ¿No fuisteis vos una de las personas que informasteis de la infamia de lady Chastity?

—Desde luego, alteza —dijo Nerissa con recato—, lo que hace que todavía sea más importante que ahora repare el mal que causé. Lord Trelyn y yo… —la bella dirigió sus ojos de cierva a su senil marido y él corrió a ponerse a su lado— dudamos antes de apoyar la historia, porque conocíamos un poco a lady Chastity y pensábamos que era virtuosa. Creíamos que, en el peor de los casos, habría sido culpable de cometer una indiscreción. Fue sólo cuando no dio ninguna señal de estar arrepentida cuando nos vimos obligados a hablar.

—Y ahora, ¿sabes algo que no sabías entonces?

—Desde luego. —Nerissa era la perfecta estampa de la mujer bella y virtuosa—. Después de que su alteza fuera tan

amable de permitirme bailar con mi marido, empecé a marearme a causa del calor y los perfumes del salón de baile.
—Bajó la cabeza con timidez—. Su alteza se hará cargo. Estoy en estado interesante...

—Ah —dijo Augusta—. Por supuesto.

Trelyn se pavoneó orgulloso.

—Fui a buscar el frescor del invernadero. Mientras estaba allí, entró gente en la pequeña estancia adyacente, dejándome sin otra salida que la que daba al exterior. Como no quise arriesgarme a coger un resfriado, oí todo lo que ocurría. El señor Vernham confesó su perversa trama y dijo que él no... no había mancillado a lady Chastity. El conde enloqueció al pensar en lo mucho que se había equivocado al juzgar a su hija, lo mismo que yo.

Augusta no era tonta y Chastity se dio cuenta de que la princesa percibía que detrás de todo aquello había algo que olía mal, pero no tenía nada que ganar oponiéndose, y se arriesgaba a ser piedra de escándalo si su presencia allí con lord Bute se ponía de manifiesto.

—Un triste caso —dijo ella—. Me pregunto que habrá sido de la desdichada chica. Tal vez podamos encontrarla y hacer algo para rehabilitar su buen nombre. Un matrimonio respetable resultaría muy adecuado.

Los ojos de Rothgar encontraron a Chastity. Ella se había quedado totalmente petrificada, llena de terror al pensar que tendría que descubrirse ante aquella multitud, que hacía corro como si estuviera viendo una representación teatral.

Pero la mano de Cyn la empujó con firmeza hacia delante. Con el corazón al galope, ella caminó temblorosa en dirección a Rothgar.

—Aquí está ella, alteza. ¿Me permite presentaros a lady Chastity Ware?

Aquél era el momento decisivo, porque la aceptación por parte de la realeza era la condición *sine qua non* de la respetabilidad.

Augusta observó a Chastity durante unos prolongados momentos. Después, sonrió, aunque sin mucha convicción, y le tendió la mano. Chastity se hundió en una profunda reverencia para besarla.

—Al parecer, querida, se te ha juzgado mal —dijo la princesa—. ¿Juras ahora, delante de testigos, que eres pura?

Chastity se incorporó, consciente de que el rostro se le había encendido. Esperó que todos lo interpretaran como una señal de timidez y trató de encontrar palabras que fueran verdaderas.

—Juro ante el cielo que era virgen cuando Henry Vernham se metió a hurtadillas en mi cama, alteza, y que yo no le invité a ello. Gracias a la divina Providencia, él no tuvo ocasión de ultrajarme antes de que me rescataran. —Se volvió hacia Nerissa Trelyn.

—No sabéis cuánto agradecí que fueseis vos la que acudisteis entonces, milady. Comprendo que no era fácil creer en mi virtud.

Nerissa consiguió que manaran lágrimas reales de sus grandes ojos, y abrazó a Chastity rodeada de una nube de perfume de rosas que a la muchacha le resultó muy familiar.

—¡Pobre inocente! —Se volvió hacia Augusta y se arrodilló con mucha teatralidad—. Alteza, debemos hacer todo lo que esté en nuestra mano para enmendar este error, o mi conciencia nunca podrá descansar en paz.

—Desde luego que sí —dijo la princesa, aunque con aire displicente. Se quedó pensativa y luego dijo—: Este suceso me ha causado una conmoción nerviosa. Me quedaré aquí unos días para descansar, lord Rothgar, si eso es posible.

—Será un honor para Rothgar Abbey, alteza.

—Y como lady Trelyn está en un estado delicado, necesitaré otras damas de compañía. Tal vez lady Chastity y lady Elfled quieran ocupar temporalmente esos puestos.

Ambas mujeres hicieron una profunda reverencia.

—Será un gran honor, alteza —dijo Elf.

—Hay que mandar información de lo que aquí se ha revelado a los periódicos que se han complacido extendiendo esas procaces falsedades. —Augusta miró a Chastity y su mirada pareció suavizarse—. lady Chastity, me doy cuenta de que ha pasado usted por una experiencia espantosa, pero lo que más le conviene es el matrimonio. Especialmente alguno que la mantenga apartada de Londres por algún tiempo.

Chastity deseó saberse el papel de aquella obra. Volvió a hacer una reverencia:

—Estoy dispuesta a dejarme guiar por usted, alteza. —Entonces vio a Augusta levantar las cejas y se dio cuenta de que sus anillos estaban a la vista. Oh, Señor.

Rothgar dio un paso al frente:

—Creo que mi hermano, el capitán Cynric Malloren, estaría dispuesto a casarse con lady Chastity. Ha prestado sus servicios al país en el ejército y, según creo, ahora está interesado en hacer lo mismo en la administración de Canadá.

—Canadá —dijo Augusta secamente mientras Cyn se adelantaba—. Una idea excelente. Y tan oportuna. No podía encajar mejor en mis planes.

Chastity quería que se la tragara la tierra. Cyn le cogió la mano y se la apretó.

—Como la dama acaba de quedarse huérfana —dijo Augusta—, convendría que el matrimonio se celebrara en privado y pronto. Supongo que eso no plantea ningún problema.

—Se hará como vos ordenéis —dijo Rothgar, con un rostro admirablemente inexpresivo. Augusta y él intercambiaron durante un segundo una chispeante mirada.

Los labios de la princesa formaron una jocosa mueca.

—Pillo —le dijo reprobadoramente—. Supongo que te propones que yo corone todo esto asistiendo como testigo al enlace. ¿Por qué no? Estoy segura que también se podrá traer a mi hijo para el evento.

Chastity miró a la princesa con gran pasmo. También el rey. Rothgar no perdió ni un ápice de su calma.

—Vuestra gracia, alteza, es, como siempre, excelsa.

—Desde luego —dijo Augusta—, lo recordaréis, milord. Y ahora, después de semejante drama, necesito una habitación en la que poder descansar.

La princesa se deslizó majestuosa hacia la puerta, pero se detuvo cerca del cuerpo cubierto por una capa, con los ojos fijos en un punto distante. El cadáver fue arrastrado rápidamente hasta que el paso quedó despejado y, en su lugar, se dejó caer una alfombra para tapar la sangre. La reina continuó entonces su camino, seguida por Chastity y Elf.

—Bien —dijo lady Fanshaw—. ¿Podemos seguir ahora con el maldito juego?

Después, mucho después, los Malloren, los Frazer y los Ware se reunieron para celebrarlo y comentarlo.

—Milord —le preguntó Chastity a Rotghar—. ¿Hasta qué punto estaba planeado?

Él sonrió levemente.

—¿Me atribuiré todo el merito y, además, me arrogaré poderes sobrenaturales? No, pero el secreto del genio consiste en estar listo para agarrar la ocasión. Confieso que esperaba presionar a tu padre para que realizara alguna maldita confesión más, pero no contaba con empujarle a la locura y a la violencia. Lo lamento.

—Pues yo no, excepto por lo la parte que le tocó a Fort. —Chastity encaró a sus pasmados interlocutores—. Pero no por todo lo que me hizo, sino por lo que era capaz de hacer. Ya sabía que estaba loco, pero se las apañaba muy bien para disimularlo. Le amenazara la espada que le amenazara, él nunca habría dejado de tejer sus tramas. Le importaban un pimiento los demás. Imaginaos que hubiera llegado a tener poder sobre Inglaterra.

—Me temo que tienes razón —dijo Rothgar—. El asunto de la falsa carta estaba planeado, desde luego. Confiaba en que, aunque todo lo demás fallara, aquello le desestabilizaría. Y así fue.

—¿Y Henry Vernham? —preguntó Verity.

Rothgar sacudió la cabeza.

—Era un estúpido lleno de codicia. Pero no le vaticiné ese final. Debo confesaros que en ese momento empecé a pensar como piensa Chastity. El conde lo mató como a un perro. Era peligroso que ese hombre anduviera suelto por el mundo.

—Y Fort disparó a padre a su vez —dijo Chastity—. Está muy abatido por ello.

Cyr le cogió la mano.

—Había que hacerlo, amor, y él era el único que lo tenía a tiro.

Chastity no estaba muy segura de aquello, pero lo dejó pasar.

—¿Qué me dices de la princesa? —preguntó la muchacha—. ¿Por qué la invitaste?

—La aceptación por parte de la realeza era esencial para mis planes —dijo Rothgar—. Admito que no se me escapó la profunda enemistad entre ella y Walgrave. Esperaba que ella nos apoyara si lo veía como un medio de oponerse al conde. Pero no esperaba, como comprenderéis, que él muriera.

Chastity sacudió la cabeza admirativamente.

—Y ahora dime, milord, ¿cómo hiciste entrar a Nerissa Trelyn en escena? ¿La carta?

—Eso lo puede contar Bryght.

Bryght Malloren sonrió con sarcasmo.

—Mi querida Nerissa se divirtió mucho seduciéndome en el invernadero. Yo no tuve que hacer nada. Sólo relajarme y disfrutar. Entonces, tal y como estaba planeado, nos pillaron. Ella se azoró mucho, porque yo soy el hombre de quien su estúpido marido tiene celos. La escuchamos, pero no sintió ningún apremio por lavar el nombre de Chastity hasta que le enseñé la carta. Me temo que Nerissa Trelyn no está muy contenta con ninguno de nosotros.

—Tampoco estoy segura de que la princesa lo esté —dijo Verity.

—Cierto, pero ella es una mujer sensata por lo general —dijo Rothgar—. Le ha molestado verse envuelta en este asunto, pero me está muy agradecida por arrojar un manto de respetabilidad sobre este latoso viaje. —Levantó una ceja

mirando a Chastity—. Tengo entendido que Cyn prometió
que si tu honor era restaurado, él no insistiría en lo del matrimonio, pero creo que te has visto obligada.

Chastity se miró los anillos.

—Por una vez, milord, él había roto su promesa.

—Sí —dijo Rothgar un tanto severo—, y esos anillos
pudieron echarlo todo a perder. En el futuro, ten la amabilidad de no embellecer mis tramas.

Cyn besó la mano de Chastity a la altura de los anillos.

—En el futuro, esperamos vernos libres de tus tramas.

—Eso sí que es gratitud de tu parte —dijo Rothgar, pero
estaba sonriendo.

Pronto Chastity y Cyn se hallaron a solas en la casa, descansando intensamente después de toda aquella agitación.
Tras la fiesta, la mayoría de las habitaciones públicas estaban en proceso de limpieza, y todos los dormitorios sobran-
tes estaban llenos invitados que habían decidido quedarse.
Así que acabaron en la alcoba de Cyn, el uno en brazos del
otro, sobre la cama.

—Pero no haremos nada impropio hasta que estemos
casados —dijo él.

—Dentro de dos días —dijo Chastity maravillada.

—Si tu hermano mantiene su palabra y da el consentimiento.

—¿Por qué iba a oponerse?

El tono de Cyn se tornó irónico.

—Porque los Malloren están una vez más enfrentados
con los Ware. Él cree que Rothgar le obligó a apretar el gatillo.

—¿Cómo puede pensar eso? Nadie podía saber que mi padre intentaría disparar a la princesa.

—No, pero Rothgar mandó a Fort a la otra punta del recibidor, cerca de la princesa. Cuando llegó el momento, tanto Rothgar como Brand podían haber usado sus armas contra tu padre, pero no lo hicieron, forzando a Fort a hacerlo.

—Vi cómo Rothgar sujetaba a Brand —dijo Chastity—. Entonces no lo entendí.

La muchacha se daba cuenta de que Cyn también estaba afligido.

—Creo que lo hizo porque nadie iba pensar que a Fort le movía la maldad, mientras que la enemistad entre Rothgar y Walgrave es conocida por todos.

Chastity se estremeció.

—Me cae bien Rothgar, pero, a veces, hace que se me hiele la sangre en las venas. Pobre Fort.

—Pobres todos nosotros. Espero que esto no signifique que el rencor se va a prolongar, pero si tu hermano y el mío se van a enseñar los dientes, doy gracias a Dios de que nosotros, por lo menos, vamos a estar bien lejos. Te gustará Acadia, amor.

Chastity se recostó hacia atrás con un suspiro de satisfacción.

—Estoy segura. Debería llamarse Arcadia, un lugar perfecto. —Se giró y alzó la cabeza, buscando un beso—. Nuestro paraíso particular.

Cyn la besó pero dijo con ironía.

—¿Te he hecho concebir falsas esperanzas? Es un bello lugar, pero salvaje y abrupto.

—Tú estarás allí —dijo ella simplemente.

El siguiente beso se tornó peligrosamente profundo, pero Cyn encontró fuerzas para finalizarlo y hacer que Chastity se pusiera en pie.

—Venga. A tu habitación. Después de todo lo pasado, no vamos a empezar otra vez haciendo que te encuentren en una situación comprometida.

—Ah —dijo Chastity maliciosamente, mientras él la conducía hacia la puerta—, pero por lo menos esta vez podrían convencerme para que me casara con usted, señor...

22

La boda fue de una magnificencia asombrosa.

Muchos de los invitados se habían quedado tras el dramático baile; otros habían sido convidados especialmente para la ceremonia, gente socialmente relevante y un pequeño número de voraces cotillas.

Espoleados por la princesa Augusta, el rey y su nueva esposa llegaron para tomar parte en el evento. La razón aparente de George era asegurarse de que su madre se había recuperado de su ordalía, pero él y su poco atractiva consorte alemana estaban obviamente encantados de asistir al acontecimiento del año.

Después de pensarlo detenidamente —porque era bastante soso pero muy meticuloso—, George consintió en que le presentaran a la infame Chastity Ware y, después, bromeó con cierto esfuerzo y dijo que, efectivamente, su belleza y su virtud eran de escándalo. Su tímida mujer se mostró muy afable e hizo un comentario sobre el anillo custodio, tan parecido al suyo.

El vestido de novia de Chastity era de gasa del más puro blanco. Ella había dudado al respecto, pero Rothgar había impuesto su punto de vista con firmeza. Debido a la escasez de tiempo, no llevaba muchos bordados de fantasía, pero, como estaba hecho de la más cara seda de encaje de Valenciennes, festoneado de perlas y diamantes, eso apenas importaba.

Rothgar lo había encargado. Y Fort lo había pagado, lo que podía ser otro motivo de enemistad. Otra familia menos pudiente se hubiera arruinado con aquel gasto. Fort había regresado —observando un luto severo— para entregar a su hermana. Su actitud hacia todos los Malloren era muy fría. En comparación, Bryght Malloren estaba absolutamente jovial, ya que al fin parecía haberse recuperado del hechizo de Nerissa Trelyn.

Elf y Verity eran las damas de compañía de Chastity, pero la madre y la esposa del rey insistieron en sentarse junto a ella para ayudarla con la cola. Chastity tenía la impresión de que la princesa Augusta esperaba ver alguna señal de intemperancia. La muchacha había sentido un profundo alivio cuando las manchas se borraron definitivamente de sus pezones.

La propia ansiedad de Chastity, su sensación de que en cualquier momento la burbuja podía estallar y dejarla de nuevo desnuda y expuesta ante la maldad del mundo, pareció convencer a Augusta de que se trataba de una novia oportunamente nerviosa.

Augusta le palmeó la mejilla antes de marcharse.

—Tal vez ha sido un enlace un tanto apresurado, querida, pero ha sido lo mejor. Parte del daño ha sido reparado, pero estarás más segura siendo una mujer bien casada, especialmente si formas parte de la familia Malloren. Pocos se atreverían a ofenderla. Y, fuera del país, tendrás tiempo para acomodarte a tu nuevo estado. Mi hijo ha nombrado a tu marido ayudante del general Lawrence, el gobernador de Acadia. He incluido un mensaje en los correos oficiales para tranquilizar a su esposa, en caso de que hayan llegado hasta allí rumores desafortunados.

La joven reina aceptó las reverencias de todas las damas al levantarse para marchar. Ella levantó a Chastity y se inclinó hasta quedar muy cerca de ella:

—De verdad —le dijo con su fuerte acento alemán—, no debes tener miedo. —Se sonrojó—. ¡Todo es… es agradable, de hecho! —Después se fue apresuradamente.

Chastity intercambió una mirada divertida con su hermana, pero, en el fondo, le había conmovido el intento de la reina de aplacar sus miedos. Aunque sus verdaderos miedos eran otros.

Que todo aquello resultara ser un sueño.

Que su padre volviera a aparecer para atormentarla.

Que alguien se pusiera en pie durante la ceremonia para acusarla.

Que alguien le preguntara abiertamente: «¿Alguna vez has hecho el amor con un hombre?» No sería capaz de mentir con convicción.

La muchacha temblaba ligeramente mientras Fort la llevaba a la capilla de Rothgar Abbey.

Él percibió su tensión y se detuvo en seco, frunciendo el ceño.

—¿No quieres hacerlo, Chastity? Dios sabe que lo que debes hacer es casarte con él, pero ya te fallé una vez y no pienso hacerlo más. Si lo deseas, lo detendré todo, y que se vayan a la porra Rothgar y los Malloren

Chastity sabía que él estaría encantado con esta contienda. Consiguió sonreír de manera tranquilizadora:

—Claro que quiero, Fort. De verdad. Simplemente tengo mucho miedo de que algo pueda impedirlo.

Él le devolvió la sonrisa, aunque con cierta tristeza.

—Entonces, vamos. Acabemos cuanto antes.

Cyn llevaba un dorado traje de terciopelo, en un tono opaco, adornado con brillantes galones. No se había empolvado el pelo. Al verla a ella, sus ojos se contagiaron de la luminosidad de su traje, como si él también hubiera temido que aquel evento nunca llegara a tener lugar.

Durante los últimos días habían estado bastante ocupados y se habían visto muy poco. Sin embargo, tal vez así había sido mejor, ya que necesitaron menos fuerza de voluntad.

Fort vaciló unos instantes antes de entregar a Chastity a Cyn.

—Hazle daño, Malloren —le dijo suavemente—, y te destruiré.

Cyn se limitó a levantar las cejas.

—¿El hermano protector? Una actitud nueva en ti.

Chastity se apresuró a poner su mano sobre la de Cyn y se colocó entre ambos. Él le sonrió indolentemente y le besó la mano.

—Hola, Charles.

Chastity sintió que se ruborizaba y fijó su atención en el capellán de la Abadía.

La muchacha apenas pudo seguir la ceremonia porque todos sus sentidos estaban pendientes de cualquier indicio de una interrupción, una interrupción que indicara que alguien iba a detener aquella boda. Contestó de memoria cuando le preguntaron y, de pronto, se encontró frente a Cyn, su marido.

—Oh —dijo ella—. ¡Pero no lo he hecho bien! ¿No podemos repetirlo?

Las risas se extendieron por toda la capilla. Los labios de Cyn se curvaron:

—¿Por qué no?

Así que volvieron a hacer las promesas y esta vez se miraron el uno al otro e hicieron los votos con solemnidad. Después se besaron tiernamente, con un levísimo roce de sus labios.

Cogidos de la mano, se mezclaron con los invitados que tomaban vino y comían tarta. Chastity detectó algunas miradas curiosas e incluso cínicas —especialmente dirigidas a su cintura— pero, a la vista de la abrumadora aceptación, sobre todo por parte de la realeza, nadie se atrevió a darle la espalda.

Ya sabía que para entonces, tímidamente en los periódicos, y de un modo más abierto en las cartas y cotilleos, la historia de la pobre Chastity Ware corría por el país, mucho más impresionante a causa de las muertes de Henry Vernham y el conde de Walgrave.

Después Cyn la llevó al vestíbulo. Aunque todavía era de día y apenas había comenzado la tarde, Chastity miró hacia las escaleras.

—No —dijo Cyn—. Estoy pensando en otra cosa. Tus baúles están en el carruaje. —Le tendió a Chastity una hermosa capa de terciopelo blanco, con los bordes de níveo armiño—. ¿Vendrás conmigo, esposa?

—A cualquier parte —dijo ella, y él la envolvió con el manto.

Subieron a un elegante coche, uno que ella conocía bastante bien. Ella vio que el escudo de armas había sido restaurado y lucía en todo su esplendor. Hoskins y un mozo de establo estaban en el pescante.

Les seguía un coche más sencillo.

—Jerome y tu nueva doncella —le dijo Cyn a modo de explicación—. Somos un respetable matrimonio y debemos comportarnos como tal.

—¿Respetable? —bromeó ella—. Qué aburrido suena.

Él hizo una mueca:

—Oh, mujer de poca fe.

Pasaron el viaje recordando sus extrañas y variopintas aventuras, volviendo a saborear el dolor y la alegría, confirmándose mutuamente que aquel sueño era realidad. Chastity no prestó mucha atención a la carretera hasta que entraron en una ajetreada población. Entonces miró por la ventana.

—Pero esto es… —Le miró a él—. ¿Winchester?

Se detuvieron en el Three Balls.

Chastity se iluminó al mirar a Cyn.

—¿La misma habitación?

Él asintió.

—Cuando estuvimos allí, yo pensé… me hubiera gustado que fuera nuestra noche de bodas.

—A mí también.

Cyn ayudó a bajar a la muchacha y la condujo hasta la posada. El mesonero hizo una profunda reverencia y pronto quedó claro que lord Cynric Malloren había alquilado para su uso toda la hospedería. Les mostraron su pequeña, bella y familiar habitación. Alguien había conseguido rosas frescas y las había colocado en un recipiente delante de la ventana, perfumando el aire.

Los sirvientes subieron el equipaje pero enseguida fueron despachados. Sobre la mesa había vino y una colación fría. Un fuego hacía que la habitación resultara acogedora.

Cyn se despojó de su enorme abrigo. Chastity se quitó la capa y acarició la piel.

—Es precioso. Debe haber costado una fortuna.

—Es el regalo de bodas que Rothgar te hace. Yo no me lo podría haber permitido. ¿Te importa haberte casado con la parte pobre de la familia?

Ella percibió el destello de sus ojos y suspiró:

—Ay de mí, no tuve elección, señor.

Él le tendió la mano y ella se le acercó para darle confiadamente la suya. Él le besó las palmas, a esas alturas impolutas, después la arrastró aún más hacia él para besarle los labios, colocándole las manos en los costados.

—Ballenas y aros —comenzó él—. Te lo advertí. Fuera con ellos.

—Pero señor —protestó ella—, usted me amenazó... esto, me prometió quitármelos.

Él evaluó el caro vestido y vio que constaba de una sola pieza y se ajustaba por la espalda. Pronto yacía desconsideradamente sobre el suelo. Él sonrió al ver el armazón de los aros.

—Estas cosas parecen bien tontas cuando no llevan nada encima. —Después, también aquello desapareció, seguido del corsé de encaje.

Ella se volvió para encararlo, vestida únicamente con una fina camisola de seda y las medias de cuadros. Le retiró el abrigo de los hombros y desabotonó su chaleco con brocados. Esta vez, sus dedos llegaron hasta el final sin desfallecer. Consiguió incluso deshacerle el nudo del fular y quitárselo lentamente.

Muy pronto se quedó únicamente con los pantalones de terciopelo dorado y una camisa de cuello abierto. Chastity estaba a la expectativa, con la boca seca por lo que se anticipaba.

Él miró en dirección a la mesa.

—Comida —dijo.

—¡Cyn!

Cogió la mano de la muchacha, la llevó hasta la mesa, se sentó y la colocó a ella sobre su regazo. Sus ágiles dedos encontraron las ligas y las desataron. Él las miró y sonrió. Ambos conocían bien aquel par.

—¿Te acuerdas…? —preguntó.

Temblando, ella escondió la cara en el hombro de Cyn.

—Sí.

Él le quitó suavemente las medias y después recorrió con la mano su pierna desnuda, por la parte externa, desde abajo en dirección a la cadera. Ella se retorció, pero él no la tocó donde ella hubiera deseado.

En lugar de ello, sacó la mano de debajo de la camisola de la muchacha y cogió un pastelillo, un dorado pastel de manzana adornado con abundante nata.

—¿Te acuerdas? —le preguntó.

Ella se rió.

—¡Claro que me acuerdo! Santo cielo, Cyn, ¿vamos a revivir el tiempo que hemos pasado juntos, momento a momento, comida a comida?

—Qué idea tan encantadora —dijo él—. Me pregunto dónde puedo encontrar galletas de Shrewsbury.

Chastity cogió el bollo y le dio un buen mordisco.

—Una moza de apetitos verdaderamente feroces —dijo él, y le lamió la nata y las migas de alrededor de la boca. Cuando ella tragó el bocado, él la besó, cumplida y profundamente.

—Mmm —dijo él—. Delicioso.

—Sólo me quieres por mis manzanas.

Con una clamorosa carcajada, él le aplicó los labios primero a un pezón y después al otro.

—Y por tus cerezas —murmuró él.

La mano de Cyn se desplazó ligera sobre la camisola de la muchacha, produciendo excitación a su paso. Él sacó un frasquito que ella recordaba bien y untó delicadamente ciertos lugares secretos.

—Me preguntaba qué habría sido de él —susurró ella.

—Lo compré pensando en este momento, aunque quizás entonces no lo sabía...

Chastity le arrebató el botecito y le ungió a él a su vez. Después de una lucha entre risas, él lo recuperó. El almizcleño perfume les envolvió mientras se peleaban por él. La mano de la muchacha bajó por el cuerpo de Cyn y descubrió algo más.

—¡Pepino! —exclamó, y se fundieron en sonoras carcajadas.

Después él salió de debajo de ella de modo que se quedó sola sentada sobre la silla. Él le colocó los restos del pastel en la mano y se quitó la ropa, observándola con ojos sombríos.

Chastity se quedó de piedra, presa de un gozo que le privó hasta del aliento y le hizo ignorar el bollo que tenía en la mano. Él era tan hermoso, su marido, que se le saltaron las lágrimas.

—Creía que tenías hambre —dijo él.

Ella miró el dulce, luego se lo tiró. Él se limitó a quedarse allí de pie mientras la dorada fruta con sus jugos y la copiosa nata amarillenta se deslizaban lentamente por su flexible torso. Aterrizó sobre su pene, osciló allí unos instantes y después cayó, dejándolo a él bien decorado.

Él miró hacia abajo e hizo un sonriente mohín:

—Creo que la cena está servida, milady.

Chastity tuvo la impresión de que aquél no era un comportamiento apropiado para una pareja casada, pero se levantó y avanzó hacia él. Cyn retrocedió hasta caer de espaldas sobre la cama.

—¡Me rindo! —declaró—. Haz conmigo lo que quieras, moza.

Chastity estaba hipnotizada por una gran gota de nata que tenía en la punta del pene. Se inclinó y la chupó. Él corcoveó.

—¡Cielos!

Cuando ella levantó la vista, sin embargo, estaba claro que él no estaba enfadado. Lenta y tiernamente siguió limpiándole con la lengua. Observó cómo el pecho de Cyn se movía con profundas respiraciones, escuchó su aliento, sintió los temblores que lo recorrían. Se colocó encima y se ensartó sobre él.

—¡No! —jadeó él, pero después, volteándose a la par que ella, se rindió y la amó con febril intensidad. Chastity ardía de júbilo por ser capaz de hacerle aquello a él, para él, con él.

Ambos rugieron enardecidos por la pasión.

Estaban empapados de un sudor que olía a dulce cuando Cyn se levantó de encima de ella, frunciendo el ceño.

—No pretendía que nuestra primera vez fuera así.

A Chastity se le encogió el corazón. La culpa era suya. Tenía que haber sabido que la gente casada no se comportaba de ese modo.

—Lo siento...

Él la hizo callar con un beso, un largo y asfixiante beso.

—Pues yo no —le aseguró—. Sólo quería que fuera perfecto para ti esta primera vez.

—Ha sido perfecto, pero lamento…

Él la hizo callar cubriéndole los labios tiernamente con la mano

—No lamentes nada. Puedes tomarme siempre que quieras. Pero ahora, querida esposa, deja que yo te tome a ti…

A través de la seda, luego bajo la seda, él estimuló sus puntos de placer, enardeciéndola hasta que ella se retorció bajo sus manos y labios anhelando el desahogo. Entonces, él la penetró con una infinita y provocadora lentitud, y la liberó.

Al día siguiente, Cyn y Chastity deambulaban por las antiguas calles de Winchester en su privado mundo de dicha. Pero, en cierto cruce, se encontraron con un chaval que les era familiar.

—Me acuerdo de usted, capitán —dijo el chico haciendo una mueca, después añadió rápidamente—. Milord.

Cyn se echó a reír y le arrojó una guinea de oro.

—Eso por tu memoria, y por que me acabo de casar.

El chico le vitoreó. Luego se acordó de hacer una reverencia.

—Mis mejores deseos para los dos.

Sin embargo, al seguir paseando, la sonrisa de Chastity se esfumó, y ella se ciñó la capa de piel un poco más cerca del cuerpo.

—La gente se acuerda de las cosas durante mucho tiempo, ¿no es cierto?

Cyn la miró y después la condujo hacia un edificio conocido por ambos: el banco de Darby.

Entraron juntos y rápidamente fueron acompañados hasta la habitación artesonada, el cuarto favorito del señor Darby, y obsequiados con jerez.

—¿Y qué puedo hacer por usted, lord Cynric? —preguntó el banquero.

—Estoy aquí para hacer ciertas disposiciones financieras a favor de mi esposa —dijo Cyn. Se volvió hacia Chastity—. Querida mía, éste es el señor Darby. Voy a arreglar las cosas para que puedas sacar fondos de aquí mientras estamos en Inglaterra.

El señor Darby hizo una reverencia y le besó la mano a Chastity.

—Lady Malloren, es desde luego un honor. Por favor, acepte mi más calurosa felicitación…

Pronto salieron otra vez al aire fresco y Cyn le sonrió a Chastity.

—¿Lo ves? La reputación de la infame Chastity Ware esta siendo reparada, pero ella también ha desaparecido. De ahora en adelante vas a ser lady Cynric Malloren y estarás a salvo de cualquier desazón, te lo aseguro.

Chastity se volvió con una radiante sonrisa.

—Volví a nacer el día que te conocí… ¡Oh, Cyn! Todo va a ir bien de verdad, ¿a que sí?

Él la rodeó con sus brazos, allí mismo, en la calle.

—Es perfecto y siempre lo será, amor mío. Sin embargo, creo que deberíamos crear un nuevo escándalo. Hagamos que todos se escandalicen de nuestra alegría y fidelidad, tan pasadas de moda. Y de la cantidad de tiempo que pasamos en privado. Si no recuerdo mal —dijo él, mientras los ojos se le

iban oscureciendo por el deseo—, tenemos unos encantado-
res aposentos esperándonos…

La feliz risa de Chastity los acompañó mientras volvían
a toda prisa a la dulce intimidad de la habitación del Three
Balls.

Otros títulos publicados en
books4pocket romántica

Jo Beverley
La dama del antifaz
Tentar a la suerte

Julia Quinn
El duque y yo

Susan Carroll
El merodeador nocturno
Novia de medianoche

Karyn Monk
La rosa y el guerrero

Patricia Ryan
Tormenta secreta
Hechizo del halcón
La espía de la corona
Viento salvaje

Mary Jo Putney
Una rosa perfecta

Linda Howard
Premonición mortal
El hombre perfecto

www.books4pocket.com